The Travel Agent's Complete Desk Reference

The Travel Agent's Complete Desk Reference

Kelly Monaghan, CTC

Additional Research by Caitlin Kingsley

The Travel Agent's Complete Desk Reference

Fifth Edition

For information contact
The Intrepid Traveler
P.O. Box 531
Branford, CT 06405

http://www.intrepidtraveler.com

ISBN: 978-1-887140-81-2
LCCN: 2008934983

Publisher's Cataloguing in Publication Data

Monaghan, Kelly
The travel agent's complete desk reference. 5th edition.
By Kelly Monaghan. Branford, CT: The Intrepid Traveler, copyright 2009.
PARTIAL CONTENTS: Airport, airline, country & currency codes. —Industry contacts &
information sources. —Reference section and bibliography. Time zones at a glance. Glossary of
travel-related terms & abbreviations.
1. Travel—Information services—Directories. 2. Tourist trade—Information services—Di-
rectories. 3. Travel—Dictionaries. 4. Tourist trade— Dictionaries. 5. Travel—Bibliography. 6.
Tourist trade—Bibliography. 7. Countries—Codes. 8. Airlines—Codes. 9. Airports—Codes. 10.
Money—Codes. 11. Time zones.
I. Title. II. Title: Travel agent's complete desk reference. III. Monaghan, Kelly.
910.2

Dedication

To the pioneering men and women who are revolutionizing the travel distribution landscape by becoming independent, outside travel agents while maintaining the highest standards of professionalism and ethics, this book is respectfully dedicated.

Table of Contents

9

Introduction

This book grew out of my efforts to learn the travel business as an outside sales rep and independent contractor. There were numerous codes to learn so I could decipher itineraries and make reservations more efficiently. There were unfamiliar terms and jargon to master so I could converse fluently with reservationists and suppliers. There was information to gather so I could serve my growing list of clients better.

While the learning process is always enjoyable, I found myself frequently frustrated by the time it took to put my hands on just the piece of information I needed. I searched through the growing pile of industry references in my office. I spent time on the phone tracking down numbers and addresses. I launched myself into cyberspace to get my questions answered. If only there was a handy, one-stop reference that would give me the information I needed quickly, when I needed it.

If necessity is the mother of invention, then frustration is its midwife. Out of my annoyance grew the book you now hold in your hands. I have designed it to help you avoid the glitches that I experienced when I first started out and to save you time as you begin to navigate the exciting world of selling travel.

The Travel Agent's Complete Desk Reference is conceived primarily as a companion piece to my book, *Home-Based Travel Agent: How To Succeed In Your Own Travel Marketing Business*. That means it is dedicated to the beginner. However, even experienced travel agents will find this a handy guide to have on their desk, near the desktop PC and the phone, ready to provide the code to that out-of-the-way destination or the toll-free number of an unfamiliar supplier. The book should also offer those who experience the travel industry as customers a window into this exciting world. It will allow them to decipher the gibberish on their airline tickets and itineraries and help them better understand the special terms and jargon used in brochures and in the ever-present fine print. Not incidentally, it will assist them as they make their own travel arrangements electronically via the Internet.

The Travel Agent's Complete Desk Reference is, like Caesar's Gaul, divided into three parts. The first is dedicated to the codes that make researching fares and schedules a breeze. If you decide to automate, you will need to become

10

familiar with these codes to make the most efficient use of your GDS (global distribution system). Even if you do not use a GDS, you will find these codes coming in handy as you work with consolidators and the growing number of research and booking tools available on the Internet.

Part Two presents a cornucopia of toll-free phone numbers and web sites that give you access to both travel industry suppliers and a wealth of free travel information. Also included are listings of travel industry organizations, consortiums, and additional web sites of particular interest to travel agents.

The reference section, Part Three, will help answer frequently asked questions by deciphering industry jargon, acronyms, and frequently used GDS abbreviations. Also here you will find an extensive bibliography pointing you towards additional sources of information that can deepen your knowledge of both the travel industry and the many exciting destinations it serves.

I would like to extend special thanks to my long-suffering wife, Sally Scanlon, who pitched in selflessly to make earlier editions of this book possible, and to Caitlin Kingsley who assisted in the often tedious job of tracking down illusive bits of information.

Kelly Monaghan, CTC
Branford, CT

Part One:

Airport, Airline, Country & Currency Codes

About The Codes

This section contains information about the primary codes used in the various global distribution systems (GDS) to identify cities, airports, airlines and other suppliers. These codes are universal, that is, they are the same no matter which GDS you happen to be using. They serve the dual purpose of making the GDSs faster and more efficient, by sharply reducing the chances of confusion or error.

You will turn to this section in one of two situations: You need to find the proper code for a destination or a carrier or you are confronted with an unfamiliar code and need to know what it stands for. With that in mind, this section has been arranged as follows:

Domestic Airports. Here are listed, alphabetically by city name, destinations in the United States (including Puerto Rico, the U.S. Virgin Islands, American Samoa, and Guam) and Canada and the universal three-letter codes used to uniquely identify them. I have used the standard two-letter abbreviations for states and provinces, which are listed at the end of this introduction. When you are constructing a domestic itinerary, you will find the codes you need here.

International Airports. Here are listed, alphabetically by city name, destinations outside the United States and Canada along with their unique three-letter codes. When you are constructing an international itinerary, you will find the codes you need here.

Airport Codes. Until you begin to learn airport codes by heart you will find yourself confronted with unfamiliar codes. Even after you have been in the business for years, you will find that you are constantly bumping into unfamiliar codes. Here are listed, alphabetically by code, all the airports included in Domestic Airports and International Airports. When confronted with an unfamiliar airport code, this listing will identify the airport.

Airlines. Here are listed, alphabetically by airline, all the world's scheduled passenger carriers and their codes. Like airports, all airlines are identified by a unique code. As this edition goes to press, airlines are identified by two-digit alphanumeric codes, that is, some combination of letters and numbers (e.g. AA or N9). Because the two-digit format limits the pos-

sible number of codes, the industry has created a three-digit code system for airlines. At some point in the not-too-far-distant future, the industry will switch over from the old two-digit codes to the new three-digit codes. Consequently, I have listed both codes for each airline. When the switch takes place, you'll be ready. Note that some airlines have not yet been assigned three-digit codes.

Airline Codes. Just as you will see unfamiliar airport codes, you will find unfamiliar airline codes cropping up on itineraries and GDS screens. Here are listed, alphabetically by code, both the two- and three-digit airline codes and the airlines to which they correspond. When confronted with an unfamiliar airline code, this listing will identify the airline.

Hotels and Rental Cars. The major car rental firms and a growing number of hotel chains have their own GDS codes which allow you to book them directly through the GDS. Here are listed, alphabetically by company name, the major car rental firms and hotels and their unique GDS codes.

Hotel and Rental Car Codes. Here are listed, alphabetically by code, the codes used for hotels and rental cars and the companies which they identify.

Countries and Currencies. There is a growing trend toward international standardization in abbreviations. Here we have listed, alphabetically by country, the nations of the world. For each, we have provided the two-letter country abbreviation, the complete name of the currency used in that country, and the three-digit code for that currency.

Country and Currency Codes. Here are listed, alphabetically by code, the two-digit country codes and the three-digit currency codes. Use this listing when you need to decipher an unfamiliar country or currency code.

Please note that codes change. This is especially true of airport and airline codes. Airports close, open or have their designation changed. Airlines start up and go out of business. All GDSs let you query the system to find a code for an airport or carrier or decipher a new or unfamiliar code.

U.S. State & Territory Abbreviations

AK	Alaska		FL	Florida
AL	Alabama		GA	Georgia
AR	Arkansas		GU	Guam
AS	American Samoa		HI	Hawaii
AZ	Arizona		IA	Iowa
CA	California		ID	Idaho
CO	Colorado		IL	Illinois
CT	Connecticut		IN	Indiana
DC	District of Columbia		KS	Kansas
DE	Delaware		KY	Kentucky

LA	Louisiana		OK	Oklahoma
MA	Massachusetts		OR	Oregon
MD	Maryland		PA	Pennsylvania
ME	Maine		PR	Puerto Rico
MI	Michigan		RI	Rhode Island
MN	Minnesota		SC	South Carolina
MO	Missouri		SD	South Dakota
MS	Mississippi		TN	Tennessee
MT	Montana		TX	Texas
NC	North Carolina		UT	Utah
ND	North Dakota		VA	Virginia
NE	Nebraska		VI	U.S. Virgin Islands
NH	New Hampshire		VT	Vermont
NJ	New Jersey		WA	Washington
NM	New Mexico		WI	Wisconsin
NV	Nevada		WV	West Virginia
NY	New York		WY	Wyoming
OH	Ohio			

Canadian Province Abbreviations

AB	Alberta		NU	Nunavut Territories
BC	British Columbia		ON	Ontario
MB	Manitoba		PE	Prince Edward Island
NB	New Brunswick		QC	Quebec
NL	Newfoundland & Labrador		SK	Saskatchewan
NT	Northwest Territories		YT	Yukon Territory
NS	Nova Scotia			

16

The Travel Agent's
Complete Desk
Reference

Domestic Airports

Abbotsford, BC	YXX	Angoon, AK	AGN
Aberdeen, SD	ABR	Aniak, AK	ANI
Abilene, TX	ABI	Anvik, AK	ANV
Adak Island, AK	ADK	Appleton, WI	ATW
Aguadilla, PR	BQN	Arcata, CA	ACV
Akhiok, AK	AKK	Arctic Village, AK	ARC
Akiachak, AK	KKI	Arviat, NT	YEK
Akiak, AK	AKI	Asheville, NC	AVL
Akron/Canton, OH	CAK	Ashland, KY	HTS
Akulivik, QU	AKV	Aspen, CO	ASE
Akutan, AK	KQA	Athens, GA	AHN
Alakanuk, AK	AUK	Atka, AK	AKB
Alamogordo, NM	ALM	Atlanta, GA	ATL
Alamosa, CO	ALS	Atlantic City (Intl), NJ	ACY
Albany, GA	ABY	Atlantic City, NJ	AIY
Albany, NY	ALB	Atmautluak, AK	ATT
Albany, OR	CVO	Atqasuk, AK	ATK
Albuquerque, NM	ABQ	Attawapiskat, ON	YAT
Aleknagik, AK	WKK	Augusta, GA	AGS
Aleneva, AK	AED	Augusta, ME	AUG
Alexandria, LA	AEX	Aupaluk, PQ	YPJ
Alitak, AK	ALZ	Austin, TX	AUS
Allakaket, AK	AET	Bagotville, PQ	YBG
Allentown, PA	ABE	Baie Comeau, PQ	YBC
Alliance, NE	AIA	Baker Lake, NU	YBK
Alma, PQ	YTF	Bakersfield, CA	BFL
Alpena, MI	APN	Baltimore, MD	BWI
Altoona, PA	AOO	Banff, AB	YBA
Amarillo, TX	AMA	Bangor, ME	BGR
Ambler, AK	ABL	Bar Harbor, ME	BHB
Amook, AK	AOS	Barrow, AK	BRW
Anacortes, WA	OTS	Barter Island, AK	BTI
Anaheim, CA	ANA	Bathurst, NB	ZBF
Anahim Lake, BC	YAA	Baton Rouge, LA	BTR
Anaktuvuk, AK	AKP	Battle Creek, MI	BTL
Anchorage, AK	ANC	Bay City, MI	MBS
Angling Lake, ON	YAX	Bearskin Lake, ON	XBE

Beaumont, TX	BPT	Cape Dorset, NT	YTE
Beaver, AK	WBQ	Cape Girardeau, MO	CGI
Beckley, WV	BKW	Cape Lisburne, AK	LUR
Bell Island, AK	KBE	Cape Newenham, AK	EHM
Bella Coola, BC	QBC	Carlsbad, CA	CLD
Bellefonte, PA	PSB	Carlsbad, NM	CNM
Bellingham, WA	BLI	Carmel, CA	MRY
Bemidji, MN	BJI	Casper, WY	CPR
Bend/Redmond, OR	RDM	Castlegar, BC	YCG
Benton Harbor, MI	BEH	Cat Lake, ON	YAC
Bethel, AK	BET	Catalina Island, CA	AVX
Bethlehem, PA	ABE	Cedar City, UT	CDC
Bettles, AK	BTT	Cedar Rapids/Iowa City, IA	CID
Big Trout Lake, ON	YTL	Center Island, WA	CWS
Billings, MT	BIL	Central, AK	CEM
Binghamton, NY	BGM	Chadron, NE	CDR
Birch Creek, AK	KBC	Chalkyitsik, AK	CIK
Birmingham, AL	BHM	Champaign, IL	CMI
Bismarck, ND	BIS	Chapleau, ON	YLD
Blakely Island, WA	BYW	Charleston, SC	CHS
Blanc Sablon, PQ	YBX	Charleston, WV	CRW
Block Island, RI	BID	Charlo, NB	YCL
Bloomington, IN	BMG	Charlotte, NC	CLT
Bloomington/Normal, IL	BMI	Charlottesville, VA	CHO
Bluefield/Princeton, WV	BLF	Charlottetown, PE	YYG
Boise, ID	BOI	Chatham, NB	YCH
Boston, MA	BOS	Chattanooga, TN	CHA
Boulder City, NV	BLD	Chefornak, AK	CYF
Boundary, AK	BYA	Chesterfield Inlet, NT	YCS
Bozeman, MT	BZN	Chevak, AK	VAK
Bradenton, FL	SRQ	Chevery, PQ	YHR
Bradford, PA	BFD	Cheyenne, WY	CYS
Brainerd, MN	BRD	Chibougamau, PQ	YMT
Brandon, MB	YBR	Chicago (Meigs), IL	CGX
Branson, MO	ZBX	Chicago (Metro), IL	CHI
Brevig Mission, AK	KTS	Chicago (Midway), IL	MDW
Bridgeport, CT	BDR	Chicago (O'Hare), IL	ORD
Bristol, VA	TRI	Chicago (Pal Waukee), IL	PWK
Brochet, MB	YBT	Chicken, AK	CKX
Broughton Island, NT	YVM	Chico, CA	CIC
Brownsville, TX	BRO	Chignik, AK	KCL
Brownwood, TX	BWD	Chino, CA	CNO
Brunswick, GA	BQK	Chisana, AK	CZN
Bryan, TX	CFD	Chisasibi, PQ	YKU
Bryce Canyon, UT	BCE	Chisholm, MN	HIB
Buckland, AK	BKC	Chuathbaluk, AK	CHU
Buffalo, NY	BUF	Churchill Falls, NF	ZUM
Bullhead City, AZ	IFP	Churchill, MB	YYQ
Burbank, CA	BUR	Cincinnati (Municipal), OH	LUK
Burlington, IA	BRL	Cincinnati, OH	CVG
Burlington, VT	BTV	Circle, AK	IRC
Butte, MT	BTM	Circle Hot Springs, AK	CHP
Calgary (Intl), AB	YYC	Clarks Point, AK	CLP
Cambridge Bay, NT	YCB	Clarksburg, WV	CKB
Campbell River, BC	YBL	Cleveland, OH	CLE
Candle, AK	CDL	Clovis, NM	CVN

Clyde River, NT	YCY	Dothan, AL	DHN
Cody, WY	COD	Dryden, ON	YHD
Coeur D'Alene, ID	COE	DuBois, PA	DUJ
Coffman Cove, AK	KCC	Dubuque, IA	DBQ
Cold Bay, AK	CDB	Duluth, MN/Superior, WI	DLH
College Station, TX	CLL	Durango, CO	DRO
Colorado Springs, CO	COS	Durham, NC	RDU
Columbia, MO	COU	Dutch Harbor, AK	DUT
Columbia, SC	CAE	Eagle, AK	EAA
Columbus, GA	CSG	East Hampton, NY	HTO
Columbus, MS	UBS	East Main, PQ	ZEM
Columbus, OH	CMH	Easton, PA	ABE
Columbus (Rickenbaker), OH	LCK	Eastsound, WA	ESD
Columbus/Strkvl/W. Pt., MS	GTR	Eau Claire, WI	EAU
Comox, BC	YQQ	Edmonton (Intl), AB	YEG
Coral Harbour, NT	YZS	Edmonton (Metro), AB	YEA
Cordova, AK	CDV	Edmonton (Muni), AB	YXD
Corpus Christi, TX	CRP	Edmonton (Namao), AB	YED
Cortez, CO	CEZ	Edna Bay, AK	EDA
Craig, AK	CGA	Eek, AK	EEK
Cranbrook, BC	YXC	Egegik, AK	EGX
Crescent City, CA	CEC	Ekuk, AK	KKU
Crested Butte, CO	CSE	Ekwok, AK	KEK
Crooked Creek, AK	CKD	El Centro/Imperial, CA	IPL
Cross Lake, MB	YCR	El Dorado, AR	ELD
Cube Cove, AK	CUW	El Paso, TX	ELP
Culebra, PR	CPX	Elfin Cove, AK	ELV
Cumberland, MD	CBE	Elim, AK	ELI
Dallas/Ft. Worth (Intl), TX	DFW	Elko, NV	EKO
Dallas/Ft. Worth (Love), TX	DAL	Elliot Lake, ON	YEL
Davenport, IA	DVN	Elmira/Corning, NY	ELM
Dawson City, YT	YDA	Ely, NV	ELY
Dawson Creek, BC	YDQ	Emmonak, AK	EMK
Dayton, OH	DAY	Enid, OK	WDG
Daytona Beach, FL	DAB	Erie, PA	ERI
Decatur, IL	DEC	Escanaba, MI	ESC
Decatur Island, WA	DTR	Eugene, OR	EUG
Deep Bay, AK	WDB	Eureka/Arcata, CA	ACV
Deer Lake, NF	YDF	Evansville, IN	EVV
Deer Lake, ON	YVZ	Excursion Inlet, AK	EXI
Deering, AK	DRG	Fairbanks, AK	FAI
Del Rio, TX	DRT	Fajardo, PR	FAJ
Delta Junction, AK	DJN	Fall River/New Bedford, MA	EWB
Deming, NM	DMN	False Island, AK	FAK
Denver, CO	DEN	False Pass, AK	KFP
Des Moines, IA	DSM	Fargo, ND	FAR
Detroit (City), MI	DET	Farmingdale (Republic), NY	FRG
Detroit (Metro), MI	DTT	Farmington, NM	FMN
Detroit (Wayne Cty), MI	DTW	Fayetteville, AR	FYV
Devils Lake, ND	DVL	Fayetteville, NC	XNA
Dickenson, ND	DIK	Fishers Island, NY	FID
Dillingham, AK	DLG	Flagstaff, AZ	FLG
Diomede Island, AK	DIO	Flat, AK	FLT
Dodge City, KS	DDC	Flin Flon, MB	YFO
Dolomi, AK	DLO	Flint, MI	FNT
Dora Bay, AK	DOF	Florence, AL	MSL

Florence, SC	FLO	Grand Rapids, MN	GPZ
Fond du Lac, SK	ZFD	Grande Prairie, AB	YQU
Fort Albany, ON	YFA	Grayling, AK	KGX
Fort Collins/Loveland, CO	FNL	Great Bend, KS	GBD
Fort Dodge, IA	FOD	Great Falls, MT	GTF
Fort Francis, ON	YAG	Green Bay, WI	GRB
Fort Hope, ON	YFH	Greensboro/H.Pt/	
Fort Huachuca/Sierra		Win-Salem, NC	GSO
Vista, AZ	FHU	Greenville, MS	GLH
Fort Lauderdale, FL	FLL	Greenville, NC	PGV
Fort McMurray, AB	YMM	Greenville/Spartanburg, SC	GSP
Fort Myers, FL	FMY	Guam, GU	GUM
Fort Myers (Regional), FL	RSW	Gulfport/Biloxi, MS	GPT
Fort Nelson, BC	YYE	Gunnison, CO	GUC
Fort Severn, ON	YER	Gustavus, AK	GST
Fort Simpson, NT	YFS	Hagerstown, MD	HGR
Fort Smith, AR	FSM	Haines, AK	HNS
Fort Smith, NT	YSM	Halifax (Intl), NS	YHZ
Fort St. John, BC	YXJ	Hall Beach, NT	YUX
Fort Wayne, IN	FWA	Hamilton, ON	YHM
Fort Worth, TX	DFW	Hampton/Newport News/	
Fort Yukon, AK	FYU	Wmsbrg, VA	PHF
Fox Harbour, NF	YFX	Hana, Maui, HI	HNM
Franklin, PA	FKL	Hancock, MI	CMX
Fredericton, NB	YFC	Harlingen, TX	HRL
Frenchville, ME	WFK	Harrisburg (Intl), PA	MDT
Fresno, CA	FAT	Harrisburg, PA	HAR
Friday Harbor, WA	FRD	Harrison, AR	HRO
Gainesville, FL	GNV	Hartford, CT	BDL
Galena, AK	GAL	Hartford, CT/Springfield,MA	HFD
Gallup, NM	GUP	Hattiesburg, MS	HBG
Gambell, AK	GAM	Havasupai, AZ	HAE
Gander, NF	YQX	Havre, MT	HVR
Garden City, KS	GCK	Havre St. Pierre, PQ	YGV
Gary, IN	GYY	Hay River, NT	YHY
Gaspe, PQ	YGP	Hayden, CO	HDN
Geraldton, ON	YGQ	Hays, KS	HYS
Gillam, MB	YGX	Healy Lake, AK	HKB
Gillette, WY	GCC	Hearst, ON	YHF
Gillies Bay, BC	YGB	Helena, MT	HLN
Gjoa Haven, NT	YHK	Hibbing/Chisolm, MN	HIB
Gladewater/Kilgore/		Hickory, NC	HKY
Longview, TX	GGG	High Level, AB	YOJ
Glasgow, MT	GGW	Hilo, Hawaii, HI	ITO
Glendive, MT	GDV	Hilton Head Island, SC	HHH
Gods Narrows, MB	YGO	Hobart Bay, AK	HBH
Gods River, MB	ZGI	Hobbs, NM	HOB
Golovin, AK	GLV	Hollis, AK	HYL
Goodnews Bay, AK	GNU	Holman Island, NT	YHI
Goose Bay, NF	YYR	Holy Cross, AK	HCR
Gore Bay, ON	YZE	Homer, AK	HOM
Grand Canyon, AZ	GCN	Honolulu (Oahu) HI	HNL
Grand Forks, ND	GFK	Hoolehua (Molokai), HI	MKK
Grand Island, NE	GRI	Hoonah, AK	HNH
Grand Junction, CO	GJT	Hooper Bay, AK	HPB
Grand Rapids, MI	GRR	Hornepayne, ON	YHN

Hot Springs, AR	HOT	Kangirsuk, PQ	YKG
Houston (Ellington), TX	EFD	Kansas City (Downtown), MO	MKC
Houston (Hobby), TX	HOU	Kansas City (Intl), MO	MCI
Houston (Intercontinental), TX	IAH	Kapalua, Maui, HI	JHM
Hughes, AK	HUS	Kapuskasing, ON	YYU
Huntington, WV/Ashland, KY	HTS	Karluk, AK	KYK
Huntsville/Decatur, AL	HSV	Kasaan, AK	KXA
Huron, SD	HON	Kasabonika, ON	XKS
Huslia, AK	HSL	Kaschechewan, ON	ZKE
Hyannis, MA	HYA	Kasigluk, AK	KUK
Hydaburg, AK	HYG	Kauai Is. (Lihue), HI	LIH
Hyder, AK	WHD	Kayenta, AZ	MVM
Idaho Falls, ID	IDA	Kearney, NE	EAR
Igiugig, AK	IGG	Keene, NH/Brattleboro, VT	EEN
Igloolik, NT	YGT	Kelowna, BC	YLW
Iles de la Madeleine, PQ	YGR	Kenai, AK	ENA
Iliamna, AK	ILI	Kenmore Air Harbor, WA	KEH
Imperial, CA	IPL	Kenora, ON	YQK
Indianapolis, IN	IND	Ketchikan, AK	KTN
Int'l Falls, MN	INL	Key West, FL	EYW
Inukjuak, PQ	YPH	Kiana, AK	IAN
Inuvik, NT	YEV	Kilgore, TX	GGG
Inyokern, CA	IYK	Killeen, TX	ILE
Iowa City, IA	IOW	King Cove, AK	KVC
Iqaluit, NT	YFB	King Salmon, AK	AKN
Iron Mountain, MI	IMT	Kingfisher Lake, ON	KIF
Ironwood, MI	IWD	Kingman, AZ	IGM
Island Lake, MB	YIV	Kingsport, TN	TRI
Islip (Macarthur), NY	ISP	Kingston, ON	YGK
Ithaca, NY	ITH	Kinston, NC	ISO
Ivanof Bay, AK	KIB	Kipnuk, AK	KPN
Jackson Hole, WY	JAC	Kirksville, MO	IRK
Jackson, MS	JAN	Kitoi Bay, AK	KKB
Jackson, TN	MKL	Kivalina, AK	KVL
Jacksonville, FL	JAX	Klamath Falls, OR	LMT
Jacksonville, NC	OAJ	Klawock, AK	KLW
Jamestown, ND	JMS	Knoxville, TN	TYS
Jamestown, NY	JHW	Kobuk, AK	OBU
Jefferson City, MO	JEF	Kodiak, AK	ADQ
Johnson City, NY	BGM	Kona, Hawaii, HI	KOA
Johnson City, TN	TRI	Kongiganak, AK	KKH
Johnstown, PA	JST	Kotlik, AK	KOT
Jonesboro, AR	JBR	Kotzebue, AK	OTZ
Joplin, MO	JLN	Koyuk, AK	KKA
Juneau, AK	JNU	Koyukuk, AK	KYU
Kahului, HI	OGG	Kuujjuaq, PQ	YVP
Kake, AK	KAE	Kuujjuarapik, PQ	YGW
Kakhonak, AK	KNK	Kwethluk, AK	KWT
Kalamazoo, MI	AZO	Kwigillingok, AK	KWK
Kalaupapa, HI	LUP	La Crosse WI/Winona, MN	LSE
Kalispell/Glacier Natl Pk, MT	FCA	La Ronge, SK	YVC
Kalskag, AK	KLG	Lac Brochet, MB	XLB
Kaltag, AK	KAL	Lafayette, IN	LAF
Kamloops, BC	YKA	Lafayette, LA	LFT
Kamuela, HI	MUE	Lake Charles, LA	LCH
Kangiqsualujjuaq, PQ	XGR	Lake Havasu City, AZ	HII

Domestic Airports

Lake Minchumina, AK	LMA	Marquette, MI	MQT
Lake Placid, NY	LKP	Marshall, AK	MLL
Lake Tahoe, CA	TVL	Martha's Vineyard, MA	MVY
Lanai City, HI	LNY	Martinsburg, WV	MRB
Lancaster, PA	LNS	Mason City, IA	MCW
Lansdowne House, ON	YLH	Massena, NY	MSS
Lansing, MI	LAN	Mattoon, IL	MTO
Laramie, WY	LAR	Mayaguez, PR	MAZ
Laredo, TX	LRD	McAllen, TX	MFE
Larsen Bay, AK	KLN	McCarthy, AK	MXY
Las Cruces, NM	LRU	McCook, NE	MCK
Las Vegas (Henderson), NV	HSH	McGrath, AK	MCG
Las Vegas (N. Terminal), NV	VGT	Medford, OR	MFR
Las Vegas, NV	LAS	Medicine Hat, AB	YXH
Latrobe, PA	LBE	Mekoryuk, AK	MYU
Laurel (Hattiesburg), MS	PIB	Melbourne, FL	MLB
Lawton, OK	LAW	Memphis, TN	MEM
Leaf Rapids, MB	YLR	Merced, CA	MCE
Lethbridge, AB	YQL	Meridian, MS	MEI
Levelock, AK	KLL	Metlakatia, AK	MTM
Lewisburg/Greenbrier		Meyers Chuck, AK	WMK
Valley, WV	LWB	Miami (Intl), FL	MIA
Lewiston, ID	LWS	Midland/Odessa, TX	MAF
Lewiston/Auburn, ME	LEW	Miles City, MT	MLS
Lewistown, MT	LWT	Milwaukee, WI	MKE
Lexington, KY	LEX	Minneapolis/St. Paul, MN	MSP
Liberal, KS	LBL	Micocqua-Woodruff, WI	AVR
Lime Village, AK	LVD	Minot, ND	MOT
Lincoln, NE	LNK	Minto, AK	MNT
Little Rock, AR	LIT	Mission, TX	MFE
Lloydminster, AB	YLL	Missoula, MT	MSO
London, ON	YXU	Moab, UT	CNY
Long Beach, CA	LGB	Mobile AL/Pascagoula, MS	MOB
Long Island, AK	LIJ	Modesto, CA	MOD
Longview, TX	GGG	Moline, IL	MLI
Lopez Island, WA	LPS	Moncton, NB	YQM
Los Alamos, NM	LAM	Monroe, LA	MLU
Los Angeles (Intl), CA	LAX	Mont Joli, PQ	YYY
Louisville, KY	SDF	Monterey/Carmel, CA	MRY
Lovell, WY	POY	Montgomery, AL	MGM
Lubbock, TX	LBB	Montpelier/Barre, VT	MPV
Ludington, MI	LDM	Montreal (Dorval), PQ	YUL
Lufkin/Nacogdoches, TX	OCH	Montreal (Metro), PQ	YMQ
Lynchburg, VA	LYH	Montreal (Mirabel), PQ	YMX
Lynn Lake, MB	YYL	Montrose, CO	MTJ
Mackinac Island, MI	MCD	Moosonee, ON	YMO
Macon, GA	MCN	Morgantown, WV	MGW
Madison, WI	MSN	Moser Bay, AK	KMY
Manchester, NH	MHT	Moses Lake, WA	MWH
Manhattan, KS	MHK	Mount Vernon, IL	MVN
Manistee, MI	MBL	Mountain Home, AR	WMH
Manley Hot Springs, AK	MLY	Mountain Village, AK	MOU
Manokotak, AK	KMO	Muscle Shoals, AL	MSL
Marathon, FL	MTH	Muskegon, MI	MKG
Marietta/Parkersburg, WV	PKB	Muskrat Dam, ON	MSA
Marion, IL	MWA	Myrtle Beach, SC	MYR

Nakina, ON	YQN	Olga Bay, AK	KOY
Naknek, AK	NNK	Omaha, NE	OMA
Nanaimo, BC	YCD	Ontario, CA	ONT
Nanisivik, NT	YSR	Opapamiska Lake, ON	YBS
Nantucket, MA	ACK	Orange County/Santa	
Napakiak, AK	WNA	Ana, CA	SNA
Napaskiak, AK	PKA	Orlando (Sanford), FL	SFB
Naples, FL	APF	Orlando (Intl), FL	MCO
Nashville, TN	BNA	Oshkosh, WI	OSH
Natashquan, PQ	YNA	Ottawa (Intl), ON	YOW
Naukiti, AK	NKI	Ottawa (Rockcliffe), ON	YRO
Nelson Lagoon, AK	NLG	Ottumwa, IA	OTM
Nemiscau, PQ	YNS	Ouzinkie, AK	KOZ
New Bern, NC	EWN	Owensboro, KY	OWB
New Haven, CT	HVN	Oxford House, MB	YOH
New London/Groton, CT	GON	Oxnard, CA	OXR
New Orleans, LA	MSY	Paducah, KY	PAH
New Stuyahok, AK	KNW	Page, AZ	PGA
New York (Dntwn H/P), NY	JRB	Pago Pago, AS	PPG
New York (E34th St. H/P), NY	TSS	Pakuashipi, PQ	YIF
New York (E60th St H/P), NY	JRE	Palm Springs, CA	PSP
New York (Kennedy), NY	JFK	Palmdale/Lancaster, CA	PMD
New York (La Guardia), NY	LGA	Panama City, FL	PFN
New York (Marine Air		Parkersburg, WV	PKB
Term.), NY	QNY	Parks, AK	KPK
New York (Metro), NY	NYC	Pascagoula, MS	PGL
New York (W30th St. H/P), NY	JRA	Pasco, WA	PSC
Newark, NJ/New York, NY	EWR	Peace River, AB	YPE
Newburgh (Stewart), NY	SWF	Peawanuk, ON	YPO
Newport News/Wmsbg., VA	PHF	Pedro Bay, AK	PDB
Newtok, AK	WWT	Pelican, AK	PEC
Nightmute, AK	NME	Pellston, MI	PLN
Nikolai, AK	NIB	Pendleton, OR	PDT
Nikolski, AK	IKO	Pensacola, FL	PNS
Noatak, AK	WTK	Penticton, BC	YYF
Nome, AK	OME	Peoria, IL	PIA
Nondalton, AK	NNL	Perryville, AK	KPV
Noorvik, AK	ORV	Petersburg, AK	PSG
Norfolk, NE	OFK	Philadelphia (Intl), PA	PHL
Norfolk, VA	ORF	Philipsburg, PA	PSB
Norman Wells, NT	YVQ	Phoenix, AZ	PHX
North Bay, ON	YYB	Pickle Lake, ON	YPL
North Bend, OR	OTH	Pierre, SD	PIR
North Platte, NE	LBF	Pikangikum, ON	YPM
Norway House, MB	YNE	Pilot Point, AK	PIP
Nuiqsut, AK	NUI	Pilot Point (Ugashik), AK	UGB
Nulato, AK	NUL	Pilot Station, AK	PQS
Nunapitchuk, AK	NUP	Pinehurst, NC	SOP
Oak Harbor, WA	ODW	Pittsburgh, PA	PIT
Oakland, CA	OAK	Platinum, AK	PTU
Ofu Island, AS	OFU	Plattsburgh, NY	PLB
Ogdensburg, NY	OGS	Pocatello, ID	PIH
Ogoki, ON	YOG	Point Baker, AK	KPB
Oil City, PA	OIL	Point Hope, AK	PHO
Oklahoma City, OK	OKC	Point Lay, AK	PIZ
Old Harbour, AK	OLH	Ponca City, OK	PNC

23

The Travel Agent's
Complete Desk
Reference

Ponce, PR	PSE	Roche Harbor, WA	RCE
Pond Inlet, NT	YIO	Rochester, MN	RST
Port Alexander, AK	PTD	Rochester, NY	ROC
Port Alsworth, AK	PTA	Rock Springs, WY	RKS
Port Angeles, WA	CLM	Rockford, IL	RFD
Port Bailey, AK	KPY	Rockland, ME	RKD
Port Clarence, AK	KPC	Rocky Mount/Wilson, NC	RWI
Port Hardy, BC	YZT	Rosario, WA	RSJ
Port Heiden, AK	PTH	Roswell, NM	ROW
Port Hope Simpson, NF	YHA	Round Lake, ON	ZRJ
Port Lions, AK	ORI	Rouyn, PQ	YUY
Port Moller, AK	PML	Ruby, AK	RBY
Port Protection, AK	PPV	Ruidoso, NM	RUI
Port Williams, AK	KPR	Russian Mission, AK	RSH
Portage Creek, AK	PCA	Rutland, VT	RUT
Portland, ME	PWM	Sachigo Lake, ON	ZPB
Portland, OR	PDX	Sacramento (Metro), CA	SMF
Poughkeepsie, NY	POU	Saginaw/Bay City/	
Powell River, BC	YPW	Midland, MI	MBS
Prescott, AZ	PRC	Salem, OR	SLE
Presque Isle, ME	PQI	Salina, KS	SLN
Prince Albert, SK	YPA	Salisbury, MD	SBY
Prince George, BC	YXS	Salluit, PQ	YZG
Prince Rupert, BC	YPR	Salt Lake City, UT	SLC
Princeville, Kauai, HI	HPV	San Angelo, TX	SJT
Providence, RI	PVD	San Antonio, TX	SAT
Provincetown, MA	PVC	San Diego (Brown Field), CA	SDM
Prudhoe Bay/Deadhorse, AK	SCC	San Diego (Lindberg), CA	SAN
Pueblo, CO	PUB	San Diego (Montgomery), CA	MYF
Pukatawagan, MB	XPK	San Francisco, CA	SFO
Pullman, WA	PUW	San Jose, CA	SJC
Qualicum, BC	XQU	San Juan (Isla Grand), PR	SIG
Quebec, PQ	YQB	San Juan (Munoz Marin), PR	SJU
Quesnel, BC	YQZ	San Luis Obispo, CA	SBP
Quincy, IL	UIN	Sand Point, AK	SDP
Quinhagak, AK	KWN	Sandspit, BC	YZP
Rainbow Lake, AB	YOP	Sandy Lake, ON	ZSJ
Raleigh/Durham, NC	RDU	Sanford, FL	SFB
Rampart, AK	RMP	Santa Barbara, CA	SBA
Rankin Inlet, NT	YRT	Santa Fe, NM	SAF
Rapid City, SD	RAP	Santa Maria, CA	SMX
Reading, PA	RDG	Santa Rosa, CA	STS
Red Devil, AK	RDV	Saranac Lake, NY	SLK
Red Lake, ON	YRL	Sarasota/Bradenton, FL	SRQ
Red Sucker Lake, MB	YRS	Sarnia, BC	YZR
Redding, CA	RDD	Saskatoon, SK	YXE
Regina, SK	YQR	Sault Ste. Marie	
Reno, NV	RNO	(Chippewa), MI	CIU
Repluse Bay, NT	YUT	Sault Ste. Marie (Metro), MI	SSM
Resolute, NT	YRB	Sault Ste. Marie, ON	YAM
Rhinelander, WI	RHI	Savannah, GA	SAV
Richmond/Wmsbrg, VA	RIC	Savoonga, AK	SVA
Riverside, CA	RAL	Scammon Bay, AK	SCM
Riverton, WY	RIW	Schefferville, PQ	YKL
Roanoke, VA	ROA	Scottsbluff, NE	BFF
Roberval, PQ	YRJ	Scranton, PA	AVP

Seal Bay, AK	SYB	Stephenville, NF	YJT	
Seattle/Tacoma, WA	SEA	Sterling/Rock Falls, IL	SQI	
Seattle (Boeing Field), WA	BFI	Stevens Point, WI	STE	
Selawik, AK	WLK	Stevens Village, AK	SVS	
Sept-Iles, PQ	YZV	Stockton, CA	SCK	
Seward, AK	SWD	Stony Rapids, SK	YSF	
Shageluk, AK	SHX	Stony River, AK	SRV	
Shaktoolik, AK	SKK	Sudbury, ON	YSB	
Shamattawa, MB	ZTM	Sugarland, TX	SGR	
Sheffield, AL	MSL	Sun Valley, ID	SUN	
Sheldon Point, AK	SXP	Superior, WI	SUW	
Sheridan, WY	SHR	Swan River, MB	ZJN	
Shishmaref, AK	SHH	Sydney, NS	YQY	
Show Low, AZ	SOW	Syracuse, NY	SYR	
Shreveport, LA	SHV	Tacoma, WA	SEA	
Shungnak, AK	SHG	Tadoule Lake, MB	XTL	
Sidney, NE	SNY	Takotna, AK	TCT	
Silver City, NM	SVC	Talkeetna, AK	TKA	
Sioux City, IA	SUX	Tallahassee, FL	TLH	
Sioux Falls, SD	FSD	Taloyoak, NT	YYH	
Sioux Lookout, ON	YXL	Tampa/St. Pete., FL	TPA	
Sitka, AK	SIT	Tanana, AK	TAL	
Skagway, AK	SGY	Tasiujuaq, PQ	YTQ	
Sleetmute, AK	SLQ	Tatalina, AK	TLJ	
Smith Cove, AK	SCJ	Tau, AS	TAV	
Smithers, BC	YYD	Teller, AK	TLA	
South Bend, IN	SBN	Telluride, CO	TEX	
South Indian Lake, MB	XSI	Tenakee Springs, AK	TKE	
South Naknek, AK	WSN	Terrace, BC	YXT	
Spencer, IA	SPW	Terre Haute, IN	HUF	
Spokane, WA	GEG	Tete-a-la-Baleine, PQ	ZTB	
Springfield, IL	SPI	Tetlin, AK	TEH	
Springfield, MA	BDL	Texarkana, AR	TXK	
Springfield, MO	SGF	The Pas, MB	YQD	
St. Anthony, NF	YAY	Thief River Falls, MN	TVF	
St. Cloud, MN	STC	Thompson, MB	YTH	
St. Croix, VI	STX	Thorne Bay, AK	KTB	
St. George Island, AK	STG	Thunder Bay, ON	YQT	
St. George, UT	SGU	Timmins, ON	YTS	
St. John, NB	YSJ	Tin City, AK	TNC	
St. Johns, NF	YYT	Togiak, AK	TOG	
St. Leonard, NB	YSL	Tok, AK	TKJ	
St. Louis (Lambert), MO	STL	Toksook Bay, AK	OOK	
St. Mary's, AK	KSM	Toledo, OH	TOL	
St. Michael, AK	SMK	Topeka, KS	TOP	
St. Paul Island, AK	SNP	Toronto (Metro), ON	YTO	
St. Paul, MN	MSP	Toronto (Pearson), ON	YYZ	
St. Petersburg/		Toronto (Toronto Is.), ON	YTZ	
Clearwater, FL	PIE	Traverse City, MI	TVC	
St. Thomas, VI	STT	Trenton, NJ	TTN	
State College, PA	SCE	Tri-City Airport, TN	TRI	
Staunton (Shenandoah		Tucson, AZ	TUS	
Valley), VA	SHD	Tulita, NT	ZFN	
Ste. Therese Point, MB	YST	Tulsa, OK	TUL	
Steamboat Springs, CO	SBS	Tuluksak, AK	TLT	
Stebbins, AK	WBB	Tuntutuliak, AK	WTL	

25

Tununak, AK	TNK	Wemindji, PQ	YNC
Tupelo, MS	TUP	Wenatchee, WA	EAT
Tuscaloosa, AL	TCL	West Palm Beach, FL	PBI
Twin Falls, ID	TWF	West Point, AK	KWP
Twin Hills, AK	TWA	Westerly, RI	WST
Tyler, TX	TYR	Westsound, WA	WSX
Uganik, AK	UGI	Whale Cove, NT	YXN
Unalakleet, AK	UNK	Whale Pass, AK	WWP
Uranium City, SK	YBE	Wheeling, WV	HLG
Utica, New York	UCA	White Mountain, AK	WMO
Utopia Creek, AK	UTO	White Plains, NY	HPN
Vail (Eagle County), CO	EGE	Whitehorse, YT	YXY
Vail (Stolport), CO	WHR	Wichita Falls, TX	SPS
Val D'Or, PQ	YVO	Wichita, KS	ICT
Valdez, AK	VDZ	Wilkes-Barre/Scranton, PA	AVP
Valdosta, GA	VLD	Williams Lake, BC	YWL
Vancouver (Intl), BC	YVR	Williamsport, PA	IPT
Venetie, AK	VEE	Williston, ND	ISN
Vernal, UT	VEL	Wilmington, DE	ILG
Vicksburg, MS	VKS	Wilmington, NC	ILM
Victoria (Intl), BC	YYJ	Windsor, ON	YQG
Victoria, TX	VCT	Winnipeg, MB	YWG
Vieques, PR	VQS	Winona, MN	ONA
Visalia, CA	VIS	Winston-Salem (Smith-	
Wabush, NF	YWK	Reynolds), NC	INT
Waco, TX	ACT	Wolf Point, MT	OLF
Wainwright, AK	AIN	Worcester, MA	ORH
Wales, AK	WAA	Worland, WY	WRL
Walla Walla, WA	ALW	Wrangell, AK	WRG
Washington (Dulles), DC	IAD	Wunnummin Lake, ON	WNN
Washington (Metro), DC	WAS	Yakima, WA	YKM
Washington (Reagan), DC	DCA	Yakutat, AK	YAK
Waskaganish, PQ	YKQ	Yankton, SD	YKN
Waterfall, AK	KWF	Yarmouth, NS	YQI
Waterloo, IA	ALO	Yellowknife, NT	YZF
Watertown, NY	ART	Yes Bay, AK	WYB
Watertown, SD	ATY	York, PA	THV
Wausau, WI	AUW	Youngstown, OH	YNG
Wausau (Wisc. Cntl.), WI	CWA	Yuma, AZ	YUM
Wawa, ON	YXZ	Zachar Bay, AK	KZB
Webequie, ON	YWP		

International Airports

Aalborg, Denmark	AAL	Airok, Marshall Islands	AIC
Aalesund, Norway	AES	Aitape, Papua New Guinea	ATP
Aarhus, Denmark	AAR	Aitutaki, Cook Islands	AIT
Abaiang, Kiribati	ABF	Ajaccio, Corsica, France	AJA
Abakan, Russia	ABA	Akieni, Gabon	AKE
Abbottabad, Pakistan	AAW	Akita, Japan	AXT
Abecher, Chad	AEH	Akmola, Kazakstan	TSE
Abemama, Kiribati	AEA	Aksu, China	AKU
Aberdeen, Scotland	ABZ	Aktau. Kazakstan	SCO
Abha, Saudi Arabia	AHB	Aktyubinsk, Kazakstan	AKX
Abidjan, Cote D'lvoire	ABJ	Akureyri, Iceland	AEY
Abu Dhabi, UAE	AUH	Al Ain, UAE	AAN
Abu Simbel, Egypt	ABS	Al Arish, Egypt	AAC
Abuja, Nigeria	ABV	Al Ghaydah, Yemen	AAY
Acapulco, Mexico	ACA	Al Hoceima, Morocco	AHU
Acarigua, Venezuela	AGV	Al-Baha, Saudi Arabia	ABT
Accra, Ghana	ACC	Al-Fujairah, UAE	FJR
Adana, Turkey	ADA	Albany, Australia	ALH
Addis Ababa, Ethiopia	ADD	Albuq, Yemen	BUK
Adelaide, Australia	ADL	Albury, Australia	ABX
Aden, Yemen	ADE	Alderney, Channel	
Adler/Sochi, Russia	AER	Islands, UK	ACI
Adrar, Algeria	AZR	Aleppo, Syria	ALP
Afutara, Solomon Islands	AFT	Alexander Bay, South Africa	ALJ
Agadir, Morocco	AGA	Alexandria, Egypt	ALY
Agartala, India	IXA	Alexandroupolis, Greece	AXD
Agatti Island, India	AGX	Alghero, Italy	AHO
Agaun, Papua New Guinea	AUP	Algiers, Algeria	ALG
Agen, France	AGF	Alicante, Spain	ALC
Agra, India	AGR	Alice Springs, Australia	ASP
Aguascalientes, Mexico	AGU	Almaty, Kazakstan	ALA
Aguni, Japan	AGJ	Almeria, Spain	LEI
Ahmedabad, India	AMD	Alor Island, Indonesia	ARD
Ahuas, Honduras	AHS	Alor Setar, Malaysia	AOR
Ahwaz, Iran	AWZ	Alotau, Papua New Guinea	GUR
Ailuk, Marshall Islands	AIM	Alta Floresta, Brazil	AFL
Aioun El Atrouss, Mauritania	AEO	Alta, Norway	ALF

The Travel Agent's Complete Desk Reference

Altamira, Brazil	ATM	Arar, Saudi Arabia	RAE
Altay, China	AAT	Araracuara, Colombia	ACR
Altenrhein, Switzerland	ACH	Arauca, Colombia	AUC
Amami O Shima, Japan	ASJ	Arba Mintch, Ethiopia	AMH
Amazon Bay, Papua New		Ardabil, Iran	ADU
Guinea	AZB	Arequipa, Peru	AQP
Ambanja, Madagascar	IVA	Arica, Chile	ARI
Ambatomainty, Madagascar	AMY	Aripuana, Brazil	AIR
Ambatondrazaka, Madagascar	WAM	Arkalyk, Kazakstan	AYK
Ambon, Indonesia	AMQ	Arkhangelsk, Russia	ARH
Amboseli, Kenya	ASV	Armenia, Colombia	AXM
Amman, Jordan	AMM	Armidale, Australia	ARM
Amritsar, India	ATQ	Arona, Solomon Islands	RNA
Amsterdam, Netherlands	AMS	Arorae Is, Kiribati	AIS
Anaa, Fr. Polynesia	AAA	Arthur's Town, Bahamas	ATC
Anadyr, Russia	DYR	Aruba, Aruba	AUA
Anapa, Russia	AAQ	Arvidsjaur, Sweden	AJR
Ancona, Italy	AOI	Asahikawa, Japan	AKJ
Andahuaylas, Peru	ANS	Ascension, Bolivia	ASC
Andenes, Norway	ANX	Ashkhabad, Turkmenistan	ASB
Andizan, Uzbekistan	AZN	Asmara, Eritrea	ASM
Andorra La Vella, Andorra	ALV	Asosa, Ethiopia	ASO
Andros Town, Bahamas	ASD	Assab, Eritrea	ASA
Anegada, BVI	NGD	Astrakhan, Russia	ASF
Aneityum, Vanuatu	AUY	Asturias, Spain	OVD
Angouleme, France	ANG	Astypalaia Is., Greece	JTY
Anguilla, West Indies	AXA	Asuncion, Paraguay	ASU
Aniwa, Vanatu	AWD	Aswan, Egypt	ASW
Ankang, China	AKA	Ataq, Yemen	AXK
Ankara (Esenboga), Turkey	ESB	Atar, Mauritania	ATR
Ankara, Turkey	ANK	Atbara, Sudan	ATB
Ankavandra, Madagascar	JVA	Athens, Greece	ATH
Annaba, Algeria	AAE	Atiu, Cook Islands	AIU
Annecy, France	NCY	Atoifi, Solomon Islands	ATD
Anqing, China	AQG	Attopeu, Laos	AOU
Antalaha, Madagascar	ANM	Atuona, Fr. Polynesia	AUQ
Antalya, Turkey	AYT	Atyrau, Kazakstan	GUW
Antananarivo, Madagascar	TNR	Auckland, New Zealand	AKL
Antigua, West Indies	ANU	Augsburg, Germany	AGB
Antofagasta, Chile	ANF	Auki, Solomon Islands	AKS
Antosohihy, Madagascar	WAI	Aumo, Papua New Guinea	AUV
Antsalova, Madagascar	WAQ	Aur, Marshall Islands	AUL
Antsiranana, Madagascar	DIE	Aurangabad, India	IXU
Antwerp, Belgium	ANR	Aurillac, France	AUR
Aomori, Japan	AOJ	Avignon, France	AVN
Apartado, Colombia	APO	Avu Avu, Solomon Islands	AVU
Apia (Fagali I.), Western Samoa	FGI	Axum, Ethiopia	AXU
Apia, Western Samoa	APW	Ayacucho, Peru	AYP
Aplay, Colombia	API	Ayers Rock, Australia	AYQ
Aqaba, Jordan	AQJ	Bacolod, Philippines	BCD
Aracaju, Brazil	AJU	Badajoz, Spain	BJZ
Aracatuba, Brazil	ARU	Bagdogra, India	IXB
Arad, Romania	ARW	Bage, RS, Brazil	BGX
Aragip, Papua New Guinea	ARP	Baghdad (Metro), Iraq	BGW
Araguaina, Brazil	AUX	Baghdad (Int'l), Iraq	SDA
Aranuka, Kiribati	AAK	Baguio, Philippines	BAG

Bahar Dar, Ethiopia	BJR	Basel, Switzerland	BSL
Bahawalpur, Pakistan	BHV	Basse-Terre, Guadeloupe	BBR
Bahia Blanca, Argentina	BHI	Bastia, Corsica, France	BIA
Bahia Pinas, Panama	BFG	Bata, Equatorial Guinea	BSG
Bahia Solano, Colombia	BSC	Batam, Indonesia	BTH
Bahrain, Bahrain	BAH	Bathurst, Australia	BHS
Baia Mare, Romania	BAY	Bathurst Is., Australia	BRT
Baimuru, Papua New Guinea	VMU	Batman, Turkey	BAL
Bakalalan, Malaysia	BKM	Batom, Indonesia	BXM
Baku, Azerbaijan	BAK	Batsfjord, Norway	BJF
Balhash, Kazakstan	BXH	Battambang, Cambodia	BBM
Bali, Papua New Guinea	BAJ	Batumi, Georgia	BUS
Balikpapan, Indonesia	BPN	Bauru, Brazil	BAU
Balimo, Papua New Guinea	OPU	Bayamo, Cuba	BYM
Ballalae, Solomon Islands	BAS	Bayreuth, Germany	BYU
Ballina, Australia	BNK	Bechar, Algeria	CBH
Balmaceda, Chile	BBA	Bedourie, Australia	BEU
Bamaga, Australia	ABM	Beef Island, BVI	EIS
Bamako, Mali	BKO	Beica, Ethiopia	BEI
Ban Me Thuot, Vietnam	BMV	Beihai, China	BHY
Banda Aceh, Indonesia	BTJ	Beijing (Capital), China	PEK
Bandar Abbas, Iran	BND	Beijing, China	BJS
Bandar Lampung, Indonesia	TKG	Beira, Mozambique	BEW
Bandar Lengeh, Iran	BDH	Beirut, Lebanon	BEY
Bandar Seri Begawan,		Bejaia, Algeria	BJA
Brunei Darussalam	BWN	Belaga, Malaysia	BLG
Bandung, Indonesia	BDO	Belem, Brazil	BEL
Bangalore, India	BLR	Belep Is., New Caledonia	BMY
Bangkok, Thailand	BKK	Belfast (City), N. Ireland, UK	BHD
Bangui, Cen. African Republic	BGF	Belfast (Intl), N. Ireland, UK	BFS
Banja Luka, Bosnia	BNX	Belgrade, Yugoslavia	BEG
Banjarmasin, Indonesia	BDJ	Belize City, Belize	BZE
Banjul, Gambia	BJL	Belize City (Municipal), Belize	TZA
Bannu, Pakistan	BNP	Bellavista, Peru	BLP
Baoshan, China	BSD	Bellona Is., Solomon Islands	BNY
Baotou, China	BAV	Belo Horizonte (Confins),	
Baracoa, Cuba	BCA	Brazil	CNF
Barakoma, Solomon Islands	VEV	Belo Horizonte (Metro),	
Barbuda, West Indies	BBQ	Brazil	BHZ
Barcaldine, Australia	BCI	Belo Horizonte	
Barcelona, Spain	BCN	(Pampulha), Brazil	PLU
Barcelona, Venezuela	BLA	Beloreck, Russia	BCX
Bardufoss, Norway	BDU	Benbecula, Scotland, UK	BEB
Bari, Italy	BRI	Benghazi, Libya	BEN
Bario, Malaysia	BBN	Bengkulu, Indonesia	BKS
Barisal, Bangladesh	BZL	Benguela, Angola	BUG
Barnaul, Russia	BAX	Benin City, Nigeria	BNI
Barquisimeto, Venezuela	BRM	Berau, Indonesia	BEJ
Barra Colorado, Costa Rica	BCL	Berbera, Somalia	BBO
Barra Do Garcas, Brazil	BPG	Berdyansk, Ukraine	ERD
Barra, Scotland, UK	BRR	Bergen, Norway	BGO
Barrancabermeja, Colombia	EJA	Bergerac, France	EGC
Barranquilla, Colombia	BAQ	Berlevag, Norway	BVG
Barreiras, Brazil	BRA	Berlin (Metro), Germany	BER
Barrow Island, Australia	BWB	Berlin (Schoenefeld),	
Basankusu, Congo, Dem. Rep.	BSU	Germany	SXF

The Travel Agent's Complete Desk Reference

Berlin (Tegel), Germany	TXL	Bonanza, Nicaragua	BZA
Berlin (Tempelhof), Germany	THF	Bondoukou, Cote D'Ivoire	BDK
Bermuda, Atlantic Ocean	BDA	Bonn, Germany	BNJ
Bern, Switzerland	BRN	Bora Bora, Fr. Polynesia	BOB
Beru, Kiribati	BEZ	Borama, Somalia	BXX
Besalampy, Madagascar	BPY	Bordeaux, France	BOD
Beziers, France	BZR	Bordj Badji Mokhtar, Algeria	BMW
Bhadrapur, Nepal	BDP	Borlange, Sweden	BLE
Bhairawa, Nepal	BWA	Bornholm, Denmark	RNN
Bhamo, Myanmar	BMO	Borroloola, Australia	BOX
Bharatpur, Nepal	BHR	Bossaso, Somalia	BSA
Bhavnagar, India	BHU	Bouake, Cote D'lvoire	BYK
Bhopal, India	BHO	Boulia, Australia	BQL
Bhubaneswar, India	BBI	Bourgas, Bulgaria	BOJ
Bhuj, India	BHJ	Bourke, Australia	BRK
Biak, Indonesia	BIK	Bournemouth, England, UK	BOH
Biarritz, France	BIQ	Bradford, England, UK	BRF
Big Creek, Belize	BGK	Braganca, Portugal	BGC
Bikini Atoll, Marshall Islands	BII	Brampton Is., Australia	BMP
Bilbao, Spain	BIO	Brasilia, Brazil	BSB
Billund, Denmark	BLL	Bratislava, Slovakia	BTS
Bima, Indonesia	BMU	Bratsk, Russia	BTK
Bimini, Bahamas	BIM	Brava, Cape Verde Islands	BVR
Biniguni, Papua New Guinea	XBN	Brazzaville, Congo	BZV
Bintulu, Malaysia	BTU	Bremen, Germany	BRE
Biratnagar, Nepal	BIR	Brest, Belarus	BQT
Birdsville, Australia	BVI	Brest, France	BES
Birmingham, England, UK	BHX	Brewarrina, Australia	BWQ
Bisha, Saudi Arabia	BHH	Bridgetown, Barbados	BGI
Bishkek, Kyrgyzstan	FRU	Brindisi, Italy	BDS
Bisho, South Africa	BIY	Brisbane, Australia	BNE
Biskra, Algeria	BSK	Bristol, England, UK	BRS
Bissau, Guinea Bissau	OXB	Brive-La-Gaillarde, France	BVE
Bitam, Gabon	BMM	Brize Norton, England, UK	BZZ
Blackall, Australia	BKQ	Brno, Czech Rep.	BRQ
Blackpool, England, UK	BLK	Broken Hill, Australia	BHQ
Blackwater, Australia	BLT	Bronnoysund, Norway	BNN
Blagoveschensk, Russia	BQS	Broome, Australia	BME
Blantyre, Malawi	BLZ	Brus Laguna, Honduras	BHG
Blenheim, New Zealand	BHE	Brussels, Belgium	BRU
Bloemfontein, South Africa	BFN	Bubaque, Guinea-Bissau	BQE
Bluefields, Nicaragua	BEF	Bucaramanga, Colombia	BGA
Blumenau, Brazil	BNU	Bucharest (Baneasa), Romania	BBU
Boa Vista, Brazil	BVB	Bucharest (Metro), Romania	BUH
Boa Vista, Cape Verde Islands	BVC	Bucharest (Otopeni), Romania	OTP
Boang, Papua New Guinea	BOV	Budapest, Hungary	BUD
Bocas Del Toro, Panama	BOC	Buenos Aires (Metro), Argentina	BUE
Bodo, Norway	BOO	Buenos Aires (Newbery), Argentina	AEP
Bodrum, Turkey	BXN	Buenos Aires (Pistarini), Argentina	EZE
Boende, Congo, Dem. Rep.	BNB		
Bogota, Colombia	BOG		
Bol, Croatia	BWK	Buffalo Range, Zimbabwe	BFO
Bologna, Italy	BLQ	Bujumbura, Burundi	BJM
Bom Jesus Da Lapa, Brazil	LAZ	Buka, Papua New Guinea	BUA
Bombay, India	BOM	Bukhara, Uzbekistan	BHK
Bonaire, Neth. Antilles	BON		

Bulawayo, Zimbabwe	BUQ	Carriacou Is., Grenada	CRU
Bulolo, Papua New Guinea	BUL	Carrillo, Costa Rica	RIK
Bumba, Congo, Dem. Rep.	BMB	Cartagena, Colombia	CTG
Bundaberg, Australia	BDB	Casablanca (Anfa), Morocco	CAS
Bunia, Congo, Dem. Rep.	BUX	Casablanca (Mohamed V),	
Burao, Somalia	BUO	Morocco	CMN
Bureta, Fiji	LEV	Cascavel, Brazil	CAC
Burketown, Australia	BUC	Casino, Australia	CSI
Burnie, Australia	BWT	Castres, France	DCM
Bushehr, Iran	BUZ	Catamarca, Argentina	CTC
Busuanga, Philippines	USU	Catania, Italy	CTA
Butaritari, Kiribati	BBG	Caticlan, Philippines	MPH
Butuan, Philippines	BXU	Caucasia, Colombia	CAQ
Cabinda, Angola	CAB	Cauquira, Honduras	CDD
Cacoal, Brazil	OAL	Caxias Do Sul, Brazil	CXJ
Caen, France	CFR	Caye Caulker, Belize	CUK
Cagayan de Oro, Philippines	CGY	Cayenne, Fr. Guiana	CAY
Cagliari, Italy	CAG	Cayman Brac Is., West Indies	CYB
Cairns, Australia	CNS	Cayo Coco, Cuba	CCC
Cairo, Egypt	CAI	Cayo Largo del Sur, Cuba	CYO
Cajamarca, Peru	CJA	Cebu, Philippines	CEB
Calabar, Nigeria	CBQ	Ceduna, Australia	CED
Calama, Chile	CJC	Chachapoyas, Peru	CHH
Calcutta, India	CCU	Chah-Bahar, Iran	ZBR
Cali, Colombia	CLO	Chandigarh, India	IXC
Calicut, India	CCJ	Changchun, China	CGQ
Calvi, Corsica, France	CLY	Changde, China	CGD
Camaguey, Cuba	CMW	Changsha, China	CSX
Cambridge, England, UK	CBG	Changuinola, Panama	CHX
Campbeltown, Scotland, UK	CAL	Changzhou, China	CZX
Campeche, Mexico	CPE	Chania, Crete, Greece	CHQ
Campina Grande, Brazil	CPV	Chaoyang, China	CHG
Campinas, Brazil	CPQ	Chapeco, Brazil	XAP
Campo Grande, Brazil	CGR	Charleroi, Belgium	CRL
Campos, Brazil	CAW	Charleville, Australia	CTL
Canaima, Venezuela	CAJ	Chatham Island, New	
Canberra, Australia	CBR	Zealand	CHT
Cancun, Mexico	CUN	Cheju, Korea	CJU
Cannes, France	CEQ	Chelyabinsk, Russia	CEK
Canouan Is., Windward		Chengdu, China	CTU
Islands	CIW	Chennai/Madras, India	MAA
Canton, China	CAN	Cherbourg, France	CER
Canton Island, Kiribati	CIS	Chetumal, Mexico	CTM
Cap Haitien, Haiti	CAP	Chiang Mai, Thailand	CNX
Cap Skirring, Senegal	CSK	Chiang Rai, Thailand	CEI
Cape Orford, Papua		Chiayi, Taiwan	CYI
New Guinea	CPI	Chichen Itza, Mexico	CZA
Cape Town, South Africa	CPT	Chiclayo, Peru	CIX
Cape Vogel, Papua		Chigorodo, Colombia	IGO
New Guinea	CVL	Chihuahua, Mexico	CUU
Capurgana, Colombia	CPB	Chimbote, Peru	CHM
Caracas, Venezuela	CCS	Chinju, Korea	HIN
Carajas, Brazil	CKS	Chios, Greece	JKH
Caravelas, Brazil	CRQ	Chita, Russia	HTA
Cardiff, Wales, UK	CWL	Chitral, Pakistan	CJL
Carnarvon, Australia	CVQ	Chitre, Panama	CTD

31

*International
Airports*

Chittagong, Bangladesh	CGP	Denmark	RKE
Choiseul Bay, Solomon Isl.	CHY	Copiapo, Chile	CPO
Chongqing, China	CKG	Cordoba, Argentina	COR
Chos Malal, Argentina	HOS	Cork, Ireland	ORK
Christchurch, New Zealand	CHC	Corn Is., Nicaragua	RNI
Christmas Is., Indian Ocean	XCH	Coro, Venezuela	CZE
Christmas Is., Kiribati	CXI	Corozal, Belize	CZH
Chub Cay, Bahamas	CCZ	Corrientes, Argentina	CNQ
Cicia, Fiji	ICI	Corumba, Brazil	CMG
Ciego De Avila, Cuba	AVI	Corvo Island, Portugal	CVU
Ciudad Bolivar, Venezuela	CBL	Cotabato, Philippines	CBO
Ciudad Del Carmen, Mexico	CME	Coto 47, Costa Rica	OTR
Ciudad Del Este, Paraguay	AGT	Cotonou, Benin	COO
Ciudad Juarez, Mexico	CJS	Coventry, England, UK	CVT
Ciudad Obregon, Mexico	CEN	Cowarie, Australia	CWR
Ciudad Victoria, Mexico	CVM	Cowra, Australia	CWT
Clermont-Ferrand, France	CFE	Cox's Bazar, Bangladesh	CXB
Cleve, Australia	CVC	Cozumel, Mexico	CZM
Cloncurry, Australia	CNJ	Craig Cove, Vanuatu	CCV
Club Makokola, Malawi	CMK	Crisciuma, Brazil	CCM
Cluj, Romania	CLJ	Crooked Is., Bahamas	CRI
Coban, Guatemala	CBV	Crotone, Italy	CRV
Cobar, Australia	CAZ	Cruzeiro Do Sul, Brazil	CZS
Cobija, Bolivia	CIJ	Cucuta, Colombia	CUC
Cochabamba, Bolivia	CBB	Cudal, Australia	CUG
Cochin, India	COK	Cue, Australia	CUY
Cocos-Keeling Is.,		Cuenca, Ecuador	CUE
Indian Ocean	CCK	Cuiaba, Brazil	CGB
Coen, Australia	CUQ	Culiacan, Mexico	CUL
Coffs Harbour, Australia	CFS	Culion, Philippines	CUJ
Coimbatore, India	CJB	Cumana, Venezuela	CUM
Colima, Mexico	CLQ	Cunnamulla, Australia	CMA
Cologne/Bonn, Germany	CGN	Curaçao, Neth. Antilles	CUR
Colombo, Sri Lanka	CMB	Curitiba, Brazil	CWB
Colon, Panama	ONX	Cuzco, Peru	CUZ
Colonia, Uruguay	CYR	Da Nang, Viet Nam	DAD
Comodoro Rivadavia,		Dakar, Senegal	DKR
Argentina	CRD	Dakhla, Morocco	VIL
Conakry, Guinea	CKY	Dalaman, Turkey	DLM
Conceicao Do Araguaia,		Dalat, Viet Nam	DLI
Brazil	CDJ	Dalbandin, Pakistan	DBA
Concepcion, Chile	CCP	Dali City, China	DLU
Concordia, Argentina	COC	Dalian, China	DLC
Condoto, Colombia	COG	Damascus, Syria	DAM
Connaught, Ireland	NOC	Dandong, China	DDG
Constanta, Romania	CND	Dangriga, Belize	DGA
Constantine, Algeria	CZL	Dar Es Salaam, Tanzania	DAR
Contadora, Panama	OTD	Daru, Papua New Guinea	DAU
Coober Pedy, Australia	CPD	Darwin, Australia	DRW
Cooktown, Australia	CTN	Davao, Philippines	DVO
Cooma, Australia	OOM	David, Panama	DAV
Coonabarabran, Australia	COJ	Dawe, Myanmar	TVY
Coonamble, Australia	CNB	Daxian, China	DAX
Cootamundra, Australia	CMD	Daydream Is., Australia	DDI
Copenhagen, Denmark	CPH	Dayong, China	DYG
Copenhagen (Roskilde),		Deadman's Cay, Bahamas	LGI

Deauville, France	DOL	Dunedin, New Zealand	DUD
Debra Marcos, Ethiopia	DBM	Dunhuang, China	DNH
Debra Tabor, Ethiopia	DBT	Dunk Is., Australia	DKI
Deirezzor, Syria	DEZ	Durango, Mexico	DGO
Delhi, India	DEL	Durban, South Africa	DUR
Dembidollo, Ethiopia	DEM	Durham Tees Valley, UK	MME
Denham, Australia	DNM	Dushanbe, Tajikistan	DYU
Denizli, Turkey	DNZ	Dzaoudzi, Mayotte	DZA
Denpasar, Indonesia	DPS	East London, South Africa	ELS
Dera Ghazi Khan, Pakistan	DEA	East Midlands, England, UK	EMA
Dera Ismail Khan, Pakistan	DSK	Easter Island, Chile	IPC
Derby, Australia	DRB	Ebon, Marshall Islands	EBO
Derim, Papua New Guinea	DER	Edinburgh, Scotland, UK	EDI
Dessie, Ethiopia	DSE	Edward River, Australia	EDR
Devonport, Australia	DPO	Efoge, Papua New Guinea	EFG
Dhahran, Saudi Arabia	DHA	Egilsstadir, Iceland	EGS
Dhaka, Bangladesh	DAC	Eindhoven, Netherlands	EIN
Dhangarhi, Nepal	DHI	Ekaterinburg, Russia	SVX
Dibaa, Oman	BYB	Ekibastuz, Kazakstan	EKB
Dibrugarh, India	DIB	El Golea, Algeria	ELG
Dien-Bien-Phu, Viet Nam	DIN	El Oued, Algeria	ELU
Dijon, France	DIJ	El Real, Panama	ELE
Dili, Indonesia	DIL	El Salvador, Chile	ESR
Dillons Bay, Vanuatu	DLY	El Yopal, Colombia	EYP
Dimapur, India	DMU	Elat, Israel	ETH
Dinard, France	DNR	Elazig, Turkey	EZS
Dipolog, Philippines	DPL	Elba Is., Italy	EBA
Dire Dawa, Ethiopia	DIR	Elista, Russia	ESL
Diu, India	DIU	Emae, Vanuatu	EAE
Divinopolis, Brazil	DIQ	Emirau, Papua New Guinea	EMI
Diyarbakir, Turkey	DIY	Enewetok, Marshall Islands	ENT
Djanet, Algeria	DJG	Enontekio, Finland	ENF
Djerba, Tunisia	DJE	Enschede, Netherlands	ENS
Djibouti, Djibouti	JIB	Entebbe/Kampala, Uganda	EBB
Dnepropetrovsk, Ukraine	DNK	Enugu, Nigeria	ENU
Dobo, Indonesia	DOB	Epinal, France	EPL
Dodoima, Papua New Guinea	DDM	Ercan, Cyprus	ECN
Dolpa, Nepal	DOP	Erechim, Brazil	ERM
Dominica (Cane), West Indies	DCF	Erfurt, Germany	ERF
Dominica, West Indies	DOM	Erigavo, Somalia	ERA
Donegal, Ireland	CFN	Errachidia, Morocco	ERH
Donetsk, Ukraine	DOK	Erzincan, Turkey	ERC
Dongola, Sudan	DOG	Erzurum, Turkey	ERZ
Doomadgee Mission, Australia	DMD	Esa'Ala, Papua New Guinea	ESA
Dortmund, Germany	DTM	Esbjerg, Denmark	EBJ
Douala, Cameroon	DLA	Esmeraldas, Ecuador	ESM
Dourados, Brazil	DOU	Esperance, Australia	EPR
Dresden, Germany	DRS	Espirtu Santo, Vanuatu	SON
Dubai, UAE	DXB	Esquel, Argentina	EQS
Dubbo, Australia	DBO	Essen, Germany	ESS
Dublin, Ireland	DUB	Eua, Tonga	EUA
Dubrovnik, Croatia	DBV	Evenes, Norway	EVE
Duesseldorf, Germany	DUS	Exeter, England, UK	EXT
Dumaguete, Philippines	DGT	Fagernes, Norway	VDB
Dundee, Scotland, UK	DND	Faisalabad, Pakistan	LYP
Dundo, Angola	DUE	Fakarava, Fr. Polynesia	FAV

International Airports

The Travel Agent's
Complete Desk
Reference

Fane, Papua New Guinea	FNE	Garden Point, Australia	GPN
Farafangana, Madagascar	RVA	Gasmata Is., Papua	
Faro, Portugal	FAO	New Guinea	GMI
Faroe Islands, Denmark	FAE	Gassim, Saudi Arabia	ELQ
Farsund, Norway	FAN	Gatokae, Solomon Islands	GTA
Fera Is., Solomon Islands	FRE	Gaua, Vanuatu	ZGU
Fergana, Uzbekistan	FEG	Gauhati, India	GAU
Fernando de Noronha, Brazil	FEN	Gavle, Sweden	GVX
Fez, Morocco	FEZ	Gaziantep, Turkey	GZT
Fianarantsoa, Madagascar	WFI	Gbadolite, Congo, Dem. Rep.	BDT
Figari, France	FSC	Gdansk, Poland	GDN
Finschhafen, Papua		Geilo, Norway	DLD
New Guinea	FIN	Gelendzik, Russia	GDZ
Flateyri, Iceland	FLI	Gemena, Congo, Dem. Rep.	GMA
Flinders Is., Australia	FLS	General Roca, Argentina	GNR
Florence, Italy	FLR	General Santos, Philippines	GES
Florencia, Colombia	FLA	Geneva, Switzerland	GVA
Flores, Guatemala	FRS	Genoa, Italy	GOA
Florianopolis, Brazil	FLN	George, South Africa	GRJ
Floro, Norway	FRO	George Town, Bahamas	GGT
Forbes, Australia	FRB	Georgetown, Guyana	GEO
Forde, Norway	FDE	Geraldton, Australia	GET
Formosa, Argentina	FMA	Ghardaia, Algeria	GHA
Fort Dauphin, Madagascar	FTU	Ghimbi, Ethiopia	GHD
Fort De France, Martinique	FDF	Gibraltar, Gibraltar	GIB
Fortaleza, Brazil	FOR	Gilgit, Pakistan	GIL
Fortuna, Costa Rica	FON	Gisborne, New Zealand	GIS
Franca, Brazil	FRC	Gizan, Saudi Arabia	GIZ
Franceville, Gabon	MVB	Gizo, Solomon Islands	GZO
Francisco Beltrao, Brazil	FBE	Gladstone, Australia	GLT
Francistown, Botswana	FRW	Glasgow (Prestwick),	
Frankfurt, Germany	FRA	Scotland, UK	PIK
Freeport, Bahamas	FPO	Glasgow, Scotland, UK	GLA
Freetown, Sierra Leone	FNA	Glen Innes, Australia	GLI
Freida River, Papua		Goa, India	GOI
New Guinea	FAQ	Goba, Ethiopia	GOB
Friedrichshafen, Germany	FDH	Gode/Iddidole, Ethiopia	GDE
Fuerteventura,Spain	FUE	Goiania, Brazil	GYN
Fukue, Japan	FUJ	Gold Coast, Australia	OOL
Fukuoka, Japan	FUK	Golfito, Costa Rica	GLF
Fukushima, Japan	FKS	Golmud, China	GOQ
Funafuti Atol, Tuvalu	FUN	Goma, Congo, Dem. Rep.	GOM
Funchal, Portugal	FNC	Gonalia, Papua New Guinea	GOE
Futuna Island, Vanuatu	FTA	Gondar, Ethiopia	GDQ
Futuna, Wallis & Futuna Is.	FUT	Gore, Ethiopia	GOR
Fuzhou, China	FOC	Goroka, Papua New Guinea	GKA
Gaborone, Botswana	GBE	Gorontalo, Indonesia	GTO
Gallivare, Sweden	GEV	Gothenburg, Sweden	GOT
Galway, Ireland	GWY	Goundam, Mali	GUD
Gamba, Gabon	GAX	Gove, Australia	GOV
Gambela, Ethiopia	GMB	Governador Valadares, Brazil	GVR
Gambier Is., Fr. Polynesia	GMR	Governors Harbour, Bahamas	GHB
Gan Island, Maldives	GAN	Gozo, Malta	GZM
Ganzhou, China	KOW	Graciosa Is., Portugal	GRW
Gao, Mali	GAQ	Grafton, Australia	GFN
Garachine, Panama	GHE	Gran Canaria, Spain	LPA

Granada, Spain	GRX	Hamilton, New Zealand	HLZ	
Grand Bahama Island, Bahamas	GBI	Hammerfest, Norway	HFT	
Grand Cayman, Cayman Islands	GCM	Hangzhou, China	HGH	
		Hanimaadhoo, Maldives	HAQ	
Grand Turk Is., Turks & Caicos	GDT	Hanoi, Viet Nam	HAN	
Graz, Austria	GRZ	Hanover, Germany	HAJ	
Great Harbour Cay, Bahamas	GHC	Hanzhong, China	HZG	
Great Keppel Is., Australia	GKL	Hao Is., Fr. Polynesia	HOI	
Grenada, Windward Islands	GND	Harare, Zimbabwe	HRE	
Grenoble, France	GNB	Harbin, China	HRB	
Griffith, Australia	GFF	Harbour Island, Bahamas	HBI	
Groennedal, Greenland	JGR	Hargeisa, Somalia	HGA	
Groningen, Netherlands	GRQ	Hassi Messaoud, Algeria	HME	
Groote Is., Australia	GTE	Hasvik, Norway	HAA	
Guadalajara, Mexico	GDL	Hat Yai, Thailand	HDY	
Guadeloupe, Leeward Islands	BBR	Hateruma, Japan	HTR	
Guanaja, Honduras	GJA	Haugesund, Norway	HAU	
Guanambi, Brazil	GNM	Havana, Cuba	HAV	
Guangzhou, China	CAN	Hay, Australia	HXX	
Guantanamo, Cuba	GAO	Hayman Is., Australia	HIS	
Guapi, Colombia	GPI	Hefei, China	HFE	
Guarapari, Brazil	GUZ	Heho, Myanmar	HEH	
Guatemala City, Guatemala	GUA	Heidelberg, Germany	HDB	
Guayaquil, Ecuador	GYE	Heihe, China	HEK	
Guayaramerin, Bolivia	GYA	Helgoland, Germany	HGL	
Guaymas, Mexico	GYM	Helsingborg, Sweden	AGH	
Guernsey, Channel Islands, UK	GCI	Helsinki, Finland	HEL	
		Hemavan, Sweden	HMV	
Guerrero Negro, Mexico	GUB	Heraklion, Greece	HER	
Guilin, China	KWL	Heringsdorf, Germany	HDF	
Guiyang, China	KWE	Hermosillo, Mexico	HMO	
Gunnedah, Australia	GUH	Hervey Bay, Australia	HVB	
Gurayat, Saudi Arabia	URY	Hiroshima, Japan	HIJ	
Gurupi, Brazil	GRP	Ho Chi Minh, Viet Nam	SGN	
Gwadar, Pakistan	GWD	Hobart, Australia	HBA	
Gwalior, India	GWL	Hodeidah, Yemen	HOD	
Gweru, Zimbabwe	GWE	Hoedspruit, South Africa	HDS	
Gyandzha, Azerbaijan	KVD	Hof, Germany	HOQ	
Gyourmi, Armenia	LWN	Hofuf, Saudi Arabia	HOF	
Ha'apai, Tonga	HPA	Hohhot, China	HET	
Hachijo Jima, Japan	HAC	Hokitika, New Zealand	HKK	
Hafr Al Batin, Saudi Arabia	HBT	Holguin, Cuba	HOG	
Hagfors, Sweden	HFS	Hong Kong, Hong Kong	HKG	
Hahn, Germany	HHN	Honiara, Solomon Islands	HIR	
Haifa, Israel	HFA	Honningsvag, Norway	HVG	
Haikou, China	HAK	Hooker Creek, Australia	HOK	
Hail, Saudi Arabia	HAS	Hornafjordur, Iceland	HFN	
Hailar, China	HLD	Horta, Portugal	HOR	
Haiphong, Viet Nam	HPH	Hoskins, Papua New Guinea	HKN	
Haiwaro, Papua New Guinea	HIT	Hotan, China	HTN	
Hakodate, Japan	HKD	Houeisay, Laos	HOE	
Halmstad, Sweden	HAD	Hua Hin, Thailand	HHQ	
Hamburg, Germany	HAM	Huahine Is., Fr. Polynesia	HUH	
Hamilton, Bermuda	BDA	Hualien, Taiwan	HUN	
Hamilton Is., Australia	HTI	Huambo, Angola	NOV	
		Huanghua, China	HHA	

International Airports

Huangyan, China	HYN	Iquitos, Peru	IQT
Huanuco, Peru	HUU	Irkutsk, Russia	IKT
Huatulco, Mexico	HUX	Isafjordur, Iceland	IFJ
Hudiksvall, Sweden	HUV	Isfahan, Iran	IFN
Hue, Viet Nam	HUI	Ishigaki, Japan	ISG
Huehuetenango, Guatemala	HUG	Isiro, Congo, Dem. Rep.	IRP
Hughenden, Australia	HGD	Islamabad, Pakistan	ISB
Hultsfred, Sweden	HLF	Islay, Scotland, UK	ILY
Humberside, England, UK	HUY	Isle of Man, UK	IOM
Humera, Ethiopia	HUE	Isle of Skye, Scotland, UK	SKL
Hurghada, Egypt	HRG	Isles of Scilly (St. Marys), UK	ISC
Husavik, Iceland	HZK	Isles of Scilly (Tresco), UK	TSO
Hwange Nat'l Park,		Istanbul, Turkey	IST
Zimbabwe	HWN	Itabuna, Brazil	ITN
Hyderabad, India	HYD	Itaituba, Brazil	ITB
Hyderabad, Pakistan	HDD	Ivalo, Finland	IVL
Iasi, Romania	IAS	Ivano-Frankovsk, Ukraine	IFO
Ibague, Colombia	IBE	Iwami, Japan	IWJ
Ibiza, Spain	IBZ	Ixtapa/Zihautenejo, Mexico	ZIH
Iboki, Papua New Guinea	IBI	Izmir (Adnan Mend), Turkey	ADB
Idre, Sweden	IDB	Izmir (Metro), Turkey	IZM
Iguassu Falls, Brazil	IGU	Izumo, Japan	IZO
Iguazu, Argentina	IGR	Jabot, Marshall Islands	JAT
Ihu, Papua New Guinea	IHU	Jacobabad, Pakistan	JAG
Ikaria Island, Greece	JIK	Jacquinot Bay, Papua	
Iki, Japan	IKI	New Guinea	JAQ
Ile Des Pins, New Caledonia	ILP	Jagdalpur, India	JGB
Ilheus, Brazil	IOS	Jaipur, India	JAI
Illizi, Algeria	VVZ	Jakarta (Halim), Indonesia	HLP
Ilo, Peru	ILQ	Jakarta (Metro), Indonesia	JKT
Iloilo, Philippines	ILO	Jakarta (Soekarno),	
Ilulissat, Greenland	JAV	Indonesia	CGK
Imperatriz, Brazil	IMP	Jaluit Is., Marshall Islands	UIT
Impfondol, Congo	ION	Jambi, Indonesia	DJB
Imphal, India	IMF	Jammu, India	IXJ
In Amenas, Algeria	IAM	Jamnagar, India	JGA
In Salah, Algeria	INZ	Janakpur, Nepal	JKR
Inagua, Bahamas	IGA	Jaque, Panama	JQE
Inchon, Korea	ICN	Jayapura, Indonesia	DJJ
Indaselassie, Ethiopia	SHC	Jeddah, Saudi Arabia	JED
Indore, India	IDR	Jeh, Marshall Islands	JEJ
Ine, Marshall Islands	IMI	Jerez de la Frontera, Spain	XRY
Inisheer, Ireland	INQ	Jersey, Channel Islands, UK	JER
Inishmaan, Ireland	IIA	Jerusalem, Israel	JRS
Inishmore, Ireland	IOR	Jessore, Bangladesh	JSR
Innsbruck, Austria	INN	Ji-Parana, Brazil	JPR
Invercargill, New Zealand	IVC	Jiamusi, China	JMU
Inverell, Australia	IVR	Jijel, Algeria	GJL
Inverness, Scotland, UK	INV	Jilin, China	JIL
Ioannina, Greece	IOA	Jimma, Ethiopia	JIM
Iokea, Papua New Guinea	IOK	Jinan, China	TNA
Ipatinga, Brazil	IPN	Jingdezhen, China	JDZ
Ipiales, Colombia	IPI	Jinghong, China	JHG
Ipoh, Malaysia	IPH	Jinka, Ethiopa	BCO
Ipota, Vanuatu	IPA	Jinzhou, China	JNZ
Iquique, Chile	IQQ	Jiujiang, China	JIU

Jiwani, Pakistan	JIW	Kansai (Osaka/Kyoto), Japan	KIX
Joacaba, Brazil	JCB	Kaohsiung, Taiwan	KHH
Joao Pessoa, Brazil	JPA	Kapit, Malaysia	KPI
Jodhpur, India	JDH	Karachi, Pakistan	KHI
Joensuu, Finland	JOE	Karaganda, Kazakstan	KGF
Johannesburg, South Africa	JNB	Karamay, China	KRY
Johnston Island,		Kariba, Zimbabwe	KAB
Pacific Ocean	JON	Karlstad, Sweden	KSD
Johor Bahru, Malaysia	JHB	Karpathos, Greece	AOK
Joinville, Brazil	JOI	Karratha, Australia	KTA
Jomsom, Nepal	JMO	Kars, Turkey	KSY
Jonkoping, Sweden	JKG	Karshi, Uzbekistan	KSQ
Jorhat, India	JRH	Karumba, Australia	KRB
Jos, Nigeria	JOS	Karup, Denmark	KRP
Jouf, Saudi Arabia	AJF	Kasane, Botswana	BBK
Juanjui, Peru	JJI	Kashi, China	KHG
Juazeiro Do Norte, Brazil	JDO	Kasos Island, Greece	KSJ
Juiz De Fora, Brazil	JDF	Kastelorizo, Greece	KZS
Jujuy, Argentina	JUJ	Kastoria, Greece	KSO
Julia Creek, Australia	JCK	Katherine, Australia	KTR
Juliaca, Peru	JUL	Kathmandu, Nepal	KTM
Jumla, Nepal	JUM	Katowice, Poland	KTW
Juzhou, China	JUZ	Kaukura Atoll, Fr. Polynesia	KKR
Jyvaskyla, Finland	JYV	Kaunas, Lithuania	KUN
Kaadedhdhoo, Maldives	KDM	Kavala, Greece	KVA
Kaben, Marshall Islands	KBT	Kavieng, Papua New Guinea	KVG
Kabri Dar, Ethiopia	ABK	Kawthaung, Myanmar	KAW
Kabul, Afghanistan	KBL	Kayes, Mali	KYS
Kadhdhoo, Maldives	KDO	Kayseri, Turkey	ASR
Kaduna, Nigeria	KAD	Kazan, Russia	KZN
Kagau, Solomon Islands	KGE	Keetmanshoop, Namibia	KMP
Kagi, Papua New Guinea	KGW	Kefallinia, Greece	EFL
Kagoshima, Japan	KOJ	Kemerovo, Russia	KEJ
Kahramanmaras, Turkey	KCM	Kemi/Tornio, Finland	KEM
Kaiserslauter, Germany	KLT	Kempsey, Australia	KPS
Kaitaia, New Zealand	KAT	Kendari, Indonesia	KDI
Kajaani, Finland	KAJ	Kengtung, Myanmar	KET
Kalamata, Greece	KLX	Kenieba, Mali	KNZ
Kalbarri, Australia	KAX	Kerama, Japan	KJP
Kalemie, Congo, Dem. Rep.	FMI	Kerema, Papua New Guinea	KMA
Kalemyo, Myanmar	KMV	Kerikeri, New Zealand	KKE
Kalgoorlie, Australia	KGI	Kerkyra, Greece	CFU
Kalibo, Philippines	KLO	Kerman, Iran	KER
Kaliningrad, Russia	KGD	Kermanshah, Iran	KSH
Kalkurung, Australia	KFG	Kerry County, Ireland	KIR
Kalmar, Sweden	KLR	Kerteh, Malaysia	KTE
Kameshli, Syria	KAC	Keshad, India	IXK
Kamusi, Papua New Guinea	KUY	Khabarovsk, Russia	KHV
Kananga, Congo, Dem. Rep.	KGA	Khajuraho, India	HJR
Kandavu, Fiji	KDV	Khamti, Myanmar	KHM
Kandla, India	IXY	Kharkov, Ukraine	HRK
Kandrian, Papua		Khartoum, Sudan	KRT
New Guinea	KDR	Khasab, Oman	KHS
Kangerlussuaq, Greenland	SFJ	Khon Kaen, Thailand	KKC
Kangnung, Korea	KAG	Khuzdar, Pakistan	KDD
Kano, Nigeria	KAN	Kiel, Germany	KEL

Kiev (Borispol), Ukraine	KBP	Koumac, New Caledonia	KOC
Kiev (Metro), Ukraine	IEV	Kowanyama, Australia	KWM
Kiffa, Mauritania	KFA	Kozani, Greece	KZI
Kigali, Rwanda	KGL	Krakow, Poland	KRK
Kigoma, Tanzania	TKQ	Kramfors, Sweden	KRF
Kikaiga Shima, Japan	KKX	Krasnodar, Russia	KRR
Kikori, Papua New Guinea	KRI	Krasnowodsk, Turkmenistan	KRW
Kili Is., Marshall Islands	KIO	Krasnoyarsk, Russia	KJA
Kilimanjaro, Tanzania	JRO	Kristiansand, Norway	KRS
Kimberley, South Africa	KIM	Kristianstad, Sweden	KID
Kindu, Congo, Dem. Rep.	KND	Kristiansund, Norway	KSU
King Is., Australia	KNS	Kuala Lumpur, Malaysia	KUL
Kingscote, Australia	KGC	Kuala Terengganu, Malaysia	TGG
Kingston, Jamaica	KIN	Kuantan, Malaysia	KUA
Kingston (Tinson), Jamaica	KTP	Kuching, Malaysia	KCH
Kinmen, Taiwan	KNH	Kudat, Malaysia	KUD
Kinshasa, Congo, Dem. Rep.	FIH	Kuito, Angola	SVP
Kirakira, Solomon Islands	IRA	Kulu, India	KUU
Kirkenes, Norway	KKN	Kulusuk Is., Greenland	KUS
Kirkwall, Scotland, UK	KOI	Kumamoto, Japan	KMJ
Kirovograd, Ukraine	KGO	Kumejima, Japan	UEO
Kiruna, Sweden	KRN	Kundiawa, Papua	
Kisangani, Congo, Dem. Rep.	FKI	New Guinea	CMU
Kishinev, Moldova	KIV	Kunming, China	KMG
Kisumu, Kenya	KIS	Kunsan, Korea	KUV
Kita Kyushu, Japan	KKJ	Kununurra, Australia	KNX
Kitadaito, Japan	KTD	Kuopio, Finland	KUO
Kitava, Papua New Guinea	KVE	Kupang, Indonesia	KOE
Kithira, Greece	KIT	Kuqa, China	KCA
Kittila, Finland	KTT	Kuri, Papua New Guinea	KUQ
Kiunga, Papua New Guinea	UNG	Kuria, Kiribati	KUC
Kiwayu, Kenya	KWY	Kushiro, Japan	KUH
Klagenfurt, Austria	KLU	Kuusamo, Finland	KAO
Kleinzee, South Africa	KLZ	Kuwait, Kuwait	KWI
Knock, Ireland	NOC	Kwajalein, Marshall Islands	KWA
Kochi, Japan	KCZ	Kwangju, Korea	KWJ
Koh Kong, Cambodia	KKZ	Kyaukpyu, Myanmar	KYP
Koh Samui, Thailand	USM	Kyzl Orda, Kazakstan	KZO
Kokkola/Pietarsaari, Finland	KOK	La Ceiba, Honduras	LCE
Kokoda, Papua New Guinea	KKD	La Coruna, Spain	LCG
Kokshetau, Kazakstan	KOV	La Desirade, Guadeloupe	DSD
Komatsu, Japan	KMQ	La Palma, Panama	PLP
Kone, New Caledonia	KNQ	La Paz, Bolivia	LPB
Konya, Turkey	KYA	La Paz, Mexico	LAP
Korhogo, Cote D'Ivoire	HGO	La Rioja, Argentina	IRJ
Korla, China	KRL	La Rochelle, France	LRH
Koro, Fiji	KXF	La Serena, Chile	LSC
Koror, Palau	ROR	Laayoune, Morocco	EUN
Kos, Greece	KGS	Labasa, Fiji	LBS
Kosice, Slovakia	KSC	Labuan, Malaysia	LBU
Kosrae, Micronesia	KSA	Lae Is., Marshall Islands	LML
Kostanay, Kazakstan	KSN	Lae, Papua New Guinea	LAE
Koszalin, Poland	OSZ	Lages, Brazil	LAJ
Kota Bharu, Malaysia	KBR	Lago Agrio, Ecuador	LGQ
Kota Kinabalu, Malaysia	BKI	Lagos, NIgeria	LOS
Koulamoutou, Gabon	KOU	Lahad Datu, Malaysia	LDU

Lahore, Pakistan	LHE	Lidkoping, Sweden	LDK
Lake Evella, Australia	LEL	Lifou, New Caledonia	LIF
Lakeba, Fiji	LKB	Lightning Ridge, Australia	LHG
Lakselv, Norway	LKL	Lihir Island, Papua	
Lalibela, Ethiopia	LLI	New Guinea	LNG
Lamap, Vanuatu	LPM	Lijiang City, China	LJG
Lambarene, Gabon	LBQ	Likiep Is., Marshall Islands	LIK
Lamen Bay, Vanuatu	LNB	Lilabari, India	IXI
Lamezia/Terme, Italy	SUF	Lille, France	LIL
Lamidanda, Nepal	LDN	Lilongwe, Malawi	LLW
Lampang, Thailand	LPT	Lima, Peru	LIM
Lampedusa, Italy	LMP	Limbang, Malaysia	LMN
Lamu, Kenya	LAU	Limoges, France	LIG
Lands End, England, UK	LEQ	Lindeman Is., Australia	LDC
Langkawi, Malaysia	LGK	Lindi, Tanzania	LDI
Lannion, France	LAI	Linkoping, Sweden	LPI
Lanzarote, Spain	ACE	Linz, Austria	LNZ
Lanzhou, China	LHW	Lisala, Congo, Dem. Rep.	LIQ
Laoag, Philippines	LAO	Lisbon, Portugal	LIS
Lappeenranta, Finland	LPP	Lismore, Australia	LSY
Larnaca, Cyprus	LCA	Liuzhou, China	LZH
Las Palmas, Canary Islands	LPA	Liverpool, England, UK	LPL
Las Piedras, Venezuela	LSP	Livingstone, Zambia	LVI
Las Tunas, Cuba	VTU	Livramento, Brazil	LVB
Lashio, Myanmar	LSH	Lizard Is., Australia	LZR
Lastourville, Gabon	LTL	Ljubljana, Slovenia	LJU
Latakia, Syria	LTK	Lockhart River, Australia	IRG
Laucala Island, Fiji	LUC	Lodja, Congo, Dem. Rep.	LJA
Launceston, Australia	LST	Loen, Marshall Islands	LOF
Laverton, Australia	LVO	Loikaw, Myanmar	LIW
Lawas, Malaysia	LWY	Lome, Togo	LFW
Lazaro Cardenas, Mexico	LZC	Loncopue, Argentina	LCP
Le Havre, France	LEH	London (City), England, UK	LCY
Le Puy, France	LPY	London (Gatwick),	
Le Touquet, France	LTQ	England, UK	LGW
Learmonth, Australia	LEA	London (Heathrow),	
Leeds, England, UK	LBA	England, UK	LHR
Legaspi, Philippines	LGP	London (Luton),	
Leguizamo, Colombia	LGZ	England, UK	LTN
Leh, India	IXL	London (Metro),	
Leigh Creek, Australia	LGH	England, UK	LON
Leinster, Australia	LER	London (Stansted),	
Leipzig, Germany	LEJ	England, UK	STN
Leknes, Norway	LKN	Londonderry, N. Ireland, UK	LDY
Lemnos, Greece	LXS	Londrina, Brazil	LDB
Leon, Mexico	LEN	Long Banga, Malaysia	LBP
Leon/Guanajuato, Mexico	BJX	Long Is., Australia	HAP
Leonora, Australia	LNO	Long Island, Bahamas	LGI
Leros, Greece	LRS	Long Lellang, Malaysia	LGL
Lese, Papua New Guinea	LNG	Long Pasia, Malaysia	GSA
Leticia, Colombia	LET	Long Semado, Malaysia	LSM
Lhasa, China	LXA	Long Seridan, Malaysia	ODN
Lianyungang, China	LYG	Long Sukang, Malaysia	LSU
Liberia, Costa Rica	LIR	Longana, Vanuatu	LOD
Libreville, Gabon	LBV	Longreach, Australia	LRE
Lichinga, Mozambique	VXC	Longyearbyen, Norway	LYR

40

*The Travel Agent's
Complete Desk
Reference*

Lonorore, Vanuatu	LNE	Majkin, Marshall Islands	MJE
Lord Howe Is., Australia	LDH	Majunga, Madagascar	MJN
Loreto, Mexico	LTO	Majuro, Marshall Islands	MAJ
Lorient, France	LRT	Makale, Ethiopia	MQX
Los Angeles, Chile	LSQ	Makemo, Fr. Polynesia	MKP
Los Cabos, Mexico	SJD	Makhachkala, Russia	MCX
Los Mochis, Mexico	LMM	Makin Is., Kiribati	MTK
Losuia, Papua New Guinea	LSA	Makokou, Gabon	MKU
Loubomo, Congo	DIS	Makung, Taiwan	MZG
Lourdes/Tarbes, France	LDE	Makurdi, Nigeria	MDI
Luanda, Angola	LAD	Malabo, Equatorial Guinea	SSG
Luang Namtha, Laos	LXG	Malacca, Malaysia	MKZ
Luang Prabang, Laos	LPQ	Malaga, Spain	AGP
Lubang, Philippines	LBX	Malalaua, Papua	
Lubango, Angola	SDD	New Guinea	MLQ
Lubumbashi, Congo,		Malang, Indonesia	MLG
Dem. Rep.	FBM	Malange, Angola	MEG
Lucknow, India	LKO	Malargue, Argentina	LGS
Luderitz, Namibia	LUD	Malatya, Turkey	MLX
Luena, Angola	LUO	Male, Maldives	MLE
Lugano, Switzerland	LUG	Malekolon, Papua	
Lukla, Nepal	LUA	New Guinea	MKN
Lulea, Sweden	LLA	Malindi, Kenya	MYD
Luoyang, China	LYA	Malmo (Metro), Sweden	MMA
Lusaka, Zambia	LUN	Malmo (Sturup), Sweden	MMX
Luxembourg, Luxembourg	LUX	Maloelap Is., Marshall	
Luxi, China	LUM	Islands	MAV
Luxor, Egypt	LXR	Malololailai, Fiji	PTF
Luzhou, China	LZO	Maloy Harbor, Norway	QFQ
Lvov, Ukraine	LWO	Malta, Malta	MLA
Lycksele, Sweden	LYC	Man, Cote D'Ivoire	MJC
Lyon, France	LYS	Mana, Fiji	MNF
M'banza Congo, Angola	SSY	Manado, Indonesia	MDC
Maastricht, Netherlands	MST	Managua, Nicaragua	MGA
MacArthur River, Australia	MCV	Manakara, Madagascar	WVK
Macau, Macau	MFM	Mananara, Madagascar	WMR
Maceio, Brazil	MCZ	Manang, Nepal	NGX
Mackay, Australia	MKY	Mananjary, Madagascar	MNJ
Madang, Papua New Guinea	MAG	Manari, Papua New Guinea	MRM
Madinah, Saudi Arabia	MED	Manaus, Brazil	MAO
Madras, India	MAA	Manchester, England, UK	MAN
Madrid, Spain	MAD	Mandalay, Myanmar	MDL
Madurai, India	IXM	Mandritsara, Madagascar	WMA
Mae Hong Son, Thailand	HGN	Mangaia, Cook Islands	MGS
Mae Sot, Thailand	MAQ	Mangalore, India	IXE
Maewo, Vanuatu	MWF	Mangrove Cay, Bahamas	MAY
Magadan, Russia	GDX	Manguna, Papua	
Magdalena, Bolivia	MGD	New Guinea	MFO
Magnitogorsk, Russia	MQF	Manihi, Fr. Polynesia	XMH
Mahe Is., Seychelles	SEZ	Manihiki Is., Cook Islands	MHX
Mahendranagar, Nepal	XMG	Manila, Philippines	MNL
Maiana, Kiribati	MNK	Maningrida, Australia	MNG
Maiduguri, Nigeria	MIU	Manizales, Colombia	MZL
Maintirano, Madagascar	MXT	Manja, Madagascar	MJA
Maio, Cape Verde Islands	MMO	Mannheim, Germany	MHG
Maitland, Australia	MTL	Manston, England, UK	MSE

Manus Is., Papua New Guinea	MAS	
Manzanillo, Cuba	MZO	
Manzanillo, Mexico	ZLO	
Manzini, Swaziland	MTS	
Maota, Savai'i Is., Western Samoa	MXS	
Mapua, Papua New Guinea	MPU	
Maputo, Mozambique	MPM	
Mar Del Plata, Argentina	MDQ	
Mara Lodges, Kenya	MRE	
Maraba, Brazil	MAB	
Maracaibo, Venezuela	MAR	
Marakei, Kiribati	MZK	
Marau Sound, Solomon Islands	RUS	
Mare, New Caledonia	MEE	
Margate, South Africa	MGH	
Marie Galante, Fr. Antilles	GBJ	
Mariehamn, Finland	MHQ	
Marilia, Brazil	MII	
Maringa, Brazil	MGF	
Mariupol, Ukraine	MPW	
Maroantsetra, Madagascar	WMN	
Maroua, Cameroon	MVR	
Marrakech, Morocco	RAK	
Marseille, France	MRS	
Marsh Harbour, Bahamas	MHH	
Marudi, Malaysia	MUR	
Maryborough, Australia	MBH	
Mascara, Algeria	MUW	
Maseru, Lesotho	MSU	
Mashad, Iran	MHD	
Masirah, Oman	MSH	
Mastic Point, Bahamas	MSK	
Masvingo, Zimbabwe	MVZ	
Matadi, Congo, Dem. Rep.	MAT	
Mataiva, Fr. Polynesia	MVT	
Matamoros, Mexico	MAM	
Mataram, Indonesia	AMI	
Matsumoto, Japan	MMJ	
Matsuyama, Japan	MYJ	
Maturin, Venezuela	MUN	
Mauke Is., Cook Islands	MUK	
Maulmyine, Myanmar	MNU	
Maumere, Indonesia	MOF	
Maun, Botswana	MUB	
Maupiti, Fr. Polynesia	MAU	
Mauritius, Mauritius	MRU	
Mayaguana, Bahamas	MYG	
Mazatlan, Mexico	MZT	
Mbambanakira, Solomon Islands	MBU	
Mbandaka, Congo, Dem. Rep.	MDK	
Mbuji-Mayi, Congo, Dem. Rep.	MJM	
Medan, Indonesia	MES	

Medellin (Cordova), Colombia	MDE
Medellin (Herrera), Colombia	EOH
Meekatharra, Australia	MKR
Mehamn, Norway	MEH
Meixian, China	MXZ
Mejit Is., Marshall Islands	MJB
Mekane Selam, Ethiopia	MKS
Melbourne (Essendon), Australia	MEB
Melbourne (Tullamarine), Australia	MEL
Melilla, Spain	MLN
Memanbetsu, Japan	MMB
Mendi, Ethiopia	NDM
Mendi, Papua New Guinea	MDU
Mendoza, Argentina	MDZ
Menongue, Angola	SPP
Menorca, Spain	MAH
Merauke, Indonesia	MKQ
Merida, Mexico	MID
Merida, Venezuela	MRD
Merimbula, Australia	MIM
Mesalia, Papua New Guinea	MFZ
Metz, France	MZM
Metz/Nancy, France	ETZ
Mexicali, Mexico	MXL
Mexico City, Mexico	MEX
Mfuwe, Zambia	MFU
Miandrivazo, Madagascar	ZVA
Mianwali, Pakistan	MWD
Middle Caicos, Turks & Caicos	MDS
Mikkeli, Finland	MIK
Mikonos, Greece	JMK
Milan (Linate), Italy	LIN
Milan (Malpensa), Italy	MXP
Milan (Metro), Italy	MIL
Milan (Orio Al Serio), Italy	BGY
Mildura, Australia	MQL
Milford Sound, New Zealand	MFN
Mili Is., Marshall Islands	MIJ
Millingimbi, Australia	MGT
Milos, Greece	MLO
Minacu, Brazil	MQH
Minami Daito, Japan	MMD
Minatitlan, Mexico	MTT
Mineralnye Vody, Russia	MRV
Minsk, Belarus	MSQ
Miri, Malaysia	MYY
Mirpur Khas, Pakistan	MPD
Misawa, Japan	MSJ
Misima Is., Papua New Guinea	MIS
Mitiaro, Cook Islands	MOI
Mitzic, Gabon	MZC
Miyake Jima, Japan	MYE

International Airports

Miyako Jima, Japan	MMY	Mosjoen, Norway	MJF
Miyazaki, Japan	KMI	Mostar, Bosnia	OMO
Mizan Teferi, Ethiopia	MTF	Mosteiros, Cape Verde	
Mmabatho, South Africa	MBD	Islands	MTI
Mo I Rana, Norway	MQN	Mota Lava, Vanuatu	MTV
Moa, Cuba	MOA	Motueka, New Zealand	MZP
Moala, Fiji	MFJ	Mouila, Gabon	MJL
Moanda, Congo, Dem. Rep.	MNB	Mount Cook (Glentanner),	
Moanda, Gabon	MFF	New Zealand	GTN
Mogadishu, Somalia	MGQ	Mount Cook, New Zealand	MON
Mohenjo Daro, Pakistan	MJD	Mount Gambier, Australia	MGB
Mokuti Lodge, Namibia	OKU	Mount Hagen, Papua	
Molde, Norway	MOL	New Guinea	HGU
Mombasa, Kenya	MBA	Mount. Isa, Australia	ISA
Monastir, Tunisia	MIR	Mount Keith, Australia	WME
Monbetsu, Japan	MBE	Mount Magnet, Australia	MMG
Monclova, Mexico	LOV	Mount Pleasant, Falkland Is.	MPN
Mong Hsat, Myanmar	MOG	Moyobamba, Peru	MBP
Monkey Mia, Australia	MJK	Mpacha, Namibia	MPA
Mono Is., Solomon Islands	MNY	Mtwara, Tanzania	MYW
Monrovia (Roberts Intl),		Mucuri, Brazil	MVS
Liberia	ROB	Mudanjiang, China	MDG
Monrovia (Sprigg Payne),		Mudgee, Australia	DGE
Liberia	MLW	Muenster, Germany	FMO
Monte Carlo (H/P), Monaco	MCM	Mukah, Malaysia	MKM
Monte Dourado, Brazil	MEU	Mulhouse, France	BSL
Montego Bay, Jamaica	MBJ	Mulhouse, France/Basel,	
Monteria, Colombia	MTR	Switzerland	MLH
Monterrey, Mexico	MTY	Multan, Pakistan	MUX
Montes Claros, Brazil	MOC	Mulu, Malaysia	MZV
Montevideo, Uruguay	MVD	Munda, Solomon Islands	MUA
Montlucon, France	MCU	Mundulkiri, Cambodia	MWV
Montpellier, France	MPL	Munich, Germany	MUC
Montserrat, Montserrat	MNI	Murcia, Spain	MJV
Moorabbin, Australia	MBW	Murmansk, Russia	MMK
Moorea, Fr. Polynesia	MOZ	Mus, Turkey	MSR
Mopti, Mali	MZI	Muscat, Oman	MCT
Mora, Sweden	MXX	Musoma, Tanzania	MUZ
Morafenobe, Madagascar	TVA	Mussau, Papua New Guinea	MWU
Moree, Australia	MRZ	Muzaffarabad, Pakistan	MFG
Morelia, Mexico	MLM	Mwanza, Tanzania	MWZ
Morioka, Japan	HNA	Myeik, Myanmar	MGZ
Mornington, Australia	ONG	Myitkyina, Myanmar	MYT
Moro, Papua New Guinea	MXH	Mysore, India	MYQ
Morombe, Madagascar	MXM	Mytilene, Greece	MJT
Morondava, Madagascar	MOQ	Mzuzu, Malawi	ZZU
Moroni, Comoros	YVA	N'Zeto, Angola	ARZ
Moroni (Hahaya), Comoros	HAH	Naberevnye Chelny, Russia	NBC
Moruya, Australia	MYA	Nadi, Fiji	NAN
Moscow (Bykovo), Russia	BKA	Nadym, Russia	NYM
Moscow (Domodedovo),		Naga, Philippines	WNP
Russia	DME	Nagasaki, Japan	NGS
Moscow (Metro), Russia	MOW	Nagoya, Japan	NGO
Moscow (Sheremetyevo),		Nagpur, India	NAG
Russia	SVO	Nairobi (Metro), Kenya	NBO
Moscow (Vnukovo), Russia	VKO	Nairobi (Wilson), Kenya	WIL

Nakashibetsu, Japan	SHB	Nepalganj, Nepal	KEP
Nakhon Phanom, Thailand	KOP	Neryungri, Russia	NER
Nakhon Ratchasima, Thailand	NAK	Neuquen, Argentina	NQN
		Nevis, Leeward Islands	NEV
Nakhon Si Thammarat, Thailand	NST	New Plymouth, New Zealand	NPL
		New Valley, Egypt	UVL
Namangan, Uzbekistan	NMA	Newcastle, Australia	NTL
Namatanai, Papua New Guinea	ATN	Newcastle (Belmont), Australia	BEO
Namdrik Is., Marshall Islands	NDK	Newcastle, England, UK	NCL
		Newman, Australia	ZNE
Namibe, Angola	MSZ	Newquay, England, UK	NQY
Nampula, Mozambique	APL	Ngaoundere, Cameroon	NGE
Namsos, Norway	OSY	Ngau Is., Fiji	NGI
Nan, Thailand	NNT	Ngukurr, Australia	RPM
Nanchang, China	KHN	Nha-Trang, Viet Nam	NHA
Nanchong, China	NAO	Niamey, Niger	NIM
Nanjing, China	NKG	Niamtougou, Togo	LRL
Nanning, China	NNG	Nice, France	NCE
Nanortalik, Greenland	JNN	Nicosia, Cyprus	NIC
Nantes, France	NTE	Niigata, Japan	KIJ
Nantong, China	NTG	Nikolaev, Ukraine	NLV
Nanyang, China	NNY	Nikunau, Kiribati	NIG
Nanyuki, Kenya	NYK	Nimes, France	FNI
Napier, New Zealand	NPE	Ningbo, China	NGB
Naples, Italy	NAP	Nioro, Mali	NIX
Narathiwat, Thailand	NAW	Niquelandia, Brazil	NQL
Nare, Colombia	NAR	Nissan Is., Papua New Guinea	IIS
Narrabri, Australia	NAA		
Narrandera, Australia	NRA	Niuafo'ou, Tonga	NFO
Narsaq, Greenland	JNS	Niuatoputapu, Tonga	NTT
Narsarsuaq, Greenland	UAK	Niue Island, Niue	IUE
Narvik, Norway	NVK	Nizhnevartovsk, Russia	NJC
Nassau, Bahamas	NAS	Nizhniy Novgorod, Russia	GOJ
Nassau (Paradise Is.), Bahamas	PID	Nkayi, Congo	NKY
		Nojabrxsk, Russia	NOJ
Nassau (SPB), Bahamas	WZY	Nonouti, Kiribati	NON
Natal, Brazil	NAT	Nordholz-Spieka, Germany	NDZ
Nauru Is., Rep. of Nauru	INU	Norfolk Is., Pacific Ocean	NLK
Navegantes, Brazil	NVT	Norilsk, Russia	NSK
Nawabshah, Pakistan	WNS	Normanton, Australia	NTN
Naxos, Greece	JNX	Norrkoping, Sweden	NRK
Ndjamena, Chad	NDJ	Norsup, Vanuatu	NUS
Ndola, Zambia	NLA	North Caicos, Turks & Caicos	NCA
Necocli, Colombia	NCI	North Eleuthera, Bahamas	ELH
Neerlerit Inaat, Greenland	CNP	Norwich, England, UK	NWI
Neftekamsk, Russia	NEF	Nosara Beach, Costa Rica	NOB
Nefteyugansk, Russia	NFG	Nossi-be, Madagascar	NOS
Neghelli, Ethiopia	EGL	Nouadhibou, Mauritania	NDB
Negril, Jamaica	NEG	Nouakchott, Mauritania	NKC
Neiva, Colombia	NVA	Noumea (Magenta), New Caledonia	GEA
Nejjo, Ethiopia	NEJ		
Nejran, Saudi Arabia	EAM	Noumea, New Caledonia	NOU
Nelson, New Zealand	NSN	Novosibirsk, Russia	OVB
Nelspruit, South Africa	NLP	Novyj Urengoj, Russia	NUX
Nema, Mauritania	EMN	Nueva Gerona, Cuba	GER

International Airports

Nueva Guinea, Nicaragua	NVG	Oslo (Gardermoen), Norway	GEN
Nuevo Laredo, Mexico	NLD	Oslo (Metro), Norway	OSL
Nuku Hiva, Fr. Polynesia	NHV	Osorno, Chile	ZOS
Nukus, Uzbekistan	NCU	Ostersund, Sweden	OSD
Numbulwar, Australia	NUB	Ostrava, Czech Rep.	OSR
Nuqui, Colombia	NQU	Otu, Colombia	OTU
Nuremberg, Germany	NUE	Ouagadougou, Burkina Faso	OUA
Nuuk, Greenland	GOH	Ouargla, Algeria	OGX
Nyaung-u, Myanmar	NYU	Ouarzazate, Morocco	OZZ
Nyngan, Australia	NYN	Oudomxay, Laos	ODY
Oaxaca, Mexico	OAX	Ouesso, Congo	OUE
Obihiro, Japan	OBO	Oujda, Morocco	OUD
Ocana, Colombia	OCV	Oulu, Finland	OUL
Ocho Rios, Jamaica	OCJ	Ouvea, New Caledonia	UVE
Odense, Denmark	ODE	Ovda, Israel	VDA
Odessa, Ukraine	ODS	Owando, Congo	FTX
Ohrid, Macedonia	OHD	Oyem, Gabon	OYE
Oita, Japan	OIT	Paama, Vanuatu	PBJ
Okayama, Japan	OKJ	Paamiut, Greenland	JFR
Oki Island, Japan	OKI	Pacific Harbour, Fiji	PHR
Okinawa, Japan	OKA	Padang, Indonesia	PDG
Okino Erabu, Japan	OKE	Paderborn, Germany	PAD
Okondja, Gabon	OKN	Pakse, Laos	PKZ
Okushiri, Japan	OIR	Palacios, Honduras	PCH
Olbia, Italy	OLB	Palanga, Lithuania	PLQ
Olpoi, Vanuatu	OLJ	Palangkaraya, Indonesia	PKY
Olympic Dam, Australia	OLP	Palembang, Indonesia	PLM
Omboue, Gabon	OMB	Palenque, Mexico	PQM
Omsk, Russia	OMS	Palermo, Italy	PMO
Ondangwa, Namibia	OND	Palma Mallorca, Spain	PMI
Ongava Game Reserve,		Palmar, Costa Rica	PMZ
Namibia	OGV	Palmas, Brazil	PMW
Onotoa, Kiribati	OOT	Palmerston N., New Zealand	PMR
Ontong Java, Solomon		Palu, Indonesia	PLW
Islands	OTV	Pamplona, Spain	PNA
Open Bay, Papua		Panama City (Paitilla),	
New Guinea	OPB	Panama	PAC
Oradea, Romania	OMR	Panama City (Tocumen	
Oran, Algeria	ORN	Intl), Panama	PTY
Orange, Australia	OAG	Pangkalpinang, Indonesia	PGK
Orange (Cudal), Australia	CUG	Panjgur, Pakistan	PJG
Oranjemund, Namibia	OMD	Pantelleria, Italy	PNL
Orebro, Sweden	ORB	Papeete, Fr. Polynesia	PPT
Orenburg, Russia	REN	Paphos, Cyprus	PFO
Ormara, Pakistan	ORW	Para Chinar, Pakistan	PAJ
Ornskoldsvik, Sweden	OER	Paraburdoo, Australia	PBO
Orsk, Russia	OSW	Paramaribo, Suriname	PBM
Orsta-Volda, Norway	HOV	Paramaribo (Zorg En Hoop),	
Osaka (Itami), Japan	ITM	Suriname	ORG
Osaka (Kansai), Japan	KIX	Paraparaumu, New Zealand	PPQ
Osaka (Metro), Japan	OSA	Parasi, Solomon Islands	PRS
Osh, Kyrgyzstan	OSS	Paris (De Gaulle), France	CDG
Oshima, Japan	OIM	Paris (Metro), France	PAR
Osijek, Croatia	OSI	Paris (Orly), France	ORY
Oskarshamn, Sweden	OSK	Parkes, Australia	PKE
Oslo (Fornebu), Norway	FBU	Parma, Italy	PMF

Parnaiba, Brazil	PHB	Plymouth, England, UK	PLH
Paro, Bhutan	PBH	Podgorica, Yugoslavia	TGD
Paros, Greece	PAS	Pohang, Korea	KPO
Pasni, Pakistan	PSI	Pohnpei, Micronesia	PNI
Passo Fundo, Brazil	PFB	Pointe A Pitre, Guadeloupe	PTP
Pasto, Colombia	PSO	Pointe Noire, Congo	PNR
Patna, India	PAT	Poitiers, France	PIS
Patos De Minas, Brazil	POJ	Pokhara, Nepal	PKR
Patras, Greece	GPA	Ponta Delgada, Portugal	PDL
Patreksfjordur, Iceland	PFJ	Ponta Grossa, Brazil	PGZ
Pau, France	PUF	Ponta Pora, Brazil	PMG
Paulo Afonso, Brazil	PAV	Pontianak, Indonesia	PNK
Pavlodar, Kazakstan	PWQ	Poona, India	PNQ
Pedro Juan Caballero,		Popayan, Colombia	PPN
Paraguay	PJC	Popondetta, Papua	
Pekanbaru, Indonesia	PKU	New Guinea	PNP
Pelly Bay, NT	YUF	Porbandar, India	PBD
Pelotas, Brazil	PET	Porgera, Papua New Guinea	RGE
Pemba, Mozambique	POL	Pori, Finland	POR
Pemba, Tanzania	PMA	Porlamar, Venezuela	PMV
Penang, Malaysia	PEN	Port Antonio, Jamaica	POT
Penneshaw, Australia	PEA	Port Au Prince, Haiti	PAP
Penrhyn Is., Cook Islands	PYE	Port Augusta, Australia	PUG
Penzance, England, UK	PZE	Port Blair, India	IXZ
Pereira, Colombia	PEI	Port Elizabeth, South Africa	PLZ
Perigueux, France	PGX	Port Elizabeth, Windward	
Perm, Russia	PEE	Islands	BQU
Perpignan, France	PGF	Port Gentil, Gabon	POG
Perth, Australia	PER	Port Harcourt, Nigeria	PHC
Perugia, Italy	PEG	Port Hedland, Australia	PHE
Pescara, Italy	PSR	Port Lincoln, Australia	PLO
Peshawar, Pakistan	PEW	Port Macquarie, Australia	PQQ
Petrolina, Brazil	PNZ	Port Moresby, Papua	
Petropavlovsk, Kazakstan	PPK	New Guinea	POM
Petropavlovsk-Kamchats,		Port of Spain, Trinidad	
Russia	PKC	& Tobago	POS
Petrozavodsk, Russia	PES	Port Sudan, Sudan	PZU
Phalaborwa, South Africa	PHW	Port Vila, Vanuatu	VLI
Phaplu, Nepal	PPL	Portland, Australia	PTJ
Phitsanulok, Thailand	PHS	Porto Alegre, Brazil	POA
Phnom Penh, Cambodia	PNH	Porto Nacional, Brazil	PNB
Phrae, Thailand	PRH	Porto, Portugal	OPO
Phuket, Thailand	HKT	Porto Santo, Portugal	PXO
Pico Island, Portugal	PIX	Porto Seguro, Brazil	BPS
Piedras Negras, Mexico	PDS	Porto Velho, Brazil	PVH
Pietermaritzburg,		Posadas, Argentina	PSS
South Africa	PZB	Potosi, Bolivia	POI
Pietersburg, South Africa	PTG	Poum, New Caledonia	PUV
Pingtung, Taiwan	PIF	Pouso Alegre, Brazil	PPY
Pisa, Italy	PSA	Poza Rica, Mexico	PAZ
Pituffik, Greenland	THU	Poznan, Poland	POZ
Piura, Peru	PIU	Prague, Czech Rep.	PRG
Placencia, Belize	PLJ	Praia, Cape Verde Islands	RAI
Playa Del Carmen, Mexico	PCM	Praslin Is., Seychelles Is.	PRI
Pleiku, Viet Nam	PXU	Pres. Prudente, Brazil	PPB
Plettenberg Bay, South Africa	PBZ	Preveza/Lefkas, Greece	PVK

45

International Airports

Principe Is., Principe Is.	PCP	Quito, Ecuador	UIO
Pristina, Yugoslavia	PRN	Rabaraba, Papua	
Proserpine, Australia	PPP	New Guinea	RBP
Providencia, Colombia	PVA	Rabat, Morocco	RBA
Providenciales, Turks		Rabaul, Papua New Guinea	RAB
& Caicos	PLS	Rafha, Saudi Arabia	RAH
Pucallpa, Peru	PCL	Rahim Yar Khan, Pakistan	RYK
Puebla, Mexico	PBC	Raiatea, Fr. Polynesia	RFP
Puerto Armuelles, Panama	AML	Raipur, India	RPR
Puerto Asis, Colombia	PUU	Rajkot, India	RAJ
Puerto Ayacucho, Venezuela	PYH	Rajshahi, Bangladesh	RJH
Puerto Barrios, Guatemala	PBR	Ramata, Solomon Islands	RBV
Puerto Berrio, Colombia	PBE	Ramingining, Australia	RAM
Puerto Cabezas, Nicaragua	PUZ	Ranchi, India	IXR
Puerto Carreno, Colombia	PCR	Rangiroa, Fr. Polynesia	RGI
Puerto Escondido, Mexico	PXM	Ranong, Thailand	UNN
Puerto Inirida, Colombia	PDA	Rarotonga, Cook Islands	RAR
Puerto Jiminez, Costa Rica	PJM	Ras Al Khaimah, UAE	RKT
Puerto Lempira, Honduras	PEU	Ras An Naqb, Egypt	RAF
Puerto Madryn, Argentina	PMY	Rasht, Iran	RAS
Puerto Maldonado, Peru	PEM	Rawala Kot, Pakistan	RAZ
Puerto Montt, Chile	PMC	Rebun, Japan	RBJ
Puerto Ordaz, Venezuela	PZO	Recife, Brazil	REC
Puerto Penasco, Mexico	PPE	Redcliffe, Vanuatu	RCL
Puerto Plata, Dominican Rep.	POP	Redencao, Brazil	RDC
Puerto Princesa, Philippines	PPS	Reggio Calabria, Italy	REG
Puerto Suarez, Bolivia	PSZ	Reims, France	RHE
Puerto Vallarta, Mexico	PVR	Renmark, Australia	RMK
Pula, Croatia	PUY	Rennell, Solomon Islands	RNL
Pumani, Papua New Guinea	PMN	Rennes, France	RNS
Punta Arenas, Chile	PUQ	Resistencia, Argentina	RES
Punta Cana, Dominican Rep.	PUJ	Retalhuleu, Guatemala	RER
Punta Del Este, Uruguay	PDP	Reunion Island, Indian Ocean	RUN
Punta Gorda, Belize	PND	Reus, Spain	REU
Punta Islita, Costa Rica	PBP	Reykjavik (Domestic), Iceland	RKV
Pusan, Korea	PUS	Reykjavik (Keflavik), Iceland	KEF
Putao, Myanmar	PBU	Reykjavik (Metro), Iceland	REK
Puttaparthi, India	PUT	Reynosa, Mexico	REX
Pyongyang, N. Korea	FNJ	Rhodes, Greece	RHO
Qaisumah, Saudi Arabia	AQI	Ribeirao Preto, Brazil	RAO
Qiemo, China	IQM	Riberalta, Bolivia	RIB
Qingdao, China	TAO	Richards Bay, South Africa	RCB
Qinhuangdao, China	SHP	Richmond, Australia	RCM
Qiqihar, China	NDG	Riga, Latvia	RIX
Queenstown, Australia	UEE	Rincon de los Sauces,	
Queenstown, New Zealand	ZQN	Argentina	RDS
Quelimane, Mozambique	UEL	Ringi Cove, Solomon Islands	RIN
Quepos, Costa Rica	XQP	Rio Branco, Brazil	RBR
Queretaro, Mexico	QRO	Rio Cuarto, Argentina	RCU
Quetta, Pakistan	UET	Rio De Janeiro (Dumont),	
Quetzaltenango, Guatemala	AAZ	Brazil	SDU
Qui Nhon, Viet Nam	UIH	Rio De Janeiro (Metro), Brazil	RIO
Quibdo, Colombia	UIB	Rio de Janeriro (Intl), Brazil	GIG
Quilpie, Australia	ULP	Rio Dulce, Guatemala	LCF
Quimper, France	UIP	Rio Gallegos, Argentina	RGL
Quine Hill, Vanuatu	UIQ	Rio Grande, Argentina	RGA

Rio Grande, Brazil	RIG	Samara, Russia	KUF	
Riohacha, Colombia	RCH	Samarinda, Indonesia	SRI	
Rioja, Peru	RIJ	Samarkand, Uzbekistan	SKD	
Rishiri, Japan	RIS	Sambava, Madagascar	SVB	
Riyadh, Saudi Arabia	RUH	Sambu, Panama	SAX	
Riyan Mukalla, Yemen	RIY	Samburu, Kenya	UAS	
Roanne, France	RNE	Samos, Greece	SMI	
Roatan, Honduras	RTB	Samsun, Turkey	SSX	
Rock Sound, Bahamas	RSD	San Andres Is., Colombia	ADZ	
Rockhampton, Australia	ROK	San Andros, Bahamas	SAQ	
Rodez, France	RDZ	San Antonio, Venezuela	SVZ	
Rodrigues Island, Mauritius	RRG	San Blas, Panama	NBL	
Roervik, Norway	RVK	San Borja, Bolivia	SRJ	
Roma, Australia	RMA	San Carlos de Bariloche,		
Rome (Ciampino), Italy	CIA	Argentina	BRC	
Rome (Fiumicino), Italy	FCO	San Carlos, Nicaragua	NCR	
Rome (Metro), Italy	ROM	San Cristobal, Ecuador	SCY	
Rondonopolis, Brazil	ROO	San Fernando De Apure,		
Ronneby, Sweden	RNB	Venezuela	SFD	
Roros, Norway	RRS	San Joaquin, Bolivia	SJB	
Rosario, Argentina	ROS	San Jose Cabo, Mexico	SJD	
Rosh Pina, Israel	RPN	San Jose, Costa Rica	SJO	
Rost, Norway	RET	San Jose, Philippines	SJI	
Rostock-Laage, Germany	RLG	San Juan, Argentina	UAQ	
Rostov, Russia	ROV	San Luis, Argentina	LUQ	
Rota, Mariana Islands	ROP	San Luis Potosi, Mexico	SLP	
Rotorua, New Zealand	ROT	San Martin de los Andes,		
Rotterdam, Netherlands	RTM	Argentina	CPC	
Rottnest Is., Australia	RTS	San Miguel, Panama	NMG	
Rotuma, Fiji	RTA	San Pedro, Belize	SPR	
Rouen, France	URO	San Pedro Sula, Honduras	SAP	
Rovaniemi, Finland	RVN	San Rafael, Argentina	AFA	
Roxas City, Philippines	RXS	San Salvador, Bahamas	ZSA	
Rundu, Namibia	NDU	San Salvador, El Salvador	SAL	
Rurutu Is., Fr. Polynesia	RUR	San Sebastian, Spain	EAS	
Saarbruecken, Germany	SCN	San Tome, Venezuela	SOM	
Saba, Neth. Antilles	SAB	San Vincente Del Caguan,		
Sadah, Yemen Arab Rep.	SYE	Colombia	SVI	
Safia, Papua New Guinea	SFU	Sana'a, Yemen Arab Rep.	SAH	
Saidpur, Bangladesh	SPD	Sandakan, Malaysia	SDK	
Saidu Sharif, Pakistan	SDT	Sandane, Norway	SDN	
Saipan, Mariana Islands	SPN	Sandefjord, Norway	TRF	
Sakon Nakhon, Thailand	SNO	Sandnessjoen, Norway	SSJ	
Sal, Cape Verde Islands	SID	Sanliurfa, Turkey	SFQ	
Salalah, Oman	SLL	Santa Ana, Solomon Islands	NNB	
Salamanca, Spain	SLM	Santa Cruz Do Sul, Brazil	CSU	
Salamo, Papua New Guinea	SAM	Santa Cruz Is., Solomon		
Sale, Australia	SXE	Islands	SCZ	
Salehard, Russia	SLY	Santa Cruz La Palma, Spain	SPC	
Salina Cruz, Mexico	SCX	Santa Cruz (Trompillo),		
Salt Cay, Turks & Caicos	SLX	Bolivia	SRZ	
Salta, Argentina	SLA	Santa Cruz (Viru Viru),		
Saltillo, Mexico	SLW	Bolivia	VVI	
Salvador, Brazil	SSA	Santa Elena, Venezuela	SNV	
Salzburg, Austria	SZG	Santa Fe, Argentina	SFN	
Sam Neua, Laos	NEU	Santa Maria, Brazil	RIA	

International Airports

Santa Maria, Portugal	SMA	Sayaboury, Laos	ZBY
Santa Marta, Colombia	SMR	Scone, Australia	NSO
Santa Rosa, Argentina	RSA	Sege, Solomon Islands	EGM
Santa Rosa, Brazil	SRA	Sehulea, Papua New Guinea	SXH
Santa Terezinha, Brazil	STZ	Sehwen Sharif, Pakistan	SYW
Santana Do Araguaia, Brazil	CMP	Seinajoki, Finland	SJY
Santander, Spain	SDR	Seiyun, Yemen	GXF
Santarem, Brazil	STM	Selibaby, Mauritania	SEY
Santiago, Chile	SCL	Selje, Norway	QFK
Santiago, Cuba	SCU	Semarang, Indonesia	SRG
Santiago De Compostela, Spain	SCQ	Semipalatinsk, Kazakstan	PLX
		Semporna, Malaysia	SMM
Santiago Del Estero, Argentina	SDE	Sendai, Japan	SDJ
		Seoul (Inchon), Korea	ICN
Santiago, Dominican Rep.	STI	Seoul (Kimpo), Korea	GMP
Santiago, Panama	SYP	Seoul (Metro), Korea	SEL
Santo Angelo, Brazil	GEL	Seville, Spain	SVQ
Santo Antao, Cape Verde Islands	NTO	Sfax, Tunisia	SFA
		Shanghai, China	SHA
Santo Domingo, Dominican Rep.	SDQ	Shannon, Ireland	SNN
		Shantou, China	SWA
Santorini (Thira), Greece	JTR	Sharjah, UAE	SHJ
Sanya, China	SYX	Sharm El Sheikh, Egypt	SSH
Sao Felix Do Araguaia, Brazil	SXO	Sharurah, Saudi Arabia	SHW
		Shashi, China	SHS
Sao Felix Do Xingu, Brazil	SXX	Shenyang, China	SHE
Sao Jorge Island, Portugal	SJZ	Shenzhen, China	SZX
Sao Jose Do Rio Preto, Brazil	SJP	Shepparton, Australia	SHT
Sao Jose Dos Campos, Brazil	SJK	Shetland Is. (Lerwick), Scotland, UK	LWK
Sao Luiz, Brazil	SLZ		
Sao Nicolau, Cape Verde Islands	SNE	Shetland Is., Scotland, UK	SDZ
		Shetland Is. (Sumburgh), Scotland, UK	LSI
Sao Paolo (Viracopas), Brazil	VCP		
Sao Paulo (Congonhas), Brazil	CGH	Shijiazhuang, China	SJW
		Shillavo, Ethiopia	HIL
Sao Paulo (Guarulhos), Brazil	GRU	Shimkent, Kazakstan	CIT
		Shiraz, Iran	SYZ
Sao Paulo (Metro), Brazil	SAO	Shonai, Japan	SYO
Sao Tome Island	TMS	Shute Harbour, Australia	JHQ
Sao Vicente, Cape Verde Islands	VXE	Sibiu, Romania	SBZ
		Sibu, Malaysia	SBW
Sapporo (Chitose), Japan	CTS	Siem Reap, Cambodia	REP
Sapporo (Metro), Japan	SPK	Sihanoukville, Cambodia	KOS
Sapporo (Okadama), Japan	OKD	Siirit, Turkey	SXZ
Sara, Vanuatu	SSR	Silchar, India	IXS
Sarajevo, Bosnia	SJJ	Simao, China	SYM
Saratov, Russia	RTW	Simferopol, Ukraine	SIP
Saravane, Laos	VNA	Simikot, Nepal	IMK
Sary, Iran	SRY	Simla, India	SLV
Satu Mare, Romania	SUJ	Simra, Nepal	SIF
Saudarkrokur, Iceland	SAK	Sindal, Denmark	CNL
Sauren, Papua New Guines	SXW	Singapore (Changi),	SIN
Saurimo, Angola	VHC	Singleton, Australia	SIX
Savannakhet, Laos	ZVK	Sinop, Brazil	OPS
Savonlinna, Finland	SVL	Sinop, Turkey	SIC
Savusavu, Fiji	SVU	Sion, Switzerland	SIR

Sitia, Greece	JSH	St. Tropez, France	JSZ
Sittwe, Myanmar	AKY	St. Vincent, Windward	
Siuna, Nicaragua	SIU	Islands	SVD
Sivas, Turkey	VAS	Stavanger, Norway	SVG
Skardu, Pakistan	KDU	Stavropol, Russia	STW
Skelleftea, Sweden	SFT	Stella Maris, Bahamas	SML
Skiathos, Greece	JSI	Stockholm (Arlanda),	
Skien, Norway	SKE	Sweden	ARN
Skiros, Greece	SKU	Stockholm (Metro), Sweden	STO
Skopje, Macedonia	SKP	Stockholm (Skavsta),	
Skovde, Sweden	KVB	Sweden	NYO
Skukuza, South Africa	SZK	Stockolm (Bromma), Sweden	BMA
Sligo, Ireland	SXL	Stokmarknes, Norway	SKN
Snake Bay, Australia	SNB	Stord, Norway	SRP
Socotra, Yemen	SCT	Stornoway, Scotland, UK	SYY
Soderhamn, Sweden	SOO	Storuman, Sweden	SQO
Sofia, Bulgaria	SOF	Strasbourg, France	SXB
Sogamoso, Colombia	SOX	Strzhewoi, Russia	SWT
Sogndal, Norway	SOG	Stung Treng, Cambodia	TNX
Sokcho, Korea	SHO	Stuttgart, Germany	STR
Sokoto, Nigeria	SKO	Suavanao, Solomon Islands	VAO
Sola, Vanuatu	SLH	Suceava, Romania	SCV
Solo City, Indonesia	SOC	Sucre, Bolivia	SRE
Son La, Viet Nam	SQH	Sui, Pakistan	SUL
Sonderborg, Denmark	SGD	Sukhothai, Thailand	THS
Sorkjosen, Norway	SOJ	Sukkertoppen, Greenland	JSU
Sorong, Indonesia	SOQ	Sukkur, Pakistan	SKZ
South Andros, Bahamas	TZN	Sule, Papua New Guinea	ULE
South Caicos, Turks		Sun City, South Africa	NTY
& Caicos	XSC	Sundsvall, Sweden	SDL
South Molle Is., Australia	SOI	Sunshine Coast, Australia	MCY
South West Bay, Vanuatu	SWJ	Sur, Oman	SUH
Southampton, England, UK	SOU	Surabaya, Indonesia	SUB
Southern Cross, Australia	SQC	Surat, India	STV
Soyo, Angola	SZA	Surat Thani, Thailand	URT
Split, Croatia	SPU	Surgut, Russia	SGC
Spring Point, Bahamas	AXP	Surkhet, Nepal	SKH
Springbok, South Africa	SBU	Suva, Fiji	SUV
Srinagar, India	SXR	Sveg, Sweden	EVG
St. Barthelemy, Guadeloupe	SBH	Svolvaer, Norway	SVJ
St. Brieuc, France	SBK	Swakopmund, Namibia	SWP
St. Etienne, France	EBU	Sydney, Australia	SYD
St. Eustatius, Neth. Antilles	EUX	Sydney (Palm Beach),	
St. George, Australia	SGO	Australia	LBH
St. Kitts, St. Kitts & Nevis	SKB	Sydney (Rose Bay), Australia	RSE
St. Lucia (Hewanorra),		Sylhet, Bangladesh	ZYL
West Indies	UVF	Syros, Greece	JSY
St. Lucia, West Indies	SLU	Szczecin, Poland	SZZ
St. Maarten (Esperance),		Taba, Egypt	TCP
Neth. Antilles	SFG	Tabarka, Tunisia	TBJ
St. Maarten, Neth. Antilles	SXM	Tabatinga, Brazil	TBT
St. Petersburg, Russia	LED	Tabiteuea North, Kiribati	TBF
St. Petersburg (Rzhevka),		Tabiteuea South, Kiribati	TSU
Russia	RVH	Tabora, Tanzania	TBO
St. Pierre, St. Pierre		Tabriz, Iran	TBZ
and Miquelon	FSP	Tabubil, Papua New Guinea	TBG

International Airports

Tabuk, Saudi Arabia	TUU	Tegucigalpa, Honduras	TGU
Tacheng, China	TCG	Tehran, Iran	THR
Tachilek, Myanmar	THL	Tel Aviv (Jaffa), Israel	TLV
Tacloban, Philippines	TAC	Tel Aviv/Jaffa (Sde Dov),	
Tacna, Peru	TCQ	Israel	SDV
Taegu, Korea	TAE	Tembagapura, Indonesia	TIM
Taichung, Taiwan	TXG	Temuco, Chile	ZCO
Taif, Saudi Arabia	TIF	Tenerife (Metro), Spain	TCI
Tainan, Taiwan	TNN	Tenerife (N. Los Rodeo),	
Taipei (Chiang Kai Shek),		Spain	TFN
Taiwan	TPE	Tenerife (Reina Sofia), Spain	TFS
Taipei (Sung Shan), Taiwan	TSA	Tennant Creek, Australia	TCA
Taitung, Taiwan	TTT	Tepic, Mexico	TPQ
Taiyuan, China	TYN	Terapo, Papua New Guinea	TEO
Taiz, Yemen	TAI	Terceira Is., Portugal	TER
Taji, Papua New Guinea	TAJ	Teresina, Brazil	THE
Takamatsu, Japan	TAK	Termez, Uzbekistan	TMJ
Takapoto, Fr. Polynesia	TKP	Ternate, Indonesia	TTE
Takaroa, Fr. Polynesia	TKX	Terre De Haut, Guadeloupe	LSS
Talara, Peru	TYL	Tete, Mozambique	TET
Tallinn, Estonia	TLL	Tetuan, Morocco	TTU
Tamana Island, Kiribati	TMN	Tezpur, India	TEZ
Tamanrasset, Algeria	TMR	Thandwe, Myanmar	SNW
Tamarindo, Costa Rica	TNO	Thangool, Australia	THG
Tamatave, Madagascar	TMM	Thargomindah, Australia	XTG
Tambor, Costa Rica	TMU	The Bight, Bahamas	TBI
Tame, Colombia	TME	Thessaloniki, Greece	SKG
Tampere, Finland	TMP	Thisted, Denmark	TED
Tampico, Mexico	TAM	Thursday Is., Australia	TIS
Tamworth, Australia	TMW	Tianjin, China	TSN
Tan Tan, Morocco	TTA	Tiaret, Algeria	TID
Tanegashima, Japan	TNE	Tidjikja, Mauritania	TIY
Tangier, Morocco	TNG	Tiga, New Caledonia	TGJ
Tanjung Pandan, Indonesia	TTR	Tijuana, Mexico	TIJ
Tanna, Vanuatu	TAH	Tikehau Atoll, Fr. Polynesia	TIH
Tapachula, Mexico	TAP	Timaru, New Zealand	TIU
Tapini, Papua New Guinea	TPI	Timbuktu (Tombouctou),	
Taplejung, Nepal	TPJ	Mali	TOM
Tarakan, Indonesia	TRK	Timimoun, Algeria	TMX
Taramajima, Japan	TRA	Timisoara, Romania	TSR
Tarapoto, Peru	TPP	Tinak Is., Marshall Islands	TIC
Tarawa, Kiribati	TRW	Tindouf, Algeria	TIN
Taree, Australia	TRO	Tingo Maria, Peru	TGI
Tari, Papua New Guinea	TIZ	Tinian, Mariana Islands	TIQ
Tarija, Bolivia	TJA	Tioman, Malaysia	TOD
Tashkent, Uzbekistan	TAS	Tippi, Ethiopia	TIE
Tatry/Poprad, Slovakia	TAT	Tirana, Albania	TIA
Taupo, New Zealand	TUO	Tiree, Scotland, UK	TRE
Tauranga, New Zealand	TRG	Tirgu Mures, Romania	TGM
Taveuni, Fiji	TVU	Tiruchirapally, India	TRZ
Tawau, Malaysia	TWU	Tirupati, India	TIR
Tbessa, Algeria	TEE	Tivat, Yugoslavia	TIV
Tbilisi, Georgia	TBS	Tlemsen, Algeria	TLM
Tchibanga, Gabon	TCH	Tobago, Trinidad & Tobago	TAB
Te Anau, New Zealand	TEU	Tokat, Turkey	TJK
Tefe, Brazil	TFF	Tokunoshima, Japan	TKN

Tokushima, Japan	TKS	Tum, Ethiopia	TUJ	
Tokyo (Haneda), Japan	HND	Tumaco, Colombia	TCO	
Tokyo (Metro), Japan	TYO	Tumbes, Peru	TBP	
Tokyo (Narita), Japan	NRT	Tumling Tar, Nepal	TMI	
Toledo, Brazil	TOW	Tunis, Tunisia	TUN	
Tomanggong, Malaysia	TMG	Tunxi, China	TXN	
Tomsk, Russia	TOF	Turaif, Saudi Arabia	TUI	
Tongatapu, Tonga	TBU	Turbat, Pakistan	TUK	
Tongoa, Vanuatu	TGH	Turbo, Colombia	TRB	
Toowoomba, Australia	TWB	Turin, Italy	TRN	
Torreon, Mexico	TRC	Turku, Finland	TKU	
Torres, Vanuatu	TOH	Tuticorin, India	TCR	
Torsby, Sweden	TYF	Tuxtla Gutierrez, Mexico	TGZ	
Tortola (Road Town), BVI	RAD	Tuy Hoa, Vietnam	TBB	
Tortola (Westend), BVI	TOV	Tyumen, Russia	TJM	
Tortuquero, Costa Rica	TTQ	Ube, Japan	UBJ	
Tottori, Japan	TTJ	Uberaba, Brazil	UBA	
Touggourt, Algeria	TGR	Uberlandia, Brazil	UDI	
Touho, New Caledonia	TOU	Ubon Ratchathani, Thailand	UBP	
Toulon, France	TLN	Udaipur, India	UDR	
Toulouse, France	TLS	Udon Thani, Thailand	UTH	
Tours, France	TUF	Ufa, Russia	UFA	
Townsville, Australia	TSV	Uige, Angola	UGO	
Toyama, Japan	TOY	Ujae Is., Marshall Islands	UJE	
Toyooka, Japan	TJH	Ujung Pandang, Indonesia	UPG	
Tozeur, Tunisia	TOE	Ukhta, Russia	UCT	
Trabzon, Turkey	TZX	Ulan Bator, Mongolia	ULN	
Trang, Thailand	TST	Ulan-Ude, Russia	UUD	
Trapani, Italy	TPS	Ulei, Vanuatu	ULB	
Traralgon, Australia	TGN	Ulgit, Mongolia	ULG	
Treasure Cay, Bahamas	TCB	Ulsan, Korea	USN	
Trelew, Argentina	REL	Ulundi, South Africa	ULD	
Trieste, Italy	TRS	Uluru, Australia	AYQ	
Trinidad, Bolivia	TDD	Umea, Sweden	UME	
Tripoli, Libya	TIP	Umtata, South Africa	UTT	
Trivandrum, India	TRV	Union Island, St. Vincent	UNI	
Trollhattan, Sweden	THN	Unst, Shetland Is.,		
Trombetas, Brazil	TMT	Scotland, UK	UNT	
Tromso, Norway	TOS	Upernavik, Greenland	JUV	
Trondheim, Norway	TRD	Upington, South Africa	UTN	
Trujillo, Honduras	TJI	Uraj, Russia	URJ	
Trujillo, Peru	TRU	Uralsk, Kazakstan	URA	
Truk, Micronesia	TKK	Urgench, Uzbekistan	UGC	
Tsaratanana, Madagascar	TTS	Urmieh, Iran	OMH	
Tshikapa, Congo, Dem. Rep.	TSH	Urrao, Colombia	URR	
Tsiroanomandidy,		Uruapan, Mexico	UPN	
Madagascar	WTS	Uruguaiana, Brazil	URG	
Tsumeb, Namibia	TSB	Urumqi, China	URC	
Tsushima, Japan	TSJ	Useless Loop, Australia	USL	
Tubuai, Fr. Polynesia	TUB	Ushuaia, Argentina	USH	
Tucuma, Brazil	TUZ	Ust-Ilimsk, Russia	UIK	
Tucuman, Argentina	TUC	Ust-Kamenogorsk,		
Tucurui, Brazil	TUR	Kazakstan	UKK	
Tufi, Papua New Guinea	TFI	Utapao, Thailand	UTP	
Tuguegarao, Philippines	TUG	Utila, Honduras	UII	
Tulear, Madagascar	TLE	Utirik Is., Marshall Islands	UTK	

51

International Airports

52

The Travel Agent's Complete Desk Reference

Uummannaq, Greenland	UMD	Vojens, Denmark	SKS
Uvol, Papua New Guinea	UVO	Volgograd, Russia	VOG
Vaasa, Finland	VAA	Vologda, Russia	VGD
Vadodara, India	BDQ	Voronezh, Russia	VOZ
Vadso, Norway	VDS	Waco Kungo, Angola	CEO
Vaeroy, Norway	VRY	Wadi-Ad-Dawasir,	
Valdivia, Chile	ZAL	Saudi Arabia	WAE
Valencia, Spain	VLC	Wagga Wagga, Australia	WGA
Valencia, Venezuela	VLN	Waingapu, Indonesia	WGP
Valesdir, Vanuatu	VLS	Wairoa, New Zealand	WIR
Valladolid, Spain	VLL	Wakkanai, Japan	WKJ
Valledupar, Colombia	VUP	Walaha, Vanuatu	WLH
Valverde, Spain	VDE	Walgett, Australia	WGE
Van, Turkey	VAN	Walker's Cay, Bahamas	WKR
Vanimo, Papua New Guinea	VAI	Wallis Is., Wallis &	
Vanuabalavu, Fiji	VBV	Futuna Islands	WLS
Varadero, Cuba	VRA	Walvis Bay, Namibia	WVB
Varanasi, India	VNS	Wanaka, New Zealand	WKA
Vardoe, Norway	VAW	Wanganui, New Zealand	WAG
Varginha, Brazil	VAG	Wangerooge, Germany	AGE
Varkaus, Finland	VRK	Wanigela, Papua	
Varna, Bulgaria	VAR	New Guinea	AGL
Vasteras, Sweden	VST	Wanxian, China	WXN
Vava'u, Tonga	VAV	Wapenamanda, Papua	
Vaxjo, Sweden	VXO	New Guinea	WBM
Venice, Italy	VCE	Wapolu, Papua New Guinea	WBC
Veracruz, Mexico	VER	Warsaw, Poland	WAW
Verona, Italy	VRN	Waspam, Nicaragua	WSP
Vestmannaeyjar, Iceland	VEY	Wasu, Papua New Guinea	WSU
Victoria Falls, Zimbabwe	VFA	Wasum, Papua New Guinea	WUM
Victoria R. Downs, Australia	VCD	Waterford, Ireland	WAT
Videira, Brazil	VIA	Wedau, Papua New Guinea	WED
Viedma, Argentina	VDM	Wedjh, Saudi Arabia	EJH
Vienna, Austria	VIE	Weifang, China	WEF
Vientiane, Laos	VTE	Weihai, China	WEH
Vigo, Spain	VGO	Weipa, Australia	WEI
Vila Rica, Brazil	VLP	Wellington, New Zealand	WLG
Vilhelmina, Sweden	VHM	Wenzhou, China	WNZ
Vilhena, Brazil	BVH	West End, Bahamas	WTD
Villa Gesell, Argentina	VLG	West Wyalong, Australia	WWY
Villa Mercedes, Argentina	VME	Westerland, Germany	GWT
Villahermosa, Mexico	VSA	Westport, New Zealand	WSZ
Villavicencio, Colombia	VVC	Westray, Scotland, UK	WRY
Vilnius, Lithuania	VNO	Wewak, Papua New Guinea	WWK
Vinh City, Vietnam	VII	Whakatane, New Zealand	WHK
Virac, Philippines	VRC	Whangarei, New Zealand	WRE
Virgin Gorda, BVI	VIJ	Whyalla, Australia	WYA
Viru, Solomon Islands	VIU	Wick, Scotland, UK	WIC
Visby, Sweden	VBY	Wilhelmshaven, Germany	WVN
Vishakhapatnam, India	VTZ	Wiluna, Australia	WUN
Vitoria Da Conquista, Brazil	VDC	Windhoek (Eros), Namibia	ERS
Vitoria, Spain	VIT	Windhoek (Intl), Namibia	WDH
Vivigani, Papua New Guinea	VIV	Windorah, Australia	WNR
Vladikavkaz, Russia	OGZ	Winton, Australia	WIN
Vladivostok, Russia	VVO	Woja, Marshall Islands	WJA
Vohemar, Madagascar	VOH	Wollogorang, Australia	WLL

Woomera, Australia	UMR	Yichang, China	YIH	
Wotho, Marshall Islands	WTO	Yinchuan, China	INC	
Wotje Is., Marshall Islands	WTE	Yining, China	YIN	
Wroclaw, Poland	WRO	Yiwu, China	YIW	
Wudinna, Australia	WUD	Yogyakarta, Indonesia	JOG	
Wuhan, China	WUH	Yola, Nigeria	YOL	
Wuyishan, China	WUS	Yonago, Japan	YGJ	
Wuzhou, China	WUZ	Yonaguni Jima, Japan	OGN	
Wyndham, Australia	WYN	Yorke Is., Australia	OKR	
Xayabury, Laos	XAY	Yoronjima, Japan	RNJ	
Xi An (Xianyang), China	XIY	Yosu, Korea	RSU	
Xi An (Xiguan), China	SIA	Young, Australia	NGA	
Xiamen, China	XMN	Yulin, China	UYN	
Xiangfan, China	XFN	Yurimaguas, Peru	YMS	
Xichang, China	XIC	Yuzhno-Sakhalinsk, Russia	UUS	
Xieng Khouang, Laos	XKH	Zacatecas, Mexico	ZCL	
Xining, China	XNN	Zadar, Croatia	ZAD	
Yakushima, Japan	KUM	Zagreb, Croatia	ZAG	
Yakutsk, Russia	YKS	Zahedan, Iran	ZAH	
Yamagata, Japan	GAJ	Zakinthos Is., Greece	ZTH	
Yamoussoukro, Cote D'Ivoire	ASK	Zamboanga, Philippines	ZAM	
Yan'an, China	ENY	Zanzibar, Tanzania	ZNZ	
Yanbo, Saudi Arabia	YNB	Zaporozhye, Ukraine	OZH	
Yandina, Solomon Islands	XYA	Zaragoza, Spain	ZAZ	
Yangon, Myanmar	RGN	Zhambyl, Kazakstan	DMB	
Yanji, China	YNJ	Zhanjiang, China	ZHA	
Yantai, China	YNT	Zhaotong, China	ZAT	
Yaounde, Cameroon	NSI	Zhengzhou, China	CGO	
Yap, Micronesia	YAP	Zhezkazgan, Kazakstan	DZN	
Yazd, Iran	AZD	Zhob, Pakistan	PZH	
Yechon, Korea	YEC	Zhuhai, China	ZUH	
Yelimane, Mali	EYL	Ziguinchor, Senegal	ZIG	
Yerevan, Armenia	EVN	Zouerate, Mauritania	OUZ	
Yibin, China	YBP	Zurich, Switzerland	ZRH	

*International
Airports*

The Travel Agent's
Complete Desk
Reference

Airport Codes

AAA	Anaa, Fr. Polynesia		ACV	Arcata/Eureka, CA
AAC	Al Arish, Egypt		ACY	Atlantic City (Intl), NJ
AAE	Annaba, Algeria		ADA	Adana, Turkey
AAK	Aranuka, Kiribati		ADB	Izmir (Adnan Mend), Turkey
AAL	Aalborg, Denmark		ADD	Addis Ababa, Ethiopia
AAN	Al Ain, UAE		ADE	Aden, Yemen
AAQ	Anapa, Russia		ADK	Adak Island, AK
AAR	Aarhus, Denmark		ADL	Adelaide, Australia
AAT	Altay, China		ADQ	Kodiak, AK
AAW	Abbottabad, Pakistan		ADU	Ardabil, Iran
AAY	Al Ghaydah, Yemen		ADZ	San Andres Is., Colombia
AAZ	Quetzaltenango, Guatemala		AEA	Abemama, Kiribati
ABA	Abakan, Russia		AED	Aleneva, AK
ABE	Allentown/Bethlehem/Easton, PA		AEH	Abecher, Chad
			AEO	Aioun El Atrouss, Mauritania
ABF	Abaiang, Kiribati		AEP	Buenos Aires (Newbery), Argentina
ABI	Abilene, TX		
ABJ	Abidjan, Cote D'lvoire		AER	Adler/Sochi, Russia
ABK	Kabri Dar, Ethiopia		AES	Aalesund, Norway
ABL	Ambler, AK		AET	Allakaket, AK
ABM	Bamaga, Australia		AEX	Alexandria, LA
ABQ	Albuquerque, NM		AEY	Akureyri, Iceland
ABR	Aberdeen, SD		AFA	San Rafael, Argentina
ABS	Abu Simbel, Egypt		AFL	Alta Floresta, Brazil
ABT	Al-Baha, Saudi Arabia		AFT	Afutara, Solomon Islands
ABV	Abuja, Nigeria		AGA	Agadir, Morocco
ABX	Albury, Australia		AGB	Augsburg, Germany
ABY	Albany, GA		AGE	Wangerooge, Germany
ABZ	Aberdeen, Scotland		AGF	Agen, France
ACA	Acapulco, Mexico		AGH	Helsingborg, Sweden
ACC	Accra, Ghana		AGJ	Aguni, Japan
ACE	Lanzarote, Spain		AGL	Wanigela, Papua New Guinea
ACH	Altenrhein, Switzerland		AGN	Angoon, AK
ACI	Alderney, Channel Islands, UK		AGP	Malaga, Spain
ACK	Nantucket, MA		AGR	Agra, India
ACR	Araracuara, Colombia		AGS	Augusta, GA
ACT	Waco, TX		AGT	Ciudad Del Este, Paraguay

AGU	Aguascalientes, Mexico	AMQ	Ambon, Indonesia
AGV	Acarigua, Venezuela	AMS	Amsterdam, Netherlands
AGX	Agatti Island, India	AMY	Ambatomainty, Madagascar
AHB	Abha, Saudi Arabia	ANA	Anaheim, CA
AHN	Athens, GA	ANC	Anchorage, AK
AHO	Alghero, Italy	ANF	Antofagasta, Chile
AHS	Ahuas, Honduras	ANG	Angouleme, France
AHU	Al Hoceima, Morocco	ANI	Aniak, AK
AIA	Alliance, NE	ANK	Ankara, Turkey
AIC	Airok, Marshall Islands	ANM	Antalaha, Madagascar
AIM	Ailuk, Marshall Islands	ANR	Antwerp, Belgium
AIN	Wainwright, AK	ANS	Andahuaylas, Peru
AIR	Aripuana, Brazil	ANU	Antigua, West Indies
AIS	Arorae Is, Kiribati	ANV	Anvik, AK
AIT	Aitutaki, Cook Islands	ANX	Andenes, Norway
AIU	Atiu, Cook Islands	AOI	Ancona, Italy
AIY	Atlantic City, NJ	AOJ	Aomori, Japan
AJA	Ajaccio, Corsica, France	AOK	Karpathos, Greece
AJF	Jouf, Saudi Arabia	AOO	Altoona, PA
AJR	Arvidsjaur, Sweden	AOR	Alor Setar, Malaysia
AJU	Aracaju, Brazil	AOS	Amook, AK
AKA	Ankang, China	AOU	Attopeu, Laos
AKB	Atka, AK	APF	Naples, FL
AKE	Akieni, Gabon	API	Aplay, Colombia
AKI	Akiak, AK	APL	Nampula, Mozambique
AKJ	Asahikawa, Japan	APN	Alpena, MI
AKK	Akhiok, AK	APO	Apartado, Colombia
AKL	Auckland, New Zealand	APW	Apia, Western Samoa
AKN	King Salmon, AK	AQG	Anqing, China
AKP	Anaktuvuk, AK	AQI	Qaisumah, Saudi Arabia
AKS	Auki, Solomon Islands	AQJ	Aqaba, Jordan
AKU	Aksu, China	AQP	Arequipa, Peru
AKV	Akulivik, QU	ARC	Arctic Village, AK
AKX	Aktyubinsk, Kazakstan	ARD	Alor Island, Indonesia
AKY	Sittwe, Myanmar	ARH	Arkhangelsk, Russia
ALA	Almaty, Kazakstan	ARI	Arica, Chile
ALB	Albany, NY	ARM	Armidale, Australia
ALC	Alicante, Spain	ARN	Stockholm (Arlanda), Sweden
ALF	Alta, Norway	ARP	Aragip, Papua New Guinea
ALG	Algiers, Algeria	ART	Watertown, NY
ALH	Albany, Australia	ARU	Aracatuba, Brazil
ALJ	Alexander Bay, South Africa	ARW	Arad, Romania
ALM	Alamogordo, NM	ARZ	N'Zeto, Angola
ALO	Waterloo, IA	ASA	Assab, Eritrea
ALP	Aleppo, Syria	ASB	Ashkhabad, Turkmenistan
ALS	Alamosa, CO	ASC	Ascension, Bolivia
ALV	Andorra La Vella, Andorra	ASD	Andros Town, Bahamas
ALW	Walla Walla, WA	ASE	Aspen, CO
ALY	Alexandria, Egypt	ASF	Astrakhan, Russia
ALZ	Alitak, AK	ASJ	Amami O Shima, Japan
AMA	Amarillo, TX	ASK	Yamoussoukro, Cote D'Ivoire
AMD	Ahmedabad, India	ASM	Asmara, Eritrea
AMH	Arba Mintch, Ethiopia	ASO	Asosa, Ethiopia
AMI	Mataram, Indonesia	ASP	Alice Springs, Australia
AML	Puerto Armuelles, Panama	ASR	Kayseri, Turkey
AMM	Amman, Jordan	ASU	Asuncion, Paraguay

ASV	Amboseli, Kenya	AZR	Adrar, Algeria	
ASW	Aswan, Egypt	BAG	Baguio, Philippines	
ATB	Atbara, Sudan	BAH	Bahrain, Bahrain	
ATC	Arthur's Town, Bahamas	BAJ	Bali, Papua New Guinea	
ATD	Atoifi, Solomon Islands	BAK	Baku, Azerbaijan	
ATH	Athens, Greece	BAL	Batman, Turkey	
ATK	Atqasuk, AK	BAQ	Barranquilla, Colombia	
ATL	Atlanta, GA	BAS	Ballalae, Solomon Islands	
ATM	Altamira, Brazil	BAU	Bauru, Brazil	
ATN	Namatanai, Papua New Guinea	BAV	Baotou, China	*Airport Codes*
		BAX	Barnaul, Russia	
ATP	Aitape, Papua New Guinea	BAY	Baia Mare, Romania	
ATQ	Amritsar, India	BBA	Balmaceda, Chile	
ATR	Atar, Mauritania	BBG	Butaritari, Kiribati	
ATT	Atmautluak, AK	BBI	Bhubaneswar, India	
ATW	Appleton, WI	BBK	Kasane, Botswana	
ATY	Watertown, SD	BBM	Battambang, Cambodia	
AUA	Aruba, Aruba	BBN	Bario, Malaysia	
AUC	Arauca, Colombia	BBO	Berbera, Somalia	
AUG	Augusta, ME	BBQ	Barbuda, West Indies	
AUH	Abu Dhabi, UAE	BBR	Basse-Terre, Guadeloupe	
AUK	Alakanuk, AK	BBU	Bucharest (Baneasa), Romania	
AUL	Aur, Marshall Islands	BCA	Baracoa, Cuba	
AUP	Agaun, Papua New Guinea	BCD	Bacolod, Philippines	
AUQ	Atuona, Fr. Polynesia	BCE	Bryce Canyon, UT	
AUR	Aurillac, France	BCI	Barcaldine, Australia	
AUS	Austin, TX	BCL	Barra Colorado, Costa Rica	
AUV	Aumo, Papua New Guinea	BCN	Barcelona, Spain	
AUW	Wausau, WI	BCO	Jinka, Ethiopa	
AUX	Araguaina, Brazil	BCX	Beloreck, Russia	
AUY	Aneityum, Vanuatu	BDA	Hamilton, Bermuda	
AVI	Ciego De Avila, Cuba	BDB	Bundaberg, Australia	
AVL	Asheville, NC	BDH	Bandar Lengeh, Iran	
AVN	Avignon, France	BDJ	Banjarmasin, Indonesia	
AVP	Wilkes-Barre/Scranton, PA	BDK	Bondoukou, Cote D'Ivoire	
AVR	Minocqua-Woodruff, WI	BDL	Hartford, CT/Springfield, MA	
AVU	Avu Avu, Solomon Islands	BDO	Bandung, Indonesia	
AVX	Catalina Island, CA	BDP	Bhadrapur, Nepal	
AWD	Aniwa, Vanatu	BDQ	Vadodara, India	
AWZ	Ahwaz, Iran	BDR	Bridgeport, CT	
AXA	Anguilla, West Indies	BDS	Brindisi, Italy	
AXD	Alexandroupolis, Greece	BDT	Gbadolite, Congo, Dem. Rep.	
AXK	Ataq, Yemen	BDU	Bardufoss, Norway	
AXM	Armenia, Colombia	BEB	Benbecula, Scotland, UK	
AXP	Spring Point, Bahamas	BEF	Bluefields, Nicaragua	
AXT	Akita, Japan	BEG	Belgrade, Yugoslavia	
AXU	Axum, Ethiopia	BEH	Benton Harbor, MI	
AYK	Arkalyk, Kazakstan	BEI	Beica, Ethiopia	
AYP	Ayacucho, Peru	BEJ	Berau, Indonesia	
AYQ	Ayers Rock/Uluru, Australia	BEL	Belem, Brazil	
AYT	Antalya, Turkey	BEN	Benghazi, Libya	
AZB	Amazon Bay, Papua New Guinea	BEO	Newcastle (Belmont), Australia	
		BER	Berlin (Metro), Germany	
AZD	Yazd, Iran	BES	Brest, France	
AZN	Andizan, Uzbekistan	BET	Bethel, AK	
AZO	Kalamazoo, MI	BEU	Bedourie, Australia	

58

BEW	Beira, Mozambique	BJM	Bujumbura, Burundi
BEY	Beirut, Lebanon	BJR	Bahar Dar, Ethiopia
BEZ	Beru, Kiribati	BJS	Beijing, China
BFD	Bradford, PA	BJX	Leon/Guanajuato, Mexico
BFF	Scottsbluff, NE	BJZ	Badajoz, Spain
BFG	Bahia Pinas, Panama	BKA	Moscow (Bykovo), Russia
BFI	Seattle (Boeing Field), WA	BKC	Buckland, AK
BFL	Bakersfield, CA	BKI	Kota Kinabalu, Malaysia
BFN	Bloemfontein, South Africa	BKK	Bangkok, Thailand
BFO	Buffalo Range, Zimbabwe	BKM	Bakalalan, Malaysia
BFS	Belfast (Intl), N. Ireland, UK	BKO	Bamako, Mali
BGA	Bucaramanga, Colombia	BKQ	Blackall, Australia
BGC	Braganca, Portugal	BKS	Bengkulu, Indonesia
BGF	Bangui, Cen. African Republic	BKW	Beckley, WV
BGI	Bridgetown, Barbados	BLA	Barcelona, Venezuela
BGK	Big Creek, Belize	BLD	Boulder City, NV
BGM	Binghamton/Johnson City, NY	BLE	Borlange, Sweden
BGO	Bergen, Norway	BLF	Bluefield/Princeton, WV
BGR	Bangor, ME	BLG	Belaga, Malaysia
BGW	Baghdad (Metro), Iraq	BLI	Bellingham, WA
BGX	Bage, RS, Brazil	BLK	Blackpool, England, UK
BGY	Milan (Orio Al Serio), Italy	BLL	Billund, Denmark
BHB	Bar Harbor, ME	BLP	Bellavista, Peru
BHD	Belfast (City), N. Ireland, UK	BLQ	Bologna, Italy
BHE	Blenheim, New Zealand	BLR	Bangalore, India
BHG	Brus Laguna, Honduras	BLT	Blackwater, Australia
BHH	Bisha, Saudi Arabia	BLZ	Blantyre, Malawi
BHI	Bahia Blanca, Argentina	BMA	Stockolm (Bromma), Sweden
BHJ	Bhuj, India	BMB	Bumba, Congo, Dem. Rep.
BHK	Bukhara, Uzbekistan	BME	Broome, Australia
BHM	Birmingham, AL	BMG	Bloomington, IN
BHO	Bhopal, India	BMI	Bloomington/Normal, IL
BHQ	Broken Hill, Australia	BMM	Bitam, Gabon
BHR	Bharatpur, Nepal	BMO	Bhamo, Myanmar
BHS	Bathurst, Australia	BMP	Brampton Is., Australia
BHU	Bhavnagar, India	BMU	Bima, Indonesia
BHV	Bahawalpur, Pakistan	BMV	Ban Me Thuot, Vietnam
BHX	Birmingham, England, UK	BMW	Bordj Badji Mokhtar, Algeria
BHY	Beihai, China	BMY	Belep Is., New Caledonia
BHZ	Belo Horizonte (Metro), Brazil	BNA	Nashville, TN
BIA	Bastia, Corsica, France	BNB	Boende, Congo, Dem. Rep.
BID	Block Island, RI	BND	Bandar Abbas, Iran
BII	Bikini Atoll, Marshall Islands	BNE	Brisbane, Australia
BIK	Biak, Indonesia	BNI	Benin City, Nigeria
BIL	Billings, MT	BNJ	Bonn, Germany
BIM	Bimini, Bahamas	BNK	Ballina, Australia
BIO	Bilbao, Spain	BNN	Bronnoysund, Norway
BIQ	Biarritz, France	BNP	Bannu, Pakistan
BIR	Biratnagar, Nepal	BNU	Blumenau, Brazil
BIS	Bismarck, ND	BNX	Banja Luka, Bosnia
BIY	Bisho, South Africa	BNY	Bellona Is., Solomon Islands
BJA	Bejaia, Algeria	BOB	Bora Bora, Fr. Polynesia
BJF	Batsfjord, Norway	BOC	Bocas Del Toro, Panama
BJI	Bemidji, MN	BOD	Bordeaux, France
BJL	Banjul, Gambia	BOG	Bogota, Colombia
		BOH	Bournemouth, England, UK

BOI	Boise, ID
BOJ	Bourgas, Bulgaria
BOM	Bombay, India
BON	Bonaire, Neth. Antilles
BOO	Bodo, Norway
BOS	Boston, MA
BOV	Boang, Papua New Guinea
BOX	Borroloola, Australia
BPG	Barra Do Garcas, Brazil
BPN	Balikpapan, Indonesia
BPS	Porto Seguro, Brazil
BPT	Beaumont, TX
BPY	Besalampy, Madagascar
BQE	Bubaque, Guinea-Bissau
BQK	Brunswick, GA
BQL	Boulia, Australia
BQN	Aguadilla, PR
BQS	Blagoveschensk, Russia
BQT	Brest, Belarus
BQU	Port Elizabeth, Windward Islands
BRA	Barreiras, Brazil
BRC	San Carlos de Bariloche, Argentina
BRD	Brainerd, MN
BRE	Bremen, Germany
BRF	Bradford, England, UK
BRI	Bari, Italy
BRK	Bourke, Australia
BRL	Burlington, IA
BRM	Barquisimeto, Venezuela
BRN	Bern, Switzerland
BRO	Brownsville, TX
BRQ	Brno, Czech Rep.
BRR	Barra, Scotland, UK
BRS	Bristol, England, UK
BRT	Bathurst Is., Australia
BRU	Brussels, Belgium
BRW	Barrow, AK
BSA	Bossaso, Somalia
BSB	Brasilia, Brazil
BSC	Bahia Solano, Colombia
BSD	Baoshan, China
BSG	Bata, Equatorial Guinea
BSK	Biskra, Algeria
BSL	Basel, Switzerland/Mulhouse, France
BSU	Basankusu, Congo, Dem. Rep.
BTH	Batam, Indonesia
BTI	Barter Island, AK
BTJ	Banda Aceh, Indonesia
BTK	Bratsk, Russia
BTL	Battle Creek, MI
BTM	Butte, MT
BTR	Baton Rouge, LA
BTS	Bratislava, Slovakia

BTT	Bettles, AK
BTU	Bintulu, Malaysia
BTV	Burlington, VT
BUA	Buka, Papua New Guinea
BUC	Burketown, Australia
BUD	Budapest, Hungary
BUE	Buenos Aires (Metro), Argentina
BUF	Buffalo, NY
BUG	Benguela, Angola
BUH	Bucharest (Metro), Romania
BUK	Albuq, Yemen
BUL	Bulolo, Papua New Guinea
BUO	Burao, Somalia
BUQ	Bulawayo, Zimbabwe
BUR	Burbank, CA
BUS	Batumi, Georgia
BUX	Bunia, Congo, Dem. Rep.
BUZ	Bushehr, Iran
BVB	Boa Vista, Brazil
BVC	Boa Vista, Cape Verde Islands
BVE	Brive-La-Gaillarde, France
BVG	Berlevag, Norway
BVH	Vilhena, Brazil
BVI	Birdsville, Australia
BVR	Brava, Cape Verde Islands
BWA	Bhairawa, Nepal
BWB	Barrow Island, Australia
BWD	Brownwood, TX
BWI	Baltimore, MD
BWK	Bol, Croatia
BWN	Bandar Seri Begawan, Brunei Darussalam
BWQ	Brewarrina, Australia
BWT	Burnie, Australia
BXH	Balhash, Kazakstan
BXM	Batom, Indonesia
BXN	Bodrum, Turkey
BXU	Butuan, Philippines
BXX	Borama, Somalia
BYA	Boundary, AK
BYB	Dibaa, Oman
BYK	Bouake, Cote D'lvoire
BYM	Bayamo, Cuba
BYU	Bayreuth, Germany
BYW	Blakely Island, WA
BZA	Bonanza, Nicaragua
BZE	Belize City, Belize
BZL	Barisal, Bangladesh
BZN	Bozeman, MT
BZR	Beziers, France
BZV	Brazzaville, Congo
BZZ	Brize Norton, England, UK
CAB	Cabinda, Angola
CAC	Cascavel, Brazil
CAE	Columbia, SC
CAG	Cagliari, Italy

CAI	Cairo, Egypt	CGD	Changde, China
CAJ	Canaima, Venezuela	CGH	Sao Paulo (Congonhas), Brazil
CAK	Akron/Canton, OH	CGI	Cape Girardeau, MO
CAL	Campbeltown, Scotland, UK	CGK	Jakarta (Soekarno), Indonesia
CAN	Guangzhou (Canton), China	CGN	Cologne/Bonn, Germany
CAP	Cap Haitien, Haiti	CGO	Zhengzhou, China
CAQ	Caucasia, Colombia	CGP	Chittagong, Bangladesh
CAS	Casablanca (Anfa), Morocco	CGQ	Changchun, China
CAW	Campos, Brazil	CGR	Campo Grande, Brazil
CAY	Cayenne, Fr. Guiana	CGX	Chicago (Meigs), IL
CAZ	Cobar, Australia	CGY	Cagayan de Oro, Philippines
CBB	Cochabamba, Bolivia	CHA	Chattanooga, TN
CBE	Cumberland, MD	CHC	Christchurch, New Zealand
CBG	Cambridge, England, UK	CHG	Chaoyang, China
CBH	Bechar, Algeria	CHH	Chachapoyas, Peru
CBL	Ciudad Bolivar, Venezuela	CHI	Chicago (Metro), IL
CBO	Cotabato, Philippines	CHM	Chimbote, Peru
CBQ	Calabar, Nigeria	CHO	Charlottesville, VA
CBR	Canberra, Australia	CHP	Circle Hot Springs, AK
CBV	Coban, Guatemala	CHQ	Chania, Crete, Greece
CCC	Cayo Coco, Cuba	CHS	Charleston, SC
CCJ	Calicut, India	CHT	Chatham Island, New Zealand
CCK	Cocos-Keeling Is., Indian Ocean	CHU	Chuathbaluk, AK
CCM	Crisciuma, Brazil	CHX	Changuinola, Panama
CCP	Concepcion, Chile	CHY	Choiseul Bay, Solomon Islands
CCS	Caracas, Venezuela	CIA	Rome (Ciampino), Italy
CCU	Calcutta, India	CIC	Chico, CA
CCV	Craig Cove, Vanuatu	CID	Cedar Rapids/Iowa City, IA
CCZ	Chub Cay, Bahamas	CIJ	Cobija, Bolivia
CDB	Cold Bay, AK	CIK	Chalkyitsik, AK
CDC	Cedar City, UT	CIS	Canton Island, Kiribati
CDD	Cauquira, Honduras	CIT	Shimkent, Kazakstan
CDG	Paris (De Gaulle), France	CIU	Sault Ste. Marie (Chippewa), MI
CDJ	Conceicao Do Araguaia, Brazil		
CDL	Candle, AK	CIW	Canouan Is., Windward Islands
CDR	Chadron, NE	CIX	Chiclayo, Peru
CDV	Cordova, AK	CJA	Cajamarca, Peru
CEB	Cebu, Philippines	CJB	Coimbatore, India
CEC	Crescent City, CA	CJC	Calama, Chile
CED	Ceduna, Australia	CJL	Chitral, Pakistan
CEI	Chiang Rai, Thailand	CJS	Ciudad Juarez, Mexico
CEK	Chelyabinsk, Russia	CJU	Cheju, Korea
CEM	Central, AK	CKB	Clarksburg, WV
CEN	Ciudad Obregon, Mexico	CKD	Crooked Creek, AK
CEO	Waco Kungo, Angola	CKG	Chongqing, China
CEQ	Cannes, France	CKS	Carajas, Brazil
CER	Cherbourg, France	CKX	Chicken, AK
CEZ	Cortez, CO	CKY	Conakry, Guinea
CFD	Bryan, TX	CLD	Carlsbad, CA
CFE	Clermont-Ferrand, France	CLE	Cleveland, OH
CFN	Donegal, Ireland	CLJ	Cluj, Romania
CFR	Caen, France	CLL	College Station, TX
CFS	Coffs Harbour, Australia	CLM	Port Angeles, WA
CFU	Kerkyra, Greece	CLO	Cali, Colombia
CGA	Craig, AK	CLP	Clarks Point, AK
CGB	Cuiaba, Brazil	CLQ	Colima, Mexico

CLT	Charlotte, NC	CRP	Corpus Christi, TX	
CLY	Calvi, Corsica, France	CRQ	Caravelas, Brazil	
CMA	Cunnamulla, Australia	CRU	Carriacou Is., Grenada	
CMB	Colombo, Sri Lanka	CRV	Crotone, Italy	
CMD	Cootamundra, Australia	CRW	Charleston, WV	
CME	Ciudad Del Carmen, Mexico	CSE	Crested Butte, CO	
CMG	Corumba, Brazil	CSG	Columbus, GA	
CMH	Columbus, OH	CSI	Casino, Australia	
CMI	Champaign, IL	CSK	Cap Skirring, Senegal	
CMK	Club Makokola, Malawi	CSU	Santa Cruz Do Sul, Brazil	
CMN	Casablanca (Mohamed V),	CSX	Changsha, China	
	Morocco	CTA	Catania, Italy	
CMP	Santana Do Araguaia, Brazil	CTC	Catamarca, Argentina	
CMU	Kundiawa, Papua New Guinea	CTD	Chitre, Panama	
CMW	Camaguey, Cuba	CTG	Cartagena, Colombia	
CMX	Hancock, MI	CTL	Charleville, Australia	
CNB	Coonamble, Australia	CTM	Chetumal, Mexico	
CND	Constanta, Romania	CTN	Cooktown, Australia	
CNF	Belo Horizonte (Confins), Brazil	CTS	Sapporo (Chitose), Japan	
CNJ	Cloncurry, Australia	CTU	Chengdu, China	
CNL	Sindal, Denmark	CUC	Cucuta, Colombia	
CNM	Carlsbad, NM	CUE	Cuenca, Ecuador	
CNO	Chino, CA	CUG	Orange (Cudal), Australia	
CNP	Neerlerit Inaat, Greenland	CUJ	Culion, Philippines	
CNQ	Corrientes, Argentina	CUK	Caye Caulker, Belize	
CNS	Cairns, Australia	CUL	Culiacan, Mexico	
CNX	Chiang Mai, Thailand	CUM	Cumana, Venezuela	
CNY	Moab, UT	CUN	Cancun, Mexico	
COC	Concordia, Argentina	CUQ	Coen, Australia	
COD	Cody, WY	CUR	Curaçao, Neth. Antilles	
COE	Coeur D'Alene, ID	CUU	Chihuahua, Mexico	
COG	Condoto, Colombia	CUW	Cube Cove, AK	
COJ	Coonabarabran, Australia	CUY	Cue, Australia	
COK	Cochin, India	CUZ	Cuzco, Peru	
COO	Cotonou, Benin	CVC	Cleve, Australia	
COR	Cordoba, Argentina	CVG	Cincinnati, OH	
COS	Colorado Springs, CO	CVL	Cape Vogel, Papua New Guinea	
COU	Columbia, MO	CVM	Ciudad Victoria, Mexico	
CPB	Capurgana, Colombia	CVN	Clovis, NM	
CPC	San Martin de los Andes,	CVO	Albany, OR	
	Argentina	CVQ	Carnarvon, Australia	
CPD	Coober Pedy, Australia	CVT	Coventry, England, UK	
CPE	Campeche, Mexico	CVU	Corvo Island, Portugal	
CPH	Copenhagen, Denmark	CWA	Wausau (Wisc. Cntl.), WI	
CPI	Cape Orford, Papua New	CWB	Curitiba, Brazil	
	Guinea	CWL	Cardiff, Wales, UK	
CPO	Copiapo, Chile	CWR	Cowarie, Australia	
CPQ	Campinas, Brazil	CWS	Center Island, WA	
CPR	Casper, WY	CWT	Cowra, Australia	
CPT	Cape Town, South Africa	CXB	Cox's Bazar, Bangladesh	
CPV	Campina Grande, Brazil	CXI	Christmas Is., Kiribati	
CPX	Culebra, PR	CXJ	Caxias Do Sul, Brazil	
CRD	Comodoro Rivadavia,	CYB	Cayman Brac Is., West Indies	
	Argentina	CYF	Chefornak, AK	
CRI	Crooked Is., Bahamas	CYI	Chiayi, Taiwan	
CRL	Charleroi, Belgium	CYO	Cayo Largo del Sur, Cuba	

61

Airport Codes

62

CYR	Colonia, Uruguay
CYS	Cheyenne, WY
CZA	Chichen Itza, Mexico
CZE	Coro, Venezuela
CZH	Corozal, Belize
CZL	Constantine, Algeria
CZM	Cozumel, Mexico
CZN	Chisana, AK
CZS	Cruzeiro Do Sul, Brazil
CZX	Changzhou, China
DAB	Daytona Beach, FL
DAC	Dhaka, Bangladesh
DAD	Da Nang, Viet Nam
DAL	Dallas/Ft. Worth (Love), TX
DAM	Damascus, Syria
DAR	Dar Es Salaam, Tanzania
DAU	Daru, Papua New Guinea
DAV	David, Panama
DAX	Daxian, China
DAY	Dayton, OH
DBA	Dalbandin, Pakistan
DBM	Debra Marcos, Ethiopia
DBO	Dubbo, Australia
DBQ	Dubuque, IA
DBT	Debra Tabor, Ethiopia
DBV	Dubrovnik, Croatia
DCA	Washington (Reagan), DC
DCF	Dominica (Cane), West Indies
DCM	Castres, France
DDC	Dodge City, KS
DDG	Dandong, China
DDI	Daydream Is., Australia
DDM	Dodoima, Papua New Guinea
DEA	Dera Ghazi Khan, Pakistan
DEC	Decatur, IL
DEL	Delhi, India
DEM	Dembidollo, Ethiopia
DEN	Denver, CO
DER	Derim, Papua New Guinea
DET	Detroit (City), MI
DEZ	Deirezzor, Syria
DFW	Dallas/Ft. Worth (Intl), TX
DGA	Dangriga, Belize
DGE	Mudgee, Australia
DGO	Durango, Mexico
DGT	Dumaguete, Philippines
DHA	Dhahran, Saudi Arabia
DHI	Dhangarhi, Nepal
DHN	Dothan, AL
DIB	Dibrugarh, India
DIE	Antsiranana, Madagascar
DIJ	Dijon, France
DIK	Dickenson, ND
DIL	Dili, Indonesia
DIN	Dien-Bien-Phu, Viet Nam
DIO	Diomede Island, AK

DIQ	Divinopolis, Brazil
DIR	Dire Dawa, Ethiopia
DIS	Loubomo, Congo
DIU	Diu, India
DIY	Diyarbakir, Turkey
DJB	Jambi, Indonesia
DJE	Djerba, Tunisia
DJG	Djanet, Algeria
DJJ	Jayapura, Indonesia
DJN	Delta Junction, AK
DKI	Dunk Is., Australia
DKR	Dakar, Senegal
DLA	Douala, Cameroon
DLC	Dalian, China
DLD	Geilo, Norway
DLG	Dillingham, AK
DLH	Duluth, MN/Superior, WI
DLI	Dalat, Viet Nam
DLM	Dalaman, Turkey
DLO	Dolomi, AK
DLU	Dali City, China
DLY	Dillons Bay, Vanuatu
DMB	Zhambyl, Kazakstan
DMD	Doomadgee Mission, Australia
DME	Moscow (Domodedovo), Russia
DMN	Deming, NM
DMU	Dimapur, India
DND	Dundee, Scotland, UK
DNH	Dunhuang, China
DNK	Dnepropetrovsk, Ukraine
DNM	Denham, Australia
DNR	Dinard, France
DNZ	Denizli, Turkey
DOB	Dobo, Indonesia
DOF	Dora Bay, AK
DOG	Dongola, Sudan
DOK	Donetsk, Ukraine
DOL	Deauville, France
DOM	Dominica, West Indies
DOP	Dolpa, Nepal
DOU	Dourados, Brazil
DPL	Dipolog, Philippines
DPO	Devonport, Australia
DPS	Denpasar, Indonesia
DRB	Derby, Australia
DRG	Deering, AK
DRO	Durango, CO
DRS	Dresden, Germany
DRT	Del Rio, TX
DRW	Darwin, Australia
DSD	La Desirade, Guadeloupe
DSE	Dessie, Ethiopia
DSK	Dera Ismail Khan, Pakistan
DSM	Des Moines, IA
DTM	Dortmund, Germany

DTR	Decatur Island, WA	ELG	El Golea, Algeria	
DTT	Detroit (Metro), MI	ELH	North Eleuthera, Bahamas	
DTW	Detroit (Wayne Cty), MI	ELI	Elim, AK	
DUB	Dublin, Ireland	ELM	Elmira/Corning, NY	
DUD	Dunedin, New Zealand	ELP	El Paso, TX	
DUE	Dundo, Angola	ELQ	Gassim, Saudi Arabia	
DUJ	DuBois, PA	ELS	East London, South Africa	
DUR	Durban, South Africa	ELU	El Oued, Algeria	
DUS	Duesseldorf, Germany	ELV	Elfin Cove, AK	
DUT	Dutch Harbor, AK	ELY	Ely, NV	
DVL	Devils Lake, ND	EMA	East Midlands, England, UK	
DVN	Davenport, IA	EMI	Emirau, Papua New Guinea	
DVO	Davao, Philippines	EMK	Emmonak, AK	
DXB	Dubai, UAE	EMN	Nema, Mauritania	
DYG	Dayong, China	ENA	Kenai, AK	
DYR	Anadyr, Russia	ENF	Enontekio, Finland	
DYU	Dushanbe, Tajikistan	ENS	Enschede, Netherlands	
DZA	Dzaoudzi, Mayotte	ENT	Enewetok, Marshall Islands	
DZN	Zhezkazgan, Kazakstan	ENU	Enugu, Nigeria	
EAA	Eagle, AK	ENY	Yan'an, China	
EAE	Emae, Vanuatu	EOH	Medellin (Herrera), Colombia	
EAM	Nejran, Saudi Arabia	EPL	Epinal, France	
EAR	Kearney, NE	EPR	Esperance, Australia	
EAS	San Sebastian, Spain	EQS	Esquel, Argentina	
EAT	Wenatchee, WA	ERA	Erigavo, Somalia	
EAU	Eau Claire, WI	ERC	Erzincan, Turkey	
EBA	Elba Is., Italy	ERD	Berdyansk, Ukraine	
EBB	Entebbe/Kampala, Uganda	ERF	Erfurt, Germany	
EBJ	Esbjerg, Denmark	ERH	Errachidia, Morocco	
EBO	Ebon, Marshall Islands	ERI	Erie, PA	
EBU	St. Etienne, France	ERM	Erechim, Brazil	
ECN	Ercan, Cyprus	ERS	Windhoek (Eros), Namibia	
EDA	Edna Bay, AK	ERZ	Erzurum, Turkey	
EDI	Edinburgh, Scotland, UK	ESA	Esa'Ala, Papua New Guinea	
EDR	Edward River, Australia	ESB	Ankara (Esenboga), Turkey	
EEK	Eek, AK	ESC	Escanaba, MI	
EEN	Keene, NH/Brattleboro, VT	ESD	Eastsound, WA	
EFD	Houston (Ellington), TX	ESL	Elista, Russia	
EFG	Efoge, Papua New Guinea	ESM	Esmeraldas, Ecuador	
EFL	Kefallinia, Greece	ESR	El Salvador, Chile	
EGC	Bergerac, France	ESS	Essen, Germany	
EGE	Vail (Eagle County), CO	ETH	Elat, Israel	
EGL	Neghelli, Ethiopia	ETZ	Metz/Nancy, France	
EGM	Sege, Solomon Islands	EUA	Eua, Tonga	
EGS	Egilsstadir, Iceland	EUG	Eugene, OR	
EGV	Eagle River, WI	EUN	Laayoune, Morocco	
EGX	Egegik, AK	EUX	St. Eustatius, Neth. Antilles	
EHM	Cape Newenham, AK	EVE	Evenes, Norway	
EIN	Eindhoven, Netherlands	EVG	Sveg, Sweden	
EIS	Beef Island, BVI	EVN	Yerevan, Armenia	
EJA	Barrancabermeja, Colombia	EVV	Evansville, IN	
EJH	Wedjh, Saudi Arabia	EWB	Fall River/New Bedford, MA	
EKB	Ekibastuz, Kazakstan	EWN	New Bern, NC	
EKO	Elko, NV	EWR	Newark, NJ/New York, NY	
ELD	El Dorado, AR	EXI	Excursion Inlet, AK	
ELE	El Real, Panama	EXT	Exeter, England, UK	

Airport Codes

63

EYL	Yelimane, Mali
EYP	El Yopal, Colombia
EYW	Key West, FL
EZE	Buenos Aires (Pistarini), Argentina
EZS	Elazig, Turkey
FAE	Faroe Islands, Denmark
FAI	Fairbanks, AK
FAJ	Fajardo, PR
FAK	False Island, AK
FAN	Farsund, Norway
FAO	Faro, Portugal
FAQ	Freida River, Papua New Guinea
FAR	Fargo, ND
FAT	Fresno, CA
FAV	Fakarava, Fr. Polynesia
FAY	Fayetteville, NC
FBE	Francisco Beltrao, Brazil
FBM	Lubumbashi, Congo, Dem. Rep.
FBU	Oslo (Fornebu), Norway
FCA	Kalispell/Glacier Natl Pk, MT
FCO	Rome (Fiumicino), Italy
FDE	Forde, Norway
FDF	Fort De France, Martinique
FDH	Friedrichshafen, Germany
FEG	Fergana, Uzbekistan
FEN	Fernando de Noronha, Brazil
FEZ	Fez, Morocco
FGI	Apia (Fagali I.), Western Samoa
FHU	Fort Huachuca/Sierra Vista, AZ
FID	Fishers Island, NY
FIH	Kinshasa, Congo, Dem. Rep.
FIN	Finschhafen, Papua New Guinea
FJR	Al-Fujairah, UAE
FKI	Kisangani, Congo, Dem. Rep.
FKL	Franklin, PA
FKS	Fukushima, Japan
FLA	Florencia, Colombia
FLG	Flagstaff, AZ
FLI	Flateyri, Iceland
FLL	Fort Lauderdale, FL
FLN	Florianopolis, Brazil
FLO	Florence, SC
FLR	Florence, Italy
FLS	Flinders Is., Australia
FLT	Flat, AK
FMA	Formosa, Argentina
FMI	Kalemie, Congo, Dem. Rep.
FMN	Farmington, NM
FMO	Muenster, Germany
FMY	Fort Myers, FL
FNA	Freetown, Sierra Leone
FNC	Funchal, Portugal

FNE	Fane, Papua New Guinea
FNI	Nimes, France
FNJ	Pyongyang, N. Korea
FNL	Fort Collins/Loveland, CO
FNT	Flint, MI
FOC	Fuzhou, China
FOD	Fort Dodge, IA
FON	Fortuna, Costa Rica
FOR	Fortaleza, Brazil
FPO	Freeport, Bahamas
FRA	Frankfurt, Germany
FRB	Forbes, Australia
FRC	Franca, Brazil
FRD	Friday Harbor, WA
FRE	Fera Is., Solomon Islands
FRG	Farmingdale (Republic), NY
FRO	Floro, Norway
FRS	Flores, Guatemala
FRU	Bishkek, Kyrgyzstan
FRW	Francistown, Botswana
FSC	Figari, France
FSD	Sioux Falls, SD
FSM	Fort Smith, AR
FSP	St. Pierre, St. Pierre and Miquelon
FTA	Futuna Island, Vanuatu
FTU	Fort Dauphin, Madagascar
FTX	Owando, Congo
FUE	Fuerteventura, Spain
FUJ	Fukue, Japan
FUK	Fukuoka, Japan
FUN	Funafuti Atol, Tuvalu
FUT	Futuna, Wallis & Futuna Is.
FWA	Fort Wayne, IN
FYU	Fort Yukon, AK
GAJ	Yamagata, Japan
GAL	Galena, AK
GAM	Gambell, AK
GAN	Gan Island, Maldives
GAO	Guantanamo, Cuba
GAQ	Gao, Mali
GAU	Gauhati, India
GAX	Gamba, Gabon
GBD	Great Bend, KS
GBE	Gaborone, Botswana
GBI	Grand Bahama Island, Bahamas
GBJ	Marie Galante, Fr. Antilles
GCC	Gillette, WY
GCI	Guernsey, Channel Islands, UK
GCK	Garden City, KS
GCM	Grand Cayman, Cayman Islands
GCN	Grand Canyon, AZ
GDE	Gode/Iddidole, Ethiopia
GDL	Guadalajara, Mexico

GDN	Gdansk, Poland	GNV	Gainesville, FL	
GDQ	Gondar, Ethiopia	GOA	Genoa, Italy	
GDT	Grand Turk Is., Turks & Caicos	GOB	Goba, Ethiopia	
		GOE	Gonalia, Papua New Guinea	
GDV	Glendive, MT	GOH	Nuuk, Greenland	
GDX	Magadan, Russia	GOI	Goa, India	
GDZ	Gelendzik, Russia	GOJ	Nizhniy Novgorod, Russia	
GEA	Noumea (Magenta), New Caledonia	GOM	Goma, Congo, Dem. Rep.	
		GON	New London/Groton, CT	
GEG	Spokane, WA	GOQ	Golmud, China	
GEL	Santo Angelo, Brazil	GOR	Gore, Ethiopia	
GEN	Oslo (Gardermoen), Norway	GOT	Gothenburg, Sweden	
GEO	Georgetown, Guyana	GOV	Gove, Australia	
GER	Nueva Gerona, Cuba	GPA	Patras, Greece	
GES	General Santos, Philippines	GPI	Guapi, Colombia	
GET	Geraldton, Australia	GPN	Garden Point, Australia	
GEV	Gallivare, Sweden	GPT	Gulfport/Biloxi, MS	
GFF	Griffith, Australia	GPZ	Grand Rapids, MN	
GFK	Grand Forks, ND	GRB	Green Bay, WI	
GFN	Grafton, Australia	GRI	Grand Island, NE	
GGG	Gladewater/Kilgore/Longview, TX	GRJ	George, South Africa	
		GRP	Gurupi, Brazil	
GGT	George Town, Bahamas	GRQ	Groningen, Netherlands	
GGW	Glasgow, MT	GRR	Grand Rapids, MI	
GHA	Ghardaia, Algeria	GRU	Sao Paulo (Guarulhos), Brazil	
GHB	Governors Harbour, Bahamas	GRW	Graciosa Is., Portugal	
GHC	Great Harbour Cay, Bahamas	GRX	Granada, Spain	
GHD	Ghimbi, Ethiopia	GRZ	Graz, Austria	
GHE	Garachine, Panama	GSA	Long Pasia, Malaysia	
GIB	Gibraltar, Gibraltar	GSO	Greensboro/H.Pt/Win-Salem, NC	
GIG	Rio de Janeriro (Intl), Brazil			
GIL	Gilgit, Pakistan	GSP	Greenville/Spartanburg, SC	
GIS	Gisborne, New Zealand	GST	Gustavus, AK	
GIZ	Gizan, Saudi Arabia	GTA	Gatokae, Solomon Islands	
GJA	Guanaja, Honduras	GTE	Groote Is., Australia	
GJL	Jijel, Algeria	GTF	Great Falls, MT	
GJT	Grand Junction, CO	GTN	Mount Cook (Glentanner), New Zealand	
GKA	Goroka, Papua New Guinea			
GKL	Great Keppel Is., Australia	GTO	Gorontalo, Indonesia	
GLA	Glasgow, Scotland, UK	GTR	Columbus/Strkvl/W. Pt., MS	
GLF	Golfito, Costa Rica	GUA	Guatemala City, Guatemala	
GLH	Greenville, MS	GUB	Guerrero Negro, Mexico	
GLI	Glen Innes, Australia	GUC	Gunnison, CO	
GLT	Gladstone, Australia	GUD	Goundam, Mali	
GLV	Golovin, AK	GUH	Gunnedah, Australia	
GMA	Gemena, Congo, Dem. Rep.	GUM	Guam, GU	
GMB	Gambela, Ethiopia	GUP	Gallup, NM	
GMI	Gasmata Is., Papua New Guinea	GUR	Alotau, Papua New Guinea	
		GUW	Atyrau, Kazakstan	
GMP	Seoul (Kimpo), Korea	GUZ	Guarapari, Brazil	
GMR	Gambier Is., Fr. Polynesia	GVA	Geneva, Switzerland	
GNB	Grenoble, France	GVR	Governador Valadares, Brazil	
GND	Grenada, Windward Islands	GVX	Gavle, Sweden	
GNM	Guanambi, Brazil	GWD	Gwadar, Pakistan	
GNR	General Roca, Argentina	GWE	Gweru, Zimbabwe	
GNU	Goodnews Bay, AK	GWL	Gwalior, India	

65

Airport Codes

66

*The Travel Agent's
Complete Desk
Reference*

GWT	Westerland, Germany
GWY	Galway, Ireland
GXF	Seiyun, Yemen
GYA	Guayaramerin, Bolivia
GYE	Guayaquil, Ecuador
GYM	Guaymas, Mexico
GYN	Goiania, Brazil
GYY	Gary, IN
GZM	Gozo, Malta
GZO	Gizo, Solomon Islands
GZT	Gaziantep, Turkey
HAA	Hasvik, Norway
HAC	Hachijo Jima, Japan
HAD	Halmstad, Sweden
HAE	Havasupai, AZ
HAH	Moroni (Hahaya), Comoros
HAJ	Hanover, Germany
HAK	Haikou, China
HAM	Hamburg, Germany
HAN	Hanoi, Viet Nam
HAP	Long Is., Australia
HAQ	Hanimaadhoo, Maldives
HAR	Harrisburg, PA
HAS	Hail, Saudi Arabia
HAU	Haugesund, Norway
HAV	Havana, Cuba
HBA	Hobart, Australia
HBG	Hattiesburg, MS
HBH	Hobart Bay, AK
HBI	Harbour Island, Bahamas
HBT	Hafr Al Batin, Saudi Arabia
HCR	Holy Cross, AK
HDB	Heidelberg, Germany
HDD	Hyderabad, Pakistan
HDF	Heringsdorf, Germany
HDN	Hayden, CO
HDS	Hoedspruit, South Africa
HDY	Hat Yai, Thailand
HEH	Heho, Myanmar
HEK	Heihe, China
HEL	Helsinki, Finland
HER	Heraklion, Greece
HET	Hohhot, China
HFA	Haifa, Israel
HFD	Hartford, CT/Springfield,MA
HFE	Hefei, China
HFN	Hornafjordur, Iceland
HFS	Hagfors, Sweden
HFT	Hammerfest, Norway
HGA	Hargeisa, Somalia
HGD	Hughenden, Australia
HGH	Hangzhou, China
HGL	Helgoland, Germany
HGN	Mae Hong Son, Thailand
HGO	Korhogo, Cote D'Ivoire
HGR	Hagerstown, MD

HGU	Mount Hagen, Papua New Guinea
HHA	Huanghua, China
HHH	Hilton Head Island, SC
HHN	Hahn, Germany
HHQ	Hua Hin, Thailand
HIB	Hibbing/Chisolm, MN
HII	Lake Havasu City, AZ
HIJ	Hiroshima, Japan
HIL	Shillavo, Ethiopia
HIN	Chinju, Korea
HIR	Honiara, Solomon Islands
HIS	Hayman Is., Australia
HIT	Haiwaro, Papua New Guinea
HJR	Khajuraho, India
HKB	Healy Lake, AK
HKD	Hakodate, Japan
HKG	Hong Kong, Hong Kong
HKK	Hokitika, New Zealand
HKN	Hoskins, Papua New Guinea
HKT	Phuket, Thailand
HKY	Hickory, NC
HLD	Hailar, China
HLF	Hultsfred, Sweden
HLG	Wheeling, WV
HLN	Helena, MT
HLP	Jakarta (Halim), Indonesia
HLZ	Hamilton, New Zealand
HME	Hassi Messaoud, Algeria
HMO	Hermosillo, Mexico
HMV	Hemavan, Sweden
HNA	Morioka, Japan
HND	Tokyo (Haneda), Japan
HNH	Hoonah, AK
HNL	Honolulu (Oahu) HI
HNM	Hana, Maui, HI
HNS	Haines, AK
HOB	Hobbs, NM
HOD	Hodeidah, Yemen
HOE	Houeisay, Laos
HOF	Hofuf, Saudi Arabia
HOG	Holguin, Cuba
HOI	Hao Is., Fr. Polynesia
HOK	Hooker Creek, Australia
HOM	Homer, AK
HON	Huron, SD
HOQ	Hof, Germany
HOR	Horta, Portugal
HOS	Chos Malal, Argentina
HOT	Hot Springs, AR
HOU	Houston (Hobby), TX
HOV	Orsta-Volda, Norway
HPA	Ha'apai, Tonga
HPB	Hooper Bay, AK
HPH	Haiphong, Viet Nam
HPN	White Plains, NY

HPV	Princeville, Kauai, HI	IFJ	Isafjordur, Iceland	
HRB	Harbin, China	IFN	Isfahan, Iran	
HRE	Harare, Zimbabwe	IFO	Ivano-Frankovsk, Ukraine	
HRG	Hurghada, Egypt	IFP	Bullhead City, AZ	
HRK	Kharkov, Ukraine	IGA	Inagua, Bahamas	
HRL	Harlingen, TX	IGG	Igiugig, AK	
HRO	Harrison, AR	IGM	Kingman, AZ	
HSH	Las Vegas (Henderson), NV	IGO	Chigorodo, Colombia	
HSL	Huslia, AK	IGR	Iguazu, Argentina	
HSV	Huntsville/Decatur, AL	IGU	Iguassu Falls, Brazil	
HTA	Chita, Russia	IHU	Ihu, Papua New Guinea	
HTI	Hamilton Is., Australia	IIA	Inishmaan, Ireland	
HTN	Hotan, China	IIS	Nissan Is., Papua New Guinea	
HTO	East Hampton, NY	IKI	Iki, Japan	
HTR	Hateruma, Japan	IKO	Nikolski, AK	
HTS	Huntington, WV/Ashland, KY	IKT	Irkutsk, Russia	
HUE	Humera, Ethiopia	ILE	Killeen, TX	
HUF	Terre Haute, IN	ILG	Wilmington, DE	
HUG	Huehuetenango, Guatemala	ILI	Iliamna, AK	
HUH	Huahine Is., Fr. Polynesia	ILM	Wilmington, NC	
HUI	Hue, Viet Nam	ILO	Iloilo, Philippines	
HUN	Hualien, Taiwan	ILP	Ile Des Pins, New Caledonia	
HUS	Hughes, AK	ILQ	Ilo, Peru	
HUU	Huanuco, Peru	ILY	Islay, Scotland, UK	
HUV	Hudiksvall, Sweden	IMF	Imphal, India	
HUX	Huatulco, Mexico	IMI	Ine, Marshall Islands	
HUY	Humberside, England, UK	IMK	Simikot, Nepal	
HVB	Hervey Bay, Australia	IMP	Imperatriz, Brazil	
HVG	Honningsvag, Norway	IMT	Iron Mountain, MI	
HVN	New Haven, CT	INC	Yinchuan, China	
HVR	Havre, MT	IND	Indianapolis, IN	
HWN	Hwange Nat'l Park, Zimbabwe	INL	Int'l Falls, MN	
HXX	Hay, Australia	INN	Innsbruck, Austria	
HYA	Hyannis, MA	INQ	Inisheer, Ireland	
HYD	Hyderabad, India	INT	Winston-Salem (Smith-Reynolds), NC	
HYG	Hydaburg, AK			
HYL	Hollis, AK	INU	Nauru Is., Rep. of Nauru	
HYN	Huangyan, China	INV	Inverness, Scotland, UK	
HYS	Hays, KS	INZ	In Salah, Algeria	
HZG	Hanzhong, China	IOA	Ioannina, Greece	
HZK	Husavik, Iceland	IOK	Iokea, Papua New Guinea	
IAD	Washington (Dulles), DC	IOM	Isle of Man, UK	
IAH	Houston (Intercontinental), TX	ION	Impfondol, Congo	
IAM	In Amenas, Algeria	IOR	Inishmore, Ireland	
IAN	Kiana, AK	IOS	Ilheus, Brazil	
IAS	Iasi, Romania	IOW	Iowa City, IA	
IBE	Ibague, Colombia	IPA	Ipota, Vanuatu	
IBI	Iboki, Papua New Guinea	IPC	Easter Island, Chile	
IBZ	Ibiza, Spain	IPH	Ipoh, Malaysia	
ICI	Cicia, Fiji	IPI	Ipiales, Colombia	
ICN	Seoul (Inchon), Korea	IPL	El Centro/Imperial, CA	
ICT	Wichita, KS	IPN	Ipatinga, Brazil	
IDA	Idaho Falls, ID	IPT	Williamsport, PA	
IDB	Idre, Sweden	IQM	Qiemo, China	
IDR	Indore, India	IQQ	Iquique, Chile	
IEV	Kiev (Metro), Ukraine	IQT	Iquitos, Peru	

Airport Codes

IRA	Kirakira, Solomon Islands	JDH	Jodhpur, India
IRC	Circle, AK	JDO	Juazeiro Do Norte, Brazil
IRG	Lockhart River, Australia	JDZ	Jingdezhen, China
IRJ	La Rioja, Argentina	JED	Jeddah, Saudi Arabia
IRK	Kirksville, MO	JEF	Jefferson City, MO
IRP	Isiro, Congo, Dem. Rep.	JEJ	Jeh, Marshall Islands
ISA	Mount. Isa, Australia	JER	Jersey, Channel Islands, UK
ISB	Islamabad, Pakistan	JFK	New York (Kennedy), NY
ISC	Isles of Scilly (St. Marys), UK	JFR	Paamiut, Greenland
ISG	Ishigaki, Japan	JGA	Jamnagar, India
ISN	Williston, ND	JGB	Jagdalpur, India
ISO	Kinston, NC	JGR	Groennedal, Greenland
ISP	Islip (Macarthur), NY	JHB	Johor Bahru, Malaysia
IST	Istanbul, Turkey	JHG	Jinghong, China
ITB	Itaituba, Brazil	JHM	Kapalua, Maui, HI
ITH	Ithaca, NY	JHQ	Shute Harbour, Australia
ITM	Osaka (Itami), Japan	JHW	Jamestown, NY
ITN	Itabuna, Brazil	JIB	Djibouti, Djibouti
ITO	Hilo, Hawaii, HI	JIK	Ikaria Island, Greece
IUE	Niue Island, Niue	JIL	Jilin, China
IVA	Ambanja, Madagascar	JIM	Jimma, Ethiopia
IVC	Invercargill, New Zealand	JIU	Jiujiang, China
IVL	Ivalo, Finland	JIW	Jiwani, Pakistan
IVR	Inverell, Australia	JJI	Juanjui, Peru
IWD	Ironwood, MI	JKG	Jonkoping, Sweden
IWJ	Iwami, Japan	JKH	Chios, Greece
IXA	Agartala, India	JKR	Janakpur, Nepal
IXB	Bagdogra, India	JKT	Jakarta (Metro), Indonesia
IXC	Chandigarh, India	JLN	Joplin, MO
IXE	Mangalore, India	JMK	Mikonos, Greece
IXI	Lilabari, India	JMO	Jomsom, Nepal
IXJ	Jammu, India	JMS	Jamestown, ND
IXK	Keshad, India	JMU	Jiamusi, China
IXL	Leh, India	JNB	Johannesburg, South Africa
IXM	Madurai, India	JNN	Nanortalik, Greenland
IXR	Ranchi, India	JNS	Narsaq, Greenland
IXS	Silchar, India	JNU	Juneau, AK
IXU	Aurangabad, India	JNX	Naxos, Greece
IXY	Kandla, India	JNZ	Jinzhou, China
IXZ	Port Blair, India	JOE	Joensuu, Finland
IYK	Inyokern, CA	JOG	Yogyakarta, Indonesia
IZM	Izmir (Metro), Turkey	JOI	Joinville, Brazil
IZO	Izumo, Japan	JON	Johnston Island, Pacific Ocean
JAC	Jackson Hole, WY	JOS	Jos, Nigeria
JAG	Jacobabad, Pakistan	JPA	Joao Pessoa, Brazil
JAI	Jaipur, India	JPR	Ji-Parana, Brazil
JAN	Jackson, MS	JQE	Jaque, Panama
JAQ	Jacquinot Bay, Papua New Guinea	JRA	New York (W30th St. H/P), NY
JAT	Jabot, Marshall Islands	JRB	New York (Dntwn H/P), NY
JAV	Ilulissat, Greenland	JRE	New York (E60th St H/P), NY
JAX	Jacksonville, FL		
JBR	Jonesboro, AR	JRH	Jorhat, India
JCB	Joacaba, Brazil	JRO	Kilimanjaro, Tanzania
JCK	Julia Creek, Australia	JRS	Jerusalem, Israel
JDF	Juiz De Fora, Brazil	JSH	Sitia, Greece

JSI	Skiathos, Greece	KFA	Kiffa, Mauritania	
JSR	Jessore, Bangladesh	KFG	Kalkurung, Australia	
JST	Johnstown, PA	KFP	False Pass, AK	
JSU	Sukkertoppen, Greenland	KGA	Kananga, Congo, Dem. Rep.	
JSY	Syros, Greece	KGC	Kingscote, Australia	
JSZ	St. Tropez, France	KGD	Kaliningrad, Russia	
JTR	Santorini (Thira), Greece	KGE	Kagau, Solomon Islands	
JTY	Astypalaia Is., Greece	KGF	Karaganda, Kazakstan	
JUJ	Jujuy, Argentina	KGI	Kalgoorlie, Australia	
JUL	Juliaca, Peru	KGL	Kigali, Rwanda	
JUM	Jumla, Nepal	KGO	Kirovograd, Ukraine	
JUV	Upernavik, Greenland	KGS	Kos, Greece	
JUZ	Juzhou, China	KGW	Kagi, Papua New Guinea	
JVA	Ankavandra, Madagascar	KGX	Grayling, AK	
JYV	Jyvaskyla, Finland	KHG	Kashi, China	
KAB	Kariba, Zimbabwe	KHH	Kaohsiung, Taiwan	
KAC	Kameshli, Syria	KHI	Karachi, Pakistan	
KAD	Kaduna, Nigeria	KHM	Khamti, Myanmar	
KAE	Kake, AK	KHN	Nanchang, China	
KAG	Kangnung, Korea	KHS	Khasab, Oman	
KAJ	Kajaani, Finland	KHV	Khabarovsk, Russia	
KAL	Kaltag, AK	KIB	Ivanof Bay, AK	
KAN	Kano, Nigeria	KID	Kristianstad, Sweden	
KAO	Kuusamo, Finland	KIF	Kingfisher Lake, ON	
KAT	Kaitaia, New Zealand	KIJ	Niigata, Japan	
KAW	Kawthaung, Myanmar	KIM	Kimberley, South Africa	
KAX	Kalbarri, Australia	KIN	Kingston, Jamaica	
KBC	Birch Creek, AK	KIO	Kili Is., Marshall Islands	
KBE	Bell Island, AK	KIR	Kerry County, Ireland	
KBL	Kabul, Afghanistan	KIS	Kisumu, Kenya	
KBP	Kiev (Borispol), Ukraine	KIT	Kithira, Greece	
KBR	Kota Bharu, Malaysia	KIV	Kishinev, Moldova	
KBT	Kaben, Marshall Islands	KIX	Kansai (Osaka/Kyoto), Japan	
KCA	Kuqa, China	KJA	Krasnoyarsk, Russia	
KCC	Coffman Cove, AK	KJP	Kerama, Japan	
KCH	Kuching, Malaysia	KKA	Koyuk, AK	
KCL	Chignik, AK	KKB	Kitoi Bay, AK	
KCM	Kahramanmaras, Turkey	KKC	Khon Kaen, Thailand	
KCZ	Kochi, Japan	KKD	Kokoda, Papua New Guinea	
KDD	Khuzdar, Pakistan	KKE	Kerikeri, New Zealand	
KDI	Kendari, Indonesia	KKH	Kongiganak, AK	
KDM	Kaadedhdhoo, Maldives	KKI	Akiachak, AK	
KDO	Kadhdhoo, Maldives	KKJ	Kita Kyushu, Japan	
KDR	Kandrian, Papua New Guinea	KKN	Kirkenes, Norway	
KDU	Skardu, Pakistan	KKR	Kaukura Atoll, Fr. Polynesia	
KDV	Kandavu, Fiji	KKU	Ekuk, AK	
KEF	Reykjavik (Keflavik), Iceland	KKX	Kikaiga Shima, Japan	
KEH	Kenmore Air Harbor, WA	KKZ	Koh Kong, Cambodia	
KEJ	Kemerovo, Russia	KLG	Kalskag, AK	
KEK	Ekwok, AK	KLL	Levelock, AK	
KEL	Kiel, Germany	KLN	Larsen Bay, AK	
KEM	Kemi/Tornio, Finland	KLO	Kalibo, Philippines	
KEP	Nepalganj, Nepal	KLR	Kalmar, Sweden	
KER	Kerman, Iran	KLT	Kaiserslauter, Germany	
KET	Kengtung, Myanmar	KLU	Klagenfurt, Austria	
		KLW	Klawock, AK	

Airport Codes

69

KLX	Kalamata, Greece
KLZ	Kleinzee, South Africa
KMA	Kerema, Papua New Guinea
KMG	Kunming, China
KMI	Miyazaki, Japan
KMJ	Kumamoto, Japan
KMO	Manokotak, AK
KMP	Keetmanshoop, Namibia
KMQ	Komatsu, Japan
KMV	Kalemyo, Myanmar
KMY	Moser Bay, AK
KND	Kindu, Congo, Dem. Rep.
KNH	Kinmen, Taiwan
KNK	Kakhonak, AK
KNQ	Kone, New Caledonia
KNS	King Is., Australia
KNW	New Stuyahok, AK
KNX	Kununurra, Australia
KNZ	Kenieba, Mali
KOA	Kona, Hawaii, HI
KOC	Koumac, New Caledonia
KOE	Kupang, Indonesia
KOI	Kirkwall, Scotland, UK
KOJ	Kagoshima, Japan
KOK	Kokkola/Pietarsaari, Finland
KOP	Nakhon Phanom, Thailand
KOS	Sihanoukville, Cambodia
KOT	Kotlik, AK
KOU	Koulamoutou, Gabon
KOV	Kokshetau, Kazakstan
KOW	Ganzhou, China
KOY	Olga Bay, AK
KOZ	Ouzinkie, AK
KPB	Point Baker, AK
KPC	Port Clarence, AK
KPI	Kapit, Malaysia
KPK	Parks, AK
KPN	Kipnuk, AK
KPO	Pohang, Korea
KPR	Port Williams, AK
KPS	Kempsey, Australia
KPV	Perryville, AK
KPY	Port Bailey, AK
KQA	Akutan, AK
KRB	Karumba, Australia
KRF	Kramfors, Sweden
KRI	Kikori, Papua New Guinea
KRK	Krakow, Poland
KRL	Korla, China
KRN	Kiruna, Sweden
KRP	Karup, Denmark
KRR	Krasnodar, Russia
KRS	Kristiansand, Norway
KRT	Khartoum, Sudan
KRW	Krasnowodsk, Turkmenistan
KRY	Karamay, China
KSA	Kosrae, Micronesia
KSC	Kosice, Slovakia
KSD	Karlstad, Sweden
KSH	Kermanshah, Iran
KSJ	Kasos Island, Greece
KSM	St. Mary's, AK
KSN	Kostanay, Kazakstan
KSO	Kastoria, Greece
KSQ	Karshi, Uzbekistan
KSU	Kristiansund, Norway
KSY	Kars, Turkey
KTA	Karratha, Australia
KTB	Thorne Bay, AK
KTD	Kitadaito, Japan
KTE	Kerteh, Malaysia
KTM	Kathmandu, Nepal
KTN	Ketchikan, AK
KTP	Kingston (Tinson), Jamaica
KTR	Katherine, Australia
KTS	Brevig Mission, AK
KTT	Kittila, Finland
KTW	Katowice, Poland
KUA	Kuantan, Malaysia
KUC	Kuria, Kiribati
KUD	Kudat, Malaysia
KUF	Samara, Russia
KUH	Kushiro, Japan
KUK	Kasigluk, AK
KUL	Kuala Lumpur, Malaysia
KUM	Yakushima, Japan
KUN	Kaunas, Lithuania
KUO	Kuopio, Finland
KUQ	Kuri, Papua New Guinea
KUS	Kulusuk Is., Greenland
KUU	Kulu, India
KUV	Kunsan, Korea
KUY	Kamusi, Papua New Guinea
KVA	Kavala, Greece
KVB	Skovde, Sweden
KVC	King Cove, AK
KVD	Gyandzha, Azerbaijan
KVE	Kitava, Papua New Guinea
KVG	Kavieng, Papua New Guinea
KVL	Kivalina, AK
KWA	Kwajalein, Marshall Islands
KWE	Guiyang, China
KWF	Waterfall, AK
KWI	Kuwait, Kuwait
KWJ	Kwangju, Korea
KWK	Kwigillingok, AK
KWL	Guilin, China
KWM	Kowanyama, Australia
KWN	Quinhagak, AK
KWP	West Point, AK
KWT	Kwethluk, AK
KWY	Kiwayu, Kenya

KXA	Kasaan, AK	LDY	Londonderry, N. Ireland, UK
KXF	Koro, Fiji	LEA	Learmonth, Australia
KYA	Konya, Turkey	LED	St. Petersburg, Russia
KYK	Karluk, AK	LEH	Le Havre, France
KYP	Kyaukpyu, Myanmar	LEI	Almeria, Spain
KYS	Kayes, Mali	LEJ	Leipzig, Germany
KYU	Koyukuk, AK	LEL	Lake Evella, Australia
KZB	Zachar Bay, AK	LEN	Leon, Mexico
KZI	Kozani, Greece	LEQ	Lands End, England, UK
KZN	Kazan, Russia	LER	Leinster, Australia
KZO	Kyzl Orda, Kazakstan	LET	Leticia, Colombia
KZS	Kastelorizo, Greece	LEV	Bureta, Fiji
LAD	Luanda, Angola	LEW	Lewiston/Auburn, ME
LAE	Lae, Papua New Guinea	LEX	Lexington, KY
LAF	Lafayette, IN	LFT	Lafayette, LA
LAI	Lannion, France	LFW	Lome, Togo
LAJ	Lages, Brazil	LGA	New York (La Guardia), NY
LAM	Los Alamos, NM	LGB	Long Beach, CA
LAN	Lansing, MI	LGH	Leigh Creek, Australia
LAO	Laoag, Philippines	LGI	Deadman's Cay/Long Island,
LAP	La Paz, Mexico		Bahamas
LAR	Laramie, WY	LGK	Langkawi, Malaysia
LAS	Las Vegas, NV	LGL	Long Lellang, Malaysia
LAU	Lamu, Kenya	LGP	Legaspi, Philippines
LAW	Lawton, OK	LGQ	Lago Agrio, Ecuador
LAX	Los Angeles (Intl), CA	LGS	Malargue, Argentina
LAZ	Bom Jesus Da Lapa, Brazil	LGW	London (Gatwick), England, UK
LBA	Leeds, England, UK	LGZ	Leguizamo, Colombia
LBB	Lubbock, TX	LHE	Lahore, Pakistan
LBE	Latrobe, PA	LHG	Lightning Ridge, Australia
LBF	North Platte, NE	LHR	London (Heathrow), England,
LBH	Sydney (Palm Beach), Australia		UK
LBL	Liberal, KS	LHW	Lanzhou, China
LBP	Long Banga, Malaysia	LIF	Lifou, New Caledonia
LBQ	Lambarene, Gabon	LIG	Limoges, France
LBS	Labasa, Fiji	LIH	Kauai Is. (Lihue), HI
LBU	Labuan, Malaysia	LIJ	Long Island, AK
LBV	Libreville, Gabon	LIK	Likiep Is., Marshall Islands
LBX	Lubang, Philippines	LIL	Lille, France
LCA	Larnaca, Cyprus	LIM	Lima, Peru
LCE	La Ceiba, Honduras	LIN	Milan (Linate), Italy
LCF	Rio Dulce, Guatemala	LIQ	Lisala, Congo, Dem. Rep.
LCG	La Coruna, Spain	LIR	Liberia, Costa Rica
LCH	Lake Charles, LA	LIS	Lisbon, Portugal
LCK	Columbus (Rickenbacker), OH	LIT	Little Rock, AR
LCP	Loncopue, Argentina	LIW	Loikaw, Myanmar
LCY	London (City), England, UK	LJA	Lodja, Congo, Dem. Rep.
LDB	Londrina, Brazil	LJG	Lijiang City, China
LDC	Lindeman Is., Australia	LJU	Ljubljana, Slovenia
LDE	Lourdes/Tarbes, France	LKB	Lakeba, Fiji
LDH	Lord Howe Is., Australia	LKL	Lakselv, Norway
LDI	Lindi, Tanzania	LKN	Leknes, Norway
LDK	Lidkoping, Sweden	LKO	Lucknow, India
LDM	Ludington, MI	LKP	Lake Placid, NY
LDN	Lamidanda, Nepal	LLA	Lulea, Sweden
LDU	Lahad Datu, Malaysia	LLI	Lalibela, Ethiopia

71

Airport Codes

72

*The Travel Agent's
Complete Desk
Reference*

LLW	Lilongwe, Malawi	LUA	Lukla, Nepal
LMA	Lake Minchumina, AK	LUC	Laucala Island, Fiji
LML	Lae Is., Marshall Islands	LUD	Luderitz, Namibia
LMM	Los Mochis, Mexico	LUG	Lugano, Switzerland
LMN	Limbang, Malaysia	LUK	Cincinnati (Municipal), OH
LMP	Lampedusa, Italy	LUM	Luxi, China
LMT	Klamath Falls, OR	LUN	Lusaka, Zambia
LNB	Lamen Bay, Vanuatu	LUO	Luena, Angola
LNE	Lonorore, Vanuatu	LUP	Kalaupapa, HI
LNG	Lese/Lihir Island, Papua New Guinea	LUQ	San Luis, Argentina
		LUR	Cape Lisburne, AK
LNK	Lincoln, NE	LUX	Luxembourg, Luxembourg
LNO	Leonora, Australia	LVB	Livramento, Brazil
LNS	Lancaster, PA	LVD	Lime Village, AK
LNY	Lanai City, HI	LVI	Livingstone, Zambia
LNZ	Linz, Austria	LVO	Laverton, Australia
LOD	Longana, Vanuatu	LWB	Lewisburg/Greenbrier Valley, WV
LOF	Loen, Marshall Islands		
LON	London (Metro), England, UK	LWK	Shetland Is. (Lerwick), Scotland, UK
LOS	Lagos, NIgeria		
LOV	Monclova, Mexico	LWN	Gyourmi, Armenia
LPA	Las Palmas, Canary Islands	LWO	Lvov, Ukraine
LPB	La Paz, Bolivia	LWS	Lewiston, ID
LPI	Linkoping, Sweden	LWT	Lewistown, MT
LPL	Liverpool, England, UK	LWY	Lawas, Malaysia
LPM	Lamap, Vanuatu	LXA	Lhasa, China
LPP	Lappeenranta, Finland	LXG	Luang Namtha, Laos
LPQ	Luang Prabang, Laos	LXR	Luxor, Egypt
LPS	Lopez Island, WA	LXS	Lemnos, Greece
LPT	Lampang, Thailand	LYA	Luoyang, China
LPY	Le Puy, France	LYC	Lycksele, Sweden
LRD	Laredo, TX	LYG	Lianyungang, China
LRE	Longreach, Australia	LYH	Lynchburg, VA
LRH	La Rochelle, France	LYP	Faisalabad, Pakistan
LRL	Niamtougou, Togo	LYR	Longyearbyen, Norway
LRS	Leros, Greece	LYS	Lyon, France
LRT	Lorient, France	LZC	Lazaro Cardenas, Mexico
LRU	Las Cruces, NM	LZH	Liuzhou, China
LSA	Losuia, Papua New Guinea	LZO	Luzhou, China
LSC	La Serena, Chile	LZR	Lizard Is., Australia
LSE	La Crosse WI/Winona, MN	MAA	Chennai/Madras, India
LSH	Lashio, Myanmar	MAB	Maraba, Brazil
LSI	Shetland Is. (Sumburgh), Scotland, UK	MAD	Madrid, Spain
		MAF	Midland/Odessa, TX
LSM	Long Semado, Malaysia	MAG	Madang, Papua New Guinea
LSP	Las Piedras, Venezuela	MAH	Menorca, Spain
LSQ	Los Angeles, Chile	MAJ	Majuro, Marshall Islands
LSS	Terre De Haut, Guadeloupe	MAM	Matamoros, Mexico
LST	Launceston, Australia	MAN	Manchester, England, UK
LSU	Long Sukang, Malaysia	MAO	Manaus, Brazil
LSY	Lismore, Australia	MAQ	Mae Sot, Thailand
LTK	Latakia, Syria	MAR	Maracaibo, Venezuela
LTL	Lastourville, Gabon	MAS	Manus Is., Papua New Guinea
LTN	London (Luton), England, UK	MAT	Matadi, Congo, Dem. Rep.
LTO	Loreto, Mexico	MAU	Maupiti, Fr. Polynesia
LTQ	Le Touquet, France	MAV	Maloelap Is., Marshall Islands

MAY	Mangrove Cay, Bahamas		MFJ	Moala, Fiji
MAZ	Mayaguez, PR		MFM	Macau, Macau
MBA	Mombasa, Kenya		MFN	Milford Sound, New Zealand
MBD	Mmabatho, South Africa		MFO	Manguna, Papua New Guinea
MBE	Monbetsu, Japan			
MBH	Maryborough, Australia		MFR	Medford, OR
MBJ	Montego Bay, Jamaica		MFU	Mfuwe, Zambia
MBL	Manistee, MI		MFZ	Mesalia, Papua New Guinea
MBP	Moyobamba, Peru		MGA	Managua, Nicaragua
MBS	Saginaw/Bay City/Midland, MI		MGB	Mount Gambier, Australia
MBU	Mbambanakira, Solomon Islands		MGD	Magdalena, Bolivia
			MGF	Maringa, Brazil
MBW	Moorabbin, Australia		MGH	Margate, South Africa
MCD	Mackinac Island, MI		MGM	Montgomery, AL
MCE	Merced, CA		MGQ	Mogadishu, Somalia
MCG	McGrath, AK		MGS	Mangaia, Cook Islands
MCI	Kansas City (Intl), MO		MGT	Millingimbi, Australia
MCK	McCook, NE		MGW	Morgantown, WV
MCM	Monte Carlo (H/P), Monaco		MGZ	Myeik, Myanmar
MCN	Macon, GA		MHD	Mashad, Iran
MCO	Orlando (Intl), FL		MHG	Mannheim, Germany
MCT	Muscat, Oman		MHH	Marsh Harbour, Bahamas
MCU	Montlucon, France		MHK	Manhattan, KS
MCV	MacArthur River, Australia		MHQ	Mariehamn, Finland
MCW	Mason City, IA		MHT	Manchester, NH
MCX	Makhachkala, Russia		MHX	Manihiki Is., Cook Islands
MCY	Sunshine Coast, Australia		MIA	Miami (Intl), FL
MCZ	Maceio, Brazil		MID	Merida, Mexico
MDC	Manado, Indonesia		MII	Marilia, Brazil
MDE	Medellin (Cordova), Colombia		MIJ	Mili Is., Marshall Islands
MDG	Mudanjiang, China		MIK	Mikkeli, Finland
MDI	Makurdi, Nigeria		MIL	Milan (Metro), Italy
MDK	Mbandaka, Congo, Dem. Rep.		MIM	Merimbula, Australia
MDL	Mandalay, Myanmar		MIR	Monastir, Tunisia
MDQ	Mar Del Plata, Argentina		MIS	Misima Is., Papua New Guinea
MDS	Middle Caicos, Turks & Caicos		MIU	Maiduguri, Nigeria
MDT	Harrisburg (Intl), PA		MJA	Manja, Madagascar
MDU	Mendi, Papua New Guinea		MJB	Mejit Is., Marshall Islands
MDW	Chicago (Midway), IL		MJC	Man, Cote D'Ivoire
MDZ	Mendoza, Argentina		MJD	Mohenjo Daro, Pakistan
MEB	Melbourne (Essendon), Australia		MJE	Majkin, Marshall Islands
			MJF	Mosjoen, Norway
MED	Madinah, Saudi Arabia		MJK	Monkey Mia, Australia
MEE	Mare, New Caledonia		MJL	Mouila, Gabon
MEG	Malange, Angola		MJM	Mbuji-Mayi, Congo, Dem. Rep.
MEH	Mehamn, Norway		MJN	Majunga, Madagascar
MEI	Meridian, MS		MJT	Mytilene, Greece
MEL	Melbourne (Tullamarine), Australia		MJV	Murcia, Spain
			MKC	Kansas City (Downtown), MO
MEM	Memphis, TN		MKE	Milwaukee, WI
MES	Medan, Indonesia		MKG	Muskegon, MI
MEU	Monte Dourado, Brazil		MKK	Hoolehua (Molokai), HI
MEX	Mexico City, Mexico		MKL	Jackson, TN
MFE	McAllen/Mission, TX		MKM	Mukah, Malaysia
MFF	Moanda, Gabon		MKN	Malekolon, Papua New Guinea
MFG	Muzaffarabad, Pakistan		MKP	Makemo, Fr. Polynesia

Airport Codes

73

*The Travel Agent's
Complete Desk
Reference*

MKQ	Merauke, Indonesia
MKR	Meekatharra, Australia
MKS	Mekane Selam, Ethiopia
MKU	Makokou, Gabon
MKY	Mackay, Australia
MKZ	Malacca, Malaysia
MLA	Malta, Malta
MLB	Melbourne, FL
MLE	Male, Maldives
MLG	Malang, Indonesia
MLH	Mulhouse, France/Basel, Switzerland
MLI	Moline, IL
MLL	Marshall, AK
MLM	Morelia, Mexico
MLN	Melilla, Spain
MLO	Milos, Greece
MLQ	Malalaua, Papua New Guinea
MLS	Miles City, MT
MLU	Monroe, LA
MLW	Monrovia (Sprigg Payne), Liberia
MLX	Malatya, Turkey
MLY	Manley Hot Springs, AK
MMA	Malmo (Metro), Sweden
MMB	Memanbetsu, Japan
MMD	Minami Daito, Japan
MME	Durham Tees Valley, England, UK
MMG	Mount Magnet, Australia
MMJ	Matsumoto, Japan
MMK	Murmansk, Russia
MMO	Maio, Cape Verde Islands
MMX	Malmo (Sturup), Sweden
MMY	Miyako Jima, Japan
MNB	Moanda, Congo, Dem. Rep.
MNF	Mana, Fiji
MNG	Maningrida, Australia
MNI	Montserrat, Montserrat
MNJ	Mananjary, Madagascar
MNK	Maiana, Kiribati
MNL	Manila, Philippines
MNT	Minto, AK
MNU	Maulmyine, Myanmar
MNY	Mono Is., Solomon Islands
MOA	Moa, Cuba
MOB	Mobile AL/Pascagoula, MS
MOC	Montes Claros, Brazil
MOD	Modesto, CA
MOF	Maumere, Indonesia
MOG	Mong Hsat, Myanmar
MOI	Mitiaro, Cook Islands
MOL	Molde, Norway
MON	Mount Cook, New Zealand
MOQ	Morondava, Madagascar
MOT	Minot, ND

MOU	Mountain Village, AK
MOW	Moscow (Metro), Russia
MOZ	Moorea, Fr. Polynesia
MPA	Mpacha, Namibia
MPD	Mirpur Khas, Pakistan
MPH	Caticlan, Philippines
MPL	Montpellier, France
MPM	Maputo, Mozambique
MPN	Mount Pleasant, Falkland Is.
MPU	Mapua, Papua New Guinea
MPV	Montpelier/Barre, VT
MPW	Mariupol, Ukraine
MQF	Magnitogorsk, Russia
MQH	Minacu, Brazil
MQL	Mildura, Australia
MQN	Mo I Rana, Norway
MQT	Marquette, MI
MQX	Makale, Ethiopia
MRB	Martinsburg, WV
MRD	Merida, Venezuela
MRE	Mara Lodges, Kenya
MRM	Manari, Papua New Guinea
MRS	Marseille, France
MRU	Mauritius, Mauritius
MRV	Mineralnye Vody, Russia
MRY	Monterey/Carmel, CA
MRZ	Moree, Australia
MSA	Muskrat Dam, ON
MSE	Manston, England, UK
MSH	Masirah, Oman
MSJ	Misawa, Japan
MSK	Mastic Point, Bahamas
MSL	Muscle Shoals/Florence/ Sheffield, AL
MSN	Madison, WI
MSO	Missoula, MT
MSP	Minneapolis/St. Paul, MN
MSQ	Minsk, Belarus
MSR	Mus, Turkey
MSS	Massena, NY
MST	Maastricht, Netherlands
MSU	Maseru, Lesotho
MSY	New Orleans, LA
MSZ	Namibe, Angola
MTF	Mizan Teferi, Ethiopia
MTH	Marathon, FL
MTI	Mosteiros, Cape Verde Islands
MTJ	Montrose, CO
MTK	Makin Is., Kiribati
MTL	Maitland, Australia
MTM	Metlakatia, AK
MTO	Mattoon, IL
MTR	Monteria, Colombia
MTS	Manzini, Swaziland
MTT	Minatitlan, Mexico

MTV	Mota Lava, Vanuatu	MZO	Manzanillo, Cuba	
MTY	Monterrey, Mexico	MZP	Motueka, New Zealand	
MUA	Munda, Solomon Islands	MZT	Mazatlan, Mexico	
MUB	Maun, Botswana	MZV	Mulu, Malaysia	
MUC	Munich, Germany	NAA	Narrabri, Australia	
MUE	Kamuela, HI	NAG	Nagpur, India	
MUK	Mauke Is., Cook Islands	NAK	Nakhon Ratchasima, Thailand	
MUN	Maturin, Venezuela	NAN	Nadi, Fiji	
MUR	Marudi, Malaysia	NAO	Nanchong, China	
MUW	Mascara, Algeria	NAP	Naples, Italy	
MUX	Multan, Pakistan	NAR	Nare, Colombia	
MUZ	Musoma, Tanzania	NAS	Nassau, Bahamas	
MVB	Franceville, Gabon	NAT	Natal, Brazil	
MVD	Montevideo, Uruguay	NAW	Narathiwat, Thailand	
MVM	Kayenta, AZ	NBC	Naberevnye Chelny, Russia	
MVN	Mount Vernon, IL	NBL	San Blas, Panama	
MVR	Maroua, Cameroon	NBO	Nairobi (Metro), Kenya	
MVS	Mucuri, Brazil	NCA	North Caicos, Turks & Caicos	
MVT	Mataiva, Fr. Polynesia	NCE	Nice, France	
MVY	Martha's Vineyard, MA	NCI	Necocli, Colombia	
MVZ	Masvingo, Zimbabwe	NCL	Newcastle, England, UK	
MWA	Marion, IL	NCR	San Carlos, Nicaragua	
MWD	Mianwali, Pakistan	NCU	Nukus, Uzbekistan	
MWF	Maewo, Vanuatu	NCY	Annecy, France	
MWH	Moses Lake, WA	NDB	Nouadhibou, Mauritania	
MWU	Mussau, Papua New Guinea	NDG	Qiqihar, China	
MWV	Mundulkiri, Cambodia	NDJ	Ndjamena, Chad	
MWZ	Mwanza, Tanzania	NDK	Namdrik Is., Marshall Islands	
MXH	Moro, Papua New Guinea	NDM	Mendi, Ethiopia	
MXL	Mexicali, Mexico	NDU	Rundu, Namibia	
MXM	Morombe, Madagascar	NDZ	Nordholz-Spieka, Germany	
MXP	Milan (Malpensa), Italy	NEF	Neftekamsk, Russia	
MXS	Maota, Savai'i Is., Western Samoa	NEG	Negril, Jamaica	
MXT	Maintirano, Madagascar	NEJ	Nejjo, Ethiopia	
MXX	Mora, Sweden	NER	Neryungri, Russia	
MXY	McCarthy, AK	NEU	Sam Neua, Laos	
MXZ	Meixian, China	NEV	Nevis, Leeward Islands	
MYA	Moruya, Australia	NFG	Nefteyugansk, Russia	
MYD	Malindi, Kenya	NFO	Niuafo'ou, Tonga	
MYE	Miyake Jima, Japan	NGA	Young, Australia	
MYF	San Diego (Montgomery), CA	NGB	Ningbo, China	
MYG	Mayaguana, Bahamas	NGD	Anegada, BVI	
MYJ	Matsuyama, Japan	NGE	Ngaoundere, Cameroon	
MYQ	Mysore, India	NGI	Ngau Is., Fiji	
MYR	Myrtle Beach, SC	NGO	Nagoya, Japan	
MYT	Myitkyina, Myanmar	NGS	Nagasaki, Japan	
MYU	Mekoryuk, AK	NGX	Manang, Nepal	
MYW	Mtwara, Tanzania	NHA	Nha-Trang, Viet Nam	
MYY	Miri, Malaysia	NHV	Nuku Hiva, Fr. Polynesia	
MZC	Mitzic, Gabon	NIB	Nikolai, AK	
MZG	Makung, Taiwan	NIC	Nicosia, Cyprus	
MZI	Mopti, Mali	NIG	Nikunau, Kiribati	
MZK	Marakei, Kiribati	NIM	Niamey, Niger	
MZL	Manizales, Colombia	NIX	Nioro, Mali	
MZM	Metz, France	NJC	Nizhnevartovsk, Russia	

NKC	Nouakchott, Mauritania		NVA	Neiva, Colombia
NKG	Nanjing, China		NVG	Nueva Guinea, Nicaragua
NKI	Naukiti, AK		NVK	Narvik, Norway
NKY	Nkayi, Congo		NVT	Navegantes, Brazil
NLA	Ndola, Zambia		NWI	Norwich, England, UK
NLD	Nuevo Laredo, Mexico		NYC	New York (Metro), NY
NLG	Nelson Lagoon, AK		NYK	Nanyuki, Kenya
NLK	Norfolk Is., Pacific Ocean		NYM	Nadym, Russia
NLP	Nelspruit, South Africa		NYN	Nyngan, Australia
NLV	Nikolaev, Ukraine		NYO	Stockholm (Skavsta), Sweden
NMA	Namangan, Uzbekistan		NYU	Nyaung-u, Myanmar
NME	Nightmute, AK		OAG	Orange, Australia
NMG	San Miguel, Panama		OAJ	Jacksonville, NC
NNB	Santa Ana, Solomon Islands		OAK	Oakland, CA
NNG	Nanning, China		OAL	Cacoal, Brazil
NNK	Naknek, AK		OAX	Oaxaca, Mexico
NNL	Nondalton, AK		OBO	Obihiro, Japan
NNT	Nan, Thailand		OBU	Kobuk, AK
NNY	Nanyang, China		OCH	Lufkin/Nacogdoches, TX
NOB	Nosara Beach, Costa Rica		OCJ	Ocho Rios, Jamaica
NOC	Connaught/Knock, Ireland		OCV	Ocana, Colombia
NOJ	Nojabrxsk, Russia		ODE	Odense, Denmark
NON	Nonouti, Kiribati		ODN	Long Seridan, Malaysia
NOS	Nossi-be, Madagascar		ODS	Odessa, Ukraine
NOU	Noumea, New Caledonia		ODW	Oak Harbor, WA
NOV	Huambo, Angola		ODY	Oudomxay, Laos
NPE	Napier, New Zealand		OER	Ornskoldsvik, Sweden
NPL	New Plymouth, New Zealand		OFK	Norfolk, NE
NQL	Niquelandia, Brazil		OFU	Ofu Island, AS
NQN	Neuquen, Argentina		OGG	Kahului, HI
NQU	Nuqui, Colombia		OGN	Yonaguni Jima, Japan
NQY	Newquay, England, UK		OGS	Ogdensburg, NY
NRA	Narrandera, Australia		OGV	Ongava Game Reserve,
NRK	Norrkoping, Sweden			Namibia
NRT	Tokyo (Narita), Japan		OGX	Ouargla, Algeria
NSI	Yaounde, Cameroon		OGZ	Vladikavkaz, Russia
NSK	Norilsk, Russia		OHD	Ohrid, Macedonia
NSN	Nelson, New Zealand		OIL	Oil City, PA
NSO	Scone, Australia		OIM	Oshima, Japan
NST	Nakhon Si Thammarat,		OIR	Okushiri, Japan
	Thailand		OIT	Oita, Japan
NTE	Nantes, France		OKA	Okinawa, Japan
NTG	Nantong, China		OKC	Oklahoma City, OK
NTL	Newcastle, Australia		OKD	Sapporo (Okadama), Japan
NTN	Normanton, Australia		OKE	Okino Erabu, Japan
NTO	Santo Antao, Cape Verde		OKI	Oki Island, Japan
	Islands		OKJ	Okayama, Japan
NTT	Niuatoputapu, Tonga		OKN	Okondja, Gabon
NTY	Sun City, South Africa		OKR	Yorke Is., Australia
NUB	Numbulwar, Australia		OKU	Mokuti Lodge, Namibia
NUE	Nuremberg, Germany		OLB	Olbia, Italy
NUI	Nuiqsut, AK		OLF	Wolf Point, MT
NUL	Nulato, AK		OLH	Old Harbour, AK
NUP	Nunapitchuk, AK		OLJ	Olpoi, Vanuatu
NUS	Norsup, Vanuatu		OLP	Olympic Dam, Australia
NUX	Novyj Urengoj, Russia		OMA	Omaha, NE

OMB	Omboue, Gabon	OUZ	Zouerate, Mauritania
OMD	Oranjemund, Namibia	OVB	Novosibirsk, Russia
OME	Nome, AK	OVD	Asturias, Spain
OMH	Urmieh, Iran	OWB	Owensboro, KY
OMO	Mostar, Bosnia	OXB	Bissau, Guinea Bissau
OMR	Oradea, Romania	OXR	Oxnard, CA
OMS	Omsk, Russia	OYE	Oyem, Gabon
ONA	Winona, MN	OZH	Zaporozhye, Ukraine
OND	Ondangwa, Namibia	OZZ	Ouarzazate, Morocco
ONG	Mornington, Australia	PAC	Panama City (Paitilla), Panama
ONT	Ontario, CA		
ONX	Colon, Panama	PAD	Paderborn, Germany
OOK	Toksook Bay, AK	PAH	Paducah, KY
OOL	Gold Coast, Australia	PAJ	Para Chinar, Pakistan
OOM	Cooma, Australia	PAP	Port Au Prince, Haiti
OOT	Onotoa, Kiribati	PAR	Paris (Metro), France
OPB	Open Bay, Papua New Guinea	PAS	Paros, Greece
OPO	Porto, Portugal	PAT	Patna, India
OPS	Sinop, Brazil	PAV	Paulo Afonso, Brazil
OPU	Balimo, Papua New Guinea	PAZ	Poza Rica, Mexico
ORB	Orebro, Sweden	PBC	Puebla, Mexico
ORD	Chicago (O'Hare), IL	PBD	Porbandar, India
ORF	Norfolk, VA	PBE	Puerto Berrio, Colombia
ORG	Paramaribo (Zorg En Hoop), Suriname	PBH	Paro, Bhutan
		PBI	West Palm Beach, FL
ORH	Worcester, MA	PBJ	Paama, Vanuatu
ORI	Port Lions, AK	PBM	Paramaribo, Suriname
ORK	Cork, Ireland	PBO	Paraburdoo, Australia
ORN	Oran, Algeria	PBP	Punta Islita, Costa Rica
ORV	Noorvik, AK	PBR	Puerto Barrios, Guatemala
ORW	Ormara, Pakistan	PBU	Putao, Myanmar
ORY	Paris (Orly), France	PBZ	Plettenberg Bay, South Africa
OSA	Osaka (Metro), Japan	PCA	Portage Creek, AK
OSD	Ostersund, Sweden	PCH	Palacios, Honduras
OSH	Oshkosh, WI	PCL	Pucallpa, Peru
OSI	Osijek, Croatia	PCM	Playa Del Carmen, Mexico
OSK	Oskarshamn, Sweden	PCP	Principe Is., Principe Is.
OSL	Oslo (Metro), Norway	PCR	Puerto Carreno, Colombia
OSR	Ostrava, Czech Rep.	PDA	Puerto Inirida, Colombia
OSS	Osh, Kyrgyzstan	PDB	Pedro Bay, AK
OSW	Orsk, Russia	PDG	Padang, Indonesia
OSY	Namsos, Norway	PDL	Ponta Delgada, Portugal
OSZ	Koszalin, Poland	PDP	Punta Del Este, Uruguay
OTD	Contadora, Panama	PDS	Piedras Negras, Mexico
OTH	North Bend, OR	PDT	Pendleton, OR
OTM	Ottumwa, IA	PDX	Portland, OR
OTP	Bucharest (Otopeni), Romania	PEA	Penneshaw, Australia
OTR	Coto 47, Costa Rica	PEC	Pelican, AK
OTS	Anacortes, WA	PEE	Perm, Russia
OTU	Otu, Colombia	PEG	Perugia, Italy
OTV	Ontong Java, Solomon Islands	PEI	Pereira, Colombia
OTZ	Kotzebue, AK	PEK	Beijing (Capital), China
OUA	Ouagadougou, Burkina Faso	PEM	Puerto Maldonado, Peru
OUD	Oujda, Morocco	PEN	Penang, Malaysia
OUE	Ouesso, Congo	PER	Perth, Australia
OUL	Oulu, Finland	PES	Petrozavodsk, Russia

Airport Codes

PET	Pelotas, Brazil		PLJ	Placencia, Belize
PEU	Puerto Lempira, Honduras		PLM	Palembang, Indonesia
PEW	Peshawar, Pakistan		PLN	Pellston, MI
PFB	Passo Fundo, Brazil		PLO	Port Lincoln, Australia
PFJ	Patreksfjordur, Iceland		PLP	La Palma, Panama
PFN	Panama City, FL		PLQ	Palanga, Lithuania
PFO	Paphos, Cyprus		PLS	Providenciales, Turks & Caicos
PGA	Page, AZ		PLU	Belo Horizonte (Pampulha), Brazil
PGF	Perpignan, France			
PGK	Pangkalpinang, Indonesia		PLW	Palu, Indonesia
PGL	Pascagoula, MS		PLX	Semipalatinsk, Kazakstan
PGV	Greenville, NC		PLZ	Port Elizabeth, South Africa
PGX	Perigueux, France		PMA	Pemba, Tanzania
PGZ	Ponta Grossa, Brazil		PMC	Puerto Montt, Chile
PHB	Parnaiba, Brazil		PMD	Palmdale/Lancaster, CA
PHC	Port Harcourt, Nigeria		PMF	Parma, Italy
PHE	Port Hedland, Australia		PMG	Ponta Pora, Brazil
PHF	Hampton/Newport News/ Wmsbrg, VA		PMI	Palma Mallorca, Spain
			PML	Port Moller, AK
PHL	Philadelphia (Intl), PA		PMN	Pumani, Papua New Guinea
PHO	Point Hope, AK		PMO	Palermo, Italy
PHR	Pacific Harbour, Fiji		PMR	Palmerston N., New Zealand
PHS	Phitsanulok, Thailand		PMV	Porlamar, Venezuela
PHW	Phalaborwa, South Africa		PMW	Palmas, Brazil
PHX	Phoenix, AZ		PMY	Puerto Madryn, Argentina
PIA	Peoria, IL		PMZ	Palmar, Costa Rica
PIB	Laurel (Hattiesburg), MS		PNA	Pamplona, Spain
PID	Nassau (Paradise Is.), Bahamas		PNB	Porto Nacional, Brazil
			PNC	Ponca City, OK
PIE	St. Petersburg/Clearwater, FL		PND	Punta Gorda, Belize
PIF	Pingtung, Taiwan		PNH	Phnom Penh, Cambodia
PIH	Pocatello, ID		PNI	Pohnpei, Micronesia
PIK	Glasgow (Prestwick), Scotland, UK		PNK	Pontianak, Indonesia
			PNL	Pantelleria, Italy
PIP	Pilot Point, AK		PNP	Popondetta, Papua New Guinea
PIR	Pierre, SD			
PIS	Poitiers, France		PNQ	Poona, India
PIT	Pittsburgh, PA		PNR	Pointe Noire, Congo
PIU	Piura, Peru		PNS	Pensacola, FL
PIX	Pico Island, Portugal		PNZ	Petrolina, Brazil
PIZ	Point Lay, AK		POA	Porto Alegre, Brazil
PJC	Pedro Juan Caballero, Paraguay		POG	Port Gentil, Gabon
			POI	Potosi, Bolivia
PJG	Panjgur, Pakistan		POJ	Patos De Minas, Brazil
PJM	Puerto Jiminez, Costa Rica		POL	Pemba, Mozambique
PKA	Napaskiak, AK		POM	Port Moresby, Papua New Guinea
PKB	Marietta/Parkersburg, WV			
PKC	Petropavlovsk-Kamchats, Russia		POP	Puerto Plata, Dominican Rep.
			POR	Pori, Finland
PKE	Parkes, Australia		POS	Port of Spain, Trinidad & Tobago
PKR	Pokhara, Nepal			
PKU	Pekanbaru, Indonesia		POT	Port Antonio, Jamaica
PKY	Palangkaraya, Indonesia		POU	Poughkeepsie, NY
PKZ	Pakse, Laos		POY	Lovell, WY
PLB	Plattsburgh, NY		POZ	Poznan, Poland
PLH	Plymouth, England, UK		PPB	Pres. Prudente, Brazil

PPE	Puerto Penasco, Mexico		PVD	Providence, RI
PPG	Pago Pago, AS		PVH	Porto Velho, Brazil
PPK	Petropavlovsk, Kazakstan		PVK	Preveza/Lefkas, Greece
PPL	Phaplu, Nepal		PVR	Puerto Vallarta, Mexico
PPN	Popayan, Colombia		PWK	Chicago (Pal Waukee), IL
PPP	Proserpine, Australia		PWM	Portland, ME
PPQ	Paraparaumu, New Zealand		PWQ	Pavlodar, Kazakstan
PPS	Puerto Princesa, Philippines		PXM	Puerto Escondido, Mexico
PPT	Papeete, Fr. Polynesia		PXO	Porto Santo, Portugal
PPV	Port Protection, AK		PXU	Pleiku, Viet Nam
PPY	Pouso Alegre, Brazil		PYE	Penrhyn Is., Cook Islands
PQI	Presque Isle, ME		PYH	Puerto Ayacucho, Venezuela
PQM	Palenque, Mexico		PZB	Pietermaritzburg, South Africa
PQQ	Port Macquarie, Australia		PZE	Penzance, England, UK
PQS	Pilot Station, AK		PZH	Zhob, Pakistan
PRC	Prescott, AZ		PZO	Puerto Ordaz, Venezuela
PRG	Prague, Czech Rep.		PZU	Port Sudan, Sudan
PRH	Phrae, Thailand		QBC	Bella Coola, BC
PRI	Praslin Is., Seychelles Is.		QFK	Selje, Norway
PRN	Pristina, Yugoslavia		QFQ	Maloy Harbor, Norway
PRS	Parasi, Solomon Islands		QNY	New York (Marine Air Term.), NY
PSA	Pisa, Italy			
PSB	Bellefonte/Philipsburg, PA		QRO	Queretaro, Mexico
PSC	Pasco, WA		RAB	Rabaul, Papua New Guinea
PSE	Ponce, PR		RAD	Tortola (Road Town), BVI
PSG	Petersburg, AK		RAE	Arar, Saudi Arabia
PSI	Pasni, Pakistan		RAF	Ras An Naqb, Egypt
PSO	Pasto, Colombia		RAH	Rafha, Saudi Arabia
PSP	Palm Springs, CA		RAI	Praia, Cape Verde Islands
PSR	Pescara, Italy		RAJ	Rajkot, India
PSS	Posadas, Argentina		RAK	Marrakech, Morocco
PSZ	Puerto Suarez, Bolivia		RAL	Riverside, CA
PTA	Port Alsworth, AK		RAM	Ramingining, Australia
PTD	Port Alexander, AK		RAO	Ribeirao Preto, Brazil
PTF	Malololailai, Fiji		RAP	Rapid City, SD
PTG	Pietersburg, South Africa		RAR	Rarotonga, Cook Islands
PTH	Port Heiden, AK		RAS	Rasht, Iran
PTJ	Portland, Australia		RAZ	Rawala Kot, Pakistan
PTP	Pointe A Pitre, Guadeloupe		RBA	Rabat, Morocco
PTU	Platinum, AK		RBJ	Rebun, Japan
PTY	Panama City (Tocumen Intl), Panama		RBP	Rabaraba, Papua New Guinea
			RBR	Rio Branco, Brazil
PUB	Pueblo, CO		RBV	Ramata, Solomon Islands
PUF	Pau, France		RBY	Ruby, AK
PUG	Port Augusta, Australia		RCB	Richards Bay, South Africa
PUJ	Punta Cana, Dominican Rep.		RCE	Roche Harbor, WA
PUQ	Punta Arenas, Chile		RCH	Riohacha, Colombia
PUS	Pusan, Korea		RCL	Redcliffe, Vanuatu
PUT	Puttaparthi, India		RCM	Richmond, Australia
PUU	Puerto Asis, Colombia		RCU	Rio Cuarto, Argentina
PUV	Poum, New Caledonia		RDC	Redencao, Brazil
PUW	Pullman, WA		RDD	Redding, CA
PUY	Pula, Croatia		RDG	Reading, PA
PUZ	Puerto Cabezas, Nicaragua		RDM	Bend/Redmond, OR
PVA	Providencia, Colombia		RDS	Rincon de los Sauces, Argentina
PVC	Provincetown, MA		RDU	Raleigh/Durham, NC

RDV	Red Devil, AK	ROB	Monrovia (Roberts Intl), Liberia
RDZ	Rodez, France		
REC	Recife, Brazil	ROC	Rochester, NY
REG	Reggio Calabria, Italy	ROK	Rockhampton, Australia
REK	Reykjavik (Metro), Iceland	ROM	Rome (Metro), Italy
REL	Trelew, Argentina	ROO	Rondonopolis, Brazil
REN	Orenburg, Russia	ROP	Rota, Mariana Islands
REP	Siem Reap, Cambodia	ROR	Koror, Palau
RER	Retalhuleu, Guatemala	ROS	Rosario, Argentina
RES	Resistencia, Argentina	ROT	Rotorua, New Zealand
RET	Rost, Norway	ROV	Rostov, Russia
REU	Reus, Spain	ROW	Roswell, NM
REX	Reynosa, Mexico	RPM	Ngukurr, Australia
RFD	Rockford, IL	RPN	Rosh Pina, Israel
RFP	Raiatea, Fr. Polynesia	RPR	Raipur, India
RGA	Rio Grande, Argentina	RRG	Rodrigues Island, Mauritius
RGE	Porgera, Papua New Guinea	RRS	Roros, Norway
RGI	Rangiroa, Fr. Polynesia	RSA	Santa Rosa, Argentina
RGL	Rio Gallegos, Argentina	RSD	Rock Sound, Bahamas
RGN	Yangon, Myanmar	RSE	Sydney (Rose Bay), Australia
RHE	Reims, France	RSH	Russian Mission, AK
RHI	Rhinelander, WI	RSJ	Rosario, WA
RHO	Rhodes, Greece	RST	Rochester, MN
RIA	Santa Maria, Brazil	RSU	Yosu, Korea
RIB	Riberalta, Bolivia	RSW	Fort Myers (Regional), FL
RIC	Richmond/Wmsbrg, VA	RTA	Rotuma, Fiji
RIG	Rio Grande, Brazil	RTB	Roatan, Honduras
RIJ	Rioja, Peru	RTM	Rotterdam, Netherlands
RIK	Carrillo, Costa Rica	RTS	Rottnest Is., Australia
RIN	Ringi Cove, Solomon Islands	RTW	Saratov, Russia
RIO	Rio De Janeiro (Metro), Brazil	RUH	Riyadh, Saudi Arabia
RIS	Rishiri, Japan	RUI	Ruidoso, NM
RIW	Riverton, WY	RUN	Reunion Island, Indian Ocean
RIX	Riga, Latvia	RUR	Rurutu Is., Fr. Polynesia
RIY	Riyan Mukalla, Yemen	RUS	Marau Sound, Solomon Islands
RJH	Rajshahi, Bangladesh		
RKD	Rockland, ME	RUT	Rutland, VT
RKE	Copenhagen (Roskilde), Denmark	RVA	Farafangana, Madagascar
		RVH	St. Petersburg (Rzhevka), Russia
RKS	Rock Springs, WY		
RKT	Ras Al Khaimah, UAE	RVK	Roervik, Norway
RKV	Reykjavik (Domestic), Iceland	RVN	Rovaniemi, Finland
RLG	Rostock-Laage, Germany	RWI	Rocky Mount/Wilson, NC
RMA	Roma, Australia	RXS	Roxas City, Philippines
RMK	Renmark, Australia	RYK	Rahim Yar Khan, Pakistan
RMP	Rampart, AK	SAB	Saba, Neth. Antilles
RNA	Arona, Solomon Islands	SAF	Santa Fe, NM
RNB	Ronneby, Sweden	SAH	Sana'a, Yemen Arab Rep.
RNE	Roanne, France	SAK	Saudarkrokur, Iceland
RNI	Corn Is., Nicaragua	SAL	San Salvador, El Salvador
RNJ	Yoronjima, Japan	SAM	Salamo, Papua New Guinea
RNL	Rennell, Solomon Islands	SAN	San Diego (Lindberg), CA
RNN	Bornholm, Denmark	SAO	Sao Paulo (Metro), Brazil
RNO	Reno, NV	SAP	San Pedro Sula, Honduras
RNS	Rennes, France	SAQ	San Andros, Bahamas
ROA	Roanoke, VA	SAT	San Antonio, TX

SAV	Savannah, GA	SFQ	Sanliurfa, Turkey
SAX	Sambu, Panama	SFT	Skelleftea, Sweden
SBA	Santa Barbara, CA	SFU	Safia, Papua New Guinea
SBH	St. Barthelemy, Guadeloupe	SGC	Surgut, Russia
SBK	St. Brieuc, France	SGD	Sonderborg, Denmark
SBN	South Bend, IN	SGF	Springfield, MO
SBP	San Luis Obispo, CA	SGN	Ho Chi Minh, Viet Nam
SBS	Steamboat Springs, CO	SGO	St. George, Australia
SBU	Springbok, South Africa	SGR	Sugarland, TX
SBW	Sibu, Malaysia	SGU	St. George, UT
SBY	Salisbury, MD	SGY	Skagway, AK
SBZ	Sibiu, Romania	SHA	Shanghai, China
SCC	Prudhoe Bay/Deadhorse, AK	SHB	Nakashibetsu, Japan
SCE	State College, PA	SHC	Indaselassie, Ethiopia
SCJ	Smith Cove, AK	SHD	Staunton (Shenandoah Valley), VA
SCK	Stockton, CA		
SCL	Santiago, Chile	SHE	Shenyang, China
SCM	Scammon Bay, AK	SHG	Shungnak, AK
SCN	Saarbruecken, Germany	SHH	Shishmaref, AK
SCO	Aktau. Kazakstan	SHJ	Sharjah, UAE
SCQ	Santiago De Compostela, Spain	SHO	Sokcho, Korea
SCT	Socotra, Yemen	SHP	Qinhuangdao, China
SCU	Santiago, Cuba	SHR	Sheridan, WY
SCV	Suceava, Romania	SHS	Shashi, China
SCX	Salina Cruz, Mexico	SHT	Shepparton, Australia
SCY	San Cristobal, Ecuador	SHV	Shreveport, LA
SCZ	Santa Cruz Is., Solomon Islands	SHW	Sharurah, Saudi Arabia
SDA	Baghdad (Int'l), Iraq	SHX	Shageluk, AK
SDD	Lubango, Angola	SIA	Xi An (Xiguan), China
SDE	Santiago Del Estero, Argentina	SIC	Sinop, Turkey
SDF	Louisville, KY	SID	Sal, Cape Verde Islands
SDJ	Sendai, Japan	SIF	Simra, Nepal
SDK	Sandakan, Malaysia	SIG	San Juan (Isla Grand), PR
SDL	Sundsvall, Sweden	SIN	Singapore (Changi), Singapore
SDM	San Diego (Brown Field), CA	SIP	Simferopol, Ukraine
SDN	Sandane, Norway	SIR	Sion, Switzerland
SDP	Sand Point, AK	SIT	Sitka, AK
SDQ	Santo Domingo, Dominican Rep.	SIU	Siuna, Nicaragua
SDR	Santander, Spain	SIX	Singleton, Australia
SDT	Saidu Sharif, Pakistan	SJB	San Joaquin, Bolivia
SDU	Rio De Janeiro (Dumont), Brazil	SJC	San Jose, CA
SDV	Tel Aviv/Jaffa (Sde Dov), Israel	SJD	Los Cabos, Mexico
SDZ	Shetland Is., Scotland, UK	SJI	San Jose, Philippines
SEA	Seattle/Tacoma, WA	SJJ	Sarajevo, Bosnia
SEL	Seoul (Metro), Korea	SJK	Sao Jose Dos Campos, Brazil
SEY	Selibaby, Mauritania	SJO	San Jose, Costa Rica
SEZ	Mahe Is., Seychelles	SJP	Sao Jose Do Rio Preto, Brazil
SFA	Sfax, Tunisia	SJT	San Angelo, TX
SFB	Sanford, FL	SJU	San Juan (Munoz Marin), PR
SFD	San Fernando De Apure, Venezuela	SJW	Shijiazhuang, China
		SJY	Seinajoki, Finland
SFG	St. Maarten (Esperance), Neth. Antilles	SJZ	Sao Jorge Island, Portugal
		SKB	St. Kitts, St. Kitts & Nevis
SFJ	Kangerlussuaq, Greenland	SKD	Samarkand, Uzbekistan
SFN	Santa Fe, Argentina	SKE	Skien, Norway
SFO	San Francisco, CA	SKG	Thessaloniki, Greece

The Travel Agent's Complete Desk Reference

SKH	Surkhet, Nepal	SPD	Saidpur, Bangladesh
SKK	Shaktoolik, AK	SPI	Springfield, IL
SKL	Isle of Skye, Scotland, UK	SPK	Sapporo (Metro), Japan
SKN	Stokmarknes, Norway	SPN	Saipan, Mariana Islands
SKO	Sokoto, Nigeria	SPP	Menongue, Angola
SKP	Skopje, Macedonia	SPR	San Pedro, Belize
SKS	Vojens, Denmark	SPS	Wichita Falls, TX
SKU	Skiros, Greece	SPU	Split, Croatia
SKZ	Sukkur, Pakistan	SPW	Spencer, IA
SLA	Salta, Argentina	SQC	Southern Cross, Australia
SLC	Salt Lake City, UT	SQH	Son La, Viet Nam
SLE	Salem, OR	SQI	Sterling/Rock Falls, IL
SLH	Sola, Vanuatu	SQO	Storuman, Sweden
SLK	Saranac Lake, NY	SRA	Santa Rosa, Brazil
SLL	Salalah, Oman	SRE	Sucre, Bolivia
SLM	Salamanca, Spain	SRG	Semarang, Indonesia
SLN	Salina, KS	SRI	Samarinda, Indonesia
SLP	San Luis Potosi, Mexico	SRJ	San Borja, Bolivia
SLQ	Sleetmute, AK	SRP	Stord, Norway
SLU	St. Lucia, West Indies	SRQ	Sarasota/Bradenton, FL
SLV	Simla, India	SRV	Stony River, AK
SLW	Saltillo, Mexico	SRY	Sary, Iran
SLX	Salt Cay, Turks & Caicos	SRZ	Santa Cruz (Trompillo), Bolivia
SLY	Salehard, Russia	SSA	Salvador, Brazil
SLZ	Sao Luiz, Brazil	SSG	Malabo, Equatorial Guinea
SMA	Santa Maria, Portugal	SSH	Sharm El Sheikh, Egypt
SMF	Sacramento (Metro), CA	SSJ	Sandnessjoen, Norway
SMI	Samos, Greece	SSM	Sault Ste. Marie (Metro), MI
SMK	St. Michael, AK	SSR	Sara, Vanuatu
SML	Stella Maris, Bahamas	SSX	Samsun, Turkey
SMM	Semporna, Malaysia	SSY	M'banza Congo, Angola
SMR	Santa Marta, Colombia	STC	St. Cloud, MN
SMX	Santa Maria, CA	STE	Stevens Point, WI
SNA	Orange County/Santa Ana, CA	STG	St. George Island, AK
SNB	Snake Bay, Australia	STI	Santiago, Dominican Rep.
SNE	Sao Nicolau, Cape Verde Islands	STL	St. Louis (Lambert), MO
SNN	Shannon, Ireland	STM	Santarem, Brazil
SNO	Sakon Nakhon, Thailand	STN	London (Stansted), England, UK
SNP	St. Paul Island, AK		
SNV	Santa Elena, Venezuela	STO	Stockholm (Metro), Sweden
SNW	Thandwe, Myanmar	STR	Stuttgart, Germany
SNY	Sidney, NE	STS	Santa Rosa, CA
SOC	Solo City, Indonesia	STT	St. Thomas, VI
SOF	Sofia, Bulgaria	STV	Surat, India
SOG	Sogndal, Norway	STW	Stavropol, Russia
SOI	South Molle Is., Australia	STX	St. Croix, VI
SOJ	Sorkjosen, Norway	STZ	Santa Terezinha, Brazil
SOM	San Tome, Venezuela	SUB	Surabaya, Indonesia
SON	Espirtu Santo, Vanuatu	SUF	Lamezia/Terme, Italy
SOO	Soderhamn, Sweden	SUH	Sur, Oman
SOP	Pinehurst, NC	SUJ	Satu Mare, Romania
SOQ	Sorong, Indonesia	SUL	Sui, Pakistan
SOU	Southampton, England, UK	SUN	Sun Valley, ID
SOW	Show Low, AZ	SUV	Suva, Fiji
SOX	Sogamoso, Colombia	SUW	Superior, WI
SPC	Santa Cruz La Palma, Spain	SUX	Sioux City, IA

SVA	Savoonga, AK	TAH	Tanna, Vanuatu	
SVB	Sambava, Madagascar	TAI	Taiz, Yemen	
SVC	Silver City, NM	TAJ	Taji, Papua New Guinea	
SVD	St. Vincent, Windward Islands	TAK	Takamatsu, Japan	
SVG	Stavanger, Norway	TAL	Tanana, AK	
SVI	San Vincente Del Caguan, Colombia	TAM	Tampico, Mexico	
		TAO	Qingdao, China	
SVJ	Svolvaer, Norway	TAP	Tapachula, Mexico	
SVL	Savonlinna, Finland	TAS	Tashkent, Uzbekistan	
SVO	Moscow (Sheremetyevo), Russia	TAT	Tatry/Poprad, Slovakia	
		TAV	Tau, AS	
SVP	Kuito, Angola	TBB	Tuy Hoa, Vietnam	
SVQ	Seville, Spain	TBF	Tabiteuea North, Kiribati	
SVS	Stevens Village, AK	TBG	Tabubil, Papua New Guinea	
SVU	Savusavu, Fiji	TBI	The Bight, Bahamas	
SVX	Ekaterinburg, Russia	TBJ	Tabarka, Tunisia	
SVZ	San Antonio, Venezuela	TBO	Tabora, Tanzania	
SWA	Shantou, China	TBP	Tumbes, Peru	
SWD	Seward, AK	TBS	Tbilisi, Georgia	
SWF	Newburgh (Stewart), NY	TBT	Tabatinga, Brazil	
SWJ	South West Bay, Vanuatu	TBU	Tongatapu, Tonga	
SWP	Swakopmund, Namibia	TBZ	Tabriz, Iran	
SWT	Strzhewoi, Russia	TCA	Tennant Creek, Australia	
SXB	Strasbourg, France	TCB	Treasure Cay, Bahamas	
SXE	Sale, Australia	TCG	Tacheng, China	
SXF	Berlin (Schoenefeld), Germany	TCH	Tchibanga, Gabon	
		TCI	Tenerife (Metro), Spain	
SXH	Sehulea, Papua New Guinea	TCL	Tuscaloosa, AL	
SXL	Sligo, Ireland	TCO	Tumaco, Colombia	
SXM	St. Maarten, Neth. Antilles	TCP	Taba, Egypt	
SXO	Sao Felix Do Araguaia, Brazil	TCQ	Tacna, Peru	
		TCR	Tuticorin, India	
SXP	Sheldon Point, AK	TCT	Takotna, AK	
SXR	Srinagar, India	TDD	Trinidad, Bolivia	
SXW	Sauren, Papua New Guines	TED	Thisted, Denmark	
SXX	Sao Felix Do Xingu, Brazil	TEE	Tbessa, Algeria	
SXZ	Siirit, Turkey	TEH	Tetlin, AK	
SYB	Seal Bay, AK	TEO	Terapo, Papua New Guinea	
SYD	Sydney, Australia	TER	Terceira Is., Portugal	
SYE	Sadah, Yemen Arab Rep.	TET	Tete, Mozambique	
SYM	Simao, China	TEU	Te Anau, New Zealand	
SYO	Shonai, Japan	TEX	Telluride, CO	
SYP	Santiago, Panama	TEZ	Tezpur, India	
SYR	Syracuse, NY	TFF	Tefe, Brazil	
SYW	Sehwen Sharif, Pakistan	TFI	Tufi, Papua New Guinea	
SYX	Sanya, China	TFN	Tenerife (N. Los Rodeo), Spain	
SYY	Stornoway, Scotland, UK			
SYZ	Shiraz, Iran	TFS	Tenerife (Reina Sofia), Spain	
SZA	Soyo, Angola	TGD	Podgorica, Yugoslavia	
SZG	Salzburg, Austria	TGG	Kuala Terengganu, Malaysia	
SZK	Skukuza, South Africa	TGH	Tongoa, Vanuatu	
SZX	Shenzhen, China	TGI	Tingo Maria, Peru	
SZZ	Szczecin, Poland	TGJ	Tiga, New Caledonia	
TAB	Tobago, Trinidad & Tobago	TGM	Tirgu Mures, Romania	
TAC	Tacloban, Philippines	TGN	Traralgon, Australia	
TAE	Taegu, Korea	TGR	Touggourt, Algeria	

Airport Codes

TGU	Tegucigalpa, Honduras
TGZ	Tuxtla Gutierrez, Mexico
THE	Teresina, Brazil
THF	Berlin (Tempelhof), Germany
THG	Thangool, Australia
THL	Tachilek, Myanmar
THN	Trollhattan, Sweden
THR	Tehran, Iran
THS	Sukhothai, Thailand
THU	Pituffik, Greenland
THV	York, PA
TIA	Tirana, Albania
TIC	Tinak Is., Marshall Islands
TID	Tiaret, Algeria
TIE	Tippi, Ethiopia
TIF	Taif, Saudi Arabia
TIH	Tikehau Atoll, Fr. Polynesia
TIJ	Tijuana, Mexico
TIM	Tembagapura, Indonesia
TIN	Tindouf, Algeria
TIP	Tripoli, Libya
TIQ	Tinian, Mariana Islands
TIR	Tirupati, India
TIS	Thursday Is., Australia
TIU	Timaru, New Zealand
TIV	Tivat, Yugoslavia
TIY	Tidjikja, Mauritania
TIZ	Tari, Papua New Guinea
TJA	Tarija, Bolivia
TJH	Toyooka, Japan
TJI	Trujillo, Honduras
TJK	Tokat, Turkey
TJM	Tyumen, Russia
TKA	Talkeetna, AK
TKE	Tenakee Springs, AK
TKG	Bandar Lampung, Indonesia
TKJ	Tok, AK
TKK	Truk, Micronesia
TKN	Tokunoshima, Japan
TKP	Takapoto, Fr. Polynesia
TKQ	Kigoma, Tanzania
TKS	Tokushima, Japan
TKU	Turku, Finland
TKX	Takaroa, Fr. Polynesia
TLA	Teller, AK
TLE	Tulear, Madagascar
TLH	Tallahassee, FL
TLJ	Tatalina, AK
TLL	Tallinn, Estonia
TLM	Tlemsen, Algeria
TLN	Toulon, France
TLS	Toulouse, France
TLT	Tuluksak, AK
TLV	Tel Aviv (Jaffa), Israel
TME	Tame, Colombia
TMG	Tomanggong, Malaysia

TMI	Tumling Tar, Nepal
TMJ	Termez, Uzbekistan
TMM	Tamatave, Madagascar
TMN	Tamana Island, Kiribati
TMP	Tampere, Finland
TMR	Tamanrasset, Algeria
TMS	Sao Tome Island
TMT	Trombetas, Brazil
TMU	Tambor, Costa Rica
TMW	Tamworth, Australia
TMX	Timimoun, Algeria
TNA	Jinan, China
TNC	Tin City, AK
TNE	Tanegashima, Japan
TNG	Tangier, Morocco
TNK	Tununak, AK
TNN	Tainan, Taiwan
TNO	Tamarindo, Costa Rica
TNR	Antananarivo, Madagascar
TNX	Stung Treng, Cambodia
TOD	Tioman, Malaysia
TOE	Tozeur, Tunisia
TOF	Tomsk, Russia
TOG	Togiak, AK
TOH	Torres, Vanuatu
TOL	Toledo, OH
TOM	Timbuktu (Tombouctou), Mali
TOP	Topeka, KS
TOS	Tromso, Norway
TOU	Touho, New Caledonia
TOV	Tortola (Westend), BVI
TOW	Toledo, Brazil
TOY	Toyama, Japan
TPA	Tampa/St. Pete., FL
TPE	Taipei (Chiang Kai Shek), Taiwan
TPI	Tapini, Papua New Guinea
TPJ	Taplejung, Nepal
TPP	Tarapoto, Peru
TPQ	Tepic, Mexico
TPS	Trapani, Italy
TRA	Taramajima, Japan
TRB	Turbo, Colombia
TRC	Torreon, Mexico
TRD	Trondheim, Norway
TRE	Tiree, Scotland, UK
TRF	Sandefjord, Norway
TRG	Tauranga, New Zealand
TRI	Tri-City Airport (Bristol, Johnson Cty, Kinsport), TN
TRK	Tarakan, Indonesia
TRN	Turin, Italy
TRO	Taree, Australia
TRS	Trieste, Italy
TRU	Trujillo, Peru
TRV	Trivandrum, India

TRW	Tarawa, Kiribati	TYR	Tyler, TX	
TRZ	Tiruchirapally, India	TYS	Knoxville, TN	
TSA	Taipei (Sung Shan), Taiwan	TZA	Belize City (Municipal), Belize	
TSB	Tsumeb, Namibia	TZN	South Andros, Bahamas	
TSE	Akmola, Kazakstan	TZX	Trabzon, Turkey	
TSH	Tshikapa, Congo, Dem. Rep.	UAK	Narsarsuaq, Greenland	
TSJ	Tsushima, Japan	UAQ	San Juan, Argentina	
TSN	Tianjin, China	UAS	Samburu, Kenya	
TSO	Isles of Scilly (Tresco), UK	UBA	Uberaba, Brazil	
TSR	Timisoara, Romania	UBJ	Ube, Japan	
TSS	New York (E34th St. H/P), NY	UBP	Ubon Ratchathani, Thailand	
TST	Trang, Thailand	UBS	Columbus, MS	
TSU	Tabiteuea South, Kiribati	UCA	Utica, New York	
TSV	Townsville, Australia	UCT	Ukhta, Russia	
TTA	Tan Tan, Morocco	UDI	Uberlandia, Brazil	
TTE	Ternate, Indonesia	UDR	Udaipur, India	
TTJ	Tottori, Japan	UEE	Queenstown, Australia	
TTN	Trenton, NJ	UEL	Quelimane, Mozambique	
TTQ	Tortuquero, Costa Rica	UEO	Kumejima, Japan	
TTR	Tanjung Pandan, Indonesia	UET	Quetta, Pakistan	
TTS	Tsaratanana, Madagascar	UFA	Ufa, Russia	
TTT	Taitung, Taiwan	UGB	Pilot Point (Ugashik), AK	
TTU	Tetuan, Morocco	UGC	Urgench, Uzbekistan	
TUB	Tubuai, Fr. Polynesia	UGI	Uganik, AK	
TUC	Tucuman, Argentina	UGO	Uige, Angola	
TUF	Tours, France	UIB	Quibdo, Colombia	
TUG	Tuguegarao, Philippines	UIH	Qui Nhon, Viet Nam	
TUI	Turaif, Saudi Arabia	UII	Utila, Honduras	
TUJ	Tum, Ethiopia	UIK	Ust-Ilimsk, Russia	
TUK	Turbat, Pakistan	UIN	Quincy, IL	
TUL	Tulsa, OK	UIO	Quito, Ecuador	
TUN	Tunis, Tunisia	UIP	Quimper, France	
TUO	Taupo, New Zealand	UIQ	Quine Hill, Vanuatu	
TUP	Tupelo, MS	UIT	Jaluit Is., Marshall Islands	
TUR	Tucurui, Brazil	UJE	Ujae Is., Marshall Islands	
TUS	Tucson, AZ	UKK	Ust-Kamenogorsk, Kazakstan	
TUU	Tabuk, Saudi Arabia	ULB	Ulei, Vanuatu	
TUZ	Tucuma, Brazil	ULD	Ulundi, South Africa	
TVA	Morafenobe, Madagascar	ULE	Sule, Papua New Guinea	
TVC	Traverse City, MI	ULG	Ulgit, Mongolia	
TVF	Thief River Falls, MN	ULN	Ulan Bator, Mongolia	
TVL	Lake Tahoe, CA	ULP	Quilpie, Australia	
TVU	Taveuni, Fiji	UMD	Uummannaq, Greenland	
TVY	Dawe, Myanmar	UME	Umea, Sweden	
TWA	Twin Hills, AK	UMR	Woomera, Australia	
TWB	Toowoomba, Australia	UNG	Kiunga, Papua New Guinea	
TWF	Twin Falls, ID	UNI	Union Island, St. Vincent	
TWU	Tawau, Malaysia	UNK	Unalakleet, AK	
TXG	Taichung, Taiwan	UNN	Ranong, Thailand	
TXK	Texarkana, AR	UNT	Unst, Shetland Is., Scotland, UK	
TXL	Berlin (Tegel), Germany			
TXN	Tunxi, China	UPG	Ujung Pandang, Indonesia	
TYF	Torsby, Sweden	UPN	Uruapan, Mexico	
TYL	Talara, Peru	URA	Uralsk, Kazakstan	
TYN	Taiyuan, China	URC	Urumqi, China	
TYO	Tokyo (Metro), Japan	URG	Uruguaiana, Brazil	

Airport Codes

URJ	Uraj, Russia
URO	Rouen, France
URR	Urrao, Colombia
URT	Surat Thani, Thailand
URY	Gurayat, Saudi Arabia
USH	Ushuaia, Argentina
USL	Useless Loop, Australia
USM	Koh Samui, Thailand
USN	Ulsan, Korea
USU	Busuanga, Philippines
UTH	Udon Thani, Thailand
UTK	Utirik Is., Marshall Islands
UTN	Upington, South Africa
UTO	Utopia Creek, AK
UTP	Utapao, Thailand
UTT	Umtata, South Africa
UUD	Ulan-Ude, Russia
UUS	Yuzhno-Sakhalinsk, Russia
UVE	Ouvea, New Caledonia
UVF	St. Lucia (Hewanorra), West Indies
UVL	New Valley, Egypt
UVO	Uvol, Papua New Guinea
UYN	Yulin, China
VAA	Vaasa, Finland
VAG	Varginha, Brazil
VAI	Vanimo, Papua New Guinea
VAK	Chevak, AK
VAN	Van, Turkey
VAO	Suavanao, Solomon Islands
VAR	Varna, Bulgaria
VAS	Sivas, Turkey
VAV	Vava'u, Tonga
VAW	Vardoe, Norway
VBV	Vanuabalavu, Fiji
VBY	Visby, Sweden
VCD	Victoria R. Downs, Australia
VCE	Venice, Italy
VCP	Sao Paolo (Viracopas), Brazil
VCT	Victoria, TX
VDA	Ovda, Israel
VDB	Fagernes, Norway
VDC	Vitoria Da Conquista, Brazil
VDE	Valverde, Spain
VDM	Viedma, Argentina
VDS	Vadso, Norway
VDZ	Valdez, AK
VEE	Venetie, AK
VEL	Vernal, UT
VER	Veracruz, Mexico
VEV	Barakoma, Solomon Islands
VEY	Vestmannaeyjar, Iceland
VFA	Victoria Falls, Zimbabwe
VGD	Vologda, Russia
VGO	Vigo, Spain
VGT	Las Vegas (N. Terminal), NV

VHC	Saurimo, Angola
VHM	Vilhelmina, Sweden
VIA	Videira, Brazil
VIE	Vienna, Austria
VII	Vinh City, Vietnam
VIJ	Virgin Gorda, BVI
VIL	Dakhla, Morocco
VIS	Visalia, CA
VIT	Vitoria, Spain
VIU	Viru, Solomon Islands
VIV	Vivigani, Papua New Guinea
VKO	Moscow (Vnukovo), Russia
VKS	Vicksburg, MS
VLC	Valencia, Spain
VLD	Valdosta, GA
VLG	Villa Gesell, Argentina
VLI	Port Vila, Vanuatu
VLL	Valladolid, Spain
VLN	Valencia, Venezuela
VLP	Vila Rica, Brazil
VLS	Valesdir, Vanuatu
VME	Villa Mercedes, Argentina
VMU	Baimuru, Papua New Guinea
VNA	Saravane, Laos
VNO	Vilnius, Lithuania
VNS	Varanasi, India
VOG	Volgograd, Russia
VOH	Vohemar, Madagascar
VOZ	Voronezh, Russia
VQS	Vieques, PR
VRA	Varadero, Cuba
VRC	Virac, Philippines
VRK	Varkaus, Finland
VRN	Verona, Italy
VRY	Vaeroy, Norway
VSA	Villahermosa, Mexico
VST	Vasteras, Sweden
VTE	Vientiane, Laos
VTU	Las Tunas, Cuba
VTZ	Vishakhapatnam, India
VUP	Valledupar, Colombia
VVC	Villavicencio, Colombia
VVI	Santa Cruz (Viru Viru), Bolivia
VVO	Vladivostok, Russia
VVZ	Illizi, Algeria
VXC	Lichinga, Mozambique
VXE	Sao Vicente, Cape Verde Islands
VXO	Vaxjo, Sweden
WAA	Wales, AK
WAE	Wadi-Ad-Dawasir, Saudi Arabia
WAG	Wanganui, New Zealand
WAI	Antosohihy, Madagascar
WAM	Ambatondrazaka, Madagascar
WAQ	Antsalova, Madagascar
WAS	Washington (Metro), DC

WAT	Waterford, Ireland	WSP	Waspam, Nicaragua	
WAW	Warsaw, Poland	WST	Westerly, RI	
WBB	Stebbins, AK	WSU	Wasu, Papua New Guinea	
WBC	Wapolu, Papua New Guinea	WSX	Westsound, WA	
WBM	Wapenamanda, Papua New Guinea	WSZ	Westport, New Zealand	
		WTD	West End, Bahamas	
WBQ	Beaver, AK	WTE	Wotje Is., Marshall Islands	
WDB	Deep Bay, AK	WTK	Noatak, AK	
WDG	Enid, OK	WTL	Tuntutuliak, AK	
WDH	Windhoek (Intl), Namibia	WTO	Wotho, Marshall Islands	
WED	Wedau, Papua New Guinea	WTS	Tsiroanomandidy, Madagascar	
WEF	Weifang, China	WUD	Wudinna, Australia	
WEH	Weihai, China	WUH	Wuhan, China	
WEI	Weipa, Australia	WUM	Wasum, Papua New Guinea	
WFI	Fianarantsoa, Madagascar	WUN	Wiluna, Australia	
WFK	Frenchville, ME	WUS	Wuyishan, China	
WGA	Wagga Wagga, Australia	WUZ	Wuzhou, China	
WGE	Walgett, Australia	WVB	Walvis Bay, Namibia	
WGP	Waingapu, Indonesia	WVK	Manakara, Madagascar	
WHD	Hyder, AK	WVN	Wilhelmshaven, Germany	
WHK	Whakatane, New Zealand	WWK	Wewak, Papua New Guinea	
WHR	Vail (Stolport), CO	WWP	Whale Pass, AK	
WIC	Wick, Scotland, UK	WWT	Newtok, AK	
WIL	Nairobi (Wilson), Kenya	WWY	West Wyalong, Australia	
WIN	Winton, Australia	WXN	Wanxian, China	
WIR	Wairoa, New Zealand	WYA	Whyalla, Australia	
WJA	Woja, Marshall Islands	WYB	Yes Bay, AK	
WKA	Wanaka, New Zealand	WYN	Wyndham, Australia	
WKJ	Wakkanai, Japan	WZY	Nassau (SPB), Bahamas	
WKK	Aleknagik, AK	XAP	Chapeco, Brazil	
WKR	Walker's Cay, Bahamas	XAY	Xayabury, Laos	
WLG	Wellington, New Zealand	XBE	Bearskin Lake, ON	
WLH	Walaha, Vanuatu	XBN	Biniguni, Papua New Guinea	
WLK	Selawik, AK	XCH	Christmas Is., Indian Ocean	
WLL	Wollogorang, Australia	XFN	Xiangfan, China	
WLS	Wallis Is., Wallis & Futuna Islands	XGR	Kangiqsualujjuaq, PQ	
		XIC	Xichang, China	
WMA	Mandritsara, Madagascar	XIY	Xi An (Xianyang), China	
WME	Mount Keith, Australia	XKH	Xieng Khouang, Laos	
WMH	Mountain Home, AR	XKS	Kasabonika, ON	
WMK	Meyers Chuck, AK	XLB	Lac Brochet, MB	
WMN	Maroantsetra, Madagascar	XMG	Mahendranagar, Nepal	
WMO	White Mountain, AK	XMH	Manihi, Fr. Polynesia	
WMR	Mananara, Madagascar	XMN	Xiamen, China	
WNA	Napakiak, AK	XNA	Fayetteville, AR	
WNN	Wunnummin Lake, ON	XNN	Xining, China	
WNP	Naga, Philippines	XPK	Pukatawagan, MB	
WNR	Windorah, Australia	XQP	Quepos, Costa Rica	
WNS	Nawabshah, Pakistan	XQU	Qualicum, BC	
WNZ	Wenzhou, China	XRY	Jerez de la Frontera, Spain	
WRE	Whangarei, New Zealand	XSC	South Caicos, Turks & Caicos	
WRG	Wrangell, AK	XSI	South Indian Lake, MB	
WRL	Worland, WY	XTG	Thargomindah, Australia	
WRO	Wroclaw, Poland	XTL	Tadoule Lake, MB	
WRY	Westray, Scotland, UK	XYA	Yandina, Solomon Islands	
WSN	South Naknek, AK	YAA	Anahim Lake, BC	

Airport Codes

YAC	Cat Lake, ON	YHA	Port Hope Simpson, NF
YAG	Fort Francis, ON	YHD	Dryden, ON
YAK	Yakutat, AK	YHF	Hearst, ON
YAM	Sault Ste. Marie, ON	YHI	Holman Island, NT
YAP	Yap, Micronesia	YHK	Gjoa Haven, NT
YAT	Attawapiskat, ON	YHM	Hamilton, ON
YAX	Angling Lake, ON	YHN	Hornepayne, ON
YAY	St. Anthony, NF	YHR	Chevery, PQ
YBA	Banff, AB	YHY	Hay River, NT
YBC	Baie Comeau, PQ	YHZ	Halifax (Intl), NS
YBE	Uranium City, SK	YIF	Pakuashipi, PQ
YBG	Bagotville, PQ	YIH	Yichang, China
YBK	Baker Lake, NU	YIN	Yining, China
YBL	Campbell River, BC	YIO	Pond Inlet, NT
YBP	Yibin, China	YIV	Island Lake, MB
YBR	Brandon, MB	YIW	Yiwu, China
YBS	Opapamiska Lake, ON	YJT	Stephenville, NF
YBT	Brochet, MB	YKA	Kamloops, BC
YBX	Blanc Sablon, PQ	YKG	Kangirsuk, PQ
YCB	Cambridge Bay, NT	YKL	Schefferville, PQ
YCD	Nanaimo, BC	YKM	Yakima, WA
YCG	Castlegar, BC	YKN	Yankton, SD
YCH	Chatham, NB	YKQ	Waskaganish, PQ
YCL	Charlo, NB	YKS	Yakutsk, Russia
YCR	Cross Lake, MB	YKU	Chisasibi, PQ
YCS	Chesterfield Inlet, NT	YLD	Chapleau, ON
YCY	Clyde River, NT	YLH	Lansdowne House, ON
YDA	Dawson City, YT	YLL	Lloydminster, AB
YDF	Deer Lake, NF	YLR	Leaf Rapids, MB
YDQ	Dawson Creek, BC	YLW	Kelowna, BC
YEA	Edmonton (Metro), AB	YMM	Fort McMurray, AB
YEC	Yechon, Korea	YMO	Moosonee, ON
YED	Edmonton (Namao), AB	YMQ	Montreal (Metro), PQ
YEG	Edmonton (Intl), AB	YMS	Yurimaguas, Peru
YEK	Arviat, NT	YMT	Chibougamau, PQ
YEL	Elliot Lake, ON	YMX	Montreal (Mirabel), PQ
YER	Fort Severn, ON	YNA	Natashquan, PQ
YEV	Inuvik, NT	YNB	Yanbo, Saudi Arabia
YFA	Fort Albany, ON	YNC	Wemindji, PQ
YFB	Iqaluit, NT	YNE	Norway House, MB
YFC	Fredericton, NB	YNG	Youngstown, OH
YFH	Fort Hope, ON	YNJ	Yanji, China
YFO	Flin Flon, MB	YNS	Nemiscau, PQ
YFS	Fort Simpson, NT	YNT	Yantai, China
YFX	Fox Harbour, NF	YOG	Ogoki, ON
YGB	Gillies Bay, BC	YOH	Oxford House, MB
YGJ	Yonago, Japan	YOJ	High Level, AB
YGK	Kingston, ON	YOL	Yola, Nigeria
YGO	Gods Narrows, MB	YOP	Rainbow Lake, AB
YGP	Gaspe, PQ	YOW	Ottawa (Intl), ON
YGQ	Geraldton, ON	YPA	Prince Albert, SK
YGR	Iles de la Madeleine, PQ	YPE	Peace River, AB
YGT	Igloolik, NT	YPH	Inukjuak, PQ
YGV	Havre St. Pierre, PQ	YPJ	Aupaluk, PQ
YGW	Kuujjuarapik, PQ	YPL	Pickle Lake, ON
YGX	Gillam, MB	YPM	Pikangikum, ON

YPO	Peawanuk, ON
YPR	Prince Rupert, BC
YPW	Powell River, BC
YQB	Quebec, PQ
YQD	The Pas, MB
YQG	Windsor, ON
YQI	Yarmouth, NS
YQK	Kenora, ON
YQL	Lethbridge, AB
YQM	Moncton, NB
YQN	Nakina, ON
YQQ	Comox, BC
YQR	Regina, SK
YQT	Thunder Bay, ON
YQU	Grande Prairie, AB
YQX	Gander, NF
YQY	Sydney, NS
YQZ	Quesnel, BC
YRB	Resolute, NT
YRJ	Roberval, PQ
YRL	Red Lake, ON
YRO	Ottawa (Rockcliffe), ON
YRS	Red Sucker Lake, MB
YRT	Rankin Inlet, NT
YSB	Sudbury, ON
YSF	Stony Rapids, SK
YSJ	St. John, NB
YSL	St. Leonard, NB
YSM	Fort Smith, NT
YSR	Nanisivik, NT
YST	Ste. Therese Point, MB
YTE	Cape Dorset, NT
YTF	Alma, PQ
YTH	Thompson, MB
YTL	Big Trout Lake, ON
YTO	Toronto (Metro), ON
YTQ	Tasiujuaq, PQ
YTS	Timmins, ON
YTZ	Toronto (Toronto Is.), ON
YUF	Pelly Bay, NT
YUL	Montreal (Dorval), PQ
YUM	Yuma, AZ
YUT	Repluse Bay, NT
YUX	Hall Beach, NT
YUY	Rouyn, PQ
YVA	Moroni, Comoros
YVC	La Ronge, SK
YVM	Broughton Island, NT
YVO	Val D'Or, PQ
YVP	Kuujjuaq, PQ
YVQ	Norman Wells, NT
YVR	Vancouver (Intl), BC
YVZ	Deer Lake, ON
YWG	Winnipeg, MB
YWK	Wabush, NF
YWL	Williams Lake, BC
YWP	Webequie, ON
YXC	Cranbrook, BC
YXD	Edmonton (Muni), AB
YXE	Saskatoon, SK
YXH	Medicine Hat, AB
YXJ	Fort St. John, BC
YXL	Sioux Lookout, ON
YXN	Whale Cove, NT
YXS	Prince George, BC
YXT	Terrace, BC
YXU	London, ON
YXX	Abbotsford, BC
YXY	Whitehorse, YT
YXZ	Wawa, ON
YYB	North Bay, ON
YYC	Calgary (Intl), AB
YYD	Smithers, BC
YYE	Fort Nelson, BC
YYF	Penticton, BC
YYG	Charlottetown, PE
YYH	Taloyoak, NT
YYJ	Victoria (Intl), BC
YYL	Lynn Lake, MB
YYQ	Churchill, MB
YYR	Goose Bay, NF
YYT	St. Johns, NF
YYU	Kapuskasing, ON
YYY	Mont Joli, PQ
YYZ	Toronto (Pearson), ON
YZE	Gore Bay, ON
YZF	Yellowknife, NT
YZG	Salluit, PQ
YZP	Sandspit, BC
YZR	Sarnia, BC
YZS	Coral Harbour, NT
YZT	Port Hardy, BC
YZV	Sept-Iles, PQ
ZAD	Zadar, Croatia
ZAG	Zagreb, Croatia
ZAH	Zahedan, Iran
ZAL	Valdivia, Chile
ZAM	Zamboanga, Philippines
ZAT	Zhaotong, China
ZAZ	Zaragoza, Spain
ZBF	Bathurst, NB
ZBR	Chah-Bahar, Iran
ZBX	Branson, MO
ZBY	Sayaboury, Laos
ZCL	Zacatecas, Mexico
ZCO	Temuco, Chile
ZEM	East Main, PQ
ZFD	Fond du Lac, SK
ZFN	Tulita, NT
ZGI	Gods River, MB
ZGU	Gaua, Vanuatu
ZHA	Zhanjiang, China

90

ZIG	Ziguinchor, Senegal
ZIH	Ixtapa/Zihautenejo, Mexico
ZJN	Swan River, MB
ZKE	Kaschechewan, ON
ZLO	Manzanillo, Mexico
ZNE	Newman, Australia
ZNZ	Zanzibar, Tanzania
ZOS	Osorno, Chile
ZPB	Sachigo Lake, ON
ZQN	Queenstown, New Zealand
ZRH	Zurich, Switzerland
ZRJ	Round Lake, ON
ZSA	San Salvador, Bahamas
ZSJ	Sandy Lake, ON
ZTB	Tete-a-la-Baleine, PQ
ZTH	Zakinthos Is., Greece
ZTM	Shamattawa, MB
ZUH	Zhuhai, China
ZUM	Churchill Falls, NF
ZVA	Miandrivazo, Madagascar
ZVK	Savannakhet, Laos
ZYL	Sylhet, Bangladesh
ZZU	Mzuzu, Malawi

Airlines

40-Mile Air	Q5	MLA	Air Astana	KC	KZR
Adria Airways	JP	ADR	Air Austral	UU	REU
Aegean	A3	AEE	Air Berlin	AB	BER
Aer Arann	RE	REA	Air Botswana	BP	BOT
Aer Lingus	EI	EIN	Air Burkina	2J	VBW
Aero Benin	EM	AEB	Air Caledonie	TY	TPC
Aero California	JR	SER	Air Caledonie Int'l	SB	ACI
Aero Condor	Q6	CDP	Air Canada	AC	ACA
Aero Contractors (Nigeria)	AJ	NIG	Air Canada Jazz	QK	JZA
Aero Lanka	QL	RLN	Air Caraibes	TX	FWI
Aero-Tropics	HC	ATI	Air Central	NV	CRF
AeroCaribbean	7L	CRN	Air Chathams	CV	CVA
AeroEjecutiva	SX	AJO	Air China	CA	CCA
Aeroflot	SU	AFL	Air Comet	A7	MPD
Aeroflot-Don	D9	DNV	Air Corridor	QC	CRD
Aeroflot-Nord	5N	AUL	Air Creebec	YN	CRQ
AeroGal	2K	GLG	Air Dolomiti	EN	DLA
Aerogaviota	KG	GTV	Air Europa	UX	AEA
Aerolimousine	N/A	LIN	Air Fiji	PC	FAJ
Aerolineas Argentinas	AR	ARG	Air Finland	OF	FIF
Aerolineas Dominicanas			Air France	AF	AFR
(Dominair)	YU	ADM	Air Greenland	GL	GRL
AeroLineas Sosa	P4	NSO	Air Guyane	3S	GUY
Aeromexico	AM	AMX	Air Iceland	NY	FXI
Aeromexico Connect	5D	SLI	Air India	AI	AIC
Aeropelican	OT	PEL	Air India Regional	CD	LLR
Aeroperlas	WL	APP	Air Inuit	3H	AIE
Aeropostal	VH	LAV	Air Ivoire	VU	VUN
AeroRepublica	P5	RPB	Air Jamaica	JM	AJM
AeroSur (Bolivia)	5L	ASU	Air Japan	NQ	AJX
Aerosvit Airlines (Ukraine)	VV	AEW	Air Kiribati	4A	AKL
Afriqiyah	8U	AAW	Air Koryo	JS	KOR
Afrique Airlines	X5	FBN	Air Link Pty.	DR	N/A
Aigle Azur	ZI	AAF	Air Macau	NX	AMU
Air Algerie	AH	DAH	Air Madagascar	MD	MDG
Air Alps Aviation	A6	LPV	Air Malawi	QM	AML
Air Arabia	G9	ABY	Air Malta	KM	AMC

Air Mandalay	6T	N/A	Angel Airlines (Thailand)	8G	NGE
Air Marshall Islands	CW	MRS	Arctic Circle Air Service	5F	CIR
Air Mauritius	MK	MAU	Ariana Afghan Airlines	FG	AFG
Air Moldova	9U	MLD	Arik Air	W3	ARA
Air Namibia	SW	NMB	Arizona Express	K7	TMP
Air New Zealand	NZ	ANZ	Arkia Israeli Airlines	IZ	AIZ
Air Nippon	EL	ANK	Armavia	U8	RNV
Air Nippon Network	EH	AKX	Aserca (Venezuela)	R7	OCA
Air Niugini	PX	ANG	Asia Pacific Airlines	N/A	MGE
Air North (Yukon Terr.)	4N	ANT	Asian Spirit	6K	RIT
Air Nostrum	YW	ANE	Asiana Airlines	OZ	AAR
Air Pacific Ltd.	FJ	FJI	Astraeus	5W	AEU
Air Philippines	2P	GAP	Astrakhan Airlines	OB	ASZ
Air Pullmantur	EB	PLM	ATA Aerocondor	2B	ARD
Air Rarotonga	GZ	RAR	Atlant-Soyuz	3G	AYZ
Air Saint-Pierre	PJ	SPM	Atlantic Airways (Faroe Is.)	RC	FLI
Air Senegal	V7	SNG	Atlas Blue	8A	BMM
Air Seychelles	HM	SEY	Atlasjet	KK	KKK
Air Sinai	4D	ASD	Augsburg Airways	IQ	AUB
Air Slovakia	GM	SVK	Aurigny Air Services	GR	AUR
Air Southwest	WO	WOW	Austral Lineas Aereas	AU	AUT
Air Sunshine	YI	RSI	Australian Air Express	XM	XME
Air Tahiti	VT	VTA	Austrian Airlines	OS	AUA
Air Tahiti Nui	TN	THT	Aviacsa	6A	CHP
Air Tanzania	TC	ATC	Aviaenergo	7U	ERG
Air Tindi	8T	N/A	Avianca	AV	AVA
Air Transat	TS	TSC	AVIATECA (Guatemala)	GU	GUG
Air Turks and Caicos	JY	IWY	Avies	U3	AIA
Air Urga	3N	URG	AVIOR	9V	ROI
Air Vallee	DO	RVL	Avirex Gabon	G2	VXG
Air Vanuatu	NF	AVN	Axis Airways	6V	AXY
Air VIA Bulgarian	VL	VIM	Azerbaijan Airlines		
Air Wisconsin	ZW	AWI	(AZAL)	J2	AHY
Air Zimbabwe	UM	AZW	B&H Airlines	JA	BON
Air-Do (Hokkaido Intl)	HD	ADO	Bahamasair	UP	BHS
AirAsia	AK	AXM	Baker Aviation	8Q	BAJ
airBaltic	BT	BTI	Bangkok Airways	PG	BKP
AirBlue Limited	ED	ABQ	Barents AirLink	8N	NKF
Aircompany SCAT	DV	VSV	Batavia Air	7P	BTV
Aires	4C	ARE	Bearskin Airlines	JV	BLS
Airlinair	A5	RLA	Belair	4T	BHP
Airlines of Tasmania	FO	ATM	Belavia	B2	BRU
Airnorth	TL	ANO	Bellview Airlines	B3	BLV
AirTran	FL	TRS	Bemidji Airlines	CH	BMJ
Aklak Air	6L	AKK	Benin Golf	A8	BGL
Alaska Airlines	AS	ASA	Bering Air	8E	BRG
Albanian Airlines	LV	LBC	Berjaya Air	J8	BVT
Alidaunia	D4	LID	Biman Bangladesh	BG	BBC
Alitalia	AZ	AZA	Binter Canarias	NT	IBB
Alitalia Express	XM	SMX	Blue Panorama Airlines	BV	BPA
All Nippon Airways	NH	ANA	Blue Wings	QW	BWG
Allegiant Air	G4	AAY	Blue1	KF	BLF
Alliance Air (Uganda)	Y2	AFJ	BMI (British Midland)	BD	BMA
Alliance Airlines	QQ	UTY	bmibaby	WW	BMI
American Airlines	AA	AAL	Brindabella Airlines	FQ	BRI
American Eagle	MQ	EGF	Brit Air	DB	BZH

British Airways	BA	BAW	Domodedovo Airlines	E3	DMO
British International			Dragonair	KA	HDA
Helicopters	BS	BIH	Druk Air	KB	DRK
Brussels Airlines	SN	BEL	Dutch Antilles Express	9H	DNL
Bulgaria Air	FB	LZB	Eagle Air Uganda	H7	EGU
Buraq Air	UZ	BRQ	Eagle Aviation (Kenya)	Y4	EQA
Calm Air	MO	CAV	East African Airlines	QU	UGX
Cambodia Airlines	Y6	KHM	East African Safari Air	B5	HSA
Canadian North (Air			East Asia Airlines	3E	EMU
NorTerra)	5T	MPE	Eastern Airways	T3	EZE
Canjet	C6	CJA	Easyjet	U2	EZY
Cape Air	9K	KAP	Egyptair	MS	MSR
Carpatair	V3	KRP	El Al Israel Airlines	LY	ELY
Caspian Airlines	RV	CPN	Emirates	EK	UAE
Cathay Pacific Airways	CX	CPA	Enkor Airlines	G8	ENK
Cayman Airways	KX	CAY	Era Aviation	7H	ERH
CCM Airlines	XK	CCM	Eritrean Airlines	B8	ERT
CEBU Pacific Air	5J	CEB	Estonian Air	OV	ELL
Central Mountain Air	9M	GLR	Ethiopian Airlines	ET	ETH
Centre-Avia Airlines	J7	CVC	Etihad Airways	EY	ETD
Chautauqua Airlines	RP	CHQ	Euro-Asia Air	5B	EAK
China Airlines	CI	CAL	Euroair	6M	EUP
China Eastern Airlines	MU	CES	Eurofly	GJ	EEZ
China Southern Airlines	CZ	CSN	EuroLOT	K2	ELO
Cielos Airlines	A2	CIU	Eurowings	EW	EWG
Cimber Air	QI	CIM	EVA Airways	BR	EVA
Cirrus Airlines	C9	RUS	Everts Air	3Z	N/A
City Airline	CF	SDR	Executive Airlines	OW	EXK
Cityjet	WX	BCY	Expo Aviation	8D	EXV
Click Mexicana	QA	CBE	ExpressJet	XE	BTA
ClubAir	6P	ISG	Finnair	AY	FIN
Coastal Air Transport	DQ	CXT	Finnish Commuter Airlines	FC	FCM
Colgan Air	9L	CJC	First Air	7F	FAB
Comair (South Africa)	MN	CAW	First Choice Airways	DP	FCA
Comair (US)	OH	COM	Flight Alaska	4Y	UYA
CommutAir	C5	UCA	Flybaboo	F7	BBO
Condor	DE	CFG	flyBE	BE	BEE
Contact Air	C3	KIS	Flyglobespan	Y2	GSM
Continental Airlines	CO	COA	Freedom Air	FP	FRE
Continental Micronesia	CS	CMI	Frontier Airlines	F9	FFT
COPA Airlines (Panama)	CM	CMP	Frontier Flying Service	2F	FTA
Corsairfly	SS	CRL	Futura International		
Cosmic Air	F5	COZ	Airways	FH	FUA
Croatia Airlines	OU	CTN	Gambia Int'l Airlines	GC	GNR
Cubana Airlines	CU	CUB	Garuda Indonesia	GA	GIA
Cyprus Airways	CY	CYP	Gazpromavia Aviation	4G	GZP
Cyprus Turkish Airlines	YK	KYV	Georgian National Airlines	QB	GFG
Czech Airlines (CSA)	OK	CSA	Germania	ST	GMI
Daallo Airlines	D3	DAO	Germanwings	4U	GWI
Dalavia	H8	KHB	GMG Airlines	Z5	GMG
Danish Air Transport	DX	DTR	Go One Airways	GK	N/A
Delta Air Lines	DL	DAL	GOL	G3	GLO
Denim Air	3D	DNM	Golden Air	DC	GAO
DirektFlyg	HS	HSV	Gomelavia	YD	GOM
Djibouti Airlines	D8	DJB	Grant Aviation	GS	N/A
Dniproavia	Z6	UDN	Great Lakes Aviation	ZK	GLA

Airlines

The Travel Agent's
Complete Desk
Reference

Gulf Air	GF	GFA	Jetstar Airways	JQ	JST
Gulfstream Int'l Airlines	3M	GFT	Jetstar Pacific	BL	PIC
Hageland Aviation	H6	HAG	Kaliningradavia	KD	KNI
Hahn Air	HR	HHN	Kam Air	RQ	KMF
Hainan Airlines	HU	CHH	Katmai Air	KT	N/A
Hamburg International	4R	HHI	Kato Air	6S	KAT
Harbour Air	H3	N/A	KD Air	XC	KDC
Hawaiian Airlines	HA	HAL	Kenmore Air	M5	KEN
Hawkair	BH	BHA	Kenya Airways	KQ	KQA
Heli Air Monaco	YO	MCM	Keystone Air Service	BZ	KEE
Heli Securite	H4	HLI	Kish Air	Y9	IRK
Helijet International	JB	JBA	Kivalliq Air	FK	N/A
Helisureste	UV	HSE	KLM Cityhopper	WA	KLC
Hellas Jet	T4	HEJ	KLM Royal Dutch Airlines	KL	KLM
Helvetic Airways	2L	OAW	KMV	KV	MVD
Hemus Air	DU	HMS	Kolavia Airlines	7K	KGL
Hewa Bora Airways	EO	ALX	Korean Air	KE	KAL
Hex'Air	UD	HER	Krasair	7B	KJC
Hong Kong Airlines	HX	CRK	Kronflyg	K4	N/A
Hong Kong Express	UO	HKE	Kuban Airlines	GW	KIL
Horizon Air	QX	QXE	Kuwait Airways	KU	KAC
Iberia	IB	IBE	Kyrgyzstan	QH	LYN
Ibex Airlines	FW	IBX	Kyrgyzstan Airlines	R8	KGA
Icaro Air	X8	ICD	L.A.B. Flying Service	JF	LAB
Icelandair	FI	ICE	Labrador Airways	WJ	LAL
Iliamna Air Taxi	V8	IAR	LACSA (Costa Rica)	LR	LRC
Imair Airline	IK	ITX	LADE	5U	LDE
Indian Airlines	IC	IAC	LagunAir	N7	LGA
Indonesia AirAsia	QZ	AWQ	LAM (Mozambique)	TM	LAM
Inland Aviation Services	7N	N/A	Lan Airlines	LA	LAN
Inter Airlines	6K	INX	Lan Ecuador	XL	LNE
Interair South Africa	D6	ILN	LAN Express	LU	LXP
Interavia Airlines	ZA	SUW	Lan Peru	LP	LPE
Interlink Airlines	ID	ITK	Lao Airlines	QV	LAO
InterSky	3L	ISK	Larry's Flying Service	J6	N/A
Iran Air	IR	IRA	LatCharter	6Y	LTC
Iran Aseman Airlines	EP	IRC	Lauda Air	NG	LDA
Iraqi Airways	IA	IAW	LGW (Germany)	HE	LGW
Island Air (Aloha)	WP	MKU	LIAT (Antigua)	LI	LIA
Island Airlines	IS	N/A	Libyan Airlines	LN	LAA
Islas Airways	IF	ISW	Lion Air	JT	LNI
Islena Airlines	WC	ISV	Lithuanian Airlines	TE	LIL
Israir Airlines	6H	ISR	Livingston	LM	LVG
ItAli Airlines	FS	ACL	LOT Polish Airlines	LO	LOT
ITEK Air	GI	IKA	LTU Billa	L3	LTO
Ivoire Airways	XV	IVW	LTU International		
JAL Express	JC	JEX	Airways	LT	LTU
JALways	JO	JAZ	Lufthansa	LH	DLH
Japan Air Commuter	3X	JAC	Lufthansa CityLine	CL	CLH
Japan Airlines	JL	JAL	Luxair	LG	LGL
Japan Transocean	NU	JTA	Lviv Airlines	5V	UKW
Jat Airways	JU	JAT	Macair	CC	MCK
Jet Airways (India)	9W	JAI	Macedonian Airlines	IN	MAK
Jet2	LS	EXS	Mahan Airlines	W5	IRM
JetBlue	B6	JBU	Malaysia Airlines	MH	MAS
JetLite	S2	RSH	Malev Hungarian Airlines	MA	MAH

Malmo Aviation	TF	SCW	Pacific Sun	FJ	FJI
Mandala Airlines	RI	MDL	Pacific Wings Airlines	LW	NMI
Mandarin Airlines	AE	MDA	Pakistan Int'l Airlines		
Martinair Holland	MP	MPH	(PIA)	PK	PIA
Maya Island Air	MW	MYD	Palestinian Airlines	PF	PNW
MenaJet	IM	MNJ	Pamir Air	NR	PIR
Meridiana	IG	ISS	Pantanal	P8	PTN
Merpati Nusantara	MZ	MNA	Papillon Airways	HI	N/A
Mesa Airlines	YV	ASH	Paradise Air	RN	N/A
Mesaba Aviation	XJ	MES	PB Air	9Q	PBA
Mexican	MX	MXA	Pelican Air	7V	PDF
MIAT-Mongolian Airlines	OM	MGL	Pelita Air	6D	PAS
Middle East Airlines			Penair	KS	PEN
(AirLiban)	ME	MEA	Perm Airlines	P9	PGP
Midwest Airlines	YX	MEP	Philippine Airlines	PR	PAL
Moldavian Airlines	2M	MDV	Phuket Airlines	9R	VAP
Monarch Airlines	ZB	MON	PLUNA (Uruguay)	PU	PUA
Montenegro Airlines	YM	MGX	PMTair	U4	PMT
Myanma Airways	UB	UBA	Polynesian	PH	PAO
Myanmar Airways	8M	MMA	Porter Airlines	PD	POE
Nakina Air Service	T2	N/A	Portugalia	NI	PGA
National Jet Systems	NC	NJS	Precision Air	PW	PRF
Nature Air	5C	NRR	President Airlines		
Nepal Airlines	RA	RNA	(Cambodia)	TO	PSK
New England Airlines	EJ	NEA	Primaris Airlines	FE	WCP
Nice Helicopteres	JX	N/A	Promech	Z3	N/A
NigerAir Continental	N9	NCN	Provincial Airlines	PB	SPR
Nok Air	DD	NOK	Qantas Airways	QF	QFA
Nordic Regional	6N	NRD	Qatar Airways	QR	QTR
Norfolk Air	O7	N/A	Regional Air Lines		
North American Airlines	NA	NAO	(Morocco)	FN	RGL
North Flying	M3	NFA	Regional Airlines (France)	YS	RAE
North-Wright Airways	HW	NWL	REX Regional Express	ZL	RXA
Northwest Airlines	NW	NWA	Rico Linhas Aereas	C7	RLE
Northwest Regional			Romavia	WQ	RMV
Airlines	FY	NWR	Rossiya	FV	SDM
Northwestern Air Lease	J3	PLR	Royal Air Maroc	AT	RAM
Norwegian Air Shuttle	DY	NAX	Royal Brunei Airlines	BI	RBA
Nouvelair Tunisie	BJ	LBT	Royal Jordanian	RJ	RJA
Novair	1I	NVR	Royal Khmer Airlines	RK	RKH
Odessa Airlines	5K	ODS	Royal Phnom Penh	RL	PPW
Olson Air Service	4B	N/A	Russian Sky Airlines	P7	ESL
OLT (Germany)	OL	OLT	Rwandair Express	WB	RWD
Olympic Airlines	OA	OAL	Ryanair	FR	RYR
Oman Air	WY	OMA	S7 Airlines	S7	SBI
Omni-Aviacao E			Saint Barth Commuter	PV	SBU
Tecnologia	OC	OAV	Salmon Air	S6	N/A
Omskavia	N3	OMS	Samara Airlines	E5	BRZ
Orenburg Airlines	R2	ORB	San Juan Airlines	2G	MRR
Orient Thai Airlines	OX	OEA	San Juan Aviation	JI	N/A
Our Airline	ON	RON	SANSA (Costa Rica)	RZ	LRS
Overland Airways	OJ	OLA	Santa Barbara Airlines	S3	BBR
P.T. Dirgantara Air			Saravia	6W	SOV
Services	AW	DIR	SAT Airlines	HZ	SHU
Pacific Airways	3F	N/A	SATA International	S4	RZO
Pacific Coastal Airlines	8P	PCO	Satena	9N	NSE

Saudi Arabian Airlines	SV	SVA	Swiftair	W3	SWT
Sayakhat Airlines	W7	SAH	SWISS	LX	SWR
Scandinavian Airlines			Sylt Air	7E	AWU
System (SAS)	SK	SAS	Syrian Arab Airlines	RB	SYR
Scenic Airlines	YR	EGJ	TAAG-Angola	DT	DTA
Scot Airways	CB	SAY	TAC - Trans Air Congo	Q8	TSG
Seaborne Airlines	BB	SBS	Taca Int'l Airlines	TA	TAI
Servicios Aereos			TACV	VR	TCV
Profesionales	5S	PSV	Tajik Air	7J	TZK
Sevenair	UG	SEN	TAM (Brazil)	JJ	TAM
Severstal Aircompany	D2	SSF	TAM Mercosur	PZ	LAP
Shaheen Air Int'l	NL	SAI	TAME (Ecuador)	EQ	TAE
Shandong Airlines	SC	CDG	Tanana Air Service	4E	TNR
Shanghai Airlines	FM	CSH	Tandem Aero	TQ	TDM
Shenzhen Airlines	ZH	CSZ	TAP Air Portugal	TP	TAP
Shuttle America	S5	TCF	TAROM Romanian Air	RO	ROT
Sibaviatrans (SIAT)	5M	SIB	Tatarstan Airlines	U9	TAK
Sichuan Airlines	3U	CSC	Tavrey Aircompany	T6	TVR
Siem Reap Airways	FT	SRH	TCI Skyking	RU	SKI
Sierra National Airlines	LJ	SLA	Thai Airways	TG	THA
SilkAir	MI	SLK	Thomas Cook Airlines	MT	TCX
Singapore Airlines	SQ	SIA	Thomas Cook Airlines		
Skippers Aviation	JW	N/A	Scandinavia	DK	VKG
Sky Airline	H2	SKU	Thomsonfly	BY	TOM
SkyEurope	NE	ESK	Tiger Airways	TR	TGW
Skymark Airlines	BC	SKY	Trans Air	P6	MUI
Skyservice Airlines	5G	SSV	Trans North Aviation	HX	N/A
Skytrans	NP	N/A	Trans States Airlines	AX	LOF
Skyway Airlines	AL	SYX	Transaero Airlines	UN	TSO
Skyways Express	JZ	SKX	Transasia Airways	GE	TNA
Skywest (Australia)	XR	OZW	Transcaraibes Air Int'l	DZ	NOE
SkyWest Airlines	OO	SKW	Transportes Aeromar	VW	TAO
SmartWings	QS	TVS	Transwest Air	9T	ABS
Smokey Bay Air	2E	N/A	Tropic Air	PM	TOS
Solomon Airlines	IE	SOL	Tropical Airways Haiti	M7	TBG
South African Airlink	4Z	LNK	TUIfly	X3	HLX
South African Airways			Tunisair	TU	TAR
(SAA)	SA	SAA	Turan Air	3T	URN
South African Express			Turkish Airlines	TK	THY
Airways	YB	EXY	Turkmenistan Airlines	T5	TUA
South Airlines (Ukraine)	YG	OTL	Twin Jet	T7	TJT
South East Asian Airlines	DG	SRQ	Tyrolean Airways	VO	TYR
Southwest Airlines	WN	SWA	Ukraine Int'l Airlines	PS	AUI
Spanair	JK	JKK	Ukrainian Mediterranean		
Spirit Airlines	NK	NKS	Airlines	UF	UKM
Sri Lankan Airlines	UL	ALK	UNI Air	B7	UIA
Sriwijaya Air	SJ	SJY	United Airlines	UA	UAL
STA Trans African	T8	STA	Ural Airlines	U6	SVR
Sterling	NB	SNB	US Airways	US	USA
Sudan Airways	SD	SUD	USA 3000	U5	GWY
Sun Air of Scandinavia	EZ	SUS	UTair Aviation	UT	TMN
Sun Country Airlines	SY	SCX	Uzbekistan Airways	HY	UZB
SunExpress	XQ	SXS	Valuair	VF	VLU
Sunshine Express	CQ	EXL	Varig	RG	VRN
Sunwing Airlines	WG	SWG	Viaggio Air	VM	VOA
Surinam Airways	PY	SLM	Vietnam Airlines	VN	HVN

Vintage Props & Jets	VQ	VPP	Wind Jet	IV	JET
Virgin America	VX	VRD	Windward Islands Airways	WM	WIA
Virgin Atlantic	VS	VIR	Wings of Alaska	K5	WAK
Virgin Blue	DJ	VOZ	Wizz Air	W6	WZZ
Virgin Nigeria	VK	VGN	World Airways	WO	WOA
Visa Airways	9A	N/A	Wright Air Service	8V	WRF
Vladivostok Air	XF	VLK	Xiamen Airlines	MF	CXA
VLM (Belgium)	VG	VLM	XL Airways	JN	XLA
Volare Airlines	VA	VLE	XL Airways France	SE	XLF
Vueling	VY	VLG	Xpressair	XN	XAR
Warbelow's Air Ventures	4W	VNA	Xtra Airways	XP	CXP
Welcome Air	2W	WLC	Yamal Airlines	YL	LLM
West Air Sweden	PT	SWN	Yangon Airways	HK	N/A
West Coast Air	8O	N/A	Yemenia Yemen Airways	IY	IYE
Westjet	WS	WJA	Zambian Airways	Q3	MBN
Wideroe's Flyveselskap	WF	WIF	Zanair	B4	TAN
Wimbi Dira Airways	9C	WDH			

Airlines

Airline Codes

1I	Novair	5D	Aeromexico Connect
2B	ATA Aerocondor	5F	Arctic Circle Air Service
2E	Smokey Bay Air	5G	Skyservice Airlines
2F	Frontier Flying Service	5J	CEBU Pacific Air
2G	San Juan Airlines	5K	Odessa Airlines
2J	Air Burkina	5L	AeroSur (Bolivia)
2K	AeroGal	5M	Sibaviatrans (SIAT)
2L	Helvetic Airways	5N	Aeroflot-Nord
2M	Moldavian Airlines	5S	Servicios Aereos Profesionales
2P	Air Philippines	5T	Canadian North (Air NorTerra)
2W	Welcome Air	5U	LADE
3D	Denim Air	5V	Lviv Airlines
3E	East Asia Airlines	5W	Astraeus
3F	Pacific Airways	6A	Aviacsa
3G	Atlant-Soyuz	6D	Pelita Air
3H	Air Inuit	6H	Israir Airlines
3L	InterSky	6K	Asian Spirit
3M	Gulfstream Int'l Airlines	6K	Inter Airlines
3N	Air Urga	6L	Aklak Air
3S	Air Guyane	6M	Euroair
3T	Turan Air	6N	Nordic Regional
3U	Sichuan Airlines	6P	ClubAir
3X	Japan Air Commuter	6S	Kato Air
3Z	Everts Air	6T	Air Mandalay
4A	Air Kiribati	6V	Axis Airways
4B	Olson Air Service	6W	Saravia
4C	Aires	6Y	LatCharter
4D	Air Sinai	7B	Krasair
4E	Tanana Air Service	7E	Sylt Air
4G	Gazpromavia Aviation	7F	First Air
4N	Air North (Yukon Terr.)	7H	Era Aviation
4R	Hamburg International	7J	Tajik Air
4T	Belair	7K	Kolavia Airlines
4U	Germanwings	7L	AeroCaribbean
4W	Warbelow's Air Ventures	7N	Inland Aviation Services
4Y	Flight Alaska	7P	Batavia Air
4Z	South African Airlink	7U	Aviaenergo
5B	Euro-Asia Air	7V	Pelican Air
5C	Nature Air	8A	Atlas Blue

8D	Expo Aviation
8E	Bering Air
8G	Angel Airlines (Thailand)
8M	Myanmar Airways
8N	Barents AirLink
8O	West Coast Air
8P	Pacific Coastal Airlines
8Q	Baker Aviation
8T	Air Tindi
8U	Afriqiyah
8V	Wright Air Service
9A	Visa Airways
9C	Wimbi Dira Airways
9H	Dutch Antilles Express
9K	Cape Air
9L	Colgan Air
9M	Central Mountain Air
9N	Satena
9Q	PB Air
9R	Phuket Airlines
9T	Transwest Air
9U	Air Moldova
9V	AVIOR
9W	Jet Airways (India)
A2	Cielos Airlines
A3	Aegean
A5	Airlinair
A6	Air Alps Aviation
A7	Air Comet
A8	Benin Golf
AA	American Airlines
AAF	Aigle Azur
AAL	American Airlines
AAR	Asiana Airlines
AAW	Afriqiyah
AAY	Allegiant Air
AB	Air Berlin
ABQ	AirBlue Limited
ABS	Transwest Air
ABY	Air Arabia
AC	Air Canada
ACA	Air Canada
ACI	Air Caledonie Int'l
ACL	ItAli Airlines
ADM	Aerolineas Dominicanas (Dominair)
ADO	Air-Do (Hokkaido Intl)
ADR	Adria Airways
AE	Mandarin Airlines
AEA	Air Europa
AEB	Aero Benin
AEE	Aegean
AEU	Astraeus
AEW	Aerosvit Airlines (Ukraine)
AF	Air France
AFG	Ariana Afghan Airlines

AFJ	Alliance Air (Uganda)
AFL	Aeroflot
AFR	Air France
AH	Air Algerie
AHY	Azerbaijan Airlines (AZAL)
AI	Air India
AIA	Avies
AIC	Air India
AIE	Air Inuit
AIZ	Arkia Israeli Airlines
AJ	Aero Contractors (Nigeria)
AJM	Air Jamaica
AJO	AeroEjecutiva
AJX	Air Japan
AK	AirAsia
AKK	Aklak Air
AKL	Air Kiribati
AKX	Air Nippon Network
AL	Skyway Airlines
ALK	Sri Lankan Airlines
ALX	Hewa Bora Airways
AM	Aeromexico
AMC	Air Malta
AML	Air Malawi
AMU	Air Macau
AMX	Aeromexico
ANA	All Nippon Airways
ANE	Air Nostrum
ANG	Air Niugini
ANK	Air Nippon
ANO	Airnorth
ANT	Air North (Yukon Terr.)
ANZ	Air New Zealand
APP	Aeroperlas
AR	Aerolineas Argentinas
ARA	Arik Air
ARD	ATA Aerocondor
ARE	Aires
ARG	Aerolineas Argentinas
AS	Alaska Airlines
ASA	Alaska Airlines
ASD	Air Sinai
ASH	Mesa Airlines
ASU	AeroSur (Bolivia)
ASZ	Astrakhan Airlines
AT	Royal Air Maroc
ATC	Air Tanzania
ATI	Aero-Tropics
ATM	Airlines of Tasmania
AU	Austral Lineas Aereas
AUA	Austrian Airlines
AUB	Augsburg Airways
AUI	Ukraine Int'l Airlines
AUL	Aeroflot-Nord
AUR	Aurigny Air Services
AUT	Austral Lineas Aereas

AV	Avianca	BOT	Air Botswana	
AVA	Avianca	BP	Air Botswana	
AVN	Air Vanuatu	BPA	Blue Panorama Airlines	
AW	P.T. Dirgantara Air Services	BR	EVA Airways	
AWI	Air Wisconsin	BRG	Bering Air	
AWQ	Indonesia AirAsia	BRI	Brindabella Airlines	
AWU	Sylt Air	BRQ	Buraq Air	
AX	Trans States Airlines	BRU	Belavia	
AXM	AirAsia	BRZ	Samara Airlines	
AXY	Axis Airways	BS	British International Helicopters	
AY	Finnair			
AYZ	Atlant-Soyuz	BT	airBaltic	
AZ	Alitalia	BTA	ExpressJet	
AZA	Alitalia	BTI	airBaltic	
AZW	Air Zimbabwe	BTV	Batavia Air	
B2	Belavia	BV	Blue Panorama Airlines	
B3	Bellview Airlines	BVT	Berjaya Air	
B4	Zanair	BWG	Blue Wings	
B5	East African Safari Air	BY	Thomsonfly	
B6	JetBlue	BZ	Keystone Air Service	
B7	UNI Air	BZH	Brit Air	
B8	Eritrean Airlines	C3	Contact Air	
BA	British Airways	C5	CommutAir	
BAJ	Baker Aviation	C6	Canjet	
BAW	British Airways	C7	Rico Linhas Aereas	
BB	Seaborne Airlines	C9	Cirrus Airlines	
BBC	Biman Bangladesh	CA	Air China	
BBO	Flybaboo	CAL	China Airlines	
BBR	Santa Barbara Airlines	CAV	Calm Air	
BC	Skymark Airlines	CAW	Comair (South Africa)	
BCY	Cityjet	CAY	Cayman Airways	
BD	BMI (British Midland)	CB	Scot Airways	
BE	flyBE	CBE	Click Mexicana	
BEE	flyBE	CC	Macair	
BEL	Brussels Airlines	CCA	Air China	
BER	Air Berlin	CCM	CCM Airlines	
BG	Biman Bangladesh	CD	Air India Regional	
BGL	Benin Golf	CDG	Shandong Airlines	
BH	Hawkair	CDP	Aero Condor	
BHA	Hawkair	CEB	CEBU Pacific Air	
BHP	Belair	CES	China Eastern Airlines	
BHS	Bahamasair	CF	City Airline	
BI	Royal Brunei Airlines	CFG	Condor	
BIH	British International Helicopters	CH	Bemidji Airlines	
		CHH	Hainan Airlines	
BJ	Nouvelair Tunisie	CHP	Aviacsa	
BKP	Bangkok Airways	CHQ	Chautauqua Airlines	
BL	Jetstar Pacific	CI	China Airlines	
BLF	Blue1	CIM	Cimber Air	
BLS	Bearskin Airlines	CIR	Arctic Circle Air Service	
BLV	Bellview Airlines	CIU	Cielos Airlines	
BMA	BMI (British Midland)	CJA	Canjet	
BMI	bmibaby	CJC	Colgan Air	
BMJ	Bemidji Airlines	CL	Lufthansa CityLine	
BMM	Atlas Blue	CLH	Lufthansa CityLine	
BON	B&H Airlines	CM	COPA Airlines (Panama)	

CMI	Continental Micronesia
CMP	COPA Airlines (Panama)
CO	Continental Airlines
COA	Continental Airlines
COM	Comair (US)
COZ	Cosmic Air
CPA	Cathay Pacific Airways
CPN	Caspian Airlines
CQ	Sunshine Express
CRD	Air Corridor
CRF	Air Central
CRK	Hong Kong Airlines
CRL	Corsairfly
CRN	AeroCaribbean
CRQ	Air Creebec
CS	Continental Micronesia
CSA	Czech Airlines (CSA)
CSC	Sichuan Airlines
CSH	Shanghai Airlines
CSN	China Southern Airlines
CSZ	Shenzhen Airlines
CTN	Croatia Airlines
CU	Cubana Airlines
CUB	Cubana Airlines
CV	Air Chathams
CVA	Air Chathams
CVC	Centre-Avia Airlines
CW	Air Marshall Islands
CX	Cathay Pacific Airways
CXA	Xiamen Airlines
CXP	Xtra Airways
CXT	Coastal Air Transport
CY	Cyprus Airways
CYP	Cyprus Airways
CZ	China Southern Airlines
CZ	China Southern Airlines
D2	Severstal Aircompany
D3	Daallo Airlines
D4	Alidaunia
D6	Interair South Africa
D8	Djibouti Airlines
D9	Aeroflot-Don
DAH	Air Algerie
DAL	Delta Air Lines
DAO	Daallo Airlines
DB	Brit Air
DC	Golden Air
DD	Nok Air
DE	Condor
DG	South East Asian Airlines
DIR	P.T. Dirgantara Air Services
DJ	Virgin Blue
DJB	Djibouti Airlines
DK	Thomas Cook Airlines Scandinavia
DL	Delta Air Lines

DLA	Air Dolomiti
DLH	Lufthansa
DMO	Domodedovo Airlines
DNL	Dutch Antilles Express
DNM	Denim Air
DNV	Aeroflot-Don
DO	Air Vallee
DP	First Choice Airways
DQ	Coastal Air Transport
DR	Air Link Pty.
DRK	Druk Air
DT	TAAG-Angola
DTA	TAAG-Angola
DTR	Danish Air Transport
DU	Hemus Air
DV	Aircompany SCAT
DX	Danish Air Transport
DY	Norwegian Air Shuttle
DZ	Transcaraibes Air Int'l
E3	Domodedovo Airlines
E5	Samara Airlines
EAK	Euro-Asia Air
EB	Air Pullmantur
ED	AirBlue Limited
EEZ	Eurofly
EGF	American Eagle
EGJ	Scenic Airlines
EGU	Eagle Air Uganda
EH	Air Nippon Network
EI	Aer Lingus
EIN	Aer Lingus
EJ	New England Airlines
EK	Emirates
EL	Air Nippon
ELL	Estonian Air
ELO	EuroLOT
ELY	El Al Israel Airlines
EM	Aero Benin
EMU	East Asia Airlines
EN	Air Dolomiti
ENK	Enkor Airlines
EO	Hewa Bora Airways
EP	Iran Aseman Airlines
EQ	TAME (Ecuador)
EQA	Eagle Aviation (Kenya)
ERG	Aviaenergo
ERH	Era Aviation
ERT	Eritrean Airlines
ESK	SkyEurope
ESL	Russian Sky Airlines
ET	Ethiopian Airlines
ETD	Etihad Airways
ETH	Ethiopian Airlines
EUP	Euroair
EVA	EVA Airways
EW	Eurowings

EWG	Eurowings	GAO	Golden Air
EXK	Executive Airlines	GAP	Air Philippines
EXL	Sunshine Express	GC	Gambia Int'l Airlines
EXS	Jet2	GE	Transasia Airways
EXV	Expo Aviation	GF	Gulf Air
EXY	South African Express Airways	GFA	Gulf Air
EY	Etihad Airways	GFG	Georgian National Airlines
EZ	Sun Air of Scandinavia	GFT	Gulfstream Int'l Airlines
EZE	Eastern Airways	GI	ITEK Air
EZY	Easyjet	GIA	Garuda Indonesia
F5	Cosmic Air	GJ	Eurofly
F7	Flybaboo	GK	Go One Airways
F9	Frontier Airlines	GL	Air Greenland
FAB	First Air	GLA	Great Lakes Aviation
FAJ	Air Fiji	GLG	AeroGal
FB	Bulgaria Air	GLO	GOL
FBN	Afrique Airlines	GLR	Central Mountain Air
FC	Finnish Commuter Airlines	GM	Air Slovakia
FCA	First Choice Airways	GMG	GMG Airlines
FCM	Finnish Commuter Airlines	GMI	Germania
FE	Primaris Airlines	GNR	Gambia Int'l Airlines
FFT	Frontier Airlines	GOM	Gomelavia
FG	Ariana Afghan Airlines	GR	Aurigny Air Services
FH	Futura International Airways	GRL	Air Greenland
FI	Icelandair	GS	Grant Aviation
FIF	Air Finland	GSM	Flyglobespan
FIN	Finnair	GTV	Aerogaviota
FJ	Air Pacific Ltd.	GU	AVIATECA (Guatemala)
FJ	Pacific Sun	GUG	AVIATECA (Guatemala)
FJI	Air Pacific Ltd.	GUY	Air Guyane
FJI	Pacific Sun	GW	Kuban Airlines
FK	Kivalliq Air	GWI	Germanwings
FL	AirTran	GWY	USA 3000
FLI	Atlantic Airways (Faroe Is.)	GZ	Air Rarotonga
FM	Shanghai Airlines	GZP	Gazpromavia Aviation
FN	Regional Air Lines (Morocco)	H2	Sky Airline
FO	Airlines of Tasmania	H3	Harbour Air
FP	Freedom Air	H4	Heli Securite
FQ	Brindabella Airlines	H6	Hageland Aviation
FR	Ryanair	H7	Eagle Air Uganda
FRE	Freedom Air	H8	Dalavia
FS	ItAli Airlines	HA	Hawaiian Airlines
FT	Siem Reap Airways	HAG	Hageland Aviation
FTA	Frontier Flying Service	HAL	Hawaiian Airlines
FUA	Futura International Airways	HC	Aero-Tropics
FV	Rossiya	HD	Air-Do (Hokkaido Intl)
FW	Ibex Airlines	HDA	Dragonair
FWI	Air Caraibes	HE	LGW (Germany)
FXI	Air Iceland	HEJ	Hellas Jet
FY	Northwest Regional Airlines	HER	Hex'Air
G2	Avirex Gabon	HHI	Hamburg International
G3	GOL	HHN	Hahn Air
G4	Allegiant Air	HI	Papillon Airways
G8	Enkor Airlines	HK	Yangon Airways
G9	Air Arabia	HKE	Hong Kong Express
GA	Garuda Indonesia	HLI	Heli Securite

The Travel Agent's
Complete Desk
Reference

Code	Airline	Code	Airline
HLX	TUIfly	IZ	Arkia Israeli Airlines
HM	Air Seychelles	J2	Azerbaijan Airlines (AZAL)
HMS	Hemus Air	J3	Northwestern Air Lease
HR	Hahn Air	J6	Larry's Flying Service
HS	DirektFlyg	J7	Centre-Avia Airlines
HSA	East African Safari Air	J8	Berjaya Air
HSE	Helisureste	JA	B&H Airlines
HSV	DirektFlyg	JAC	Japan Air Commuter
HU	Hainan Airlines	JAI	Jet Airways (India)
HVN	Vietnam Airlines	JAL	Japan Airlines
HW	North-Wright Airways	JAT	Jat Airways
HX	Hong Kong Airlines	JAZ	JALways
HX	Trans North Aviation	JB	Helijet International
HY	Uzbekistan Airways	JBA	Helijet International
HZ	SAT Airlines	JBU	JetBlue
IA	Iraqi Airways	JC	JAL Express
IAC	Indian Airlines	JET	Wind Jet
IAR	Iliamna Air Taxi	JEX	JAL Express
IAW	Iraqi Airways	JF	L.A.B. Flying Service
IB	Iberia	JI	San Juan Aviation
IBB	Binter Canarias	JJ	TAM (Brazil)
IBE	Iberia	JK	Spanair
IBX	Ibex Airlines	JKK	Spanair
IC	Indian Airlines	JL	Japan Airlines
ICD	Icaro Air	JM	Air Jamaica
ICE	Icelandair	JN	XL Airways
ID	Interlink Airlines	JO	JALways
IE	Solomon Airlines	JP	Adria Airways
IF	Islas Airways	JQ	Jetstar Airways
IG	Meridiana	JR	Aero California
IK	Imair Airline	JS	Air Koryo
IKA	ITEK Air	JST	Jetstar Airways
ILN	Interair South Africa	JT	Lion Air
IM	MenaJet	JTA	Japan Transocean
IN	Macedonian Airlines	JU	Jat Airways
INX	Inter Airlines	JV	Bearskin Airlines
IQ	Augsburg Airways	JW	Skippers Aviation
IR	Iran Air	JX	Nice Helicopteres
IRA	Iran Air	JY	Air Turks and Caicos
IRC	Iran Aseman Airlines	JZ	Skyways Express
IRK	Kish Air	JZA	Air Canada Jazz
IRM	Mahan Airlines	K2	EuroLOT
IS	Island Airlines	K4	Kronflyg
ISG	ClubAir	K5	Wings of Alaska
ISK	InterSky	K7	Arizona Express
ISR	Israir Airlines	KA	Dragonair
ISS	Meridiana	KAC	Kuwait Airways
ISV	Islena Airlines	KAL	Korean Air
ISW	Islas Airways	KAP	Cape Air
ITK	Interlink Airlines	KAT	Kato Air
ITX	Imair Airline	KB	Druk Air
IV	Wind Jet	KC	Air Astana
IVW	Ivoire Airways	KD	Kaliningradavia
IWY	Air Turks and Caicos	KDC	KD Air
IY	Yemenia Yemen Airways	KE	Korean Air
IYE	Yemenia Yemen Airways	KEE	Keystone Air Service

KEN	Kenmore Air	LM	Livingston
KF	Blue1	LN	Libyan Airlines
KG	Aerogaviota	LNE	Lan Ecuador
KGA	Kyrgyzstan Airlines	LNI	Lion Air
KGL	Kolavia Airlines	LNK	South African Airlink
KHB	Dalavia	LO	LOT Polish Airlines
KHM	Cambodia Airlines	LOF	Trans States Airlines
KIL	Kuban Airlines	LOT	LOT Polish Airlines
KIS	Contact Air	LP	Lan Peru
KJC	Krasair	LPE	Lan Peru
KK	Atlasjet	LPV	Air Alps Aviation
KKK	Atlasjet	LR	LACSA (Costa Rica)
KL	KLM Royal Dutch Airlines	LRC	LACSA (Costa Rica)
KLC	KLM Cityhopper	LRS	SANSA (Costa Rica)
KLM	KLM Royal Dutch Airlines	LS	Jet2
KM	Air Malta	LT	LTU International Airways
KMF	Kam Air	LTC	LatCharter
KNI	Kaliningradavia	LTO	LTU Billa
KOR	Air Koryo	LTU	LTU International Airways
KQ	Kenya Airways	LU	LAN Express
KQA	Kenya Airways	LV	Albanian Airlines
KRP	Carpatair	LVG	Livingston
KS	Penair	LW	Pacific Wings Airlines
KT	Katmai Air	LX	SWISS
KU	Kuwait Airways	LXP	LAN Express
KV	KMV	LY	El Al Israel Airlines
KX	Cayman Airways	LYN	Kyrgyzstan
KYV	Cyprus Turkish Airlines	LZB	Bulgaria Air
KZR	Air Astana	M3	North Flying
L3	LTU Billa	M5	Kenmore Air
LA	Lan Airlines	M7	Tropical Airways Haiti
LAA	Libyan Airlines	MA	Malev Hungarian Airlines
LAB	L.A.B. Flying Service	MAH	Malev Hungarian Airlines
LAL	Labrador Airways	MAK	Macedonian Airlines
LAM	LAM (Mozambique)	MAS	Malaysia Airlines
LAN	Lan Airlines	MAU	Air Mauritius
LAO	Lao Airlines	MBN	Zambian Airways
LAP	TAM Mercosur	MCK	Macair
LAV	Aeropostal	MCM	Heli Air Monaco
LBC	Albanian Airlines	MD	Air Madagascar
LBT	Nouvelair Tunisie	MDA	Mandarin Airlines
LDA	Lauda Air	MDG	Air Madagascar
LDE	LADE	MDL	Mandala Airlines
LG	Luxair	MDV	Moldavian Airlines
LGA	LagunAir	ME	Middle East Airlines (AirLiban)
LGL	Luxair	MEA	Middle East Airlines (AirLiban)
LGW	LGW (Germany)	MEP	Midwest Airlines
LH	Lufthansa	MES	Mesaba Aviation
LI	LIAT (Antigua)	MF	Xiamen Airlines
LIA	LIAT (Antigua)	MGE	Asia Pacific Airlines
LID	Alidaunia	MGL	MIAT-Mongolian Airlines
LIL	Lithuanian Airlines	MGX	Montenegro Airlines
LIN	Aerolimousine	MH	Malaysia Airlines
LJ	Sierra National Airlines	MI	SilkAir
LLM	Yamal Airlines	MK	Air Mauritius
LLR	Air India Regional	MKU	Island Air (Aloha)

105

Airlines

MLA	40-Mile Air	N/A	Visa Airways
MLD	Air Moldova	N/A	Norfolk Air
MMA	Myanmar Airways	N3	Omskavia
MN	Comair (South Africa)	N7	LagunAir
MNA	Merpati Nusantara	N9	NigerAir Continental
MNJ	MenaJet	NA	North American Airlines
MO	Calm Air	NAO	North American Airlines
MON	Monarch Airlines	NAX	Norwegian Air Shuttle
MP	Martinair Holland	NB	Sterling
MPD	Air Comet	NC	National Jet Systems
MPE	Canadian North (Air NorTerra)	NCN	NigerAir Continental
MPH	Martinair Holland	NE	SkyEurope
MQ	American Eagle	NEA	New England Airlines
MRR	San Juan Airlines	NF	Air Vanuatu
MRS	Air Marshall Islands	NFA	North Flying
MS	Egyptair	NG	Lauda Air
MSR	Egyptair	NGE	Angel Airlines (Thailand)
MT	Thomas Cook Airlines	NH	All Nippon Airways
MU	China Eastern Airlines	NI	Portugalia
MUI	Trans Air	NIG	Aero Contractors (Nigeria)
MVD	KMV	NJS	National Jet Systems
MW	Maya Island Air	NK	Spirit Airlines
MX	Mexican	NKF	Barents AirLink
MXA	Mexican	NKS	Spirit Airlines
MYD	Maya Island Air	NL	Shaheen Air Int'l
MZ	Merpati Nusantara	NMB	Air Namibia
N/A	Asia Pacific Airlines	NMI	Pacific Wings Airlines
N/A	Aerolimousine	NOE	Transcaraibes Air Int'l
N/A	Grant Aviation	NOK	Nok Air
N/A	Papillon Airways	NP	Skytrans
N/A	Harbour Air	NQ	Air Japan
N/A	Promech	NR	Pamir Air
N/A	Everts Air	NRD	Nordic Regional
N/A	Olson Air Service	NRR	Nature Air
N/A	Larry's Flying Service	NSE	Satena
N/A	Island Airlines	NSO	AeroLineas Sosa
N/A	Air Link Pty.	NT	Binter Canarias
N/A	Air Mandalay	NU	Japan Transocean
N/A	Go One Airways	NV	Air Central
N/A	Yangon Airways	NVR	Novair
N/A	West Coast Air	NW	Northwest Airlines
N/A	Inland Aviation Services	NWA	Northwest Airlines
N/A	Air Tindi	NWL	North-Wright Airways
N/A	Skytrans	NWR	Northwest Regional Airlines
N/A	Pacific Airways	NX	Air Macau
N/A	San Juan Aviation	NY	Air Iceland
N/A	Katmai Air	NZ	Air New Zealand
N/A	Kivalliq Air	O7	Norfolk Air
N/A	Kronflyg	OA	Olympic Airlines
N/A	Salmon Air	OAL	Olympic Airlines
N/A	Nakina Air Service	OAV	Omni-Aviacao E Tecnologia
N/A	Nice Helicopteres	OAW	Helvetic Airways
N/A	Skippers Aviation	OB	Astrakhan Airlines
N/A	Smokey Bay Air	OC	Omni-Aviacao E Tecnologia
N/A	Paradise Air	OCA	Aserca (Venezuela)
N/A	Trans North Aviation	ODS	Odessa Airlines

OEA	Orient Thai Airlines	PPW	Royal Phnom Penh	
OF	Air Finland	PR	Philippine Airlines	
OH	Comair (US)	PRF	Precision Air	
OJ	Overland Airways	PS	Ukraine Int'l Airlines	
OK	Czech Airlines (CSA)	PSK	President Airlines (Cambodia)	
OL	OLT (Germany)	PSV	Servicios Aereos Profesionales	
OLA	Overland Airways	PT	West Air Sweden	
OLT	OLT (Germany)	PTN	Pantanal	
OM	MIAT-Mongolian Airlines	PU	PLUNA (Uruguay)	
OMA	Oman Air	PUA	PLUNA (Uruguay)	
OMS	Omskavia	PV	Saint Barth Commuter	
ON	Our Airline	PW	Precision Air	
OO	SkyWest Airlines	PX	Air Niugini	
ORB	Orenburg Airlines	PY	Surinam Airways	
OS	Austrian Airlines	PZ	TAM Mercosur	
OT	Aeropelican	Q3	Zambian Airways	
OTL	South Airlines (Ukraine)	Q5	40-Mile Air	
OU	Croatia Airlines	Q6	Aero Condor	
OV	Estonian Air	Q8	TAC - Trans Air Congo	
OW	Executive Airlines	QA	Click Mexicana	
OX	Orient Thai Airlines	QB	Georgian National Airlines	
OZ	Asiana Airlines	QC	Air Corridor	
OZW	Skywest (Australia)	QF	Qantas Airways	
P4	AeroLineas Sosa	QFA	Qantas Airways	
P5	AeroRepublica	QH	Kyrgyzstan	
P6	Trans Air	QI	Cimber Air	
P7	Russian Sky Airlines	QK	Air Canada Jazz	
P8	Pantanal	QL	Aero Lanka	
P9	Perm Airlines	QM	Air Malawi	
PAL	Philippine Airlines	QQ	Alliance Airlines	
PAO	Polynesian	QR	Qatar Airways	
PAS	Pelita Air	QS	SmartWings	
PB	Provincial Airlines	QTR	Qatar Airways	
PBA	PB Air	QU	East African Airlines	
PC	Air Fiji	QV	Lao Airlines	
PCO	Pacific Coastal Airlines	QW	Blue Wings	
PD	Porter Airlines	QX	Horizon Air	
PDF	Pelican Air	QXE	Horizon Air	
PEL	Aeropelican	QZ	Indonesia AirAsia	
PEN	Penair	R2	Orenburg Airlines	
PF	Palestinian Airlines	R7	Aserca (Venezuela)	
PG	Bangkok Airways	R8	Kyrgyzstan Airlines	
PGA	Portugalia	RA	Nepal Airlines	
PGP	Perm Airlines	RAE	Regional Airlines (France)	
PH	Polynesian	RAM	Royal Air Maroc	
PIA	Pakistan Int'l Airlines (PIA)	RAR	Air Rarotonga	
PIC	Jetstar Pacific	RB	Syrian Arab Airlines	
PIR	Pamir Air	RBA	Royal Brunei Airlines	
PJ	Air Saint-Pierre	RC	Atlantic Airways (Faroe Is.)	
PK	Pakistan Int'l Airlines (PIA)	RE	Aer Arann	
PLM	Air Pullmantur	REA	Aer Arann	
PLR	Northwestern Air Lease	REU	Air Austral	
PM	Tropic Air	RG	Varig	
PMT	PMTair	RGL	Regional Air Lines (Morocco)	
PNW	Palestinian Airlines	RI	Mandala Airlines	
POE	Porter Airlines	RIT	Asian Spirit	

Airlines

RJ	Royal Jordanian
RJA	Royal Jordanian
RK	Royal Khmer Airlines
RKH	Royal Khmer Airlines
RL	Royal Phnom Penh
RLA	Airlinair
RLE	Rico Linhas Aereas
RLN	Aero Lanka
RMV	Romavia
RN	Paradise Air
RNA	Nepal Airlines
RNV	Armavia
RO	TAROM Romanian Air
ROI	AVIOR
RON	Our Airline
ROT	TAROM Romanian Air
RP	Chautauqua Airlines
RPB	AeroRepublica
RQ	Kam Air
RSH	JetLite
RSI	Air Sunshine
RU	TCI Skyking
RUS	Cirrus Airlines
RV	Caspian Airlines
RVL	Air Vallee
RWD	Rwandair Express
RXA	REX Regional Express
RYR	Ryanair
RZ	SANSA (Costa Rica)
RZO	SATA International
S2	JetLite
S3	Santa Barbara Airlines
S4	SATA International
S5	Shuttle America
S6	Salmon Air
S7	S7 Airlines
SA	South African Airways (SAA)
SAA	South African Airways (SAA)
SAH	Sayakhat Airlines
SAI	Shaheen Air Int'l
SAS	Scandinavian Airlines System (SAS)
SAY	Scot Airways
SB	Air Caledonie Int'l
SBI	S7 Airlines
SBS	Seaborne Airlines
SBU	Saint Barth Commuter
SC	Shandong Airlines
SCW	Malmo Aviation
SCX	Sun Country Airlines
SD	Sudan Airways
SDM	Rossiya
SDR	City Airline
SE	XL Airways France
SEN	Sevenair
SER	Aero California

SEY	Air Seychelles
SHU	SAT Airlines
SIA	Singapore Airlines
SIB	Sibaviatrans (SIAT)
SJ	Sriwijaya Air
SJY	Sriwijaya Air
SK	Scandinavian Airlines System (SAS)
SKI	TCI Skyking
SKU	Sky Airline
SKW	SkyWest Airlines
SKX	Skyways Express
SKY	Skymark Airlines
SLA	Sierra National Airlines
SLI	Aeromexico Connect
SLK	SilkAir
SLM	Surinam Airways
SMX	Alitalia Express
SN	Brussels Airlines
SNB	Sterling
SNG	Air Senegal
SOL	Solomon Airlines
SOV	Saravia
SPM	Air Saint-Pierre
SPR	Provincial Airlines
SQ	Singapore Airlines
SRH	Siem Reap Airways
SRQ	South East Asian Airlines
SS	Corsairfly
SSF	Severstal Aircompany
SSV	Skyservice Airlines
ST	Germania
STA	STA Trans African
SU	Aeroflot
SUD	Sudan Airways
SUS	Sun Air of Scandinavia
SUW	Interavia Airlines
SV	Saudi Arabian Airlines
SVA	Saudi Arabian Airlines
SVK	Air Slovakia
SVR	Ural Airlines
SW	Air Namibia
SWA	Southwest Airlines
SWG	Sunwing Airlines
SWN	West Air Sweden
SWR	SWISS
SWT	Swiftair
SX	AeroEjecutiva
SXS	SunExpress
SY	Sun Country Airlines
SYR	Syrian Arab Airlines
SYX	Skyway Airlines
T2	Nakina Air Service
T3	Eastern Airways
T4	Hellas Jet
T5	Turkmenistan Airlines

T6	Tavrey Aircompany	U4	PMTair	
T7	Twin Jet	U5	USA 3000	
T8	STA Trans African	U6	Ural Airlines	
TA	Taca Int'l Airlines	U8	Armavia	
TAE	TAME (Ecuador)	U9	Tatarstan Airlines	
TAI	Taca Int'l Airlines	UA	United Airlines	
TAK	Tatarstan Airlines	UAE	Emirates	
TAM	TAM (Brazil)	UAL	United Airlines	
TAN	Zanair	UB	Myanma Airways	
TAO	Transportes Aeromar	UBA	Myanma Airways	
TAP	TAP Air Portugal	UCA	CommutAir	
TAR	Tunisair	UD	Hex'Air	
TBG	Tropical Airways Haiti	UDN	Dniproavia	
TC	Air Tanzania	UF	Ukrainian Mediterranean	
TCF	Shuttle America		Airlines	
TCV	TACV	UG	Sevenair	
TCX	Thomas Cook Airlines	UGX	East African Airlines	
TDM	Tandem Aero	UIA	UNI Air	
TE	Lithuanian Airlines	UKM	Ukrainian Mediterranean	
TF	Malmo Aviation		Airlines	
TG	Thai Airways	UKW	Lviv Airlines	
TGW	Tiger Airways	UL	Sri Lankan Airlines	
THA	Thai Airways	UM	Air Zimbabwe	
THT	Air Tahiti Nui	UN	Transaero Airlines	
THY	Turkish Airlines	UO	Hong Kong Express	
TJT	Twin Jet	UP	Bahamasair	
TK	Turkish Airlines	URG	Air Urga	
TL	Airnorth	URN	Turan Air	
TM	LAM (Mozambique)	US	US Airways	
TMN	UTair Aviation	USA	US Airways	
TMP	Arizona Express	UT	UTair Aviation	
TN	Air Tahiti Nui	UTY	Alliance Airlines	
TNA	Transasia Airways	UU	Air Austral	
TNR	Tanana Air Service	UV	Helisureste	
TO	President Airlines (Cambodia)	UX	Air Europa	
TOM	Thomsonfly	UYA	Flight Alaska	
TOS	Tropic Air	UZ	Buraq Air	
TP	TAP Air Portugal	UZB	Uzbekistan Airways	
TPC	Air Caledonie	V3	Carpatair	
TQ	Tandem Aero	V7	Air Senegal	
TR	Tiger Airways	V8	Iliamna Air Taxi	
TRS	AirTran	VA	Volare Airlines	
TS	Air Transat	VAP	Phuket Airlines	
TSC	Air Transat	VBW	Air Burkina	
TSG	TAC - Trans Air Congo	VF	Valuair	
TSO	Transaero Airlines	VG	VLM (Belgium)	
TU	Tunisair	VGN	Virgin Nigeria	
TUA	Turkmenistan Airlines	VH	Aeropostal	
TVR	Tavrey Aircompany	VIM	Air VIA Bulgarian	
TVS	SmartWings	VIR	Virgin Atlantic	
TX	Air Caraibes	VK	Virgin Nigeria	
TY	Air Caledonie	VKG	Thomas Cook Airlines	
TYR	Tyrolean Airways		Scandinavia	
TZK	Tajik Air	VL	Air VIA Bulgarian	
U2	Easyjet	VLE	Volare Airlines	
U3	Avies	VLG	Vueling	

Airlines

VLK	Vladivostok Air
VLM	VLM (Belgium)
VLU	Valuair
VM	Viaggio Air
VN	Vietnam Airlines
VNA	Warbelow's Air Ventures
VO	Tyrolean Airways
VOA	Viaggio Air
VOZ	Virgin Blue
VPP	Vintage Props & Jets
VQ	Vintage Props & Jets
VR	TACV
VRD	Virgin America
VRN	Varig
VS	Virgin Atlantic
VSV	Aircompany SCAT
VT	Air Tahiti
VTA	Air Tahiti
VU	Air Ivoire
VUN	Air Ivoire
VV	Aerosvit Airlines (Ukraine)
VW	Transportes Aeromar
VX	Virgin America
VXG	Avirex Gabon
VY	Vueling
W3	Arik Air
W3	Swiftair
W5	Mahan Airlines
W6	Wizz Air
W7	Sayakhat Airlines
WA	KLM Cityhopper
WAK	Wings of Alaska
WB	Rwandair Express
WC	Islena Airlines
WCP	Primaris Airlines
WDH	Wimbi Dira Airways
WF	Wideroe's Flyveselskap
WG	Sunwing Airlines
WIA	Windward Islands Airways
WIF	Wideroe's Flyveselskap
WJ	Labrador Airways
WJA	Westjet
WL	Aeroperlas
WLC	Welcome Air
WM	Windward Islands Airways
WN	Southwest Airlines
WO	World Airways
WO	Air Southwest
WOA	World Airways
WOW	Air Southwest
WP	Island Air (Aloha)
WQ	Romavia
WRF	Wright Air Service
WS	Westjet
WW	bmibaby
WX	Cityjet

WY	Oman Air
WZZ	Wizz Air
X3	TUIfly
X5	Afrique Airlines
X8	Icaro Air
XAR	Xpressair
XC	KD Air
XE	ExpressJet
XF	Vladivostok Air
XJ	Mesaba Aviation
XK	CCM Airlines
XL	Lan Ecuador
XLA	XL Airways
XLF	XL Airways France
XM	Alitalia Express
XM	Australian Air Express
XME	Australian Air Express
XN	Xpressair
XP	Xtra Airways
XQ	SunExpress
XR	Skywest (Australia)
XV	Ivoire Airways
Y2	Alliance Air (Uganda)
Y2	Flyglobespan
Y4	Eagle Aviation (Kenya)
Y6	Cambodia Airlines
Y9	Kish Air
YB	South African Express Airways
YD	Gomelavia
YG	South Airlines (Ukraine)
YI	Air Sunshine
YK	Cyprus Turkish Airlines
YL	Yamal Airlines
YM	Montenegro Airlines
YN	Air Creebec
YO	Heli Air Monaco
YR	Scenic Airlines
YS	Regional Airlines (France)
YU	Aerolineas Dominicanas (Dominair)
YV	Mesa Airlines
YW	Air Nostrum
YX	Midwest Airlines
Z3	Promech
Z5	GMG Airlines
Z6	Dniproavia
ZA	Interavia Airlines
ZB	Monarch Airlines
ZH	Shenzhen Airlines
ZI	Aigle Azur
ZK	Great Lakes Aviation
ZL	REX Regional Express
ZW	Air Wisconsin

Hotel Companies

Abba Hotels	AB	City Partners Hotels	CF
AC Hoteles	AR	Clarion Hotels	CC
ACC-Nifos	IF	Classic British Hotels	KB
Accor Hotels	RT	Classic Int'l Hotels	IH
Adams Mark Hotels	AM	Club Quarters	CQ
Affinia	NY	ClubHouse Inns	KL
Akzent Hotels	AK	Coast Hotels & Resorts	WX
Allegiance Services	AV	Columbus Res Service	BX
Aloft	AL	Comfort Inn	CI
AmericInn	AA	Comfort Suites	CZ
AmeriHost Inn	AE	Concorde Hotels	CD
Amerisuites	AJ	Conrad Hotels	CN
ANA Hotels	AN	Constellation Group	TH
ATAhotels	AQ	Corus Hotels	CL
Atel Hotels Network	AC	Country Inns & Suites	CX
Austrotel Hotels	SX	Courtyard by Marriott	CY
Axcess Hotels	AZ	Crowne Plaza Hotels	CP
Barcelo Hotels	BN	Days Inn	DI
Baymont Inns & Suites	BU	De Vere Hotels	DV
Best Inns & Suites	BI	Delta Hotels	DE
Best Value Inn	BV	Design Hotels	DS
Best Western Int'l	BW	Destination Hotels & Resorts	DN
Boscolo Hotels	BA	Distinguished Hotels	DH
Boutique Hotels	BC	Domina Hotels	DM
Bulgari Hotels & Resorts	BG	Doral Conference Ctrs & Rsts	DL
Caesar Park Hotels	CJ	Dorchester Group	DC
Camberley Hotels	QC	Doubletree Hotels	DT
Cambria Suites	EZ	Drury Hotels	DR
Camino Real Hotels	CM	Dusit Hotels	GA
Candlewood Suites	YO	E.D.S.	ED
Carlson Hotel Brands	CW	Econolodge	EO
Cendant Hotel Brands	TR	Element	EL
Charming Hotels & Resorts	CU	Embassy Suites	ES
Chateaux & Hotels de France	CE	Epoque Hotels	EP
Choice Hotels	EC	Exclusive Hotels	EU

Executive Hotels & Resorts	EI	K Hotels	KH
Extended Stay America	EA	Kempinski Hotels	KI
Extra Holidays	XH	Keytel	KY
Fairfield Inn	FN	Kimpton Hotel Group	KC
Fairmont Hotels	FA	Knights Inn	KG
Fiesta Americana	FH	KSL Resorts	KO
Flag Hotels	FW	La Quinta Inns	LQ
Fontainebleau Resort	FB	Langham Hotels	LO
Four Seasons	FS	Le Meridien	MD
Gaylord Hotels	GE	Leading Hotels of the World	LW
GenaRes	GZ	LeisureLink, Inc.	LI
Global Conextions	GX	Lexington Collection	LP
Golden Tulip Hotels	GT	Loews Hotels	LZ
Gouverneur Hotels	HQ	Louvre Hotels	NN
Grand Heritage	GH	Luxe Worldwide Hotels	LE
Grand Hospitality	GG	Luxury Collection	LC
Grand Traditions	GD	Luxury Resorts	XO
Graves Hotels	GV	Macdonald Hotel Group	GB
Great Hotels of the World	GW	Magnolia Hotels	MG
GuestHouse International	GO	MainStay Suites	MZ
Hampton Inn	HX	Malmaison (UK)	MI
Harrahs Hotels & Resorts	HR	Mandarin Oriental	MO
Hawthorn Suites	BH	Marco Polo Hotels	MH
Hilton Garden Inn	GI	Maritim Hotels	MM
Hilton Hotel Brands	EH	Marriott Conference Centers	ET
Hilton Hotels	HH	Marriott Hotel Brands	EM
Hilton International	HL	Marriott Hotels	MC
Historic Hotels of America	HE	Marriott Vacation Club	MB
Holiday Inn Worldwide	HI	Maybourne Hotel Group	VY
Homestead Studio Suites	BE	Melrose Hotel Company	ML
Homewood Suites	HG	Mercure Hotels	RT
Hospitality Solutions	GR	Meritus Hotels & Resorts	GM
Hot Key International	HK	MGM Mirage	MV
Hotel Indigo	IN	Microtel Inns & Suites	MT
Hotel Port	DJ	Millennium & Copthorne	MU
Hotelred	HD	Minto Suite Hotel	MS
HotelREZ	HO	Moore Reservation Systems	MW
Hotelzon	XZ	Motel 6	MX
Hotusa Hotels	HA	Mövenpick Hotels	MK
Howard Johnson	HJ	Myfidelio	IQ
Hyatt Hotels & Resorts	HY	N H Hotels	NS
Hyatt Place	HP	New Otani Hotels	NO
Hyatt Vacation Club	HU	Nikko Hotels International	NK
Ibis Hotels	RT	Noble House Hotels	NC
Independent Hotels	IM	Novotel	RT
InnLink Hotels	SM	Oberoi Hotels	OB
InnPoints Worlwide	IP	Okura Hotels & Resorts	OC
Intercontinental Hotel Brands	6C	Omni Hotels	OM
Intercontinental Hotels	IC	Orient Express Hotels	OE
Interstate Hotels & Resorts	BK	Otedis	OI
ITS/Magellan Services	TS	Othon Hotels	OT
Jameson Inns/Signature Inns	SJ	Outrigger Hotels & Resorts	OR
Joie de Vivre Hospitality	JV	Pacific International	PI
Jolly Hotels	JH	Pan Pacific Hotels	PF
Jumeirah International	JT	Park Inn	PD
Jurys Doyle Hotel Group	JD	Park Plaza Hotels & Resorts	PK

Payless Lodging	PA	Small Luxury Hotels	LX
Peabody Hotel Group	PY	Sofitel	RT
Peninsula Hotels	PN	Sol/Melia Group	SM
Performance Connections	PX	Sonesta Hotels	SN
Preferred Boutique	PV	Sorat Hotels	ST
Preferred Hotels	PH	Special Properties	SP
Prince Resorts of Hawaii	PJ	SpringHill Suites	XV
Protea Hotels	PR	Stamford Hotels	YS
Qhotels	QH	StarHotels	SY
Quality Inns & Suites	QI	Starwood	SW
Quality Reservations	QR	Staybridge Suites	YZ
Radisson Hotels & Resorts	RD	Steigenberger Hotels	SR
Raffles International	YR	Sterling Hotels & Resorts	WR
Ramada Inn	RA	Studio 6	SS
Ramada International	NR	Suburban Lodge	UB
Reconline	ON	Summerfield Suites	HY
Red Lion Hotels	RL	Summit Int'l Htls & Rsrts	XL
Red Roof Inns	RF	Super 8	OZ
Regal Hotels International	RQ	Supranational Hotels	SX
Regent Hotels & Resorts	RE	Sutton Place Hotels	SF
Registry Resort	RH	Swissotel	SL
Relais & Chateaux	WB	Synxis	YX
Renaissance Hotels	BR	Taj Hotels	TJ
Reservhotel	TA	Thistle Hotels	TI
Residence Inn	RC	Top International Hotels	TP
Resort Bookings	RB	TownePlace Suites	TO
ResortQuest Hawaii	AH	Travelodge	TL
ResortQuest International	QV	Travelodge Australia	LT
Rezlink Intl	RK	Travelodge UK	TG
Rihga Royal Hotels	RR	Unirez	UZ
RingHotels	RX	Utell Hotels	UI
Ritz Carlton Club	ZC	Vacation Click	VK
Ritz-Carlton Hotels	RZ	Vagabond Inns	VA
Rocco Forte Collection	FC	Vantage Hospitality	VH
RockResorts	RS	Vantis Hotels	VE
Rodeway Inn	RI	W Hotels	WH
Rosewood Hotels & Resorts	RW	Waldorf Astoria	WA
Rydges Hotel Group	RG	Walt Disney Hotels	DW
Sarova Hotels	SV	Warwick Int'l Hotels	WK
Scandic Hotels	SH	WestCoast Hotel Partners	WC
Sceptre Hospitality Resources	SC	Westin Hotels and Resorts	WI
Select Marketing Hotels	SQ	Westmark Hotels	WM
Sercotel Hotels	SE	Wingate Inns	WG
Shangri-La Hotels & Resorts	SG	Woodfin Suite Hotels	WD
Sheraton Hotels	SI	Worldhotels	EW
Shilo Inns	BP	Wyndham Hotels	WY
Sierra Suites	US	XN Global Res	XN
Sleep Inns	SZ		

Note: Some hotels share a GDS code because they have common owner-ship or belong to the same group.

Rental Car Companies

Ace	AC	Hertz	ZE
Advantage	AD	Its	TS
Alamo	AL	L&M	LM
Americar	AF	Midway	MW
Auto Europe	ZU	National	ZL
Avis	ZI	New Frontier	NF
Budget	ZD	Payless	ZA
Capps Vans	CV	Practical Car	ZP
Continental	CO	Rent Rite	RR
Discount	DS	Sakura Rent A Car	RT
Dollar	ZR	Simply Wheelz	ZH
Enterprise	ET	Sixt	SX
EuropCar	EP	Specialty	VR
EZ Rent	EZ	Thrifty	ZT
Fox	FX	U-save	SV

Hotel & Rental Car Codes

Hotel Codes

6C	Intercontinental Hotel Brands	CL	Corus Hotels
AA	AmericInn	CM	Camino Real Hotels
AB	Abba Hotels	CN	Conrad Hotels
AC	Atel Hotels Network	CP	Crowne Plaza Hotels
AE	AmeriHost Inn	CQ	Club Quarters
AH	ResortQuest Hawaii	CU	Charming Hotels & Resorts
AJ	Amerisuites	CW	Carlson Hotel Brands
AK	Akzent Hotels	CX	Country Inns & Suites
AL	Aloft	CY	Courtyard by Marriott
AM	Adams Mark Hotels	CZ	Comfort Suites
AN	ANA Hotels	DC	Dorchester Group
AQ	ATAhotels	DE	Delta Hotels
AR	AC Hoteles	DH	Distinguished Hotels
AV	Allegiance Services	DI	Days Inn
AZ	Axcess Hotels	DJ	Hotel Port
BA	Boscolo Hotels	DL	Doral Conference Centers &
BC	Boutique Hotels		Resorts
BE	Homestead Studio Suites	DM	Domina Hotels
BG	Bulgari Hotels & Resorts	DN	Destination Hotels & Resorts
BH	Hawthorn Suites	DR	Drury Hotels
BI	Best Inns & Suites	DS	Design Hotels
BK	Interstate Hotels & Resorts	DT	Doubletree Hotels
BN	Barcelo Hotels	DV	De Vere Hotels
BP	Shilo Inns	DW	Walt Disney Hotels
BR	Renaissance Hotels	EA	Extended Stay America
BU	Baymont Inns & Suites	EC	Choice Hotels
BV	Best Value Inn	ED	E.D.S.
BW	Best Western Int'l	EH	Hilton Hotel Brands
BX	Columbus Res Service	EI	Executive Hotels & Resorts
CC	Clarion Hotels	EL	Element
CD	Concorde Hotels	EM	Marriott Hotel Brands
CE	Chateaux & Hotels de France	EO	Econolodge
CF	City Partners Hotels	EP	Epoque Hotels
CI	Comfort Inn	ES	Embassy Suites
CJ	Caesar Park Hotels	ET	Marriott Conference Centers

EU	Exclusive Hotels	KH	K Hotels
EW	Worldhotels	KI	Kempinski Hotels
EZ	Cambria Suites	KL	ClubHouse Inns
FA	Fairmont Hotels	KO	KSL Resorts
FB	Fontainebleau Resort	KY	Keytel
FC	Rocco Forte Collection	LC	Luxury Collection
FH	Fiesta Americana	LE	Luxe Worldwide Hotels
FN	Fairfield Inn	LI	LeisureLink, Inc.
FS	Four Seasons	LO	Langham Hotels
FW	Flag Hotels	LP	Lexington Collection
GA	Dusit Hotels	LQ	La Quinta Inns
GB	Macdonald Hotel Group	LT	Travelodge Australia
GD	Grand Traditions	LW	Leading Hotels of the World
GE	Gaylord Hotels	LX	Small Luxury Hotels
GG	Grand Hospitality	LZ	Loews Hotels
GH	Grand Heritage	MB	Marriott Vacation Club
GI	Hilton Garden Inn	MC	Marriott Hotels
GM	Meritus Hotels & Resorts	MD	Le Meridien
GO	GuestHouse International	MG	Magnolia Hotels
GR	Hospitality Solutions	MH	Marco Polo Hotels
GT	Golden Tulip Hotels	MI	Malmaison (UK)
GV	Graves Hotels	MK	Mövenpick Hotels
GW	Great Hotels of the World	ML	Melrose Hotel Company
GX	Global Conextions	MM	Maritim Hotels
GZ	GenaRes	MO	Mandarin Oriental
HA	Hotusa Hotels	MS	Minto Suite Hotel
HD	Hotelred	MT	Microtel Inns & Suites
HE	Historic Hotels of America	MU	Millennium & Copthorne
HG	Homewood Suites	MV	MGM Mirage
HH	Hilton Hotels	MW	Moore Reservation Systems
HI	Holiday Inn Worldwide	MX	Motel 6
HJ	Howard Johnson	MZ	MainStay Suites
HK	Hot Key International	NC	Noble House Hotels
HL	Hilton International	NK	Nikko Hotels International
HO	HotelREZ	NN	Louvre Hotels
HP	Hyatt Place	NO	New Otani Hotels
HQ	Gouverneur Hotels	NR	Ramada International
HR	Harrahs Hotels & Resorts	NS	N H Hotels
HU	Hyatt Vacation Club	NY	Affinia
HX	Hampton Inn	OB	Oberoi Hotels
HY	Hyatt Hotels & Resorts	OC	Okura Hotels & Resorts
HY	Summerfield Suites	OE	Orient Express Hotels
IC	Intercontinental Hotels	OI	Otedis
IF	ACC-Nifos	OM	Omni Hotels
IH	Classic Int'l Hotels	ON	Reconline
IM	Independent Hotels	OR	Outrigger Hotels & Resorts
IN	Hotel Indigo	OT	Othon Hotels
IP	InnPoints Worlwide	OZ	Super 8
IQ	Myfidelio	PA	Payless Lodging
JD	Jurys Doyle Hotel Group	PD	Park Inn
JH	Jolly Hotels	PF	Pan Pacific Hotels
JT	Jumeirah International	PH	Preferred Hotels
JV	Joie de Vivre Hospitality	PI	Pacific International
KB	Classic British Hotels	PJ	Prince Resorts of Hawaii
KC	Kimpton Hotel Group	PK	Park Plaza Hotels & Resorts
KG	Knights Inn	PN	Peninsula Hotels

PR	Protea Hotels	SW	Starwood	
PV	Preferred Boutique	SX	Austrotel Hotels	
PX	Performance Connections	SX	Supranational Hotels	
PY	Peabody Hotel Group	SY	StarHotels	
QC	Camberley Hotels	SZ	Sleep Inns	
QH	Qhotels	TA	Reservhotel	
QI	Quality Inns & Suites	TG	Travelodge UK	
QM	Queens Moat Houses	TH	Constellation Group	
QR	Quality Reservations	TI	Thistle Hotels	
QV	ResortQuest International	TJ	Taj Hotels	
RA	Ramada Inn	TL	Travelodge	
RB	Resort Bookings	TO	TownePlace Suites	
RC	Residence Inn	TP	Top International Hotels	
RD	Radisson Hotels & Resorts	TR	Cendant Hotel Brands	
RE	Regent Hotels & Resorts	TS	ITS/Magellan Services	
RF	Red Roof Inns	UB	Suburban Lodge	
RG	Rydges Hotel Group	UI	Utell Hotels	
RH	Registry Resort	US	Sierra Suites	
RI	Rodeway Inn	UZ	Unirez	
RK	Rezlink Intl	VA	Vagabond Inns	
RL	Red Lion Hotels	VE	Vantis Hotels	
RQ	Regal Hotels International	VH	Vantage Hospitality	
RR	Rihga Royal Hotels	VK	Vacation Click	
RS	RockResorts	VY	Maybourne Hotel Group	
RT	Accor Hotels	WA	Waldorf Astoria	
RT	Ibis Hotels	WB	Relais & Chateaux	
RT	Mercure Hotels	WC	WestCoast Hotel Partners	
RT	Novotel	WD	Woodfin Suite Hotels	
RT	Sofitel	WG	Wingate Inns	
RW	Rosewood Hotels & Resorts	WH	W Hotels	
RX	RingHotels	WI	Westin Hotels and Resorts	
RZ	Ritz-Carlton Hotels	WK	Warwick Int'l Hotels	
SC	Sceptre Hospitality Resources	WM	Westmark Hotels	
SE	Sercotel Hotels	WR	Sterling Hotels & Resorts	
SF	Sutton Place Hotels	WX	Coast Hotels & Resorts	
SG	Shangri-La Hotels & Resorts	WY	Wyndham Hotels	
SH	Scandic Hotels	XH	Extra Holidays	
SI	Sheraton Hotels	XL	Summit Int'l Htls & Rsrts	
SJ	Jameson Inns/Signature Inns	XN	XN Global Res	
SL	Swissotel	XO	Luxury Resorts	
SM	InnLink Hotels	XV	SpringHill Suites	
SM	Sol/Melia Group	XZ	Hotelzon	
SN	Sonesta Hotels	YO	Candlewood Suites	
SP	Special Properties	YR	Raffles International	
SQ	Select Marketing Hotels	YS	Stamford Hotels	
SR	Steigenberger Hotels	YX	Synxis	
SS	Studio 6	YZ	Staybridge Suites	
ST	Sorat Hotels	ZC	Ritz Carlton Club	
SV	Sarova Hotels			

Note: Some hotels share a GDS code because they have common ownership or belong to the same group.

Rental Car Codes

AC	Ace	RT	Sakura Rent A Car
AD	Advantage	SV	U-save
AF	Americar	SX	Sixt
AL	Alamo	TS	Its
CO	Continental	VR	Specialty
CV	Capps Vans	ZA	Payless
DS	Discount	ZD	Budget
EP	EuropCar	ZE	Hertz
ET	Enterprise	ZH	Simply Wheelz
EZ	EZ Rent	ZI	Avis
FX	Fox	ZL	National
LM	L&M	ZP	Practical Car
MW	Midway	ZR	Dollar
NF	New Frontier	ZT	Thrifty
RR	Rent Rite	ZU	Auto Europe

Note: The layout of this section differs from that of other sections in *Part I*. Whereas other sections are laid out two columns per page, this section contains only one column, with each entry containing four items of information. The information in each line is meant to be read straight across the page, as follows: first the country name, then the two-digit code for that country, then the unit of currency for that country, and, finally, the three-digit code for that currency.

Afghanistan	AF	Afghani	AFA
Albania	AL	Lek	ALL
Algeria	DZ	Algerian Dinar	DZD
American Samoa	AS	US Dollar	USD
Andorra	AD	Euro	EUR
Angola	AO	Kwanza	AOA
Anguilla	AI	East Caribbean Dollar	XCD
Antarctica	AQ		
Antigua & Barbuda	AG	East Caribbean Dollar	XCD
Argentina	AR	Argentine Peso	ARS
Armenia	AM	Dram	AMD
Aruba	AW	Aruban Guilder	AWG
Australia	AU	Australian Dollar	AUD
Austria	AT	Euro	EUR
Azerbaijan	AZ	Manat	AZM
Bahamas	BS	Bahamian Dollar	BSD
Bahrain	BH	Bahrani Dinar	BHD
Bangladesh	BD	Taka	BDT
Barbados	BB	Barbados Dollar	BBD
Belarus	BY	Belorussian Ruble	BYR
Belgium	BE	Euro	EUR
Belize	BZ	Belize Dollar	BZD
Benin	BJ	CFA Franc BCEAO	XOF
Bermuda	BM	Bermudian Dollar	BMD
Bhutan	BT	Ngultrum	BTN
Bolivia	BO	Boliviano	BOB
Bosnia Hercegovina	BA	Bosnian Mark	BAM
Botswana	BW	Pula	BWP
Bouvet Island	BV	Norwegian Krone	NOK
Brazil	BR	Real	BRL
British Indian Ocean	IO	U.S. Dollar	USD
Britsh Virgin Islands	VG	U.S. Dollar	USD
Brunei Darussalam	BN	Brunei Dollar	BND
Bulgaria	BG	Lev	BGN
Burkina Faso	BF	CFA Franc BCEAO	XOF
Burundi	BI	Burundi Franc	BIF
Cambodia	KH	Riel	KHR
Cameroon	CM	CFA Franc BEAC	XAF
Canada	CA	Canadian Dollar	CAD
Cape Verde	CV	Escudo	CVE
Cayman Islands	KY	Cayman Islands Dollar	KYD
Central African Republic	CF	CFA Franc BEAC	XAF
Chad	TD	CFA Franc BEAC	XAF

Chile	CL	Chilean Peso	CLP
China	CN	Yuan Renminbi	CNY
Christmas Islands	CX	Australian Dollar	AUD
Cocos (Keeling) Islands	CC	Australian Dollar	AUD
Colombia	CO	Colombian Peso	COP
Comoros	KM	Comoro Franc	KMF
Congo	CG	CFA Franc BEAC	XAF
Congo, Dem. Rep.	CD	New Zaire	ZRN
Cook Islands	CK	New Zealand Dollar	NZD
Costa Rica	CR	Costa Rican Colon	CRC
Cote d'Ivoire	CI	CFA Franc BCEAO	XOF
Croatia	HR	Kuna	HRK
Cuba	CU	Cuban Peso	CUP
Cyprus	CY	Euro	EUR
Czech Republic	CZ	Koruna	CZK
Denmark	DK	Danish Krone	DKK
Djibouti	DJ	Djibouti Franc	DJF
Dominica	DM	East Caribbean Dollar	XCD
Dominican Republic	DO	Dominican Peso	DOP
East Timor	TL	Escudo	TPE
Ecuador	EC	Sucre	ECS
Egypt	EG	Egyptian Pound	EGP
El Salvador	SV	El Salvador Colon	SVC
Equatorial Guinea	GQ	CFA Franc BEAC	XAF
Eritrea	ER	Ethiopian Nakfa	ERN
Estonia	EE	Kroon	EEK
Ethiopia	ET	Ethiopian Birr	ETB
Falkland Islands	FK	Falkland Island Pound	FKP
Faroe Islands	FO	Danish Krone	DKK
Fiji	FJ	Fiji Dollar	FJD
Finland	FI	Euro	EUR
France	FR	Euro	EUR
French Guiana	GF	Euro	EUR
French Polynesia	PF	CFP Franc	XPF
French Southern Territories	TF	Euro	EUR
Gabon	GA	CFA Franc BEAC	XAF
Gambia	GM	Dalasi	GMD
Georgia	GE	Lari	GEL
Germany	DE	Euro	EUR
Ghana	GH	Cedi	GHC
Gibraltar	GI	Gibraltar Pound	GIP
Greece	GR	Euro	EUR
Greenland	GL	Danish Krone	DKK
Grenada	GD	East Caribbean Dollar	XCD
Guadeloupe	GP	Euro	EUR
Guam	GU	US Dollar	USD
Guatemala	GT	Quetzal	GTQ
Guinea	GN	Guinea Franc	GNF
Guinea-Bissau	GW	Guinea-Bissau Peso	GWP
Guyana	GY	Guyana Dollar	GYD
Haiti	HT	Gourde	HTG
Heard & McDonald Isl.	HM	Australian Dollar	AUD
Honduras	HN	Lempira	HNL
Hong Kong	HK	Hong Kong Dollar	HKD
Hungary	HU	Forint	HUF
Iceland	IS	Iceland Krona	ISK
India	IN	Indian Rupee	INR
Indonesia	ID	Indonesian Rupiah	IDR
Iran	IR	Iranian Rial	IRR
Iraq	IQ	Iraqi Dinar	IQD
Ireland	IE	Euro	EUR
Israel	IL	Shekel	ILS
Italy	IT	Euro	EUR
Jamaica	JM	Jamaican Dollar	JMD
Japan	JP	Yen	JPY
Jordan	JO	Jordanian Dinar	JOD
Kazakhstan	KZ	Tenge	KZT

Kenya	KE	Kenyan Shilling	KES
Kiribati	KI	Australian Dollar	AUD
Korea, North	KP	North Korean Won	KPW
Korea, South	KR	Korean Won	KRW
Kuwait	KW	Kuwaiti Dinar	KWD
Kyrgyzstan	KG	Som	KGS
Laos	LA	Kip	LAK
Latvia	LV	Latvian Lats	LVL
Lebanon	LB	Lebanese Pound	LBP
Lesotho	LS	Loti	LSL
Liberia	LR	Liberian Dollar	LRD
Libya	LY	Libyan Dinar	LYD
Liechtenstein	LI	Swiss Franc	CHF
Lithuania	LT	Litas	LTL
Luxembourg	LU	Euro	EUR
Macau	MO	Pataca	MOP
Macedonia	MK	Denar	MKD
Madagascar	MG	Malagasy Franc	MGF
Malawi	MW	Kwacha	MWK
Malaysia	MY	Malaysian Ringgit	MYR
Maldives	MV	Rufiyaa	MVR
Mali	ML	CFA Franc BCEAO	XOF
Malta	MT	Euro	EUR
Marshall Islands	MH	US Dollar	USD
Martinique	MQ	Euro	EUR
Mauritania	MR	Ouguiya	MRO
Mauritius	MU	Mauritius Rupee	MUR
Mayotte	YT	Euro	EUR
Mexico	MX	Mexican Peso	MXN
Micronesia	FM	US Dollar	USD
Moldova	MD	Moldovan Leu	MDL
Monaco	MC	Euro	EUR
Mongolia	MN	Tugrik	MNT
Montenegro	ME	Euro	EUR
Montserrat	MS	East Caribbean Dollar	XCD
Morocco	MA	Moroccan Dirham	MAD
Mozambique	MZ	Metical	MZM
Myanmar	MM	Kyat	MMK
Namibia	NA	Namibian Dollar	NAD
Nauru	NR	Australian Dollar	AUD
Nepal	NP	Nepalese Rupee	NPR
Netherlands	NL	Euro	EUR
Netherlands Antilles	AN	Netherlands Antillian Guilder	ANG
New Caledonia	NC	CFP Franc	XPF
New Zealand	NZ	New Zealand Dollar	NZD
Nicaragua	NI	Cordoba Oro	NIO
Niger	NE	CFA Franc BCEAO	XOF
Nigeria	NG	Naira	NGN
Niue	NU	New Zealand Dollar	NZD
Norfolk Island	NF	Australian Dollar	AUD
Northern Mariana Islands	MP	US Dollar	USD
Norway	NO	Norwegian Krone	NOK
Oman	OM	Rial Omani	OMR
Pakistan	PK	Pakistani Rupee	PKR
Palau	PW	US Dollar	USD
Panama	PA	Balboa	PAB
Papua New Guinea	PG	Kina	PGK
Paraguay	PY	Guarani	PYG
Peru	PE	Nuevo Sol	PEN
Philippines	PH	Philippine Peso	PHP
Pitcairn Island	PN	New Zealand Dollar	NZD
Poland	PL	Zloty	PLZ
Portugal	PT	Euro	EUR
Puerto Rico	PR	US Dollar	USD
Qatar	QA	Qatari Rial	QAR
Reunion	RE	Euro	EUR
Romania	RO	Leu	ROL

Countries &
Currencies

The Travel Agent's
Complete Desk
Reference

Russian Federation	RU	Russian Ruble	RUR
Rwanda	RW	Rwanda Franc	RWF
Saint Helena	SH	St. Helena Pound	SHP
Saint Kitts & Nevis	KN	East Caribbean Dollar	XCD
Saint Lucia	LC	East Caribbean Dollar	XCD
Saint Pierre & Miquelon	PM	Euro	EUR
Saint Vincent & Grenadines	VC	East Caribbean Dollar	XCD
Samoa, Western	WS	Tala	WST
San Marino	SM	Euro	EUR
Sao Tome & Principe	ST	Dobra	STD
Saudi Arabia	SA	Saudi Riyal	SAR
Senegal	SN	CFA Franc BCEAO	XOF
Serbia	RS	Serbian Dinar	RSD
Seychelles	SC	Seychelles Rupee	SCR
Sierra Leone	SL	Leone	SLL
Singapore	SG	Singapore Dollar	SGD
Slovakia	SK	Euro	EUR
Slovenia	SI	Euro	EUR
Solomon Islands	SB	Solomon Islands Dollar	SBD
Somalia	SO	Somali Shilling	SOS
South Africa	ZA	South African Rand	ZAR
Spain	ES	Euro	EUR
Sri Lanka	LK	Sri Lanka Rupee	LKR
Sudan	SD	Sudanese Dinar	SDD
Suriname	SR	Suriname Dollar	SRD
Svalbard & Jan Mayen Isl.	SJ	Norwegian Krone	NOK
Swaziland	SZ	Lilangeni	SZL
Sweden	SE	Swedish Krona	SEK
Switzerland	CH	Swiss Franc	CHF
Syria	SY	Syrian Pound	SYP
Taiwan (China)	TW	New Taiwan Dollar	TWD
Tajikistan	TJ	Somoni	TJS
Tanzania	TZ	Tanzanian Shilling	TZS
Thailand	TH	Thai Baht	THB
Togo	TG	CFA Franc BCEAO	XOF
Tokelau	TK	New Zealand Dollar	NZD
Tonga	TO	Pa'anga	TOP
Trinidad & Tobago	TT	Trinidad Dollar	TTD
Tunisia	TN	Tunisian Dinar	TND
Turkey	TR	Turkish Lira	TRL
Turkmenistan	TM	Manat	TMM
Turks & Caicos Is.	TC	US Dollar	USD
Tuvalu	TV	Australian Dollar	AUD
Uganda	UG	Uganda Shilling	UGX
Ukraine	UA	Hryvnia	UAH
United Arab Emirates	AE	UAE Dirham	AED
United Kingdom (England)	GB	Pound Sterling	GBP
United States	US	US Dollar	USD
United States (minor outlying islands)	UM	US Dollar	USD
Uruguay	UY	Peso Uruguayo	UYU
Uzbekistan	UZ	Sum	UZS
Vanuatu	VU	Vatu	VUV
Vatican City	VA	Euro	EUR
Venezuela	VE	Bolivar	VEB
Vietnam	VN	Dong	VND
Virgin Islands (British)	VG	US Dollar	USD
Virgin Islands (US)	VI	US Dollar	USD
Wallis & Futuna Islands	WF	CFP Franc	XPF
Western Sahara	EH	Moroccan Dirham	MAD
Yemen	YE	Yemeni Rial	YER
Zambia	ZM	Kwacha	ZMK

Country & Currency Codes

AD	Andorra
AE	United Arab Emirates
AED	UAE Dirham
AF	Afghanistan
AFA	Afghani
AG	Antigua & Barbuda
AI	Anguilla
AL	Albania
ALL	Lek
AM	Armenia
AMD	Dram
AN	Netherlands Antilles
AO	Angola
AOA	Kwanza
AQ	Antarctica
AR	Argentina
ARS	Argentine Peso
AS	American Samoa
AT	Austria
AU	Australia
AUD	Australian Dollar
AW	Aruba
AWG	Aruban Guilder
AZ	Azerbaijan
AZM	Manat
BA	Bosnia Hercegovina
BAM	Bosnian Mark
BB	Barbados
BBD	Barbados Dollar
BD	Bangladesh
BDT	Taka
BE	Belgium
BF	Burkina Faso
BG	Bulgaria
BGN	Lev
BH	Bahrain
BHD	Bahrani Dinar

BI	Burundi
BIF	Burundi Franc
BJ	Benin
BM	Bermuda
BMD	Bermudian Dollar
BN	Brunei Darussalam
BND	Brunei Dollar
BO	Bolivia
BOB	Boliviano
BR	Brazil
BRL	Real
BS	Bahamas
BSD	Bahamian Dollar
BT	Bhutan
BTN	Ngultrum
BV	Bouvet Island
BW	Botswana
BWP	Pula
BY	Belarus
BYR	Belorussian Ruble
BZ	Belize
BZD	Belize Dollar
CA	Canada
CAD	Canadian Dollar
CC	Cocos (Keeling) Islands
CD	Congo, Dem. Rep.
CF	Central African Republic
CG	Congo
CH	Switzerland
CHF	Swiss Franc
CI	Cote d'Ivoire
CK	Cook Islands
CL	Chile
CLP	Chilean Peso
CM	Cameroon
CN	China
CNY	Yuan Renminbi

CO	Colombia
COP	Colombian Peso
CR	Costa Rica
CRC	Costa Rican Colon
CU	Cuba
CUP	Cuban Peso
CV	Cape Verde
CVE	Escudo
CX	Christmas Islands
CY	Cyprus
CZ	Czech Republic
CZK	Koruna
DE	Germany
DJ	Djibouti
DJF	Djibouti Franc
DK	Denmark
DKK	Danish Krone
DM	Dominica
DO	Dominican Republic
DOP	Dominican Peso
DZ	Algeria
DZD	Algerian Dinar
EC	Ecuador
ECS	Sucre
EE	Estonia
EEK	Kroon
EG	Egypt
EGP	Egyptian Pound
EH	Western Sahara
ER	Eritrea
ERN	Ethiopian Nakfa
ES	Spain
ET	Ethiopia
ETB	Eritrean Birr
EUR	Euro
FI	Finland
FJ	Fiji
FJD	Fiji Dollar
FK	Falkland Islands
FKP	Falkland Island Pound
FM	Micronesia
FO	Faroe Islands
FR	France
GA	Gabon
GB	United Kingdom (England)
GBP	Pound Sterling
GD	Grenada
GE	Georgia
GEL	Lari
GF	French Guiana
GH	Ghana
GHC	Cedi
GI	Gibraltar
GIP	Gibraltar Pound
GL	Greenland
GM	Gambia

GMD	Dalasi
GN	Guinea
GNF	Guinea Franc
GP	Guadeloupe
GQ	Equatorial Guinea
GR	Greece
GT	Guatemala
GTQ	Quetzal
GU	Guam
GW	Guinea-Bissau
GWP	Guinea-Bissau Peso
GY	Guyana
GYD	Guyana Dollar
HK	Hong Kong
HKD	Hong Kong Dollar
HM	Heard & McDonald Isl.
HN	Honduras
HNL	Lempira
HR	Croatia
HRK	Kuna
HT	Haiti
HTG	Gourde
HU	Hungary
HUF	Forint
ID	Indonesia
IDR	Indonesian Rupiah
IE	Ireland
IL	Israel
ILS	Shekel
IN	India
INR	Indian Rupee
IO	British Indian Ocean
IQ	Iraq
IQD	Iraqi Dinar
IR	Iran
IRR	Iranian Rial
IS	Iceland
ISK	Iceland Krona
IT	Italy
JM	Jamaica
JMD	Jamaican Dollar
JO	Jordan
JOD	Jordanian Dinar
JP	Japan
JPY	Yen
KE	Kenya
KES	Kenyan Shilling
KG	Kyrgyzstan
KGS	Som
KH	Cambodia
KHR	Riel
KI	Kiribati
KM	Comoros
KMF	Comoro Franc
KN	Saint Kitts & Nevis
KP	Korea, North

KPW	North Korean Won	MW	Malawi	
KR	Korea, South	MWK	Kwacha	
KRW	Korean Won	MX	Mexico	
KW	Kuwait	MXN	Mexican Peso	
KWD	Kuwaiti Dinar	MY	Malaysia	
KY	Cayman Islands	MYR	Malaysian Ringgit	
KYD	Cayman Islands Dollar	MZ	Mozambique	
KZ	Kazakhstan	MZM	Metical	
KZT	Tenge	NA	Namibia	
LA	Laos	NAD	Namibian Dollar	
LAK	Kip	NC	New Caledonia	
LB	Lebanon	NE	Niger	
LBP	Lebanese Pound	NF	Norfolk Island	
LC	Saint Lucia	NG	Nigeria	
LI	Liechtenstein	NGN	Naira	
LK	Sri Lanka	NI	Nicaragua	
LKR	Sri Lanka Rupee	NIO	Cordoba Oro	
LR	Liberia	NL	Netherlands	
LRD	Liberian Dollar	NO	Norway	
LS	Lesotho	NOK	Norwegian Krone	
LSL	Loti	NP	Nepal	
LT	Lithuania	NPR	Nepalese Rupee	
LTL	Litas	NR	Nauru	
LU	Luxembourg	NU	Niue	
LV	Latvia	NZ	New Zealand	
LVL	Latvian Lats	NZD	New Zealand Dollar	
LY	Libya	OM	Oman	
LYD	Libyan Dinar	OMR	Rial Omani	
MA	Morocco	PA	Panama	
MAD	Moroccan Dirham	PAB	Balboa	
MC	Monaco	PE	Peru	
MD	Moldova	PEN	Nuevo Sol	
MDL	Moldovan Leu	PF	French Polynesia	
ME	Montenegro	PG	Papua New Guinea	
MG	Madagascar	PGK	Kina	
MGF	Malagasy Franc	PH	Philippines	
MH	Marshall Islands	PHP	Philippine Peso	
MK	Macedonia	PK	Pakistan	
MKD	Denar	PKR	Pakistani Rupee	
ML	Mali	PL	Poland	
MM	Myanmar	PLZ	Zloty	
MMK	Kyat	PM	Saint Pierre & Miquelon	
MN	Mongolia	PN	Pitcairn Island	
MNT	Tugrik	PR	Puerto Rico	
MO	Macau	PT	Portugal	
MOP	Pataca	PW	Palau	
MP	Northern Mariana Islands	PY	Paraguay	
MQ	Martinique	PYG	Guarani	
MR	Mauritania	QA	Qatar	
MRO	Ouguiya	QAR	Qatari Rial	
MS	Montserrat	RE	Reunion	
MT	Malta	RO	Romania	
MU	Mauritius	ROL	Leu	
MUR	Mauritius Rupee	RS	Serbia	
MV	Maldives	RSD	Serbian Dinar	
MVR	Rufiyaa	RU	Russian Federation	

*Country &
Currency Codes*

RUR	Russian Ruble
RW	Rwanda
RWF	Rwanda Franc
SA	Saudi Arabia
SAR	Saudi Riyal
SB	Solomon Islands
SBD	Solomon Islands Dollar
SC	Seychelles
SCR	Seychelles Rupee
SD	Sudan
SDD	Sudanese Dinar
SE	Sweden
SEK	Swedish Krona
SG	Singapore
SGD	Singapore Dollar
SH	Saint Helena
SHP	St. Helena Pound
SI	Slovenia
SJ	Svalbard & Jan Mayen Isl.
SK	Slovakia
SL	Sierra Leone
SLL	Leone
SM	San Marino
SN	Senegal
SO	Somalia
SOS	Somali Shilling
SR	Suriname
SRD	Suriname Dollar
ST	Sao Tome & Principe
STD	Dobra
SV	El Salvador
SVC	El Salvador Colon
SY	Syria
SYP	Syrian Pound
SZ	Swaziland
SZL	Lilangeni
TC	Turks & Caicos Is.
TD	Chad
TF	French Southern Territories
TG	Togo
TH	Thailand
THB	Thai Baht
TJ	Tajikistan
TJS	Somoni
TK	Tokelau
TL	East Timor
TM	Turkmenistan
TMM	Manat
TN	Tunisia
TND	Tunisian Dinar
TO	Tonga
TOP	Pa'anga
TPE	Escudo

TR	Turkey
TRL	Turkish Lira
TT	Trinidad & Tobago
TTD	Trinidad Dollar
TV	Tuvalu
TW	Taiwan (China)
TWD	New Taiwan Dollar
TZ	Tanzania
TZS	Tanzanian Shilling
UA	Ukraine
UAH	Hryvnia
UG	Uganda
UGX	Uganda Shilling
UM	United States (minor islands)
US	United States
USD	US Dollar
UY	Uruguay
UYU	Peso Uruguayo
UZ	Uzbekistan
UZS	Sum
VA	Vatican City
VC	Saint Vincent & Grenadines
VE	Venezuela
VEB	Bolivar
VG	Virgin Islands (British)
VI	Virgin Islands (US)
VN	Vietnam
VND	Dong
VU	Vanuatu
VUV	Vatu
WF	Wallis & Futuna Islands
WS	Samoa, Western
WST	Tala
XAF	CFA Franc BEAC
XCD	East Caribbean Dollar
XOF	CFA Franc BCEAO
XPF	CFP Franc
YE	Yemen
YER	Yemeni Rial
YT	Mayotte
ZA	South Africa
ZAR	South African Rand
ZM	Zambia
ZMK	Kwacha
ZRN	New Zaire
ZW	Zimbabwe
ZWD	Zimbabwe Dollar

II

Part Two:

Industry Contacts & Information Sources

Supplier Contacts

This section contains toll free telephone numbers and web site URLs for suppliers of the major travel products: airlines, hotels, rental cars, tours, and cruises. I have attempted to be more rather than less inclusive, but I have made no attempt to be encyclopedic. In other words, there are companies in each category that are not listed, either intentionally or unintentionally.

This is especially true in the tour operators category. There are thousands of tour operators and any attempt to list them all would be futile. Consequently, the listing is limited primarily to operators that have toll-free numbers, on the theory that those are the ones you will be most likely to call. There are many excellent tour operators who, for one reason or another, have opted not to have toll-free numbers. That fact alone should not disqualify them from your consideration.

Also included are the phone numbers of some non-scheduled charter airlines which are not carried on GDSs and consequently were not listed in the previous section on airline codes.

The listings in this section are not intended to be a substitute for specialized directories such as *The Official Hotel Guide*, *The Official Tour Directory* or any of the other excellent guides which provide in-depth information and exhaustive listings of the travel industry segments they cover. Rather, this section is intended as a sort of shorthand phone book to be used when you need to contact a specific supplier but don't remember the number. There is also space for you to jot down the numbers of additional suppliers with which you may be doing business. That way, this book will become an ongoing resource.

The Travel Agent's
Complete Desk
Reference

40-Mile Air	907-883-5191	www.40-mileair.com
Adria Airways	888-792-3742	www.adria-airways.com
Aegean		www.aegeanair.com
Aer Arann		www.aerarann.com
Aer Lingus	800-223-6537	www.aerlingus.com
Aero California	800-237-6225	www.aerocalifornia.com.mx
Aero Condor		www.aerocondor.com/index_english_reservations.htm
Aero Contractors (Nigeria)		www.acn.aero
Aero Lanka		www.aerolanka.aero
Aero-Tropics		www.aero-tropics.com.au
Aeroflot	888-340-6400	www.aeroflot.ru
Aeroflot-Don		www.aeroflot-don.ru
Aeroflot-Nord		www.aeroflot-nord.ru
AeroGal	888-723-7642	www.aerogal.com.ec
Aerogaviota		www.aerogaviota.com
Aerolimousine		www.avcom.ru
Aerolineas Argentinas	800-333-0276	www.aerolineas.com
AeroLineas Sosa		www.laceibaonline.net/aerososa
Aeromexico	800-237-6639	www.aeromexico.com
Aeromexico Connect	800-237-6639	www.aeromexicoconnect.com
Aeropelican		www.aeropelican.com.au
Aeroperlas	800-535-8780	www.aeroperlas.com
Aeropostal	888-912-8466	www.aeropostal.com
AeroRepublica		www.aerorepublica.com
AeroSur (Bolivia)	866-903-2885	www.aerosur.com
Aerosvit Airlines (Ukraine)	212-661-1620	www.aerosvit.com
Afriqiyah	877-359-0999	www.afriqiyah.aero
Aigle Azur		www.aigleazur.net
Air Algerie		www.airralgerie.dz
Air Alps Aviation		www.airalps.com
Air Arabia		www.airarabia.com
Air Astana	888-855-1557	www.airastana.com
Air Austral		www.air-austral.com
Air Berlin	866-266-5588	www.airberlin.com
Air Botswana	800-518-7781	www.airbotswana.co.bw
Air Burkina		www.air-burkina.com
Air Caledonie		www.air-caledonie.nc
Air Caledonie Int'l	800-254-7251	www.aircalin.com
Air Canada	888-247-2262	www.aircanada.com
Air Canada Jazz	902-873-5000	www.flyjazz.ca
Air Caraibes		www.aircaraibes.com
Air Central	800-235-9262	www.air-central.co.jp
Air Chathams		www.airchathams.co.nz
Air China	800-982-8802	www.airchina.com.cn
Air Comet		www.aircomet.com
Air Corridor		www.aircorridor.co.mz
Air Creebec	819-825-8375	www.aircreebec.ca
Air Dolomiti		www.airdolomiti.it
Air Europa		www.air-europa.com
Air Fiji	877-247-3454	www.airfiji.com.fj
Air Finland		www.airfinland.fi
Air France	800-237- 2747	www.airfrance.com

Air Greenland		www.airgreenland.com
Air Guyane		www.airguyane.com
Air Iceland		www.airiceland.is
Air India	800-223-7776	www.airindia.com
Air India Regional	800-223-7776	www.airindia.com
Air Inuit	800-361-5933	www.airinuit.com
Air Ivoire		www.airivoire.com
Air Jamaica	800-523-5585	www.airjamaica.com
Air Japan	800-235-9262	www.air-japan.co.jp
Air Kiribati		www.kiritours.com/Travel/ AirKiribati/Index.html
Air Koryo		www.korea-dpr.com/users/
switzerland/korea_enterprise_airkoryo/airkoryo_fr.php		
Air Link Pty.		www.airlinkairlines.com.au
Air Macau		www.airmacau.com.mo
Air Madagascar	866-933-5963	www.airmadagascar.mg
Air Malawi		www.airmalawi.com
Air Malta	866-357-4155	www.airmalta.com
Air Mandalay		www.airmandalay.com
Air Marshall Islands		www.airmarshallislands.com
Air Mauritius	800-537-1182	www.airmauritius.com
Air Moldova		www.airmoldova.md
Air Namibia	800-626-4242	www.airnamibia.com.na
Air New Zealand	800-262-1234	www.airnz.co.nz
Air Nippon	800-235-9262	www.air-nippon.co.jp
Air Nippon Network	800-235-9262	www.ank-net.co.jp
Air Niugini	675-327-3555	www.airniugini.com.pg
Air North (Yukon Terr.)	800-661-0407	www.flyairnorth.com
Air Nostrum	800-772-4642	www.airnostrum.es
Air Pacific Ltd.	800-227-4446	www.airpacific.com
Air Philippines		www.airphils.com
Air Pullmantur	800-937-6362	www.pullmanturair.com
Air Rarotonga		www.airraro.com
Air Saint-Pierre	877-277-7765	www.airsaintpierre.com
Air Senegal		www.air-senegal-international.com
Air Seychelles	800-677-4277	www.airseychelles.com
Air Sinai	800-334-6787	www.egyptair.com.eg
Air Slovakia		www.airslovakia.sk
Air Southwest		www.airsouthwest.com
Air Sunshine	800-327-8900	www.airsunshine.com
Air Tahiti		www.airtahiti.aero
Air Tahiti Nui	877-824-4846	www.airtahitinui.com
Air Tanzania		www.airtanzania.com
Air Tindi	867-669-8200	www.airtindi.com
Air Transat	800-388-5836	www.airtransat.com
Air Turks and Caicos		www.flyairtc.com
Air Urga		www.urga.com.ua
Air Vallee		www.airvallee.com
Air Vanuatu	800-677-4277	www.airvanuatu.com
Air VIA Bulgarian		www.air-via.com
Air Wisconsin	920-739-5123	www.airwis.com
Air Zimbabwe	800-742-3006	www.airzimbabwe.aero
Air-Do (Hokkaido Intl)		www.airdo21.com
AirAsia		www.airasia.com
airBaltic	877-359-2258	www.airbaltic.com
AirBlue Limited		www.airblue.com

131

Supplier Contacts

The Travel Agent's Complete Desk Reference

Aircompany SCAT		www.scat.kz
Aires		www.aires.com.co
Airlinair		www.airlinair.com
Airlines of Tasmania		www.airtasmania.com.au
Airnorth		www.airnorth.com.au
AirTran	800-247-8726	www.airtrain.com
Aklak Air	867-777-3777	www.aklakair.ca
Alaska Airlines	800-426-0333	www.alaskaair.com
Albanian Airlines		www.albanianairlines.com.al
Alidaunia		www.alidaunia.it
Alitalia	800-223-5730	www.alitalia.com
Alitalia Express	800-223-5730	www.alitalia.it
All Nippon Airways	800-235-9262	www.anaskyweb.com
Allegiant Air	800-432-3810	www.allegiantair.com
Alliance Air (Uganda)		www.saallianceair.com
Alliance Airlines	800-227-4500	www.allianceairlines.com.au
American Airlines	800-433-7300	www.aa.com
American Eagle	800-433-7300	www.aa.com
Arctic Circle Air Service	907-245-1382	www.arcticcircleair.com
Ariana Afghan Airlines	866-330-3431	www.flyariana.com
Arik Air		www.arikair.com
Arizona Express	866-435-9872	www.azxpress.com
Arkia Israeli Airlines		www.arkia.com
Armavia		www.u8.am
Aserca (Venezuela)		www.asercaairlines.com
Asia Pacific Airlines		www.flyapa.com
Asian Spirit		www.asianspirit.com
Asiana Airlines	800-227-4262	www.flyasiana.com
Astraeus		www.flystar.com
ATA Aerocondor		www.aerocondor.com
Atlant-Soyuz		www.atlant-soyuz.ru
Atlantic Airways (Faroe Is.)		www.atlantic.fo
Atlas Blue		www.atlas-blue.com
Atlasjet		www.atlasjet.com/en
Augsburg Airways	800-645-3880	www.augsburgair.de
Aurigny Air Services		www.aurigny.com
Austral Lineas Aereas	800-333-0276	www.austral.com.ar
Australian Air Express		www.aae.com.au
Austrian Airlines	800-843-0002	www.aua.com
Aviacsa	866-246-0961	www.aviacsa.com
Aviaenergo		www.aviaenergo.ru
Avianca	800-284-2622	www.avianca.com
AVIATECA (Guatemala)	888-477-8222	www.aviateca.aero
Avies		www.avies.ee
AVIOR		www.avior.com.ve
Avirex Gabon		www.flyavirex.com
Axis Airways		www.axis-airways.com
Azerbaijan Airlines (AZAL)		www.azal.co.uk
B&H Airlines		www.airbosna.ba
Bahamasair	800-222-4262	www.bahamasair.com
Bangkok Airways	866-226-4565	www.bangkokair.com
Barents AirLink		www.barentsairlink.se
Batavia Air		www.batavia-air.co.id
Bearskin Airlines	800-465-2327	www.bearskinairlines.com
Belair	866-366-5588	www.airberlin.com
Belavia		www.belavia.by

Bellview Airlines		www.flybellviewair.com
Bemidji Airlines	800-332-7133	www.bemidjiaviation.com
Benin Golf		www.benin-golf-air.com
Bering Air	907-443-5464	www.beringair.com
Berjaya Air		www.berjaya-air.com
Biman Bangladesh	212-808-4476	www.bimanair.com
Binter Canarias	800-772-4642	www.bintercanarias.com
Blue Panorama Airlines		www.blue-panorama.com
Blue Wings		www.bluewings.com
Blue1	800-221-2350	www.blue1.com
BMI (British Midland)	800-788-0555	www.flybmi.com
bmibaby		www.bmibaby.com
Brindabella Airlines		www.brindabellaairlines.com.au
Brit Air	800-375-8723	www.britair.fr
British Airways	800-247-9297	www.britishairways.com
British International Helicopters		www.scillyhelicopter.co.uk
Brussels Airlines	516-740-5200	www.brusselsairlines.com
Bulgaria Air	888-462-8542	www.air.bg
Buraq Air		www.buraqair.com
Calm Air	800-839-2256	www.calmair.com
Canadian North (Air NorTerra)	800-661-1505	www.cdn-north.com
Canjet	800-809-7777	www.canjet.com
Cape Air	800-352-0714	www.flycapeair.com
Carpatair		www.carpatair.com
Caspian Airlines		www.caspian.aero
Cathay Pacific Airways	800-233-2742	www.cathaypacific.com
Cayman Airways	800-422-9626	www.caymanairways.com
CCM Airlines		www.ccm-airlines.com
CEBU Pacific Air		www.cebupacificair.com
Central Mountain Air	888-865-8585	www.flycma.com
Centre-Avia Airlines		www.centreavia.ru
Chautauqua Airlines	317-484-6000	www.flychautauqua.com
China Airlines	800-227-5118	www.china-airlines.com
China Eastern Airlines	800-200-5118	www.ce-air.com
China Southern Airlines	323-653-8088	www.flychinasouthern.com
Cielos Airlines		www.cielos-airlines.com
Cimber Air		www.cimber.dk
Cirrus Airlines		www.cirrus-world.de
City Airline		www.cityairline.com
Cityjet	800-992-3932	www.cityjet.com
Click Mexicana		www.clickmx.com
ClubAir		www.clubair.it
Coastal Air Transport		www.coastalair.com
Colgan Air	703-368-8880	www.colganair.com
Comair (South Africa)		www.comair.co.za
Comair (US)	800-221-1212	www.comair.com
CommutAir	518-562-2700	www.commutair.com
Condor	800-524-6975	www.condor.com
Contact Air	800-645-3880	www.contactair.de
Continental Airlines	800-525-0280	www.continental.com
Continental Micronesia	800-525-0280	www.continental.com
COPA Airlines (Panama)	800-359-2672	www.copaair.com
Corsairfly		www.corseairfly.com
Cosmic Air		www.cosmicair.com

Croatia Airlines		www.croatiaairlines.hr
Cubana Airlines	888-667-1222	www.cubana.cu
Cyprus Airways	718-267-6882	www.cyprusairways.com
Cyprus Turkish Airlines		www.kthy.net
Czech Airlines (CSA)	800-223-2365	www.czechairlines.com
Daallo Airlines	312-822-9105	www.daallo.com
Dalavia		www.dalavia.ru
Danish Air Transport		www.dat.dk
Delta Air Lines	800-221-1212	www.delta.com
Denim Air		www.denimair.com
DirektFlyg		www.direktflyg.com
Djibouti Airlines		www.djiboutiairlines.com
Dniproavia		www.dniproavia.com
Domodedovo Airlines		www.akdal.ru
Dragonair	800-233-2742	www.dragonair.com
Druk Air		www.drukair.com.bt
Dutch Antilles Express		www.flydae.com
Eagle Air Uganda		www.flyeagleuganda.com
Eagle Aviation (Kenya)		www.eaglekenya.com
East African Airlines		www.flyeastafrican.com
East African Safari Air		www.bookeastafrican.com
East Asia Airlines		www.helihongkong.com
Eastern Airways		www.easternairways.com
Easyjet		www.easyjet.com
Egyptair	800-334-6787	www.egyptair.com
El Al Israel Airlines	800-223-6700	www.elal.com
Emirates	800-777-3999	www.emirates.com
Enkor Airlines		www.chelavia.ru
Era Aviation	800-866-8394	www.flyera.com
Eritrean Airlines	877-374-8732	www.flyeritrea.com
Estonian Air		www.estonian-air.com
Ethiopian Airlines	800-445-2733	www.flyethiopian.com
Etihad Airways	888-838-4423	www.etihadairways.com
Euro-Asia Air		www.euroasiaair.kz
Euroair		www.euroair.gr
Eurofly	800-459-0581	www.euroflyusa.com/US
EuroLOT		www.eurolot.com.pl
Eurowings	800-645-3880	www.eurowings.de
EVA Airways	800-695-1188	www.evaair.com
Everts Air	907-450-2350	www.evertsair.com
Executive Airlines		www.executive-airlines.com
Expo Aviation		www.expoavi.com
ExpressJet	888-958-9538	www.expressjet.com
Finnair	800-950-5000	www.finnair.com
Finnish Commuter Airlines		www.finncomm.com
First Air	800-267-1247	www.firstair.ca
First Choice Airways		www.firstchoice.co.uk
Flight Alaska	907-543-3003	www.yuteair.com
Flybaboo		www.flybaboo.com
flyBE		www.flybe.com
Flyglobespan	800-663-8614	www.flyglobespan.com
Freedom Air		www.freedomairguam.com
Frontier Airlines	800-432-1359	www.frontierairlines.com
Frontier Flying Service	800-478-6779	www.frontierflying.com
Futura Intl Airways		www.futura-aer.com
Gambia Int'l Airlines		www.gia.gm

Garuda Indonesia	800-342-7832	www.garuda-indonesia.com
Gazpromavia Aviation		www.gazpromavia.ru
Georgian National Airlines		www.national-avia.com
Germania		www.germania.aero
Germanwings		www.germanwings.com
GMG Airlines		www.gmgairlines.com
GOL		www.voegol.com.br
Golden Air		www.goldenair.se
Gomelavia		www.gomelavia.com
Grant Aviation	877-890-4321	www.flygrant.com
Great Lakes Aviation	800-554-5111	www.greatlakesav.com
Gulf Air	888-359-4853	www.gulfair.com
Gulfstream Int'l Airlines	954-985-1500	www.gulfstreamair.com
Hageland Aviation	866-239-0119	www.hageland.com
Hahn Air	646-322-7834	www.hahnair.de
Hainan Airlines		www.hnair.com
Hamburg International		www.hamburg-international.de
Harbour Air	800-665-0212	www.harbourair.com
Hawaiian Airlines	800-367-5320	www.hawaiianair.com
Hawkair	800-487-1216	www.hawkair.ca
Heli Air Monaco		www.heliairmonaco.com
Heli Securite		www.helicopter-saint-tropez.com
Helijet International	800-665-4354	www.helijet.com
Helisureste		www.helisureste.com
Hellas Jet		www.hellas-jet.com
Helvetic Airways		www.helvetic.com
Hemus Air	888-462-8542	www.air.bg
Hewa Bora Airways		www.hba.cd
Hex'Air		www.hexair.com
Hong Kong Airlines		www.hkairlines.com
Hong Kong Express		www.hongkongexpress.com
Horizon Air	800-547-9308	www.alaskaair.com
Iberia	800-772-4642	www.iberia.com
Ibex Airlines		www.ibexair.co.jp
Icaro Air		www.icaro.aero
Icelandair	800-223-5500	www.icelandair.com
Iliamna Air Taxi	907-571-1248	www.iliamnaair.com
Imair Airline		www.imair.com
Indian Airlines	800-223-7776	www.indian-airlines.nic.in
Indonesia AirAsia		www.airasia.com
Inland Aviation Services	907-675-4624	www.inlandaviation.com
Inter Airlines		www.interekspres.com
Interair South Africa		www.interair.co.za
Interavia Airlines		www.inter-avia.ru
Interlink Airlines		www.interlinkairlines.com
InterSky		www.intersky.biz
Iran Air		www.iranair.com
Iran Aseman Airlines		www.iaa.ir
Iraqi Airways		www.iraqiairways.co.uk
Island Air (Aloha)	800-323-3345	www.islandair.com
Island Airlines	800-248-7779	www.islandair.net
Islas Airways		www.islasairways.com
Islena Airlines	800-535-8780	www.flyislena.com
Israir Airlines	877-477-2471	www.israirairlines.com
ItAli Airlines		www.italiweb.it
ITEK Air		www.itekair.kg

Supplier
Contacts

JAL Express		www.jal.co.jp/jex
JALways		www.jalways.co.jp
Japan Air Commuter	800-525-3663	www.ar.jal.com
Japan Airlines	800-525-3663	www.jal.com
Japan Transocean		www.jal.co.jp/jta
Jat Airways	212-689-1677	www.jat.com
Jet Airways (India)	877-835-9538	www.jetairways.com
Jet2		www.jet2.com
JetBlue	800-538-2583	www.jetblue.com
JetLite		www.jetlite.com
Jetstar Airways	866-397-8170	www.jetstar.com
Jetstar Pacific	866-397-8170	www.jetstar.com/ve
Kaliningradavia		www.kdavia.eu
Kam Air		www.flykamair.com
Katmai Air	800-544-0551	www.katmaiair.com
Kato Air		www.katoair.no
KD Air	800-665-4244	www.kdair.com
Kenmore Air	800-543-9595	www.kenmoreair.com
Kenya Airways	866-536-9224	www.kenya-airways.com
Keystone Air Service	800-665-3975	www.keystoneair.mb.ca
Kish Air		www.kishairline.com
Kivalliq Air	204-888-0100	www.kivalliqair.com
KLM Cityhopper	800-225-2525	www.klm.com/passage/cityhopper/nl/index.html
KLM Royal Dutch Airlines	800-374-7747	www.klm.com
KMV		www.kmvavia.aero
Kolavia Airlines		www.kolavia.ru
Korean Air	800-438-5000	www.koreanair.com
Krasair		www.krasair.ru
Kuban Airlines		www.alk.ru
Kuwait Airways	800-458-9248	www.kuwaitairways.com
Kyrgyzstan		www.air.kg
L.A.B. Flying Service	907-766-2222	www.labflying.com
Labrador Airways	800-563-3042	www.airlabrador.com
LACSA (Costa Rica)	800-225-2272	www.taca.com
LADE		www.lade.com.ar
LagunAir		www.lagunair.com
LAM (Mozambique)		www.airmozambique.eu
Lan Airlines	866-435-9526	www.lan.com
Lan Ecuador	866-435-9526	www.lan.com
LAN Express	866-435-9526	www.lan.com
Lan Peru	866-435-9526	www.lan.com
Lao Airlines		www.laoairlines.com
Larry's Flying Service	907-474-9169	www.larrysflying.com
LatCharter		www.latcharter.com
Lauda Air		www.laudaair.com
LGW (Germany)	866-266-5588	www.lgw.de
LIAT (Antigua)	888-844-5428	www.liatairline.com
Libyan Airlines		www.ln.aero
Lion Air		www.lionair.co.id
Lithuanian Airlines		www.flylal.com
Livingston		www.livingstonair.it
LOT Polish Airlines	212-7890970	www.lot.com
LTU Billa	866-266-5588	www.ltu.at
LTU International Airways	866-266-5588	www.ltu.de
Lufthansa	800-645-3880	www.lufthansa.com

Lufthansa CityLine	800-645-3880	www.lufthansacityline.com
Luxair		www.luxair.lu
Lviv Airlines		www.avia.lviv.ua
Macair	800-227-4500	www.macair.com.au
Macedonian Airlines		www.mat.com.mk
Mahan Airlines		www.mahan.aero
Malaysia Airlines	800-552-9264	www.malaysiaairlines.com
Malev Hungarian Airlines	800-223-6884	www.malev.hu
Malmo Aviation		www.malmoaviation.se
Mandala Airlines		www.mandalaair.com
Mandarin Airlines		www.mandarin-airlines.com
Martinair Holland	800-627-8462	www.martinair.com
Maya Island Air		www.mayaairways.com
MenaJet		www.menajet.com
Meridiana	800-881-1422	www.meridiana.it
Merpati Nusantara		www.merpati.co.id
Mesa Airlines	800-637-2247	www.mesa-air.com
Mesaba Aviation	651-367-5000	www.mesaba.com
Mexican	800-531-7921	www.mexicana.com
MIAT-Mongolian Airlines	303-757-1929	www.miat.com
Middle East Airlines (AirLiban)	212-244-6850	www.mea.com.lb
Midwest Airlines	800-452-2022	www.midwestairlines.com
Moldavian Airlines		www.mdv.md
Monarch Airlines		www.flymonarch.com
Montenegro Airlines		www.montenegro-airlines.com
Myanma Airways		www.mot.gov.mm/ma/index.html
Myanmar Airways		www.maiair.com
Nakina Air Service	807-329-5341	
National Jet Systems		www.nationaljet.com.au
Nature Air	800-235-9272	www.natureair.com
Nepal Airlines		www.royalnepal-airlines.com
New England Airlines	800-243-2460	www.block-island.com/nea
Nice Helicopteres		www.nicehelicopteres.com
Nok Air		www.nokair.com
Nordic Regional		www.nordicregional.se
Norfolk Air		www.norfolkair.com
North American Airlines	800-359-6222	www.northamericanair.com
North Flying		www.northflying.com
North-Wright Airways	867-587-2333	www.north-wrightairways.com
Northwest Airlines	800-225-2525	www.nwa.com
Northwest Regional Airlines		www.northwestregional.com.au
Northwestern Air Lease	877-872-2216	www.nwal.ca
Norwegian Air Shuttle		www.norwegian.no
Nouvelair Tunisie		www.nouvelair.com
Novair		www.novair.net
Odessa Airlines		www.odessaonline.com.ua
Olson Air Service		www.olsonair.com
OLT (Germany)		www.olt.de
Olympic Airlines	800-223-1226	www.olympicairlines.com
Oman Air		www.oman-air.com
Omni-Aviacao E Tecnologia		www.omni.pt
Omskavia		www.omskavia.ru
Orenburg Airlines		www.orenair.ru
Orient Thai Airlines		www.orient-thai.com
Our Airline		www.ourairline.com.au
Overland Airways		www.overland.aero

P.T. Dirgantara Air Services		www.schreiner.nl
Pacific Airways	877-360-3500	www.flypacificairways.com
Pacific Coastal Airlines	800-663-2872	www.pacificcoastal.com
Pacific Sun	800-227-4446	www.pacificsun.com.fj
Pacific Wings Airlines	888-575-4546	www.pacificwings.com
Pakistan Int'l Airlines (PIA)	800-578-6786	www.piac.com.pk
Palestinian Airlines		www.palairlines.com
Pamir Air		www.pamirairways.af
Pantanal		www.pantanal-airlines.com.br
Papillon Airways	800-528-2418	www.papillon.com
Paradise Air	877-412-0877	www.flywithparadise.com
PB Air		www.pbair.com
Pelican Air		www.pelicanair.co.za
Pelita Air		www.pelita-air.com
Penair	800-448-4226	www.penair.com
Perm Airlines		www.savino.perm.ru
Philippine Airlines	800-435-9725	www.philippineairlines.com
Phuket Airlines		www.phuketairlines.com
PLUNA (Uruguay)		www.pluna.com.uy
PMTair		www.pmtair.com
Polynesian	800-644-7659	www.polynesianairlines.com
Porter Airlines	888-619-8622	www.flyporter.com
Portugalia	800-221-7370	www.flytap.com
Precision Air		www.precisionairtz.com
Primaris Airlines	702-270-0999	www.primarisairlines.com
Promech	800-860-3845	www.promechair.com
Provincial Airlines	800-563-2800	www.provincialairlines.ca
Qantas Airways	800-227-4500	www.qantas.com.au
Qatar Airways	877-777-2827	www.qatarairways.com
Regional Air Lines (Morocco)		www.regionalmaroc.com
Regional Airlines (France)	800-237- 2747	www.regional.com
REX Regional Express		www.regionalexpress.com.au
Rico Linhas Aereas		www.voerico.com.br
Romavia		www.romavia.ro
Rossiya		www.rossiya-airlines.ru/en
Royal Air Maroc	800-344-6726	www.royalairmaroc.com
Royal Brunei Airlines		www.bruneiair.com
Royal Jordanian	800-223-0470	www.rja.com.jo
Royal Khmer Airlines		www.royalkhmerairlines.com
Royal Phnom Penh		
Russian Sky Airlines		www.rusky.ru
Rwandair Express		www.rwandair.com
Ryanair		www.ryanair.com
S7 Airlines		www.s7.ru
Saint Barth Commuter		www.stbarthcommuter.com
Salmon Air	800-448-3413	www.salmonair.com
Samara Airlines		www.samara-airlines.ru
San Juan Airlines	800-874-4434	www.sanjuanairlines.com
SANSA (Costa Rica)	877-767-2672	www.flysansa.com
Santa Barbara Airlines	866-213-2457	www.santabarbaraairlines.com
Saravia		www.saravia.ru
SAT Airlines		www.satairlines.ru
SATA International	800-762-9995	www.sata.pt
Satena		www.satena.com
Saudi Arabian Airlines	800-472-8342	www.saudiairlines.com
Sayakhat Airlines		www.sayakhat.kz

Scandinavian Airlines System (SAS)	800-221-2350	www.flysas.com
Scenic Airlines	800-634-6801	www.scenic.com
Scot Airways	800-237-2747	www.scotairways.co.uk
Seaborne Airlines	888-359-8687	www.seaborneairlines.com
Servicios Aereos Profesionales	809-826-4117	www.sapair.com
Sevenair		www.sevenair.com.tn
Severstal Aircompany		www.airport.cpv.ru
Shaheen Air Int'l		www.shaheenair.com
Shandong Airlines		www.shandongair.com
Shanghai Airlines		www.shanghai-air.com
Shenzhen Airlines		www.shenzhenair.com
Shuttle America	317-484-6000	www.shuttleamerica.com
Sibaviatrans (SIAT)		www.siat.ru
Sichuan Airlines		www.scal.com.cn
Siem Reap Airways		www.siemreapairways.com
Sierra National Airlines		www.flysna.com
SilkAir		www.silkair.com
Singapore Airlines	800-742-3333	www.singaporeair.com
Skippers Aviation		www.skippers.com.au
Sky Airline		www.skyairline.cl
SkyEurope		www.skyeurope.com
Skymark Airlines		www.skymark.co.jp
Skyservice Airlines	800-701-9448	www.skyserviceairlines.com
Skytrans		www.skytrans.com.au
Skyway Airlines	800-452-2022	www.midwestairlines.com
Skyways Express		www.skyways.se
Skywest (Australia)		www.skywest.com.au
SkyWest Airlines	435-634-3400	www.skywest.com
SmartWings		www.smartwings.net
Smokey Bay Air	888-482-1511	www.smokeybayair.com
Solomon Airlines	800-677-4277	www.solomonairlines.com.au
South African Airlink		www.saairlink.co.za
South African Airways	800-852-9256	www.flysaa.com
South African Express Airways	800-722-9675	www.flysax.com
South Airlines (Ukraine)		www.otlavia.com
South East Asian Airlines		www.flyseair.com
Southwest Airlines	800-435-9792	www.southwest.com
Spanair	888-545-5757	www.spanair.com
Spirit Airlines	800-772-7117	www.spiritair.com
Sri Lankan Airlines	877 915 2652	www.srilankan.aero
Sriwijaya Air		www.sriwijayaair-online.com
STA Trans African		www.sta-airlines.com
Sterling		www.sterling.dk
Sudan Airways		www.sudanair.com
Sun Air of Scandinavia	800-247-9297	www.sun-air.dk
Sun Country Airlines	800-359-6786	www.suncountry.com
SunExpress		www.sunexpress.com
Sunwing Airlines	877-786-9464	www.flysunwing.com
Surinam Airways	800-327-6864	www.slm.nl
Swiftair		www.swiftair.com
SWISS	877-359-7947	www.swiss.com
Sylt Air		www.syltair.eu
Syrian Arab Airlines		www.syrian-airlines.com

*Supplier
Contacts*

TAAG-Angola		www.taagangola.pages.web.com
TAC - Trans Air Congo		www.transaircongo.org
Taca Int'l Airlines	800-535-8780	www.taca.com
TACV	866-359-8228	www.flytacv.com
TAM (Brazil)	888-235-9826	www.tamairlines.com
TAM Mercosur	888-235-9826	www.tam.com.py
TAME (Ecuador)		www.tame.com.ec
Tanana Air Service	907-524-3330	www.fairbanks-alaska.com/ tanana-air-service.htm
TAP Air Portugal	800-221-7370	www.tap.pt
TAROM Romanian Air	212-560-0840	www.tarom.ro
Tatarstan Airlines		www.avia-tatarstan.ru
Tavrey Aircompany		www.tavrey.com
TCI Skyking	649-941-3136	www.skyking.tc
Thai Airways	800-426-5204	www.thaiair.com
Thomas Cook Airlines		www.thomascookairlines.co.uk
Thomas Cook Airlines Scandinavia		www.thomascookairlines.dk
Thomsonfly		www.thomsonfly.com
Tiger Airways		www.tigerairways.com
Trans Air	808-836-8080	www.transairhawaii.com
Trans North Aviation	800-451-6442	www.transnorth.com
Trans States Airlines	314-222-4300	www.transstates.net
Transaero Airlines		www.transaero.ru
Transasia Airways		www.tna.com.tw
Transcaraibes Air Int'l		www.air-tropical.com
Transportes Aeromar		www.aeromar.com.mx
Transwest Air	800-667-9356	www.transwestair.com
Tropic Air	800-422-3435	www.tropicair.com
Tropical Airways Haiti		www.tropical-haiti.com
TUIfly		www.tuifly.com
Tunisair		www.tunisair.com
Turan Air		www.turan-air.com
Turkish Airlines	800-874-8875	www.turkishairlines.com
Turkmenistan Airlines		www.turkmenistanembassy.org/ turkmen/travel/airline.html
Twin Jet		www.twinjet.fr
Tyrolean Airways	800-843-0002	www.aua.com.at
Ukraine Int'l Airlines	800-876-0114	www.ukraine-international.com
Ukrainian Mediterranean Airlines		www.umairlines.com
UNI Air		www.uniair.com.tw
United Airlines	800-241-6522	www.united.com
Ural Airlines		www.uralairlines.ru
US Airways	800-428-4322	www.usairways.com
USA 3000	877-872-3000	www.usa3000.com
UTair Aviation		www.utair.ru
Uzbekistan Airways		www.uzairways.com
Valuair	866-397-8170	www.valuair.com
Varig	800-468-2744	www.varig.com
Viaggio Air	888-462-8542	www.air.bg
Vietnam Airlines	415-677-0888	www.vietnamair.com.vn
Vintage Props & Jets	800-852-0275	www.vpj.com
Virgin America	877-359-8474	www.virginamerica.com
Virgin Atlantic	800-862-8621	www.virgin-atlantic.com
Virgin Blue		www.virginblue.com.au

Virgin Nigeria		www.virginnigeria.com
Visa Airways		www.visaairways.com
Vladivostok Air	206-443-1614	www.vladavia.ru
VLM (Belgium)		www.flyvlm.com
Volare Airlines		www.volareweb.com
Vueling		www.vueling.com
Warbelow's Air Ventures	800-478-0812	www.warbelows.com
Welcome Air		www.welcomeair.com
West Air Sweden		www.westair.se
West Coast Air	604-606-6800	www.westcoastair.com
Westjet	800-538-5696	www.westjet.com
Wideroe's Flyveselskap	800-221-2350	www.wideroe.no
Wimbi Dira Airways		www.wda.cd
Wind Jet		www.volawindjet.it
Windward Islands Airways	866-466-0410	www.fly-winair.com
Wings of Alaska	907-789-0790	www.wingsofalaska.com
Wizz Air		www.wizzair.com
World Airways	770-632-8000	www.worldair.com
Wright Air Service	907-474-0502	www.wrightair.net
Xiamen Airlines		www.xiamenair.com.cn
XL Airways		www.xl.com
XL Airways France		www.xl.com
Xtra Airways	775-738-6040	www.xtraairways.com
Yamal Airlines		www.yamal-airlines.ru
Yangon Airways		www.yangonair.com
Yemenia Yemen Airways	800-936-8300	www.yemenia.com
Zambian Airways		www.zambianairways.com
Zanair		www.zanair.com

Supplier
Contacts

*Supplier
Contacts*

Abba Hotels		www.abbahotels.com
Abotel		www.ati-abotel.com
AC Hoteles		www.ac-hoteles.com
ACC-Nifos		www.nifos.cz
Accor Hotels	800-221-4542	www.accorhotels.com
Adams Mark Hotels	800-444-2326	www.adamsmark.com
Affinia	866-246-2203	www.affinia.com
Akzent Hotels		www.akzent.de
Allstar Hotels	800-285-9834	www.allstarhotels
Aloft	877-462-5638	www.alofthotels.com
Alp'Azur Hotels		www.alpazurhotels.com
Althoff Hotels		www.althoffhotels.de
Amari Hotels		www.amari.com
AmericInn	800-396-5007	www.americinn.com
AmeriHost Inn	800-434-5800	www.amerihostinn.com
Amerisuites	800-833-1516	www.amerisuites.com
ANA Hotels	800-262-4683	www.anahotels.com
Arcantis Hotels		www.arcantis-hotels.com
Arcotel Hotels		www.arcotel.at
Astotel		www.astotel.com
ATAhotels		www.atahotels.it
Atel Hotels Network		www.atel-hotels.com
Austrotel Hotels		www.austrotel.at
Barcelo Hotels	800-227-2356	www.barcelo.com
Baymont Inns & Suites	877-229-6668	www.baymontinns.com
Best Inns & Suites	800-237-8466	www.americasbestinns.com
Best Value Inn	888-315-2378	www.bestvalueinn.com
Best Western Int'l	800-780-7234	www.bestwestern.com
Bilderberg Hotels		www.bilderberg.nl
Boscolo Hotels	888-626-7265	www.boscolohotels.com
Boutique Hotels	877-847-4444	www.boutiquehg.com
Bulgari Hotels & Resorts		www.bulgarihotels.com
Caesar Park Hotels		www.caesar-park.com
Camberley Hotels	800-555-8000	www.camberleyhotels.com
Cambria Suites	877-424-6423	www.cambriasuites.com
Camino Real Hotels	800-722-6466	www.caminoreal.com
Campanile Hotels		www.campanile.com
Candlewood Suites	877-226-3539	www.candlewoodsuites.com
Cendant Hotel Brands	973-428-9700	
Charming Hotels & Resorts	212-588-1877	www.thecharminghotels.com
Chateaux & Hotels de Charme		www.ila-chateau.com
Chateaux & Hotels de France		www.chateauxhotels.com
Choice Hotels	877-424-6423	www.choicehotels.com
Choice Hotels Europe		www.choicehotelseurope.com
Citadines Apart'hotels		www.citadines.com
City Lodge Hotels		www.citylodge.co.za
City Partners Hotels		www.cph-hotels.com
Clarion Hotels	877-424-6423	www.choicehotels.com
Classic British Hotels		www.classicbritishhotels.com
Classic Int'l Hotels	212-279-6311	www.cihotels.com

Club Quarters		www.clubquarters.com
ClubHouse Inns	800-258-2466	www.clubhouseinn.com
Coast Hotels & Resorts	800-663-1144	www.coasthotels.com
Coastal Hotels	800-716-6199	www.coastalhotel.com
Columbus Res Service	800-843-3311	
Comfort Inn	877-424-6423	www.comfortinn.com
Comfort Suites	877-424-6423	www.comfortsuites.com
Concorde Hotels	800-888-4747	www.concorde-hotels.com
Conrad Hotels	800-266-7237	www.conradhotels.com
Corinthia Hotels Int'l		www.corinthiahotels.com
Corus Hotels		www.corushotels.co.uk
Country Comfort		www.countrycomforthotels.com
Country Hearth Inn	888-444-2784	www.countryhearth.com
Country Inns & Suites	888 201 1746	www.countryinns.com
Countryside Hotels		www.countrysidehotels.se
Courtyard by Marriott	888-236-2427	www.courtyard.com
Crowne Plaza Hotels	800-227-6963	www.crowneplaza.com
Dai-Ichi Hotels		www.daiichihotel.com
Dan Hotels	800-223-7773	www.danhotels.com
Dansk Kroer & Hoteller		www.dansk-kroferie.dk
Days Inn	800-329-7466	www.daysinn.com
De Vere Hotels		www.devereonline.co.uk
Dedeman Hotels		www.dedemanhotels.com
Delta Hotels	888-778-5050	www.deltahotels.com
Design Hotels	800-337-4685	www.designhotels.com
Destination Hotels & Resorts	800-434-7347	www.destinationhotels.com
Distinguished Hotels	877-545-3478	www.distinguishedhotels.com
Domina Hotels		www.dominahotels.com
Doral Conference Centers & Resorts	866-463-6725	www.doral.com
Dorchester Group	800 650 1842	www.thedorchester.com
Dorint Hotels		www.dorint.de
Doubletree Hotels	800-222-8733	www.doubletree.com
Drury Hotels	800-378-7946	www.druryhotels.com
Dusit Hotels		www.dusit.com
Econolodge	877-424-6423	www.econolodge.com
Element	877-353-6368	www.elementhotels.com
Embassy Suites	800-362-2779	www.embassysuites.com
Epoque Hotels	866-376-7831	www.epoquehotels.com
eSuites	813-882-0410	www.esuiteshotels.com
Etap Hotel		www.etaphotel.com
Evergreen Int'l Hotels		www.evergreen-hotels.com
Exclusive Hotels		www.exclusive-hotels.com
Execustay	888-340-2565	www.execustay.com
Executive Hotels & Resorts	888-388-3932	www.executivehotels.net
Extended Stay America	800-804-3724	www.extendedstayhotels.com
Extra Holidays	800-347-8182	www.extraholidays.com
Fairfield Inn	800-228-2800	www.fairfieldinn.com
Fairmont Hotels	866-326-6875	www.fairmont.com
Fiesta Americana	800-343-7821	www.fiestamericana.com
First Hotels		www.firsthotels.com
Flag Hotels	877-424-6423	www.choicehotels.com.au
Fontainebleau Resort	305-538-2000	www.fontainebleau.com
Formule1		www.hotelformule1.com
Four Seasons	800-819-5053	www.fourseasons.com

Gaylord Hotels	866-972-6779	www.gaylordhotels.com
GenaRes	(GDS only)	g-resdirect.com
Global Conextions	(GDS only)	www.globalconextions.com
Global Hotel Alliance		www.globalhotelalliance.com
Golden Leaf Hotels		www.golden-leaf-hotel.com
Golden Tulip Hotels	800-448-8355	www.goldentulip.com
Gouverneur Hotels	888-910-1111	www.gouverneur.com
Grand Heritage	888-934-7263	www.grandheritage.com
Grand Hospitality	800-965-3000	www.grandhospitality.com
Grand Traditions	312-214-3566	www.grandtraditionhotels.com
Graves Hotels	866-523-1100	www.graveshotelsresorts.com
Great Hotels of the World	888-222-8859	www.ghotw.com
Great Southern Hotels		www.gsh.ie
Grecotel		www.grecotel.gr
Grupo Posadas		www.posadas.com
GuestHouse International	800-214-8378	www.guesthouseintl.com
Hampton Inn	800-426-7866	www.hamptoninn.com
Hard Rock Hotels	800-473-7625	www.hardrockhotels.com
Harrahs Hotels & Resorts	800-427-7247	www.harrahs.com
Hawthorn Suites	800-527-1133	www.hawthorn.com
Hilton Garden Inn	877-782-9444	www.hiltongardeninn.com
Hilton Hotels	800-445-8667	www.hilton.com
Hilton International	800-445-8667	www.hilton.com
Historic Hotels of America	800-678-8946	www.historichotels.org
Historic Hotels of Europe		www.historichotelsofeurope.com
Holiday Inn Worldwide	888-465-4329	www.holiday-inn.com
Homestead Studio Suites	800-804-3724	www.homesteadhotels.com
Homewood Suites	800-225-5466	www.homewood-suites.com
HongKong & Shanghai Htl		www.hshgroup.com
Hotel du Vin		www.hotelduvin.com
Hotel Equatorial Int'l		www.equatorial.com
Hotel Indigo	877-846-3446	www.hotelindigo.com
Hotelbook	800-446-8357	www.hotelbook.com
Hoteles Catalonia		www.hoteles-catalonia.es
Hotusa Hotels		www.hotusahotels.com
Howard Johnson	800-446-4656	www.hojo.com
Husa Hoteles		www.husa.es
Hyatt Hotels & Resorts	888-591-1234	www.hyatt.com
Hyatt Place	888-591-1234	www.hyattplace.com
Hyatt Vacation Club	800-926-4447	www.hyatt.com/hvc
Iberostar Hotels		www.iberostar.com
Ibis Hotels	800-221-4542	www.ibishotel.com
InnLink Hotels	800-525-4658	www.innlink.com
InnPoints Worlwide	800-401-2262	www.innpointsworldwide.com
Intercontinental Hotels	800-424-6835	www.intercontinental.com
Interstate Hotels & Resorts	703-387-3100	www.ihrco.com
InTown Suites	800-553-9338	www.intownsuites.com
Island Outpost	800-688-7678	www.islandoutpost.com
ITS/Magellan Services	800-521-0643	www.its-cars-hotels.com
Jameson Inns/Signature Inns	800-822-5252	www.jamesoninns.com
Joie de Vivre Hospitality	800-738-7477	www.jdvhospitality.com
Jolly Hotels	800-221-2626	www.jollyhotels.com
Jumeirah International		www.jumeirah.com
Jurys Doyle Hotel Group	617-532-2815	www.jurysdoyle.com
K Hotels	786-253-4906	www.k-hotels.com

145

Supplier
Contacts

The Travel Agent's Complete Desk Reference

Kempinski Hotels	800-426-3135	www.kempinski.com
Key West Inn	800-833-0555	www.keywestinn.net
Keytel		www.keytel.co.uk
Kimpton Hotel Group	800-546-7866	www.kimptonhotels.com
Knights Inn	800-843-5644	www.knightsinn.com
Kor Hotel Group	800 439 3719	www.korhotelgroup.com
KSL Resorts	800-950-0086	www.kslresorts.com
La Quinta Inns	800-753-3757	www.lq.com
Langham Hotels		www.langhamhotels.com
Le Meridien	800-543-4300	www.lemeridien.com
Leading Hotels of the World	800-745-8883	www.lhw.com
Leisure Resource	800-729-9051	www.leisureresource.com
LeisureLink, Inc.	626-696-4500	www.leisurelink.com
Lexington Collection	877-539-7171	www.lexingtoncollection.com
Lindner Hotels		www.lindner.de
Loews Hotels	866-563-9792	www.loewshotels.com
Louvre Hotels		www.louvrehotels.com
LTI International Hotels		www.lti.de
Luxe Worldwide Hotels	866-589-3411	www.luxehotels.com
Luxury Collection	800-325-3589	www.luxurycollection.com
Luxury Resorts	877-597-9696	www.luxuryresorts.com
Macdonald Hotel Group	888-892-0038	www.macdonaldhotels.co.uk
Magnolia Hotels	888-915-1110	www.magnoliahotels.com
MainStay Suites	877-424-6423	www.mainstaysuites.com
Malmaison (UK)		www.malmaison.com
Mandarin Oriental	800-526-6567	www.mandarin-oriental.com
Marco Polo Hotels		www.marcopolohotels.com
Maritim Hotels	800-843-3311	www.maritim.de
Marriott Conf. Centers	800-228-9290	www.marriott.com/conference-centers
Marriott Hotels	888-236-2427	www.marriott.com
Marriott Vacation Club		www.vacationclub.com
Maybourne Hotel Group	866-599-6991	www.maybourne.com
Melrose Hotel Company	800-635-7673	www.melrosehotel.com
Menzies Hotels (UK)		www.menzies-hotels.co.uk
Mercure Hotels	800-221-4542	www.mercure.com
Meritus Hotels & Resorts	866 598 8718	www.meritus-hotels.com
MGM Mirage	877-880-0880	www.mgmmirage.com
Microtel Inns & Suites	888-222-2142	www.microtelinn.com
Millennium & Copthorne	866 866 8086	www.millenniumhotels.com
Minotel	800-365-3346	www.minotel.com
Minto Suite Hotel	800-267-3377	www.mintosuitehotel.com
Monte-Carlo SBM		www.montecarloresort.com
Morgan's Hotel Group	800-697-1791	www.morganshotelgroup.com
Motel 6	800-466-8356	www.motel6.com
Mövenpick Hotels	800-344-6835	www.moevenpick-hotels.com
Myfidelio	(GDS only)	www.myfidelio.net
New Hotel (France)		www.new-hotel.com
New Otani Hotels	800-421-8795	www.newotani.co.jp
NH Hoteles	888-726-0528	www.nh-hotels.com
Nikko Hotels International	800-645-5687	www.nikkohotels.com
Noble House Hotels	866-662-5348	www.noblehousehotels.com
Nordic Hotels Group		www.nhg.dk
Novotel	800-668-6835	www.novotel.com
Oberoi Hotels	800-562-3764	www.oberoihotels.com
Occidental Hotels	800-858-2258	www.occidentalhotels.com

Okura Hotels & Resorts	800-526-2281	www.okura.com
Omni Hotels	800-444-6664	www.omnihotels.com
Orbis Hotels (Poland)		www.orbis.pl
Orient Express Hotels	800-237-1236	www.orient-express.com
Othon Hotels		www.hoteis-othon.com.br
Outrigger Hotels & Resorts	800-688-7444	www.outrigger.com
Pacifica Hotels	800-720-0223	www.pacificahotels.com
Pan Pacific Hotels		www.panpacific.com
Park Inn	888-201-1801	www.parkinn.com
Park Plaza Hotels & Resorts	888-201-1803	www.parkplaza.com
Peabody Hotel Group	901-762-5400	www.peabodyhotelgroup.com
Peninsula Hotels	866-382-8388	www.peninsula.com
Per Aquuam Resorts		www.peraquum.com
Pestana Hotels		www.pestana.com
Preferred Hotels	800-323-7500	www.preferredhotels.com
Prima Hotels & Resorts	800-447-7462	www.inisrael.com/prima
Prince Resorts of Hawaii	888-977-4623	www.princeresortshawaii.com
Private Selection		www.alpineclassics.ch
Protea Hotels		www.proteahotels.com
Pueblo Bonito Hotels	800-990-8250	www.pueblobonito.com
Quality Inns & Suites	877-424-6423	www.qualityinn.com
Radisson Edwardian (UK)	888-201-1719	www.radissonedwardian.com
Radisson Hotels & Resorts	888-201-1718	www.radisson.com
Raffles International	800-768-9009	www.raffles.com
Ramada Inn	800-272-6232	www.ramada.com
Ramada International	800-272-6232	www.ramadainternational.com
Ramada Jarvis		www.ramadajarvis.co.uk
Red Lion Hotels	800-733-5466	www.redlion.com
Red Roof Inns	800-733-5466	www.redroof.com
Regal Hotels International	800-457-4000	www.regal-hotels.com
Regent Hotels & Resorts	800-545-4000	www.regenthotels.com
Registry Resort	888-422-6177	www.registryresort.com
Relais & Chateaux	800-735-2478	www.relaischateaux.com
Renaissance Hotels	800-468-3571	www.renaissancehotels.com
Reservhotel	800-521-5200	www.reservhotel.com
Residence Inn	800-331-3131	www.residenceinn.com
Resort Bookings	888-724-6060	www.resortbook.com
ResortQuest Hawaii	877-997-6667	www.resortquesthawaii.com
ResortQuest International	800-468-3529	www.resortquest.com
Reval Hotels		www.revalhotels.com
RezRez	888-611-6911	www.rezrez.com
Rihga Royal Hotels		www.rihga.com
RingHotels		www.ringhotels.de
Ritz Carlton Club	877-201-4290	www.ritzcarltonclub.com
Ritz-Carlton Hotels	800-241-3333	www.ritzcarlton.com
RIU Hotels	888-666-8816	www.riu.com
Rocco Forte Collection	888-667-9477	www.roccofortecollection.com
RockResorts	800-367-7625	www.rockresorts.com
Rodeway Inn	877-424-6423	www.rodewayinn.com
Romantik Hotels	800-650-8018	www.romantikhotels.com
Rosewood Hotels & Resorts	888-767-3966	www.rosewoodhotels.com
Rotana Hotels		www.rotana.com
Rydges Hotel Group		www.rydges.com
Sandals Resorts	800-726-3257	www.sandals.com
Sandman Hotels	800-726-3626	www.sandmanhotels.com

Supplier
Contacts

Sarova Hotels	800-524-7979	www.sarovahotels.com
Scandic Hotels	800-448-8355	www.scandichotels.com
Sceptre Hospitality	800-252-0522	www.esceptre.com
Select Marketing Hotels		www.selectmarketinghotels.com
Sercotel Hotels		www.sercotel.es
Serena Hotels		www.serenahotels.com
Shangri-La Hotels & Resorts	866-565-5050	www.shangri-la.com
Sheraton Hotels	800-325-3535	www.sheraton.com
Shilo Inns	800-222-2244	www.shiloinns.com
Shoney's Inn	800-552-4667	www.shoneysinn.com
Sierra Suites	888-695-7608	www.sierrasuites.com
Signature Inns	800-526-3766	www.signatureinn.com
Sino Hotels		www.sino-hotels.com
Sleep Inns	877-424-6423	www.sleepinn.com
Small Luxury Hotels	800-525-4800	www.slh.com
Sofitel	800-221-4542	www.sofitel.com
Sol/Melia Group	800-336-3542	www.solmelia.com
Sonesta Hotels	800-766-3782	www.sonesta.com
Sorat Hotels		www.sorat-hotels.com
Southern Sun		www.southernsun.com
Special Properties	800-424-6835	www.intercontinental.com
SpringHill Suites	800-831-1000	www.springhillsuites.com
St. Regis Hotels & Resorts	888-201-4482	www.stregis.com
Stamford Hotels		www.stamford.com.au
StarHotels		www.starhotels.it
Starwood	800-325-3535	www.starwood.com
Staybridge Suites	877-238-8889	www.staybridge.com
Steigenberger Hotels		www.steigenberger.com
Sterling Hotels & Resorts	800-637-7200	www.sterlinghotels.com
Studio 6	888-897-0202	www.staystudio6.com
Suburban Lodge	877-424-6423	www.suburbanlodge.com
Suitehotel	800-221-4542	www.suite-hotel.com
Summerfield Suites	866-974-9288	www.summerfieldsuites.com
Summit Int'l Htls & Rsrts	800-457-4000	www.summithotels.com
Sun International		www.suninternational.com
Super 8	800-800-8000	www.super8.com
Supranational Hotels	800-843-3311	www.snrhotels.com
Sutton Place Hotels	866-378-8866	www.suttonplace.com
Swallow Hotels		www.swallow-hotels.com
Swiss-Belhotel		www.swiss-belhotel.com
Swissotel	800-637-9477	www.swissotel.com
Synxis	303-595-2500	www.synxis.com
Tablet Hotels		www.tablethotels.com
Taj Hotels	866-969-1825	www.tajhotels.com
Thistle Hotels	800-847-4358	www.thistlehotels.com
Tokyu Hotels (Japan)	800-428-6598	www.tokyuhotels.co.jp
Top City & Country		www.topccl-hotels.de
Top International Hotels	800-448-8355	www.topinternational.com
TownePlace Suites	800-257-3000	www.towneplacesuites.com
Travelodge	800-578-7878	www.travelodge.com
Travelodge Australia		www.travelodge.com.au
Travelodge UK		www.travelodge.co.uk
Treff Hotels (Germany)		www.ramada.de
Trident Hotels (India)	866-706-5888	www.tridenthotels.com
Unirez	888-431-0700	

Utell Hotels	800-448-8355	www.utell.com
Vagabond Inns	800-522-1555	www.vagabondinn.com
Value Place	800-825-8375	www.myvalueplace.com
Vantage Hospitality	888-582-2378	www.vantagehospitality.com
Village Hotels (UK)		www.villagehotelsonline.co.uk
von Essen Hotels (UK)		www.vonessenhotels.co.uk
W Hotels	888-625-5144	www.whotels.com
Warwick Int'l Hotels	800-203-3232	www.warwickhotels.com
WestCoast Hotel Partners	800-325-4000	www.westcoasthotelpartners.com
Westin Hotels and Resorts	800-937-8461	www.westin.com
Westmark Hotels	800-544-0970	www.westmarkhotels.com
Whitbread Hotels (UK)		www.whitbread.co.uk
Wingate Inns	800-228-1000	www.wingateinns.com
Woodfin Suite Hotels	800-966-3346	www.woodfinsuitehotels.com
Worldhotels	800-223-5652	www.worldhotels.com
Worldres		www.worldres.com
Wyndham Hotels	877-999-3223	www.wyndham.com

*Supplier
Contacts*

Additional Hotel Contacts

Rental Cars

Ace	800-323-3221	www.acerentacar.com
Advantage	800-777-5500	www.arac.com
Alamo	800-424-3687	www.ta.alamo.com
Americar		www.americar.com
Auto Europe	800-223-5555	www.autoeurope.com
Auto Venture	800-426-7502	www.autoventure.com
Avis	800-331-2212	www.avis.com
Budget	800-527-0707	www.unlimitedbudget.com
Budget of Canada	800-435-7100	www.budget.ca
Carey International	800-336-4646	www.ecarey.com
Continental	800-327-3791	www.continentalcar.com
Cruise America RVs	800-327-7799	www.cruiseamerica.com
Dan Dooley Car Hire	800-331 9301	www.dan-dooley.ie
Dollar	800-800-1000	www.dollar.com
E-Z Rent A Car	800-277-5171	www.e-zrentacar.com
Enterprise	800-325-8007	www.enterprise.com
Europcar	877-940-6900	www.europcaramericas.com
Europe By Car	800-223-1516	www.europebycar.com
Fox Rent-a-Car	800-225-4369	www.foxrentacar.com
Hertz	800-654-8881	www.hertz.com
Holiday Res Systems	800-729-5378	www.holidaycar.com
Int'l Travel Services	800-521-0643	www.its-cars-hotels.com
Kemwel	800-678-0678	www.kemwel.com
L and M	800-666-0807	www.lmcarrental.com
Midway Rent A Car	800-824-5260	www.midwaycarrental.com
National Car Rental	800-227-7368	www.nationalcar.com
New Frontier (Canada)	800-567-2837	www.newfrontiercar.com
Payless	800-541-1566	www.paylesscarrental.com
Preferred	702-894-9936	www.preferredrentacar.com
Renault Eurodrive	800-221-1052	www.renaultusa.com
Rent-A-Wreck	800-421-7253	www.rentawreck.com
RentRite	800-318-8974	www.allriterentacar.com
Sixt		www.sixtusa.com
Specialty Vans	866-825-7005	www.rentvans.com
Thrifty	800-822-8257	www.thrifty.com
U Save Auto Rental	800-272-8728	www.usave.net

Additional Rental Car Contacts

206 Tours	800-2068687	www.206tours.com
A Touch of Class Tours	800-203-0438	www.atoctours.com
A&A Holidays	800-611-7783	www.aaholidays.com
AAT King's Australian Tours	866-240-1659	www.aatkings.com
Abel Tasman Tours	800-388-1828	www.attours.com
Abercrombie & Kent	800-323-7308	www.abercrombiekent.com
Aberdeen Tours	800-282-8321	www.aberdeentours.com
Above & Beyond Tours	800-397-2681	www.abovebeyondtours.com
Above the Clouds Trekking	800-233-4499	www.aboveclouds.com
Abrams Travel	800-338-7075	www.abramstravel.com
Abreu Tours	800-223-1580	www.abreu-tours.com
Absolute Asia	800-736-8187	www.absoluteasia.com
Academic Tours	800-875-9171	www.academictours.com
Accessible Journeys	800-846-4537	www.disabilitytravel.com
ACIS	800-888-2247	www.acis.com
Action Whitewater Adven.	800-453-1482	www.riverguide.com
Adriatic Tours	800-262-1718	www.adriatictours.com
Adrift Adventures	800-874-4483	www.adrift.net
Adventure Alaska	800-365-7057	www.adventurealaskatours.com
Adventure Assocs.	800-527-2500	www.adventure-associates.com
Adventure Center	800-228-8747	www.adventurecenter.com
Adventures on Skis	800-628-9655	www.advonskis.com
Adventures Unlimited	800-239-6864	www.adventuresunlimited.com
Aegean Med Tours	888-968-0355	www.aegeanmedtours.com
AER World Tours	800-492-0254	www.aertours.com
AeroMexico Vacations	800-245-8585	www.aeromexicovacations.com
AESU Travel	800-695-2378	www.aesu.com
Afloat in France	800-524-2420	www.afloatinfrance.com
Africa Experts	800-245-0920	www.africaexperts.com
African Safari	800-414-3090	www.africansafarico.com
African Travel	800-421-8907	www.africantravelinc.com
AfricaTours	800-235-3692	www.africasafaris.com
AIMS Travel Services	800-935-0935	www.aimstravel.com
Air Canada Vacations	877-752-9910	www.aircanadavacations.com
Air France Holidays	800-237-2623	www.airfranceholidays.com
Air Jamaica Vacations	800-568-3247	www.airjamaicavacations.com
Alaska Airlines Vacations	800-468-2248	www.alaskaair.com
Alaska Discovery	800-586-1911	www.akdiscovery.com
Alaska Heritage Tours	877-258-6877	www.alaskaheritagetours.com
Alaska Highway Cruises	800-323-5757	www.alaskarv.com
Alaska Reel Adventures	800-877-2661	www.alaskareel.com
Alaska Wildland	800-334-8730	www.alaskawildland.com
Albatross Travel	800-553-1113	www.albatross-tours.us
Alken Tours	800-221-6686	www.alkentours.com
All About Tours	800-274-8687	www.allabouthawaii.com
Allied Tour & Travel	800-672-1009	www.alliedtt.com
Alpine Adventures	888-478-4004	www.swisshiking.com
Alta Tours	800-338-4191	www.altatours.com
Altura Tours	800-242-4122	www.alturatours.com
Alumni Holidays	800-323-7373	www.ahitravel.com
Amazon Tours & Cruises	800-892-1035	www.amazontours.net
Amazonia Expeditions	800-262-9669	www.perujungle.com
Ambassador Tours	800-989-9000	www.ambassadortours.com

American Airlines Vacations	800-321-2121	www.aavacations.com
American Overland Exp.	800-598-1325	www.aoeadventures.com
American Travel Abroad	800-228-0877	www.amta.com
AMI Travel	800-821-8947	www.amitravel.com
AMNH Expeditions	800-462-8687	www.amnhexpeditions.org
Amtrak Vacations	800-268-7252	www.amtrakvacations.com
Andean Treks	800-683-8148	www.andeantreks.com
Another Land	888-334-7559	www.anotherland.com
Antipodes Tours	800-354-7471	www.antipodestours.com
ANZ Tours	888-909-1940	www.anztours.com
Apollo Tours	800-228-4367	www.apollotours.com
Applause Theatre Service	800-451-9930	www.applause-tickets.com
Apple Vacations	800-727-3400	www.applevacations.com
Aqua Dreams	888-322-3483	www.aquadreams.com
Aqua Trek	800-541-4334	www.aquatrek.com
Arctic Odysseys	800-574-3021	www.arcticodysseys.com
ARI Tours	800-227-2887	www.ari-tours.com
Ariel Tours	800-262-1818	www.arieltours.com
Arizona River Runners	800-477-7238	www.raftarizona.com
Asia Transpacific Journeys	800-642-2742	www.asiatranspacific.com
Asia Voyages	800-914-9133	www.asiavoyages.com
Asian Pacific Adventures	800-825-1680	www.asianpacificadventures.com
Aspen Ski Tours	800-525-2052	www.ski.com
Astro Tours	800-543-7717	www.astrotours-greecetravel.com
ATC Anadolu Travel	888-262-3658	www.atc-anadolu.com
ATI Tours	800-417-1430	www.atitours.com
Atlantic Tours	800-565-7173	www.atlantictours.com
AtlanticGolf	800-542-6224	www.atlanticgolf.com
ATS Tours	800-423-2880	www.atstours.com
Austin Lehman Adventures	800-575-1540	www.austinlehman.com
Australia New Zealand Golf	800-622-6606	www.golfaustralianewzealand.com
Australian Pacific Touring	800-290-8687	www.aptouring.com
Austravel		www.aus-vacations.com
Auto Venture	800-426-7502	www.autoventure.com
Avalon Waterways	877-380-1544	www.avalonwaterways.com
Avanti Destinations	800-422-5053	www.avantidestinations.com
Aventours	800-888-6639	www.mexico-experts.com
Aviatours	888-574-2566	www.aviatours.net
Avila Tours	800-661-2221	www.avilatours.ca
Ayelet Tours	800-237-1517	www.ayelet.com
Backroads	800-462-2848	www.backroads.com
Baja Expeditions	800-843-6967	www.bajaex.com
Belize It Tours	800-627-8227	www.belizeittours.com
Best Catholic Pilgrimages	800-908-2378	www.bestcatholic.com
Bhutan Travel	800-950-9908	www.bhutantravel.com
Bicycle Adventures	800-443-6060	www.bicycleadventures.com
Big Bend River Tours	800-545-4240	www.bigbendrivertours.com
Big Five Tours	800-244-3483	www.bigfive.com
Bill Russell's Mtn Tours	800-669-4453	www.russelltours.com
Blue Danube Holidays	800-268-4155	www.bluedanubeholidays.com
Blue Marble Travel	215-923-3788	www.bluemarble.org
Blue Planet Journeys	888-334-3782	www.blueplanetjourneys.com
Blue Sky Tours	800-678-2787	www.blueskytours.com
Blue Voyage Turkish Tours		www.bluevoyage.com
Born Free Safaris	800-472-3274	www.bornfreesafaris.com
Borton Overseas	800-843-0602	www.bortonoverseas.com

Bound To Travel	714-773-0222	www.boundtotravel.com
Branson Country Tours	800-841-2376	www.bransoncountrytours.com
Branson Vacation Tours	800-417-6122	www.bvtamerica.com
BransonUSA	800-871-9494	www.bransonusa.com
Bravo Tours	800-272-8674	www.bravotours.com
Brazil Nuts Tours	800-553-9959	www.brazilnuts.com
Brazilian Wave Tours	800-682-3315	www.brazilianwavetours.com
Brekke Scandinavia	800-437-5302	www.brekketours.com
Brendan Worldwide Vac.	800-421-8446	www.brendanvacations.com
Brennan Vacations	800-237-7249	www.brennanvacations.com
Brewster Tours	800-661-1152	www.brewster.ca
Brian Moore Int'l	800-982-2299	www.bmit.com
British Airways Holidays	800-247-9297	www.britishairways.com
Buddy Bombard's Europe	800-862-8537	www.buddybombard.com
Butterfield & Robinson	800-678-1147	www.butterfield.com
Calif. Parlor Car Tours	800-227-4250	www.calpartours.com
Calif. Tour Consultants	800-227-4276	www.catour.com
California Native	800-926-1140	www.calnative.com
CampAlaska	800-376-9438	www.campalaska.com
Campioni Italiani	888-483-6386	www.campioni-italiani.com
Canyoneers	800-525-0924	www.canyoneers.com
Caradonna Caribbean	800-328-2288	www.caradonna.com
Caravan Tours	800-227-2826	www.caravantours.com
Caravan-Serai	800-451-8097	www.caravan-serai.com
Caribbean Selections	800-282-3941	www.caribbeanselections.com
Cartan Tours	800-818-1998	www.cartan.com
CBT Tours	800-736-2453	www.cbttours.com
Celebrity Alaska Tours	888-307-8401	www.celebritycruises.com
Celtic Dream Tours	813-317-6039	www.celticdreamtours.com
Celtic Tours	800-833-4373	www.celtictours.com
CenPac Dive Travel	800-846-3483	www.cenpacdive.com
Central Holidays	800-935-5000	www.centralholidays.com
Champion Holidays	800-868-7658	www.china-discovery.com
CHAT Tours	800-268-1180	www.travelinechatours.com
China Professional Tours	800-252-4462	www.chinaprofessional.com
China Silk Tours	800-945-7960	www.chinasilktour.com
China Travel Service	800-899-8618	www.chinatravelservice.com
Chinasmith	800-872-4462	www.chinasmith.com
Christian Tours	800-476-3900	www.burkechristiantours.com
Ciao Travel	800-942-2426	www.ciaotravel.com
Ciclismo Classico	800-866-7314	www.ciclismoclassico.com
CIE Tours	800-243-8687	www.cietours.com
CIT Tours	800-387-0711	www.cittours.ca
City Escape Holidays	800-222-0022	www.cityescapeholidays.com
Classic Custom Vacations	800-221-3949	www.classiccustomvacations.com
Classic Golf & Leisure	800-283-1619	www.classic-golf.com
Classic Journeys	800-200-3887	www.classicjourneys.com
Classical Movements	800-882-0025	www.classicalmovements.com
Cloud Tours	800-223-7880	www.cloudtours.com
Club Europa	800-331-1882	www.clubeuropatravel.com
Club Toscana	866-563-4248	www.clubtoscana.com
Cobblestone Small Gp Trs	800-227-7889	www.cobblestonetours.com
Collette Vacations	800-832-4656	www.collettevacations.com
Comtours	800-248-1331	www.comtours.com
Consolidated Tours	800-554-4556	www.ctoinc.com
Contiki Holidays	800-266-8454	www.contiki.com

Continental Journeys	800-601-4343	www.continentaljourneys.com
Continental Vacations	800-634-5555	www.coolvacations.com
Corporate Sport	800-700-1357	www.corpsport.com
Cortez Travel	800-854-1029	www.cortez-usa.com
Cosmopolitan Adv. Tours	800-569-6228	www.cosmopolitanadventure tours.com
Cosmos	800-221-0090	www.cosmosvacations.com
Costa Rica Connection	800-345-7422	www.crconnect.com
Costa Rica Experts	800-827-9046	www.costaricaexperts.com
Country Squire Tours	800-759-6820	www.newenglandtours.com
Country Walkers	800-464-9255	www.countrywalkers.com
Cox & Kings	800-999-1758	www.coxandkingsusa.com
Creative Leisure Int'l	800-413-1000	www.creativeleisure.com
Creative Safaris	800-768-9020	www.creativesafaris.com
Creative Travel Group	800-345-5195	www.creativetravelgroup.com
Cross Country Int'l	800-828-8768	www.walkingvacations.com
Cross-Culture	800-491-1148	www.ccjourneys.com
Crown Peters Travel	800-321-1199	www.crownpeters.com
Crystal Tours	888-823-0055	www.crystal-tours.com
Cultural Folk Tours	800-935-8875	www.boraozkok.com
Cultural Vacations	800-953-8111	www.culturalvacations.com
Culture Quest Tours	800-678-6877	www.cqtours.com
Cyclevents	808-443-0152	www.cyclevents.com
Dailey-Thorp Travel	800-998-4677	www.daileythorp.com
Daman-Nelson Travel	800-343-2626	www.skirun.com
Dan Dipert Tours	800-433-5335	www.dandipert.com
David Anderson Safaris	800-927-4647	www.davidanderson.com
Delight Travel	800-328-6638	www.delighttravel.com
Delta Vacations	800-221-6666	www.deltavacations.com
Desert Adventures	888-440-5337	www.red-jeep.com
Design Trav. & Tours	800-543-7164	www.designtraveltours.com
DER	800-782-2424	www.der.com
Destinations Ireland	800-832-1848	www.destinations-ireland.com
DFW Tours	800-527-2589	www.dfwtours.com
DIA World Tours	800-342-8258	www.diatravel.com
Discovery Treks	888-256-8731	www.discoverytreks.com
Distinctive Travel & Tours	888-843-7914	www.distinctiveeurotours.com
Distrav	877-334-7872	www.distrav.com
Dive Discovery	800-886-7321	www.divediscovery.com
Donna Franca Tours	800-225-6290	www.donnafranca.com
Dream Voyages	800-241-4070	www.dreamvoyages.com
Driving Tours of France	800-717-1703	www.dtof.com
EastQuest	800-638-3449	www.east-quest.com
Easy Rider Bicycle Tours	800-488-8332	www.easyridertours.com
EC Tours	800-388-0877	www.ectours.com
Echo River Trips	800-652-3246	www.echotrips.com
Ecosummer Expeditions	800-465-8884	www.ecosummer.com
Ecotours Expeditions	800-688-1822	www.naturetours.com
Educational Tours	800-275-4109	www.ed-tours.com
Educational Travel Svcs.	800-929-4387	www.ets.travelwithus.com
EEI Travel	800-927-3876	www.eeitravel.com
EEI Travel	800-927-3876	www.europeexpress.com
EF Educational Tours	800-637-8222	www.eftours.com
EF Explore America	800-503-2323	www.efamerica.com
Egypt Tours	800-523-4978	www.egypttours.com
Elegant Adventures	800-451-4398	www.elegantadventures.com

Encore Tours	877-460-3801	www.encoretours.com
English Lakeland Ramblers	800-724-8801	www.ramblers.com
Equitours	800-545-0019	www.equitours.com
Escapade Vacations	800-356-2405	www.escapadevacations.com
Escape Adventures	800-596-2953	www.escapeadventures.com
Escape Holidays	800-428-7390	www.escapeholidays.com
Esoteric Sports	800-321-8008	www.esotericsports.com
Especially 4-U Tours	800-331-4968	www.especially4utours.com
Esperienze Italiane	800-480-2426	www.lidiasitaly.com
Esplanade Tours	800-426-5492	www.esplanadetours.com
ET Educational Tours	800-962-0060	www.educationaltours.com
ETM Travel Group	800-992-7700	www.etmtravelgroup.com
Euro Bike & Walking Tours	800-321-6060	www.eurobike.com
Euro Lloyd Tours	800-334-2724	www.eurolloyd.com
Euro River Cruises	800-543-4504	www.eurorivercruises.com
Eurobound	888-672-7476	www.eurobound.com
EuroGroups	800-462-2577	www.eurogroups.com
Europe At Cost (EAC)	800-322-3876	www.europeatcost.com
Europe-Bound	888-733-3876	www.europe-bound.com
European Incoming Svcs.	800-443-1644	www.eistours.com
European Tours Ltd.	800-882-3983	www.europtours.com
European Travel Service	800-466-1713	www.eurotrvl.com
Europeds	877-388-6633	www.europeds.com
Eurovacations	877-387-6822	www.eurovacations.com
Exeter International	800-633-1008	www.exeterinternational.com
Exotic Journeys	800-554-6342	www.exoticjourneys.com
Extra Holidays	800-438-6493	www.extraholidays.com
Far Flung Adventures	800-359-4138	www.farflung.com
Far North Tours	800-478-7480	www.farnorthtours.com
Festival Tours	800-225-0117	www.festivaltours.com
Fishing Int'l	800-950-4242	www.fishinginternational.com
Five Star Touring	800-792-7827	www.fivestartouring.com
Five Stars of Scandinavia	800-722-4126	www.5stars-of-scandinavia.com
Florida Tour Connection	800-956-8687	www.floridatourconnection.com
Fly Tahiti	866-982-4484	www.flytahiti.com
Foreign Indep. Tours	800-248-3487	www.foreign-independent-tours.com
Forum Travel	800-252-4475	www.foruminternational.com
FOS Tours & Travel	800-367-3450	www.fostours.com
Four Seasons Vacations	800-328-4298	www.4-seasonsvacations.com
France Vacations	800-332-5332	www.francevacations.net
FreeGate Tourism	800-223-0304	www.freegatetours.com
French Experience	800-283-7262	www.frenchexperience.com
Friendly Planet Travel	800-555-5765	www.friendlyplanet.com
Friendship Tours	800-213-9155	www.friendshiptours.com
Frontier Travel & Tours	800-647-0800	www.frontiertraveltours.com
Funjet Vacations	800-558-3060	www.funjet.com
Future Vacations	800-456-2323	www.futurevacations.com
Gabriele's Travels Italy	888-287-8733	www.travelingtoitaly.com
Gadabout Tours	800-952-5068	www.gadabouttours.com
Galapagos Inc	800-327-9854	www.galapagoscruises.net
Galapagos Network	800-633-7972	www.ecoventura.com
GAP Adventures	800-708-7761	www.gapadventures.com
Gate 1	800-682-3333	www.gate1travel.com
Gem Travel	800-948-3548	www.gemtravel.com
General Tours	800-221-2216	www.generaltours.com
Geographic Expeditions	800-777-8183	www.geoex.com

Supplier
Contacts

Gerber Tours	800-645-9145	www.gerbertours.com
Getaway Bicycle Tours	800-499-2453	www.getawayadventures.com
Gil Travel	800-223-3855	www.giltravel.com
GL Tours	800-334-5832	www.gltours.com
Glavs Travel USA	800-336-5727	www.glavs.com
Global Spectrum	800-419-4446	www.asianpassages.com
Globus	800-221-0090	www.globusjourneys.com
Glory Tours	877-424-5679	www.glory-tours.com
GM Tours	800-836-6836	www.gmtours.com
Go Ahead Vacations	800-242-4686	www.goaheadvacations.com
Go Classy Tours	800-329-8145	www.goclassy.com
GoGo Worldwide	800-899-2558	www.gogowwv.com
Golden Sports Tours	800-966-8258	www.goldensports.com
Golf Destinations	800-774-6531	www.golfdestinations.com
Golf Int'l	800-833-1389	www.golfinternational.com
Golf & Wine Australia	619-405-4015	www.golfwineaustralia.com
GoPlay Sports Tours	877-795-0814	www.goplaytours.com
GoWay.com	800-387-8850	www.goway.com
Grand European Tours	800-552-5545	www.getours.com
Grand Prix Tours	800-400-1998	www.gptours.com
Grand Slam Tennis	800-289-3333	www.grandslamtennistours.com
Grandtravel	800-247-7651	www.grandtrvl.com
Gray Line	800-472-9546	www.grayline.com
Great Escape Tours	800-365-1833	www.greatescapetours.com
Great Spas of the World	800-772-8463	www.greatspas.com
Group Tour Company	800-424-8895	www.grouptourcompany.com
Gutsy Women Travel	866-464-8879	www.gutsywomentravel.com
GWV International	866-797-0038	www.gwvtravel.com
Hanns Ebensten Travel	866-294-8174	www.hetravel.com
Happy Holidays	800-884-2779	www.worldgrouptravel.com
Happy Vacations	800-877-4277	www.happy-vacations.com
Hawaii World	800-442-9244	www.hawaiiworld.com
Heavenly Int'l Tours	800-322-8622	www.heavenlytours.com
Hellenic Adventures	800-851-6349	www.hellenicadventures.com
Heritage Fest./Bowl Games	800-999-7676	www.heritagefestivals.com
Heritage Tours	800-378-4555	www.heritagetoursonline.com
Himalayan Int'l Tours	800-421-8975	www.himalayantours.com
HLO Tours	800-736-4456	www.hlotours.com
Holbrook Travel	800-451-7111	www.holbrooktravel.com
Holidaze Ski Tours	800-526-2827	www.holidaze.com
Holland America Tours	800-426-0327	www.hollandamerica.com
Homeric Tours	800-223-5570	www.homerictours.com
Hometours Int'l	866-367-4668	thor.he.net/~hometour
Hotard Vacations	800-535-2732	www.hotard.com
Icelandair Holidays	800-779-2899	www.icelandair.com
Il Viaggio	888-864-8362	www.ilviaggio.com
Image Tours	800-968-9161	www.imagetours.com
In Quest of the Classics	800-227-1393	www.iqotc.com
InnovAsian Travel	800-553-4665	www.innovasian.com
Insight Vacations	800-582-8380	www.insightvacations.com
Int'l Curtain Call	800-669-9070	www.iccoperatours.com
Int'l Expeditions	800-633-4734	www.ietravel.com
Int'l Kitchen	800-945-8606	www.theinternationalkitchen.com
Int'l Ventures	800-727-5475	www.internationalventures.com
Inter Island Tours	800-245-3434	www.interislandtours.com
InterGolf Vacations	800-468-0051	www.intergolfvacations.com

Intourist USA	800-556-5305	www.intourist-usa.com
Irish-American Int'l	800-633-0505	www.ireland411.com
Island Destinations	888-454-4422	www.islanddestinations.com
Island Dreams Travel	800-346-6116	www.islandream.com
Island Resort Tours	800-251-1755	www.islandresorttours.com
Islands Escapes	800-667-6601	www.islandsescapes.com
Islands in the Sun	888-828-6877	www.islandsinthesun.com
Isle Inn Tours	800-237-9376	www.isleinntours.com
Israel Tour Connection	800-247-7235	www.israeltour.com
Isram World	800-223-7460	www.isram.com
IST Cultural Tours	800-833-2111	www.ist-tours.com
ITC Golf Tours	800-257-4981	www.itcgolf-africatours.com
ITS Tours	800-533-8688	www.supersavertours.com
Ivory Photo Safaris	877-723-2748	www.ivorynet.com
JC Travel	800-227-3920	www.jc-travel.com
Jerry Quinlan's Celtic Golf	800-535-6148	www.jqcelticgolf.com
Jolivac	888-565-4822	www.jolivac.com
Journeys Int'l	800-255-8735	www.journeys-intl.com
Journeys Unlimited	800-486-8359	www.journeys-unlimited.com
Karell's African Dream	800-327-0373	www.karell.com
Kenai Fjord Tours	800-478-8068	www.kenaifjords.com
Ker & Downey	800-423-4236	www.kerdowney.com
Key Holidays	800-783-0783	www.keyholidays.com
Key Tours	800-576-1784	www.keytours.com
King Tut Tours	800-398-1888	www.kingtuttours.com
Knightly Tours	800-426-2123	www.knightlytours.com
Koala Tours	800-535-0316	www.koalaworld.com
Kompas Holidays	800-233-6422	www.kompas.net
Kutrubes Travel	800-878-8566	www.kutrubestravel.com
Ladatco Tours	800-327-6162	www.ladatco.com
Latour	800-825-0825	www.latour.com
Legend Tours	800-333-6114	www.legendtours.com
Leisure Resource Tours	800-729-9051	www.leisureresource.com
Lindblad Expeditions	800-397-3348	www.expeditions.com
Lismore Tours	800-547-6673	www.lismoretours.com
Lost World Adventures	800-999-0558	www.lostworldadventures.com
Lotus Int'l Tours	888-329-7848	www.lotustravel.com
Lotus Travel	800-956-8873	www.lotustours.net
Lynott Tours	800-221-2474	www.lynotttours.com
Madison Int'l Travel	800-424-2422	www.madisontravel.com
Maduro Dive Fanta-Seas	800-327-6709	www.maduro.com
Magellan Tours	856-786-6969	www.magellantours.com
Magnum Belize	800-447-2931	www.magnumbelize.com
Maiellano Travel	800-223-1616	www.maiellano.com
Marakesh Tourist	800-458-1722	www.marakeshtouristco.com
Maranatha Tours	800-545-5533	www.maranathatours.com
Mariah Wilderness Exp.	800-462-7424	www.mariahwe.com
Maupintour	800-255-4266	www.maupintour.com
Mayatour	800-690-2072	www.mayatour.com
Mayflower Tours	800-323-7604	www.mayflowertours.com
Meander Adventures	888-616-7272	www.meanderadventures.com
Mediterranean Dest.	800-247-3323	www.ibrcusa.com
Mena Tours & Travel	800-937-6362	www.menatours.net
Metro Tours	800-221-2810	www.metrotours.com
Mexico Adventures	800-206-8132	www.coppercanyon.com.mx
MGM Mirage Vacations	800-360-7111	www.mgmmiragevacations.com

Supplier
Contacts

Micato Safaris	800-642-2861	www.micato.com
Midwest Airlines Vacations	800-444-4479	www.midwestairlinesvacations.com
MILA Tours	800-367-7378	www.milatours.com
MIR Corporation	800-424-7289	www.mircorp.com
MISR Travel	800-223-4978	www.misrtravel.us
Mosaic Tours	800-862-2060	www.mosaictours.com
Mountain Equestrian Tvl	800-838-3918	www.metbelize.com
Mountain Travel-Sobek	888-831-7526	www.mtsobek.com
MTS Travel	800-418-2929	www.mtstravel.com
Mythic Travel	831-688-6550	www.mythic-travel.com
Myths & Mountains	800-670-6984	www.mythsandmountains.com
Nabila Tours	800-443-6453	www.nabilatours.com
Natural Habitat Adventures	800-543-8917	www.nathab.com
Nature Expeditions	800-869-0639	www.naturexp.com
NauticBlue	800-416-0224	www.nauticblue.com
New England Vac. Tours	800-742-7669	www.sover.net/~nevt
New York City Vacation	888-692-8701	www.nycvp.com
Newman's South Pacific	800-421-3326	www.newmansvacations.com
Nomadic Expeditions	800-998-6634	www.nomadicexpeditions.com
Nordic Saga Tours	800-848-6449	www.nordicsaga.com
NWA World Vacations	800-800-1504	www.nwaworldvacations.com
O.A.R.S.	800-346-6277	www.oars.com
Odysseys Unlimited	888-370-6765	www.odysseys-unlimited.com
Olympia Tours	800-367-6718	www.olympiatours.com
On The Scene	800-621-5327	www.onthescenechicago.com
OnSafari.com	800-700-3677	www.onsafari.com
Open Road Tours	800-766-7117	www.openroadtours.com
Orbis Polish Travel	800-876-7247	www.orbistravel.com
Orient Flexi-Pax	800-545-5540	www.orientflexipax.com
Outer Edge Expeditions	800-322-5235	www.outer-edge.com
Owenoak Int'l Golf	800-426-4498	www.owenoak.com
Ozark Country Vacations	800-463-4254	www.ozarkcountryvacations.com
Pacha Tours	800-722-4288	www.pachatours.com
Pacific Bestour	800-688-3288	www.bestour.com
Pacific Delight	800-221-7179	www.pacificdelighttours.com
Pacific Destination Ctr	800-227-5317	www.pacific-destinations.com
Pacific Holidays	800-355-8025	www.pacificholidaysinc.com
Pacific Protour	800-776-8882	www.pacificprotour.com
Pan American Travel	800-364-4359	www.panamtours.com
Panorama Holidays	800-475-9339	www.panoramaholidays.com
Parker Tours	800-833-9600	www.parkertours.com
Passage Tours Scandinavia	800-548-5960	www.passagetours.com
Passport Costa Rica	877-772-6782	www.passportcostarica.com
Passports	800-332-7277	www.passports.com
Patrician Journeys	800-344-1443	www.patricianjourneys.com
Perillo Tours	800-431-1515	www.perillotours.com
PerryGolf	800-344-5257	www.perrygolf.com
Peter Hughes Diving	800-932-6237	www.peterhughes.com
Peter's Way Tours	800-225-7662	www.petersway.com
Petrabax	800-634-1188	www.petrabax.com
Pharos Travel	800-999-5511	www.pharostravel.com
Pinto Basto Tours	800-526-8539	www.pousada.com
Pleasant Holidays	800-448-3333	www.pleasantagent.com
Poseidon Ventures	800-854-9334	www.poseidontours.com
Preferred Adventures	800-840-8687	www.preferredadventures.com
Premier Travel Services	800-545-1910	www.premiertours.com

Presley Tours	800-621-6100	www.presleytours.com
Pride World	866-774-3336	www.prideworldtravel.com
Princess Tours	800-426-0442	www.princess.com
Qantas Vacations	800-252-4162	www.qantasvacations.com
Quark Expeditions	800-356-5699	www.quarkexpeditions.com
Quasar Nautica	800-247-2925	www.quasarnauticausa.com
Rail Europe	800-438-7245	www.raileurope.com
Rail Source Europe	800-294-1650	www.railsourceeurope.com
Rail Source International	800-551-2085	www.rsiworld.com
Rail Travel Center	800-458-5394	www.railtravelcenter.com
Rama Tours	800-835-7262	www.ramatoursindia.com
Randonnee	800-242-1825	www.randonneetours.com
Rascals in Paradise	800-872-7225	www.rascalsinparadise.com
Rebel Tours	800-732-3588	www.rebeltours.com
Red Star Travel	800-215-4378	www.travel2russia.com
Reef & Rainforest	800-794-9767	www.reefrainforest.com
Reel Wilderness Adventures	800-726-8323	www.reelwild.com
Religious Tours	800-752-8090	www.religious-tours.com
Remote Odysseys Worldwide	800-451-6034	www.rowinternational.com
Rim Tours	800-626-7335	www.rimtours.com
Rim-Pac Int'l	800-701-8687	www.rim-pac.com
Ritz Tours	800-900-2446	www.ritztours.com
Roatan Charter	800-282-8932	www.roatan.com
Roberts Hawaii	800-831-5541	www.robertshawaii.com
Rocky Mountaineer Rail	800-665-7245	www.rockymountaineer.com
Rod & Reel Adventures	800-356-6982	www.rodreeladventures.com
Russian National Group	877-221-7120	www.russia-travel.com
Sacca Tours	800-326-5170	www.saccatours.com
Safari Brokers	877-723-2748	www.safaribrokers.com
Safari Ventures	888-341-7771	www.safariventures.com
Safariline	866-466-0301	www.safarilinetravel.com
Sanborn Tours	800-395-8482	www.sanborns.com
Sand Dollar Tours	800-397-2674	www.sanddollartours.com
Saranjan	800-858-9594	www.saranjan.com
Scantours	800-223-7226	www.scantours.com
Sceptre Ireland	800-221-0924	www.sceptretours.com
Scots-American Travel	800-247-7268	www.scotsamerican.com
Scuba Voyages	800-544-7631	www.scubavoyages.com
Sea Fiji Travel	800-854-3454	www.seafiji.com
Sea Kayak Adventures	800-616-1943	www.seakayakadventures.com
Sea Paradise Scuba	800-322-5662	www.seaparadise.com
Select Int'l	800-842-4842	www.select-intl.com
Select Travel Service	800-752-6787	www.selecttravel.com
SGH Golf	800-284-8884	www.sghgolf.com
Shenandoah Tours	800-572-3303	www.shenandoahtours.com
Sheri Griffith Exped.	800-332-2439	www.griffithexp.com
ShoreTrips	888-355-0220	www.shoretrips.com
Silk Road Tours	888-881-7455	www.silkroadtours.com
SITA World Travel	800-421-5643	www.sitatours.com
Ski Vacation Planners	800-822-6754	www.skivacationplanners.com
Ski.com	800-525-2052	www.ski.com
SkiEurope	800-333-5533	www.ski-europe.com
Skyline Travel	800-645-6198	www.skylinetravel.com
Slickrock Adventures	800-390-5715	www.slickrock.com
Smolka Tours	800-722-0057	www.smolkatours.com
Snow Lion Expeditions	800-525-8735	www.snowlion.com

Supplier Contacts

160

The Travel Agent's
Complete Desk
Reference

Sol International	800-765-5657	www.solintl.com
Solar Tours	800-388-7652	www.solartours.com
Somak Safaris	800-757-6625	www.somaksafaris.com
South American Fiesta	800-334-3782	www.southamericafiesta.com
South Fishing Travel	800-882-4665	www.southfishing.com
South Star Tours	800-654-4468	www.southstartours.com
Southwest Vacations	800-423-5683	www.swavacations.com
Southwind Adventures	800-377-9463	www.southwindadventures.com
Spa Finder	800-255-7727	www.spafinder.com
Spa Trek Travel	800-272-3480	www.spatrek.com
Space Adventures	888-857-7223	www.spaceadventures.com
SpaFariAdventures	800-488-8747	www.globalfitnessadventure.com
Spanish Heritage Tours	800-456-5050	www.shtours.com
SpaQuest	800-772-7837	www.spa-quest.com
Specialty Tours	800-342-4299	www.specialtytours.com
Sports Empire	800-255-5258	www.sports-empire.com
Sportstours	800-488-0463	www.sportstours.com
SRI Travel	888-451-9399	www.sritravel.com
ST Tours	800-780-8877	www.sttours.com
Star Destinations	800-284-4440	www.stardestinations.com
Starr Tours	800-314-8411	www.starrtours.com
Stockler Expeditions	800-591-2955	www.stocklerexpeditions.net
Sunny Land Tours	800-783-7839	www.sunnylandtours.com
Sunquest Vacations	800-268-8899	www.sunquest.ca
Sunrise Tours	800-881-8804	www.travelsunrise.com
Sunspots International	800-334-5623	www.sunspotsintl.com
Suntrek Tours	800-786-8735	www.suntrek.com
Suntrips	800-514-5194	www.suntrips.com
Superclubs	877-467-8737	www.superclubs.com
Swain Tours	800-227-9246	www.swaintours.com
Synagogue Travel		www.synagoguetravel.com
Tahiti Bound	888-672-7476	www.tahitibound.com
Tahiti Legends	800-200-1213	www.tahitilegends.com
Tahiti Vacations	800-553-3477	www.tahitivacations.net
TAL Tours	800-825-9399	www.taltours.com
Tara Tours	800-327-0080	www.taratours.com
Tatra Travel	800-321-2999	www.tatratravel.com
Tauck Bridges	800-788-7885	www.tauckbridges.com
Tauck World Discovery	800-468-2825	www.tauck.com
TCS Expeditions	800-727-7477	www.tcs-expeditions.com
TEI Tours & Travel	800-435-4334	www.teiglobal.com
Terry Flynn Tours	800-678-7848	www.terryflynntours.com
The Moorings	800-535-7289	www.moorings.com
Third Eye Travel	800-456-3393	www.thirdeyetravel.com
Thomason Safaris	800-235-0289	www.thomsonsafaris.com
Tierra Mar Travel	800-525-5524	www.tierramartravel.com
TNT Vacations	800-262-0123	www.tntvacations.com
Toto Tours	800-565-1241	www.tototours.com
Tour Designs	800-432-8687	www.tourdesignsinc.com
Tourco	800-537-5378	www.tourco.com
Tourcrafters	800-621-2259	www.tourcrafters.com
Tourlite Int'l	800-272-7600	www.tourlite.com
Tourmasters	800-729-1406	www.tourmasters.com
Tours in the Sun	800-987-8669	www.toursinthesuntravel.com
Tours Specialists	800-223-7552	www.toursspecialists.com
Tourtech International	800-882-2636	www.tourtech.net

Tova Gilead	800-242-8682	www.tovagilead.com
Tradesco Tours	800-448-4321	www.tradescotours.com
Trafalgar Tours	800-854-0103	www.trafalgartours.com
Travcoa	800-992-2003	www.travcoa.com
Travel Beyond	800-876-3131	www.travelbeyond.com
Travel Bound	800-808-9543	www.booktravelbound.com
Travel Charter	800-711-0080	www.travelcharter.com
Travel Connection	800-862-0862	www.tvlconn.com
Travel Impressions	800-284-0044	www.travelimpressions.com
Travel Plans Int'l	800-323-7600	www.travelplansintl.com
Traveline/CHAT	800-268-1180	www.travelinechatours.com
TravelMarvel	800-290-8687	www.aptouring.com
Trek America	800-873-5872	www.trekamerica.com
Trek Holidays	800-661-7265	www.trekholidays.com
Trip-N-Tour Pacific	800-348-0842	www.trip-n-tour.com
Tropical Travel Reps.	800-451-8017	www.tropicaltravel.com
Ulysses Tours	800-431-1424	www.ulyssestours.com
Undersea Expeditions	800-669-0310	www.underseax.com
Unique Journeys	800-421-1981	www.uniquejourney.com
Unique World Cruises	800-669-0757	www.uniqueworldcruises.com
United Travel Group	800-223-6486	www.unitedtouring.com
United Vacations	800-328-6877	www.unitedvacations.com
Unitours	800-777-7432	www.unitours.com
Universal Studios Vacations	800-331-3134	www.universalstudiosvacations.com
Universal Travel Systems	800-255-4338	www.uts-travel.com
Uniworld	800-733-7820	www.uniworld.com
US Airways Vacations	800-455-0123	www.usairwaysvacations.com
VacationLand	800-245-0050	www.vacation-land.com
Vacations by Adv. Tours	800-999-9046	www.atusa.com
Vacations for Less	800-200-2423	www.vacations4less.com
Valor Tours	800-842-4504	www.valortours.com
Value Holidays	800-558-6850	www.valhol.com
Van Gogh Tours	800-435-6192	www.vangoghtours.com
Vantage Adventures	800-826-8268	www.travelvantage.com
Villas of the World	888-728-4552	www.villasoftheworld.com
Virgin Vacations	888-937-8474	www.virgin-vacations.com
Visit Italy Tours	800-255-3537	www.visititalytours.com
Vytis Tours	800-778-9847	www.vytistours.com
Walking the World	970-498-0050	www.walkingtheworld.com
Walt Disney Travel	800-854-3104	www.disneytravelagents.com
Way To Go Costa Rica	800-835-1223	www.waytogocostarica.com
Wayfarers, The	800-249-4620	www.thewayfarers.com
Weissman Teen Tours	800-942-8005	www.weissmantours.com
Werner Tours	800-532-9800	www.wernercoach.com
Western River Exped.	800-453-7450	www.westernriver.com
Westmar Tours & Travel	800-336-7963	www.wstmr.com
Wide World of Golf	800-214-4653	www.wideworldofgolf.com
Wild Rivers Expeditions	800-422-7654	www.riversandruins.com
Wilderness Travel	800-368-2794	www.wildernesstravel.com
Wildland Adventures	800-345-4453	www.wildland.com
Wildlife Safari	800-221-8118	www.wildlife-safari.com
Witte Travel & Tours	800-469-4883	www.wittetravel.com
World Express Tours	800-544-2235	www.worldexpresstours.com
World Express Travel	800-441-8908	www.worldexpresstravel.com
World of Diving	800-900-7657	www.worldofdiving.com
World Strides	800-468-5899	www.worldstrides.com

Supplier
Contacts

Worry-Free Vacations	888-225-5658	www.worryfreevacations.com
XO Travel Consultants	888-262-9682	www.xotravelconsultants.com
Ya'lla Tours	800-644-1595	www.yallatours.com
Yankee Holidays	800-225-2550	www.yankee-holidays.com
Your Man Tours	800-922-9000	www.ymtvacations.com
Zegrahm Expeditions	800-628-8747	www.zeco.com

Supplier
Contacts

Cruise Lines

Adventure Canada	800-363-7566	www.adventurecanada.com
Afloat in France	800-524-2420	www.afloatinfrance.com
Aggressor Fleet	800-348-2628	www.aggressor.com
Amadeus Waterways	800-626-0126	www.amadeuswaterways.com
Ambassador Cruise Lines	800-255-5551	www.ambassadorcruiseline.com
American Canadian Caribbean	800-556-7450	www.accl-smallships.com
American Cruise Lines	800-814-6880	www.americancruiselines.com
American Safari Cruises	888-862-8881	www.amsafari.com
Arctic Umiaq Line		www.aul.gl
Canadian Sailing Expediations	877-429-9463	www.cansailexp.com
Captain Cook Cruises		www.captcookcrus.com.au
Carnival Cruise Lines	800-327-9501	www.carnival.com
Celebrity Cruises	800-437-3111	www.celebritycruises.com
Clipper Stad Amsterdam		www.stadamsterdam.nl
Club Med	800-248-5463	www.clubmedta.com
Color Line		www.colorline.com
Coral Princess Cruises	800-441-6880	www.coralprincesscruises.com
Costa Cruises	800-462-6782	www.costacruises.com
CruiseWest	800-426-7702	www.cruisewest.com
Crystal Cruises	800-446-6620	www.crystalcruises.com
Cunard Line	800-528-6273	www.cunard.com
DFDS Seaways	800-533-3755	www.dfdsseaways.com
Discovery Cruise Line	800-866-8687	www.discoverycruise.com
Disney Cruise Line	800-511-1333	www.disneytravelagents.com
Fjord Line		www.fjordline.com
Fred Olsen Cruise Lines		www.fredolsencruises.com
Freighter World Cruises	800-531-7774	www.freighterworld.com
French Country Waterways	800-222-1236	www.fcwl.com
Galapagos Cruises	800-327-9854	www.galapagoscruises.net
Golden Star Cruises		www.goldenstarcruises.com
Gota Canal Cruises		www.gotacanal.se
Great Lakes Cruise Co.	888-891-0203	www.greatlakescruising.com
Hapag-Lloyd Cruises	800-782-3924	www.eurolloyd.com
Hebredian Island Cruises	800-659-2648	www.hebridean.co.uk
Holland America Line	800-426-0327	www.hollandamerica.com
Hurtigruten	800-323-7436	www.hurtigruten.us
Imperial Majesty	800-394-3865	www.imperialmajesty.com
Island Cruises		www.islandcruises.com
Kristina Cruises		www.kristinacruises.com
Lindblad Expeditions	800-397-3348	www.expeditions.com
Louis Cruise Lines		www.louiscruises.com
Majestic America Line	800-434-1232	www.majesticamericaline.com
MSC Italian Cruises	800-666-9333	www.msccruises.com
Nekton Diving Cruises	800-899-6753	www.nektoncruises.com
North Star Cruises		www.northstarcruises.com.au
Norwegian Cruise Line	800-327-7030	www.ncl.com
Oceania Cruises	800-531-5658	www.oceaniacruises.com
Oceanwide Expeditions	800-453-7245	www.oceanwide-expeditions.com
Odyssey Cruises	888-741-0281	www.odysseycruises.com
P&O Cruises		www.pocruises.com

Paradise Cruises	800-334-6191	www.paradisecruises.com
Pearl Seas Cruises	800-983-7462	www.pearlseascruises.com
Peter Deilmann Europ-	800-348-8287	www.deilmann-cruises.com
Phillips Cruises	800-544-0529	www.26glaciers.com
Princess Cruises	800-421-1700	www.princess.com
Quark Expeditions	800-356-5699	www.quarkexpeditions.com
Radisson Seven Seas	800-285-1835	www.rssc.com
RiverBarge Excursions	888-462-2743	www.riverbarge.com
Royal Caribbean Int'l	800-327-6700	www.royalcaribbean.com
Saga Cruises		www.saga.co.uk
Saint Lawrence Cruise Lines	800-267-7868	www.stlawrencecruiselines.com
Sea Cloud Cruises	888-732-2568	www.seacloud.com
Sea Escape Cruises	877-732-3722	www.seaescape.com
Seabourn Cruises	800-929-9391	www.seabourn.com
SiamCruise		www.siamcruise.com
Silja Line		www.silja.fi
Silversea Cruises	800-722-9955	www.silversea.com
SongLine Cruises of Indonesia		www.songlinecruises.com
Spirit Cruises	800-877-4748	www.spiritcruises.com
Star Clippers	800-442-0551	www.starclippers.com
Star Cruises	800-327-9020	www.starcruises.com
Swan Hellenic Cruises	866-923-9182	www.swanhellenic.com
Variety Cruises	800-319-7776	www.varietycruises.com
Victoria Clipper	877-679-1650	www.victoriaclipper.com
Victoria Cruises	800-348-8084	www.victoriacruises.com
Viking River Cruises	877-668-4546	www.rivercruises.com
Viking Yacht Cruises	800-341-3030	www.vikings.gr
Windstar Cruises	800-258-7245	www.windstarcruises.com
Yangtze River Cruises	800-510-4002	www.yangtzerivercruises.com

Additional Cruise Line Contacts

Travel Insurance Providers

Access America	866-807-3982	www.accessamerica.com
CSA Travel Protection	800-711-1197	www.csatravelprotection.com
Columbus Direct (UK)		www.columbusdirect.com
HTH Worldwide	888-243-2358	www.hthworldwide.com
Int'l Medical Group	800-628-4664	www.imglobal.com
MEDEX International	800-527-2029	www.medexassist.com
MedJet Assistance	800-963-3538	www.medjetassistance.com
MultiNational Underwriters	800-605-2282	www.mnui.com
Travel Assistance Int'l	800-821-2828	www.travelassistance.com
Travel Guard	800-826-4919	www.travel-guard.com
Travel Insured	800-243-3174	www.travelinsured.com
Travelex	800-537-8052	www.travelex-insurance.com
TravelSafe	800-523-8020	www.travelsafe.com

Additional Travel Insurance Contacts

Web Sites for Travel Agents

This section contains web sites that are of particular interest to travel agents and that are not listed elsewhere in the book (although for the sake of convenience I have repeated a number of web addresses here). I make no pretense to being encyclopedic. With the Internet growing exponentially, that would be impossible. Instead, I hope to whet your appetite and provide you with enough knowledge to get you started and empower you to conduct your own explorations of this amazing and ever-expanding resource. Searching the Internet is both a challenge and a pleasure and it can be just a little bit addictive.

In these listings, the "http://" that begins all Internet addresses has been omitted. Be aware that, while most Internet addresses continue with "www.", many do not, especially ones on servers overseas. So the fact that an address does not begin "http://www." does not mean it is a typographical error.

Search Engines & Directories

The Internet is so vast that it cries out for some organization and enterprising computer whizzes have responded with a bewildering variety of search engines and directories. A **search engine** is a computer program that automatically logs on to one site and then follows every hyperlink it encounters until it exhausts all the possibilities. Along the way, it examines and indexes the contents of every page it encounters, using powerful subprograms called "algorithms" that determine the relevance and importance of the contents of each page. When you type in keywords in the "search" box at a search engine site, the engine retrieves with astounding speed hundreds or perhaps thousands of pages that contain the keywords you have specified. My favorite search engine is Google (www.google.com) and I am not alone in my admiration for this powerful research tool. Microsoft, never content to let others grab market share, has fought back and its search site (live.com) has its adherents. The most popular search engines are:

AltaVista	www.altavista.com

Once extremely popular, now a shadow of its former self.

AOL Search	search.aol.com

Good for searching AOL content; less useful for other things.

Ask Jeeves	www.ask.com
DogPile	www.dogpile.com

Dogpile aggregates search results from several different search engines.

FAST Search	www.alltheweb.com
Google	www.google.com
Live Search	www.live.com

Brought to you by the wonderful folks at Microsoft.

Lycos	www.lycos.com

While search engines use robot programs to catalog the Web, **directories** rely on old-fashioned human intelligence to examine sites and place them in the appropriate category. The original and still the most popular directory of the Web is Yahoo (www.yahoo.com). Because they are limited by human endurance, directories often do not have the depth of coverage of search engines. That is why Yahoo supplements searches of its own directory with results from Google. Another important directory is the Open Directory Project (dmoz.org). Google has its own directory (directory.google.com).

There are many more search engines and Web directories. To find them go to one of the sites mentioned and type "search engines" into the search box. To learn more about search engines and how to use them visit Search Engine Watch (www.searchenginewatch.com).

As you might have guessed, not every Web directory and search engine attempts to cover the entire Internet. Some have made an attempt to specialize in travel, with mixed results. Here are a few:

Johnny Jet	www.johnnyjet.com

The best of this group.

Kasbah	www.kasbah.com
Kayak	www.kayak.com

Searches booking engines.

Travigator	www.travigator.com

Consolidators

Consolidators are making the move to the Internet, some with online booking capabilities. Here are some of them. Many of these sites require registration and an ARC/IATA or TRUE number.

American Travel Abroad	www.amta.com
Arrow Travel	www.arrowtravel.com
Aussie Adventures	www.aussie-adventures.com
C&H International	www.cnhintl.com

Crown Peters	www.crownpeters.com/airfares.html
DFW Tours	www.dfwtoursagent.com
Downunder Direct	www.downunderdirect.com
Eurofly Vacations	www.euroflyvacations.com
Extra Value Air	www.extravalueair.com
Gateway Travel	www.gttglobal.com
Hari World	www.hariworld.com
International Travel Exchange	www.ratedesk.com
Ireland-UK Consolidated	www.agentsair.com
Pan Express Travel	www.panexpresstravel.com
PremierGateway	www.premiergateway.com
Picasso Travel	www.picassotravel.com
Skybird Travel	www.skybirdtravel.com
Skylink	www.skylinkus.com
Solar Tours	www.solartours.com
TransAm Travel	www.transamtravel.com
Up and Away	www.upandaway.com

Other Useful Airline Sites

Here, in no particular order, are some sites that you may find useful for researching air travel and air fares.

Airlines on the Web	www.flyaow.com
Smilin' Jack	www.smilinjack.com/airlines.htm

Smilin' Jack is one of our favorite sites and a great place to locate airline web sites not listed above.

ITA Software	beta.itasoftware.com

ITA provides the underlying software for a number of booking engines. This site is a handy research tool; it does not offer booking capabilities.

Destinations Unlimited	www.air-fare.com

This site tracks fares among the fifty major markets in the United States and calls out major price breaks.

SeatGuru	www.seatguru.com

A fun site for those who obsess about getting the best possible seat on every flight. Well designed and packed with information about every single seat on most major airlines.

Hotels & Hospitality

eHotelier	www.ehotelier.com

A portal site for the industry.

Hospitalitynet	www.hospitalitynet.org

An excellent site for resources on and discussion of the hotel and hospitality industry.

Hotel Interactive	www.hotelinteractive.com

A slick site covering news and trends in the hotel business.

170

The Travel Agent's Complete Desk Reference

Cruise Industry

About Cruises	cruises.about.com
Cruise Addicts	www.cruise-addicts.com
Cruise Critic	www.cruisecritic.com
Cruise Diva	www.cruisediva.com
Cruise Reports	www.cruise-reports.com
Cruise Tip Calculator	cruisetip.tpkeller.com

This fun little page lets you estimate the cost of tips based on number of people traveling and length of cruise.

Just for Travel Agents

Home-Based Travel Agent
   Resource Center   www.hometravelagency.com

Articles, tips, techniques, and a free newsletter for home-based agents.

OSSN   www.ossn.com

The Outside Sales Support Network (OSSN) site has many resources, including a bulletin board, for members only. You can download a discounted membership application form at:

www. hometravelagency.com / ossnapp.pdf

Positive Space   www.positivespace.com

A "vertical portal" for travel agents. Registration required and they will market to you aggressively. Good information, though.

Travel Agent Events   www.travelagentevents.com
Travel Agent Specials   www.travelagentspecials.com

Travel agents from around the world can post special offers on this site. A possible outlet for unused group space.

Travel Hacker   www.travelhacker.com

Home of the "Travel Agent-Digest," an Internet mailing list for travel agents. Tips and information are traded but sometimes the conversation turns nasty. There is some bias against home-based agents within this community.

Travel Research Online   www.travelresearchonline.com

Sign uop for their daily newletter summarizing news of the travel industry. Also allows you to send customized e-postcards and destinatiuon reports to your clients.

Travel News & Blogs

Christopher Elliott   www.elliott.org
e-tid.com   www.e-tid.com
Europe by Mouse   www.europebymouse.com
Gadling   www.gadling.com
Jaunted   www.jaunted.com
Joe Sent Me   www.joesentme.com
JourneyWoman   www.journeywoman.com
Modern Agent   www.modernagent.com
Rick Seaney   www.rickseany.com
Travel Agent Central   www.travelagentcentral.com
Travel Mole   www.travelmole.com
Travel Research Online   www.travelresearchonline.com
Travel Trade   www.traveltrade.com
Travel Weekly   www.travelweekly.com
Travel Wire News   www.travelwirenews.com

Government Sites

Federal Aviation Admin.   www.faa.gov
   *A portal to information about airport status, airline on-time
   performance, and more.*
Dept. of Homeland Security   www.dhs.gov
Transportation Security Admin. www.tsa.gov
   *Check here for the latest information on security screening
   procedures for airports. It can save you and your clients from
   unpleasant surprises.*
Travel Registration   https://travelregistration.state.gov
   *This service of the U.S. State Department allows travelers to
   register online with the U.S. Embassy in countries they will
   be visiting, a wise move in case of emergency.
   (Note the https in the URL.)*
U.S. State Department   travel.state.gov
   *An extensive resource including the latest information on
   getting passports, travel advisories and warnings, and tips
   for Americans traveling abroad.*

Sources of Tourist Information: United States

There are hundreds, if not thousands, of soures of free tourist information about states, cities, regions, and resort areas across the United States. Some are listed here.

First, I have listed all of the state tourist offices. These governmental organizations have the job of attracting tourists to their states. They all produce informational materials about the attractions and recreational activities their states have to offer. Some are more lavish or more helpful than others. Some are more prompt in responding to queries than others.

Many states publish guides which are targeted specifically at those in the travel industry, containing information of special interest to travel agents and tour operators. Make sure, when requesting information, that you identify yourself as a travel agent.

Within some of the states, I have listed, alphabetically by location, the names and addresses of major local sources of information, usually a convention and visitors bureau. Again, this listing is not exhaustive. It is limited to the major tourist destinations. Obviously, any selection of "major tourist destinations" will be somewhat subjective. You will find listings for major cities and areas which, according to industry statistics, are the most visited by tourists. So please don't take offense if your local area or favorite destination is not included. No slight was intended.

Finding sources of information on cities or areas not listed is an easy task. Start with 800-number information (1-800-555-1212) to see if there is a toll-free number for tourist information. Failing that, call directory information in the local area code, specify the city, and ask for the convention and visitors bureau or the chamber of commerce listing. Or do a Google search for the city or region, adding keywords like "tourism" or "cvb."

Another excellent source of information is the Tourism Offices Worldwide Directory (www.towd.com) on the Internet.

ALABAMA
Alabama Bureau of Tourism and Travel
P.O. Box 4927
Montgomery, AL 36103-4927
800-ALABAMA
www.touralabama.org

ALASKA
Alaska Tourism Office
P.O. Box 110801
Juneau, AK 99811-0801
907-465-2012
907-465-5442 fax
www.dced.state.ak.us/tourism

Anchorage Convention and Visitors
Bureau
524 West Fourth Avenue
Anchorage, AK 99501
907-276-4118
907-278-5559 fax
800-478-1255
www.anchorage.net

ARIZONA
Arizona Office of Tourism
1110 West Washington Street
Suite 155
Phoenix, AZ 85007
888-520-3433
www.arizonaguide.com

Phoenix Convention and Visitors
Bureau
400 East Van Buren Street
1 Arizona Center, Suite 600
Phoenix, AZ 85004-2290
602-254-6500
877-CALL-PHX
www.phoenixcvb.com

Scottsdale Chamber of Commerce
7343 Scottsdale Mall
Scottsdale, AZ 85251-4498
480-945-8481
480-947-4523 fax
www.scottsdalechamber.com

Metropolitan Tucson Convention and
Visitors Bureau
110 South Church Avenue
Tucson, AZ 85701
520-624-1817
520-884-7804 fax
www.visittucson.org

ARKANSAS
Arkansas Department of Parks and
Tourism
One Capitol Mall
Little Rock, AR 72201
800-628-8725
www.arkansas.com

CALIFORNIA
California Division of Tourism
P.O. Box 1499
Sacramento, CA 95812-1499
800-462-2543
http://gocalif.ca.gov

Anaheim / Orange County Convention
and Visitors Bureau
800 Katella Avenue
Anaheim, CA 92802
714-765-8888
714-991-8963 fax
www.anaheimoc.org

Los Angeles Convention and Visitors
Bureau
685 Figueroa Street
Los Angeles, CA 90017
213-689-8822
www.visitlosangeles.info

Palm Springs Desert Resorts
Convention and Visitors Bureau
70-100 Highway 111
Rancho Mirage, CA 92270
760-770-9000
760-770-9001 fax
800-967-3767
www.palmspringsusa.com

San Diego Convention and Visitors
Authority
401 B Street / Suite 1400
San Diego, CA 92101-4237
619-236-1212
619-230-7084 fax
www.sandiego.org

San Francisco Convention and Visitors
Bureau
900 Market Street
San Francisco, CA 94103-2804
415-391-2000
415-362-7323 fax
www.sfvisitor.org

Sonoma County Tourism Program
520 Mendocino Avenue / Suite 210
Santa Rosa, CA 95401
707-565-5383
800-5-SONOMA
707-565-5385 fax
www.sonomacounty.com

COLORADO
Colorado Tourism Office
1625 Broadway / Suite 1700
Denver, CO 80202
303-892-3885
800-265-6723
www.colorado.com

Denver Metro Convention and Visitors
Bureau
1555 California
Denver, CO 80210
303-892-1112
800-462-5280
www.denver.org

Vail Valley Tourism and Convention
Bureau
100 East Meadow Drive
Vail, CO 81657
970-476-1000
800-653-4523
www.visitvailvalley.com

CONNECTICUT
Connecticut Office of Tourism
Department of Economic and
Community Development
505 Hudson Street
Hartford, CT 06106
860-270-8080
800-CT-BOUND
www.tourism.state.ct.us

Greater New Haven Convention &
Visitors Bureau
59 Elm Street
New Haven, CT 06510
203-777-8550
800-332-STAY
203-782-7755 fax
www.newhavencvb.org

DELAWARE
Delaware Tourism Office
99 Kings Highway
Dover, DE 19901
302-739-4271

302-739-5749 fax
866-2-VISIT-DE
www.visitdelaware.net

DISTRICT OF COLUMBIA
Washington DC Convention and Visitors
Association
1212 New York Avenue NW
Suite 600
Washington, DC 20005
202-789-7000
202-789-7037 fax
www.washington.org

FLORIDA
Visit Florida
661 East Jefferson Street
Tallahassee, FL 32301
850-488-5607
888-7-FLA-USA
www.flausa.com

Greater Fort Lauderdale Convention
and Visitors Bureau
1850 Eller Drive
Ft. Lauderdale, FL 33316
954-765-4466
954-765-4467
www.sunny.org

Kissimmee-St. Cloud Convention and
Visitors Bureau
P.O. Box 422007
Kissimmee, FL 34742-2007
407-847-5000
800-327-9159
www.floridakiss.com

Florida Space Coast Office of Tourism
2725 Judge Fran Jamieson Way
Viera, FL 32940
321-637-5483
321-637-5494 fax
800-93-OCEAN
www.space-coast.com

Greater Miami Convention and Visitors
Bureau
701 Brickell Avenue
Suite 2700
Miami, FL 33131
305-539-3000
305-539-3113 fax
800-933-8448
www.miamibeaches.com

176

The Travel Agent's
Complete Desk
Reference

Orlando-Orange County Convention
and Visitors Bureau
6700 Forum Drive
Orlando, FL 32821
407-363-5872
800-646-2087
www.orlandoinfo.com

St. Petersburg-Clearwater Convention
and Visitors Bureau
14450 46th Street North / Suite 108
Clearwater, FL 33762
727-464-7200
727-464-7222 fax
877-352-3224
www.stpete-clearwater.com

Tampa Bay Convention and Visitors
Bureau
400 North Tampa Street / Suite 2800
Tampa, FL 33602
813-223-2752
813-229-6616 fax
800-44-TAMPA
www.visittampabay.com

GEORGIA
Georgia Department of Industry, Trade
and Tourism
285 Peachtree Center Avenue / Suite 1100
Atlanta, GA 30303
404-656-3590
800-VISIT-GA
www.georgia.org

Atlanta Convention and Visitors Bureau
233 Peachtree Street NE / Suite 100
Atlanta, GA 30303
404-521-6600
404-577-3293 fax
800-ATLANTA
www.atlanta.net

Savannah Area Convention and Visitors
Bureau
P.O. Box 1628
Savannah, GA 31402
912-644-6400
877-SAVANNAH
www.savannahvisit.com

HAWAII
Hawaii Visitors and Convention Bureau
2270 Kalakaua Avenue
Honolulu, HI 96815
808-923-1811

808-924-0290 fax
800-464-2924
www.hvcb.org

IDAHO
Idaho Department of Commerce
700 West State Street
P.O. Box 83720
Boise, ID 83720-0093
208-334-2470
208-334-2631 fax
800-VISIT-ID
www.visitid.org

ILLINOIS
Illinois Bureau of Tourism
100 West Randolph Street
Suite 3-400
Chicago, IL 60602
800-2-CONNECT
312-814-4723
www.enjoyillinois.com

Chicago Convention and Tourism
Bureau
2301 South Lake Shore Drive
Chicago, IL 60616-1490
312-567-8500
312-567-8533 fax
877-CHICAGO
www.chicago.il.org

INDIANA
Indiana Department of Commerce/
Tourism
One North Capitol Street
Suite 700
Indianapolis, IN 46204-2288
800-ENJOY-IN
317-232-8860
317-233-6887 fax
www.enjoyindiana.com

IOWA
Iowa Division of Tourism
Department of Economic Development
200 East Grand Avenue
Des Moines, IA 50309
515-242-4705
515-242-4718 fax
888-472-6035
www.traveliowa.com

KANSAS
Kansas Travel and Tourism Division
1000 SW Jackson Street

Suite 100
Topeka, KS 66612-1354
785-296-2009
785-296-6988 fax
800-252-6727
www.travelks.com

KENTUCKY
Kentucky Department of Travel
Development
500 Mero Street / Suite 2200
Frankfort, KY 40601
502-564-4930
502-564-5695 fax
800-225-8747
www.kytourism.com

LOUISIANA
Louisiana Office of Tourism
P.O. Box 94291
Baton Rouge, LA 70804
225-342-8110
800-227-4386
www.louisianatravel.com

New Orleans Metropolitan Convention
and Visitors Bureau
2020 St. Charles Avenue
New Orleans, LA 70130
504-566-5011
800-672-6124
www.neworleanscvb.com

MAINE
Maine Office of Tourism
59 State House Station
Augusta, ME 04333-0059
207-287-5711
888-642-6345
www.visitmaine.com

MARYLAND
Maryland Office of Tourism
Development
217 East Redwood Street
Baltimore, MD 21202-0059
800-MD-IS-FUN
410-767-3400
www.mdisfun.org

MASSACHUSETTS
Massachusetts Office of Travel and
Tourism
10 Park Plaza / Suite 4510
Boston, MA 02116
617-973-8500

617-973-8525 fax
800-227-MASS
www.mass-vacation.com

Greater Boston Convention and Visitors
Bureau
2 Copley Place / Suite 105
Boston, MA 02116-6501
617-424-7664 fax
888-SEE-BOSTON
www.bostonusa.com

MICHIGAN
Travel Michigan
P.O. Box 30226
Lansing MI 48909
888-78-GREAT
517-373-0670
517-373-0059 fax
www.michigan.org/

MINNESOTA
Minnesota Office of Tourism
100 Metro Square
121 7th Place East
St. Paul, MN 55101
651-296-5029
800-657-3700
www.exploreminnesota.com

MISSISSIPPI
Mississippi Division of Tourism
P.O. Box 849
Jackson, MS 39205
601-359-3297
601-359-5757 fax
800-WARMEST
www.visitmississippi.org

MISSOURI
Missouri Division of Tourism
P.O. Box 1055
Jefferson City, MO 65102
573-751-4133
573-751-5160 fax
800-810-5500
www.missouritourism.org

Branson Lakes Area CVB
P.O. Box 1897
Branson, MO 65615
800-214-3661
www.bransonchamber.com

*US Tourist
Information*

MONTANA
Montana Travel /
Montana Department of Commerce
1424 9th Avenue
P.O. Box 200533
Helena, Montana 59620-0533
800-548-3390
406-444-1800 fax
1-800-VISIT-MT
www.visitmt.com

NEBRASKA
Nebraska Division of Travel and
Tourism
P.O. Box 98907
Lincoln, NE 68509
800-228-4307
402-471-3026 fax
www.visitnebraska.org

NEVADA
Nevada Commission on Tourism
401 North Carson Street
Carson City, NV 89701
775-687-4322
775-687-6779 fax
800-638-2328
www.travelnevada.com

Las Vegas Convention and Visitors
Authority
3150 Paradise Road
Las Vegas, NV 89109-9096
702-892-7575
877-VISIT-LV
www.lasvegasfreedom.com

NEW HAMPSHIRE
New Hampshire Office of Travel and
Tourism
P.O. Box 1856
Concord, NH 03302
603-271-2665
603-271-6870 fax
800-FUN-IN-NH
www.visitnh.gov

NEW JERSEY
New Jersey Division of Travel and
Tourism
20 West State Street
Trenton, NJ 08625
609-777-0885
800-VISIT-NJ
www.state.nj.us/travel

NEW MEXICO
New Mexico Department of Tourism
491 Old Santa Fe Trail
P.O. Box 20002
Santa Fe, NM 87501
800-733-6396
www.newmexico.org

NEW YORK
New York State Division of Tourism
P.O. Box 2603
Albany, NY 12220-0603
518-474-4116
800-225-5697
www.iloveny.com

NYC & Company (CVB)
810 Seventh Avenue
New York, NY 10019
212-484-1200
212-245-5943 fax
www.nycvisit.com

NORTH CAROLINA
North Carolina Division of Tourism
P.O. Box 29571
Raleigh, NC 27826-0571
919-733-8372
919-733-8582 fax
800-VISIT-NC
www.visitnc.org

NORTH DAKOTA
North Dakota Tourism Division
Century Center
1600 E. Century Ave. Suite 2
PO Box 2057
701-328-2525
701-328-4878
800-HELLO-ND
www.ndtourism.com

OHIO
Ohio Division of Travel and Tourism
P.O. Box 1001
Columbus, OH 43216-1001
614-466-8844
614-466-6744 fax
800-282-5393
www.ohiotourism.com

OKLAHOMA
Oklahoma Tourism and Recreation
Department
15 North Robinson / Suite 801
P.O. Box 52002

Oklahoma City, OK 73105-2002
405-521-2409
405-521-3992 fax
800-652-OKLA
www.travelok.com

OREGON
Oregon Tourism Commission
775 Summer Street NE
Salem, OR 97310-1282
503-986-0000
503-986-0001 fax
800-547-7842
www.traveloregon.com

PENNSYLVANIA
Pennsylvania Tourism Office
400 North Street
Harrisburg, PA 17120
717-787-5453
717-787-0687 fax
800-847-4872
www.visitpa.com

Philadelphia Convention and Visitors
Bureau
1515 Market Street / Suite 2020
Philadelphia, PA 19102
215-636-3300
800-CALL-PHL
www.pcvb.org

RHODE ISLAND
Rhode Island Tourism Division
One West Exchange Street
Providence, RI 02903
401-222-2601
401-273-8270 fax
800-556-2484
www.visitrhodeisland.com

SOUTH CAROLINA
South Carolina Department of Parks,
Recreation and Tourism
1205 Pendleton Street
Columbia, SC 29201-0071
803-734-1700
800-346-3634
www.discoversouthcarolina.com

Myrtle Beach Convention & Visitors
Bureau
1200 North Oak Street
Myrtle Beach, SC 29577
843-626-7444

800-356-3016
www.mbchamber,com

SOUTH DAKOTA
South Dakota Department of Tourism
711 East Wells Avenue
Pierre, SD 57501-3369
605-773-3301
800-732-5682
www.travelsd.com

TENNESSEE
Tennessee Department of Tourism
Development
320 Sixth Avenue North
5th FL / Rachel Jackson Building
Nashville, TN 37243
615-741-2159
800-GO2TENN
www.state.tn.us/tourdev/

Nashville Convention & Visitors Bureau
211 Commerce Street / Suite 100
Nashville, TN 37201
615-259-4730
615-244-6278 fax
800-657-6910
www.nashvillecvb.com

TEXAS
Texas Department of Commerce, Tourist
Division
P.O. Box 12728
Austin, TX 78711-2728
512-462-9191
800-888-8839
www.traveltex.com

Dallas Convention and Visitors Bureau
325 North St. Paul Street / Suite 700
Dallas, TX 75201
214-571-1000
214-571-1008 fax
800-232-5527
www.dallascvb.com

San Antonio Convention and Visitors
Bureau
203 South St. Mary's Street
San Antonio, TX 78205
210-207-6700
800-447-3372
www.sanantoniocvb.com

US Tourist Information

The Travel Agent's Complete Desk Reference

UTAH
Utah Travel Council
P.O. Box 147420
Salt Lake City, UT 84114
800-UTAH-FUN
801-538-1030
www.utah.com

Salt Lake Convention and Visitors Bureau
90 South West Temple
Salt Lake City, UT 84101-1406
801-521-2822
801-355-9323 fax
800-541-4955
www.visitsaltlake.com

VERMONT
Vermont Department of Tourism
6 Baldwin Street, Drawer 33
Montpelier, VT 05633-1301
802-828-0587
802-828-3233 fax
800-VERMONT
www.1-800-vermont.com

VIRGINIA
Virginia Division of Tourism
901 East Byrd Street
Richmond, VA 23219
804-786-4484
800-VISIT-VA
www.virginia.org

Williamsburg Area Convention and Visitors Bureau
P.O. Box 3585
201 Penniman Road
Williamsburg, VA 23187
757-253-0192
800-368-6511
www.visitwilliamsburg.com

WASHINGTON
Washington State Tourism Development Division
P.O. Box 42500
Olympia, WA 98504-2500
800-544-1800
www.tourism.wa.gov

Seattle - King County Convention and Visitors Bureau
One Convention Place
701 Pike Street / Suite 800
Seattle, WA 98101
206-461-5840
206-461-5855 fax
www.seeseattle.org

WEST VIRGINIA
West Virginia Division of Tourism
90 MacCorkle Avenue SW
South Charleston, WV 25303
304-558-2200
800-CALL-WVA
www.callwva.com

WISCONSIN
Wisconsin Department of Tourism
201 West Washington Avenue
P.O. Box 7976
Madison WI 53707-7976
608-266-2161
800-432-8747
www.travelwisconsin.com

WYOMING
Wyoming Division of Tourism
Frank Norris Jr. Travel Center
I-25 at College Drive
Cheyenne, WY 82002
307-777-7777
800-225-5996
www.wyomingtourism.org

Sources of Tourist Information: International

This listing of international tourism information is very similar to the one in the last section, with one major difference. In this section are listed, in abbreviated form, the visa and entry requirements for each foreign country.

On the line immediately following the country name you will find one or more of the following codes:

P: Passport required for entry. In the past, proof of U.S. citizenship, such as a drivers licence or birth certificate, was sufficient for travel to some countries. Now **all** U.S. citizens are required to have a passport when traveling abroad.

PV: Passport and visa required for entry. When a visa is required, the length of stay and cost of the *typical* tourist visa is given. Be aware that many countries that do not require a visa for short stays, require them for stays of longer than 15, 30, 90, or more days. Note, too, that some countries have different requirements for different types of visas (e.g. tourist, business, study, resident, etc.). That may mean that while no visa may be required for tourists, business trips may require a visa with a hefty fee. So we have provided contact information for the office issuing visas, even if no visa is required for tourists. Make sure you check on the applicable requirements so you can advise your client accordingly.

NT: No tourist visas issued. Some countries issue no tourist visas, but only admit visitors with a valid business visa and business reason for entry.

TC: Tourist card required.

✈ : Proof of a return/onward ticket required. In other words, they want to make sure you won't wind up stranded in their country.

$:   Proof of sufficient funds required. Many countries want some assurance you have enough money to support yourself during your stay. What constitutes "sufficient funds" will vary from country to country.

✚ :   Vaccinations or other medical measures required.

In addition to this basic information on passports, visas, and other entry requirements, you will find a contact for additional information about each country. Sometimes that will be the embassy, other times it will be a separate tourist bureau with separate offices.

When a country has more that one tourist office, the primary office is listed first, then other cities in which offices are located. When no source of tourist information is listed, you may be able to obtain tourist brochures from the embassy or consulates.

AFGHANISTAN
PV
Embassy of Afghanistan
2341 Wyoming Avenue, NW
Washington, DC 20008
202-483-6410
www.embassyofafghanistan.org
Travel documents to Afghanistan were not being issued at press time.

ALBANIA
P (entry card; 10 euros, 30 days)
For visa information:
Embassy of the Republic of Albania
2100 S Street, NW
Washington DC 20008
202-223-4942
www.albanianembassy.org

ALGERIA
PV (90 days, $100) ✈
For visa information:
Embassy of the Democratic and Popular Republic of Algeria
2118 Kalorama Rd, NW
Washington DC 20008
202-265-0880
www.algeria-us.org
(Travel by U.S. citizens not recommended.)

ANDORRA
P
For visa information:
Embassy of the Principality of Andorra
2 United Nations, 27th floor
New York, NY 10017
212-750-8064

ANGOLA
PV (90 days, $110) ✈ **$ ✚**
For visa information:
The Embassy of Angola
2100 16th Street, NW
Washington, DC 20009
202-452-1042
www.angola.org
Consulates in:
New York
(Travel by U.S. citizens not recommended.)

ANTIGUA AND BARBUDA
P ✈ **$**
For visa information:
Embassy of Antigua and Barbuda
3216 New Mexico Avenue, NW
Washington, DC 20016
202-362-5122
For tourism information:
Antigua and Barbuda Tourist Board
610 Fifth Avenue / Suite 311
New York, NY 10020
888-268-4227 toll free
212-541-4117

ARGENTINA
P
For visa information:
Argentine Embassy
1811 Q Street, NW
Washington, DC 20009
202-238-6401
www.embassyofargentina-usa.org
Consulates in:
Atlanta, Chicago, Houston, Los Angeles, Miami, New York

For tourism information:
Argentina Government Tourist
Information
12 West 56th Street
New York, NY 10019
212-603-0443
Other offices in:
Coral Gables, Los Angeles

ARMENIA
PV (21 days, $60-$95)
For visa information:
Embassy of the Republic of Armenia
2225 R Street, NW
Washington, DC 20008
202-319-1976
www.armeniaemb.org
Consulates in:
Beverly Hills
For tourism information:
146 Deer Creek Road
Fredonia, TX 76842
915-429-6288
www.tourarmenia.com

ARUBA
P ✈ $
For visa information:
(See Netherlands Antilles)
For tourism information:
Aruba Tourism Authority
1200 Harbor Boulevard
Weehawken, NJ 07087
800-862-7822
www.aruba.com
Other offices in:
Atlanta, Chicago, Coral Gables, Ft.
Lauderdale, Houston, Woodbridge
(Ontario, CANADA)

AUSTRALIA
PV (12 months, AUS$20) ✈ **$**
For visa information:
Embassy of Australia
1601 Massachusetts Avenue, NW
Washington, DC 20036-2273
202-797-3145
www.usa.embassy.gov.au
Consulates in:
Honolulu, Los Angeles, New York, San
Francisco, Toronto, Vancouver
For tourism information:
Australian Tourist Commission
2049 Century Park East
Los Angeles, CA 90067
310-229-4870

www.australia.com
Other offices in:
New York

AUSTRIA
P
For visa information:
Embassy of Austria
3524 International Court, NW
Washington, DC 20008
202-895-6767
www.austria.org
Consulates in:
Chicago, Los Angeles, New York
For tourism information:
Austrian National Tourist Office
500 Fifth Avenue / Suite 800
New York, NY 10110
212-575-7723
www.austria-tourism.at
Other offices in:
Los Angeles, Toronto

AZERBAIJAN
PV (3 days, $20; 90 days, $131)
For visa information:
Embassy of the Republic of Azerbaijan
2741 34th Street, NW
Washington, DC 20008
202-337-3500
www.azembassy.com

BAHAMAS
P ✈
For visa information:
Embassy of the Bahamas
2220 Massachusetts Avenue, NW
Washington DC 20008
202-319-2660
Consulates in:
New York, Miami
For tourism information:
Bahamas Tourist Office
150 East 52nd Street
New York, NY 10022
212-758-2777
www.bahamas.com
Other offices in:
Aventura (FL), Chicago, Dallas, Los
Angeles

BAHRAIN
PV (2 weeks, $48) ✈
For visa information:
Embassy of the Kingdom of Bahrain
3502 International Drive, NW

*International
Tourist
Information*

184

*The Travel Agent's
Complete Desk
Reference*

Washington, DC 20008
202-342-1111
www.bahrainembassy.org
Consulates in:
New York

BANGLADESH
PV ($100) ✈
For visa information:
Embassy of the People's Republic of
Bangladesh
3510 International Drive, NW
Washington, DC 20008
202-244-2745
www.bangladoot.org

BARBADOS
P ✈ **$**
For visa information:
Embassy of Barbados
2144 Wyoming Avenue, NW
Washington, DC 20008
202-939-9200
washington@foreign.gov.bb
Consulates in:
Los Angeles, New York
For tourism information:
Barbados Tourism Authority
800 Second Avenue
New York, NY 10017
800-221-9831
212-986-6516
www.barbados.org
Other offices in:
Los Angeles, Toronto

BELARUS
PV (30 days, $131)
For visa information:
Embassy of Belarus
1619 New Hampshire Avenue, NW
Washington, DC 20009
202-986-1606
www.belarusembassy.org
Consulates in:
New York

BELGIUM
P ✈ **$**
For visa information:
Embassy of Belgium
3330 Garfield Street, NW
Washington, DC 20008
202-333-6900
www.diplobel.us
Consulates in:

Atlanta, Chicago, Los Angeles, New
York
For tourism information:
Belgian Tourist Office
220 East 42nd Street, Suite 3402
New York, NY 10017
212-758-8130
www.visitbelgium.com

BELIZE
P ✈ **$**
For visa information:
Embassy of Belize
2535 Massachusetts Avenue, NW
Washington, DC 20008
202-332-9636
www.embassyofbelize.org
Consulates in:
New York
For tourism information:
800-624-0686
www.travelbelize.org

BENIN
PV (36 months, $100) ✈ ✚
For visa information:
Embassy of the Republic of Benin
2124 Kalorama Road, NW
Washington DC 20008
202-232-6656
www.beninembassy.us

BERMUDA
P ✈
For visa information:
British Embassy
19 Observatory Circle, NW
Washington, DC 20008
202-588-7800
For tourism information:
Bermuda Department of Tourism
205 East 42nd Street, 16th Floor
New York, NY 10017
212-818-9800
www.bermudatourism.com
Other offices in:
Atlanta, Boston, Chicago, Toronto

BHUTAN
PV ($165-$200 per day, all-incl) ✚
For visa information:
Bhutan Mission to the United Nations
2 United Nations Plaza, 27th floor
New York, NY 10017
212-826-1919
For tourism information:

Bhutan Travel
120 East 56th Street
New York, NY 10022
800-950-9908
www.tourism.gov.bt

BOLIVIA
PV ($100)
For visa information:
Consular Section of the Embassy of
Bolivia
1819 H Street, NW
Washington, DC 20006
202-232-4828
www.bolivia-usa.org
Consulates in:
New York, Miami, San Francisco

BONAIRE
P ✈
For visa information:
(See Netherlands Antilles)
For tourism information:
Bonaire Tourism Office
10 Rockefeller Plaza
New York, NY 10020
800-266-2473
www.bonaire.org

BOSNIA AND HERZEGOVINA
P
For visa information:
Embassy of Bosnia and Herzegovina
2109 E Street, NW
Washington, D.C. 20037
202-337-1500
www.bosnianembassy.org
Consulates in:
Chicago
For tourism information:
www.bhtourism.ba

BOTSWANA
P ✈ **$**
For visa information:
Embassy of the Republic of Botswana
1531 New Hampshire Avenue, NW
Washington DC 20036
202-244-4990
www.botswanaembassy.org
Consulates in:
Houston, Los Angeles
For tourism information:
Botswana Tourism
631 Commack Road
Commack, NY 11725

877-445-7447
www.botswanatourism.co.bw

BRAZIL
PV (90 days, $140)
For visa information:
Brazilian Embassy
Consular Section
3009 Whitehaven Street, NW
Washington, D.C. 20008
202-238-2828
www.brazilemb.org
Consulates in:
Atlanta, Boston, Chicago, Houston, Los
Angeles, Miami, NYC, San Francisco
For tourism information:
Brazilian Tourism Offices
New York 646-378-2126
Los Angeles 310-341-8394
www.braziltour.com

BRITISH VIRGIN ISLANDS
P ✈ **$**
For visa information:
Chief Immigration Officer
Immigration Department
Road Town, Tortola
British Virgin Islands
284-494-3701
For tourism information:
British Virgin Islands Tourist Board
370 Lexington Avenue
New York, NY 10017
800-835-8530
www.bviwelcome.com
Other offices in:
Los Angeles

BRITISH WEST INDIES
P ✈ **$**
For visa information:
British Embassy
3100 Massachusetts Avenue, NW
Washington, DC 20008
202-588-7800
For tourism information:
(See various islands)

BRUNEI DARUSSALAM
PV ✈ (3 months, $14)
For visa information:
Embassy of Brunei Darussalam
3520 International Court, NW
Washington, D.C. 20008
202-237-1838
www.bruneiembassy.org

Consulates in:
New York

BULGARIA
P ✚
For visa information:
Embassy of the Republic of Bulgaria
1621 22nd Street, NW
Washington, DC 20008
202-387-0174
www.bulgaria-embassy.org
Consulates in:
Chicago, New York, Los Angeles

BURKINA FASO
PV (6 months, $100)
For visa information:
Embassy of Burkina Faso
2340 Massachusetts Avenue, NW
Washington, DC 20008
202-332-5577
www.burkinaembassy-usa.org

BURUNDI
PV (2 months, $40) ✈ ✚
For visa information:
Embassy of the Republic of Burundi
2233 Wisconsin Avenue, NW
Washington, DC 20007
202-342-2574
www.burundiembassy-usa.org
Consulates in:
New York

CAMBODIA
PV (3 months, $20)
For visa information:
Royal Embassy of Cambodia
4530 16th Street, NW
Washington, DC 20011
202-726-7742
www.embassyofcambodia.org

CAMEROON
PV (3 months, $99) ✈ $ ✚
For visa information:
Embassy of the Republic of Cameroon
2349 Massachusetts Avenue, NW
Washington, DC 20008
202-265-8790
www.ambacam-usa.org
Consulates in:
New York, San Francisco

CANADA
P
For visa information:
Canadian Embassy
501 Pennsylvania Avenue, NW
Washington, DC 20001
202-682-1740
www.canadianembassy.org
Consulates in:
Anchorage, Atlanta, Boston, Buffalo,
Chicago, Dallas, Detroit, Houston, Los
Angeles, Miami, Minneapolis, New
York, Philadelphia, Phoenix, Raleigh,
San Diego, San Francisco, Seattle,
Tucson
For tourism information:
www.travelcanada.ca

CAPE VERDE
PV ($11)
For visa information:
Embassy of the Republic of Cape Verde
3415 Massachusetts Avenue, NW
Washington, DC 20007
202-965-6820
Consulates in:
Boston, New York

CAYMAN ISLANDS
P ✈ $
For visa information:
British Embassy
3100 Massachusetts Avenue, NW
Washington, DC 20008
202-588-7800
For tourism information:
Cayman Islands Department of Tourism
3 Park Avenue, 39th Floor
New York, NY 10016
212-889-9009
www.caymanislands.ky
Other offices in:
Boston, Chicago, Dallas, Houston,
Miami, Toronto

CENTRAL AFRICAN REPUBLIC
PV (1 year, $150) ✈ ✚
For visa information:
Embassy of Central African Republic
1618 22nd Street, NW
Washington, DC 20008
202-483-7800

CHAD
PV (1 month, $100) ✈ ✚
For visa information:
Embassy of the Republic of Chad
2002 R Street, NW
Washington, DC 20009
202-462-4009

CHILE
P ($100 entry fee)
For visa information:
Embassy of Chile
1732 Massachusetts Avenue, NW
Washington, DC 20036
202-785-1746
www.chile-usa.org
Consulates in:
Boston, Chicago, Houston, Los Angeles,
Miami, New York, Philadelphia, San
Francisco, San Juan

CHINA
PV (3 to 6 months, $130)
For visa information:
Embassy of the People's Republic of China
2201 Wisconsin Avenue, NW
Washington, DC 20007
202-338-6688
www.china-embassy.org
Consulates in:
Chicago, Houston, New York, Los
Angeles, San Francisco, Toronto,
Vancouver
For tourism information:
China National Tourist Office
550 North Brand Boulevard
Glendale, CA 91203
818-545-7507
www.cnto.org
Other offices in:
New York

COLOMBIA
PV ✈
For visa information:
Embassy of Colombia
2118 Leroy Place NW
Washington, DC 20008
202-387-8338
www.colombiaemb.org
Consulates in:
Atlanta, Boston, Chicago, Houston,
Los Angeles, Miami, New York, San
Francisco
For tourism information:
www.turismocolombia.com

COMOROS ISLANDS
P ✈
For visa information:
Embassy of the Federal and Islamic
Republic of Comoros
420 East 50th Street
New York, NY 10022
212-750-1637

**CONGO, DEMOCRATIC REPUBLIC
OF THE (formerly Zaire)**
PV (1 month, $75) ✈
For visa information:
Embassy of the Democratic Republic of
the Congo
1726 M Street, NW
Washington, DC 20036
202-234-7690

CONGO, REPUBLIC OF THE
PV (1 month, $120) ✈ ✚
For visa information:
Embassy of the Republic of the Congo
4891 Colorado Avenue, NW
Washington, DC 20011
202-726-5500

COOK ISLANDS
P ✈ **$**
For visa information:
Consulate for the Cook Islands
Kamehameha Schools #16
Kapalama Heights
Honolulu, HI 96817
808-847-6377

COSTA RICA
P ✈
For visa information:
Embassy of Costa Rica
Consular Section
2112 S Street, NW
Washington, DC 20008
202-234-2945 or
202-234-2946
costarica-embassy.org
Consulates in:
Atlanta, Chicago, Denver, Houston,
Los Angeles, Miami, New York, San
Francisco, San Juan
For tourism information:
www.visitcostarica.com

*International
Tourist
Information*

COTE D'IVOIRE
P
For visa information:
Embassy of the Republic of Cote d'Ivoire
2424 Massachusetts Avenue, NW
Washington, DC 20008
202-797-0300
Consulates in:
San Francisco
415-391-0176
For tourism information:
Cote d'Ivoire Tourist Office
2424 Massachusetts Avenue, NW
Washington, DC 20008
202-797-0344

CROATIA
P
For visa information:
Embassy of the Republic of Croatia
to the United States of America
2343 Massachusetts Avenue, NW
Washington D.C., 20008
202-588-5899
www.croatiaemb.org
Consulates in:
Chicago, Kansas City, Los Angeles, New
Orleans, New York, Pittsburgh, Seattle

CUBA
PV (90 days, $26) ✈
For visa information:
Cuban Interests Section
2630 16th Street, NW
Washington, DC 20009
202-797-8518
embacu.cubaminrex.cu
(Treasury Dept. license required for
travel by U.S. citizens. See www.treas.
gov/ofac)
For tourism information:
Cuba Tourist Board
1200 Bay Street
Toronto, ON M5R 2A5
CANADA
(416) 362-0700
www.gocuba.ca
Other offices in:
Montreal

CURACAO
P ✈ **$**
For visa information:
(See Netherlands Antilles)
For tourism information:
Curaçao Tourism Corporation

800-328-7222
www.curacao-tourism.com

CYPRUS
P ✈
For visa information:
Embassy of the Republic of Cyprus
2211 R Street, NW
Washington, DC 20008
202-462-5772
www.cyprusembassy.net
Consulates in:
New York, Toronto
For tourism information:
Cyprus Tourism Organization
13 East 40th Street
New York, NY 10016
212-683-5280
www.visitcyprus.com

CZECH REPUBLIC
P
For visa information:
Embassy of the Czech Republic
3900 Spring of Freedom Street, NW
Washington, DC 20008
202-274-9123
www.mzv.cz/washington
Consulates in:
Chicago, Los Angeles, New York
For tourism information:
Czech Tourist Authority
1109 Madison Avenue
New York, NY 10028
212-288-0830
www.czechtourism.com

DENMARK
P
For visa information:
Royal Danish Embassy
3200 Whitehaven Street, NW
Washington, DC 20008
202-234-4300
www.denmarkemb.org
Consulates in:
Atlanta, Boston, Chicago, Cleveland,
Dallas, Denver, Detroit, Honolulu,
Houston, Indianapolis, Kansas City,
Los Angeles, Miami, Montreal, New
Orleans, New York, Philadelphia, San
Diego, San Francisco, Seattle, Toronto,
Vancouver, and others
For tourism information:
Danish Tourist Board
P.O. Box 4649

New York, NY 10163
212-885-9700
www.visitdenmark.com

DJIBOUTI
PV (3 months, $50) ✈ ✚
Embassy of the Republic of Djibouti
1156 15th Street, NW
Washington, DC 20005
202-331-0270
Consulates in:
New York

DOMINICA
P ✈
For visa information:
Consulate of the Commonwealth of
Dominica
3216 New Mexico Avenue, NW
Washington, DC 20016
202-364-6781
For tourism information:
Dominica Tourist Office
110-64 Queens Boulevard
New York, NY 11375
718-261-9615
www.dominica.dm

DOMINICAN REPUBLIC
P TC
For visa information:
Embassy of the Dominican Republic
1715 22nd Street, NW
Washington, DC 20008
202-332-6280
www.domrep.org
Consulates in:
Boston, Chicago, Miami, New Orleans,
New York, Philadelphia, San Francisco,
San Juan
For tourism information:
Dominican Republic Tourism Board
136 East 57th Street, Suite 803
New York, NY 10022
888-374-6361
www.dominicana.com.do

DUBAI
(See United Arab Emirates)

EAST TIMOR
P
4201 Connecticut Avenue, NW
Washington DC 20008
202-966-3202
(Travel by U.S. citizens not recommended.)

ECUADOR
P
For visa information:
Embassy of Ecuador
2535 15th Street, NW
Washington, DC 20009
202-234-7166
www.ecuador.org
Consulates in:
Atlanta, Boston, Chicago, Dallas,
Houston, Miami, Minneapolis, New
York, Newark, San Francisco, San Juan,
Toronto, Vancouver
For tourism information:
www.vivecuador.com

EGYPT
PV (90 days, $15)
For visa information:
Embassy of the Arab Republic of Egypt
3521 International Court, NW
Washington, DC 20008
202-895-5400
www.egyptembassy.net
Consulates in:
Chicago, New York, San Francisco
For tourism information:
Egyptian Tourist Authority
630 Fifth Avenue
New York, NY 10111
212-332-2570
www.egypt.travel
Other offices in:
Beverly Hills, Chicago, Montreal

EL SALVADOR
P TC ($10)
For visa information:
Embassy of El Salvador
2308 California Street, NW
Washington, DC 20008
202-265-9671
www.elsalvador.org
Consulates in:
Boston, Chicago, Coral Gables, Dallas,
Houston, Los Angeles, New York, San
Francisco, and others
For tourism information:
www.elsalvador.travel

ENGLAND
(See United Kingdom)

*International
Tourist
Information*

190

The Travel Agent's Complete Desk Reference

EQUATORIAL GUINEA
P ✛
For visa information:
Embassy of the Republic of Equatorial Guinea
2020 16th Street, NW
Washington, DC 20009
202-518-5700

ERITREA
PV (3 months, $40) ✈ **$**
For visa information:
Embassy of Eritrea
1708 New Hampshire Avenue, NW
Washington, DC 20009
202-319-1991
www.embassyeritrea.org

ESTONIA
P
Embassy of Estonia
2131 Massachusetts Avenue, NW
Washington, DC 20008
202-588-0101
www.estemb.org
For visa information:
Consulate General of Estonia
305 East 47th Street
New York, NY 10017
212-883-0636
www.nyc.estemb.org
For tourism information:
www.visitestonia.com

ETHIOPIA
PV (2 years, $70) ✛
For visa information:
Embassy of Ethiopia
3506 International Drive, NW
Washington, DC 20008
202-364-1200
www.ethiopianembassy.org
Consulates in:
New York
For tourism information:
www.tourismethiopia.org

FIJI
P ✈ $
For visa information:
Embassy of the Republic of the Fiji Islands
2233 Wisconsin Avenue, NW
Washington, DC 20007
202-337-8320

www.fijiembassydc.com
Consulates in:
New York
For tourism information:
Fiji Visitors Bureau
5777 West Century Boulevard
Los Angeles, CA 90045
800-932-3454
www.bulafijinow.com

FINLAND
P
For visa information:
Embassy of Finland
3301 Massachusetts Avenue, NW
Washington, DC 20008
202-298-5800
www.finland.org
Consulates in:
Los Angeles, New York
For tourism information:
Visit Finland
1 Penn Plaza
New York, NY 10119
646-467-9876
www.visitfinland.com

FRANCE
P
For visa information:
Embassy of France
4101 Reservoir Road, NW
Washington, DC 20007
202-944-6000
www.consulfrance-washington.org
Consulates in:
Atlanta, Boston, Chicago, Houston, Los Angeles, Miami, New Orleans, New York, San Francisco
For tourism information:
French Government Tourist Office
825 Third Avenue
New York, NY 10022
514-288-6989
www.franceguide.com
Other offices in:
Chicago, Los Angeles, Montreal, Toronto

FRENCH GUIANA
P
For visa information:
Embassy of France
4101 Reservoir Road, NW
Washington, DC 20007
202-944-6200
www.consulfrance-washington.org

FRENCH POLYNESIA
P

For visa information:
Embassy of France
4101 Reservoir Road, NW
Washington, DC 20007
202-944-6200
www.consulfrance-washington.org
For tourism information:
Tahiti Tourisme
877-468-2448
www.tahiti-tourisme.com

FRENCH WEST INDIES
P

For visa information:
Embassy of France
4101 Reservoir Road, NW
Washington, DC 20007
202-944-6200
www.consulfrance-washington.org
For tourism information:
French West Indies Tourist Board
444 Madison Avenue
New York, NY 10022
212-838-3486

GABON
PV (4 months, $100) ✈ ✚

For visa information:
Embassy of the Gabonese Republic
2034 20th Street, NW
Washington, DC 20009
202-797-1000
Consulates in:
New York
For tourism information:
Gabon Tourist Information Office
347 Fifth Avenue
New York, NY 10016
212-447-6700

GALAPAGOS ISLANDS
(See Ecuador)

GAMBIA
PV (3 months, $100)

For visa information:
Embassy of the Gambia
1424 K Street, NW
Washington, DC 20005
202-785-1399
www.gambiaembassy.us
Consulates in:
New York

GEORGIA
PV (90 days, $30-$50)

For visa information:
Embassy of the Republic of Georgia
1615 New Hampshire Avenue, NW
Washington, DC 20009
202-387-2390
202-387-9153 consulate
embassy.mfa.gov.ge

GERMANY
P

For visa information:
Embassy of the Federal Republic of
Germany
4645 Reservoir Road, NW
Washington, DC 20007
202-298-4393
www.germany.info
Consulates in:
Atlanta, Boston, Chicago, Houston, Los
Angeles, Miami, Montreal, New York,
San Francisco, Toronto, Vancouver
For tourism information:
German National Tourist Office
122 East 42nd Street, Suite 2000
New York, NY 10168
212-661-7200
www.visits-to-germany.com

GHANA
PV (3 months, $50) ✈ ✚

For visa information:
Embassy of Ghana
3512 International Drive, NW
Washington, DC 20008
202-686-4520
www.ghanaembassy.org
Consulates in:
Houston, New York

GIBRALTAR
P

For visa information:
British Embassy
3100 Massachusetts Avenue, NW
Washington, DC 20008
202-588-7800
www.britainusa.com

GILBERT ISLANDS
(See Kiribati)

GREAT BRITAIN
(See United Kingdom)

GREECE
P
For visa information:
Embassy of Greece
2221 Massachusetts Avenue, NW
Washington, DC 20008
202-939-5818
www.greekembassy.org
Consulates in:
Atlanta, Boston, Chicago, Houston, Los
Angeles, Montreal, New Orleans, New
York, San Francisco, Tampa, Toronto
For tourism information:
Greek National Tourist Board
168 North Michigan Avenue
Chicago, IL 60601
312-782-1084
www.gnto.gr
Other offices in:
Los Angeles, Montreal, New York,
Toronto

GREENLAND
(See Denmark)

GRENADA
P
For visa information:
Embassy of Grenada
1701 New Hampshire Avenue, NW
Washington, DC 20009
202-265-2561
www.grenadaembassyusa.org
Consulates in:
New York, Miami, Toronto
For tourism information:
Grenada Board of Tourism
317 Madison Avenue
New York, NY 10017
800-927-9554
www.grenada.travel

GUADELOUPE
(See French West Indies.)

GUATEMALA
P
For visa information:
Embassy of Guatemala
2220 R Street, NW
Washington, DC 20008
202-745-4952
Consulates in:
Chicago, Coral Gables, Houston, Los
Angeles, New York, Philadelphia,
Providence

GUINEA
PV (2 months, $100) ✈ ✚
For visa information:
Embassy of the Republic of Guinea
2112 Leroy Place, NW
Washington, DC 20008
202-986-4300

GUINEA-BISSAU
PV ✈
For visa information:
Embassy of the Republic of Guinea-
Bissau
15929 Yukon Lane
Rockville, MD 20855
301-947-3958

GUYANA
P ✈
For visa information:
Embassy of Guyana
2490 Tracy Place, NW
Washington, DC 20008
202-265-6900

HAITI
P ✈
For visa information:
Embassy of Haiti
2311 Massachusetts Avenue, NW
Washington, DC 20008
202-332-4090
www.haiti.org
Consulates in:
Boston, Miami, New York, Puerto Rico

HONDURAS
P ✈
For visa information:
3007 Tilden Street, NW
Washington, DC 20008
202-966-7702
www.hondurasemb.org
Consulates in:
Chicago, Houston, Los Angeles, Miami,
New Orleans, New York, San Francisco,
and others
For tourism information:
Honduras Institute of Tourism
2828 Coral Way
Miami, FL 33145
800-410-9608
www.honduras.travel

HONG KONG
P ✈

For visa information:
Embassy of the People's Republic of China
2300 Connecticut Avenue, NW
Washington, DC 20008
202-328-2500
www.china-embassy.org
For tourism information:
Hong Kong Tourist Association
10940 Wilshire Boulevard
Los Angeles, CA 90024
310-208-4582
www.discoverhongkong.com
Other offices in:
New York, Toronto

HUNGARY
P ✈ **$**

For visa information:
Embassy of the Republic of Hungary
3910 Shoemaker Street, NW
Washington, DC 20008
202-362-6730
www.huembwas.org
Consulates in:
Chicago, Los Angeles, New York
For tourism information:
Hungarian Tourist Board
350 Fifth Avenue
New York, NY 10118
212-695-1221
www.gotohungary.com

ICELAND
P

For visa information:
Embassy of Iceland
1156 15th Street, NW
Washington, DC 20005
202-265-6653
www.iceland.org/us
Consulates in:
New York, Winnipeg
For tourism information:
Icelandic Tourist Board
655 Third Avenue
New York, NY 10017
212-885-9700
www.icelandtouristboard.com

INDIA
PV (6 months, $150) ✈ **$**
For visa information:

Embassy of India
2107 Massachusetts Avenue, NW
Washington, DC 20008
202-939-7000
www.indianembassy.org
Consulates in:
Chicago, Houston, New York, San Francisco, Toronto, Vancouver
For tourism information:
Government of India Tourist Office
1270 Avenue of the Americas
New York, NY 10020
800-953-9399
212-586-4901
www.incredibleindia.org
Other offices in:
Los Angeles, Toronto

INDONESIA
P (6 months, $45) ✈ **$**

For visa information:
Embassy of the Republic of Indonesia
2020 Massachusetts Avenue, NW
Washington, DC 20036
202-775-5200
www.embassyofindonesia.org
Consulates in:
Chicago, Houston, Los Angeles, New York, San Francisco, Toronto, Vancouver
For tourism information:
Indonesian Council of Tourism Partners
P.O. Box 208
Haleiwa, HI 96712
877-717-7700
www.indonesia-tourism.com

IRAN
PV

For visa information:
Embassy of Pakistan
Iranian Interests Section
2209 Wisconsin Avenue, NW
Washington, DC 20007
202-965-4990
www.daftar.org
For tourism information:
Iran Travel and Tour Organization
www.itto.org

IRAQ
PV
Embassy of Iraq
1801 P Street, NW
Washington DC 20036
202-483-7500
Travel documents to Iraq were not being

issued when this edition went to press.

IRELAND
P ✈
For visa information:
Embassy of Ireland
2234 Massachusetts Avenue, NW
Washington, DC 20008
202-462-3939
www.embassyofireland.org
Consulates in:
Boston, Chicago, New York, San
Francisco
For tourism information:
Irish Tourist Board
345 Park Avenue
New York, NY 10154
212-418-0800
www.tourismireland.com
Other offices in:
Toronto

ISRAEL
P ✈ **$**
For visa information:
Embassy of Israel
3514 International Drive, NW
Washington, DC 20008
202-364-5527
www.israelemb.org
Consulates in:
Atlanta, Boston, Chicago, Houston, Los
Angeles, Miami, Montreal, New York,
Philadelphia, San Francisco, Toronto
For tourism information:
Israel Government Tourist Office
6380 Wilshire Boulevard
Los Angeles, CA 90048
323-658-7463
888-77-ISRAEL
www.goisrael.com
Other offices in:
Atlanta, Chicago, New York, Toronto

ITALY
P
For visa information:
Embassy of Italy
3000 Whitehaven Street, NW
Washington DC 20009
202-612-4400
www.ambwashingtondc.esteri.it
Consulates in:
Boston, Chicago, Detroit, Houston,
Los Angeles, Miami, New York,
Philadelphia, San Francisco, and others
For tourism information:

Italian Government Tourist Board
630 Fifth Avenue
New York, NY 10111
212-245-5618
www.italiantourism.com
Other offices in:
Chicago, Los Angeles, Toronto

IVORY COAST
(See Cote d'Ivoire)

JAMAICA
P ✈ **$**
For visa information:
Embassy of Jamaica
1520 New Hampshire Avenue, NW
Washington, DC 20036
202-452-0660
www.embassyofjamaica.org
Consulates in:
Chicago, Miami, New York
For tourism information:
Jamaica Tourist Board
5201 Blue Lagoon Drive
Miami, FL 33126
800-233-4JTB
www.visitjamaica.com
Other offices in:
Toronto

JAPAN
P ✈
For visa information:
Embassy of Japan
2520 Massachusetts Avenue, NW
Washington, DC 20008
202-238-6700
www.embjapan.org
Consulates in:
Anchorage, Atlanta, Boston, Chicago,
Detroit, Honolulu, Houston, Guam,
Kansas City (MO), Los Angeles,
Montreal, New Orleans, New York,
Portland (OR), San Francisco, Seattle,
Toronto, Vancouver
For tourism information:
Japan National Tourist Organization
One Rockefeller Plaza
New York, NY 10020
212-757-5640
www.japantravelinfo.com
Other offices in:
Los Angeles, Toronto

JORDAN
PV (6 months, $17)
For visa information:
Embassy of the Hashemite Kingdom of Jordan
3504 International Drive, NW
Washington, DC 20008
202-966-2861
www.jordanembassyus.org
Consulates in:
Lathrup Village (MI), New York, San Francisco
For tourism information:
Jordan Tourism Board
6867 Elm Street, Suite 102
McLean, VA 22101
877-733-5673
www.seejordan.org

KAZAKHSTAN
PV (90 days, $30-$60)
For visa information:
Embassy of the Republic of Kazakhstan
1401 16th Street, NW
Washington, DC, 20036
202-232-5488
www.kazakhembus.com
For tourism information:
www.kazakhembus.com/Tourism.html

KENYA
PV (6 months, $50) ✈ ✚
For visa information:
Embassy of Kenya
2249 R Street, NW
Washington, DC 20008
202-387-6101
www.kenyaembassy.com
Consulates in:
New York
For tourism information:
Kenya Tourist Office
6442 City West Parkway
Minneapolis, MN 55344
866-44-KENYA
www.magicalkenya.com

KIRIBATI
PV ✈ $
For visa information:
Consulate of the Republic of Kiribati
95 Nakolo Place, Room 265
Honolulu, HI 96819
808-834-6775
For tourism information:
www.visit-kiribati.com

KOREA (NORTH)
(Treasury Dept. license required for travel by U.S. citizens.)

KOREA (SOUTH)
P ✈
For visa information:
Embassy of the Republic of Korea
2320 Massachusetts Avenue, NW
Washington, DC 20008
202-939-5663
www.koreaembassyusa.org
Consulates in:
Atlanta, Boston, Chicago, Guam, Honolulu, Houston, Los Angeles, Montreal, New York, San Francisco, Seattle, Toronto, Vancouver
For tourism information:
Korea National Tourism Organization
2 Executive Drive
Fort Lee, NJ 07024
800-868-7567
kto.visitkorea.or.kr
Other offices in:
Los Angeles

KUWAIT
P ($12)
For visa information:
Embassy of the State of Kuwait
2940 Tilden Street, NW
Washington, DC 20008
202-966-0702
Consulates in:
New York

KYRGYZ REPUBLIC
PV (1 month, $80)
For visa information:
Embassy of the Kyrgyz Republic
2360 Massachusetts Avenue, NW
Washington, DC 20008
202-449-9822
www.kgembassy.org

LAOS
PV (30 days, $50) ✈ $
For visa information:
Embassy of the Lao People's Democratic Republic
2222 S Street, NW
Washington, DC 20008
202-667-0076
www.laoembassy.com
For tourism information:

*International
Tourist
Information*

www.visit-laos.com

LATVIA
P
For visa information:
Embassy of Latvia
2306 Massachusetts Avenue, NW
Washington, DC 20008
202-328-2840
www.latvia-usa.org
For tourism information:
www.latviatourism.lv

LEBANON
PV (1 month, $35)
For visa information:
Embassy of Lebanon
2560 28th Street, NW
Washington, DC 20008
202-939-6300
www.lebanonembassyus.org
Consulates in:
Detroit, Los Angeles, Montreal, New
York
For tourism information:
www.destinationlebanon.gov.lb

LESOTHO
P ✈ **$**
For visa information:
Embassy of the Kingdom of Lesotho
2511 Massachusetts Avenue, NW
Washington, DC 20008
202-797-5533
www.lesothoemb-usa.gov.ls
For tourism information:
www.seelesotho.com

LIBERIA
PV (3 months, $131) ✈ ✚
For visa information:
Embassy of the Republic of Liberia
5201 16th Street, NW
Washington, DC 20011
202-723-0437
www.embassyofliberia.org
Consulates in:
Atlanta, Chicago, Detroit, Los Angeles,
New Orleans, New York, Montreal,
Philadelphia, San Francisco

LIBYA
PV
For visa information:
Mission of Libya to the United Nations
309 East 48th Street
New York, NY 10017

212-752-5775
LIECHTENSTEIN
P
For visa information:
Embassy of the Principality of
Liechtenstein
888 17th Street, NW
Washington, DC 20006
202-331-0590
www.liechtenstein.li/en/fl-aussenstelle-
washington-home
For tourism information:
www.tourismus.li

LITHUANIA
P
For visa information:
Embassy of Lithuania
2622 16th Steet, NW
Washington, DC 20009
202-234-5860
www.ltembassyus.org
Consulates in:
Chicago, New York
For tourism information:
www.tourism.lt/en

LUXEMBOURG
P
For visa information:
Embassy of Luxembourg
2200 Massachusetts Avenue, NW
Washington, DC 20008
202-265-4171
www.luxembourg-usa.org
Consulates in:
New York, Montreal, San Francisco
For tourism information:
Luxembourg National Tourist Office
17 Beekman Place
New York, NY 10022
212-935-8888
www.visitluxembourg.com

MACAU
P
For visa information:
Embassy of the People's Republic of
China
2201 Wisconsin Avenue, NW
Washington, DC 20008
202-265-4171
For tourism information:
www.macautourism.gov.mo

MACEDONIA
P
For visa information:
Embassy of the Republic of Macedonia
1101 30th Street, NW
Washington, DC 20007
202-337-3063
Consulates in:
New York
For tourism information:
www.turizam.com.mk

MADAGASCAR
PV (90 days, $120) ✈ $ ✚
For visa information:
Embassy of Madagascar
2374 Massachusetts Avenue, NW
Washington, DC 20008
202-265-5525
Consulates in:
Berkeley (CA), New York, Philadelphia
For tourism information:
Contact the embassy.

MALAWI
P ✚
For visa information:
Embassy of Malawi
1029 Vermont Avenue, NW
Washington, DC 20005
202-721-0274
www.malawiembassy-dc.org
Consulates in:
New York
For tourism information:
www.malawiembassy-dc.org/Tourism.htm

MALAYSIA
P ✚
For visa information:
Embassy of Malaysia
3516 International Court, NW
Washington, DC 20008
202-328-2700
www.kln.gov.my/perwakilan/washington
Consulates in:
Los Angeles, New York
For tourism information:
www.tourism.gov.my

MALDIVES
P ✈ $
For visa information:
Embassy of the Maldives
8o0 Second Avenue
New York, NY 10017
212-599-6194
www.maldivesmission-ny.com/
For tourism information:
www.visitmaldives.com

MALI
PV (5 years, $131) ✈
For visa information:
Embassy of the Republic of Mali
2130 R Street, NW
Washington, DC 20008
202-332-2249
www.maliembassy.us

MALTA
P
For visa information:
Embassy of Malta
2017 Connecticut Avenue, NW
Washington, DC 20008
202-462-3611
Consulates in:
Carnegie (PA), Garden City (MI),
Houston, Independence (MO), New
York, Pompano Beach (FL), San
Francisco, St. Paul
For tourism information:
www.visitmalta.com

MARSHALL ISLANDS
P ✈ $ ✚
For visa information:
Embassy of the Republic of the Marshall
Islands
2433 Massachusetts Avenue, NW
Washington, DC 20008
202-234-5414
www.rmiembassyus.org
Consulates in:
Honolulu
For tourism information:
www.visitmarshallislands.com

MARTINIQUE
(See French West Indies.)

MAURITANIA
PV (3 months, $60) ✈ ✚
For visa information:
Embassy of the Republic of Mauritania
2129 Leroy Place, NW
Washington, DC 20008
202-232-5700

197

International Tourist Information

MAURITIUS
P ✈ $ ✚
For visa information:
Embassy of Mauritius
4301 Connecticut Avenue, NW
Washington, DC 20008
202-244-1491
www.maurinet.com/embasydc.html
For tourism information:
www.mauritius.net

MEXICO
P
For visa information:
Embassy of Mexico
1911 Pennsylvania Avenue, NW
Washington, DC 20006
202-736-1000
www.embassyofmexico.org
Consulates in:
Albuquerque, Atlanta, Austin, Chicago,
Dallas, Denver, Houston, Laredo,
Los Angeles, Miami, New Orleans,
New York, Phoenix, Puerto Rico, San
Antonio, and others
For tourism information:
Mexican Tourism Board
800-446-3942
www.visitmexico.com
Other offices in:
Houston, Montreal, Toronto

MICRONESIA
P ✈ $
For visa information:
Embassy of the Federated States of
Micronesia
1725 N Street, NW
Washington, DC 20036
202-223-4383
www.fsmembassydc.org
Consulates in:
Guam, Honolulu
For tourism information:
www.visit-fsm.org

MOLDOVA
P
For visa information:
Embassy of the Republic of Moldova
2101 S Street, NW
Washington, DC 20008
202-667-1130
www.embassyrm.org
For tourism information:

www.turism.md
MONACO
P
For visa information:
Consulate General of Monaco
565 Fifth Avenue
New York, NY 10017
212-286-0500
www.monaco-consulate.com
For tourism information:
Monaco Government Tourist
565 Fifth Avenue
New York, NY 10017
212-286-3330
www.visitmonaco.com

MONGOLIA
P ✈
For visa information:
Embassy of Mongolia
2833 M Street, NW
Washington, DC 20007
202-333-7117
www.mongolianembassy.us
Consulates in:
New York
For tourism information:
Mongolian Tourism Corporation
6 East 77th Street
New York, NY 10021
212-861-9460
www.travelmongolia.org

MONTENEGRO
P
For visa information:
Embassy of the Republic of Montenegro
1610 New Hampshire Avenue, NW
Washington DC 20009
202-234-6108
For tourism information:
www.visit-montenegro.com

MOROCCO
P
For visa information:
Embassy of the Kingdom of Morocco
1601 21st Street, NW
Washington, DC 20009
202-462-7979
Consulates in:
New York
For tourism information:
Moroccan National Tourist Office
Epcot Center, Box 22663
Lake Buena Vista, FL 32830

407-827-5337
www.tourisme-marocain.com

MOZAMBIQUE
PV (2 months, $20) **$**
For visa information:
Embassy of the Republic of Mozambique
1525 New Hampshire Avenue, NW
Washington, DC 20036
202-293-7146
www.embamoc-usa.org
Consulates in:
New York

MYANMAR
PV (3 months, $20)
For visa information:
Embassy of the Union of Myanmar
2300 S Street, NW
Washington, DC 20008
202-332-3344
www.mewashingtondc.com
Consulates in:
New York
For tourism information:
www.mewashingtondc.com/tourism.htm

NAMIBIA
P ✈ $
For visa information:
Embassy of Namibia
1605 New Hampshire Avenue, NW
Washington, DC 20009
202-986-0540
www.namibianembassyusa.org
For tourism information:
www.namibiatourism.com.na

NAURU
P ✈
For visa information:
Embassy of the Republic of Nauru
800 2nd Avenue
New York NY 10017
212-937-0004

NEPAL
PV (15 days, $25)
For visa information:
Royal Nepalese Embassy
2131 Leroy Place, NW
Washington, DC 20008
202-667-4550
www.nepalembassyusa.org
Consulates in:
New York

For tourism information:
www.welcomenepal.com

NETHERLANDS
P ✈ $
For visa information:
Royal Netherlands Embassy
4200 Linnean Avenue, NW
Washington, DC 20008
877-388-2443
www.netherlands-embassy.org
Consulates in:
Chicago, Los Angeles, Miami, Montreal,
New York, Toronto, Vancouver
For tourism information:
Netherlands Board of Tourism
355 Lexington Avenue
New York, NY 10017
212-370-7360
us.holland.com

NETHERLANDS ANTILLES
(Aruba, Bonaire, Curaçao, Saba, Statia,
St. Maarten)
P P ✈ $
For visa information:
Royal Netherlands Embassy
4200 Linnean Avenue, NW
Washington, DC 20008
877-388-2443
For tourism information:
Caribbean Tourism Organization
80 Broad Street
New York, NY 10004
212-635-9530
www.onecaribbean.org
(See also, Aruba, Bonaire, Curaçao)

NEW ZEALAND
P ✈ $
For visa information:
Embassy of New Zealand
37 Observatory Circle, NW
Washington, DC 20008
202-328-4800
www.nzembassy.com
Consulates in:
Los Angeles, New York, Vancouver
For tourism information:
Tourism New Zealand
501 Santa Monica Boulevard
Santa Monica, CA 90401
866-639-9325
www.purenz.com
Other offices in:
New York

NICARAGUA
P ✈
For visa information:
Embassy of Nicaragua
1627 New Hampshire Avenue, NW
Washington, DC 20009
202-939-6531
Consulates in:
Houston, Los Angeles, Miami, New
York, San Francisco
For tourism information:
www.intur.gob.ni

NIGER
PV (1 year, $100) ✈ $ ✚
For visa information:
Embassy of the Republic of Niger
2204 R Street, NW
Washington, DC 20008
202-483-4224
www.nigerembassyusa.org
For tourism information:
www.nigerembassyusa.org/travel.html

NIGERIA
PV (3 months, $20-$85) ✈ ✚
For visa information:
Embassy of the Federal Republic of
Nigeria
1333 16th Street, NW
Washington, DC 20036
202-986-8400
www.nigeriaembassyusa.org
Consulates in:
New York
For tourism information:
www.nigeriatourism.net

NIUE
P ✈
For visa information:
(See New Zealand)
For tourism information:
www.niueisland.com

NORFOLK ISLAND
PV
For visa information:
(See Australia)
For tourism information:
www.pitcairners.org

NORWAY
P
For visa information:

Royal Norwegian Embassy
2720 34th Street, NW
Washington, DC 20008
202-333-6000
www.norway.org
Consulates in:
Houston, Minneapolis, New York, San
Francisco
For tourism information:
Norwegian Tourist Board
655 Third Avenue
New York, NY 10017
212-885-9700
www.visitnorway.com

OMAN
PV (1 month, $36) ✈
For visa information:
Embassy of the Sultanate of Oman
2535 Belmont Road, NW
Washington, DC 20008
202-387-1980
www.omani.info
For tourism information:
www.omantourism.gov.om

PAKISTAN
PV ($124) ✈
For visa information:
Embassy of the Islamic Republic of
Pakistan
3517 International Court, NW
Washington, DC 20008
202-243-6500
www.pakistan-embassy.org
Consulates in:
Boston, Chicago, Houston, Los Angeles,
New York
For tourism information:
www.tourism.gov.pk

PALAU, REPUBLIC OF
P ✈
For visa information:
Republic of Palau Embassy
1700 Pennsylvania Avenue, NW
Washington, DC 20036
202-452-6814
www.palauembassy.com
For tourism information:
www.visit-palau.com

PANAMA
P TC (30 days, $10) ✈ $
For visa information:
Embassy of Panama

2862 McGill Terrace, NW
Washington, DC 20008
202-483-1407
www.embassyofpanama.org
Consulates in:
Honolulu, Houston, Miami, Montreal,
New Orleans, New York, Philadelphia,
San Diego, San Juan, Tampa
For tourism information:
www.visitpanama.com

PAPUA NEW GUINEA
PV (60 days, $25) ✈ **$**
For visa information:
Embassy of Papua New Guinea
1779 Massachusetts Avenue, NW
Washington, DC 20036
202-745-3689
www.pngembassy.org
Consulates in:
New York
For tourism information:
www.pngtourism.org.pg

PARAGUAY
PV (90 days, $45) **$** ✈
For visa information:
Embassy of Paraguay
2400 Massachusetts Avenue, NW
Washington, DC 20008
202-483-6960
www.embaparusa.gov.py
Consulates in:
Los Angeles, Miami, New York

PERU
P ✈
For visa information:
Embassy of Peru
1700 Massachusetts Avenue, NW
Washington, DC 20036
202-833-9860
www.peruvianembassy.us
Consulates in:
Boston, Chicago, Denver, Hartford, New
York, Paterson (NJ), San Francisco
For tourism information:
www.peru.info

PHILIPPINES
PV (3 months, $30) ✈ **$**
For visa information:
Embassy of the Philippines
1600 Massachusetts Avenue, NW
Washington, DC 20036
202-467-9300

www.philippineembassy-usa.org
Consulates in:
Chicago, Guam, Honolulu, Los Angeles,
New York, San Francisco, Toronto,
Vancouver
For tourism information:
Philippine Department of Tourism
556 Fifth Avenue
New York, NY 10036
212-575-7915
www.philippinetourism.us
Other offices in:
Chicago, Los Angeles, San Francisco

POLAND
P $
For visa information:
Embassy of the Republic of Poland
Consular Division
2224 Wyoming Avenue, NW
Washington, DC 20008
202-234-3800
www.polandembassy.org
Consulates in:
Chicago, Los Angeles, Montreal, New
York, Toronto, Vancouver
For tourism information:
Polish National Tourist Office
5 Marine View Plaza
Hoboken, NJ 07030
201-420-9910
www.poland.travel

PORTUGAL
P
For visa information:
Embassy of Portugal
2125 Kalorama Road, NW
Washington, DC 20008
202-328-8610
www.embassyportugal-us.org
Consulates in:
Boston, Montreal, New Bedford (MA),
Newark (NJ), New York, Providence,
San Francisco, Toronto, Vancouver
For tourism information:
Portugal Business Development Agency
590 Fifth Avenue
New York, NY 10036
646-723-0200
www.visitportugal.com

QATAR
PV (6 months, $131)
For visa information:
Embassy of the State of Qatar

*International
Tourist
Information*

202

*The Travel Agent's
Complete Desk
Reference*

2555 M Street, NW
Washington, DC 20037
202-274-1603
www.qatarembassy.net
Consulates in:
Houston
For tourism information:
www.experienceqatar.com

ROMANIA
P
For visa information:
Embassy of Romania
1607 23rd Street, NW
Washington, DC 20008
202-232-4747
www.roembus.org
Consulates in:
Chicago, Los Angeles, New York
For tourism information:
Romanian National Tourist Office
355 Lexington Avenue
New York, NY 10017
212-545-8484
www.romaniatourism.com

RUSSIA
PV (1 month, $131-$350) ✈
For visa information:
Embassy of Russia
Consular Section
2641 Tunlaw Road, NW
Washington, DC 20007
202-939-8907
www.russianembassy.org
Consulates in:
Houston, New York, San Francisco,
Seattle
For tourism information:
Russian National Tourist Office
224 West 30th Street
New York, NY 10001
877-221-7120
www.russia-travel.com

RWANDA
P ✚
Embassy of the Republic of Rwanda
1714 New Hampshire Avenue, NW
Washington, DC 20009
202-232-2882
www.rwandaembassy.org
Consulates in:
Northbrook (IL)
For tourism information:
www.rwandatourism.com

SAINT BARTS
(See French West Indies.)

SAINT KITTS AND NEVIS
P ✈
For visa information:
Embassy of St. Kitts and Nevis
3216 New Mexico Avenue, NW
Washington, DC 20016
202-686-2636
www.embassy.gov.kn
Consulates in:
New York
For tourism information:
St. Kitts and Nevis Tourist Board
414 East 75th Street
New York, NY 10021
800-582-6208
www.stkittstourism.kn

SAINT LUCIA
P ✈
For visa information:
Embassy of Saint Lucia
3216 New Mexico Avenue, NW
Washington, DC 20016
202-364-6792
Consulates in:
New York
For tourism information:
St. Lucia Tourist Board
800 Second Avenue
New York, NY 10017
800-456-3984
www.stlucia.org
Other offices in:
Toronto

SAINT MAARTEN
(See Netherlands Antilles)
For tourism information:
St. Maarten Tourist Bureau
675 Third Avenue
New York, NY 10017
800-786-2278
212-953-2084
www.st-maarten.com
Other offices in:
Toronto

SAINT MARTIN
(See French West Indies.)

SAINT VINCENT
P ✈ $

For visa information:
Embassy of Saint Vincent and the
Grenadines
3216 New Mexico Avenue, NW
Washington, DC 20016
202-364-6730
Consulates in:
New York
For tourism information:
St. Vincent Tourism Information
801 Second Avenue
New York, NY 10017
800-729-1726
www.svgtourism.com

SAMOA
P ✈

For visa information:
Independent State of Samoa Mission to
the United Nations
800 Second Avenue
New York, NY 10017
212-599-6196
For tourism information:
www.samoa.travel

SAN MARINO
P

For visa information:
Honorary Consulate of the Republic of
San Marino
1899 L Street, NW
Washington, DC 20036
202-223-3517
Consulates in:
Detroit, New York

SAO TOME AND PRINCIPE
PV (3 months, $65) ✚

For visa information:
Sao Tome and Principe Consulate
General
400 Park Avenue
New York, NY 10022
212-317-0533

SAUDI ARABIA
PV NT ✈ ✚

For visa information:
Royal Embassy of Saudi Arabia
601 New Hampshire Avenue, NW
Washington, DC 20037
202-944-3126
www.saudiembassy.net
Consulates in:
Houston, Los Angeles, New York

SENEGAL
P ✈ ✚

For visa information:
Embassy of the Republic of Senegal
2112 Wyoming Avenue, NW
Washington, DC 20008
202-234-0540
For tourism information:
Senegal Tourist Office
350 Fifth Avenue
New York, NY 10118
800-443-2527
www.senegal-tourism.com

SERBIA
P

For visa information:
Embassy of Serbia
2134 Kalorama Road, NW
Washington, DC 20008
202-332-0333
www.yuembusa.org
Consulates in:
Chicago
For tourism information:
www.serbia-tourism.org

SEYCHELLES
P ✈ **$**

For visa information:
Embassy of the Republic of Seychelles
800 Second Avenue, Suite 400
New York, NY 10017
212-687-9766
For tourism information:
Seychelles Tourist Office
820 Second Avenue
New York, NY 10017
212-687-9766
www.seychelles.travel

SIERRA LEONE
PV (1 year, $131) ✈ ✚

For visa information:
Embassy of Sierra Leone
1701 19th Street, NW
Washington, DC 20009
202-939-9261
www.embassyofsierraleone.org
For tourism information:
www.visitsierraleone.org

SINGAPORE
P ✈ **$**

For visa information:

*International
Tourist
Information*

Embassy of Singapore
3501 International Place, NW
Washington, DC 20008
202-537-3100
www.mfa.gov.sg/washington
Consulates in:
New York, San Francisco
For tourism information:
Singapore Tourism Board
1156 Avenue of the Americas
New York, NY 10036
212-302-4861
www.singapore.travel
Other offices in:
Chicago, Los Angeles, Toronto

SLOVAK REPUBLIC
P
For visa information:
Embassy of the Slovak Republic
3523 International Court, NW
Washington, DC 20008
202-237-1054
www.mzv.sk/washington
Consulates in:
New York
For tourism information:
www.slovakia.travel

SLOVENIA
P
For visa information:
Embassy of Slovenia
2410 California Street, NW
Washington, DC 20008
202-386-6601
washington.embassy.si
Consulates in:
Cleveland, New York
For tourism information:
www.slovenia.info

SOLOMON ISLANDS
P ✈ $
For visa information:
Solomon Islands Mission to the United
Nations
800 Second Avenue
New York, NY 10017
212-599-6192
www.commerce.gov.sb
For tourism information:
www.visitsolomons.com.sb

SOMALIA
P
For visa information:
Consulate of the Somali Democratic
Republic
425 East 61st Street
New York, NY 10021
212-688-9410

SOUTH AFRICA
P ✈ $
For visa information:
Embassy of South Africa
3051 Massachusetts Avenue, NW
Washington, DC 20008
202-232-4400
www.saembassy.org
Consulates in:
Chicago, Los Angeles, Montreal, New
York, Toronto
For tourism information:
South African Tourism Board
500 Fifth Avenue
New York, NY 10110
212-730-2929
www.southafrica.net

SPAIN
P
For visa information:
Embassy of Spain
2375 Pennsylvania Avenue, NW
Washington, DC 20037
202-452-0100
Consulates in:
Boston, Chicago, Houston, Los Angeles,
Miami, New Orleans, New York, San
Francisco, San Juan, Toronto
For tourism information:
Tourist Office of Spain
845 North Michigan Avenue
Chicago, IL 60611
312-642-1992
www.spain.info/us/tourspain
www.spain.travel
Other offices in:
Los Angeles, New York, Miami, Toronto

SRI LANKA
PV (3 months, $100) **✈ $**
For visa information:
Embassy of Sri Lanka
2148 Wyoming Avenue, NW
Washington, DC 20008
202-483-4025

www.slembassyusa.org
Consulates in:
Los Angeles, New York

SUDAN
PV (3 months, $150) ✈ $ ✚
For visa information:
Embassy of the Republic of the Sudan
2210 Massachusetts Avenue, NW
Washington, DC 20008
202-338-8565
www.sudanembassy.org
Consulates in:
New York

SURINAME
PV (1 year, $100) ✈
For visa information:
Embassy of the Republic of Suriname
4301 Connecticut Avenue, NW
Washington, DC 20008
202-244-7488
www.surinameembassy.org

SWAZILAND
P ✚
For visa information:
Embassy of the Kingdom of Swaziland
1712 New Hampshire Avenue, NW
Washington, DC 20009
202-234-5002
For tourism information:
www.welcometoswaziland.com

SWEDEN
P
For visa information:
Embassy of Sweden
1501 M Street, NW
Washington, DC 20005-1702
202-467-2600
www.swedenabroad.com
Consulates in:
Los Angeles, New York, San Francisco,
Toronto, Vancouver
For tourism information:
Swedish Travel and Tourism Council
P.O. Box 4649
New York, NY 10163-4649
212-885-9700
www.visit-sweden.com

SWITZERLAND
P
For visa information:
Embassy of Switzerland

2900 Cathedral Avenue, NW
Washington, DC 20008
202-745-7900
www.swissemb.org
Consulates in:
Atlanta, Chicago, Los Angeles,
Montreal, New York, San Francisco,
Toronto, Vancouver
For tourism information:
Switzerland Tourism
608 Fifth Avenue
New York, NY 10020
877-794-8037
www.myswitzerland.com

SYRIA
PV (3 months, $131) ✈
For visa information:
Embassy of the Syrian Arab Republic
2215 Wyoming Avenue, NW
Washington, DC 20008
202-232-6313
www.syrianembassy.us
Consulates in:
Houston
For tourism information:
www.syriatourism.org

TAHITI
(See French Polynesia)
For tourism information:
Tahiti Tourisme
300 Continental Boulevard
El Segundo, CA 90245
310-414-8484
www.gototahiti.com

TAIWAN
P ✈
For visa information:
Taipei Economic and Cultural
Representative
4201 Wisconsin Avenue, NW
Washington, DC 20016
202-895-1800
www.taiwanembassy.org/US
Other offices in:
Atlanta, Boston, Chicago, Guam,
Houston, Kansas City (MO), Los
Angeles, Miami, New York, San
Francisco, Seattle
For tourism information:
Taiwan Visitors Association
3731 Wilshire Boulevard
Los Angeles, CA 90010
626-802-7038

International Tourist Information

www.taiwan.net.tw
Other offices in:
New York, San Francisco

TAJIKISTAN
PV (2 weeks, $80) ✈
For visa information:
Embassy of the Republic of Tajikistan
1005 New Hampshire Avenue, NW
Washington, DC 20037
202-223-6090
www.tjus.org

TANZANIA
PV (6 months, $100) ✈ $
For visa information:
Embassy of Tanzania
2139 R Street, NW
Washington, DC 20008
202-939-6125
www.tanzaniaembassy-us.org
Consulates in:
New York
For tourism information:
Tanzania Tourist Board
205 East 42nd Street
New York, NY 10017
212-972-9160
www.tourismtanzania.go.tz

THAILAND
P
For visa information:
Royal Thai Embassy
1024 Wisconsin Avenue, NW
Washington, DC 20007
202-944-3600
www.thaiembdc.org
Consulates in:
Atlanta, Boston, Chicago, Coral Gables
(FL), Dallas, Denver, El Paso (TX),
Honolulu, Houston, Los Angeles,
Montgomery (AL), New Orleans, New
York, Portland (OR), Toronto, Vancouver
For tourism information:
Tourism Authority of Thailand
611 North Larchmont Boulevard
Los Angeles, CA 90004
323-461-9814
www.tourismthailand.org
Other offices in:
Chicago, New York

TOGO
PV (3 months, $131) ✈ ✚
For visa information:

Embassy of the Republic of Togo
2208 Massachusetts Avenue, NW
Washington, DC 20008
202-234-4212

TONGA
P ✈
Consulate General of Tonga
360 Post Street
San Francisco, CA 94108
415-781-0365
www.tongaconsul.com
For tourism information:
Tonga Visitors Bureau
360 Post Street
San Francisco, CA 94108
415-781-0365
www.tongaholiday.com

TRINIDAD AND TOBAGO
P ✈
For visa information:
Embassy of Trinidad and Tobago
1708 Massachusetts Avenue, NW
Washington, DC 20036
202-467-6490
www.ttembassy.org
Consulates in:
Miami, New York
For tourism information:
www.gotrinidadandtobago.com

TUNISIA
P ✈
For visa information:
Embassy of Tunisia
1515 Massachusetts Avenue, NW
Washington, DC 20005
202-862-1850
Consulates in:
New York, San Francisco
For tourism information:
Contact the embassy.
www.tourismtunisia.com
Other offices in:
Montreal

TURKEY
PV ($100)
For visa information:
Embassy of the Republic of Turkey
2525 Massachusetts Avenue, NW
Washington, DC 20008
202-612-6740
www.turkishembassy.org
Consulates in:

Chicago, Houston, Los Angeles, New York
For tourism information:
Turkish Government Tourism Office
2525 Massachusetts Avenue, NW
Washington, DC 20008
202-612-6800
www.tourismturkey.org
Other offices in:
New York, Los Angeles

TURKMENISTAN
PV (10 days, $51; 20 days, $71; up to 1 month, $91; longer stays available) ✈
For visa information:
Embassy of Turkmenistan
2207 Massachusetts Avenue, NW
Washington, DC 20008
202-588-1500
www.turkmenistanembassy.org
For tourism information:
Contact the embassy

TURKS AND CAICOS
(See British West Indies)
For tourism information:
Turks and Caicos Tourist Board
60 East 42nd Street
New York, NY 10165
646-375-8830
www.turksandcaicostourism.com
Other offices in:
Miami, Toronto

TUVALU
P ✈ **$**
For visa information:
(See United Kingdom.)

UGANDA
PV (3 months, $50) ✈ ✚
For visa information:
Embassy of the Republic of Uganda
5911 16th Street, NW
Washington, DC 20011
202-726-7100
www.ugandaembassy.com
Consulates in:
New York
For tourism information:
www.visituganda.com

UKRAINE
P
For visa information:
Embassy of Ukraine

3550 M Street, NW
Washington, DC 20007
202-333-0606
www.mfa.gov.ua/usa/en
Consulates in:
Chicago, New York, San Francisco
For tourism information:
www.ukraine.org/tourism.html

UNITED ARAB EMIRATES
P
For visa information:
Embassy of the United Arab Emirates
3522 International Court, NW
Washington, DC 20008
202-243-2400
www.uae-embassy.org
Consulates in:
New York
For tourism information:
Dubai Commerce and Tourism Board
8 Penn Center
Philadelphia, PA 19103
215-751-9750
www.dubaitourism.co.ae

UNITED KINGDOM
P
For visa information:
British Embassy
3100 Massachusetts Avenue, NW
Washington, DC 20008
202-588-6500
ukinusa.fco.gov.uk
Consulates in:
Atlanta, Boston, Chicago, Dallas, Denver, Houston, Los Angeles, Miami, New York, Orlando, Phoenix, San Francisco, Seattle
For tourism information:
British Tourist Authority
551 Fifth Avenue
New York, NY 10019
800-462-2748 (US)
888-847-4885 (Canada)
www.visitbritain.us

URUGUAY
P
For visa information:
Embassy of Uruguay
1913 I Street, NW
Washington, DC 20006
202-331-1313
www.uruwashi.org
Consulates in:

International Tourist Information

Chicago, Los Angeles, Miami, New York
For tourism information:
www.turismo.gub.uy

UZBEKISTAN
PV (3 months, $131) ✈
For visa information:
Embassy of the Republic of Uzbekistan
1746 Massachusetts Avenue, NW
Washington, DC 20036
202-887-5300
www.uzbekistan.org
Consulates in:
New York
For tourism information:
Uzbekistan Tourist Board
60 East 42nd Street
New York, NY 10165
212-983-0382
www.uzbektourism.uz

VANUATU
P ✈ **$**
For visa information:
Vanuatu Mission to the United Nations
42 Broadway
New York, NY 10004
212-425-9600
For tourism information:
www.vanuatutourism.com

VENEZUELA
P ✈ **$**
For visa information:
Embassy of Venezuela
1099 30th Street, NW
Washington, DC 20007
202-342-2214
www.embavenez-us.org
Consulates in:
Boston, Chicago, Houston, Miami, New
Orleans, New York, San Francisco, San
Juan
For tourism information:
Venezuelan Tourism Association
P.O. Box 3010
Sausalito, CA 94966
415-331-0100
www.think-venezuela.net

VIETNAM
PV (1 month, $65) ✈
For visa information:
Embassy of the Socialist Republic of
Vietnam
1233 20th Street, NW
Washington, DC 20037
202-861-0737
www.vietnamembassy-usa.org
For tourism information:
www.vietnamtourism.com

YEMEN
PV (3 months, $27) ✈ **$** ✚
For visa information:
Embassy of the Republic of Yemen
2319 Wyoming Avenue, NW
Washington, DC 20008
202-965-4760
www.yemenembassy.org
Consulates in:
New York
For tourism information:
www.yementourism.com

ZAIRE
(See Congo, Democratic Republic)

ZAMBIA
PV (3 years, $135) ✈ ✚
For visa information:
Embassy of the Republic of Zambia
2419 Massachusetts Avenue, NW
Washington, DC 20008
202-265-9717
www.zambiaembassy.org
For tourism information:
www.zambiatourism.com

ZIMBABWE
PV (90 days, $30) ✈ **$**
For visa information:
Embassy of Zimbabwe
1608 New Hampshire Avenue, NW
Washington, DC 20009
202-332-7100
www.zimbabwe-embassy.us
For tourism information:
www.zimbabwetourism.co.zw

Consortiums and co-ops offer small, independent agencies a chance to match the clout wielded by major chains and franchises. By pooling the selling power of a large number of small agencies, consortiums can provide the preferred pricing and commission overrides enjoyed by the "big boys."

Independent and home-based agents can take advantage of consortium buying power in two ways: by affiliating with a host agency that is a member of a consortium or by signing up directly with a consortium. Generally speaking, an independent agent must have minimum annual sales volume of anywhere from $500,000 to several million dollars before a consortium will be interested in working with him or her. Companies willing to work with home-based agents are indicated with an asterisk (*) in the listing below.

Definitions are somewhat slippery in this area. Some companies that present themselves as consortiums are, in fact, host agencies or franchises. The most noticeable distinction is that consortiums do not require a participating agency to change its name, while franchises most often require that the franchisee operate under the franchise's brand name. However, franchises and consortiums are similar in the access they provide to better commissions rates and, sometimes, better pricing. Franchises and hosts in the listing below are called out by bold italics.

While the major attraction in joining a consortium is the good deals you can get for both your clients and yourself, many consortiums offer additional benefits, such as marketing aids, sales training, and advertising. This is especially true of franchises.

ABC Corporate Services
6400 Shafer Court
Rosemont, IL 60018
800-722-5179
402-885-8900
www.abccst.com

*Cruise Holidays**
Carlson Parkway
P.O. Box 59159
Minneapolis, MN 55459-8207
800-866-7245
www.cruiseholidays.com

*Cruise Network Plus**
32614 Seven Mile Road
Livonia, MI 48152
800-478-7811
248-478-9696
248-478-9231 fax
www.cruisenetworkplus.com

*Cruise Planners**
3300 University Drive
Suite 602
Coral Springs, FL 33065
888-582-2150

954-344-0875 fax
www.cruiseagents.com
www.cruiseplanners.com

Cruise Shoppes America*
3323 West Commercial Boulevard
Suite 112
Ft. Lauderdale, FL 33309
877-391-3181
954-714-3260
877-391-3185 fax
www.cruiseshoppes.com

CruiseOne*
1415 NW 62nd Street
Suite 205
Ft. Lauderdale, FL 33309
800-892-3925
954-958-3703
www.cruiseonefranchise.com
www.cruiseone.com

Cruises, Inc.*
1415 NW 62nd Street
Suite 205
Ft. Lauderdale, FL 33309
877-714-4072
954-958-3697 fax
www.sellcruises.com

Ensemble Travel*
29 West 36th Street
New York, NY 10018
800-442-6871
212-545-7460
www.ensembledirect.com

eTravCo*
2171 Sandy Drive
Suite 110
State College, PA 16803
814-238-2860
814-231-0709 fax
www.e-travco.com

Hickory Travel Systems
(HTS Holdings)
Park 80 Plaza East
Saddle Brook, NJ 07663-5291
800-448-0350
201-843-0820
www.hickorytravelsystems.com

IT Group*
100 Executive Way
Suite 202
Ponte Vedra, FL 32802
888-482-4636
904-285-9794 fax
www.itgroupnetwork.com

MAST Vacation Partners (MVP)*
17 West 635 Butterfield Road
Suite 150
Oakbrook Terrace, IL 60181
630-889-9817
630-889-9832 fax
www.mvptravel.com

NEST*
(Network of Entrepreneurs Selling
     Travel)
243 South Street
Oyster Bay, NY 11771
888-245-6378
516-624-6378 fax
www.jointhenest.com

Oneminutebooking.com*
220 East Central Parkway
Suite 4010
Altamonte Springs, FL 32701
800-524-9109
407-667-8700
www.oneminutebooking.com

Radius
4330 East West Highway
Suite 1100
Bethesda, MD 20814-4408
301-718-9500
301-718-4290 fax
www.radiustravel.com

Results! Travel*
Carlson Parkway
P.O. Box 59159
Minneapolis, MN 55459-8207
888-523-2200
763-212-2302 fax
www.resultstravel.com

Riverside Travel Group
13343 SE Stark Street
Portland, OR 97233
800-772-2228
503-255-2950
www.riversidetravel.com

SeaMaster Cruises*
6442 City West Parkway
Eden Prairie, MN 55344
800-824-1481
www.seamastercruises.com

Signature Travel Network*
4640 Admiralty Way
Marina Del Rey, CA 90292
310-574-0883
310-574-0804 fax
www.signaturetravelnetwork.com

Thor Inc.
12202 Airport Way
Suite 150
Broomfield, CO 80021
303-439-4100
www.thor24.com

Travelsavers*
71 Audrey Avenue
Oyster Bay, NY 11771
800-366-9895
516-624-0500
www.travelsavers.com

Vacation.com*
1650 King Street
Suite 450
Alexandria, VA 22314
800-843-0733
703-548-6815 fax
www.joinvacation.com

Virtuoso*
500 Main Street
Suite 400
Fort Worth, TX 76102-3941
866-401-7974
817-870-0300
817-870-1050 fax
www.virtuoso.com

Consortiums

Travel Associations

There are many, many organizations that involve themselves with the travel industry in one way or another, as this list proves. Some represent travel agents, some represent suppliers, others represent business travelers who deal with travel agents and suppliers, some represent people who work in the travel industry, some provide services to the trade. Some are non-profit associations, some are for-profit corporations, some are government agencies.

There will probably be a number of associations and organizations listed here that you will want to contact for one reason or another — part of any trade organization's mission, after all, is to dispense information about its area of expertise to the general public. There may well be some organizations listed here that you will want to join.

Adventure Travel Society
332 West Sackett Avenue
Salida, CO 81201
719-530-0171
719-530-0172 fax
www.adventuretravel.com
This non-profit organization "promotes adventure travel and ecotourism while integrating responsible natural resource management."

Africa Travel Association (ATA)
347 Fifth Avenue
Suite 610
New York, NY 10016
212-447-1926
212-725-8253 fax
www.africa-ata.org
A "non-profit, nonpolitical" educational organization that promotes "the tourist attractions of the continent of Africa to the travel industry in North America."

Air Carriers Association of America
1500 K Street NW
Suite 250
Washington, DC 20005
202-639-7502
202-639-7505 fax

Air Line Pilots Association (ALPA)
1625 Massachusetts Avenue NW
Washington, DC 20036
202-797-4010
202-797-4052 fax
www.alpa.org
As a labor union, ALPA represents 59,000 pilots of 49 American airlines. It also works to promote airline safety.

Air Transport Association of America (ATA)
1301 Pennsylvania Avenue NW
Suite 1100
Washington, DC 20004-1707
202-626-4000
202-626-4181 fax

214

*The Travel Agent's
Complete Desk
Reference*

www.airlines.org
A lobbying and trade organization which represents the interests of the airline industry. "Its members collectively account for 97 percent of the revenue passenger miles flown in the United States and over 95 percent of the freight ton miles."

Airlines Reporting Corporation (ARC)
4100 North Fairfax Drive
Suite 600
Arlington, VA 22203
703-816-8000
703-816-8104 fax
www.arccorp.com
A separate corporate entity established by the major airlines to administer the accreditation of travel agencies, the collection of payments for fares, and the disbursement of commissions to agents.

Airports Council International, North America (ACI-NA)
1775 K Street NW
Suite 500
Washington, DC 20006
202-293-8500
202-331-1362 fax
www.aci-na.org
A membership organization representing "165 local, regional, and state governing bodies that own and operate the principal airports served by scheduled air carriers in the United States and Canada. ACI-NA member airports service more than 97 percent of the domestic and virtually all of the international air passenger traffic and cargo traffic in North America."

American Association for Nude Recreation (AANR)
1703 North Main Street
Suite E
Kissimmee, FL 34744
800-TRY-NUDE
407-933-2064
407-933-7577 fax
www.aanr.com
"A trusted source for nudist infor-mation on such topics as what to expect at a nudist club, a nudist resort, or even from a skinny dipping experience."

American Association of Golf Tour Operators (AAGTO)
14 East 38th Street
New York, NY 10016
212-986-9176
212-986-3270 fax
www.aagto.org

Association of Canadian Travel Agents (ACTA)
130 Albert Street
Suite 1705
Ottawa, ON K1P-5G4
CANADA
613-237-3657
613-237-7052 fax
www.acta.ca
"An industry-led, not-for-profit trade association representing the retail travel community and it's many stakeholders in Canada. Our membership includes travel agencies, tour operators, travel wholesalers, and suppliers such as, airlines, hotels, destination marketing organizations, cruise and rail lines, and automobile rental companies."

American Aid Society of Paris
2, Rue St. Florentin
75001 Paris
FRANCE
01-43-12-48-07
or 01-43-12-47-90
Provides aid, in the form of loans, to financially strapped Americans living or traveling in France.

American Association of Airport Executives (AAAE)
601 Madison Street
Alexandria, VA 22314
703-824-0500
703-820-1395 fax
www.airportnet.org
Represents those who manage "airports which enplane 99 percent of passengers in the United States."

American Automobile Association (AAA)
1000 AAA Drive
Heathrow, FL 32746-5063
407-444-8000
407-444-8030 fax
www.aaa.com
A vast membership organization providing services to and representing the

interests of the American motorist. AAA provides emergency road service, maps, guide books, and trip planning services.

American Bus Association (ABA)
700 13th Street
Suite 575
Washington, DC 20005-3934
800-283-2877
202-842-1645
202-842-0850 fax
www.buses.org
A trade association for the intercity bus industries in North America. "The oldest bus association in the United States."

American Car Rental Association (ACRA)
12324 East 86th Street North
Suite 130
Owasso, OK 74055-2543
888-200-2795
www.acraorg.com
"The Voice of the American Auto Rental Industry."

American Highway Users Alliance
601 Pennsylvania Avenue
North Building, Suite 540
Washington, DC 20004
202-857-1200 (voice and fax)
www.highways.org
An organization lobbying for new roads and better traffic patterns.

American Hotel and Lodging Association (AHLA)
1201 New York Avenue NW
Suite 600
Washington, DC 20005-3931
202-289-3100
202-289-3199 fax
www.ahma.com
"The largest national trade association for the U.S. hotel and lodging industry. AH&LA is comprised of 52 member state associations, including Washington, DC, and New York City." It lobbies federal legislators and offers services at the state level such as free legal and accounting services, employee benefit and workers' compensation discounts.

American Public Transit Association (APTA)
1666 K Street NW
Suite 1100
Washington, DC 20006
202-496-4800
202-496-4321 fax
www.apta.com
An international industry group representing more than 1,100 private businesses providing public transit. "More than 95 percent of the people who use transit in the U.S. and Canada are carried by APTA members."

American Recreation Coalition (ARC)
1225 New York Avenue NW
Suite 450
Washington, DC 20005
800-257-6370
202-682-9530
202-682-9529 fax
www.funoutdoors.com
A non-profit educational organization serving the recreation industry and recreation enthusiasts.

American Sightseeing International (ASI)
2727 Steeles Avenue West
Suite 301
Toronto, ON M3J 3G9
CANADA
866-399-0899
416-663-4495
416-663-4495 fax
A non-profit sales and marketing association for the sightseeing industry. Will help travel agents arranging multi-destination tours for groups by putting them in touch with appropriate suppliers. Complete worldwide services manual is now on the Internet.

American Society of Travel Agents (ASTA)
1101 King Street
Alexandria, VA 22314-2944
800-440-2782
703-739-2782
703-684-8319 fax
www.astanet.com
The largest travel trade organization with 26,000 members seeks "to enhance the professionalism and profitability of member agents through effective repre-

sentation ... education and training, and by identifying and meeting the needs of the traveling public."

American Tourism Society (ATS)
545 Madison Avenue
Suite 505
New York, NY 10022
212-893-8111
212-893-8153 fax
www.americantourismsociety.org
A non-profit association of travel agencies, tour operators and hotels promoting tourism between the United States and Russia, Central and Eastern Europe, and the Baltic and Nordic countries.

Assist Card International (ACI)
1001 Brickell Bay Drive
Suite 2302
Miami, FL 33131
800-874-2223
305-381-9959
305-375-8135 fax
Provides assistance for travelers from South America.

Association for the Promotion of Tourism to Africa (APTA)
21761 Via Del Lago
Trabuco Canyon, California 92679
949-400-9989
949-635-0110 fax
www.apta.biz
"It is the goal and purpose of APTA to promote tourism to the Continent of Africa and its Islands. APTA will seek to improve tourism to Africa through the education of its members."

Association of American Railroads (AAR)
50 F Street NW
Washington, DC 20001
202-639-2100
202-639-2558 fax
www.aar.org
A lobbying and research group representing the railroad industry. "AAR's corporate members haul 91 percent of the nation's rail carloads and 100 percent of the rail passengers."

Association of British Travel Agents (ABTA)
68-71 Newman Street
London, W1T 3AH
UNITED KINGDOM
011-44-(0)-20-7637-2444
011-44-(0)-20-7637-0713 fax
"The Association of British Travel Agents is the UK's Premier Trade Association for Tour Operators and Travel Agents. ABTA's 600 plus tour operators and 2300 travel agency companies have over 7000 offices and are responsible for the sale of more than 90% of UK-sold package holidays."

Association of Business Travellers
Suite A
Building 11
106 Old Pittwater Road
Brookvale
Sydney, N.S.W. 2100
AUSTRALIA
612-9905-7377
612-905-7744 fax
www.abt-travel.com
For business travelers, membership provides many benefits from a comprehensive free online hotel reservation service, discounts, exclusive benefits at hotels and many other benefits, domestic and worldwide.

Association of Certified Travel Agents (ACTA)
1209 Park Avenue
New York, NY 10128
212-427-6938
212-427-6931 fax
A non-profit travel trade school association.

Association of Corporate Travel Executives (ACTE)
515 King Street
Suite 340
Alexandria, VA 22314
800-375-2283
703-683-5322
703-683-2720 fax
www.acte.org
A professional association offering "educational and networking opportunities for those involved with the business travel industry."

Association of Flight Attendants (AFA)
1275 K Street NW
Suite 500
Washington, DC 20005
202-712-9799
202-712-9792 fax
www.afa.org
This labor union is "the collective bargaining agent for 50,000 flight attendants on 7 air carriers. AFA is the largest flight attendant union in the world."

Association of National Tourist Office Representatives (ANTOR)
P.O. Box 5017
Hove, East Sussex
BN23 3ZD
UNITED KINGDOM
011-44-870-241-9084
www.antor.com

Association of Retail Travel Agents (ARTA)
c/o Travel Destinations
4320 North Miller Road
Scottsdale, AZ 85251
800-969-6069
615--985-0600 fax
www.artaonline.com
A feisty trade and lobbying organization representing travel agents. "The Association that fights for the rights and dignity of travel."

Association of Travel Marketing Executives (ATME)
2005 Palmer Avenue
Suite 193
New York, NY 10538
800-526-0041
800-525-3087 fax
www.atme.org
"One-stop resource for travel marketing news, tips and trends."

Bank Travel
Salem, OH 44460
330-332-3841
330-337-1118 fax
www.banktravel.com
"The national organization for bank loyalty program directors."

Business Travel Coalition
214 Grouse Lane
Suite 210
Radnor, PA 19087
610-341-1850
www.btctravelogue.com

California Coalition of Travel Organizations (CCTO)
c/o Desmond & Desmond
925 L Street
Suite 220
Sacramento, CA 95814
916-441-4166
916-441-3520 fax
A government watchdog group and political action committee which seeks to ensure that the California legislature will enact laws "favorable" to the travel industry. They were instrumental in the passage of California's oppressive Sellers of Travel Law.

Canadian Institute of Travel Counsellors (CITC)
55 Eglinton Avenue East
Suite 209
Toronto, ON M4P 1G8
CANADA
800-589-5776
416-484-4450
416-484-4140 fax
www.citc.ca
The Canadian equivalent of The Travel Institute

Caribbean Hotel Association (CHA)
1000 Ponce de León Avenue
San Juan, PR 00907-1672
787-725-9139
787-725-9108 fax
www.caribbeanhotels.org
A marketing organization which promotes the tourism interests of the entire Caribbean area.

Caribbean Tourism Organization (CTO)
80 Broad Street
32nd Floor
New York, NY 10004
212-635-9530
212-635-9511 fax
www.doitcaribbean.com
This association promotes travel and tourism to the Caribbean area as a whole.

Center for Responsible Tourism (CRT)
1765 D Leroy Avenue
Berkeley, CA 94709
510-540-0742
CRT seeks "to open the minds of North American travelers toward an appreciation of cultural and environmental differences and encourage their use of responsible alternate forms of travel."

Central Ohio Travel Professionals
c/o McMurray Travel Service
787-C South State Street
Westerville, OH 43081
614-899-1979
614-899-1970 fax
www.mcmurraytravel.com
A professional educational, networking, and support group for travel professionals in the central Ohio region, including outside sales reps.

Citizens Emergency Center
U.S. State Department
2201 C Street NW
Room 4811
Washington, DC 20520
202-647-5225
202-647-6201 fax
Acts as a liaison between Congress and citizens overseas, providing assistance in cases of illness, legal problems, and destitution of Americans traveling abroad. Also issues periodic Consular Information Sheets (formerly called "Travel Advisories") alerting the public to potential dangers and hazards in foreign countries.

Commercial Travelers Association (CTA)
P.O. Box 76400
Atlanta, GA 30358-1400
800-392-2856
770-993-1155
Representing the "average business traveler," CTA describes itself as "a non-profit contract negotiation and advocacy group." It is seeking, among other things, to end the airlines' requirement of a Saturday stay-over to qualify for the lowest fares.

Community Marketing, Inc.
584 Castro Street
PMB 834
San Francisco, CA 94114
415-437-3800
www.communitymarketinginc.com
A gay and lesbian marketing organization with a subspecialty in travel marketing. Publishes an annual *Gay and Lesbian Travel Industry Directory*.

Council on International Educational Exchange (CIEE)
3 Copley Place
2nd Floor
Boston, MA 02116
888-268-6245
617-247-0350
617-247-2911 fax
www.councilexchanges.org
An information clearinghouse and sponsoring organization for student travel and international student exchanges.

Cruise Lines International Association (CLIA)
80 Broad Street
Suite 1800
New York, NY 10004
212-921-0066
212-921-0549 fax
www.cruising.org
An organization sponsored by the cruise industry, providing training and marketing support to travel agents. Works with nearly 20,000 affiliated travel agencies.

Department of Commerce
International Trade Administration
Trade Development, Tourism Industries
Room 1860
14th Street & Constitution Avenue NW
Washington, DC 20230
202-482-4028
202-482-2887 fax
This office has taken over some of the functions of the defunct United States Travel and Tourism Administration.

Department of Transportation (DOT)
400 7th Street SW
Room 3248
Washington, DC 20590
202-366-4000
202-488-7876 fax
The United States government agency responsible for handling consumer complaints about the travel industry.

Dive Travel Industry Association (DTIA)
27041 SW 119 Court
Miami, FL 33032
305-257-2072 fax
A trade group that promotes dive travel, that is, travel for the purposes of scuba diving. Yearly dues are $25.

Dude Ranchers' Association (DRA)
P.O. Box 2307
Cody, WY 82414
307-587-2339
307-587-2776 fax
www.duderanch.org
A non-profit association that offers a wealth of information about dude ranch vacations, employment, merchandise and travel services for 12 states as well as Alberta and British Columbia.

East Asia Travel Association (EATA)
c/o Japan National Tourist Organization
One Rockefeller Plaza
Suite 1250
New York, NY 10020
212-757-5640
212-307-6754 fax
www.japantravelinfo.com
A marketing association which promotes travel to its member countries — Japan, Korea, Hong Kong, Macau, Thailand, and Taiwan.

Elderhostel
11 Avenue de Lafayette
Boston, MA 02111-1746
877-426-8056 (toll-free)
877-426-2166 fax
www.elderhostel.org
Elderhostel sponsors educational travel programs for senior citizens with accommodations provided by colleges and universities worldwide.

European Travel Commission (ETC)
c/o Donald N. Martin Company
One Rockefeller Plaza
Suite 214
New York, NY 10020
212-208-1200
212-218-1205 fax
www.visiteurope.com
This association promotes travel and tourism to Europe and provides information to U.S. media.

Federal Aviation Administration (FAA)
APA 200 - FAA
800 Independence Avenue SW
Washington, DC 20591
800-322-7873
202-366-2220
www.faa.gov
"The FAA is the element of the U.S. government with primary responsibility for the safety of civil aviation."

Florida-Caribbean Cruise Association (FCCA)
11200 Pines Boulevard
Suite 201
Pembroke Pines, FL 3302
954-441-8881
954-441-3171 fax
A trade association of cruise lines "created to discuss and exchange views on issues relating to legislation, tourism development, ports, safety, security and other cruise industry issues."

Globetrotters' Club
BCM/Roving
London WC1N 3XX
United Kingdom
www.globetrotters.co.uk
A club for those interested in "economical international travel and opportunities to meet people of other countries."

Greater New Orleans Black Tourism Network
2020 St. Charles Avenue
New Orleans, LA 70130-5139
800-725-5652
504-523-5652
504-522-0785 fax
www.soulofneworleans.com
Functions like a convention and visitors bureau, providing tourist information to visitors with an interest in African-American culture.

Group Leaders of America (GLAMER)
P.O. Box 129
Salem, OH 44460
800-628-0993
330-337-1027
330-337-1118 fax
www.glamer.com
"The only national organization for leaders of traveling senior groups" with a membership of 38,000.

Helicopter Association International (HAI)
1635 Prince Street
Alexandria, VA 22314
703-683-4646
703-683-4745 fax
www.rotor.com
A trade association "dedicated to promoting the helicopter as a safe and efficient method of transportation."

Hospitality Sales and Marketing Association International (HSMAI)
8201 Greensboro Drive
Suite 300
McLean, VA 22102
703-610-9024
703-610-9005 fax
www.hsmai.org
An educational and informational association servicing the hotel industry. Seeks to educate hotel executives "to better service hotel users."

Hotel Electronic Distribution Network Association (HEDNA)
7600 Leesburg Pike
Suite 430
Falls Church, VA 22043
703-970-2052
703-970-4488 fax
www.hedna.org
HEDNA is a trade association of more than 100 member companies that seeks to "promote the use of electronic distribution systems for hotel reservation sales . . . enhance automated applications and use [and] provide support to members on electronic distribution functionality and operational issues."

InterAmerican Travel Agents Society
c/o CWT Almeda Travel
450 Meyerland Plaza
Suite 96
Houston, TX 77096
800-992-5112
713-592-8000
713-592-8080 fax
www.almedatravel.com
An association of some 300 minority travel agents founded in 1953. Seeks to assist minorities in increasing their business.

International Airline Passengers Association (IAPA)
P.O. Box 700188
Dallas, TX 75370-0188
800-821-4272
972-404-9980
972-233-5348 fax
www.iapa.com
A membership organization "dedicated to the concerns and safety of frequent travelers." IAPA helps members resolve problems with suppliers, runs a full-service travel agency, and publishes Travel Safety Alert.

International Air Transport Association (IATA)
International Airlines Travel Agent Network (IATAN)
800 Place Victoria
Suite 800
P.O. Box 123
Montreal, Quebec
CANADA H42 1C3
514-844-6311
514-844-5286 fax
U.S. Office:
300 Garden City Plaza
Suite 342
Garden City, NY 11530
800-294-2826
516-663-6000
516-747-4462 fax
www.iatan.org
This association, founded by a consortium of international airlines, administers the codes which identify all the world's airports and air carriers. They also certify travel agencies and issue an identification card which has become the de facto mark of the "professional travel agent."

International Association for Medical Assistance to Travellers (IAMAT)
417 Center Street
Lewiston, NY 14092-3633
716-754-4883
519-836-3412 fax
www.iamat.org
A membership association that provides members with access to medical care around the world at fixed rates. With sufficient notice, members can contact IAMAT and receive a wide variety of health-related information. Their

information is especially helpful on the health hazards of foreign countries to which your clients might be traveling. Membership is free, although donations are welcomed.

International Association of Amusement Parks and Attractions
1448 Duke Street
Alexandria, VA 22314
703-836-4800
703-836-9678 fax
www.iaapa.org
Represents the amusement industry and services.

International Association of Conference Centers (IACC)
243 North Lindbergh Boulevard
St. Louis, MO 63141
314-993-8575
314-993-8919 fax
www.iacconline.org
"IACC is a not-for-profit association whose mission is to promote a greater awareness of conference centers as a distinct and unique segment of the training, education, hospitality and travel industries."

International Association of Convention and Visitor Bureaus (IACVB)
2025 M Street NW
Suite 500
Washington, DC 20036-4990
202-296-7888
202-296-7889 fax
www.iacvb.org
Promotes "an awareness of the convention and visitor industry's contribution to communities around the world." Works to improve professionalism within the industry.

International Association of Fairs and Expositions
P.O. Box 985
Springfield, MO 65801
417-862-5771
417-862-0156 fax
www.iafenet.org
The trade association for the agricultural fair industry.

International Association of Tour Managers
397 Walworth Road
London SE17 2AW
UNITED KINGDOM
011-44-171-703-9154
011-44-171-703-0358 fax

International Council of Cruise Lines (ICCL)
2111 Wilson Boulevard
8th Floor
Arlington, VA 22201
800-595-9338
703-522-8463
703-522-3811 fax
www.iccl.org
A trade organization founded to fight perceived government over-regulation of the cruise industry. "ICCL membership represents the interests of 15 passenger cruise lines in the North American cruise market and a growing number of important cruise industry strategic business partners."

International Council of Tourism Partners (ICTP)
P.O. Box 208
Haleiwa, HI 96712-0208
www.tourismpartners.org
Describes itself as "a worldwide force of socially responsible tourism and travel professionals." The organization supports "fair tourism trade, disaster relief, [and] sustainable tourism" among other initiatives. Fifteen percent of membership dues goes to the "UN programme on HIV Aids."

International Council on Hotel, Restaurant and Institutional Education (CHRIE)
2613 North Parham Road
2nd Floor
Richmond, VA 23294
804-346-4800
804-346-5009 fax
www.chrie.org
A non-profit educational association which brings together educational institutions offering degrees in the hospitality industry with representatives of the industry they serve. CHRIE seeks to "establish an accreditation process for education programs and identify

Travel Associations

skills standards or outcomes required for success in positions throughout the industry," which is broadly defined as comprising the food, lodging, travel and tourism segments.

International Culinary Tourism Association (ICTA)
4110 SE Hawthorne Boulevard
Suite 440
Portland, OR 97214
503-750-7200
www.culinarytourism.org
An association that helps the food and beverage industry, destinations, and travel professionals "promote their culinary treasures as marketable and sellable attractions."

The International Ecotourism Society
733 15th Street NW
Suite 1000
Washington, DC 20005
202-347-9203
202-387-7915 fax
www.ecotourism.org
An international non-profit organization that strives to make tourism a viable tool for conservation and sustainable development.

International Festivals and Events Association
2601 Eastover Terrace
Boise, ID 83706
208-433-0950
208-433-9812 fax
www.ifea.com
A professional development and educational group serving the sponsored and special events industry. "Membership ranges from the Kentucky Derby Festival . . . to the Barbecue Goat Cook-off in Brady, TX."

International Forum of Travel and Tourism Advocates (IFTTA)
2107 Van Ness Avenue
Suite 200
San Francisco, CA 94109-2572
415-673-3333
415-673-3548 fax
www.travellaw.com
This association of lawyers and travel professionals provides information, to its members and others, about legisla-

tion and regulations affecting the travel industry. It seeks to "foster research on the legal aspects of travel and tourism [and] foster a spirit of collegiality amongst the members."

International Gay and Lesbian Travel Association (IGLTA)
4331 North Federal Highway
Suite 304
FT. Lauderdale, FL 33308
800-448-8550
954-776-2626
954-776-3303 fax
www.iglta.org
IGTA is "dedicated to encouraging and assisting in the promotion of gay and lesbian travel. Membership is open to all travel and travel-related businesses."

International Hotel & Restaurant Association (IH&RA)
251, rue Jean Jacques Rousseau
75010 Paris
FRANCE
011-33-1-4488-9220
011-33-1-4488-9230 fax
An association of hotel associations, hotel chains, and individuals from 140 countries. "Works to raise the standards and reputation of the international hotel industry."

International Institute for Peace Through Tourism
Fox Hill
13 Cottage Club Road
Stowe, VT 05672
802-253-2658
802-253-2645 fax
www.iipt.org
This non-profit organization is "dedicated to fostering and facilitating tourism initiatives which contribute to international understanding and cooperation, an improved quality of environment, the preservation of heritage, and through these initiatives, helping to bring about a peaceful and sustainable world."

International Society of Travel Medicine (ISTM)
2386 Clower Street
Suite A-102
Snellville, GA 30078
770-736-7060

770-736-0313 fax
www.istm.org
The ISTM "is committed to the promotion of healthy and safe travel."

International Society of Travel and Tourism Educators (ISTTE)
23220 Edgewater
ST. Claire Shores, MI 48082
586-294-0208 (voice & fax)
www.istte.org
An association of those teaching and providing training in and to the tourism industry.

International Special Events Society
401 North Michigan Avenue
Chicago, IL 60611-4267
800-688-4737
312-321-6853
312-673-6953 fax
www.ises.com
An organization of the many different professionals who contribute to the special events industry — "from festivals to trade shows" — with a mission to "educate, advance and promote the special events industry and its network of professionals along with related industries."

Long Island Travel Agents
c/o Here and There Travel
1249 Melville Road
Farmingdale, NY 11735
516-777-1790
516-777-1791 fax
www.litaa.com
A regional association of approximately 125 -owners of local retail travel agencies.

Meeting Professionals International (MPI)
4455 LBJ Freeway
Suite 1200
Dallas, TX 75244
972-702-3000
972-702-3070 fax
www.mpiweb.org
A trade association for those who organize meetings and conventions and the companies that supply them.

Metropolitan Association of Professional Travel Agents (MAPTA)
337 West 57th Street
Suite 151
New York, NY 10019
212-332-1256
212-332-1251 fax
A continuing education and networking association of travel industry professionals in the metropolitan New York area.

Midwest Agents Selling Travel (MAST)
17 West 635 Butterfield Road
Oakbrook Terrace, IL 60181
800-762-9657
630-889-9817
630-889-9832 fax
www.mast.org
A regional association of travel agencies that promotes "professionalism and ethical conduct in the travel agency industry" and provides "educational programs for travel agents on industry issues."

Mobility International USA (MIUSA)
P. O. Box 10767
Eugene, OR 97440
541-343-1284
541-343-6812 fax
www.miusa.com
This non-profit membership organization, affiliated with Mobility International in Belgium, seeks to "promote and facilitate opportunities for people with disabilities to participate in international educational exchange and travel."

National Academy Foundation
39 Broadway
Suite 1640
New York, NY 10006
212-635-2400
212-635-2409 fax
www.naf-education.org
A non-profit organization that develops travel career prep programs for high school students.

National Air Carrier Association (NACA)
1000 Wilson Boulevard
Suite 1700
Arlington , VA 22209
703-358-8060
"NACA represents U.S. certificated

Travel
Associations

airlines which specialize in low-cost scheduled and charter services . . . in domestic and international markets."

National Air Transportation Association (NATA)
4226 King Street
Alexandria, VA 22302
800-808-6282
703-845-9000
703-845-8176 fax
www.nata-online.aero
A lobbying organization representing "the business interests of the aviation service industry." Members are "general aviation service companies providing fueling, flight training, maintenance and repair, and on-demand charter service by more than 1,700 member companies with more than 100,000 employees."

National Association of Commissioned Travel Agents (NACTA)
1101 King Street
Alexandria, VA 22314
703-739-6826
703-739-6861 fax
www.nacta.com
Formed in 1990 to "furnish a voice in the industry for independent agents." Publishes a quarterly newsletter, offers fam trips, group insurance, and other benefits for its membership.

National Association of Cruise Only Agencies (NACOA)
7600 Red Road
Suite 126
South Miami. FL 33143
305-663-5626
305-663-5625 fax
www.nacoaonline.com
"A non-profit trade association ... founded in 1985 to provide a forum to address the needs and concerns of cruise only agencies." Open to full-service agencies and independent contractors, NACOA offers educational and networking opportunities as well as errors and omissions insurance.

National Association of Railroad Passengers
900 Second Street NE
Suite 308
Washington, DC 20002

202-408-8362
202-408-8287 fax
www.narprail.org
A non-profit educational group founded in 1967 that seeks to increase government spending for rail transportation to create a more balanced mix of transportation alternatives.

National Association of RV Parks and Campgrounds (ARVC)
113 Park Avenue
Falls Church, VA 22046
703-241-8801
703-241-1004 fax
www.gocampingamerica.com
The only national association representing commercial RV parks and campgrounds in the U.S. More than 3,500 members nationwide.

National Association of Senior Travel Planners
44 Cushing Street
P.O. Box 212
Hingham, MA 02043
617-740-1185
617-749-4099 fax
An association of "pied pipers" and others who plan travel for senior citizens.

National Business Travel Association (NBTA)
110 North Royal Street
4th Floor
Alexandria, VA 22314
703-684-0836
703-684-0263 fax
www.nbta.org
A lobbying and educational organization servicing corporate business travel managers who are "responsible for over 70% of the $185 billion spent each year on business travel and entertainment."

National Council of Area and Regional Tourism Organizations
1004 Main Street
Stroudsburg, PA 18360
717-421-5791
717-421-6927 fax

National Council of Travel Attractions
Six Flags Fiesta Texas
17000 I-10 West
San Antonio, TX 78257

800-697-4258
210-697-5457
210-697-5444

National Council of Urban Tourism
Organizations
P.O. Box 4270
Anaheim, CA 92803
714-991-8963 fax

National Golf Foundation (NGF)
1150 South US Highway 1
Suite 401
Jupiter, FL 33477
800-733-6006
561-744-6006
561-744-6107 fax
www.ngf.org
The major trade association of the golf
industry. Members comprise facilities,
manufacturers and turf companies.

National Motorcoach Network, Inc.
Patriot Square
10527C Braddock Road
Fairfax, VA 22032
888-733-5287
703-250-7897
703-250-1477 fax
www.motorcoach.com
A for-profit marketing support group of
"leading independent motorcoach operators throughout the United States."
Publishes the National Motorcoach
Directory and Byways magazine. Operates a national reservation center for
motorcoach charter.

National Park Foundation
11 DuPont Circle NW
Suite 600
Washington, DC 20036
202-238-4200
202-234-3180 fax
www.nationalparks.org
The National Park Foundation describes itself as "the official non-profit
partner of the National Park Service." It
awards "more than $2 million in grants
each year to support education, visitor
services, volunteer activities," and other
services for the Parks.

National Tour Association (NTA)
546 East Main Street
Lexington, KY 40508

800-682-8886
859-226-4444
859-226-4447 fax
www.ntaonline.com
Trade association of tour operators
offering packaged travel vacations,
as well as tour suppliers and destination marketing organizations. Offers a
Consumer Protection Plan that protects
travelers in the case of a tour operator's
bankruptcy.

National Travel and Tourism Awareness
Council
1133 21st Street NW
Suite 800
Washington, DC 20036
202-293-1433
An industry coalition which promotes
and publicizes the economic contribution of travel and tourism.

National Trust for Historic Preservation
(NTHP)
1785 Massachusetts Avenue NW
Washington, DC 20036
800-944-6847
202-588-6000
202-588-6038 fax
www.nthp.org
A non-profit membership organization
leading the national preservation movement. The NTHP funds preservation
activities and operates historic house
museums.

Niche Cruise Marketing Alliance
(NCMA)
12920 NE 32nd Place
Bellevue, WA 98005
425-867-0399
425-867-0589
www.nichecruise.com
"A collection of cruise lines [that seeks]
to increase awareness about the concept
of niche cruises [and] to get the message
out [about] exciting alterna-tives to the
standard Caribbean cruise or the typical
mass-market cruise."

NorthWest Cruise ship Association
(NWCA)
100 - 1111 West Hastings Street
Vancouver, BC V6E 2J3
CANADA
604-681-9515

*Travel
Associations*

604-681-4364 fax
www.nwcruiseship.org
A non-profit trade association representing cruise lines that serve the Pacific Northwest, Canada, Alaska, and Hawaii.

Organization of Accredited Travel Hosts (OATH)
No contact information available
www.oathtravel.com
"For all your travel needs-hotels, airfare, car rentals and vacation rentals."

Pacific Asia Travel Association (PATA)
1611 Telegraph Avenue
Suite 550
Oakland, CA 94612
510-625-2055
510-625-2044 fax
www.pata.org
A trade organization which promotes travel and tourism to the nations of the Pacific Rim.

Partners in Responsible Tourism (PIRT)
P.O. Box 237
San Francisco, California 94104-0237
415-675-0420
www.pirt.org
A network of individuals and representatives of tourism companies who are concerned about the impact of tourism and tourism development on local environments and cultures, particularly those of indigenous peoples.

Passenger Vessel Association (PVA)
801 N Quincy Street
Suite 200
Arlington, VA 22203
703-807-0100
703-807-0103 fax
www.p-v-a.com
A trade association representing American-owned tour boats.

Pegasus Fear of Flying Foundation
8 Horseshoe Trail
Suite 384
Barnardsville, NC 28709
800-332-7668
828-332-7668
828-626-3061 fax
www.pegasus-fear-fly.com

Recreation Vehicle Dealers Association of North America (RVRA)
3930 University Drive
Fairfax, VA 22030-2515
800-336-0355
703-591-7130
703-591-0734 fax
www.rvda.org
An association of RV dealers who rent vehicles to the consumer.

Recreational Vehicle Industry Association (RVIA)
1896 Preston White Drive
P.O. Box 2999
Reston, VA 20195-0999
800-GO-RVING
703-620-6003
703-620-5071 fax
www.rvia.org
The trade association for RV manufacturers and parts suppliers. RVIA provides industry statistics to government and promotes RV travel to the general public.

Regional Airline Association (RAA)
2025 M Street NW
Suite 800
Washington, DC 20036-3309
202-367-1170
202-367-2170 fax
www.raa.org
A trade association representing "airlines engaged in short and medium haul scheduled airline transportation of passengers and cargo, as well as suppliers of products and services for the industry."

RV Rental Association
3930 University Drive
Fairfax, VA 22030
800-336-0355
703-591-7130
703-359-0152 fax
www.rura.org
A division of the RV Dealers Association, this organization represents companies that rent and lease recreational vehicles for a variety of uses including tourism.

Society for Accessible Travel & Hospitality (SATH)
347 Fifth Avenue
Suite 610

New York, NY 10016-5010
212-447-7284
212-725-8253 fax
www.sath.org
An association promoting the needs and interests of disabled travelers. Provides information on facilities available to the disabled in foreign countries.

Society of American Travel Writers (SATW)
4101 Lake Boone Trail
Suite 201
Raleigh, NC 27607
919-787-5181
919-787-4916 fax
www.satw.org
A professional organization for published travel writers. Conducts continuing education programs and upholds the standards of the profession.

Society of Corporate Meeting Professionals (SCMP)
217 Ridgemont Avenue
San Antonio, TX 78209
210-822-6522
210-822-9838 fax
www.scmp.org
A networking and professional development association for those in the meeting planning and convention services field.

Society of Incentive Travel Executives (SITE)
21 West 38th Street
401 North Michigan Avenue
Chicago, IL 60611
312-321-5148
312-527-6783 fax
www.site-intl.org
Provides "a network, research, professional development and ethics" to the $5 billion incentive travel industry. Members range from travel agents, to official tourist organizations, to incentive houses, and cruise lines.

Society of Government Travel Professionals (SGTP)
6935 Wisconsin Avenue NW
Suite 200
Bethesda, MD 20815-6109
301-654-8595
301-654-6663 fax

www.government-travel.org
SGTP describes itself as "a non-profit educational forum [of] travel agencies, suppliers, federal and other government travel managers and contractors throughout the U.S." Government travel is a $22.5 billion market, according to SGTP.

Student & Youth Travel Association (SYTA)
936 South Baldwin Road
Suite 104
Clarkston, MI 48348
248-814-7982
248-814-7150 fax
www.syta.com
SYTA is the non-profit, professional trade association that promotes student & youth travel and seeks to foster integrity and professionalism among student and youth travel service providers.

Tourism Industry Association of Canada (TIAC)
803-130 Albert Street
Ottawa, ON K1P 5G4
CANADA
613-238-3883
613-238-3878 fax
www.tiac-aitc.ca
A lobbying group representing the interests of the tourism industry to all levels of Canadian government.

Trade Show Exhibitors Association (TSEA)
2301 South Lake Shore Drive
Suite 1105
Chicago, IL 60616
312-842-8732
312-842-8744 fax
www.tsea.org
An association "representing exhibit marketing managers domestically and abroad." Offers educational and informational services, sponsors a certification program and an annual trade show.

Travel Agents of the Carolinas
P.O. Box 99398
Raleigh, NC 27624-9398
919-359-1590
919-676-8211 fax
A regional association of travel agencies.

Travel Associations

Travel and Tourism Research Association (TTRA)
P.O. Box 2133
Boise, ID 83701
208-429-9511
208-429-9512 fax
www.ttra.com
TTRA is comprised of "providers and users of travel and tourism research to the travel and tourism industry." It "advocates standards and promotes the application of quality travel and tourism research and marketing information."

Travel Business Roundtable
1100 New York Avenue NW
Suite 450
Washington, DC 20005
202-408-2137
202-408-1255 fax
www.tbr.org
A "strategic partner" of TIA that lobbies Congress on issues of importance to the travel industry.

Travel Industry Association of America (TIA)
1100 New York Avenue NW
Suite 450
Washington, DC 20005-3934
202-408-8422
202-408-1255 fax
www.tia.org
Promotes travel to and within the United States. Membership consists of hotels, attractions, state travel councils, and other members of the travel industry. Publishes a useful series of special reports and directories.

The Travel Institute
148 Linden Street
P.O. Box 812059
Wellesley, MA 02482
800-542-4282
781-237-0280
781-237-3860 fax
www.icta.com
Formerly, the Institute of Certified Travel Agents (ICTA), The Travel Institute is an international non-profit organization dedicated to educating and certifying travel industry professionals. Administers the Certified Travel Counselor (CTC), Certified Travel Associate (CTA) and Destination Specialist (DS) pro-

grams. Also administers the TAP test.

Travel Professionals of Color (TPOC)
P.O. Box 39895
Denver, CO 80239
866-901-1259
303-297-1402 fax
www.tpoc.org
"An organization that promotes training, networking and support of minority travel professionals."

Travel South USA
3400 Peachtree Road NE
Atlanta, GA 30326
404-231-1790
404-231-2364 fax
www.travel-south.com
Promotes travel to and within 12 Southern states. Sponsors periodic "Showcases" in which travel buyers meet with Southern suppliers.

United Motorcoach Association (UMA)
113 South West Street
Alexandria, VA 22314-2824
703-838-2929
703-838-2950 fax
www.uma.org
UMA is comprised of "more than 900 professional bus and motorcoach companies and 200 associate members, suppliers and manufacturers."

United States Tour Operator's Association (USTOA)
275 Madison Avenue
Suite 2014
New York, NY 10016
212-599-6599
212-599-6744 fax
www.ustoa.com
A trade association of many of the larger tour operators, including such heavyweights as Colette, Contiki and Globus. Represents the interests of the industry and insures travelers against member default.

Universal Federation of Travel Agents Associations (UFTAA)
1 Avenue des Castelans
Entree H
MC-98000
MONACO
011-377-92-052829

011-377-92-052987 fax
An association of travel agency organizations, individual travel agencies, and tourism enterprises from 81 countries. Promotes ethical conduct and helps members collect commissions.

Vacation Rental Managers Association
P.O. Box 1202
Santa Cruz, CA 95061-1202
831-426-8762
831-458-3637 fax
www.vrma.com
This association was formed to "increase awareness of vacation rental lodging and enhance members' business through education, professional standards, marketing, political involvement and networking." Publishes a free directory of members.

World Association of Travel Agencies (WATA)
37, rue Riant Coteau
Geneva
SWITZERLAND
011-41-22-995-1545
011-41-22-995-1546 fax
www.wata.net
WATA exists "to bring local (preferably privately-owned) travel agencies into an international network." They have 196 members in 83 countries.

World Federation of Tourist Guides Associations
President Rosalind Newlands
c/o STGA
18b Broad Street
Stirling FK8 1EF
004-41-31-477-2204
www.wftga.org
"The WFTGA's main purpose is to promote, market and ensure that tourist guides are recognised as the ambassadors of a region."

World Tourism Organization (WTO)
Calle Capitan Haya 42
E-28020 Madrid
SPAIN
011-34-567-8100
011-34-571-3733 fax
www.world-tourism.org
"Serves as a global forum for tourism policy issues and practical source of tourism know-how."

World Travel and Tourism Council (WTTC)
1-2 Queen Victoria Terrace
Sovereign Court
London E1W 3HA
UNITED KINGDOM
011-44-870-727-9882
011-44-870-728-9882 fax
www.wttc.org
"The forum for global business leaders comprising the presidents, chairs and CEOs of 100 of the world's foremost companies. It is the only body representing the private sector in all parts of the Travel & Tourism industry worldwide."

Travel Associations

230

*The Travel Agent's
Complete Desk
Reference*

III

Part Three:

Reference Section & Bibliography

From time to time, you will find it helpful to know what time it is in Hong Kong. Or Paris. Or wherever. This chart will help you do that. To use it, first locate, in the left column, the country you are interested in. (We also list Alaska, Hawaii, and American Samoa.) Then find the column for your time zone. Reading from left to right, as you would see them on a map of the United States, they are Pacific Standard Time (PST), Mountain Standard Time (MST), Central Standard Time (CST), and Eastern Standard Time (EST).

The number in the appropriate time zone column opposite the appropriate country will tell you how many hours to add or subtract to determine the corresponding time in the foreign country. An equal sign (=) indicates that there is no difference in time.

For larger countries, which span several time zones, we have listed major cities to assist you in determining the correct local time.

COUNTRY	PST	MST	CST	EST
Alaska (AKDT)	-1	-2	-3	-4
Albania	+9	+8	+7	+6
Algeria	+9	+8	+7	+6
American Samoa	-3	-4	-5	-6
Andorra	+9	+8	+7	+6
Angola	+9	+8	+7	+6
Antigua	+4	+3	+2	+1
Argentina	+5	+4	+3	+2
Armenia	+12	+11	+10	+9
Aruba	+3	+2	+1	=
Australia				
Sydney, Melbourne	+18	+17	+16	+15
Perth	+16	+15	+14	+13
Austria	+9	+8	+7	+6
Azerbaijan	+12	+11	+10	+9

234

The Travel Agent's Complete Desk Reference

COUNTRY	PST	MST	CST	EST
Bahamas	+3	+2	+1	=
Bahrain	+11	+10	+9	+8
Bangladesh	+14.5	+13.5	+12.5	+11.5
Barbados	+4	+3	+2	+1
Belarus	+10	+9	+8	+7
Belgium	+9	+8	+7	+6
Belize	+2	+1	=	-1
Benin	+9	+8	+7	+6
Bermuda	+4	+3	+2	+1
Bhutan	+13.5	+12.5	+11.5	+10.5
Bolivia	+4	+3	+2	+1
Bonaire	+4	+3	+2	+1
Bosnia	+9	+8	+7	+6
Botswana	+10	+9	+8	+7
Brazil	+5	+4	+3	+2
British Virgin Is.	+3	+2	+1	=
British W. Indies	+3	+2	+1	=
Brunei	+16	+15	+14	+13
Bulgaria	+10	+9	+8	+7
Burkina Faso	+8	+7	+6	+5
Burundi	+10	+9	+8	+7
Cambodia	+15	+14	+13	+12
Cameroon	+9	+8	+7	+6
Canada				
St. Johns	+4.5	+3.5	+2.5	+1.5
Toronto, Quebec	+3	+2	+1	=
Winnipeg	+2	+1	=	-1
Calgary	+1	=	-1	-2
Vancouver	=	-1	-2	-3
Cape Verde	+7	+6	+5	+4
Cayman Islands	+3	+2	+1	=
Central African Rep.	+9	+8	+7	+6
Chad	+9	+8	+7	+6
Chile	+4	+3	+2	+1
China (People's Rep.)	+16	+15	+14	+13
Colombia	+3	+2	+1	=
Comoros Islands	+11	+10	+9	+8
Congo	+9	+8	+7	+6
Cook Islands	-2	-3	-4	-5
Costa Rica	+2	+1	=	-1
Cote D'Ivoire	+8	+7	+6	+5
Croatia	+9	+8	+7	+6
Cuba	+3	+2	+1	=
Curaçao	+4	+3	+2	+1
Cyprus	+10	+9	+8	+7
Czech Republic	+9	+8	+7	+6

COUNTRY	PST	MST	CST	EST
Denmark	+9	+8	+7	+6
Djibouti	+11	+10	+9	+8
Dominica	+4	+3	+2	+1
Dominican Republic	+4	+3	+2	+1
Ecuador	+3	+2	+1	=
Egypt	+10	+9	+8	+7
El Salvador	+2	+1	=	-1
Equatorial Guinea	+9	+8	+7	+6
Eritrea	+11	+10	+9	+8
Estonia	+10	+9	+8	+7
Ethiopia	+11	+10	+9	+8
Fiji	+20	+19	+18	+17
Finland	+10	+9	+8	+7
France	+9	+8	+7	+6
French Guiana	+5	+4	+3	+2
French Polynesia	-2	-3	-4	-5
French West Indies	+4	+3	+2	+1
Gabon	+9	+8	+7	+6
Galapagos Islands	+2	+1	=	-1
Gambia	+8	+7	+6	+5
Georgia	+12	+11	+10	+9
Germany	+9	+8	+7	+6
Ghana	+8	+7	+6	+5
Gibraltar	+9	+8	+7	+6
Greece	+10	+9	+8	+7
Greenland	+5	+4	+3	+2
Grenada	+4	+3	+2	+1
Guadeloupe	+4	+3	+2	+1
Guatemala	+2	+1	=	-1
Guinea	+8	+7	+6	+5
Guinea-Bissau	+8	+7	+6	+5
Guyana	+4	+3	+2	+1
Haiti	+3	+2	+1	=
Hawaii (HDT)	-3	-4	-5	-6
Honduras	+2	+1	=	-1
Hong Kong	+16	+15	+14	+13
Hungary	+9	+8	+7	+6
Iceland	+8	+7	+6	+5
India	+13.5	+12.5	+11.5	+10.5
Indonesia	+15	+14	+13	+12
Iran	+11.5	+10.5	+9.5	+8.5
Iraq	+11	+10	+9	+8
Ireland	+8	+7	+6	+5
Israel	+10	+9	+8	+7
Italy	+9	+8	+7	+6
Jamaica	+3	+2	+1	=

*Time Zones
At A Glance*

COUNTRY	PST	MST	CST	EST
Japan	+17	+16	+15	+14
Jordan	+10	+9	+8	+7
Kazakhstan	+14	+13	+12	+11
Kenya	+11	+10	+9	+8
Kiribati	-3	-4	-5	-6
Korea, North & South	+17	+16	+15	+14
Kuwait	+11	+10	+9	+8
Kyrgyz Republic	+14	+13	+12	+11
Laos	+16	+15	+14	+13
Latvia	+10	+9	+8	+7
Lebanon	+10	+9	+8	+7
Lesotho	+10	+9	+8	+7
Liberia	+8	+7	+6	+5
Libya	+9	+8	+7	+6
Liechtenstein	+9	+8	+7	+6
Lithuania	+10	+9	+8	+7
Luxembourg	+9	+8	+7	+6
Macau	+16	+15	+14	+13
Macedonia	+9	+8	+7	+6
Madagascar	+11	+10	+9	+8
Malawi	+10	+9	+8	+7
Malaysia	+16	+15	+14	+13
Maldives	+13	+12	+11	+10
Mali	+8	+7	+6	+5
Malta	+9	+8	+7	+6
Marshall Islands	+20	+19	+18	+17
Martinique	+4	+3	+2	+1
Mauritania	+8	+7	+6	+5
Mauritius	+12	+11	+10	+9
Mexico				
Cancun, Mex. City	+2	+1	=	-1
La Paz	+1	=	-1	-2
Micronesia	+18	+17	+16	+15
Moldova	+10	+9	+8	+7
Monaco	+9	+8	+7	+6
Mongolia	+16	+15	+14	+13
Morocco	+8	+7	+6	+5
Mozambique	+10	+9	+8	+7
Myanmar	+14.5	+13.5	+12.5	+11.5
Namibia	+10	+9	+8	+7
Nauru	+20	+19	+18	+17
Nepal	+13.5	+12.5	+11.5	+10.5
Netherlands	+9	+8	+7	+6
Netherlands Antilles	+4	+3	+2	+1
New Zealand	+20	+19	+18	+17
Nicaragua	+2	+1	=	-1

COUNTRY	PST	MST	CST	EST
Niger	+9	+8	+7	+6
Nigeria	+9	+8	+7	+6
Norway	+9	+8	+7	+6
Oman	+12	+11	+10	+9
Pakistan	+13	+12	+11	+10
Palau, Republic of	+17	+16	+15	+14
Panama	+3	+2	+1	=
Papua New Guinea	+18	+17	+16	+15
Paraguay	+4	+3	+2	+1
Peru	+3	+2	+1	=
Philippines	+16	+15	+14	+13
Poland	+9	+8	+7	+6
Portugal	+8	+7	+6	+5
Qatar	+11	+10	+9	+8
Romania	+10	+9	+8	+7
Russia				
Moscow	+11	+10	+9	+8
Vladivostok	+15	+14	+13	+12
Rwanda	+10	+9	+8	+7
St. Kitts & Nevis	+4	+3	+2	+1
St. Lucia	+4	+3	+2	+1
St. Maarten	+4	+3	+2	+1
St. Martin	+4	+3	+2	+1
St. Vincent	+4	+3	+2	+1
San Marino	+9	+8	+7	+6
Sao Tome & Principe	+9	+8	+7	+6
Saudi Arabia	+11	+10	+9	+8
Senegal	+8	+7	+6	+5
Serbia	+9	+8	+7	+6
Seychelles	+12	+11	+10	+9
Sierra Leone	+8	+7	+6	+5
Singapore	+16	+15	+14	+13
Slovak Republic	+9	+8	+7	+6
Slovenia	+9	+8	+7	+6
Solomon Islands	+19	+18	+17	+16
Somalia	+11	+10	+9	+8
South Africa	+10	+9	+8	+7
Spain	+9	+8	+7	+6
Sri Lanka	+13.5	+12.5	+11.5	+10.5
Sudan	+10	+9	+8	+7
Suriname	+5	+4	+3	+2
Swaziland	+10	+9	+8	+7
Sweden	+9	+8	+7	+6
Switzerland	+9	+8	+7	+6
Syria	+11	+10	+9	+8
Tahiti	-2	-3	-4	-5

Time Zones
At A Glance

COUNTRY	PST	MST	CST	EST
Taiwan	+16	+15	+14	+13
Tajikistan	+14	+13	+12	+11
Tanzania	+11	+10	+9	+8
Thailand	+16	+15	+14	+13
Togo	+8	+7	+6	+5
Tonga	+21	+20	+19	+18
Trinidad & Tobago	+4	+3	+2	+1
Tunisia	+9	+8	+7	+6
Turkey	+10	+9	+8	+7
Turkmenistan	+13	+12	+11	+10
Turks & Caicos	+3	+2	+1	=
Tuvalu	+20	+19	+18	+17
Uganda	+11	+10	+9	+8
Ukraine	+10	+9	+8	+7
United Arab Emirates	+12	+11	+10	+9
United Kingdom	+8	+7	+6	+5
Uruguay	+5	+4	+3	+2
Uzbekistan	+13	+12	+11	+10
Vanuatu	+19	+18	+17	+16
Venezuela	+4	+3	+2	+1
Vietnam	+16	+15	+14	+13
Western Samoa	-3	-4	-5	-6
Yemen	+11	+10	+9	+8
Zaire				
Kinshasa	+9	+8	+7	+6
Kisangani	+10	+9	+8	+7
Zambia	+10	+9	+8	+7
Zimbabwe	+10	+9	+8	+7

Glossary of Travel Industry Terms & Abbreviations

This glossary is intended to serve as a ready reference for all the varied and sundry bits of industry jargon, GDS (or CRS) abbreviations, and organizational acronyms you might come across in the course of your business as a travel agent. I have not attempted to define the thousands of geographical terms that you might come across from time to time; specialized geographical dictionaries exist should you want to expand your knowledge in this area.

The following abbreviations are used in the glossary:

Abr.	Abbreviation.
adj.	Adjective.
Brit.	British English.
Cap.	Capitalized.
Fr.	French.
GDS.	Code used in global distribution systems, formerly known as computerized reservations systems (CRS).
Ger.	German.
It.	Italian.
Lat.	Latin.
n.	Noun.
Sp.	Spanish.
qv	*quod vide*, or *See* separate entry.
v.	Verb.

A, a

A. *GDS*. 1. Availability; will display flights with seats available. 2. An arunk (qv) or surface segment of a trip. 3. American plan (qv). 4. Code for a class of service, usually superior.

a la carte. *Fr.* Literally, "from the menu." Indicates that each dish ordered will have a separate price. Also, used in tour literature to indicate a choice of dishes will be available.

AA. 1. American Airlines. 2. Alcoholics Anonymous.

AAA. American Automobile Association.

AAAE. American Association of Airport Executives.

AAD. *GDS*. Agent automated deduction.

AAPA. American Association of Port Authorities.

AAR. Association of American Railroads.

AARP. American Association of Retired Persons.

AATTA. African-American Travel and Tourism Association.

ABA. American Bus Association.

Abacus. Asian GDS.

abaft. *adj.* On a ship, behind. For example, "abaft the bridge."

ABC. 1. *GDS*. Advanced booking charters. 2. *Slang*. The islands of the Netherlands Antilles — Aruba, Bonaire, and Curacao.

abeam. Off to the side of a ship or at right angles to its length.

above board. On a cruise ship, cabins above water level.

ABTA. Association of British Travel Agents.

AC. 1. *Abr.* Alternating current. 2. *GDS*. Access card.

ACAP. Aviation Consumer Action Project.

a/c. *Abr.* 1. Air conditioned. 2. Additional collection.

acceleration clause. A provision in a promissory note (qv) calling for the immediate payment of the balance in the event of a default (qv) by the borrower.

access code. Password to gain entry into a computer or a computer file.

accessible pedestrian signal. A device that transmits information about the timing of traffic signals in a non-visual manner, such as by sound or vibration.

ACCL. American Canadian Caribbean Line.

accommodation. Any seat, berth, room, or service sold to a passenger.

accommodation ladder. A portable, external ladder on the side of a ship, used for shore or tender (qv) access.

accountable document. Any piece of paper that, when validated by a travel agency, has a monetary value and that must be accounted for to the ARC (qv).

accountable manual documents. Blank ARC (qv) ticket stock used to hand-write tickets.

accreditation. Approval given by various trade associations to a travel agency allowing the sale of tickets and other accommodations.

accrual method. An accounting system in which the recording of income and expenses is adjusted to reflect the time periods to which they apply, as opposed to the time monies were received or disbursed. *See also* cash method.

Acela. An Amtrak train running between New York and Boston, offering faster service at a higher fare.

ACI. Assist Card International.

ACI-NA. Airports Council International, North America.

ACK. *GDS.* Acknowledge.

ACON. *GDS.* Air conditioned.

ACRA. American Car Rental Association.

acrophobia. Fear of heights.

act of God. A meteorological or seismic event over which a travel provider has no control and, hence, no legal responsibility. *See also* force majeure.

ACTA. Alliance of Canadian Travel Associations.

ACTE. Association of Corporate Travel Executives.

actual flying time. Total time spent in the air, as opposed to scheduled flight time or time spent waiting on the ground.

ACV. *Abr.* Air-cushioned vehicle. Hovercraft (qv).

AD. 1. *GDS.* Agent's discount. When followed by a number, indicates the percentage amount of the discount. For example: AD75 indicates a discount to travel agents of 75% off unrestricted coach fares. 2. *Abr. Lat.* Anno Domini, "year of our Lord."

ADA room. A hotel room that complies with the requirements of the Americans with Disabilities Act.

ad hoc. *Lat.* Of tours, put together on a customized or one-time basis, usually from existing options.

ADB. *GDS.* 1. Advise if duplicate booking. 2. Air discount bulletin.

ADCOL. *Abr.* Additional collection.

add/coll. *Abr.* Additional collection.

add-on(s). Anything optional purchased by a passenger, as in tour arrangements.

add-on fare. Amount added to a gateway fare (qv) to arrive at a through fare (qv). Sometimes called a proportional fare.

adiabatic rate. Rule of thumb that holds that temperature decreases as altitude increases (3.5°F per 1,000 ft.).

adjoining rooms. Hotel rooms that, while next to each other, have no connecting doors. *See also* connecting rooms.

ADNO. *GDS.* Advise if not okay.

ADOA. *GDS.* Advise on arrival.

ADR. *GDS.* Average daily rate.

ADS. *Abr.* Approved destination status (qv).

ADT. *Abr.* Atlantic Daylight Time; Alaska Daylight Time.

ADTK. *GDS.* Advise if ticketed.

aduane. *Fr.* Customs.

ADV. *GDS.* Advise.

advance passenger information. Data on those flying on an aircraft provided by the airline to customs officials in the destination country.

advance passenger information system. A technological solution for

the electronic transmission of passenger and crew manifests to the U.S. Customs data Center.

advertised tour. Specifically, a travel package meeting the airline requirements needed to be assigned an IT (inclusive tour) number.

advance purchase rate. Price for a product or service purchased or guaranteed a specified number of days prior to arrival or use.

ADVN. *GDS.* Advise as to names.

ADVR. *GDS.* Advise as to rate.

AER. Association of European Regions.

aerospace. Concerning the earth's atmosphere and its immediate environs, typically with an emphasis on aviation and astronautics, as in "Aerospace Museum."

AF. *GDS.* Added phone.

AFA. Association of Flight Attendants.

affinity card. A credit card marketed by a company, charity, or other group in association with the credit card company.

affinity charter. A charter (of a bus, airplane, ship, etc.) arranged by or for an affinity group.

affinity group. A group of people linked by a common bond, such as ethnicity or membership in an organization.

affinity group airfare. A fare set aside specifically for affinity groups.

AFT. *GDS.* Actual flying time (qv).

aft. Toward the rear of a ship.

AFTA. Australian Federation of Travel Agents.

agency. 1. A legal relationship in which one person acts for another in a business dealing with a third party. 2. A travel agency.

Agency Agreement, The. The contract used by IATAN (qv) to govern its dealings with travel agencies.

agency check. A check drawn on the business account of a travel agency and bearing the agency's name.

agency list. The list maintained by ARC (qv) and IATAN (qv) of appointed travel agencies.

agency manager. The person in a travel agency who holds appointment from ARC (qv), IATA (qv), etc. The person who runs an agency's day-to-day affairs.

agent. 1. A person who represents another to a third party. 2. A travel agent.

agent bypass. The practice of suppliers dealing directly with the public *See also* agentless booking.

agent eligibility list. A list prepared by the travel agency and submitted to ARC (qv) or IATAN (qv) of agency employees eligible for travel benefits. Also referred to as "the ARC list."

Agent Reporting Agreement, The. The contract used by ARC (qv) to govern its dealings with travel agencies.

agent sine. *GDS.* An agent's two-letter personal identification code.

agentless booking. A booking made by a consumer using an automated system and bypassing a travel agent.

agoraphobia. Fear of open spaces or public places.

agritourism. Recreational travel undertaken to agricultural areas or to participate in agricultural activities.

AGT. *GDS.* Agent.

ahead. In front of the ship's bow.

AHMA. American Hotel and Motel Association.

air boat. A shallow draft vessel powered by a large propeller mounted on the stern, often used for tours of swamps and rivers in the southern United States and elsewhere.

air courier. 1. A person who accompanies time-sensitive cargo being shipped as passengers' baggage, usually in exchange for a deep discount on the air fare, a practice which is increasingly rare. 2. A company that provides expedited air shipments.

air marshal. An armed law enforcement officer traveling on an airplane (usually anonymously) as a security measure.

air mile. A unit of distance measuring approximately 6,076 feet.

air piracy. The forcible appropriation or hijacking of an aircraft.

air rage. A phenomenon in which airline passengers become unruly or violent toward crew members or fellow travelers.

air taxi. An aircraft with a limited seating capacity (19 or fewer), operating within a limited range (250 miles).

air traffic controller. Person in the control tower of an airport charged with monitoring and directing the takeoff and landing of planes.

Air Travel Card. An airline-sponsored credit card, good for airline tickets only. Also known as the Universal Air Travel Plan Card.

Air Travel Organisers' Licensing. A UK government licensing scheme intended to protect traveler's from financial default by tour operators.

air walls. Moveable panels used to subdivide a larger area, such as a hotel ballroom, into smaller rooms.

airdrome. Airport, now generally obsolete.

AIRIMP. *GDS.* ARC/IATAN reservations interline message procedures/passenger.

airline appointed agency. A U.S. travel agency that holds airline ticket stock or has e-ticketing capabilities.

airline codes. Specifically, the unique two- or three-digit indicators that identify specific airlines in GDS systems. More loosely, all such unique indicators, including those that identify airports.

airline designator. Two- or three-digit alphanumeric code for an air carrier, administered by IATA (qv).

airline plate. A metal plate given to travel agencies by an airline for the purpose of imprinting and thereby validating tickets. *See also* plates.

Airlines Reporting Corporation (ARC). An autonomous corporation created by the domestic airlines. Appoints travel agencies to sell airline tickets and oversees the financial details of tracking payments to airlines and the disbursement of commissions to travel agencies.

airport access fee. The fee paid to an airport management by a car rental company for the privilege of operating its vans and buses on the airport grounds, usually passed on to the consumer.

airport codes. Three-letter codes used to uniquely identify all airports.

airport tax. A local tax imposed on air tickets and passed along to passengers, ostensibly used to fund airport maintenance, expansion, and similar expenditures.

airport transfer. Transportation provided by a tour operator to a passenger to/from an airport, usually to/from a hotel.

air/sea. Trips, tickets, or fares that include both air and sea components, as in a cruise package.

airsickness. Nausea or other discomfort caused by the motion of an aircraft.

airsickness bag. A small, sealable container provided by airlines in case of in-flight nausea.

airway. *See* jetway.

airworthy. Capable of being flown. Safe, of an aircraft.

aka. *Abr.* Also known as.

Alberta clipper. A storm system so named because it originates in the mountains of Alberta, Canada, and then moves across the northeastern United States bringing snow, strong winds, and chilly weather.

alcove. A small section of a room, indented into the wall or otherwise set apart.

alfresco. *It.* In the open air, as in alfresco dining.

all inclusive. One price covers all listed elements of the package.

alleyway. A corridor or passage on a ship.

alliance fare. A round-the-world fare offered by a group of airlines (an "alliance").

all-in. *Slang.* All inclusive, as a tour.

allotment. The number of seats, cabins, berths, etc. available for sale by a supplier or agent.

all-suite. *adj.* Describing a hotel in which all rooms have a separate living room and/or kitchen facilities.

all-terrain vehicle. A one- or two-person motorized vehicle with large wheels designed for recreational use on uneven ground or sand.

aloha. The Hawaiian word for both "hello" and "good-bye."

alongside. Describing a ship when next to a pier or another vessel.

ALPA. Airline Pilots Association.

alphanumeric. Composed of both letters and numbers, as in a record locator number (qv).

alternate distribution system. Any system that bypasses travel agencies in selling travel arrangements. Usually used to refer to the distribution of tickets through personal computers and ETDNs (qv).

alternate restaurant. On a cruise ship, a restaurant at which the passenger must pay either the full cost of the meal or a service charge, as opposed to those dining rooms whose meals are included in the price of the cruise.

altiport. An airport or airstrip in a high, mountainous region.

altitude. Height above sea level.

alumni rates. Fares reserved for passengers who have previously sailed with a cruise line.

a.m. *Abr. Lat.* Ante meridian. Morning; between midnight and noon.

Amadeus®. A computerized reservations system (qv).

ambassador. The highest ranking diplomatic representative of one country to the government of another. The executive in charge of an embassy, typically located in the capital city.

ambiance. *n.* The overall look and feel of a restaurant, hotel, or destination, or the mood or atmosphere it creates.

amenities. The facilities and features of a property, usually a hotel.

American plan. A meal plan at a hotel or resort in which three meals a day are included in the price. Sometimes referred to as Full American Plan.

AMEX, AMEXCO. American Express.

amidships. Toward the middle of a ship; the imaginary line that runs down the center of a ship.

amphibious. Capable of operating on land as well as sea.

Amtrak. Trade name of the U.S. National Railroad Passenger Corporation.

amusement park. A recreational attraction featuring mechanical rides and other forms of active entertainment. *See also* theme park.

AN. *GDS.* Added name.

anchor ball. A black ball hoisted over a ship's bow to indicate that it is anchored.

Anglophone. 1. *adj.* English-speaking. 2. *n.* A person who speaks English.

Anglosphere. That portion of the world community that speaks English and subscribes to certain principles of law and human rights.

antebellum. Built or in existence prior to the American Civil War. Used primarily to describe historic buildings.

antipode. A point on the earth's surface exactly opposite another point.

antipodean day. The day gained by crossing the International Date Line (qv). Also, called meridian day.

ANTOR. Association of National Tourist Office Representatives in Australasia.

AOC. *Brit.* Air operator's certificate.

AOG. *Abr.* Act of God (qv).

AP. *Abr.* American plan (qv).

apartheid. The former racist policy of South Africa, mandating the rigid separation of peoples by race.

APEX. *GDS.* Advance purchase excursion fare.

APHIS. Animal and Plant Health Inspection Service.

API. Advance passenger information (qv).

APIS. Advance passenger information system (qv).

Apollo®. A global distribution system owned by United Airlines and the Covia Corp.

appetizer. First course of a meal, designed to whet the appetite while awaiting the main course.

appointment. The process whereby an air carrier or other supplier certifies a travel agency to act as its agent.

apres-ski. *Fr.* Any activity that is scheduled after skiing.

approved destination status. A designation by the government of the People's Republic of China, allowing its citizens to visit a specific country

Glossary of Terms

as tourists.

APS. *Abr.* Accessible pedestrian signal (qv).

APT. *GDS.* Airline passenger tariff.

aqueduct. A bridge-like structure, usually raised, designed to carry water or a canal.

arbiter, travel agent. An individual selected by a committee representing travel agents and air carriers and charged with the responsibility of settling disputes between travel agents and ARC (qv) and enforcing terms of The Agent Reporting Agreement (qv).

arbitrary fare. *See* add-on fare.

arbitration. A method of dispute resolution intended to avoid the high costs of legal action, typically conducted under rules established by the American Arbitration Association.

arbitration clause. A provision in a contract requiring any disputes between the parties involved to be submitted to arbitration, typically under rules established by the American Arbitration Association.

ARC. Airlines Reporting Corporation (qv).

ARC list. A list prepared by a travel agency and submitted to ARC (qv) or IATAN (qv) of agency employees eligible for travel benefits. Also referred to as "the agent eligibility list."

architectural bias. The tendency of a GDS (qv) to make it easier to find and book the flights of its sponsor by virtue of the way the system is designed.

archipelago. A string of islands.

archive. 1. *v.* To store in computerized form, as travel records. 2. *n.* A repository for documents or records.

area bank. *See* Area Settlement Plan.

Area Settlement Plan. System administered by ARC on a regional basis to handle the processing of airline tickets, payments, and the disbursement of commissions to travel agencies. Also referred to as a Bank Settlement Plan.

ARINC. An airline-owned corporation providing communications and other services to the airline industry. Originally called Aeronautical Radio, Inc.

ARNK. *GDS.* (Pronounced "arunk.") Arrival unknown. Used to indicate the land portion of an air itinerary.

ARR. *GDS.* Arrival.

ARTA. Association of Retail Travel Agents.

articles of incorporation. The formal legal description of a business's activities, required for registration by the state.

arunk. Pronunciation of the acronym, ARNK (qv).

AS. *GDS.* Added segment.

ASAP. *Abr.* As soon as possible.

ASC. *GDS.* Advising schedule change.

ASP. *Abr.* Area Settlement Plan (qv).

asset. Any property, real (i.e. real estate), personal, or intellectual (e.g. a trademark or copyright), that has a cash value.

AST. *Abr.* 1. Atlantic Standard Time (qv). 2. Alaska Standard Time.

ASTA. American Society of Travel Agents.

ASTAPAC. ASTA Political Action Committee.

astern. 1. Behind a ship or other craft. 2. In casual usage, toward the back of a ship.

asylum. *See* political asylum.

AT. *GDS.* Travel to be via the Atlantic Ocean.

ATA. Air Transport Association.

ATB. *Abr.* Automated ticket/boarding pass. An electronically generated ticket that also includes the boarding pass.

ATC. Air Traffic Conference of America, the predecessor to ARC.

ATEC. Australian Tourism Export Council.

ATFDS. *Abr.* Automated ticket and fare determination system.

athwart. *adj.* At right angles to a ship's keel.

Atlantic Standard Time. A Canadian time zone. Also called Provincial Standard Time.

ATM. Automated teller machine.

ATME. Association of Travel Marketing Executives.

ATO. *Abr.* Airport ticket office.

ATOL. Air Travel Organisers' Licensing (qv).

atoll. A ring-shaped tropical island or coral reef with a lagoon in the middle.

ATP. Airline Tariff Publishing Company.

atrium. A large open space in a building, usually topped by a glass roof, sometimes containing elaborate landscaping and ponds. A popular style of hotel lobby.

ATV. *Abr.* All-terrain vehicle (qv).

ATW. Around the world.

au pair. *Fr.* A young person, usually foreign, hired to provide child care and household help in exchange for room, board, a modest salary, and a chance to learn a new language.

audit. 1. *v.* To examine financial or performance records. 2. *n.* Any such examination.

auditorium style. In a meeting, a configuration in which seats are arranged in rows, facing front, as in a theater.

aurora australis. "The Southern Lights." A colorful geomagnetic and electric display visible near the South Pole.

aurora borealis. "The Northern Lights." The Northern hemisphere's equivalent of the aurora australis.

Australasia. The region including Australia, New Zealand, and the major South Pacific islands.

auto drop PNR. A passenger name record (PNR) (qv) that has been flagged for automatic queuing on a GDS.

Autobahn. A network of high-speed superhighways in Germany and other European countries.

automated reservation system. Global distribution system (qv).

avail. *Slang.* Availability.

availability. The current inventory of seats, rooms, cabins, etc. that can be sold or reserved.

Glossary of Terms

available rooms. In a hotel, the number of rooms actually available for use on a given day, eliminating rooms not available due to damage, repairs, and so forth.

available seat miles. One seat, occupied or not, moved one mile. Used as a measure of airline capacity.

average daily rate. Statistical unit used to measure a hotel's pricing scale. Figure derived by dividing actual daily revenue by the total number of available rooms (qv).

Aviation Trust Fund. A federal reserve of tax monies levied on airline tickets and operations and set aside to improve the U.S. air transportation system.

AVIH. *GDS.* Animal in hold.

AVS. *GDS.* Availability status messages.

AWOL. *Abr.* Absent without leave. Pronounced both as individual letters and as an acronym. Term used to indicate the unauthorized absence of a crew member, as on a cruise ship.

AX. *GDS.* American Express.

AXESS. Japanese GDS.

B&B. *n.* Bed and breakfast. Traditionally, a private home that takes in guests, with breakfast included in the price of lodging. B&Bs can range from modest homes with one spare room to elaborately restored historic houses with luxury prices. Used increasingly to describe any lodging arrangement that includes breakfast, even in a hotel.

b2b. *Abr.* Business-to-business, typically used to refer to Internet sites or businesses.

BA. *GDS.* BankAmericard.

back of the house. Support and service areas usually not seen by guests of a hotel or theme park.

back office. *adj.* Describing business activities, such as accounting, that typically take place out of the view of customers.

back to back. Sequential booking of two different tours, so that the traveler has a continuous journey. Also used to describe arrangements in which one group arrives as another departs.

back-to-back ticketing. A strategy used to reduce the cost of a roundtrip involving no Saturday stay when the cost of two excursions is less than the cost of one unrestricted fare. For example, if a traveler wants to fly from New York to Denver on Monday and return Thursday, he would purchase two excursions, one from New York to Denver beginning on the Monday and the other from Denver to New York departing on the Thursday. The traveler then uses only the outbound portion of each excursion. The itinerary can be designed in such a way that the return portions of each excursion can be used on another trip. A technically illegal practice discouraged by the airlines. Also called "nested excursions."

backhaul. 1. The movement of an airliner, or other vehicle, from a destination to the point of origin. 2. The shipment of cargo on a returning vehicle.

backwash. 1. A disturbance of the water caused by a ship's propellers turning in reverse. 2. The turbulence caused by the exhaust of a jet plane.

Baedecker. Originally, a series of guidebooks published in Germany in the late nineteenth century, now used generically or metaphorically for guides in general.

baggage. All of a passenger's or traveler's personal belongings, whether checked or unchecked. *See also* checked baggage and unchecked baggage.

baggage check. The claim check (qv) or receipt, usually numbered, issued to a passenger for his or her luggage.

baggage claim. The area at an airport or other terminal where passengers retrieve their checked luggage.

bagonize. *Slang.* To wait in agony at the airport luggage carousel for your luggage to appear.

bait and switch. An illegal sales tactic in which a consumer is lured by a low price only to be told that the "special offer" is no longer available and steered to a higher priced product.

baksheesh. Arabic. Literally, "gift." A constant refrain of street beggars, the

word is also used to refer to "gifts" or bribes paid to facilitate business.

balance sheet. A financial report detailing a company's assets and liabilities as of a specific date.

balcony. An open-air space or platform off a room. The uppermost level of a theater.

ballast. Any weight placed in a ship's hold, or other special compartment, to increase stability or reduce motion. Weight used in a hot air balloon to control altitude.

bank rate. The official rate at which currency trades between banks. Usually more favorable than the rate that can be obtained by the traveler from the bank.

Bank Settlement Plan. *See* Area Settlement Plan.

bankruptcy. A legal proceeding in which a company seeks protection from its creditors while it either reorganizes in the hope of surviving or liquidates its assets. Thus, a bankrupt company may or may not still be conducting business.

banquet event order. A document providing complete and precise instructions to a hotel for the running of a banquet, meeting, or other event to be held in the hotel. Also called a function sheet.

banqueting room. A room, typically at a hotel, available for rent for a public function at which food may or may not be served.

bar. 1. A retail establishment or a counter in a restaurant that sells or dispenses alcohol. 2. In navigation, a sandbar.

bare bones. A service or facility providing only the basics, with no additional frills or amenities. *See also* no frills.

bareboat charter. A charter of a boat or yacht that does not include supplies or crew.

barf bag. *Slang.* Airsickness bag (qv). Considered offensive.

barge. A low draft (qv) vessel, often towed or pushed, used to transport cargo. A vessel designed for use on inland waterways and canals.

barge cruising. Pleasure cruises along canal systems, using converted commercial barges or new vessels built to resemble them.

barometer. A instrument that measures air pressure. Used to forecast weather.

barometric pressure. The density of the atmosphere, which varies according to altitude and weather conditions.

barrier island. A narrow strip of land lying just offshore that protects the main coastline from high waves.

barrier reef. A line of coral that protects the main shore line, usually of an island, from high waves.

barter. Buying and selling without the exchange of money. Purchasing by means of the exchange of goods or services. Typically, airlines will exchange airline seats for goods or services rendered by various suppliers.

base fare. The fare, as of an airline ticket, before tax has been added. Commissions are calculated on the base fare.

basis two. Another term for double occupancy.

bass boat. A speedy motorboat with a raised platform, used for bass fishing in the southern United States and elsewhere.

bassinet. A small, portable crib for an infant.

batch mode. A computer operation in which a specific task, ticketing, for example, is performed on a group of records.

BB. *GDS.* Buffet breakfast.

BBML. *GDS.* Baby meal.

BBR. *GDS.* Bank buying rate.

BCHFT. *GDS.* Beachfront.

beam. A measurement of a ship's width at its widest point.

bearing. The compass direction in which a vessel is traveling.

Beaufort Scale. A scientific scale from zero to 17 measuring wind force.

bed and breakfast. *See* B&B.

bed night. In the hotel industry, a measurement of occupancy. One person for one night.

bedienung. *Ger.* Gratuity included.

bedroom. A railway compartment for two, with toilet and sink.

bedsit. *Brit.* Short for "bed-sitting room." Accommodation with minimal cooking facilities and usually with shared bath. Typically used for longer-term rentals. *See also* self-catering.

beeper. A paging device that alerts the user that a telephone message has been received.

bell captain. The person in charge of a shift of a hotel's bellhops (qv).

bellhop. In a hotel, the person who carries a guest's luggage to or from the room and performs sundry other services. The term, short for "bell-hop-per," derives from the bell used in hotels to summon someone to carry a guest's luggage.

bellman and bellstaff. *See* "bellhop."

below. *n.* On a ship, any area underneath the main deck.

belvedere. *It.* (literally, "beautiful view") A scenic overlook (qv).

benchmarking. The practice of studying the methods of an acknowledged leader in an industry as a way of setting standards for one's own operation.

Benelux. Nickname for the area comprised by Belgium, the Netherlands, and Luxembourg.

BEO. *Abr.* Banquet event order (qv).

bereavement fare. A lower airline fare offered to those traveling due to a death or illness in their immediate family.

Bermuda Plan. A hotel arrangement that includes a full breakfast with the room rate.

Bermuda Triangle. A triangular area of the Atlantic whose apices are Bermuda, Miami, and the Lesser Antilles. Reputed to be the site of numerous mysterious disappearances of planes and ships.

berth. 1. A bed on a ship, usually attached to the bulkhead (qv). 2. By extension, a passenger's stateroom. 3. The space on a dock at which a ship or boat is moored. *See also* slip.

beyond rights. *See* freedom rights.

BG. *Abr.* Business group.

BHC. *GDS.* Backhaul check (qv).

BIC. Bank identifier code. *See also* SWIFT Code.

bicentenary. The 200th anniversary.

bidet. A porcelain bathroom fixture, common in European hotels, designed to bathe a woman's external genitalia and for douching.

Big Five, the. 1. The five most popular game animals in Africa: lion, leopard. rhinoceros, buffalo, elephant. 2. The five most popular costumed characters at Walt Disney theme parks: Mickey Mouse, Minnie Mouse, Donald Duck, Pluto, Goofy.

BIKE. *GDS.* Bicycle.

bike lane. A portion of a roadway that is marked off for use by bicyclists.

bikeway. A path , trail, road, or lane designated for bicycle use.

bilateral agreement. A treaty or other agreement, usually between sovereign nations, detailing their mutual understanding, policies, and obligations on a particular matter, such as trade or airline landing rights.

bilge. The bottommost part of a ship's interior. In seaman's slang, worthless talk.

bilingual. Written in or speaking two languages.

bill of fare. A menu.

bimini. A weather-proof fabric stretched over the open spaces of a sailing vessel to provide shade and weather protection to the pilot and/or passengers.

binnacle. On a ship, the holder for the compass.

biodegradable. Capable of being broken down into its constituent elements by natural processes. Used to describe "environmentally friendly" products.

biodiversity. The range of animal and plant life in an ecosystem.

biometric identifiers. Unique physical characteristics, such as patterns on the retina or hand geometry, used to identify individuals and used in passports and at theme parks.

biorhythms. The natural cycles of the human body, said to vary from person to person and to be affected by travel. *See also* jet lag.

bioterrorism. The use of biological agents by terrorists or others to cause death and panic.

bird dog. *n.* A person who drums up or brings in business for a travel agency.

birdcage. *Slang.* Air traffic control term for the airspace in the immediate vicinity of an airport.

bistro. *Fr.* A small restaurant featuring simple fare, sometimes with entertainment.

black box. *Slang.* Flight data recorder (qv).

black market. Illegal trade, commerce, or currency exchange that evades taxes, governmental oversight, or both.

black-water rafting. Riding inner tubes or other inflatables on rivers that run into or through caves.

blacked out. Not available. *See also* blackout dates.

blackout dates, blackout periods. Dates on which tickets or certain fares are not available. Blackout dates usually coincide with holidays and peak travel seasons.

BLCY. *GDS.* Balcony (qv).

blimp. A lighter-than-air airship. Used primarily as an advertising vehicle or a camera platform for sporting events; occasionally used for tourist excursions.

BLND. *GDS.* Passenger is blind.

block booking. The practice of allocating groups of airline seats, hotel rooms, or other travel products to service a specific group or for a specific use. *See also* blocked space.

block(ed) space. *n.* Seats, berths, or rooms set aside for group sale. Also, *v.*, to reserve such space.

board. 1. To get on a plane, train, or ship. 2. Meals, as in a hotel stay.

board of directors setup. Configuration of a meeting room in which chairs are placed around rectangular or oval conference tables.

boarding pass. A ticket-like form or stub, usually containing a seat assignment, issued to a boarding passenger. Serves as an additional check in the boarding process.

boat bite. *Slang.* An injury, typically minor, sustained while on a recreational sailing vessel.

boat deck. The deck on a cruise ship on which the lifeboats are located.

boat station. A ship's passenger's assigned space during lifeboat drills or an actual emergency.

boatel. Combining "boat" and "hotel." A motel for boaters.

bodega. *Sp.* A wine cellar. By extension, a winery. In some Spanish speaking countries, a bar or grocery store.

bon voyage. *Fr.* Literally, "good voyage." The traditional farewell for those departing by ship.

bond. A sum of money held in escrow to assure full payment or to indemnify a party against financial loss. An insurance agreement that accomplishes the same ends.

bonded. Protected or guaranteed by a bond.

bonnet. *Brit.* The hood of a car.

booking. A reservation.

booking code. The code used to make a booking on a GDS (qv) for a specific fare. Also called a fare code (qv).

booking engine. A computer program, accessed via the Internet, that allows the making of reservations and the purchase of travel products such as airline tickets and hotel rooms.

booking fee. The charge levied by a GDS on a supplier for handling a reservation.

boondocker. A recreational vehicle user who prefers to camp in free and/or secluded locations, as opposed to regular campgrounds that charge a fee.

boondocks, the. A mildly derogatory term for rural or unsettled land. Primarily U.S. usage.

boot. *Brit.* The trunk of a car.

booth. An exhibit area at a trade show. A covered-over stall in a market.

bordello. A house of prostitution.

bottom line. The net profit or result in a transaction. By extension, the final word or the outcome.

boutique hotel. A small property, typically offering an enhanced level of service and marketed to the affluent.

boutique operation. Any business venture that seeks to provide an enhanced level of service, at a premium price, to a select clientele.

bow. The front of a ship.

bow rider. A recreational motorboat providing access to a lounging area near the front (bow).

BP. *GDS.* Breakfast plan or Bermuda Plan (qv).

BPR. *GDS.* Boarding Pass Reserved or Boarding Pre-Reserved. A boarding pass with seating assignment arranged at the time of booking.

brasserie. *Fr.* A restaurant serving hearty fare, usually with a liquor and coffee bar.

breakage. A budget line item for items that will be broken and have to be replaced during a specific time period, for example glasses in a restaurant.

breakdown. The process of clearing and cleaning a meeting room, as in a hotel, after a function.

break-even, break-even point. The dollar figure at which an enterprise begins to show a profit. The amount of sales that must be reached for a project to become worthwhile.

break-out room. A smaller room, near a larger meeting room, for use when a larger group breaks into sections.

brewpub. A bar or restaurant that brews its own beer and ale on the premises.

bricks-and-mortar. Used to refer to a business that has a physical location, as opposed to one that operates solely on the Internet.

bridge. On a ship, the navigational center. Where the captain stands.

bridge officers. On a cruise ship, the personnel charged with the navigation of the ship.

briefing. An informational talk, usually given to those with a professional need to know the information being dispensed.

briefing tour. A tour, usually for travel agents and other industry personnel, intended to acquaint them with a new destination or new procedures.

brioche. *Fr.* A type of breakfast roll.

Brit. *Slang.* A Briton. A citizen of the British Isles.

Britannia. The mythical female personification of Britain.

BritRail. British Railways.

brochure. Any piece of promotional literature.

brown bagging. Bringing one's own food. In a restaurant, bringing wine or liquor when the restaurant is not licensed to serve alcohol.

browser. A software program enabling users to navigate the World Wide Web and the Internet.

BSI. *GDS.* Basic Sine In.

BSO. *GDS.* Basic Sine Out.

BSP. *GDS.* Bank Settlement Plan. *See* Area Settlement Plan.

BTC. Business Travel Coalition.

BTD. Business Travel Department, usually of a large corporation.

BTH. *GDS.* Bath.

BTS. Bureau of Transportation Statistics.

bubble car. A train car with a domed plexiglass top for sightseeing. Also called a dome car (qv).

bucket shop. *Brit.* slang. A consolidator (qv). Any retail outlet dealing in discounted airfares.

budget. 1. *adj.* Accommodations, tours, restaurants, etc. that are low in price and appeal to the frugal traveler. 2. *n.* A written plan outlining limits on expenditures. 3. *v.* To cost out an itinerary or trip.

budget fare. Any of a number of heavily restricted airline fares offering a substantial discount off the normal fare (qv).

buffer zone. 1. A demilitarized zone between two countries, intended to decrease the likelihood of hostilities. 2. An imaginary area extending 225 miles north and south of the United States border. Flights within this area are subject to U.S. tax.

buffet. A serve-yourself meal featuring several choices in each course.

bug. A defect or malfunction in a computer program. By extension, any glitch in a system.

Buginese schooner. A two-masted sailing vessel or schooner of Indonesian design, accommodating 12 to 18 passengers, used by some soft-adventure tour operators.

bulk contract. An agreement whereby an airline sells large blocks of seats at a discount for resale by a third party.

bulk fare. A fare available only when buying blocks of seats.

bulk mail. A U.S. Post Office category of presorted third-class mail that enjoys a special low rate.

bulkhead. The walls on a ship or airplane that divide the vessel into sections or compartments.

bulkhead seats. On an airplane, the seats immediately aft (qv) of a bulkhead, usually with limited legroom.

bullet train. A high speed train, specifically in Japan.

bumping. The practice of denying seats, usually on an airline, to ticketed passengers due to overbooking or in favor of other passengers with a higher priority.

bundling. The practice of combining a number of different products or services for sale at a single price.

bungaloft. A bungalow or other small building with a sleeping loft. Primarily Canadian usage.

bungalow. A cottage. A small house. In hotels, a room or suite that is a separate building.

bunker. On a ship, a storage place for fuel.

buoy. A floating navigational marker, used to mark channels or warn of danger.

-burg. *Ger.* suffix. A fortified place. A medieval city.

burgher. A resident of a town. A solid citizen.

burgomaster. In several European countries, a mayor or chief magistrate of a town.

burro. A small pack animal, a donkey.

bus. 1. *n.* A multi-seated vehicle used for inter- and intracity transportation. Sometimes called a "motorcoach," especially when specially designed for

255

256

*The Travel Agent's
Complete Desk
Reference*

carrying tourists. 2. *v.* To transport by bus. 3. *v.* To clear tables, as in a restaurant.

busboy. A low-level restaurant employee who clears tables, serves water, etc. Sometimes "busman" or "busperson."

bush, the bush. Wild, unsettled land; by extension, any rural locale. Frequently used in Australia and other former British colonial countries to indicate "the country" as opposed to "the city."

Bushman. 1. A member of a nomadic tribe in Southern Africa. 2. In Australia, one who lives in "the bush," the rural areas of the country.

business class. A relatively new class of airline service, positioned in marketing as between first-class and coach. Designed to appeal to the business traveler. The amenities provided in business class vary from carrier to carrier.

business mix. In a travel agency, the percentage of corporate to leisure travel booked.

bust-out, bust-out operation. A scheme in which an ARC-appointed agency sells large numbers of airline tickets in a short period but does not deposit the funds with ARC. The agency then goes out of business and the owners abscond with the funds.

buy forward. Enter into a forward transaction (qv).

buyback agreement. In the rental car industry, a practice in which automobile companies repurchase their cars at a set price after a negotiated period of time.

buyer's market. An economic condition in which supply exceeds demand, resulting in very favorable prices for buyers.

buyer's remorse. A tendency to have second thoughts about a purchase, which often leads to cancelling the sale.

buying market share. A practice in which a company offers goods or services at extremely low prices or at a loss to attract large numbers of customers, in the expectation that many of these customers will remain loyal even when prices move upwards in the future.

BVI. British Virgin Islands.

BWI. British West Indies. Sometimes pronounced "BeeWee."

bypass. 1. A route that goes around a city or other congested area. 2. *v.* To skip or avoid a destination on a trip. 3. The practice of marketing or selling direct to the public, without travel agents. *See also* agent bypass.

C, c

C. *Abr.* Celsius. *See* Celsius scale.

CAA. Civil Aeronautics Authority.

CAB. Civil Aeronautics Board. Absorbed into the DOT (Department of Transportation) in 1985.

cab. 1. A taxi (qv). 2. The driver's compartment of a vehicle.

cabana. *Sp.* 1. A hotel room that is a separate building, typically near the beach or a pool. 2. A private changing room near a hotel beach or pool.

cabaret. 1. A type of entertainment performed in a club or restaurant, usually small-scale featuring singing and/or comedy sketches. 2. A club or restaurant offering such entertainment.

cabin. 1. The passenger compartment of an airplane. 2. A ship's stateroom. 3. A rustic hotel room separate from the main building.

cabin attendant. 1. A flight attendant (qv). 2. A cabin steward (qv).

cabin steward. A ship's employee responsible for cleaning staterooms.

cable. 1. The heavy metal anchor chain on a ship. 2. Any thick rope used aboard a ship. 3. A text message sent by wire. A telegram.

cable car. 1. A trolley operated by underground cables. 2. An aerial tramway.

cable length. On ships, a distance of 600 feet (100 fathoms).

cablegram. An overseas telegram, specifically one transmitted by undersea cables.

cabotage. 1. Trade between two points in a country, usually prohibited to carriers of another nation. 2. The right to engage in such trade. *See also* freedom rights.

cabriolet. A one-seat, horse-drawn carriage.

cache. 1. *n.* A hiding place for supplies, as on a hiking trip, or any supplies so hidden. 2. *n.* Supplies suspended in the air to prevent animals from getting to them. 3. *v.* To hide supplies in this manner.

cachet. *Fr. adj.* Possessed of charm, allure, or attraction. Enjoying a good reputation.

caddy. A person who carries a golfer's clubs.

cafe. 1. *Fr.* and *Sp.* Coffee. 2. A small restaurant serving coffee. Sometimes with outdoor seating, as in "sidewalk cafe."

cafe au lait. *Fr.* Coffee with milk.

cafe noir. *Fr.* Black coffee.

CAI. Computer-assisted instruction.

call brand. Any brand of liquor that a customer must ask for by name in a restaurant; as opposed to more generic, less expensive house brands (qv).

call sign. A code identifying a ship's radio.

cambio. *Sp.* Literally, "change." By extension, a currency exchange bureau.

canal. An artificial inland waterway originally built to connect one body of water with another and allow commercial barge traffic. Now also used for recreational purposes.

258

*The Travel Agent's
Complete Desk
Reference*

canal barge. A vessel designed to carry freight on a canal, now often converted to passenger use for leisure cruising.

cancel. 1. To void, as a reservation. 2. To indicate an item has been processed, as a check.

cancellation clause. In a contract, a provision that allows for cancellation by one of the parties, usually upon payment of a penalty.

cancellation penalty. An amount deducted by a supplier from a refund of prepaid funds when a reservation is cancelled.

canoe. 1. *n.* A slender oared vessel of Native American origin. 2. *v.* To travel by or navigate a canoe.

canton. An administrative district in Switzerland or France.

capacity controlled. With limited space or seating at a specific price.

capacity dumping. The airline strategy of adding additional flights to a route in an attempt to drive a competitor out of business or off the route.

capital. The seat of government of a state, province, or country.

capitol. 1. A building housing and symbolizing a seat of government. 2. The decorative portion surmounting a column.

caps. *See* commission cap.

capstan. A device used aboard ships for winding ropes used in lifting cargo and other heavy weights.

capsule hotel. A Japanese lodging featuring small, coffin-like sleeping compartments. Often found near railway stations and usually accepting men only. Pronounced "capseru hoteru" in Japanese.

captain. 1. The commanding officer on a ship. 2. The pilot of an airplane.

CAPPS. Computer Assisted Passenger Prescreening System (qv).

car class. The specific size, style, and rental price of a rental car.

car ferry. A ship transporting automobiles and passengers.

car for hire. *Brit.* A rental car.

caravan. 1. *Brit.* A mobile home or van. 2. A group traveling together. Typically, Arab merchants and their camels. 3. By extension, a convoy of vehicles traveling together, especially military vehicles.

card mill. Derogatory term for a travel agency that recruits outside salespeople with the lure of instant travel benefits said to be obtainable with the photo ID card the agency issues.

carfare. 1. Money given, as to an employee, to cover the cost of local transportation. 2. The fare charged on a municipal transportation system.

cargo. Freight carried by a ship or airplane.

cargo liner. A ship that transports freight. *See also* freighter.

carhop. A waiter or waitress at a drive-in restaurant, where people eat in their cars.

Caribbean Basin Initiative. A U.S. government program established in 1983 to promote economic growth in the region through lower tariffs.

carnet. A customs document authorizing the transport of a car or other motor vehicle from one country to another.

carnival. 1. *U.S.* A traveling show featuring rides, games of chance, and displays of oddities. 2. A celebration preceding Lent, celebrated most prominently in New Orleans and Rio de Janeiro. 3. By extension, any large party-like outdoor celebration.

carousel. 1. A circular amusement park ride, typically with wooden horses that go up and down. 2. A mechanized device at airports to which passenger baggage is delivered and on which it is displayed while awaiting pickup.

carrier. Any company that transports passengers or freight.

carrying capacity. The maximum number of people a destination can accommodate without endangering the ecology or the supporting infrastructure.

carry-on. A piece of luggage designed to be taken aboard an airplane and fit into the space allotted for such luggage.

carry-on baggage or luggage. Baggage that is taken aboard an airplane by the passenger, as opposed to being checked and carried in the hold (qv).

cartographer. A person who creates maps.

cartography. The art and science of map-making.

CAS. *Abr.* Computer-assisted selling.

casbah. Traditionally, the old (or "native") quarter of a North African city.

cash advance. An amount given to an employee prior to a trip to cover anticipated cash outlays.

cash bar. An arrangement at a party where guests must pay for their drinks.

cash method. An accounting system in which income and expenses are recorded at the actual time received or disbursed. *See also* accrual method.

cash stipend. An amount paid by some educational tour operators to tour organizers as compensation for signing up passengers over and above those needed to qualify for a free ticket for the organizer.

cashless cruising. A system in which all purchases made on a cruise ship are signed for, with the bill presented for payment, by cash or credit card, at the end of the cruise.

casino. A gambling establishment offering a variety of gaming choices.

castaway. A person who has been shipwrecked.

casual courier. A person serving as an air courier (qv) on a one-time basis.

category. On a cruise ship, a class of cabin or fare level.

caveat emptor. *Lat.* Literally, let the buyer beware.

cay. A small island. A term used primarily in the Caribbean and pronounced "key."

CBBG. *GDS.* Cabin baggage.

CBI. *Abr.* Computer-based instruction.

CBN. *GDS.* Cabin (qv).

CBP. U.S. Customs and Border Protection, a bureau of the Department of Homeland Security (qv).

CCAR. *GDS.* Compact car.

CCRN. *GDS.* Credit card return notice.

CCS. *GDS.* Change segment status.

CCTE. *Abr.* Certified Corporate Travel Executive.

CCTV. Closed circuit television.

CDC. Centers for Disease Control and Prevention.

CD-ROM. *Abr.* Compact disc, read-only memory. A high-density storage medium for computer programs and data.

CDT. *Abr.* Central Daylight Time.

CDW. Collision Damage Waiver (qv).

ceiling. 1. The altitude of the lowest clouds. 2. The upper limit of operation of an aircraft. 3. By extension, any limit, as on expenditures.

Celsius scale. The metric scale for measuring temperature in which zero is the freezing point of water and 100 is the boiling point. Used in most countries of the world instead of the Fahrenheit scale (qv).

central reservation office. Location at which reservations are taken for a chain or group of hotels, car rental agencies, etc.

centralization. The process of consolidating certain types of activities or decision making in one place, as opposed to spreading them across corporate divisions or geographical locations.

centralized billing. A system in which a travel agent sends a single bill for travel by several or many people, as when a corporation is billed once for travel by all its employees.

centralized commissions. A system in which a supplier such as a hotel chain sends commission payments from a central office, rather than having individual properties pay commissions separately.

centralized payment plan. *See* centralized commissions.

CEO. Chief Executive Officer.

certification. A document attesting that a person or organization meets minimum standards or qualifications in a specified area. Usually issued by an organization with recognized expertise in the area.

certified mail. A premium category of mail delivery that provides proof of receipt by the addressee. Notifications required by contract are often sent certified mail.

Certified Niche Specialist (CNS). One who has taken a course in the areas of either Mature Adult, Family, or Special Interest Travel administered by the American Society of Travel Agents.

Certified Travel Counselor (CTC). One who has passed a series of rigorous tests of professional competency administered by the Institute of Certified Travel Agents.

CFCs. Chlorofluorocarbons, chemical compounds found in aerosol spray cans, refrigerators, air conditioners, and styrofoam cups among other products. In their gaseous forms they are said to be responsible for the depletion of the ozone layer (qv).

CFMD. *GDS.* Confirmed.

CFO. Chief Financial Officer.

CFY. *GDS.* Clarify.

CH. *GDS.* Child.

CHA. Caribbean Hotel Association.

chain. 1. A group of hotels, or other businesses, sharing a common name and ownership. 2. A group of islands.

chair. 1. *n.* The gender-neutral version of "chairman." The head of a committee or similar group. 2. *v.* To head such a group.

chair lift. A motor-driven cable from which hang chair-like seats for passengers. Typically found at ski resorts and used to transport people up steep inclines.

chalet. 1. A style of house associated with the ski regions of Europe. 2. By extension, any accommodation at a ski or mountain resort, especially if detached from the main building.

Chamber of Commerce. An association of businesses in a city, region, or state, devoted in part to promoting the business interests of its members. Chambers of commerce are often active in promoting tourism to their areas.

chambermaid. In hotels, a woman who cleans the rooms.

change of equipment. A change of aircraft that occurs without a change in the flight number.

change of gauge. *See* change of equipment.

channel. 1. A designated passage in a harbor, often dredged to allow safe passage of ships. Any navigable ship route. 2. A relatively narrow sea lane between two land masses.

channel-based pricing. A system in which the amount charged for a product or service differs according to the means of delivery. For example, a GDS company might charge airlines a lower per-segment fee to encourage use of a specific electronic booking tool.

charge d'affaires. *Fr.* A diplomatic rank below ambassador but accredited to the host government. The charge d'affaires often handles embassy business in the ambassador's absence.

chargeback. An amount of money deducted from monies otherwise due a merchant from a credit card company to cover the amount of disallowed charges.

chart. 1. *n.* A "map" of coastal or open waters, showing depths and hazards, used for navigation. 2. *v.* To plan, as to chart a course. 3. *n.* A graphical display of information or statistics.

charter. 1. *v.* To lease an aircraft or other mode of transport for the use of a group. 2. *n.* Any craft so used or any trip taken by such means. 3. *n.* A written document setting forth the governing principles of a group or organization.

chateau. A palatial European residence, sometimes remodeled as a hotel. Sometimes used of a hotel that is built in such a style.

chauffeur. A hired driver, usually of a limousine.

CHD. *GDS.* Child.

check. *v.* To place in the care of another, usually a carrier (qv), for retrieval at a later time upon presentation of a receipt, as in "to check luggage."

checked baggage. Baggage that a traveler has given over to the care of the carrier or other responsible party. An important distinction when liability for loss or damage is to be determined. *See also* unchecked baggage.

checker. 1. A person who receives baggage, coats, or other items to be checked. 2. *Cap.* A roomy make of New York taxicab, now obsolete.

check-in. A procedure whereby a hotel guest or airline passenger is registered as having arrived. Check-in may require the presentation of payment, reservations, or other documentation or identification.

check-in time. 1. In hotels, the earliest time at which a room will be avail-

able. 2. At airline terminals, the latest time at which a passenger may arrive for the flight without risk of losing his seat.

check-out. A procedure whereby a hotel guest formally leaves the hotel and settles his or her bill.

check-out time. In hotels, the latest time a guest may leave without being charged for another night's lodging.

checkpoint. A place on a road or at a terminal at which vehicles or people are stopped for inspection.

chevron setup. In a meeting, an arrangement in which chairs are aligned in a "V" along a central aisle.

child. In the travel industry, a designation used to determine fares and other rates. The precise definition varies from carrier to carrier and hotel to hotel. Generally, a "child" is at least two years old, as opposed to an "infant" (qv) who is younger. The upper limit can be anywhere from 9 to 18 years of age.

chit. A piece of paper or voucher (qv) that can be exchanged for food, drink, or other amenities. A raincheck (qv).

CHNG. *GDS.* Change.

CHNT. *GDS.* Change name to.

CHRIE. Council on Hotel, Restaurant, and Institutional Education.

Christian name. *Brit.* First name, of a person.

chronological order. Arranged in sequence by time of occurrence.

chronology. A list of events in their order of occurrence.

chronometer. Any instrument that measures time. A watch.

CHTR. *GDS.* Charter (qv).

Chunnel. *Slang.* Nickname for the railway tunnel beneath the English Channel linking Britain and France.

churning. The practice of repeatedly making the same booking in a GDS to avoid the 24-hour ticketing deadline.

ciao. *It.* Word for both hello and good-bye.

CIEE. Council on International Educational Exchange.

circle trip. Any trip that involves more than one destination, returning to the point of departure, as opposed to a "roundtrip" (qv).

circle trip minimum. The lowest allowable fare for a circle trip, which cannot be less than any roundtrip fare between any two cities on the itinerary.

circumnavigate. To sail around, as an island or the world.

CIS. Confederation of Independent States (qv).

citadel. A fort in a city used for the city's defense.

CITC. Canadian Institute of Travel Counselors.

city codes. Three-letter codes used to uniquely identify cities and/or their airports.

city pair. In airline bookings, the departure and arrival cities on an itinerary. The number of city pairs served by an airline is sometimes used as a measure of its size.

city terminal. *See* city ticket office.

city ticket office. An airline sales and ticketing office located anywhere other than the airport.

civil aviation. Any flight activity conducted by the private sector, as opposed to military aviation.

civil law. The law regulating non-criminal activities between and among individuals and corporations.

claim check. The receipt or stub, usually numbered, issued to a passenger for his or her luggage.

claim PNR booking. A booking that occurs when a travel agency issues a ticket for a reservation made by the passenger and entered into the GDS by the airline reservationist.

Class I to VI. A classification system used to rate the difficulty of rapids in whitewater rafting (qv). The higher the Roman numeral, the more difficult it is to negotiate the rapid.

class of service. 1. The level of amenities provided in a travel product. 2. A semi-arbitrary division determined by the fare paid, as in the multiple "classes" offered in coach by an airline. 3. An alphanumerical code indicating either (1) or (2), above.

clearance. 1. Permission, as for an airplane to take off. 2. The height of a bridge or overpass. 3. The distance between the highest point on a vessel and a bridge.

CLIA. Cruise Lines International Association.

clicks-and-mortar. Used to refer to a business, such as a travel agency chain, that combines an Internet strategy with storefront locations.

clicks-to-bricks. Used to refer to a business, such as a travel agency, that generates business via the Internet and services customers through storefront locations.

client. A term used for a customer, usually to indicate an ongoing relationship.

climate. The prevailing long-term weather conditions in a geographical region.

close. 1. *v.* To finalize or complete a sale. 2. *v.* To ask a closing question (qv). 3. *n. Brit.* A dead-end street.

closed dates. Dates on which travel or hotel rooms are unavailable due to prior sale or booking.

closing question. Any question that requires the client to make a commitment or decision that leads them closer to making a purchase.

club car. A car on a train serving liquor and refreshments.

club floor. In a hotel, a separate floor providing a higher level of service and security for a premium price. Also called Concierge Floor or Level.

clustering. In the hotel industry, a business strategy in which a number of properties are located in the same geographic area.

CMP. *Abr.* 1. Certified Meeting Professional. 2. Complete meeting package.

CNL. *GDS.* Cancel.

CNS. *Abr.* Certified Niche Specialist (qv).

coach. 1. The economy class on an airline. Also referred to as "economy" or "tourist." 2. The section of the plane designated for this class of passenger. 3. A motorcoach (qv).

coaching inns. Small hotels, often of historic significance, that were origi-

263

Glossary of Terms

nally stops along a stagecoach route; more common in Europe.

coastal cruise. A journey on a cruise ship that stays close to shore, as opposed to one that visits several islands or crosses significant distances of open water.

COC. *GDS.* Country of commencement (i.e. where travel begins).

cockpit. The pilot's compartment in a plane.

COD. *Abr.* Cash on delivery.

Code Blue. Under the Department of Homeland Security's Homeland Security Advisory System, a condition of "Guarded" risk indicating a "general risk of terrorist attack."

Code Green. Under the Department of Homeland Security's Homeland Security Advisory System, a condition of "Low" risk indicating a "low risk of terrorist attack."

Code Orange. Under the Department of Homeland Security's Homeland Security Advisory System, a condition of "High" alert, indicating "high risk of terrorist attack." The second highest level of warning.

Code Red. Under the Department of Homeland Security's Homeland Security Advisory System, a condition of "Severe" alert, indicating "severe risk of terrorist attack." The highest level of warning.

code sharing. An agreement whereby airlines permit the use of their GDS code in the flight schedule displays of other airlines.

Code Yellow. Under the Department of Homeland Security's Homeland Security Advisory System, a condition of "Elevated" risk, indicating "significant risk of terrorist attack."

cog railway. A railway system, usually used on short, very steep grades, in which a series of teeth on the rail mesh with the vehicle to insure traction.

co-host carrier. An airline that pays another to display its flights on a GDS.

COLA. *Abr.* 1. Cost of living allowance (qv). 2. Cost of living adjustment (qv).

cold call. A sales call to a prospective client with whom you have no prior contact.

cold wave. A period of abnormally cold weather.

collision damage waiver. Daily insurance that covers damage to a rental car.

colors. The flag or ensign flown from the mast or stern of a ship.

COMM. *GDS.* Commission (qv).

commercial agency. A travel agency that specializes in corporate travel.

commercial airline. An airline that carries passengers.

Commercial Sabre®. Term used to distinguish the full version of the Sabre® GDS from easySabre®, a now-defunct simplified version.

commission. 1. A percentage of the sale price paid to a salesperson as payment for making the sale. 2. An official investigative body. 3. *v.* To contract for the production of something, as to commission a work of art.

commission cap. The maximum dollar amount an airline, or other supplier, will pay as commission regardless of the actual price of the ticket or the standard commission rate.

commission split. An agreed upon division of commission income between two entities, such as a travel agency and an outside salesperson.

commissionable. Denoting the portion of total cost on which a travel agent can receive a commission.

commode. A portable toilet, usually one containing a removable bed pan or other receptacle.

common carrier. Any company engaged in the transport of people or goods for profit.

common law. Unwritten law that has become generally accepted by the formal legal system through long-standing practice.

Common Market. Obsolete term for the European Economic Community (qv).

common rated. Describing two identical fares to geographically close destinations.

commonwealth. A political entity with representative government. A voluntary association of sovereign states.

commuter. 1. *n.* A person who travels to work each day. 2. *adj.* Used to describe short-haul airlines.

comp. *Slang.* A free ticket or other complimentary extra.

comp rooms. Free rooms provided to a group of hotel guests based on total occupancy by the group.

companionway. A stairway connecting two decks on a ship.

compartment. A distinct section on a railroad car, airplane, ship, or other vehicle.

compass. A magnetic device used to determine direction aboard ship.

Computer Assisted Passenger Prescreening System (CAPPS). A U.S. national database that performs background checks on all those boarding planes or other modes of transport.

computer virus. A malicious and destructive program designed to be passed unwittingly from machine to machine via floppy disks, downloading, email, or other means.

computerized reservation system. Any of several proprietary computer systems allowing real-time access to airline fares, schedules, and seating availability and offering the capability of booking reservations and generating tickets. Now increasingly referred to as a global distribution system (qv).

complimentary. Free. Without charge.

concentrated hub. An airport where a single airline controls most of the passenger capacity.

concession. A shop or other place of business within a larger area, such as an airport or cruise ship, which has paid a fee in exchange for exclusivity.

concierge. A hotel employee charged with providing advice and additional services to the guests.

concierge level. *See* club floor.

Concorde. The supersonic jet jointly developed by Britain and France.

concourse. 1. A public area in an airport. 2. The section of the airport containing the gates.

COND. *GDS.* Conditional.

conditional fare. A fare that guarantees passage on the next available flight if the flight for which the ticket was purchased is full.

condo. Short for condominium (qv).

condo vacation. A travel product featuring lodging in a condominium (qv), typically one in a resort area, and providing additional amenities such as pools, tennis courts, golf courses, and so forth.

condominium. A form of ownership of real estate. In travel, generally used to refer to accommodations that are similar to or identical to furnished, private apartments or townhouses and that are available for rent by the day or week. Such properties are frequently rented out when the owner is not present. *See also* time share.

conductor. 1. A railway employee who collects tickets on board. 2. The person nominally in charge of a tour group. 3. The director of a symphony orchestra.

conductor's ticket. On a cruise ship, a free ticket awarded based on the size of a group booking. The ticket can be used by the travel agent who put the group together or given to a person in the group who was instrumental in making the booking happen.

Confederation of Independent States (CIS). The now independent satellite states of the former Soviet Union.

conference center. A hotel-like property designed specifically for hosting conventions and meetings.

confidential tariff. Wholesale rates intended for markup (qv) to retail pricing.

configuration. Arrangement or layout, as of an airplane's interior.

confirmation. The official acceptance of a booking by the supplier.

confirmation number. An alphanumeric code used to identify and document the confirmation of a booking.

confiscate. Take away or seize, as contraband goods.

congress. Another term for convention (qv), used most frequently in Europe.

conjunction tickets. Two or more tickets used on a single itinerary.

connecting flight. A flight that requires a passenger to change from one plane to another. *See also* connection.

connecting rooms. Hotel rooms that are next to each other and have a connecting door, in addition to the doors that open onto the hallway.

connection. A stop on a journey that requires a change of planes or other mode of transportation. *See also* connecting flight.

consent decree. A legal document whereby the target of a government lawsuit ends the suit by agreeing to take or refrain from specific actions specified in the decree.

consignment. 1. An arrangement whereby a supplier allots merchandise to a retailer who needs pay for it only upon sale. 2. Goods allotted under such an arrangement.

consolidation. 1. A business tactic in which a company concentrates its purchases with fewer suppliers to effect cost savings. 2. The process in which an industry comes to be served by fewer and fewer suppliers as companies merge or succumb to bankruptcy and competitive pressures;

the airline industry is a prime example.

consolidator. A company or individual who negotiates bulk contracts (qv) with an airline (or other travel supplier) and sells that space to the general public, usually at a discount.

consortium. A group of companies that enter into a voluntary association to share resources in order to gain a market advantage. In travel, usually used to refer to groups of suppliers that offer higher commissions and other incentives to travel agencies that enter into "preferred supplier" (qv) relationships with them.

construction fare. A round-the-world fare created by a specialist, usually a consolidator, by stitching together a series of one way fares on a number of airlines. *See also* alliance fare.

consul. A diplomatic representative of one country to another. The executive in charge of a consulate (qv).

Consular Information Sheet. One of a series of publications of the United States Department of State, providing essential travel information for each of the world's countries.

consulate. A subsidiary office of a foreign government, usually in a location other than the host nation's capital. Consulates typically handle visa applications and other business affairs of the foreign government.

consultant. An expert in a particular field who provides technical and other forms of assistance to companies or individuals on a fee basis.

continental breakfast. A breakfast of rolls, fruit and coffee or tea. Often provided on a complimentary basis by hotels and motels.

continental code. International Morse code (qv).

continental plan. A hotel rate that includes a continental breakfast (qv).

contour map. A map showing gradations in altitude.

contraband. Merchandise or substances that are illegal to import or export.

contract. A legal and enforceable agreement between two or more parties.

contract of carriage. The small print on the passenger's coupon of an airline ticket detailing the legal relationship, rights, and liabilities of the passenger and the carrier.

control tower. A central, raised operational center that supervises and directs all traffic into and out of an airport.

CONV. *GDS.* Convertible (car).

convention. A gathering of professionals or others to discuss matters of common interest.

conventioneer. A person participating in a convention.

conversion. 1. In the hotel industry, the change of a property from one brand to another. 2. The process of switching from one vendor to another. *See also* convert.

conversion agency. A formerly independent travel agency that has joined a chain. Typically, the conversion agency's name will be changed to or blended with the name of the chain.

conversion payment. A fee paid by a travel agency to a consortium upon joining.

conversion rate. The rate at which one currency is exchanged for an-

Glossary of Terms

other.

convert. *v.* 1. To switch vendors, as when an agency moves from one GDS to another. 2. To convince a customer to switch vendors.

converter. An electrical device that allows appliances designed for one type of current to be used with another.

convoy. 1. *n.* A group of ships (or other vehicles) traveling together, usually for purposes of mutual safety or defense. 2. *v.* To accompany or lead a group of vehicles to assure safe passage.

COO. *Abr.* Chief Operating Officer.

co-op advertising. An arrangement in which a supplier underwrites a portion of a travel agency's advertising expenses when such advertising features the supplier's products.

cooperative. A group of individuals or organizations that have joined together, usually to increase their buying or negotiating power.

coordinated universal time. A timekeeping system based on highly accurate atomic clocks.

cork charge, corkage. A fee charged by a restaurant for opening a bottle of wine, especially one not purchased on the premises.

corporate agency. 1. A travel agency physically located on the premises of a corporation that it services. 2. A travel agency that specializes in corporate clients.

corporate apartment. A condominium owned by a corporation for the exclusive use of its employees and guests.

corporate rate. 1. A lower hotel rate negotiated by a specific corporation for the use of its employees and guests. 2. A rate extended by a hotel to all business travelers.

corporate travel manager. A middle management position. Corporate travel managers are tasked with setting corporate travel policy and standardizing and overseeing all travel by corporate employees on company business. Many corporate travel managers function as in-house travel agents.

cost of living adjustment. The percentage by which Social Security recipients' monthly benefits are increased each year to adjust for increases in the cost of living. Intended to ensure that beneficiaries don't lose purchasing power due to inflation.

cost of living allowance. An additional sum provided to a corporate employee to offset higher prices in certain countries or cities.

cost-reimbursable contractor. A person or company working as an independent contractor for a governmental agency, whose costs, including travel, are reimbursed by the contracting agency.

cot. 1. *Abr.* Cottage. 2. A small folding bed used to provide additional sleeping space in a hotel room.

coterminous. Sharing a common boundary.

couchette. *Fr.* A sleeping compartment on a train with up to six beds.

counterfeit. 1. *adj.* False, forged. 2. *n.* An illegal copy, as of paper currency.

country of registry. The nation in which a ship's ownership is formally registered. The country of registry need not reflect the nationality of the crew or the cruise area in which the ship operates and is often chosen for tax reasons.

coup, coup d'etat. *Fr.* (Pronounced coo-day-TAH) The usually quick overthrow of a country's government, typically by assassination or forcible removal from office of the top leaders.

coupon. 1. The portion of an airline ticket collected from the passenger at the time of boarding. 2. A prepaid voucher (qv) that can be exchanged for certain specified goods or services, as a hotel room. 3. Any printed voucher providing for free or reduced cost services or goods.

coupon broker. A person or company that buys and resells airline frequent flyer awards in contravention of airline regulations.

courier. 1. Any person who accompanies cargo or hand-delivered documents. 2. *Brit.* A guide or tour escort.

course. The direction in which a ship or plane is headed. Expressed in degrees of the compass (qv).

cover charge. An admission charge, especially to a nightclub or cabaret (qv).

cover letter. A business letter that accompanies other documents or goods and explains the contents and purpose of what is being sent.

CP. *GDS.* Continental plan (qv).

CPM. *Abr.* Cost per thousand.

CPU. *Abr.* Central processing unit. Your computer's "brain."

CR. *GDS.* Change record.

credit memo. An informal document indicating that one company has a specific dollar amount credit with another, typically as a result of overpayment.

crew. All the members of the staff of a ship, airplane, or other form of transportation.

crew to passenger ratio. The number of passengers on a cruise ship divided by the number of crew members. In theory, the lower the number, the higher the level of service.

CRN. *GDS.* Cash refund notice.

croak fare. *Slang.* An airline's bereavement fare (qv) or other fare based on compassionate reasons. The implication is that one has to die to qualify for the fare.

cross-border ticketing. Writing a ticket in such a way that it appears that the travel commences in a different country than is actually the case. Used to take advantage of lower fare structures.

crossing. A cruise journey across an ocean.

Crown Colony. *Brit.* A colonial territory over which Great Britain still exerts some degree of direct control.

crow's nest. A lookout's station at the top of a ship's highest mast.

CRS. *Abr.* Computerized reservation system (qv).

CRT. *Abr.* Cathode ray tube. The screen of a computer.

cruise. In travel, any ocean, river, or lake voyage undertaken for pleasure.

cruise broker. Term used for a travel agent or other person who specializes in the sale of last-minute cruise berths.

cruise director. The person on a cruise ship charged with ensuring the enjoyment of all the passengers.

cruise fare. The actual cost of a cruise, excluding any extras, such as port taxes and gratuities.

cruise host. A gentleman recruited by the cruise ship, and usually traveling at a reduced cost, to serve as a dancing and social partner for single ladies on the cruise.

cruise line. A company that maintains a fleet of cruise ships and markets cruises to the public.

cruise ship. A seagoing vessel designed to carry passengers on leisure voyages.

cruise to nowhere. A cruise, typically of short duration and with an emphasis on partying and gambling, with no ports of call (qv).

cruiseship. *See* cruise ship.

cruising altitude. The height above the ground at which an aircraft operates most efficiently and at which it spends the bulk of its flying time.

cruising area. The general geographic location in which a cruise ship operates.

CSM. *Abr.* Convention services manager.

CSML. *GDS.* Child's meal.

CST. 1. *Abr.* Central Standard Time. 2. California Seller of Travel.

CT. *GDS.* 1. Circle trip (qv). 2. Central time.

CTC. 1. *Abr.* Certified Travel Counselor (qv). 2. *GDS.* Contact. 3. Canadian Tourism Commission.

CTCA. *GDS.* Contact's address.

CTCB. *GDS.* Contact's business phone.

CTCH. *GDS.* Contact's home phone.

CTD. *Abr.* Corporate Travel Department.

CTG. *GDS.* Cottage.

CTIP. Coalition for Travel Industry Parity.

CTM. 1. *GDS.* Circle trip minimum (qv). 2. *Abr.* Consolidated tour manual.

CTO. *GDS.* City ticket office (qv).

culture shock. The state of being overwhelmed by the differences in customs and behavior in a foreign place.

curator. The person in charge of one or more of a museum's collections.

curbside check in. A service that allows passengers to check their bags and/or get seat assignments outside a terminal building. Most common at airports.

curfew. A police or military regulation requiring people to be off the streets during a certain period, generally at night.

currency adjustment. A discontinued method of figuring fares in local currency using fare construction units (qv).

currency restriction. Any rule or law imposed by a country to regulate the flow of currency into or out of its territory.

current. 1. Any measurable movement of air or water in a specific direction. 2. A major steady movement of water in the ocean, as in the Humboldt Current (qv).

customer-activated ticketing. A vending machine that allows passengers to purchase airline tickets with a credit card.

customs. 1. A government agency that monitors the flow of goods, commodities, and substances into and from its territory and levies fees, fines, and other charges according to posted regulations. 2. The inspection area maintained by such an agency at an airport or other port of entry.

customs declaration. A form completed by an arriving passenger on which are listed the dutiable goods being imported.

customs duty. *See* duty.

customs user fee. A fee added to international airline tickets to benefit the U.S. customs service.

cut-off date. A date beyond which an offer, fare, request, or availability will no longer apply or be honored.

CV. *Abr.* Container vessel.

CVB. *Abr.* Convention and Visitors Bureau.

CVR. *Abr.* Cockpit voice recorder.

CWGN. *GDS.* Compact station wagon.

CWO. *Abr.* Cash with order.

CYBA. Charter Yacht Brokers Association.

D,d

dabble agent. Derogatory term for a part-time travel agent. Sometimes applied to any outside agent or independent contractor as a slur on their professionalism.

daily program. On a cruise ship, a listing of the day's activities.

dais. Raised platform in a room or hall on which a speaker's lectern (qv) or table for VIPs is situated.

DAPO. *GDS.* Do all possible.

database. 1. Any collection of information on a specific subject or area. Specifically, a computerized collection of such information. 2. A computer program designed to store such information.

DATAS II. A computer reservation system that is now part of Worldspan®.

Davey Jones' locker. *Slang.* The bottom of the ocean.

davit. A crane on a ship that's used to raise and lower anchors, lifeboats, and cargo.

day rate. 1. In hotels, the fee charged for a stay of limited duration, typically during daylight hours. 2. A fee charged for the use of a facility during a twenty-four hour period.

day tripper. *Brit.* A person whose roundtrip travel will be completed on the same day. On a longer leisure trip, a day tripper will make a series of one-day excursions to different locales to avoid changing hotels.

daylight savings time. An artificial forward adjustment of the clock in the Spring. Instituted to increase business by adding more hours of daylight in the evening.

d.b.a. *Abr.* Doing business as (qv).

dbl. *Abr.* Double (qv).

DBLB. *GDS.* Double room with bath.

DBLN. *GDS.* Double room without shower or bath.

DBLS. *GDS.* Double room with shower.

DC. *Abr.* Direct current.

DCSN. *GDS.* Decision.

DEA. Drug Enforcement Agency.

dead ahead. Straight in front of the ship's bow.

dead calm. No wind. Zero on the Beaufort Scale (qv).

dead reckoning. In navigation, a way of calculating a ship's or plane's position without reference to sun or stars, based on speed, direction, and drift.

deadend booking. A booking that is completed on a GDS but never ticketed. Deadend bookings can result from training new hires, forgetfulness, or fraud on the part of the travel agent.

deadhead. *v.* To return without paying cargo, whether freight or passengers. Used of commercial vehicles.

deadlight. A ventilated porthole cover that prevents light from entering.

DEAF. *GDS.* Deaf passenger.

debark. To get off a plane or ship.

debit memo. An informal invoice (qv) from a supplier showing an additional amount due. ARC (qv) will issue a debit memo when it feels the agency has made an error.

debug. A computer term meaning to identify and correct mistakes in a computer program. By extension, to correct mistakes in other contexts.

deck. The floor of a ship. A level on a ship.

deck chair. On a cruise ship, a reclining chair designed for lounging.

deck plan. Drawing or "map" that shows the layout of a ship's decks, cabins, and other areas.

deck steward. Member of a ship's crew who provides passengers with drinks, towels, deck chairs, etc.

decode. Translate from code into ordinary language.

decommission. To remove a ship from active service.

dedicated line. A telephone line that is used for ("dedicated to") a single purpose, such as a fax machine. May also refer to an electrical line.

deductible. 1. *n.* In insurance, the amount the customer must pay before the insurance kicks in. 2. *adj.* Used to describe business and other expenditures that you may subtract from your gross income in figuring your income tax liability.

deep six. *Slang.* To throw overboard. By extension, to throw away anything, usually with the motive of concealing its existence.

deep vein thrombosis. A potentially fatal medical condition brought about or aggravated by prolonged sitting in a cramped position, as on a long flight in coach class.

default. 1. *v.* To fail to supply contracted goods or services or refund the money paid for them. 2. *n.* In a computer program, a pre-programmed setting, that can sometimes be changed or modified by the user.

default protection plan. An insurance policy that protects the holder against a supplier's failure to deliver products or services or refund the money paid for them.

deluxe. *Fr.* Literally, "of luxury." Room or hotel in an excellent location with luxurious furnishings or accommodations.

demi-pension. *Fr.* Half pension (qv).

demo. 1. *Slang.* Demonstration. 2. Video or other visual or hands-on unit used in a sales demonstration.

demonstration effect. The phenomenon of local residents adopting the styles and manners they have observed in visiting tourists.

demographics. Age, income, marital status, ethnicity, and other statistical characteristics of populations. Used in marketing to analyze and identify markets.

denied boarding certificate. A coupon or other document issued by an airline and entitling the holder to compensation resulting from involuntary bumping from an overbooked flight.

denied-boarding compensation. Payment given passengers who've been bumped from a flight, cruise, or land-tour. May be a free trip, money, or accommodations.

dep. *Abr.* 1. Departure. 2. Deposit (qv).

DEP. *GDS.* 1. Scheduled departure time. 2. After departure, the time the flight departed.

Glossary of Terms

Department of Homeland Security. The U.S. government agency tasked with securing the country against terrorist attack.

departure tax. Tax levied on travelers when they leave a country.

deplane. *v.* To get off a plane.

deplate. *v.* Withdraw the right of a travel agency to issue tickets for a particular airline.

deposit. Payment made to hold space on a tour or accommodations. May be fully or partially refundable if the passenger cancels with enough advance notice.

depot. 1. Bus or train station. 2. Storage place for goods or motor vehicles.

depreciable asset. Any property owned by a business that is subject to depreciation (qv) for tax purposes.

depreciation. In taxation, a deduction taken to account for the decline in value of assets, such as machines used in a business, over a period of time. Used to offset the cost of acquiring the asset. *See also* expense.

dereg. *Slang.* Deregulation (qv).

deregulation. Elimination of regulation. In travel, usually used to refer to the U.S. government's elimination of restrictions on airlines' fares, routes, etc. Enacted in 1978.

designated driver. Member of a group who refrains from drinking alcoholic beverages in order to drive the group home safely.

designator, designator code. A two- or three-digit alphanumeric code uniquely identifying airlines and airports throughout the world. Administered by IATA (qv).

destination. Place to which a person is traveling or a thing is sent.

destination management company. A local company that handles arrangements for tours, meetings, transportation, and so forth, for groups originating elsewhere.

destination marketing organization. A company or other entity involved in the business of increasing tourism to a destination or improving its public image.

destination specialist. A person who has passed a test administered by an accrediting body certifying that he or she possesses an expert level of knowledge about a specific tourist destination or region.

destination wedding. A wedding that takes place in a location other than the bride and groom's home, typically a popular tourist destination.

DET. *GDS.* Domestic escorted tour (qv).

detached interface. A computer configuration that allows additional functions (such as accounting) to be performed while primary functions (such as ticketing) are in progress.

detente. *Fr.* A state of lessened tension or hostility between nations.

devaluation. The decrease in value of one currency in relation to another, usually by action of the government. When a currency is devalued, it buys less in foreign markets.

DEW Line. *Abr.* Distant Early Warning line. A line of radar stations set up to give advance warning of enemy air attack.

DHS. Department of Homeland Security (qv).

differential. 1. The difference in price, quality, etc. between comparable products or services. 2. The quantified amount of the difference. 3. Amount owed or credited due to a change in the class of service.

dig. *Slang.* An area of archeological excavation.

digs. *Brit.* slang. Living accommodations.

dine-around plan. Prepaid plan (such as a modified American plan) that allows guests to choose among a number of restaurants. Typically, the restaurants will all be owned by the same company.

diner. 1. The restaurant car on a train. 2. A small, usually very informal restaurant. 3. Person eating in a restaurant.

dinghy. A small oared boat.

diplomatic immunity. A provision of international law that exempts the diplomats of one country from the laws of a country to which they are assigned.

diplomatic plates. Automobile license plates, usually of a distinct design, issued to the vehicles of accredited diplomats.

direct access. System or program that gives the user the capability of tapping directly into a vendor's computer system to get last-minute information about seat or product availability.

direct billing. System in which a corporation's travel agency bills employees for their business travel. The employee must then submit an expense accounting and be reimbursed by the corporation.

direct flight. Any flight between two places that carries a single flight number. Unlike a nonstop, a direct flight will make one or more stops between the two places. The passenger may have to change planes or even change airlines. This is a change in meaning. In the past, direct flights made stops but required no change of plane.

direct mail. 1. A form of marketing in which sellers offer their products or services to buyers by mail, instead of (or in addition to) through agents or stores. 2. A form of advertising in which sellers promote their products or services by mail. Many recipients consider direct mail ads "junk mail."

direct spending. In the tourism industry, any money that goes directly from a tourist's pocket into the local economy. *See also* indirect spending.

directional selling. Booking with suppliers with whom the agency has a preferred supplier relationship.

directional tariff. A lower fare for one segment of an itinerary, usually requiring roundtrip travel or available only during certain time periods.

dirigible. A blimp (qv).

dirty bomb. An explosive device using conventional explosives designed to spread radioactive contamination. A dirty bomb is not a nuclear device.

dis. *Abr.* Discontinued.

disburse. To pay out (money).

disclaimer, disclaimer of liability. A formal denial of legal and financial responsibility for monetary losses or other injury incurred as a result of advice given or products or services sold. Example: A travel agent would use a disclaimer to ward off claims for injuries or losses a client might incur while traveling, as a result, say, of a charter cancellation or an accident while white-water rafting.

disclosure. The act of making something known. Example: By law, airline

ads must disclose all the restrictions on the special fares they advertise.

discontinued date. The date on which a fare, or other offer, expires.

discotheque. Nightclub for dancing.

discount fare. A special fare, usually offered for a limited time and in a limited quantity.

discretionary income. The amount a person has left to spend, save, or invest after paying all bills.

disembark. To get off a plane, ship, or train.

disintermediation. 1. The process of removing middlemen (qv) from the sales process, as when a travel product supplier bypasses travel agents to sell directly to the consumer. 2. The movement of money from lower yielding investments to higher yielding investments.

disk. A magnetic file used in computers.

display bias. A discontinued practice in which a GDS (qv) would display it's owners' flights first. *See also* architectural bias.

distribution. 1. The process of delivering products or services to customers. 2. The full extent of a supplier's distribution network.

district sales manager. The individual responsible for managing sales at the district level for a hotel, airline, cruise line, or other supplier. Depending on the company, may be primarily a salesperson or a manager of salespeople.

DIT. *GDS.* Domestic Independent Tour/Traveler.

dive boat. A small vessel outfitted for the needs of scuba divers. May or may not have accommodations.

divestiture. The compulsory transfer of title or disposal of interests (for example, in a corporation or real estate) upon government order, often to satisfy antitrust legislation and ensure competition. Example: In the early eighties, the federal government required the divestiture of the regional telephone companies by AT&T.

DLX. *GDS.* Deluxe room.

DM. *Abr.* 1. District manager. 2. Deutschemark.

D-Mark. *Abr.* Deutschemark.

DMC. 1. *GDS.* Directional Minimum Check. The check a travel agent must make to be sure that the fare (charged) isn't lower than the minimum applicable fare (in either direction). 2. Destination management company (qv) or consultants.

DMO. *Abr.* 1. Destination marketing organization. 2. District marketing office.

DO. *GDS.* Drop-off.

docent. A guide in a museum or art gallery.

dock. 1. *n.* The waterway between piers (qv) for the reception of ships. 2. *n.* A place for loading or unloading cargo or other materials. 3. A berth, pier, or quay. 4. *v.* To come into dock; to become docked.

docs. *Slang.* Documents.

docs rec'd. *Abr.* Documents received.

dog and pony show. *Slang.* A derogatory term for a sales presentation.

doing business as. A phrase indicating that a corporation has registered with the state to conduct business under a name other than its official corporate name. Typically abbreviated dba. A corporation might have several dba's.

dom. *Abr.* Domestic.

dome car. A train car with a domed plexiglass top for sightseeing. Also called a bubble car (qv).

domestic airline. An air carrier that provides service within its own country. Also called a domestic carrier.

domestic escorted tour. A packaged tour, with guide, that takes place in your own country.

domestic fare. Fare charged for travel within a country.

domicile. Place of residence, home.

dormette. An airline seat that reclines to sleeping position. Used on some carriers for long-distance runs. Also called a sleeperette.

DOT. Department of Transportation.

dot-matrix printer. A printer, used with a computer, that forms letters and numbers with a series of ink dots. Dot-matrix printers produce a lower print quality than laser printers.

double. A room designed to be shared by two people. It may have one double (or larger) bed, two twin beds, or two double (or larger) beds. Rooms with two double beds are sometimes called a "double double."

double booking. The practice of booking and confirming two or more reservations when only one will be used.

double-double. A hotel room with two double beds, sometimes called a twin double.

double occupancy rate. The rate charged when two people will occupy a room, suite, apartment, etc. For example, a hotel might charge an individual $100 per night for a room (single occupancy) but charge two people only $130 for double occupancy of the same room.

double-decker. A bus, or other conveyance, with two levels; used as public transportation in some cities, and exclusively for sightseeing and other special uses in other areas.

down. *Slang.* Inoperable (as in "The computer is down."). Often used of computers and computer networks when they shut down as a result of power failures, system crashes, operator errors, quirks in the system, or downtime (qv) on networks or reservation systems.

Down East. *Slang.* Extreme northeast New England. Maine.

Down Under. *Slang.* An affectionate term for Australia and, to a lesser extent, New Zealand.

downgrade. To move to a lower grade or quality of services or accommodations.

downline. 1. All segments, legs, or cities listed below the originating or headline city (on a schedule or GDS). 2. The members, in rank order, of a multi-level marketing program.

download. *v.* To transfer a file or files from a remote computer to a local computer electronically.

downsizing. A corporate restructuring aimed at making the organization smaller, more efficient, and more profitable by selling ("spinning off") or eliminating various product lines and/or business units and permanently

278

The Travel Agent's
Complete Desk
Reference

eliminating many jobs.

downtime. 1. Time during which production is stopped for repairs or alterations to a system, network, machine, or program. 2. *Slang.* Time a person spends sleeping or vegging out.

downtown. The business district of a city.

downwind. In the direction of the wind. Any location "downwind" will receive odors or emissions from an object or location "upwind" (qv).

DPLX. *GDS.* Duplex (qv).

DPP. *Abr.* Default protection plan (qv).

DPST. *GDS.* Deposit (qv).

dptr. *Abr.* Departure.

draft. (*Brit.* draught) Measurement in feet from a ship's waterline (qv) to the lowest point of its keel (qv).

drag. The aerodynamic force that slows a plane in flight.

dram shop legislation. Any law regulating the sale of alcoholic beverages in bars and restaurants.

draw. An amount paid to a salesperson on a regular basis and deducted from his or her commission earnings. Also referred to as a "draw against commission."

drayage. The charge assessed for transporting goods.

dress circle. The mezzanine (qv) or first balcony of a theater, especially an opera house.

drill. A practice exercise, as a lifeboat drill on a cruise ship.

drive-away company. A company that transports automobiles and other vehicles by finding people who will drive them to their destination.

drive-in. 1. *n.* An outdoor movie theater where people watch from their cars. 2. *adj.* Any service designed to be provided to customers in their cars.

drive market. 1. Potential travelers within driving distance of a city, port or attraction. 2. Travelers within a travel agency's local area who tend to drive to vacation destinations.

drop-off charge. An add-on fee that may be assessed when a rental car or other rental vehicle is dropped off at a location other than the one where it was rented. Usually a flat amount.

DRS. *GDS.* Direct reference system.

dry dock. 1. *n.* Dock (qv) that can be emptied of water while a ship is being repaired. 2. *v.* To put into dry dock.

dry lease. The rental of a boat, or other vehicle, without a crew or supplies.

DSM. *Abr.* District sales manager (qv).

DSO. *Abr.* District sales office. May also be called a DMO (qv).

DSPL. *GDS.* Display.

DTIA. Dive Travel Industry Association.

dual designated carrier. Air carrier that uses another airline's code in flight schedule displays. *See also* code sharing.

duck boats. World War II-vintage boats that are sometimes used for river tours.

DUI. *Abr.* Driving under the influence (of alcohol or another drug).

dumbwaiter. A small, hand-operated elevator system used to transport food and dishes from one level to another, as between the kitchen and dining room.

dune buggy. An off-road vehicle designed for travel on sandy soil.

dungeon. A prison or chamber that's dark and usually underground.

duplex. 1. A two-family house. A house that contains two separate dwelling units. 2. An apartment with rooms on two floors. 3. Separate accommodations that share walls.

dutiable. Subject to duty (qv).

duty. A tax; most often applied to imported goods.

duty-free. *adj.* Being exempt from import tax. Most often applied to goods bought in special airport shops just before boarding for a trip to another country.

DVT. *Abr.* Deep vein thrombosis (qv).

DWB. *GDS.* Double (qv) room with bath.

DXA. *GDS.* Deferred cancellation area.

Glossary of Terms

E, e

E&O. *Abr.* Errors and omissions insurance (qv).

easySABRE. A discontinued simplified version of the Sabre® GDS (qv).

EATA. East Asia Travel Association.

EB. *GDS.* 1. Eastbound. 2. English breakfast.

ECAR. *GDS.* Economy car.

eclipse. The partial or total obscuring of one heavenly body by another, especially of the sun by the moon.

ecology. 1. The study of the environment and the interaction of its various elements. 2. The flora, fauna, climate, etc. of a region or location.

economy class. 1. Coach class. 2. Y class.

economy hotel. A hotel offering few amenities (qv).

ecosystem. *See* ecology, def. 2.

ecotourism. A style of travel in which an emphasis is placed on unspoiled, natural destinations and on disturbing the environment as little as possible.

ECU. *Abr.* European currency unit. Term is obsolete with the introduction of the Euro (qv).

EDI. *Abr.* Electronic data interchange.

EDT. *GDS.* Eastern Daylight Time.

EEC. European Economic Community (qv).

eff. *Abr.* Effective.

effective date. The date on which a fare, or other offer, becomes valid.

efficiency. A hotel room with a small kitchen area and dining table.

elapsed flying time. Actual time an airplane spends in the air, as opposed to time spent taxiing to and from the gate and during stopovers.

elastic. *adj.* Expanding or contracting according to demand or economic conditions, as a fare or room rate.

ELD. *Abr.* Electronic liquor dispenser (qv).

electronic liquor dispenser. A device that serves alcoholic beverages in precisely determined amounts.

elderhostel. 1. Hostel that caters to senior citizens. 2. Special travel-study program for seniors offered by a college or university. Participants stay in college dormitories and may generally take a short course of study if they so desire.

electronic mail. *See* e-mail.

Electronic Reservations Service Provider (ERSP). Also, ERSP#. An ARC designator that identifies airline bookings made online.

electronic ticket delivery network. A network, national or regional, of ticket printing machines that are not operated by an ARC-accredited agency but instead by a company that sells its ticket distribution services. Also called "electronic ticket distribution network." An ETDN delivers flight and passenger coupons after an agent generates the ticket.

electronic ticketing. A computerized system used by airlines in which no physical ticket or boarding pass is generated.

elite status. The highest level of an airline frequent flyer program as determined by number of miles flown per year. By extension, the highest level of any loyalty program.

EMA. *Abr.* Extra mileage allowance.

e-mail, email. 1. A communications system that allows people to exchange messages via computer networks, the Internet, or wireless devices. 2. A message sent or received in this manner.

EMAN. *GDS.* Economy car with manual transmission.

embargo. A government order forbidding the departure of a commercial vehicle from an airport, port, or whatever or prohibiting commerce. Example: an embargo on rice shipments.

embark. 1. To board a ship, plane, or other transportation vehicle. 2. To start out.

EMER. *GDS.* Emergency travel.

emigrant. A person who leaves the country where he or she lives to settle in another. *See also* immigrant.

emigrate. *v.* To leave one country to assume permanent residence in another country.

emissary. A person who is sent out on a mission on behalf of another person or a country.

EMS. 1. *Abr.* Emergency medical service. 2. *GDS.* Excess mileage surcharge.

en suite. *Fr.* In the hotel industry, a phrase indicating that an amenity or feature is in the room itself or immediately adjacent.

enclave. A small area of a country or city, usually occupied by people ethnically or culturally distinct from their neighbors.

encode. To put into code. To substitute a short set of letters or numbers for a longer word or words.

encroach. 1. To gradually advance beyond the usual limits or take possession of what belongs to another. Example: A forest might encroach on a meadow; a lion might encroach on a jackal's kill.

ENDI. *GDS.* End item.

English breakfast. A breakfast of cereal or juice, eggs, meats, breads, and beverages.

English Channel. The body of water separating England from France.

enhancement. 1. An added feature to a product, as a tour. 2. In a software program, added capabilities.

enplane. To board an airplane.

enroute. On the way; while one is traveling.

ensign. The flag flown by a cruise ship.

entree. 1. In the U.S., the main dish of a meal. 2. In France, the appetizer (qv) course.

entrepreneur. A person who starts and runs a usually small business, risking capital.

entry. An input into a computer program, such as a data entry or a request for information.

entry fee. 1. The price charged for admission to a place, a competition, or an attraction. 2. The duty levied on a person entering a country.

entry requirements. 1. The payments required of and the official docu-

Glossary of Terms

ments needed by a traveler entering a country for business or pleasure. Examples: passport, visa, proofs of inoculation, proofs of duty (qv) paid.

environs. The area around a place.

EP. *GDS.* European plan. Accommodations that do not include meals.

equator. Imaginary line around the center of the earth, dividing it into northern and southern hemispheres.

equinox. Either of the two times a year (around March 21 and September 22) when the sun crosses the celestial equator and day and night are equally long.

equity club. A non-profit group, such as a country club, organized by its members for their own benefit or enjoyment. *See also* proprietary club.

EQUIV. *Abr.* Equivalent amount.

ERQ. *GDS.* Endorsement request.

errors and omission insurance. Insurance that pays for damages incurred by a client because of an agent's mistake or omission. Example: listing the wrong departure time on an itinerary or forgetting to check whether pets are allowed.

ERSP. *Abr.* Electronic Reservations Service Provider.

escort. 1. A person who accompanies an individual or group to protect or guide the other party or parties. 2. A guide who travels with a tour group. 3. A woman's date. 4. Euphemistically used of a prostitute.

escort service. A company that provides "dates" for social engagements. Often, thinly disguised call girl operations.

escorted tour. A tour offering an escort's services.

escrow account. A special account opened with a bank or other financial institution to hold funds in trust until some condition is met by the person or company for whom the funds are designated; for example, until a service has been rendered or a legal dispute settled. Example: Tenants on a rent strike to protest inadequate heat or maintenance would open an escrow account to hold their rent payments until their grievance with the landlord was settled. By paying into the escrow account, the tenants would be legally protected from eviction for nonpayment of rent.

EST. *Abr.* Eastern Standard Time.

ETA. *GDS.* Estimated time of arrival.

ETC. European Travel Commission.

ETD. *GDS.* Estimated time of departure.

ETDN. *Abr.* Electronic ticket delivery (distribution) network (qv).

E-ticket. Electronic ticket. *See* electronic ticketing.

EU. 1. European Union. 2. *GDS.* A global indicator meaning via Europe.

Eurailpass. A special-fare train ticket that entitles the purchaser to unlimited train travel in many European countries for a specified number of days or weeks.

Euro. The common unit of currency shared by many members of the European Economic Community.

European Economic Community. A bloc of European countries that have adopted common trading rules.

European plan. A hotel rate that includes no meals.

Eurotunnel. *See* Chunnel.

EWGN. *GDS.* Economy station wagon.

ex-. *Abr.* Departing from.

excess baggage. Luggage that exceeds the allowed limits for weight, size, or number of pieces. Carriers usually charge extra for excess baggage and, in some cases, may have to ship it later rather than with the passenger.

exchange order. 1. A voucher issued by a carrier or travel agent requesting that a ticket be issued. 2. The ARC document that entitles a travel agent to receive a commission.

exchange rate. The current value of one currency compared with another.

exclusive. 1. *adj.* Catering to a select clientele, not open to everyone, deluxe. 2. Sometimes used in tour brochures in the sense of "not included."

excursion. A side trip, usually optional and at an additional cost, from a main destination.

excursion fare. A special-price fare that comes with restrictions, such as advance purchase requirements and a minimum stay. Usually a roundtrip fare.

excursionist. A traveler spending less than 24 hours in a country.

executive club. A private lounge area at an airport, provided by an airline for the use of its preferred passengers.

executive housekeeper. The head of a hotel's housekeeping department.

exhibit or exhibition. A display of art, artifacts, or skill open to the public. A public showing.

expatriate. A person living in a foreign country.

expedition. In tourism, a journey with few amenities, usually to a remote area, sometimes for a scientific purpose.

expense. *v.* To elect to deduct, for the purposes of taxation, the entire cost of an asset in the current tax year, rather than depreciating it over a period of years. *See also* depreciation.

expense account. Funds allocated to cover the travel and entertainment expenses of an employee.

export. *n.* A product shipped from one country for sale in another.

exposition. A large exhibit, usually sponsored by a government or trade group, to showcase the products and services of a particular company, region, or country.

expressway. A limited-access highway or toll road (qv).

EXST. *GDS.* Extra seat.

extended stay. A hotel stay of more than seven days.

extension ladder. A form used on a manual airline ticket to extend the fare area when more than 13 cities must be listed on an itinerary.

extension tours. Tours that can be added to an existing tour, before or after, to create a longer trip.

extra section. A second aircraft used on a given flight schedule to accommodate additional passengers, usually during peak travel periods such as holidays.

EZS. *Abr.* easySABRE (qv).

Glossary of Terms

F, f

F. *Abr.* Fahrenheit. *See* Fahrenheit scale.

FAA. Federal Aviation Administration.

Fahrenheit scale. A method of measuring temperature in which water boils at 212 degrees above zero and freezes at 32 degrees above zero under normal atmospheric pressure. Commonly used in the United States.

fair market value. The price something is actually worth, assuming a free market of willing buyers and sellers acting in their own best interests.

fait accompli. *Fr.* An accomplished fact. Something that has been done and seemingly may not be reversed.

false booking. *See* deadend booking.

fam, fam trip. *Abr.* Familiarization trip or tour (qv).

familiarization trip or tour. A low-cost trip or tour offered to travel agents by a supplier or group of suppliers to familiarize the agents with their destination and services. Example, a resort property or group of hotels and restaurants in Aruba might team up with an airline or tour operator to offer a discount fam trip to the resort or to Aruba. Generally referred to as a "fam trip."

family plan. Arrangement under which family members traveling together are entitled to discounts. Example: Many motels let children under 12 stay free in their parents' room.

family style. A style of serving meals in which food is brought to the table in serving dishes, for people to help themselves, rather than put on individual plates in the kitchen.

fantail. The rear or overhang of a ship.

FAP. *Abr.* Full American plan. *See* American plan.

fare. 1. The price charged for transportation. 2. A paying passenger on a plane, train, or other public means of transport. 3. Range of food, for example, the fare served by a restaurant.

fare basis. The specific fare for a ticket at a designated level of service; specified by one or more letters or by a combination of letters and numbers. Example: The letter "Y" designates coach service on an airline.

fare break point. The destination where a given fare ends. Example: The fare break point for a passenger flying from Washington DC to Kansas City via Cleveland is Kansas City.

fare code. The code used to make a booking on a GDS (qv) for a specific fare. *See also* booking code.

fare construction unit or point. *See* fare break point.

fathom. *n.* A unit of length equalling six feet, primarily used to measure the depth of water.

FCCA. Florida-Caribbean Cruise Association.

FCU. *Abr.* Fare construction unit (qv).

FDOR. *GDS.* Four-door car.

feasibility study. Research carried out to determine whether to go ahead with a project that is under consideration, based on such factors as the marketplace, the competition, available technology, manpower, and financial resources.

Federal Aviation Administration. An agency of the federal government that administers and monitors airline safety regulations.

Federal Trade Commission. An agency of the federal government that monitors and regulates trade within the United States.

fee-based pricing. A compensation plan in which a corporation pays its travel agency a portion of the commissions generated by the corporation's travel volume, according to a negotiated schedule.

feeder airline. An air carrier that services a local market and "feeds" traffic to the national and international carriers.

ferry. 1. *n. Abr.* Ferryboat. A boat that carries people, and/or vehicles and other cargo across a body of water. 2. *v.* To carry by boat over a given body of water. 3. *v.* To cross a body of water by ferryboat.

FET. *Abr.* Foreign escorted tour. *See* escorted tour.

fete. *Fr.* A party.

FFP. *Abr.* Frequent flyer program (qv).

FHTL. *GDS.* First-class hotel.

fictitious point principle. A technique used in constructing international fares, whereby the travel agent uses a fare to a city to which the passenger is not actually traveling in order to obtain a lower fare.

fiduciary. *adj.* Relating to financial guardianship, as in "a fiduciary relationship."

field. In computer programs, an area for recording specific information, such as the client's name, address, phone number, destination, travel date, and so on. The software generally provides one field for each item of information.

fifth freedom. *See* freedom rights.

FIJET. French acronym of the World Federation of Travel Writers.

file. 1. *n.* A collection of related information, for example, about a specific client or destination. 2. *n.* A PNR (qv) in a GDS (qv). 3. *n.* An item of furniture designed to hold files. 4. *v.* To put records into a file.

FIM. *Abr.* Flight Interruption Manifest.

final payment. A payment that brings the balance owed to zero. Example: If a client pays a deposit and then two installments, the second installment is the final payment.

fingersan, fingerscanning. The electronic recording of a person's fingerprint, typically used at international points of entry as a security measure.

firm up. To confirm what has been discussed. Example: A travel agent will "firm up" the itinerary for an upcoming trip before booking space for the client or ticketing transportation.

first class. Top quality seats or services. Generally, first-class service is the best (and the most expensive) the supplier has to offer. However, some vendors offer an even more expensive "luxury class" (qv).

first seating, first sitting. On shipboard and in some restaurants, the earlier of two times a given meal is served.

first-class hotel. A hotel offering top quality services and, usually, a prime location and extensive amenities (qv).

fiscal year. A twelve-month period used for accounting or taxation purposes, that may or may not coincide with the calendar year.

FIT. *Abr./GDS.* Foreign independent tour. The acronym is now generally used to indicate any independent travel, domestic or international, that does not involve a package tour.

FITYO. Federation of International Youth Travel Organizations.

fixed costs. Costs that remain constant independent of income. Example: Rent and utilities are fixed costs for business owners, while the cost of processing orders varies with the number of orders received. To stay in business, the owner must be able to cover his or her fixed costs.

fjord. A narrow inlet from the sea, usually bounded by cliffs.

flag of convenience. The flag of a country with easy or lax maritime regulations and low fees and taxes, flown by ships that register their vessels in such countries, even though their ownership and main cruising areas are elsewhere.

flagstaff. On a ship, a pole at the stern (qv) where the flag of the ship's country of registry is flown.

flambé. *Fr.* Literally, "flaming." A cooking technique in which liquor is added at the last minute and then lit before serving.

flaps. Surfaces on the wing of an airplane that can be raised or lowered during takeoff or landing to increase lift (qv) or drag (qv).

flat. *Brit.* Apartment.

flat rate. A fixed rate that may include fees for several different services.

fleabag. *Slang.* An inferior hotel or motel.

FLIFO. *Abr.* Flight information.

flight attendant. 1. A trained person who is responsible for looking after the passengers on an aircraft. In addition to serving food and drinks, the flight attendant is responsible for seeing that safety regulations are obeyed and passengers know what to do in case of emergency. 2. A gender-neutral alternative to "steward" or "stewardess" (qv).

flight coordinator. An employee of a cruise line responsible for arranging air travel for cruise passengers paying air-inclusive fares.

flight crew. All the employees — pilot, co-pilot, and flight attendants — working on an aircraft.

flight data recorder. A crash-proof device installed in airplanes that retains a record of cockpit instrumentation. Used to determine cause in the event of a crash. See also black box, cockpit recorder.

flight deck. On a commercial airliner, the cockpit of the airplane.

flight kitchen. Where food is prepared for serving on an airplane.

flight number. A unique alphanumerical designator that identifies a specific airplane's journey from one destination to another in a single direction, sometimes with intermediate stops.

float. *n.* 1. A floating platform that's anchored near the shore for the use of boats or swimmers. 2. The sum of money represented by checks outstanding that have not yet been cashed. 3. The time between writing a check or charging a purchase on a credit card and the actual withdrawal of funds to cover it.

floatel. A vessel, that may or may not be permanently docked, that has been converted into a hotel.

floodplain. 1. An area of flat land that may be covered by flood waters. 2. A land area built up by deposits from a stream or river.

floppy disk. A small, portable magnetic disk that is used to store and transport computer data. Sometimes called a diskette.

flotilla. A fleet of ships.

flowchart. A diagram that's used to illustrate the logical or chronological sequence of tasks in a job or process. May also be referred to as a "flow sheet."

flt or FLT. GDS/*Abr.* Flight.

fly-drive package. An offering that bundles airfare, car rental, and sometimes, land accommodations into a single package, offered for a fixed price.

flyer. A single-sheet, printed advertisement.

FMC. Federal Maritime Commission.

F.O.B. *Abr.* Freight on board (qv).

FOC. *Abr.* Flag of convenience (qv).

foghorn. Any device that emits a deep booming sound as a warning to shipping.

folio. The written record of a hotel guest's account.

FONE. *GDS.* Telephone.

FOP. *GDS.* Form of payment.

force majeure. *Fr.* Literally, "superior force." An occurrence that cannot be anticipated or controlled by the travel agent, airline, cruise ship, or whatever and for which, therefore, the agent, etc. is not legally responsible.

fore and aft. Lengthwise of a ship: from stem to stern.

foredeck. The forward part of a ship's main deck.

foreign exchange rate. *See* exchange rate.

foreign independent tour. A foreign itinerary that is individually constructed and does not involve a package tour. *See also* FIT.

foreign-flag vessel. A ship owned by or registered in a country other than the United States.

fortnight. *Brit.* A period of two weeks.

fortress. A fortified place, especially a large, permanent fortification.

fortress hub. *See* concentrated hub.

forum. 1. A public place or marketplace in an ancient Roman city. 2. A public meeting place, radio or TV program, or area in a newspaper or computer bulletin board in which two or more people may openly discuss ideas.

forward. Toward the front of a ship.

forward transaction. The purchase or sale of an item or service at a specified price for delivery at a future date.

FP. *GDS.* Final payment (qv) or full pension (qv).

FQTV. *GDS.* Frequent traveler.

FRAG. *Abr.* Fragile.

franchise. A business contract in which an independent business (the franchisee) sells or markets the products and/or services of a larger firm (the franchisor). The franchisee receives training and marketing support from the franchisor and pays a fee for ongoing support.

Glossary of Terms

FRAV. *GDS.* First available.

free hits. The number of times an agency can access and query a GDS before triggering per-use charges.

free port. A port where no customs duty or regulations are imposed on goods shipped in and out.

free pouring. The dispensing of alcoholic beverages without using any measuring devices, which typically results in generous servings.

free sale. Indicates that reservations may be made without checking the availability.

free trade. The untrammeled international exchange of products and commodities with tariffs used to produce reasonable revenue and not to hinder commerce.

freebie. A product or service that is given away without charge.

freeboard. The distance from a ship's deck to the waterline.

freedom of the seas. The right of a commercial ship to cruise any waters, except territorial waters of other nations, in either peace or war.

freedom rights. A set of guiding principles governing air-service rights under international agreements. The seven freedom rights are: 1. The right to overfly another country. 2. The right to land in another country. 3. The right to carry revenue traffic to another country. 4. The right to carry revenue traffic from another country. 5. The right to carry revenue traffic between two foreign countries. 6. The right to use one's own country as a transit point when exercising other freedom rights. 7. Cabotage. (qv).

freedoms of the air. *See* freedom rights.

freestanding. *adj.* Describing an independent organization or business that is not affiliated with another establishment.

freight. 1. Cargo; goods to be shipped. 2. Shipment by common carrier as opposed to by an express service, as in "Ship it freight."

freight on board. A term used in shipping to refer to the place where the buyer becomes responsible for the shipment and the shipping charges. Example: If the buyer lives in Des Moines and buys a product F.O.B. New York, the buyer must pay the shipping charges from New York to Des Moines and is responsible for seeing that it is properly insured during that shipment.

freighter. A ship designed primarily to carry cargo. Some also carry passengers.

French service. A style of serving meals in which the waiter brings the serving dishes to the table and dishes up the food there, rather than serving plates prepared in the kitchen.

frequency. The number of flights by a given airline or other carrier on a given route during a given period of time.

frequency marketing, frequency marketing program. Any marketing plan designed to reward customers who buy on a regular basis or to encourage customers to do so, as in a frequent flyer program (qv).

frequent flyer. A person who flies frequently. Specifically, a person who is enrolled in an airline's frequent flyer program (qv).

frequent flyer program. A program offered by various airlines to promote passenger loyalty. Participants earn credits good for free travel or upgraded service based on the number of miles they fly with the carrier. They are also entitled to special services. Participation is optional.

frequent lodger. A person who frequently stays at a property or at properties belonging to a particular hotel chain. Specifically, a person who is enrolled in a hotel's frequent lodger program (qv).

frequent lodger program. A program offered by various hotels and hotel chains to promote customer loyalty. Participants earn credits good for free lodging or upgraded service based on the number of nights they stay at the hotel. They are also entitled to special services. Participation is optional.

front desk. The reception desk at a hotel.

front office. *adj.* Referring to those business activities that take place with customers or the general public. *See also* back office.

FS. *GDS.* Free sale (qv).

FTC. Federal Trade Commission (qv).

fuel charge. The amount charged by a rental car company to refill the tank of a returned vehicle.

fuel surcharge. An additional per-ticket fee added to a fare by an airline or other carrier, ostensibly to cover the cost to the carrier of a rapid rise in the price of fuel. Fuel surcharges are seldom quoted in the fare.

full house. 1. A theater, restaurant, or lodging in which all the seats or rooms are taken. 2. A poker hand consisting of three of a kind and a pair.

full pension. *See* American plan.

full service agency location. A branch of an agency that provides customers both reservations and ticketing.

full service hotel. A hotel with a restaurant.

fully appointed agency. A travel agency that is accredited to sell airline, cruise, and other travel services.

function book. In a hotel or conference center, the official record that controls room assignments for meetings and other events.

function sheet. *See* banquet event order.

functional image. For a tourist destination, the activities that tourists associate with that destination.

funnel. A ship's chimney or smokestack

funnel flight. 1. A flight on a feeder airline (qv) that connects with another flight on a larger aircraft. *See also* change of equipment. 2. The use of a single flight number for an itinerary that actually involves an online connection (qv) with two separate flight numbers, with the presumed intent to make the itinerary appear to be a direct flight as opposed to a connection with a change of aircraft.

fuselage. The main body of an aircraft to which the wings, tail, and landing gear are attached.

FYI. *Abr.* For your information.

Glossary of Terms

G, g

G-7. *See* Group of Seven.

G-8. *See* Group of Eight.

GAAT. *Abr.* Generally accepted accounting procedures.

gaijin. Japanese word for "foreigner." Considered derogatory by some.

Galileo®. A global distribution system (qv).

galley. The kitchen in a ship.

gaming. Gambling. Any casino style activities offered on a cruise ship or at a resort.

gangway. A movable ramp or stairway between a ship and a pier; used for boarding and deboarding. Also called a "gangplank."

garden side room. A hotel room on the same level as the garden, with a door that opens onto the garden.

garden view room. A hotel room that overlooks the garden but that provides no direct access to the garden.

garni. *Fr. adj.* Designates a hotel without meal service. *See also* limited service hotel.

gastronaut. One who travels primarily or exclusively to enjoy the restaurants and specialty foods of a region. *See also* gastro-tourism.

gastro-tourism. Recreational travel undertaken solely or primarily to experience the food and wine of a region. *See also* gastronaut.

gate. Area in an airport where passengers board an airplane.

gateway city. 1. A city that serves as a departure or arrival point for international flights. 2. A city that serves as an airline's entry or departure point to or from a country.

gateway fare. The fare to a major foreign city, or "gateway."

Gay Nineties. The 1890s. Used to refer to a style of entertainment, costume, or decoration evocative of that period.

gazebo. A small, open-sided structure designed for sitting and taking in the view.

gazetteer. 1. A geographical dictionary. 2. A directory in which the entries are arranged by geographical location. For example, a gazetteer of restaurants.

GDN. *GDS.* Room with a garden or a garden view. Also designated GDN-VW.

GDP. *Abr.* Gross domestic product (qv).

GDS. *Abr.* Global distribution system.

GDS new entrant. Any of a number of so-called "alternative" GDSs.

Gemini®. A global distribution system (qv).

genealogy. 1. The study of family history. 2. A listing of a person's ancestors.

Genesis®. Travel-agent-owned GDS.

gentleman's agreement. An unwritten agreement backed solely by the honor of the participants.

GETS. *Abr.* Gabriel Extended Travel Services. A global system for booking air travel, car rentals, hotels, and some ferry services that is unaffiliated with any airline or other travel provider.

GFAX. *Abr.* General facts.

GG rate. Guaranteed group rate (qv).

GI. *Abr.* Global indicator (qv).

GIANTS. Greater Independent Association of National Travel Services.

GIT. *Abr.* Group inclusive tour. A group tour that is offered only if a minimum number of people book it.

GIT fares. Airfares that apply when sold in conjunction with a group inclusive tour.

GLAMER. Group Leaders of America.

glider. An aircraft without an engine that is towed to a given height and then set free to glide on air currents. Used for sport and sightseeing.

global distribution system. Any of several proprietary computer systems allowing real-time access to airline fares, schedules, and seating availability and offering the capability of booking reservations and generating tickets. Formerly known as a computerized distribution system (qv), a term still used by many in the industry.

global indicator. A code that appears next to the fare and tells what route the travel must take.

global positioning device. *See* global positioning system.

global positioning satellite. A device orbiting the earth in middle earth orbit that broadcasts signals enabling earth-based receiving stations to provide precise geographical location information to global positioning devices.

global positioning system. Any of a number of electronic devices, many handheld or dashboard-mounted, that communicate with global positioning satellites to provide the user with geographical location information and mapping services. Now being introduced in rental cars.

G.M. *Fr. Abr.* "Gentil membre." A guest at a Club Med resort.

GM. *Abr.* General manager.

GMT. *Abr.* Greenwich mean time (qv).

GNE. *Abr.* GDS new entrant (qv).

GNP. Gross national product (qv).

GNR. *GDS.* Guest name record.

G.O. *Fr. Abr.* "Gentil organisateur." A staff member at a Club Med resort.

GO. *GDS.* Value car rental company.

Golden Age Passport. An identification card sold by the U.S. National Park Service that gives persons who are 62 or older unlimited access/entrance to the sites it operates.

gondola. 1. Passenger car suspended from a cable; used to transport skiers and sightseers. 2. Flat-bottomed Venetian boat with a high bow and stern.

GPS. *Abr.* Global positioning system (qv).

GPST. *GDS.* Group seat request.

gradient. A measure, in degrees, of how steep a slope is.

Gran Prix. *Fr.* One of several automobile races.

grand tour. A lengthy journey that takes in the major sights of a continent. Usually used to refer to "The Grand Tour of Europe," on which people of

Glossary of Terms

means saw all of the best the continent had to offer.

grand travel. The phenomenon of older travelers traveling with their grandchildren.

grandfather. *v.* To exempt a person or company from new laws or regulations based on circumstances that existed in the past. Example: A travel agency might decide to cut outside agents' share of total commissions earned from 60% to 50%, but grandfather those agents with whom it is already working. If that were the case, agents already on the books would continue to earn 60%, while new agents would be paid 50%.

gratuity. A voluntary payment above the stated cost of a product or service given in appreciation for the service rendered. A tip.

graveyard shift. The late-night or overnight work shift.

greasy spoon. A inexpensive restaurant or coffee shop that doesn't look particularly clean.

green. *adj.* Friendly to the environment or using recycled materials. For example, a "green hotel room."

green card. Identity card issued by the U.S. government to noncitizens who are permanent residents of the United States.

greenback. Any denomination of U.S. paper money.

Greenwich mean time. Solar time in Greenwich, England, which is used as the basis of standard time throughout the world. Also called "Greenwich time."

gridlock. A situation in which cars totally block city streets bringing traffic to a standstill.

gringo. A foreigner, especially an English or American person, in Spain or Latin America. Sometimes used as a slur.

grogshop. *Brit.* Bar, usually low class.

gross. The total amount (usually of money), before any deductions have been made.

gross domestic product. The total value of the products and services a nation produces for its own use during a given time period, say one year.

gross national product. The total value of the products and services a nation produces during a given time period, including exports.

gross profit. Net sales minus the cost of goods or services sold and before payment of taxes and operating expenses.

gross registered tonnage. A measurement of the enclosed space in a ship. Port officials use it to calculate harbor dues.

gross sales. Total sales receipts before subtracting any expenses or deductions for returns or other post-sale adjustments.

ground arrangements. Services covering the land portion of a trip, such as lodging, visits to museums, sightseeing tours, and transfers between airport and hotel.

ground operator. A company that provides land services such as sightseeing tours, transfers from airport to hotel, limos, taxis, and so on.

group ceiling. The maximum number of available spaces on a particular tour.

group desk. The department or counter of an airline, travel agency, hotel, or other supplier that handles group reservations.

group house. A hotel that caters primarily to the convention and meetings market.

Group of Eight. The Group of Seven (qv) and Russia.

Group of Seven. The seven most industrialized nations of the world: Canada, France, Germany, Japan, the United Kingdom, the United States, and the European Community.

group rate. The fare or room rate offered to a group of travelers.

group sales. 1. The act of marketing travel to affinity groups. 2. A department of an agency devoted to this type of sale.

GRPS. *GDS.* Groups.

GRT. *Abr.* Gross registered tonnage (qv).

GST. *Abr.* Goods and services tax.

GTIA. Golf and Travel Industry Association.

gtd. *Abr.* Guaranteed.

guar. *Abr.* Guarantee or guaranteed.

guarantee. 1. *n.* An assurance that a product or service will be provided at an agreed-upon time and/or meet stated specifications, often with a promise that the purchaser will be reimbursed if the product or service fails to meet the customer's expectations. 2. *v.* To answer for a product or service meeting agreed-upon conditions. 3. *v.* To pay for a guarantee of product or service performance.

guaranteed group rate. On a cruise ship, a group rate extended to a travel agency on a negotiated basis that will be honored regardless of the number of bookings made.

guaranteed reservation. A reservation that will be held all night, whether or not the party arrives on time. Generally, the buyer pays for the privilege by guaranteeing payment whether or not the reservation is used.

guaranteed share. A cruise line rate for a single passenger based on the line's promise to find the passenger a roommate to share a cabin. The rate will be honored even if no roommate is found.

guaranteed single. A cruise line rate for a single passenger who does not wish to share. The passenger is guaranteed a cabin in a specific category, but will be upgraded depending on availability.

guest house. A home that offers rooms to travelers. *See also* B&B.

guide. A person who takes visitors on tours of sites, such as museums, cities, wilderness areas, etc. and shares his knowledge about places, objects, or flora and fauna of interest.

Gulf Stream. A warm-water current that flows from the Caribbean North and East to the British Isles.

gunwale. The upper edge of the side of a boat.

gwailo. Chinese word for a foreigner, specifically a European. Translated variously as "ghost person" and "white devil." Considered derogatory by some.

Glossary of Terms

H, h

hacienda. *Sp.* A country house or estate.

HAI. Helicopter Association International.

HAL. Holland America Line.

halal. *adj.* Conforming to Islamic dietary laws.

half pension. Hotel rate that includes breakfast and one additional meal, typically dinner. Also called Modified American Plan and demi-pension.

halo effect. The extra business an agency gives the airline that owns the GDS system it uses, above and beyond what that airline might expect to get based on it's share of the overall market. Industry observers consider the halo effect a result of the agent's tendency to trust the GDS's accuracy, as well as what critics call the GDS's "architectural bias" (qv). The system lists the owner-airline's flights first, which some say leads to more bookings of those flights.

hamlet. A small village.

hand luggage. Baggage carried by the passenger, as on a plane. Often defined and limited by airline regulations.

hand-measured pouring. The dispensing of alcoholic beverages using shot glasses, jiggers, or other measuring tools; as opposed to free pouring (qv).

hansom cab. A horse-drawn carriage, typically used for sightseeing.

harbor. A naturally or artificially protected area where ships dock.

harbor master. The official who oversees port operations.

hard copy. A printed version of a document, as opposed to the data in the computer.

hard-dollar savings. Easily identifiable savings, such as free tickets, reduced rates, or revenue-sharing (qv). *See also* soft-dollar savings.

hatch. A hinged door covering an opening in a ship's deck.

hatchway. The opening covered by a hatch.

hawker stand. In Singapore, an outdoor or indoor stall serving cooked food.

hawser. A heavy rope used to tow or tie up a ship to a dock.

hazmat. Abr. Hazardous material.

HCC. Hotel Clearing Corporation.

head. A toilet on a boat or ship.

head count. The physical counting of passengers, as by a flight attendant, to compare a manifest (qv) with the actual number of passengers. *See also* nose count.

head tax. A fee assessed by some cities and countries on every passenger who arrives or leaves.

head wind. A strong air current blowing in the opposite direction of the course of an airplane or ship, thus decreasing the speed and/or increasing the fuel consumption of the vessel. *See also* tail wind.

HEDNA. Hotel Electronic Distribution Network Association.

heliport. A landing pad for helicopters.

heli-skiing. An excursion by helicopter to remote, pristine skiing areas.

helm. The apparatus for steering a ship. A ship's steering mechanism.

herringbone setup. *See* chevron setup.

hidden city ploy, hidden city ticketing. A stratagem used to get a lower airfare when the fare for a flight from A to C with a stop in B is cheaper than a fare directly from A to B. The passenger who wants to travel to B, buys a ticket from A to C and then gets off at B. Considered unethical by airlines and many travel agencies.

high season. The season of the year when travel to an area peaks and rates are at their highest.

higher intermediate point. When a city between the city of origin and the fare break point (qv) has a higher fare than the destination city, the higher fare must be used.

hijack. *v.* To take over a vessel or airplane by force.

HIP. *Abr.* Higher intermediate point.

hire car. *Brit.* A rented car.

history. In bookings, a detailed record of what has been done.

HITIS. Hospitality Industry Technology Integration Standards.

HK. *GDS.* Hold confirmed.

HL. *GDS.* Holds list.

HMS. *Abr.* Her (or His) Majesty's Ship.

HNML. *GDS.* Hindu meal.

hold. 1. *v.* Reserve or set aside. 2. *n.* The storage compartment of a ship or plane.

hold time. In the hospitality industry, the hour at which hotel rooms that have been reserved but not guaranteed are released for general sale, usually 4:00 or 6:00 p.m.

Holocaust. 1. The murder of six million Jews by the Nazis during World War II. 2. Generically, any great loss of human life or any almost total destruction, especially by fire.

hologram. A laser-generated image with three-dimensional properties, increasingly used to deter counterfeiting of currency, credit cards, and identification.

hollow square setup. A seating arrangement for meetings in which tables or chairs are arranged in a square (or rectangle) with an open space in the center.

home exchange. The swapping of personal residences by people in different cities or countries as a strategy to reduce the costs of vacation travel.

home port bonus. An additional commission, typically 5%, paid by cruise lines on cruise-only bookings made by agents in Florida. The commission, now being phased out by some cruise lines, is ostensibly justified by the fact that Florida-based agents receive no commissions on related airfares, as do agents in other states.

Homeland Security Advisory System. A color-coded system devised by the Department of Homeland Security (qv) to estimate the likelihood of a terrorist attack on the United States. *See also* Threat Advisory.

homepage. The first "page" or screen you *See* at a web site, typically containing a table of contents for the site.

homesickness. An intense longing for home experienced by some travelers,

especially on extended journeys.

honor system. A unsupervised system in which customers help themselves to goods and services, and then are expected to pay for what they used.

honorarium. A fee paid to a guest speaker or lecturer.

hooker. *Slang.* A prostitute or streetwalker.

hors d'oeuvres. *Fr.* Light snacks or finger food served before a meal or at the beginning of the meal.

horseshoe setup. A seating arrangement for meetings in which tables or chairs are arranged in a U shape.

hospitality industry. Term applied to the hotel, restaurant, entertainment, and resort industry.

hospitality suite. A hotel room, or suite, reserved by a company or group in which to greet customers or others. Typically, refreshments are served.

host. 1. Person leading or in charge of a tour. 2. In computer lingo, the system to which a travel agent's terminal is connected for GDS services. In some cases, the host is an airline's central computer system.

hosted tour. A tour that features the services of a person, sometimes a hotel employee, who is available to perform certain services for members of the group.

hostel. An inexpensive accommodation, typically in dormitory style. Usually used by younger travelers, as in "youth hostel."

hostelry. A hotel or inn.

hot air ballooning. An increasingly popular form of excursion in which a small number of people are carried aloft in a basket suspended from a large balloon made lighter than the surrounding air by being filled with heated air.

hot line. Any phone number used to provide fast help or customer service.

hotel. Any establishment offering overnight accommodations.

hotel register. A book, or other record, that guests sign and that becomes the permanent record of an establishment's guests.

hotel rep firm. An independent company that provides marketing support or group reservations support for a hotel or hotel chain.

hotel representative. A booking agent or agency for hotels.

hotel voucher. A pre-paid coupon that can be exchanged at certain hotels for a night's lodging.

hotelier. The owner or manager of a hotel. Someone in the hotel business.

hotelling. An office arrangement in which very mobile staffers do not have a permanent assigned office, but must reserve one whenever they are not traveling.

house brand. Any brand of liquor served when a customer requests a drink by its generic name (e.g. gin and tonic, scotch and soda). The least expensive brand served, as opposed to more expensive call brands (qv).

house flag. The flag denoting the company to which a ship belongs. A shipping company's flag.

house limit. 1. In a casino, the maximum wager permitted. 2. In a hotel or other establishment, the maximum extent to which credit will be extended before payment is requested. 3. In restaurants and bars, the maximum number of alcoholic beverages that will be served to a single customer.

house plan. 1. A diagram of a property's function spaces. 2. A property's floor plan.

houseboat. A flat-bottomed or twin hulled recreational boat that resembles a small house or apartment.

housekeeping. The department of a hotel charged with cleaning and maintaining rooms and public spaces.

hovercraft. A water-borne vessel that floats on a cushion of air.

HRU. *Abr.* Hydrostatic release units (qv).

HSAC. Homeland Security Advisory Council .

HSAS. Homeland Security Advisory System (qv).

HSMA. Hospitality Sales and Marketing Association International.

HTL. *GDS.* Hotel.

hub. A city or an airport in which an airline has major operations and many gates. For example: American has a hub in Dallas, United in Chicago, Delta in Atlanta, TWA in St. Louis.

hub-and-spoke. *adj.* A system many airlines have adopted to maximize the amount of time their planes spend in the air, thus make money for them. They designate certain cities as hubs, schedule many flights to them, and offer connecting flights from the hubs to smaller cities, which can be served by smaller aircraft.

hub and spoke tour. The hub and spoke concept applied to tours. Tour members travel out of and return to a central point each day.

hull. A ship's frame or body, not including masts and rigging.

Humboldt Current. A cold water stream flowing in a northerly direction along the coasts of Chile and Peru.

hurricane. A tropical storm (qv) with winds in excess of 75 mph.

hurricane season. A period in which hurricanes are most likely to occur, roughly from June to October in the Northern hemisphere.

hush kit. *Slang.* Added equipment used to make existing aircraft engines quieter.

HX. *GDS.* Have cancelled.

hydrofoil. 1. A ship or boat design that lifts the hull above the water as speed increases, thereby lessening friction and increasing speed. 2. Any ship or boat so designed.

hydrostatic release units. Automatically deployed life rafts used on cruise ships.

Glossary of Terms

I, i

IACC. International Association of Conference Centers.

IACVB. International Association of Convention and Visitors Bureaus.

IAFE. International Association of Fairs and Expositions.

IAMAT. International Association for Medical Assistance to Travellers.

IAPA. International Air Passenger Association.

IAR. *Abr.* Interactive agent reporting system (qv).

IAS. *GDS.* Insert a segment.

IATA. International Air Transport Association.

IATA accredited passenger agent. A non-U.S. travel agency appointed to sell tickets on behalf of members of IATA.

IATA number. An 8-digit numerical code that uniquely identifies travel agencies and other entities engaged in the sale of travel.

IATAN. International Airlines Travel Agency Network.

IATAN card. Photo identification issued by IATAN. Widely accepted as the only identification for travel agents. Sometimes called, erroneously, "IATA card."

IATAN endorsed location. A U.S. travel agency that is either an airline appointed agency (qv) or a TSI (qv) agency.

IATAN list. A record maintained by a travel agency listing those employees and independent contractors who qualify for travel benefits, as determined by IATAN.

IATAN registered personnel. Employees or owners of U.S. IATAN-accredited travel agencies who are listed in IATAN's database of travel counselors.

IAWT. International Association of World Tourism.

IC. *Abr.* Independent contractor. An outside sales representative for a travel agency.

IC-friendly. Used to describe a travel supplier willing to pay commissions directly to an independent, non-ARC/IATAN travel agent, often a home-based travel agent.

ICAO. International Civil Aviation Organization.

ICAR. *GDS.* Intermediate-size car.

ICCL. International Council of Cruise Lines.

ICTA. Institute of Certified Travel Agents.

ID. *Abr.* Identification.

IDL. *Abr.* International date line (qv).

IFR. *Abr.* Instrument flight rules (qv).

IFTAA. International Forum of Travel and Tourism Advocates.

IFUN. *GDS.* If unable.

IFWTO. International Federation of Women's Travel Organizations.

IGN. *GDS.* Ignore.

immigrant. A person who enters a country of which he is not native to settle. *See also* emigrant.

immigrate. *v.* To enter a country to assume permanent residence in it.

immunity. 1. Exemption from the laws of a country, as in "diplomatic immunity." 2. An acquired state of resistance to a disease.

IMO. International Maritime Organization.

import. 1. *v.* To bring goods from one country into another. 2. *n.* A product brought into one country from another.

IN. *GDS.* 1. International. 2. Infant. 3. Check-in.

in bond. Held until departure, as duty-free goods which, once purchased, are not delivered to the buyer until departure from the airport.

in plant. *adj.* Referring to a travel agency physically located on the premises of a corporation it services, and limited to 3% commissions. An outdated ARC (qv) term. *See also* corporate agency.

in season. Available only at certain times of the year. For example, "fresh fruit, in season."

in transit. En route. Traveling.

INAD. *GDS.* Inadmissible passenger.

inaugural. The first, as in "the inaugural sailing."

inbound. 1. Arriving. 2. Of an airline itinerary, the return leg. 3. Relating to travel services provided to passengers arriving to a travel agent's location from elsewhere.

inbound operator. A person or company providing inbound services.

incentive. Merchandise, travel, cash, service, or intangible offered to an employee or customer as a reward for taking a specified action.

incentive house. A company that runs incentive programs, often including travel programs, for other companies.

incentive travel. Travel that is given to employees or distributors as a reward for outstanding performance.

incidentals. Small items or miscellaneous expenditures.

inclusive tour. A tour package that bundles transportation and lodging along with additional services such as transfers, sightseeing, museum admissions, and so forth.

inclusive tour fare. A fare, as on an airline, that is based on the purchase of an inclusive tour.

independent contractor. An independent individual who performs services for a company for an agreed-on fee. Legally distinct from an employee.

independent tour. A tour that does not include a guide or a host or a set routine of daily activities.

indirect spending. In the tourism industry, the money spent by tourists that is respent within the local economy. *See also* direct spending.

indirect tax. Any tax or fee that is levied on one entity but passed along to another.

INF. *GDS.* Infant.

infant. In the travel industry, a designation used to determine fares and other rates. Generally, an infant is less than two years of age. Infants often travel for free.

inflation. In simplest terms, the tendency of prices to go up.

in-flight. *adj.* Describing goods or services provided during an airline flight, as in-flight magazines, in-flight duty-free shopping, and so forth.

infrastructure. 1. The underlying framework of an enterprise. 2. The network of transportation and other services provided by a government

— roads, bridges, and so forth.

in-house sales. Sales made to the employees of a company. *See also* self sales.

inlet. A narrow expanse of water, hemmed in by land. A small bay.

inn. A small hotel or guest house. Generally, used to describe accommodations possessing a certain intimacy and charm. A tavern.

inner city. An urban slum, as distinct from downtown (qv).

innkeeper. A person who owns or manages an inn.

in-out dates. Dates on which a guest arrives and leaves.

in-room messaging. System that allows hotel guests to receive electronic mail and faxes on their room televisions.

INS. Immigration and Naturalization Service.

inside cabin. On a ship, a cabin away from the ship's hull that has no windows.

instrument flight rules. A set of procedures that govern the piloting of a plane when weather conditions do not allow the pilot to *See* the ground or the natural horizon or maintain distance from other aircraft. *See also* visual flight rules.

interactive agent reporting system (IAR). An ARC program in which weekly sales reports are submitted electronically.

Intercoastal Waterway. Common misspelling of "Intracoastal Waterway" (qv).

intercontinental. Spanning more than one continent.

interface. The juncture between two computer systems or between a user and a computer system. Generically, the juncture between any two systems or organizations.

interline agreements. Contractual or formal agreements between airlines governing such matters as ticketing, baggage transfers, and so forth.

interline connection. A change of planes that also involves a change of airlines.

intermodal. Combining two forms of transportation. For example, air and sea.

international carrier. An airline or other transportation company that moves passengers between countries.

International Date Line. 180 degrees of longitude. The date is different on either side of this imaginary line located in the Pacific Ocean.

international Morse code. *See* Morse code.

Internet. A world-wide network of computers linked by telephone lines, allowing for the global dissemination of information.

interstate. Involving travel or trade between states of the United States.

intl. *Abr.* International.

Intracoastal Waterway. A 3000-mile long sheltered passage, maintained by the U.S. government, running from Maine to Florida along the eastern seaboard and from northwest Florida to the Texas-Mexico border.

intranet. A private computer network.

intrastate. Referring to travel or commerce that doesn't cross a state line.

in-vehicle travel information (safety) systems. Any of a number of inter-related technologies such as cellular phones, global positioning systems (qv), digital mapping, and others offered in rental cars.

invoice. A business document detailing goods or services provided and requesting payment.

IRC. *GDS.* International route charge.

Iron Curtain. Now obsolete term used to refer to the border between the Communist states of Eastern Europe and the West.

iron horse. Affectionate term for railroad locomotives.

IS. *GDS.* If not holding, sell.

I/S. *Abr.* Inside, as of a ship's cabin.

ISDN. Integrated services digital network. A high-speed telephone line capable of sending large amounts of data quickly.

island hopping. Visiting a number of islands in quick succession, as on a cruise.

ISLVW. *GDS.* Island view.

ISO. International Standards Organization.

ISP. Internet service provider.

isthmus. A narrow piece of land, with water on each side, connecting two larger landmasses.

isobar. A line on a weather map separating areas of different barometric pressure.

ISTTE. International Society of Travel and Tourism Educators.

IT. *GDS.* Inclusive tour.

IT fare. Inclusive tour fare (qv).

IT number. Number used in airline GDS systems to indicate that a tour has met certain requirements.

ITAG. International Travel Agent Guild.

itinerary. The route of travel. In an airline booking, a list of flights, times, etc.

ITTA. Independent Travel Technology Association.

ITX. *GDS.* Inclusive tour excursion fare.

IWGN. *GDS.* Intermediate-size station wagon.

Glossary of Terms

J, j

JAA. [European] Joint Aviation Authorities.

jack. On a ship, a small flag that denotes the ship's nationality, typically flown from the bow.

jai alai. (pronounced "high-lie") A ball game of Basque origin, played on an indoor court. Players hurl the ball from wicker baskets. A popular sport for betting in some regions.

jamboree. 1. Cap. A national or international gathering of the Boy Scouts of America. 2. Any festivity featuring music, dancing, and refreshments; typically held outdoors.

jargon. The informal or technical language used by members of the same profession or industry.

JATO. *Abr.* Jet-assisted takeoff.

jaunting car. A small horse-drawn carriage, used for tourist excursions in Ireland.

jaywalk. To cross the street in the middle of the block or against traffic signals.

JCB. A Japanese credit card brand.

jeepney. In the Philippines, a converted jeep used for public transportation. The term is a corruption of jitney (qv).

jet card. A program allowing a traveler to purchase blocks of flying time on a fractionally owned aircraft and pay a fixed hourly rate. The term derives from the card, which is similar to a credit card in appearance, that identifies the traveler.

jet lag. A physiological condition caused by the disorientation of a person's biological clock due to travel across several time zones. Characterized by irritability, lethargy, insomnia, and other symptoms.

jet loader. *See* jetway.

jet port. A synonym for airport. Seldom used.

jet ski. A one-person, motorized water vehicle on which the driver stands upright on ski-like pads.

jet stream. 1. Any high-altitude, strong wind current that can aid or hinder jet flight depending on its direction. 2. The trail of condensation left by a jet flying at high altitude.

jetiquette. *Slang.* Proper behavior while flying.

jetliner. A passenger jet.

jetty. A wooden or stone platform, projecting into the water, used for the docking of boats and ships.

jetway. An enclosed gangway that provides access from the terminal to an aircraft.

jitney. Any small motorized vehicle used for public transportation.

joint fare. The fare charged for travel that utilizes more than one airline. This fare is agreed on by the airlines involved.

joint notice of change. A form submitted to IATA (qv) when the ownership of a travel agency changes hands.

joint tenancy. A legal form of ownership involving two people, typically spouses.

Jones Act. A protectionist law of 1886 forbidding foreign flag vessels from carrying passengers between United States ports.

J-rig. A type of inflatable boat in which a central platform is mounted astride two inflated pontoons; often used in Colorado River rafting expeditions.

JRSTE. *GDS.* Junior suite (qv).

JT. *GDS.* Joint. Joint fare (qv).

jumbo jet. Any large, wide-body jet aircraft.

junior suite. A hotel room that features a separate living-sitting area (although not a separate room), in addition to the bedroom.

junk. A traditional Chinese sailing vessel, of distinctive design, with elliptical sails reinforced with bamboo; often used for tourist excursions in East Asian destinations such as Hong Kong.

junket. 1. A trip ostensibly taken for business purposes, that is primarily for pleasure. Usually used to refer to trips taken by elected officials. 2. A legitimate sponsored trip in which the expenses of the travelers are paid for by the sponsors, as when a foreign destination invites travel writers to visit.

K, k

K. *Abr.* Kilobyte. A measure of memory size in computers.

kamal. A simple celestial navigation device of Arabic origin used to determine latitude.

Karachi crouch. *Slang.* Traveler's diarrhea. Considered offensive.

karaoke. (Pronounced "carry-okey.") Japanese name for a form of entertainment in which patrons take turns singing the lyrics to prerecorded music.

karaoke bar. A bar featuring karaoke entertainment.

karaoke system. The equipment needed to provide karaoke.

kayak. A small one- or two-person rowed craft with a completely enclosed topside. Kayaks are sometimes used for shooting river rapids; some models are seagoing.

keel. The structural element that runs the length of a ship's bottom.

kg. *Abr.* Kilogram.

kilo. Short for kilogram. A metric unit of weight, approximately 2.2 pounds.

kilobyte. A measure of memory size in computers. A kilobyte can store the equivalent of 1,000 typewritten characters.

kilometer. A metric measure of distance, approximately five-eighths of a mile. The standard measure of distance and speed (kph) in most countries outside the U.S.

king post. On a ship, a tall shaft that supports a cargo boom, sometimes doubling as a ventilation shaft.

king room. A hotel room with a king-size bed.

kiosk. 1. A small vendor's stall or cart. 2. A public booth dispensing information, usually via an interactive television interface.

KIP. *GDS.* Keep alone if possible.

KK. *GDS.* Confirmed.

KL. *GDS.* Confirmed waitlist (qv).

km. *Abr.* Kilometer (qv).

knot. A nautical measure of speed, approximately 1.5 miles per hour.

kosher. Conforming to Jewish dietary laws.

KP. *GDS.* Commission percentage.

kph. *Abr.* Kilometers per hour.

Kremlin. 1. The offices of the Russian government in Moscow. 2. The historic fortress complex in Moscow containing government offices and museums.

KSML. *GDS.* Kosher meal.

lagoon. A body of water protected by a reef. Any small, calm body of water connected to a larger body of water.

lanai. In Hawaii and other tropical destinations, a porch or patio.

land arrangements. All travel elements provided to a client after arrival at the destination, such as hotel, sightseeing, and so forth.

land only. A fare rate that doesn't include air transportation.

landau. A four-wheeled, horse-drawn carriage.

landfall. The first sight of land, as from a cruise ship.

landing fee. A charge levied by an airport on an airline for the right to land a plane at its facility.

landing strip. A basic, often unpaved, runway for small planes.

landlocked. *adj.* Having no access to the sea.

landlubber. A person new to ships and sailing.

landmark. 1. A famous historical building or location. 2. A prominent geographical feature used for finding one's way.

larboard. Obsolete term for the left side of a ship, now commonly referred to as "port" (qv).

last-room availability. A feature of a GDS allowing up-to-the minute information on the number of rooms available at a hotel.

last-seat availability. A GDS capability similar to last-room availability but pertaining to airline seats.

late booking fee. An additional charge levied by some tour operators for reservations made shortly before departure.

latitude. Angular distance measured in degrees north or south of the equator.

launch. *n.* A small boat that ferries cruise passengers to and from the shore.

lavatory. A toilet. Rest room.

layover. A stop on a trip, usually overnight and usually associated with a change of planes or other transportation.

LCAR. *GDS.* Luxury car.

LDW. *Abr.* Loss damage waiver (qv).

lead time. The amount or period of time before the announcement of an event and its occurrence, or between the notification that a task must be undertaken and the time at which it must be completed.

league. A measure of distance, primarily nautical, of approximately three miles.

lectern. A small stand used by speakers at formal meetings to hold notes and such. *See also* podium.

lee. The side of a ship or island away from the wind direction.

leeward. (Pronounced "LOO-erd") *See* lee.

leg. A single segment of an itinerary.

legacy carrier. A mildly derogatory term applied to older, larger airlines with higher fares and extensive route networks. *See also* network carrier.

lei. In Hawaii, a flower necklace given in greeting.

leisure travel. Travel undertaken for pleasure, as opposed to business travel. Often used to indicate a trip of seven days or longer, regardless of its purpose.

letter of agreement. A contract in the form of a letter from one person or company to another; both parties must sign for the agreement to become binding.

letter of credit. A document issued by a bank or other financial institution attesting to an individual's or company's ability to borrow money within specific limits.

letter of intent. Typically, a letter from a potential buyer to a seller indicating the seriousness of the potential buyer's interest and agreeing to hold in strict confidence any data provided by the seller to assist the buyer in evaluating the property or business being sold. Usually required by the owner of an agency from a prospective buyer before sharing proprietary information.

LHTL. *GDS.* Luxury hotel.

liability. Exposure to damage, legal or financial.

liability coverage. Insurance providing protection from claims by third parties.

license. 1. A permit obtained from local government authorities to conduct certain types of business activities, such as a restaurant, or events, such as a parade. 2. An agreement under which one company may use the logo or other property of another, as on a tee shirt.

lido deck. On a cruise ship, the area around the swimming pool.

lifeboat. Any small rowed or motorized craft carried aboard a ship and used to remove passengers from a ship in emergencies.

lifeboat drill. A required test of a cruise ship's emergency procedures to be carried out before or within 24 hours of sailing.

lift. 1. The maximum number of airline seats available to a specific destination during a specific period. 2. The aerodynamic force that makes it possible for a plane to fly. 3. *Brit.* An elevator.

limited purpose card. A credit card that can be used only for travel expenditures, for example, and not for general purchases.

limited service agency location. A branch of a travel agency that takes reservations but doesn't provide ticketing.

limited service hotel. A hotel without a restaurant. *See also* garni.

limousine. A large chauffeured vehicle for hire, as opposed to a taxi.

line. A rope on a ship.

linen. In a hotel, sheets and towels.

liner. A large passenger-carrying ship.

liquidated damages clause. In a contract between a travel agency and a GDS vendor, a stipulation that should the agency switch vendors before the contract expires, the original vendor will be due payment for the fees it would have received had the contract remained in effect for its full length.

liveried. In uniform, as a liveried chauffeur.

livery. The uniform worn by some employees, such as chauffeurs and doormen.

llama. A long-necked animal native to South America; used as a pack animal on some trekking and hiking vacations.

LNI. *GDS.* Lanai (qv).

LO. *GDS.* Domestic transportation tax.

load factor. The percentage of available space on a plane or other mode of transportation that has been sold to date.

load lines. *See* plimsoll line.

local. *n.* or *adj.* Stopping at every station, as a train.

local fare. 1. The fare on a direct flight. 2. A fare for transportation on a single carrier.

lodge. A type of hotel, typically of a rustic character in a national park or similar setting.

lodging. Any accommodation. A room in a hotel.

log. An official record of events on a minute-by-minute or hour-by-hour basis, as a ship's log.

logo. The trademarked symbol of a business.

longitude. Angular distance measured in degrees east or west of the prime meridian (qv).

longshoreman. A dock worker.

loo. *Brit.* A toilet.

look-to-book ratio. The number of people who visit a travel agency or agency web site, compared to the number who actually make a purchase.

loss damage waiver. Daily insurance that covers theft and vandalism of a rented car in addition to damage caused by accident.

loss leader. An item sold below breakeven in the hope that customers will buy other items at full price.

loss ratio. In travel insurance, the amount paid out in claims versus the amount collected in premiums expressed as a percentage. A typical travel agency will have a loss ratio in the 30% to 40% range.

low fare search. A continuous, computerized search for the lowest current available fares designed to lower the cost of trips already booked but not yet taken.

low season. The time of year when travel to a destination is at its lowest and prices decline.

lower bed, lower berth. On a ship, the lower of two bunk beds.

lowest logical airfare. The lowest fare that is consistent with a corporation's travel policy.

loyalty marketing. Term applied to frequent flyer and similar programs designed to create repeat business.

LSF. *GDS.* Local selling fare.

LUX. *GDS.* Luxury.

luxury class. The most expensive accommodations or fare category.

M, m

MAAS. *GDS.* Meet and assist.

maglev. *Abr.* Magnetic levitation. A technology used in high-speed trains.

magrodome. On a cruise ship, a retractable glass skylight over a swimming pool.

maid service. Room cleaning services, such as those provided in a hotel, that are offered separately as in a condo (qv) or villa (qv).

maiden voyage. The first voyage of a ship.

maitre d'. *Fr.* The host or head waiter at a restaurant; supervises the waiters. Also maitre d'hotel.

major carrier. By definition of the U.S. Bureau of Transportation Statistics, an airline with annual gross revenue exceeding $1 billion. *See also* national carrier

mal de mer. *Fr.* Seasickness.

management contract. An arrangement whereby a hotel's owner contracts with a separate company to run the hotel.

management report. A report prepared by a travel agency for a corporate client detailing all travel activity and expenditures during the reporting period. Used to analyze patterns of travel usage.

manifest. A document listing the contents of a shipment or the passengers on a ship.

manual. 1. A book of instructions, computer documentation. 2. A car with a manual transmission.

MAP. *Abr.* Modified American plan (qv).

MAPTA. Metropolitan Association of Professional Travel Agents.

Mardi Gras. From the French phrase meaning "Fat Tuesday." A pre-Lenten celebration, marked by street revelry and parades, most notably observed in New Orleans.

market share. The volume of sales, expressed as a percentage, achieved by one company in a specific geographic area, compared to all sales of similar products or of similar companies.

market share override program. An enhanced commission system in which a supplier (typically an airline) will pay a travel agency an override (qv) only when the agency's percentage of sales of the supplier's product exceeds by a specified amount the supplier's market share in the travel agency's market. In other words, a travel agency's sales of an airline's tickets might have to reach 33% of the agency's total airline sales before the airline, with a market share of 30% in the agency's market, would pay the agency an override.

marketing. The process of identifying and reaching specific segments of a population for the purposes of selling them a product or service.

marketing information data tapes. Electronically recorded data from GDS activity allowing airlines to analyze sales patterns of individual travel agencies.

markup. The sum of money or percentage added to a wholesale or purchase price to arrive at the retail or resale price.

marquee. 1. A sign over a theater entrance listing the current attraction. 2. A large tent, usually without some or all the sides, used during outdoor events.

MARS. *Abr.* Multi-access reservations system.

martial law. The suspension of normal civil law and its replacement by strict military control. Often declared during times of civil unrest.

Mason-Dixon line. The boundary between Pennsylvania and Maryland. The traditional boundary between the Northern and Southern United States.

masseur, masseuse. *Fr.* The male and female variants for a person who gives massages.

MAST. Midwest Agents Selling Travel.

master. On a ship, the captain or other officer with executive authority over passengers and crew.

maximum authorized amount. The largest sum of money a bank can withdraw from a travel agency's account to settle its weekly sales report.

Mayday. 1. A radio signal word used to denote a distress call. 2. By extension, a distress call.

MCO. *GDS. Abr.* Miscellaneous charge order (qv).

MCT. *GDS.* Minimum connecting time (qv).

MDT. *Abr.* Mountain Daylight Time.

meal sitting. *See* sitting.

medical tourism. Travel that includes arrangements for medical procedures, most often elective plastic surgery.

meet and greet. *Slang.* Term for a service that greets and assists members of a group on their arrival at the airport.

meeting fare. Special fare negotiated with an airline for passengers traveling to attend a specific meeting or convention.

meeting planner. A person who specializes in the planning and organization of conventions and other business meetings.

meeting rate. Special rate offered by a hotel for guests attending a meeting, usually one being held at the hotel.

mega-agency. *Slang.* A very large travel agency with nationwide operations. There are currently about seven such agencies in the United States.

megalopolis. An extended urban area caused by the tendency of large cities to grow together.

megaship. An extremely large cruise vessel, typically with a passenger capacity of greater than 2,000.

menu engineering. In the hospitality industry, a process that analyzes the entire menu (as opposed to individual menu items) as a measure of profitability.

merchant marine. 1. The commercial shipping industry of a given nation. 2. Those involved in that industry.

merchant model pricing. A system in which suppliers sell space to travel agents at a net price, allowing the agency to set a retail price of its choosing.

merchant status. The relationship between a company, such as a travel agency, and a bank that allows the company to accept credit card payments

Glossary of Terms

from its customers.

merger. The legal process whereby one corporation acquires or joins with another.

meridians. The imaginary lines of longitude on a globe.

metal. *Slang.* An airplane.

metal detector. A hand-held or walk-through device, such as those used at airport security checkpoints, used to detect concealed metal objects.

Me-Too. Nickname for a web site, jointly owned by 11 European airlines, that would sell a variety of travel products directly to the public, bypassing travel agents; so named for its resemblance to a similar web site owned by five U.S. airlines. *See also* T-2.

metro. A public rail transportation system. A subway system.

Metroliner. An Amtrak train running between New York and Washington, offering faster service at a higher fare.

mezzanine. The first balcony level above the orchestra in a theater. *See also* dress circle.

microbrewery. A beer maker with limited capacity whose products are typically distributed within a restricted geographic region.

microjet. A small, short-range, jet-powered aircraft seating up to five passengers. Often used for air taxi service.

mid-air passenger exchange. *Slang.* Tasteless air traffic control term for a collision between two planes.

middleman. A person or company that facilitates the movement of product from supplier to end consumer, usually adding value and cost in the process. A travel agent can be seen as a middleman.

mid-office system. The management information (or MIS) portion of a travel agency's computer system, as distinct from the GDS (front office) and accounting functions (back office).

midship(s). *See* amidships.

MIDT. Marketing information data tapes (qv).

migration. 1. The periodic movement of animals from one location to another. 2. The movement of large groups of ethnically similar peoples from one area to another.

mile. A measure of distance equal to 5,280 feet or approximately 1.6 kilometers (qv). The standard measurement of distance in the U.S.

mileage allowance, mileage cap. The mileage a rental car may be driven on a single day without additional charge.

mileage charge. The per mile fee charged by a car rental company.

mileage millionaire. A person who has accumulated over a million frequent flyer miles.

mileage run. A multi-segment airline trip taken during periods of special promotions for the sole or primary purpose of accruing frequent flyer miles.

mileage system, mileage based pricing. An airfare system allowing stopovers up to a specific maximum permitted mileage.

milk run. *Slang.* A trip, usually by a train and late at night, that makes many stops along the way.

millennium. 1. A period of 1,000 years. 2. Informally, January 1, 2000.

millibar. A measure of atmospheric pressure.

MIN. *GDS.* Minimum room (qv).

minibar. A hotel room amenity consisting of a small, stocked refrigerator containing beverages and snacks that are inventoried daily and paid for as they are used.

minimum connecting time. The legally defined minimum time necessary to change planes at a given airport.

minimum land package. The minimum cost of land arrangements that must be purchased to qualify for a special air fare.

minimum room. An inexpensive hotel room booked with the understanding that the booking can be upgraded if other rooms are available on arrival.

miniple. A travel agency with a small number of branches. *See also* multiple.

minshuku. An inexpensive Japanese inn, with fewer amenities and a lower level of service than a ryokan (qv).

MINR. *GDS.* Minimum rate.

MIS. *Abr.* Management information system.

miscellaneous charge order. An ARC document used to process the payment of travel arrangements other than airfares.

MLM. *Abr.* Multi-level marketing (qv).

M/M. *GDS.* Mr. and Mrs.

mobile. 1. *adj.* Moving or capable of being moved from place to place. 2. *Brit. n.* Short for mobile phone. A cell phone.

mobile speed bump. *Slang.* A car traveling at exactly the speed limit, in an attempt by the driver to force those behind to slow down.

MOD. *GDS.* Moderate room.

modem. A device that allows computers to exchange data over phone lines.

modified American plan. A hotel rate that includes two meals daily, usually breakfast and dinner.

MODR. *GDS.* Moderate rate.

modular. In sections. Designed for easy expansion, as a modular computer system.

MOML. *GDS.* Muslim meal.

monohull. A conventional sailing or motor vessel with a single hull, as opposed to a catamaran or trimaran.

Montezuma's revenge. *Slang.* Traveler's diarrhea (qv), especially when experienced in Mexico. Named after the Aztec king of Mexico conquered by the Spanish. Considered derogatory by Mexicans.

moor. To secure a ship to a dock.

Moorish. *adj.* Denoting a style of architecture and decoration associated with northwestern Africa and southern Spain.

Morse code. A communications system consisting of letters coded into dots and dashes, and used in telegraphs.

mortality rate. 1. Of humans, the rate of deaths per thousand or hundred thousand of population. 2. Of businesses, the rate at which they cease operations or the amount of time between inception and failure.

motel. A type of hotel in which parking is provided at or near the room and the room door gives out onto the parking lot.

motor court, motor hotel. *See* motel.

motor home. A recreational vehicle that is self-driving (as opposed to towed) and that contains complete living accommodation.

motor yacht. A motorized vessel, 30 to 70 feet in length, used for luxury recreational cruising.

motorbike. A small, easily-operated motorcycle.

motorboat. A power boat. A boat with an inboard or outboard gasoline or diesel engine.

motorcoach. A bus specifically designed for touring, featuring large windows and a large luggage compartment. May include toilet facilities.

moving sidewalk. A motorized, belt-like people mover that operates flush to the floor. Often found in long corridors at airports.

mph. *Abr.* Miles per hour.

MPI. Meeting Professionals International, formerly Meeting Planners International.

MPM. *Abr.* Maximum permitted mileage. *See also* mileage system.

MS. *Abr.* Motor ship. A designation for many cruise liners.

MSCN. *GDS.* Misconnection.

MST. *Abr.* Mountain Standard Time.

MT. *Abr. GDS.* Mountain Time.

MTS. *Abr.* Motor turbine ship.

multi-access system. A GDS that can directly access the computers of several airlines or other travel suppliers.

multi-level. Having more than one floor or level.

multi-level marketing. A distribution scheme in which individuals are compensated for sales volume generated by people they have recruited into the distribution network; often a feature of referral agencies (qv).

multiple. A travel agency with a large number of branches. *See also* miniple.

mural. A large-scale painting on an interior or exterior wall.

Murphy bed. A bed designed to fold up into the wall when not in use. Found in some hotel rooms.

mustering station. A place on a ship where passengers or crew must gather in case of emergency.

MV. *Abr.* Motorized vessel.

MY. *Abr.* Motorized yacht.

N, n

NA. *Abr.* Not available. Not applicable. No answer. Need alternative.

NABHOOD. National Association of Black Hotel Owners, Operators and Developers.

NABTA. National Association of Business Travel Agents.

NAC. *GDS.* No action taken on communication.

NACA. National Air Carrier Association.

NACOA. National Association of Cruise Only Agencies.

NACTA. National Association of Commissioned Travel Agents.

NAFTA. North American Free Trade Agreement.

NAOAG. *North American Official Airline Guide.*

NAR. *GDS.* New arrival information.

narco-tourism. Recreational travel undertaken to use drugs that are illegal in the traveler's home country and that may or may not be legal in the country visited.

narrow body. *adj.* Referring to any aircraft with a single center aisle.

NATA. National Air Transportation Association.

national carrier. By definition of the U.S. Bureau of Transportation Statistics, an airline with annual gross revenue between $100 million and $1 billion. *See also* major carrier.

national park. An area set aside by a country for preservation and recreation due to its outstanding natural beauty.

nautical mile. A measure of distance used in air and sea transportation of approximately 1.1 miles.

navigable. Open to commercial shipping.

navigate. 1. To pilot, steer, or direct a vehicle such as a plane or ship on a particular course. 2. *Slang.* To find one's way.

navigation lights. *See* running lights.

NAVSTAR. Navigation System with Timing and Ranging, operated by the U.S. Department of Defense, the precursor to today's global positioning systems.

NB. *GDS.* Northbound.

NBR. *GDS.* Number.

NBTA. National Business Travel Association.

NC. *GDS.* No charge.

NCL. Norwegian Cruise Lines.

NCMA. Niche Cruise Marketing Association.

NCVM. National Cruise Vacation Month.

nested excursions. *See* back-to-back ticketing.

Net. Informal term for the Internet (qv).

net amount. The amount due the supplier after commissions have been deducted.

net fare, net rate. 1. The wholesale price that is marked up for sale to the customer. 2. The fare after commission. 3. The price at which a consolidator sells a ticket to a travel agent.

net profit. Profit after all expenses have been taken into account.

netiquette. From "net etiquette," the unwritten code of what is acceptable in email communication.

network carrier. An airline, typically a large one, characterized by an extensive route system allowing multiple connections. *See also* legacy carrier.

network premium. The fare differential an airline can command due to its dominant position at an airport.

networking. The process of using one contact to gain others.

neutral unit of construction. A common denominator used to calculate a total when adding fares in different currencies.

NIBS. *Abr.* Neutral Industry Booking System.

NO. *GDS.* No action taken (on segment).

no-fly list. A database maintained by an airline or government entity containing the names of people suspected of terrorist or other illegal activities who should, therefore, be denied boarding on an airplane.

no frills. *adj.* Bare bones. A service, as an airline flight, providing only the basics with no additional amenities.

no go. *Slang.* 1. Not possible. 2. A cancelled flight or other service.

no name. *v.* To make a reservation even though you don't have the passenger's name yet.

no show. *n.* A passenger who doesn't arrive for a flight or a hotel guest who reserves but never arrives.

NOCN. *GDS.* No connection.

non-commissionable. *adj.* Referring to elements of a travel product for which the passenger must pay but for which the travel agent receives no commission. For example, port fees.

non-compete agreement, non-compete clause. A clause in an employment contract that prevents the employee from establishing a competing business for a period of time after leaving the company's employ. Often unenforceable.

non-refundable. Of a ticket, no moneys will be returned should the trip be cancelled. The amount of the ticket, minus a service fee, may be applied to another trip in many cases.

non-scheduled. Of an airline or other carrier, having no fixed timetable of operations. Operating on an irregular schedule. Non-scheduled carriers may have lower fares than scheduled ones.

non-sked. *See* non-scheduled.

non-transferable. Cannot be used by anyone other than the person to which it was issued, as a ticket.

nonstop. Transportation comprising a single segment. Without intermediate stops.

NOOP. *GDS.* Not operating.

NOREC. *GDS.* No record.

normal fare. An airline fare for a completely unrestricted ticket.

norovirus. Any of a number of gastrointestinal viruses causing acute gastroenteritis in humans. Easily transmissible, noroviruses are an occasional problem on cruise ships.

Northern Lights, The. *See* aurora borealis.

Norwalk virus. *See* norovirus.

nose count. The physical counting of passengers, as by a flight attendant, to compare a manifest with the actual number of passengers. *See also* head count.

NOSH. *GDS.* No show (qv).

notarize. To have a document or a signature verified as genuine.

notary public. A person who has been authorized by the courts to attest to the authenticity of documents and signatures, usually for a fee. Sometimes referred to as a "notary."

NOTR. *GDS.* No traffic rights.

NPS. National Park Service.

NPTA. National Passenger Traffic Association.

NR. *GDS.* No rate. No payment required.

NRC. *GDS.* No record.

NRCF. *GDS.* Not reconfirmed.

NRP. *GDS.* Non-revenue (i.e. not paying) passenger.

NRS. *GDS.* No rate specified. (i.e. none available at time of reservation.)

NSEERS. National Security Entry Exit Registration System, a program of the Department of Homeland Security (qv).

NSML. *GDS.* No-salt meal.

NSST. *GDS.* Non-smoking seat.

NTA. National Tour Association.

NTBA. 1. *GDS.* Name to be announced (i.e. name will be provided later). 2. *Abr.* National Tour Brokers Association. *See* NTA.

NTHP. National Trust for Historic Preservation.

NTI. *GDS.* Need ticketing information.

NTSB. National Transportation Safety Board.

NUC. *Abr.* Neutral unit of construction (qv).

NV. *Abr.* Nuclear vessel.

NWCA. North West Cruiseship Association.

Glossary of Terms

316

The Travel Agent's
Complete Desk
Reference

O, o

O. *GDS.* Stopover.

O&D traffic. Origin and destination traffic. The passengers on a flight who are either boarding or deplaning at a particular stop, as distinct from those remaining on the plane to go to another destination.

OAG. *Official Airline Guide.*

occupancy rate. The percentage of hotel rooms occupied during a specific time period, omitting rooms not available for one reason or another.

OCNFT. *GDS.* Oceanfront.

OCNVW. *GDS.* Ocean view.

off airport location. A car rental company that does not have a counter in the terminal building. *See also* on airport location.

offline airline, offline carrier. Any airline other than the one or ones that own and/or control a particular global distribution system.

offline connection. A change of planes that also involves a change of airlines.

offline point. A destination with no service from a particular airline or other carrier.

off-peak. *adj.* Occurring or applicable during a period of less travel or demand, as in a flight or a fare.

off-season. *n.* A period of the year when demand for a destination decreases and prices go down. Also used as an adjective, as to describe a price or fare applicable during such a period.

OHG. *Official Hotel Guide.*

OJ. *GDS.* Open jaw (qv).

OK. *GDS.* Confirmed.

Old Glory. Nickname for the U.S. flag.

OMFG. *Official Meeting Facilities Guide.*

omnibus. Obsolete term for a bus, motorcoach, or similar mode of transportation.

on airport location. A rental car company with a counter in the terminal building. *See also* off airport location.

on site, onsite. n. 1. A branch of a travel agency located in the offices of a major customer. 2. A supplier to a tour operator that is located in the country or region in which the tour operator specializes.

onboard revenue. In the cruise industry, income derived from shipboard activities such as casinos, spas, shore excursions, shops, specialty restaurants, and so forth. As opposed to revenue generated from the sale of cabins.

one-way trip. Any trip for which a return leg has not been booked.

online carrier. An airline that can provide immediate access through a global distribution system (qv).

online connection. A change of planes that does not involve a change of airlines.

OP. *GDS.* Other person.

open bar. Beverage service that is free for guests.

open jaw. A trip that has no air travel between two points on the itinerary. *See also* arunk.

open jaw with side trip. An open jaw itinerary with an additional roundtrip from one of the cities on the itinerary.

open pay, open rate. A rate of payment or compensation that is subject to or will be determined by negotiation.

open segment, open ticket. An airline ticket with no date specified.

open seating, open sitting. Seats or tables are not assigned and will be occupied on a first-come basis.

open skies. Referring to an agreement between two countries allowing unrestricted air services between them.

open ticket. A valid ticket that does not specify flight numbers, dates, or times. The holder of the ticket makes arrangements at a later date.

open water. Portions of the sea that are far from land in which a cruise ship might experience greater motion or rougher seas.

operator. Any company providing airline, cruise, hotel, or other services.

OPNS. *GDS.* Operations.

OPT. *GDS.* Option (qv). Option date (qv).

option. 1. An additional excursion or other element that need not be taken. 2. Option date (qv).

option date. Date by which payment must be made to secure a reservation.

optional. *adj.* Used to describe any product or service that is not included in the base price but which may be added at the customer's discretion for an additional cost.

orchestra. 1. A large group of musicians. 2. The orchestra level of a theater.

orchestra pit. The sunken area between stage and audience in which orchestra members sit and play.

orchestra level. The main level of a theater. *See also* stalls.

ORG. *Official Recreation Guide.*

orientation. A meeting or training session designed to provide a basic understanding or overview of a subject.

ORIG. *GDS.* Origin. Originating. Originated.

origin. The starting point of travel.

origin and destination traffic. *See* O&D traffic.

ORML. *GDS.* Asian meal.

O/S. *Abr.* On a ship, an insider cabin.

OS. *Abr.* Outside sales. Outside sales representative.

OSI. *GDS.* Other service information (qv).

OSSN. Outside Sales Support Network.

OTA. Open Travel Alliance.

OTC. *Abr.* One-stop inclusive tour charter.

OTD. *Official Tour Directory.*

other service information. Notes attached to a PNR (qv) that do not require attention by the airline.

OTHS. *GDS.* Other services. Other service information (qv).

OUT. *GDS.* Departure date, as from a hotel.

Glossary of Terms

out plant. *adj.* Referring to a travel agency office on the premises of a corporate client at which reservations may be made. The actual ticketing is handled at another location.

outback. In Australia, extremely remote or desert areas.

outbound. *adj.* Referring to the leg of the journey departing the city of origin to the destination or destinations.

outfitter. 1. Any company that sells equipment for any of a broad range of outdoor activities. 2. A company that provides guided group or individual outdoor activities, such as whitewater rafting, trekking, camping, etc., including the use or rental of appropriate transportation and equipment.

outrigger canoe. A Polynesian style, oared vessel with an extending arm that provides stability.

outside cabin. On a ship, a cabin with a porthole, window, or occasionally a private terrace.

outside sales. A department or activity devoted to developing business through direct solicitation of potential customers away from a retail location.

outside sales representative. A person engaged in outside sales. May be an employee or an independent contractor.

outskirts. The outlying areas of a city.

outsource. To retain a separate specialist company to handle certain internal business functions.

overbooking. The practice of taking more reservations than there are seats, rooms, or space in the expectation that no shows (qv) will bring the number of reservations actually used below maximum occupancy.

overhead. 1. A storage compartment located above head level, as on an airplane. 2. The fixed expenses, such as rent and utilities, of a business.

overland. 1. Taking place on land. 2. Referring to travel that takes place off roads.

overlook. A turnoff on a highway or other location offering a scenic view.

override, override commission. An additional commission percentage paid when a certain volume level is achieved.

oversale. *See* overbooking.

oversell. 1. *See* overbooking. 2. *v.* To sell too aggressively; to exaggerate the features or benefits of a product.

oversupply. Excess capacity, as of airline seats or hotel rooms.

OW. *GDS.* One-way.

OX. *GDS.* Cancel if requested segment is available, otherwise hold.

ozone layer. A high atmosphere phenomenon providing shielding from the sun's ultraviolet rays. Degradation of the ozone layer in some areas (such as extreme southern South America and Australia) requires travelers to take additional precautions against overexposure to the sun.

P-8. The Group of Eight (qv).

PA. *GDS.* Via the Pacific.

PAC. *GDS.* Personal accident coverage. *See also* PAI, PIP.

pacing. The practice of making travel arrangements in such a way that sufficient time will be allotted for various activities.

package. A travel product bundling several distinct elements, such as air travel, a rental car, and a hotel. A package is distinguished from a tour by virtue of the fact that it combines fewer elements.

packager. A person or company that puts together travel packages.

page. *v.* To call for a person, especially over a public address system in a public place, as an airport.

PAHO. Pan-American Health Organization.

PAI. *GDS.* Personal accident insurance (qv).

P&L. *Abr.* Profit and loss.

Pan-American. *adj.* Embracing North, Central, and South America, as the Pan-American Highway.

panhandle. A section of a nation, state or territory that resembles a panhandle when viewed on a map, as the panhandle of Oklahoma.

par. 1. Equality or a level of equality. 2. A standard commonly accepted in most instances. 3. The number of strokes allotted to complete a hole in golf.

parador. *Sp.* A hotel, especially one that has been converted from a historic building such as a castle or monastery.

parcel. 1. A piece of undeveloped land. 2. A package such as might be carried or sent through the mail.

parish. 1. A geopolitical division, equivalent to a county, notably in the state of Louisiana. 2. A church district.

parliamentary procedure. A system for running meetings patterned on the rules of Britain's Parliament.

parlor car. On a train, a car providing more comfortable seating and/or food service.

PARS®. A former global distribution system (qv).

partnership. A legal form of business ownership comprising two or more individuals.

passenger facility charge. A fee imposed by a facility owner, as an airport, on those using the facility; typically added to the cost of a fare.

passenger mile. A statistical norm comprising one passenger traveling one mile. Passenger mileage for airlines is determined by multiplying the total number of miles flown by the total number of passengers carried.

passenger name record. A file on a global distribution system containing all the information relating to a specific booking. Also called "personal name record."

Passenger Network Services Corporation. Former name of International Airlines Travel Agent Network (IATAN) (qv).

passenger sales agent. Travel agent.

passenger service agent. An airline employee assigned to assist passengers checking in and boarding.

passenger service representative. An airline employee assigned to providing information and other services, such as wheelchair assistance.

passenger space ratio. A statistical measure that compares the total public space of a cruise ship to the passenger capacity, resulting in the theoretical amount of public space allotted to each passenger. A high passenger space ratio indicates a roomy ship.

passenger terminal indicator. A one- or two-digit code, administered by IATA (qv), that identifies specific passenger terminals at airports having more than one passenger terminal.

passenger traffic manager. 1. An airport-based airline manager. 2. Individual in a company who handles travel arrangements for other employees.

passive booking, passive segment. A segment entered in a GDS (qv) that does not result in a ticket being issued. Typically used by agents to generate itineraries or make notes.

passport. A document identifying an individual as a citizen of a specific country and attesting to his or her identity and ability to travel freely.

password. Any alphanumeric string used to identify a specific individual to a computer, computer program, computer network, or similar system.

PATA. Pacific Asia Travel Association.

pat-down. A screening procedure used by the Transportation Security Administration in which screeners may touch the breasts, buttocks, genitals, and other sensitive areas of those being screened.

pavilion. 1. An exhibit hall at an exposition. 2. Any open sided building or tent. 3. A section of a building projecting out from that building.

PAWOB. *Abr.* Passenger arriving without baggage.

pax. *Abr.* Passenger. Passengers.

payload. 1. The percentage of total weight, as in an airplane, that represents revenue-producing passengers and/or cargo.

PC. *Abr.* Public charter (qv).

PDM. *GDS.* Possible duplicate message.

PDQ. *Abr.* Immediately, as soon as possible. (Literally, "pretty darn quick.")

PDR. *Abr.* People's Democratic Republic (of China).

PDT. *Abr.* Pacific Daylight Time. Provincial Daylight Time.

PDW. *Abr.* Personal damage waiver. *See* collision damage waiver.

peak fare. A higher fare that applies during periods of maximum demand for a destination.

PEC. *Abr.* Personal effects coverage (qv).

penalty fare. Fare subject to a deduction or other fee should the passenger change the itinerary or cancel.

pension. *Sp.* A small hotel or boarding house.

penthouse. 1. An apartment or suite on the top floor of a hotel or top deck of a cruise ship. 2. The top floor of a hotel.

people mover. Any motorized device for moving people over short distances. Typically, a flat escalator-like rubber mat in the corridors of an airport terminal. *See also* moving sidewalk.

per diem. 1. *Lat.* by the day. 2. A sum of money paid or given to an employee to cover daily expenses. 3. In the cruise industry, the daily cost of a cruise to the passenger.

perk. *Abr.* Short for perquisite. A privilege or extra benefit associated with a person's position in a company.

personal accident insurance. Individual coverage for accidents. Also called personal injury protection (PIP) or personal accident coverage (PAC).

personal effects coverage. Insurance covering the loss of personal property from a rented car.

personal name record. *See* passenger name record.

personal watercraft. Small, noisy vessels offering straddle seating for one, two or (rarely) three passengers. Sold under brand names such as JetSki or SkiDoo. Often rented to tourists in resort destinations.

PETC. *GDS.* Pet in cabin.

petit dejeuner. *Fr.* Breakfast.

petrol. *Brit.* Gasoline.

PF. *Fr. Abr.* Prix fixe (qv).

PFC. *Abr.* Passenger facility charge (qv).

photo safari. An excursion designed to bring tourists close to wildlife, a staple of tours to African game parks.

piazza. *It.* An open square.

pidgin, pidgin English. Any of a number of dialects combining English and a local language, spoken in various parts of the world.

pier. A dock for the mooring of ships or boats.

pier head jump. The practice of booking a cruise at the very last minute, often on the dock, to get a lower fare.

pilgrimage. A journey undertaken to a religious shrine or for a religious purpose.

pilot. 1. *n.* The person in control of an aircraft. 2. The person who steers a ship; helmsman. 3. Port official responsible for guiding ships into and out of the harbor. 4. *v.* To control a plane in flight or a ship in water. 5. *n. See* pilot program.

pilot berth. On a yacht, a compact, single-person sleeping area near the helm.

pilot house. The enclosed area from which the steering mechanism of a ship is operated.

pilot program. A test or trial of a system or methodology used to detect and correct flaws or to determine suitability.

Pineapple Express. *Slang.* A winter weather system originating in the Hawaiian tropics that brings higher temperatures and heavy rains to Alaska.

pinisi. A two-masted sailing vessel or schooner of Indonesian design, accommodating 12 to 18 passengers, used by some soft-adventure tour operators.

PIP. *Abr.* Personal injury protection. *See also* personal accident insurance.

PITA. Professional Internet Travel Alliance.

pitch. 1. *n.* The measurement between identical points on seats of an airplane; the greater the pitch, the greater the degree of comfort. 2. *v.* To move

Glossary of Terms

sharply up or down, as in an airplane or boat. 3. *n.* The sharp, uncomfortable up or down motion of a plane or ship.

plan to go deposit. A fee, usually non-refundable, charged to a client by a travel agent or tour operator as a prerequisite for consulting on their travel plans. If the client books, the fee becomes a down payment; if the client does not book, the fee is forfeited.

plate. A metal stamp used to impress the name of an airline on a manual ticket when issuing a ticket for that carrier.

plates. Imprints, usually specific to a supplier, that are distributed to travel agencies and used to create tickets. *See also* airline plate.

plating away. The practice of avoiding issuing tickets for a particular carrier in the belief that the carrier may be financially unstable and cease flight operations.

Plimsoll line. A line on the hull of a ship indicating the ship has reached its maximum cargo load.

plunge pool. A small pool in a hotel room or in a private courtyard adjacent to a hotel room.

PLVW. *GDS.* Pool view.

p.m. *Abr.* Post meridian. Afternoon or evening. The time between 12 noon and 12 midnight.

PMS. *Abr.* Property management system (qv).

PNR. *Abr.* Passenger name record (qv). Passenger now recorded. Personal name record.

PNSC. Passenger Network Services Corporation (qv).

podium. 1. A lectern. 2. A raised platform, specifically one used in a public meeting for the speaker or speakers.

POE. *GDS.* Point of embarkation (qv).

point. A city or other stop on an itinerary.

point of embarkation, point of origin. Where a journey begins.

point of turnaround. The place at which an airplane or other vehicle begins its return journey to its point of origin.

point to point. *adj.* 1. Referring to fares between two cities. 2. Referring to service between two cities only, without any additional segments or continuation.

political asylum. Sanctuary given by one country to a citizen of another to protect that person from arrest or persecution.

Political Eight. *See* Group of Eight.

polyglot. A person who speaks many languages.

pontoon. 1. A hollow compartment used to float a flat-bottomed boat. 2. Any boat so designed. 3. The landing pad of a seaplane.

pontoon boat. A flat, railed platform, usually covered with an awning and offering comfortable seating, mounted on two or more hollow tubes. Used for recreational cruising in smooth waters; sometimes used as a tour boat.

pool deck. The deck on a cruise ship where the swimming pool is located.

pool route. A route on which two carriers equally share revenues and facilities and exchange equipment and crew on an as-needed basis.

poop, poop deck. A raised deck at the rear of some ships.

port. 1. The complex of buildings and facilities where ships dock. 2. In nautical parlance, left. The left side of a ship. 3. a door in the side of a ship.

port authority. A local or regional governmental entity that oversees transportation facilities such as airports, ship ports, bus terminals, and so forth.

port charges, port tax. A fee levied by the local government on departing or visiting cruise passengers. Typically, listed as a separate charge in cruise brochures.

port-intensive. *adj.* Visiting many ports; used to describe a cruise itinerary with few or no days at sea.

port of call. Any of the ports at which a ship will be stopping on a cruise.

port of entry. 1. The point at which a person or vessel enters a country. 2. A port or city designated as one at which a foreign ship or other vessel can enter a country's territory.

portal. Door. Tunnel entrance.

porte cochere. A covered entranceway, as to a hotel, designed to accommodate cars.

porter. A baggage handler. *See also* skycap.

porterage. The act or process of baggage handling.

porthole. A window, usually round, on a ship.

posada. *Sp.* A small country hotel.

posh. *Brit.* Elegant, high-class, as in a posh hotel. Its origins lie in the abbreviation for "port out, starboard home," indicating the best berths on sailings from England to India and back.

position, positioning. The act of moving aircraft or ships from one location to another so as to utilize them more efficiently or for greater revenue. *See also* repositioning.

positive space. Seating or rooms that can actually be occupied, as opposed to space reserved on a standby or if-available basis.

post audit. A detailed review of a company's employee's completed travel to determine whether or not the billed amount is accurate. Sometimes conducted by a third party which retains a percentage of any overbilled amount detected.

post code, postal code. An alphanumerical code used to facilitate the delivery of mail; primarily used in the United Kingdom, Canada, and other Commonwealth countries. *See also* ZIP code.

postdate. To place a date on a document, as a check, later than the current date.

POT. *GDS.* Point of turnaround (qv).

potable. Safe to drink.

pow wow. 1. A Native American meeting or festivity, now frequently a tourist attraction. 2. By extension, any meeting, especially one involving high level people, arranged to conclude business or make decisions.

PP. *Abr.* Per person.

PPDO. *GDS.* Per person, double occupancy.

PPR. *GDS.* Passenger profile record.

PRC. *Abr.* People's Republic of China. *See also* PDR.

pre- (or post-) convention tour. A tour or excursion sold in conjunction

with attendance at a convention or meeting.

predesignated point. A system of unique telecommunications addresses, administered by IATA, used to ensure that reservations to specific airlines are properly routed.

preferred supplier. A supplier with which a travel agency has negotiated or earned a higher commission rate.

preferred supplier agreement. An arrangement between a corporation and supplier in which, in return for discounts or other advantages, the corporation requires its employees to use the products and services of the supplier.

premiere class. First-class or an elaboration thereof. The precise definition varies according to supplier.

prepaid. Paid in full in advance.

prepaid ticket advice. The form used when a person is buying a ticket that will be issued at the airport of the same or another city.

preregistration. A service offered for some conventions, whereby room assignments and other arrangements can be made prior to arrival.

preserve. An area set aside by the government, or other entity, specifically to conserve animal life or vegetation.

press release. A formal printed announcement by a company about its activities that is written in the form of a news article and given to the media to generate or encourage publicity.

pre-trip auditing. Review of proposed travel itineraries, usually by a corporate travel manager, to spot potential savings or avoid excessive or unauthorized expenditures.

PRF. *GDS.* Partial refund message.

price fixing. An illegal practice in which competing companies agree, formally or informally, to restrict prices within a specified range.

price-point packaging. Offering a bundle of products at a single, attractive price, as opposed to pricing each component separately (a la carte).

price signaling. The practice, now declared illegal, in which competing companies alert each other to proposed changes in their pricing structure, in order to control pricing within an industry. *See also* price fixing.

prime meridian. The imaginary line through Greenwich, England, designated as zero degrees longitude (qv).

prix fixe. *Fr.* Literally, "fixed price." A meal of several courses, with no substitutions allowed, offered for a special price.

PRM. *GDS.* Premium.

productivity based pricing. An incentive provided by a GDS vendor to encourage maximum use of its service and discourage the agency from using more than one GDS.

productivity pricing. Overrides paid to travel agencies by airlines to reward volume.

professional liability insurance. *See* errors and omissions insurance.

profile. A record of information about a travel agent's customer used for qualifying (qv).

profit and loss statement. An accounting report detailing revenue and expenses.

promenade. 1. A leisurely stroll. 2. A place designed for taking such strolls. 3. A deck on a ship.

promissory note. A written promise to pay a specified sum either on demand or on a specific date.

promo. 1. *Abr.* Promotion, promotional. 2. *Slang.* A promotional announcement or advertisement.

promotional fare. A discount fare designed to increase volume.

proof of citizenship. Any documentation that indicates the citizenship of an individual, including birth certificates, voter's registration cards, or passports.

prop. 1. *Abr.* Property, proprietor. 2. A propeller. 3. *adj.* Describing a propeller driven aircraft.

property management system. A computer program used to administer a hotel.

proportional fare. *See* add-on fare.

proposal. 1. A formal written document soliciting business and spelling out what will be delivered, the costs, terms, conditions, and so forth. 2. A suggestion for a course of action.

proposal vacation. A trip to a romantic destination for the specific purpose of proposing marriage.

proprietary club. A for-profit group, such as a health club, that sells memberships to the general public. *See also* equity club.

prorate. 1. *v.* Adjust proportionally. 2. *n.* In the educational tour market, the number of paying customers required to earn a tour conductor pass (qv).

prospect. 1. *n.* A potential customer who meets certain minimum qualifications. *See also* suspect. 2. *v.* To search for potential customers.

prospecting cycle. The period of time after which a travel agent will recontact individuals or groups previously contacted to solicit business.

PROT. *GDS.* Protected reservation.

protected commission. A commission that will be paid even if the passenger cancels and the travel doesn't occur.

protocol. *n.* 1. A series of software conventions enabling computers to communicate with one another. 2. The proper form and format for conducting business, ceremonies, and so forth, as in diplomatic protocol.

prototype. A single or limited-edition working version of an aircraft or other device used for testing and demonstration purposes.

Provincial Daylight Time. Canadian term for Atlantic Daylight Time.

Provincial Standard Time. Canadian term for Atlantic Standard Time.

provisioned charter. A charter, as of a boat, that includes food and other supplies but no crew.

provisioning. The act of loading food supplies onto a ship or sailboat.

prow. The foremost part of a ship.

PSA. *Abr.* Passenger service agent (qv).

PSCZ. Puget Sound Convergence Zone.

pseudo ARC number. An alphanumeric designator, often a telephone number, used by suppliers to identify travel agencies that do not have an ARC number.

Glossary of Terms

pseudo city, pseudo city code. A GDS code used to identify a travel agency location.

pseudo PNR. A record stored in a GDS that does not contain an airline reservation. *See also* passenger name record.

pseudo-agent. 1. Someone who claims to be a travel agent but isn't. 2. Derogatory term for an outside sales representative not deemed to have sufficient training in travel.

psgr. *Abr.* Passenger.

PSR. *Abr.* Passenger service representative (qv).

PST. *Abr.* Pacific Standard Time. Provincial Standard Time.

PT. *Abr.* Port taxes. Pacific Time. Physical training.

PTA. *GDS.* Prepaid ticket advice (qv).

PTHSE. *GDS.* Penthouse.

PTM. Passenger traffic manager (qv).

PTP. *Abr.* Point-to-point (qv).

Pty. Proprietary. Designating a business; the equivalent of Inc. or Ltd.

P/U. *Abr.* Pick up.

public charter. An aircraft or other vessel that may be leased by the general public.

published fare. Any fare specifically listed in the carrier's tariff (qv).

Puget Sound Convergence Zone (PSCZ). A weather phenomenon in which northwest winds are split by the Olympic mountain range and rejoin in the Seattle area, causing unsettled weather.

pullman. A sleeping car on a railroad.

pullman berth. A sleeping compartment or pull-down bunk on a pullman train. By extension, any sleeping arrangement that is similarly configured.

pullman train. A train equipped with sleeping cars.

PUP. *GDS.* Pick up.

purser. On a ship, the person responsible for providing a wide array of passenger services, including mail, information, check cashing, safety deposit boxes, and so forth.

PWCT. *GDS.* Passenger will contact.

Q, q

QADB. *GDS.* Quad (qv) with bath.

QADN. *GDS.* Quad without bath or shower.

QADS. *GDS.* Quad with shower.

qd. *Abr.* Quad.

QINB. *GDS.* Quin (qv) with bath.

QINN. *GDS.* Quin without bath or shower.

QINS. *GDS.* Quin with shower.

QTD. *Abr.* Quarter to date.

quad. Hotel room for four people.

qualifying. 1. In sales, the process of determining if a prospect will make a good customer. 2. Process of determining which travel product is right for a customer by asking questions.

qualifying code. An alphanumeric designator that identifies a special fare, promotion, level of amenities, etc., on a ticket or other travel document.

quality assurance. In travel agency operations, the process of checking an itinerary, PNR (qv), or other reservation to insure its completeness and accuracy.

quarter deck. The stern section of the upper deck of a ship, traditionally officers' quarters.

quay. (Pronounced "key.") A pier.

queen room. A hotel room with a queen size bed.

query letter. A business letter requesting information.

queue. (Pronounced "cue.") *Brit.* 1. *v.* To line up to await service in turn, as at a bus stop. 2. *n.* A line of people waiting for service or admittance. 3. *n.* A communications area or subsystem within a networked computer system. 4. *v.* To route a communication, such as a PNR (qv), on a GDS to a specific destination, such as a travel agency.

quid. *Brit.* A pound sterling.

quin. Hotel room for five people.

quota. 1. The maximum number allowed. 2. A target number to be achieved, as a sales quota.

quote. 1. *v.* To state a price. 2. *n.* The price so stated.

R, r

R&R. *Abr.* Rest and relaxation/rehabilitation/recreation.

RAA. Regional Airline Association.

rack rate. The price a hotel charges for a room before any discount has been taken into account. The published rate for a room, sometimes set artificially high and used to calculate a variety of discounts. *See also* run of the house, walk-up rate.

raincheck. A slip or chit given to a customer in compensation for services promised but not received, usually redeemable for the identical service at a later date. For example, patrons of a rained-out sporting event will receive a coupon good for admission to a game later in the season.

ramp. *n.* Any sloping surface accommodating foot or vehicular traffic.

ramp agent. An employee of an airline charged with bringing cargo, luggage, and food supplies to the aircraft.

range. The maximum distance an aircraft can fly or a ship cruise without refueling.

ranger. An official of a National Park. A Park Ranger.

rapids. Section of a river where water flows swiftly over rocks; often navigated by rubber rafts as a recreational activity.

rate and service structure. The prices a carrier charges and the services and amenities it provides, considered as a whole system.

rate desk. The office of an airline that calculates fares for travel agents and passengers.

rate hike. An increase in fares or other costs.

rate of the day. A hotel pricing system in which the rack rate (qv) varies from day to day.

RCCL. Royal Caribbean Cruise Line.

RCVD. *GDS.* Received.

RDB. *GDS.* Reply to duplicate booking enquiry.

re. *Abr.* Regarding, about.

rebate. 1. *v.* To deduct or return a portion of moneys otherwise due, as a portion of a travel agent's commission. 2. *n.* A sum so returned.

recall commission statement. An ARC document generated by an airline to retrieve a commission paid on a ticket that the airline has refunded to the passenger.

receivership. The state of being in the control of a court, as a business in bankruptcy.

receiving agent. A contractor that provides services to incoming passengers, as those on a tour.

reception. 1. The front desk of a hotel. 2. A party or event to greet a person or persons.

receptive service operator. *See* receiving agent.

receptive services. Services provided by a receiving agent, including transfers, currency exchange, interpreters, and so forth. *See also* meet and greet.

recheck system. An automated feature of a GDS or a separate software package that continuously checks the lowest fares on a route.

reconciliation. Matching one set of records against another. For example, an employee's expense account against credit card slips and other receipts.

reconfirm. To check again, as an airline reservation. Some reservations may be cancelled unless reconfirmed.

record. *n.* In a GDS, all the information about a single booking. A PNR (qv).

record locator, record locator number. An alphanumeric string that serves as a unique identifier of a booking or a PNR (qv) in a GDS (qv).

recreation management. The process or profession of maintaining and administering the physical facilities and personnel involved in leisure-based recreational activities.

recreational vehicle. 1. A self-contained, self-driven motor home. 2. Any vehicle, such as a dune buggy (qv) or all-terrain vehicle (qv), used primarily for enjoyment.

red and green. A system used by customs in which passengers with nothing to declare follow the green symbols, while passengers with dutiable items to declare follow the red symbols through the customs area.

Red Book, The. A now-defunct hotel reference guide. The term is commonly used to refer to any hotel reference guide.

red light district. A part of a city set aside, either by municipal ordinance or informal custom, for prostitution and other sex-related businesses.

red-eye, red-eye flight. 1. A late-night flight, usually of some length and usually offering a lower fare. 2. An overnight flight that arrives at the destination early in the morning.

referral. A prospect (qv) recommended to a travel agent by another person, usually a current customer. The act of recommending such a person.

referral agency. A travel agency using a network of outside sales agents to funnel travel requests to an inside sales force that makes the actual sale. Typically, these agencies seek to recruit as large an outside sales force as possible. *See also* card mill.

refund/exchange notice. An ARC form and process for making an adjustment in money owed to the travel agency or due ARC.

regatta. A boat race.

regional carrier. An airline that serves only one clearly defined area of a country.

regional jet. A jet powered aircraft, typically with 50 seats or fewer, designed to serve smaller airports.

registered traveler. A frequent traveler who has submitted to a background check by the Transportation Security Administration and is consequently exempt from routine searches at airports.

registry. A ship's formal registration of ownership. *See also* country of registry.

regular fare. An unrestricted, full-price fare, such as "coach" (Y class) or "first" (F class).

reissue. Write or generate a new ticket due to changes in itinerary or fare.

remittance. The sending of money to pay for a product or service. Any sum

sent for this purpose.

REML. *GDS.* Reference my letter.

remote check-in. A service that allows air travelers to get boarding passes and check bags at a location away from the airport, such as a hotel.

remote ticketing. Refers to the practice of making a reservation at one location and generating the ticket at another.

REMT. *GDS.* Reference my telegram.

REN. *Abr.* Refund/exchange notice (qv).

rent a plate. *Slang.* An off premises travel agency operated by employees of the corporation at which it is located.

repeat customer. Any customer who buys again. Generally used to refer to a customer who buys repeatedly or frequently.

replacement cost. The current price of a piece of equipment if it were to be purchased new, as opposed to the present, depreciated value of the equipment.

repositioning. The act of moving a vessel, such as a cruise ship, from one area to another, usually at a specific time of year, to maximize efficiency of use. *See also* positioning.

REQ. *GDS.* Request.

request for information. A preliminary step to a request for proposal (RFP) (qv), in which a company solicits a number of potential vendors for information about their products and services.

request for proposal. A formal request by a company, containing detailed specifications, to a potential vendor asking for a bid on satisfying those specifications.

res. (Pronounced "rez.") *Abr.* Reservation.

res vendor. 1. A global distribution system company. 2. A sales representative of such a company.

residential. *adj.* Consisting of homes rather than commercial buildings, as a section of a city.

resort. 1. A city or other destination known for its leisure attractions. 2. A hotel featuring a broad range of amenities, sports facilities, and other leisure attractions, designed to provide a total vacation experience.

responsibility clause. *See* disclaimer.

rest area. On a limited-access highway, a parking area allowing drivers to rest without leaving the highway. May have amenities such as rest rooms, vending machines, full restaurant service, tourist information booths, picnic tables, and so forth.

restaurateur. A person who owns and operates restaurants.

restricted access. Not open to everyone, as a travel agency that is not open to the public.

retailer. 1. Anyone who sells goods or services to the general public. 2. In the travel industry, used to refer to a travel agent or travel agency.

retroactive. Encompassing a time period prior to execution or announcement, as a retroactive fare increase.

retrofit. Add machinery or equipment to an existing piece of equipment or system to correct a defect or add capability.

revalidation sticker. A self-adhesive form placed over the coupon portion of an airline ticket and used to record a change in carrier, flight number, date, time, class, and so forth.

revenue passenger mile. A statistical unit in the airline industry; one fare-paying passenger carried one mile.

revenue sharing. A term used to describe rebating to a corporation by a travel agency. *See* rebate.

REYL. *GDS.* Reference your letter.

REYT. *GDS.* Reference your telegram.

RFD. 1. *GDS.* Refund. 2. *Abr.* Rural free delivery.

RFI. 1. *GDS.* Request further information. 2. *Abr.* Request for information (qv).

RFP. *Abr.* Request for proposal (qv).

RHYA. *GDS.* Release for handling by your agency.

Richter scale. A logarithmic scale recording the severity of earthquakes. Because the scale is logarithmic, a 5.0 quake is ten times stronger than a 4.0 quake.

Ricknik. *Slang.* A fan of the guide books written by Rick Steves and the travel philosophy they espouse.

right of search. The right, under international maritime law, to stop a merchant ship to determine if it is in violation of revenue laws.

right of way. 1. The order of precedence in passing or proceeding, as of ships in a channel. 2. The right of one person to cross land owned by another.

riptide. A strong current flowing outward from the shore, endangering swimmers.

risk inventory. Exclusive space on a tour or cruise that a travel agency contracts to purchase, usually at an attractive discount, whether it sells the space or not.

RJ. *Abr.* Regional jet (qv).

RLNG. *GDS.* Releasing.

RLOC. *GDS.* Record locator (qv).

RLSE. *GDS.* Release.

RMKS. *GDS.* Remarks.

RMS. *Abr.* Royal mail steamship.

RNP. *GDS.* Reduce number in party.

road rat. *Slang.* A person who makes his or her living delivering recreational vehicles.

ROC. 1. *GDS.* Record of charge. 2. *Abr.* Republic of China (Taiwan).

rodeo. An entertainment featuring displays of cowboy riding and roping skills.

ROE. *GDS.* Rate of exchange.

ROH. *GDS.* Run of the house (qv).

ROK. *Abr.* Republic of Korea.

roll. 1. A list of those present. 2. The side to side motion of a ship.

rollaway. In a hotel, a cot-like bed that can be folded and rolled from place to place.

rollover clause. A now-disallowed provision of GDS contracts that triggered a new contract term any time a new piece of equipment was purchased from the vendor.

332

The Travel Agent's Complete Desk Reference

room block. In a hotel, a number of rooms set aside or reserved for a group.

room night. One hotel room occupied for one night; a statistical unit of occupancy.

room service. Meal service to a hotel room.

room tax. Local and state taxes on hotel rooms that are added to the guest's bill.

roomette. On a train, a single compartment with a fold-down bed and a toilet.

rooming list. A roster of guests and their lodging needs presented to a hotel by a group prior to a meeting.

rope tow. A continuous, moving rope used to pull skiers up a slope.

roster. A list, as of those on duty at a particular time.

rostrum. *See* podium.

rotary phone. An old type of telephone with a circular dial that when turned produces pulses corresponding to the number dialed. *See also* touch-tone phone.

roundabout. *Brit.* A traffic circle.

roundtrip, round trip. *n.* A trip, as on an airline, to a single destination and back. *adj.* Referring to fares, typically indicates that the fare is the same regardless of which of the two cities is the departure point.

routing. The sequence of cities used to construct a fare.

royalty. A payment made to a company or individual for the use of its/her property, usually an intellectual property.

RPM. *Abr.* Revenue passenger mile (qv).

RPT. *GDS.* Repeat previous transaction.

RQ. *GDS.* On request.

RQID. *GDS.* Request is desired.

RQR. *GDS.* Request for reply.

RQST. *GDS.* Request seat.

RR. *GDS.* Reconfirmed.

RS. *GDS.* Reserved seat.

RSA. *Abr.* Reservations sales agent.

RSO. *Abr.* Receptive service operator (qv).

RSVP. *Fr. Abr.* Repondez s'il vous plait. Literally, "respond if you please." Often included in written invitations, and when included, etiquette demands a response.

RT. *GDS.* Roundtrip.

rudder. The steering device of a ship.

run of the house. *See* rack rate.

running lights. A series of colored lights required on a ship during the night to prevent collisions.

Ruta Maya. *Sp.* Literally, "Mayan route" or "road." Used to denote the Mayan areas of Mexico, Belize, Honduras, and Guatemala and the tourist sites therein.

RV. *Abr.* Recreational vehicle (qv).

ryokan. A traditional Japanese inn.

S corp. *Abr.* Subchapter S Corporation (qv).

S&T. *GDS.* Shower and toilet.

SA. *GDS.* Space available.

SAB. *Abr.* Sleep aboard (qv).

Sabre®. A global distribution system (qv).

safari. 1. An adventure trip, typically in Africa, using off-road vehicles and tent-like accommodations for the purpose of viewing and photographing wildlife. 2. Originally, a hunting trip.

SAI. *Abr.* System assisted instruction.

sail 'n' stay program. A travel product combining a cruise to a destination with a one- or two-week stay at that destination, after which the passenger rejoins the cruise ship for the remainder of the cruise or to return to the point of departure.

salon. 1. An elegantly appointed reception room, as aboard a cruise ship. 2. A beauty parlor.

sampan. A small river vessel common in China.

Samson's Pillar. *See* "king post."

satellite ticket printer. 1. A branch of an ARC-accredited agency that contains a ticket printer, either attended or unattended. 2. The printer in any such branch.

satellite ticket printer network. A network of attended ticket printers, typically in hotels, maintained by an ARC-accredited entity that sells its ticket distribution services to other ARC agencies. When an agent requests a ticket to be delivered through such a system, the STPN issues the ticket, receives money from the customer, deducts the appropriate commission, and sends it to ARC (qv).

SATH. Society for the Advancement of Travel for the Handicapped.

SATO. *Abr.* Scheduled airline ticket offices.

SATW. Society of American Travel Writers.

sauna. 1. A dry heat bath in which steam can be produced by pouring water on hot coals. 2. A cabinet or room for such a bath.

SB. *Abr.* Steamboat.

SC. *GDS.* Schedule change.

SCAR. *GDS.* Standard (full-size) car.

scenic route. A secondary road designated as being especially scenic and, typically, longer.

scheduled carrier. An airline or other carrier that operates according to a regular and published timetable.

schoolroom setup. In a meeting, a configuration in which tables are lined up on either side of an aisle, with all chairs on one side of the tables, facing front.

scooter. A small motor bike available for rental in some resort areas.

screen scraping. The practice of downloading or otherwise extracting fare and schedule information from a GDS for use on another technological platform or in another medium.

screener. A person tasked with questioning, examining, or searching travelers and their baggage, as at an airport security checkpoint.

screw. The propeller of a ship.

script. 1. A GDS feature that leads and prompts an agent through the booking process. 2. An outline or word-for-word script used by someone making a telemarketing sales call.

scupper. A hole in a ship's side or deck allowing water to drain out.

SDR. *GDS.* Special drawing right (qv).

sea legs. *Slang.* The ability to move easily around a ship, without seasickness or loss of balance.

seaboard. The coast. The area near the ocean.

seagate. A small channel opening onto the sea.

seagoing. Capable of and safe for travel on the open seas.

seaplane. An airplane equipped with pontoons (qv) for landing on water.

search engine. An Internet-based computer program that enables users to locate information on the World Wide Web.

seasickness. Nausea and allied discomfort caused by the effect of a ship's motions on an individual's inner ear.

seat-on-bus. *adj.* Not private or exclusive. In other words, if transportation is sold on a seat-on-bus basis, the passenger should expect to ride with people not on the same tour or with the same group.

seat pitch. *See* pitch.

seat rotation. A practice on tours in which passengers are moved from seat to seat so as to give all travelers equal access to the "good seats."

seating. On a cruise ship, the specified time at which a passenger eats the evening meal. Typically, there are two seatings each night.

seating times. On a cruise ship, the specified hours at which meal services begin.

seatmate. One's next-door neighbor on an airplane.

seatrain. A ship that transports railway cars.

seaward. In the direction of the ocean.

seaway. 1. A designated traffic lane in the ocean. 2. An inland waterway.

seaworthy. Able to float. Safe for sea travel.

second seating, second sitting. The later of two meal seatings on a cruise ship.

second-tier airports. Airports that are not located in major cities, that are not major hubs of any airline, and that traditionally enjoy only limited service.

second world. Nations once allied to or aligned with the former Soviet Union. Now generally obsolete.

secret shopper. A person, usually hired by management, who visits a hotel or restaurant anonymously to test the level of customer service.

sector bonus. An extra commission offered for booking certain airline segments, usually international, offered for limited periods of time.

Secure Flight. A program of the Transportation Security Administration to create a database to identify "passengers known or reasonably suspected to be engaged in terrorist activity."

security. 1. Any measures taken to insure the safety of facilities, property, or personnel. 2. The screening checkpoint through which passengers must pass before boarding an airplane or other vehicle.

security surcharge. An additional fee levied on an airline ticket to pay for increased security measures at airports.

SEDM. *GDS.* Schedule exchange data message.

segment. 1. A discreet portion of a trip, typically between two cities. *See also* leg. 2. A portion of the total market. 3. *v.* To divide the total market into demographic groups, so as to offer a slightly different product or product mix to each one.

self sales. Sales of a company's products or services made to employees of that company.

self-catering. *Brit.* Referring to an apartment or efficiency (qv) in which guests can take care of their own meal and laundry needs.

self-drive. *Brit.* A rental car.

selling away. The purposeful act of promoting the products of one supplier rather than another, usually as a form of protest.

selling fare. The unrestricted coach fare.

selling up. The practice of selling a more expensive alternative or selling more optional elements of a product. Not to be confused with bait and switch (qv).

seminar. A meeting designed to instruct or impart information.

senior, senior citizen. In the travel industry, a designation used to determine fares and other rates. The age at which a customer becomes a "senior" varies with the supplier and can range from 50 to 62 to 65 years of age.

seqno. *Abr.* Sequential number.

server. A computer on which files and data are stored for retrieval by other computers.

servi-bar. A European term for minibar (qv).

service bureau. Typically, a company offering computer services on a contract basis.

service charge. 1. An additional charge, usually levied in lieu of a tip. 2. A fee charged by travel agencies for providing non-commissionable services. *See also* service fee.

service compris. *Fr.* Literally, "service included," that is, there is no need for an additional tip.

service encounter. The discreet period of time in which a customer interacts with a member of the staff of a travel provider such as a hotel.

service fee. A charge to the customer levied by a travel agency, typically to cover the time and expense of arranging air travel; a reaction to commission cuts and caps by the airlines. *See also* service charge.

service non compris. *Fr.* Literally, "service not included," that is, an additional tip is expected.

setups. Non-alcoholic mixers, glasses, ice, and garnishes provided by an establishment, such as a hotel or restaurant, with alcohol to be provided either by the guest or by the establishment for an extra charge.

Seven Continents, the. Africa, Antarctica, Asia, Australia, Europe, North America, and South America.

Seven Seas, the. 1. A general term for all the oceans of the world. 2. More

specifically, the seven seas are generally agreed to comprise the Atlantic (North and South), the Pacific (North and South), the Indian, the Arctic, and the Antarctic.

SEVIS. Student and Exchange Visitor Information System, a program of the Department of Homeland Security (qv).

sextant. A measuring device used in celestial navigation (qv) at sea to measure the angle of elevation of an object such as the sun above the horizon.

SFML. *GDS.* Sea food meal.

SG. *Abr.* School group.

sgl. *Abr.* Single (qv).

SGLB. *GDS.* Single room with bath.

SGLN. *GDS.* Single room without bath.

SGLS. *GDS.* Single room with shower.

SGMT. *GDS.* Segment (qv).

shakedown cruise. A cruise undertaken to test a ship's systems, mechanical and human, sometimes made with passengers traveling at a discount.

Shangri-La. A fictional paradise where people live without care and never age. Used to describe any especially beautiful vacation destination.

shared code carrier. An airline that is listed on a GDS under the code of another airline.

shared use path. A trail, usually two-way, separated from vehicular traffic and designated for use by pedestrians, bicyclists, joggers, skaters, and so forth. Access may be limited to specific categories of use.

sheikdom. A country or territory ruled by a sheik.

shell. A pre-printed brochure or flyer produced by a supplier that has empty space in which a travel agency may have its own logo and address imprinted.

Sherpa. 1. A Tibetan ethnic group. 2. Informally, a member of this group working as an aide or porter to a mountaineering expedition.

ship to shore. The radio system used to communicate with ships at sea.

shoji screen. A sliding rice-paper and wood room divider found in Japanese style hotels.

shopper. *Slang.* A customer who asks a travel agent for recommendations or quotes but who never actually makes a booking. *See also* tirekicker.

shore excursion. A sightseeing excursion offered in conjunction with a cruise, often for an additional charge.

shortest operated mileage. Under the mileage system (qv) of computing fares, the shortest distance between two points on an itinerary, omitting any intermediate connections.

short-haul. Of airline routes, of limited length and duration, often to, from, or between second-tier airports (qv).

shoulder season. An abbreviated season that falls between the high and low seasons (qv) and offers fares and rates between those of the other seasons.

showboat. A paddle steamer on which musical entertainment, often with a "Gay Nineties" (qv) theme, is provided.

SHTL. *GDS.* Second-class hotel.

shuttle. A short-run conveyance, sometimes provided free of charge, operating on a frequent schedule, usually between two points, such as a hotel and the airport, the airport and a car rental agency, and so forth.

SI. *GDS.* Service information. Supplementary information.

sic. *Lat.* Literally, "thus it is written," usually used to indicate that a misspelling or other questionable element in a quotation is exactly as it appeared in the original.

SIC. Standard Industrial Classification.

SIC code. Numerical designator that identifies specific industries.

siesta. An afternoon nap or rest period observed in many Spanish-speaking countries. Shops and other businesses are typically closed during this period.

simplified commissions. Supplier doublespeak for commission structures that, effectively, lower the amount of money due travel agents.

sine. A code used to identify a user or a travel agency in a GDS.

single. 1. A hotel room for one person, that may actually be able to accommodate more people. 2. One empty seat or one ticket in a theater.

single entity charter. An airplane, vessel, or other carrier that is chartered to a single company or group for the exclusive use by its employees or members.

single supplement. A charge added to a per-person occupancy rate that is based on an assumption of double occupancy, as on a cruise ship.

SIPP. *GDS.* Standard interline passenger procedures.

SITA. Societe Internationale Telecommunications Aeronautiques.

SITE. Society of Incentive Travel Executives.

site guide. 1. A guide who works at or specializes in a specific attraction, such as a museum, historical site, or ruin. 2. A page on a web site that gives visitors an overview of the contents of the site.

site inspection. 1. A visit to a hotel property or other establishment for the purpose of evaluation, as on a fam trip (qv). 2. A fam trip.

SITI. *GDS.* Sold inside, ticketed inside. A ticket sold and issued in the same country.

SITO. *GDS.* Sold inside, ticketed outside. A ticket sold in one country and issued in a country not included in the itinerary.

sitting. On a cruise ship, one of the designated meal times. There are generally two sittings for each meal.

sixth freedom. *See* freedom rights

SKD. *GDS.* Schedule. Schedule change.

SKED. *GDS.* Schedule.

ski lift. A series of seats or bars suspended from a moving overhead cable, used to move skiers up a slope.

skid row. An inner city area of seedy hotels and bars.

Ski-Doo®. A brand name for a jet ski (qv), often used generically.

skiff. A small sailboat.

skipper. *Slang.* The captain of a vessel.

skycap. A baggage carrier or porter at an airport.

skyjacking. The forcible takeover of an airplane, as by terrorists. Air piracy (qv).

337

Glossary of Terms

sleep aboard. n. In yacht chartering, a night spent aboard the chartered vessel prior to sailing, typically booked at a reduced rate.

sleeper. 1. Sleeping compartment on a train. *See also* pullman and sleeperette. 2. *Slang.* In the hotel industry, a room marked as occupied when it was actually available for sale.

sleeper berth. *See* sleeperette.

sleeperette. 1. On an aircraft, a seat designed to recline nearly horizontally so as to approximate a bed. 2. On a train, a small sleeping compartment.

sleeping policeman. *Brit.* slang. A speed bump (qv).

slip. A docking space, as at a marina.

sloop. A one-masted sailing vessel, rigged fore and aft.

slot. 1. *Slang.* A slot machine (qv). 2. A parking space for planes at an airport. 3. A takeoff or landing time for a plane. 4. *v.* To schedule or fit into a schedule of events.

slot machine. A gambling device that pays out when symbols on a number of reels align horizontally.

SLPR. *GDS.* Sleeperette (qv).

SM. *Abr.* Sales manager.

smart roads. Major traffic arteries equipped with technology such as variable electronic signs and monitoring cameras in an effort to reduce traffic congestion.

SMERF. *Abr.* In the hospitality industry, an acronym for Social, Military, Educational, Religious, Fraternal, indicating a market segment for the sales of banqueting rooms and meeting facilities.

smokestack. A ship's funnel (qv).

smorgasbord. A Swedish-style buffet. By extension, any buffet service.

SMST. *GDS.* Smoking seat.

smuggle. To transport contraband or concealed dutiable items across an international border.

snail mail. Mildly derogatory term for regular postal service mail, as opposed to the much faster email.

snowbird. *Slang.* A person from a northern country or area who travels south during the winter.

snowboard. A surfboard-like device used on ski slopes.

soft adventure. An outdoor or adventure travel experience that is not overly demanding physically.

soft class. In certain Far Eastern countries, a designation for first class.

soft departure, soft sailing. A departure date for which there are relatively few bookings.

soft opening. 1. A period of time when a new hotel, which may not be fully complete, is open for business but has not formally announced its opening. 2. The practice of many theme parks of opening the gates before the scheduled opening time in response to demand.

soft-dollar savings. Savings realized by not spending money or by saving time. *See also* hard-dollar savings.

soiree. *Fr.* A dance party. Any evening function.

SOLAS. *Abr.* Safety of life at sea. A set of international procedures designed to enhance safety aboard ships.

sole proprietorship. A legal definition of ownership in which the owner's profits are taxed as personal income.

solstice. The precise moment at which the sun is the farthest North or South from the Equator. There are two solstices each year (December 21 and June 21 in the northern hemisphere) marking, respectively, the shortest and longest days of the year (as measured from sunrise to sunset).

SOM. *GDS.* Shortest operated mileage (qv). Start of message.

sommelier. *Fr.* Wine steward, responsible for the opening, decanting, and serving of wine in a restaurant.

son et lumière. *Fr.* Literally, "sound and light." A form of entertainment in which the history of a tourist attraction is told through recorded dialogue and music and the artful lighting of the attraction itself.

SOS. *Abr.* "Save our souls," the international Morse code distress signal.

SOTI. *GDS.* Sold outside, ticketed inside. A ticket sold in one country but issued in another country on the itinerary.

SOTO. *GDS.* Sold outside, ticketed outside. A ticket sold and issued in a country not included in the itinerary.

souk. Arabic. A traditional North African marketplace.

sound. A long body of water separating an island from the mainland or connecting two larger bodies of water.

sounding. *n.* 1. The measured depth of the sea, as beneath a ship. 2. The measuring of the depth of the sea, as in "to take a sounding."

Southern Lights, The. *See* aurora australis.

SP. *Abr.* Special operations.

spa. 1. Traditionally, a resort town or area centered around mineral springs believed to have restorative powers; named after the town of Spa in Belgium. 2. A resort specifically designed to appeal to the health- or diet-conscious. 3. A room or area in a hotel or resort property offering such amenities as steam baths, saunas, massage, and so forth.

SpA. *It. abr.* Societa per Azioni. Designating a business; the equivalent of Inc. or Ltd.

spa cuisine, spa food. Light, healthy, low-calorie fare.

space. Generic term for any room, seat, table, or so forth available for sale.

space available. Term used to refer to any remaining seating or lodging sold at the last minute, generally at a discount.

space ratio. *See* passenger space ratio.

Spanglish. A mixture of Spanish and English or the use of English words in Spanish.

SPCL. *GDS.* Special class (of rental car).

spec book. A document used by a meeting planner to record all the specifications and detailed supplier instructions for a specific event.

special drawing right. A fictitious unit of currency used to devise international air fares.

special fare. Any fare other than those normally offered.

special interest tour. A tour that combines elements designed to appeal to those with certain narrow interests.

340

The Travel Agent's
Complete Desk
Reference

special operations. In the motorcoach industry, services such as airport bus routes or transportation to special events.

special service requirement. A request to an airline for services or amenities other than standard, such as wheelchair usage, meals for special diets, and so forth.

specialty vehicle. Typically, any form of conveyance other than an automobile available for rental to tourists, including all-terrain vehicles, jet skis, and so forth.

specification. A detail of a product or service included in a written document detailing the features of such a product or service.

speed bump. A raised asphalt or concrete ridge in a road used to discourage excessive speeds.

speed trap. 1. An effort by local police to catch speeding motorists, ostensibly motivated more by a desire to raise cash than a concern for safety. 2. By extension, any town or location on a highway where such efforts are mounted on a regular basis.

spelunking. The recreational exploration of caves. *See also* caving.

spinner. *Slang.* A passenger, as on an airplane, who finds his seat already taken because a duplicate boarding pass has been issued.

split. 1. An agreed-on division, as of a commission between a travel agency and an outside sales representative. 2. A half bottle of wine.

split payment transaction. A transaction in which full payment is made in two parts, each by a different method. For example, by cash and credit card or by two separate credit cards.

split ticketing. 1. Creating two separate tickets for a single journey, usually to obtain a lower fare. 2. A ticket issuing procedure in which the flight coupon goes to one location, while the auditor's and agency coupons go to another, usually a host agency.

SPML. *GDS.* Special meal.

sports bar. A pub or restaurant in which multiple television monitors feature live broadcasts of sporting events.

SQ. *GDS.* Space requested.

SR. *Abr.* Senior, seniors.

SRO. *Abr.* Standing room only, as in a theater.

SRVS. *GDS.* Serves. Servicing.

SS. 1. *GDS.* Sold segment. 2. *Abr.* Steamship.

SSM. *GDS.* Segment status message.

SSR. *GDS.* Special service requirement (qv).

SST. *Abr.* 1. Supersonic transport. The Concorde (qv). 2. Self-service terminal.

stabilizer. A fin-like projection from a ship's hull designed to reduce roll (qv).

stack. *n.* Short for smokestack. An exhaust funnel (qv) on a ship; on modern cruise ships many stacks are purely ornamental.

staff captain. The second in command on a cruise ship.

STAG. Society of Travel Agents in Government.

staging guide. *See* spec book.

stair tower. A stairway connecting several decks on a larger ship.

stalls. The orchestra seats of a British theater.

standard hotel. A tourist or economy class hotel.

standard mileage rate. The amount, in cents per mile, that the Internal Revenue Service allows for deductions for business travel using a personal vehicle.

standard passenger capacity. The number of passengers that the manufacturer or operator of a vessel or vehicle determines is optimal; the maximum safe capacity may be higher.

standard room. A lesser quality, lower priced room at a hotel.

standby. 1. *adj.* Available at a reduced cost on a space-available (qv) basis, as an airline fare. 2. *n.* A person traveling on a standby basis or waiting for a seat to open up on a flight.

starboard. A nautical term for the right-hand direction or side of a ship.

stateroom. A berth or cabin aboard a ship.

statute mile. A mile (5,280 feet or approximately 1.6 kilometers).

STCR. *GDS.* (Passenger on a) stretcher.

STD. 1. *GDS.* Standard room (qv). 2. *Abr.* Sexually-transmitted disease.

steamer, steamship. A steam-powered ship.

steeplechase. A horse race across open country with obstacles.

steerage. An extremely low-cost and uncomfortable class of sea travel, typically well below decks with few if any amenities.

Stendahl's syndrome. A condition of disorientation, dizziness, or swooning caused by too much touring, especially of historic or artistic attractions. Named for the 19th century French novelist who is said to have suffered from it.

step-on guide. A guide who joins a longer bus tour for a period of time to provide commentary on a specific locale or region.

stern. The rear portion of a ship.

steward. A ship's employee responsible for the care of passengers. *See also* cabin steward.

stewardess. Name given to flight attendants in the days when all flight attendants were women.

stiff. *Slang. v.* To deliberately not tip a waiter or other service person.

STO. *GDS.* Studio (qv).

stopover. A planned overnight (or longer) stop on a ticketed journey.

stowaway. 1. *n.* An illegal, non-paying passenger on a ship or airplane. 2. *v.* To hide on a ship so as to avoid paying.

STP. *Abr.* Satellite ticket printer (qv).

STPC. *Abr.* Stopover accommodation provided at airline's expense.

STPN. *Abr.* Satellite ticket printer network (qv).

strait. A narrow stretch of water bounded by land between two larger bodies of water.

straphanger. A commuter by bus or subway, so called from the strap-like handholds that hung in old subway cars in New York City.

streetcar. An electrified light rail vehicle used for public transportation.

stretched vessel. A cruise ship that has been retrofitted with a new midsection to increase its length and passenger capacity.

strip. *Slang.* A street or area of town featuring a concentration of nightclubs,

casinos, bars, and other forms of adult-oriented entertainment.

strip mall. A shopping center consisting of a continuous line of one-story shops.

stripped package. A tour product that meets the minimum qualifications for an IT (inclusive tour) designation on a GDS.

STTE. The former Society of Travel and Tourism Educators. Now ISTTE, the International Society of Travel and Tourism Educators.

student visa. A visa (qv) issued to those attending an accredited educational institution.

studio. An efficiency (qv). A one-room apartment.

STVR. *GDS.* Stopover (qv).

subchapter S corporation. A form of incorporation in which profits are taxed on the owner's or owners' individual tax returns, much as they would be in a sole proprietorship (qv) or partnership (qv).

subsidiary. A company wholly controlled by another through stock ownership.

subtropical. *adj.* Describing an area near the tropics but enjoying four distinct seasons.

subway. 1. An underground urban rail system. 2. *Brit.* An underground walkway or pedestrian passageway.

suite. In a hotel, an accommodation comprising more then one room; occasionally a single large room with clearly defined sleeping and sitting areas.

summit. *n.* The top of a mountain. *v.* To reach the top of a mountain.

sun deck. 1. An open area on an upper story of a building for sunbathing. 2. A similar area on a ship.

sundries. Personal toiletries or grooming items.

sunstroke. Heat stroke caused by over-long exposure to the sun.

SUP. *GDS.* Superior room (qv).

superior room. In a hotel, a more desirable and more expensive room, perhaps with a better exposure, view, or other amenities.

super-jumbo jet. A plane that carries more than 500 passengers. None is currently in service.

superliner. 1. A large luxury cruise vessel. 2. A luxury train.

supersonic transport. A plane capable of exceeding the speed of sound. The Concorde (qv).

superstructure. On a cruise ship, the part above the waterline.

supertax. A surtax (qv).

supl. info. *Abr.* Supplementary information.

supplement. An additional charge or payment, as a single supplement (qv).

supplemental carrier. 1. An air charter operator providing non-scheduled service on a for-hire basis. 2. An insurance provider providing coverage that is additional too that provided by another, "primary" insurance provider.

supplemental liability coverage. Insurance coverage providing protection from injury and damage claims that is not automatically provided under a rental car contract.

supplier. In the travel industry, any company providing travel services to the public.

supply-side fare. A fare set especially low in the expectation (or hope) that resulting volume will produce more revenue than a previous, higher fare

SUR. *GDS.* Surface.

surcharge. An additional charge levied for the provision of certain additional features or because of special or extenuating circumstances.

surety. A bond that guarantees performance or completion, as of a contract.

surface. On land. In an itinerary, referring to travel over land that does not involve an aircraft.

surfboard. Long board on which an individual can stand and ride waves as they break on the shore.

surname. *Brit.* Last name, of a person.

surtax. An additional tax levied on certain categories of goods or transactions or during a limited period of time. In some cases, funds raised by a surtax will be earmarked for specific purposes.

survey. *n.* A series of verbal questions or a questionnaire used to gather data about consumer attitudes or behavior.

suspect. An individual who may or may not meet the minimum qualifications necessary to make him a good prospect (qv).

sustainable development. New construction and business activity, including tourism, that will not adversely impact or degrade the natural environment of the area in which it occurs or deplete that area's non-renewable resources.

sustainable tourism. The development of a region's tourism industry in such a way as to not damage or deplete the resources and attractions that make the region attractive to tourists.

SV. *Abr.* Sailing vessel.

SVW. *GDS.* Sea view.

SWAP. *Abr.* Severe weather avoidance procedure.

SWATH. *Abr.* Small waterplane area twin hull. A twin-hulled ship design said to reduce turbulence and, thus, seasickness.

SWB. *GDS.* Single room with bath.

SWIFT Code. An 8- or 11-digit alphanumeric identifier that uniquely identifies a financial institution. Used in international wire transfers.

swing shift. The work period from 4 p.m. until 12 midnight. Any work shift that overlaps the day and night shifts.

System One®. A global distribution system (qv).

system-wide revenue. In the hotel industry, the total amount of revenue realized at all of a hotel company's locations, both company-owned and franchised.

T, t

T-2. Informal pre-launch code name or nickname for Orbitz, a web site owned jointly by five U.S. airlines, that would sell a variety of travel products to the public and bypass travel agents. *See also* Me-Too.

T&D. *Abr.* Training and development.

T&E. *Abr.* Travel and entertainment.

TA. *Abr.* Travel agent.

TAAD. *Abr.* Travel agent automated deduction.

TAANZ. Travel Agents Association of New Zealand.

tab. The bill, as in a restaurant.

table assignment. On a cruise ship, a specified seat at a specified table for a specified seating.

table d'hote. *Fr.* Literally, "table of the host." A meal option, as on a tour, offering a full meal with a limited choice of dishes for a fixed price.

table tent. A folded place card on a restaurant table used to list specials, advertise a featured brand, or provide other information.

TAC. *GDS.* Travel agency commission.

tail wind. A strong current of air blowing in the same direction as the course of an airplane or ship, thus increasing the speed and/or decreasing the fuel consumption of the vessel. *See also* head wind.

tandem bicycle. A bicycle built for two.

tapas. *Sp.* Snacks or hors d'ouevres served at a bar.

tariff. A schedule of fares or prices.

tarmac. The paved area of an airport.

TASC. Travel Agents of Suffolk County (NY).

TASF. Travel Agent Service Fee, an ARC program.

TAT. *GDS.* Transitional automated ticket.

TAW. *Abr.* Ticket at will-call.

taxi. 1. *n.* A vehicle with driver available for hire in metropolitan areas, which usually charges a mileage-based fare. A taxicab. 2. *v.* To drive an airplane on the ground.

taxiway. A right of way at an airport used by planes to get to and from the runway.

TBA. *Abr.* To be announced.

T-bar. A type of ski lift (qv) in which skiers grasp or lean on a horizontal bar while keeping their skis on the ground.

TBR. Travel Business Roundtable.

TC1, TC2, TC3. Traffic Conference Areas (qv).

TCP. *GDS.* To complete party.

TD. *Abr.* Ticket designator (qv).

TDOR. *GDS.* Two-door car.

technology butler. A staff member of a hotel who assists guests with computer questions and problems.

TEE. Trans-European Express.

telecommute. *v.* To work at home using a computer link to the office. Hence, telecommuter, one who works in this manner.

teleconference. A meeting in which some or all of the participants are in different locations linked by telephone.

teleferic. A cable car system.

telegram. A text message sent by wire.

telegraph. A device used to send coded messages by wire.

telemarketing. Selling via the telephone.

teleticketing. A now-discontinued automated method of ticketing used by the airlines.

temperate zone. In the Northern hemisphere, the area between the Arctic Circle and the Tropic of Cancer. In the Southern hemisphere, the area between the Antarctic Circle and the Tropic of Capricorn.

TEN. *Abr.* Ticket exchange notice.

tentalow. A cross between a tent and a bungalow, sometimes used as lodging in warm-weather resorts and campsites. Typically, a framed canvas structure on a wooden platform that might have electricity and plumbing.

tender. A small boat used to supply a larger vessel. A boat used to ferry passengers between a cruise ship and the shore.

tercentenary. The 300th anniversary.

terminal. An airport, train station, or bus station. Of train and bus stations, one at which routes end and vehicles are stored.

terms and conditions. The section of a tour or cruise document in which legal details of liability and responsibility are spelled out.

terra firma. *Lat.* Dry land.

terra incognita. *Lat.* Unknown territory.

TFC. *GDS.* Traffic.

TGC. *Abr.* Travel group charters.

TGV. *Fr. Abr.* Initials for the French phrase, "tren a grand vitesse." High speed French train system.

theater setup. In a meeting, a configuration in which seats are arranged in rows, facing front, as in a theater.

theme cruise. A cruise designed to appeal to a specific clientele with specific interests.

theme park. An amusement park that follows a particular motif or that incorporates rides based on characters or situations proprietary to the owner of the park.

theme restaurant. A restaurant designed around a particular sport, era, style of music, or entertainment industry personality. Such establishments are typically designed in a theatrical fashion, with as much attention paid to décor and memorabilia as to the food. The Hard Rock Café is a good example of a theme restaurant.

thermal neutron analysis. A baggage screening technology.

third world. 1. Term applied to any undeveloped nation or area of the world. 2. (now generally obsolete) As distinct from the first world (non-Communist, developed nations) and the second world (the Communist nations of the world).

Threat Advisory. A color-coded system devised by the Department of Homeland Security (qv) to estimate the likelihood of a terrorist attack on the United States. *See also* Homeland Security Advisory System.

346

The Travel Agent's
Complete Desk
Reference

through fare. Fare to a foreign destination reached via a gateway city (qv).

through passenger. Any passenger who is not disembarking at a particular stop.

through service. An airline flight that makes stops but does not require a change of planes.

throwaway. 1. An element of a travel product or package that is purchased but not used. 2. Any item given away for free, either as a way of rewarding a purchase or to attract business.

THRU. *GDS.* Through.

THTL. *GDS.* Tourist hotel.

TIA. Travel Industry Association.

TIAA. Travel Industry Association of America. (Same as TIA.)

TIAC. Travel Industry Association of Canada.

TIAG. Travel Industry Association of Georgia.

Tianguis. From the ancient Aztec for "outdoor market." Short for Tianguis Turistico, a major Mexican trade show for the tourism industry.

ticket. A formal travel document representing a contract between the traveler and the supplier.

ticket designator. An airline code, usually indicating a discounted fare.

ticket on departure. A ticket that will be picked up by the passenger at the airport; primarily European usage. *See also* prepaid ticket advice.

ticket stock. Blank airline tickets.

ticketed. Having purchased and issued travel documents.

ticketed point mileage. The actual distance between two cities on an itinerary.

ticketless travel. *See* electronic ticketing.

tickler file. A reminder system that links activities or deadlines with dates.

tidal wave. An abnormally large and destructive wave caused by a storm, earthquake, or other natural event.

TIDS. *Abr.* Travel Intermediary Designator Service. An IATAN (qv) program to provide unique identifiers to certain categories of non-ARC entities.

tie-in. The linking of one product or promotion with another, as when frequent flyer miles can be earned by using a credit card.

tier. 1. A quality ranking, as of hotels. 2. A balcony in a theater.

tie-up. 1. A place to secure a small boat. A boat slip (qv). 2. A temporary halt in business or traffic caused by accident or congestion.

time share, time sharing. A form of shared property ownership in which a purchaser acquires the right to occupy a piece of property, such as a condominium in a resort area, for a specific period of time, typically two weeks, each year.

time window. The period of time before and after a desired departure time in which a customer will accept a flight should the ideal flight not be available.

tirekicker. *Slang.* A customer who asks a travel agent for recommendations or quotes but who never actually makes a booking. *See also* shopper.

Titanic, The. Supposedly unsinkable British luxury liner that sank on its maiden voyage in 1912 after striking an iceberg.

TKNO. *GDS.* Ticket number.

tkt, tktd. *Abr.* Ticketed (qv).

TKTL. *GDS.* Ticket time limit.

TMIP. Travel Model Improvement Program, a project of the U.S. Department of Transportation.

TN. *GDS.* Telephone number.

TNA. *Abr.* Thermal neutron analysis (qv).

TO. *GDS.* Tour order.

TOD. *Abr.* 1. Total overall dimensions (qv), of luggage. 2. Ticket on departure (qv), primarily European. 3. Tour of duty, of airline pilots or other personnel.

TOE. *GDS.* Ticket order exception.

togethering. The practice of traveling or vacationing with family, close friends, or other affinity groups.

toll call. Any phone call other than one to the local dialing area. A long-distance call.

toll road. A highway system charging a fee, typically based on type of vehicle and total distance traveled.

tonnage. The carrying capacity of a ship.

TOP. *Abr.* Tour Operator Program (qv).

torrid zone. *See* tropics, the.

total overall dimensions. The combined length, width, and depth of a piece of luggage, typically used to determine whether a piece of luggage qualifies either as carry-on or regular baggage.

TOTL. *GDS.* Total.

touch-tone phone. A telephone on which push buttons produce a distinct tone for each number. As distinct from a rotary phone (qv).

touchdown center (or centre). A location, commercial or otherwise, designed for business travelers and providing an array of telecommunications and Internet services.

tour. A travel product in which several elements are bundled together and sold as a unit. Tours typically involve the use of a guide, host, or escort (as opposed to packages (qv) which do not).

tour boat. Any vessel used to carry passengers on sightseeing excursions.

tour conductor. 1. An employee of or contractor to a tour operator who accompanies and is in overall charge of a tour. 2. A member of a group taking a tour who is designated as that group's leader and who might have played a key role in bringing the group together for the tour.

tour conductor pass. A free passage, as on a cruise, awarded for a specific number of bookings. Typically, a tour conductor pass is controlled by the travel agent responsible for the bookings and can be used at the agent's discretion for personal use or for the tour conductor (*See* def. 2, above).

tour desk. A counter at a hotel where local tours can be booked.

tour documents. A packet of tickets, vouchers, itineraries, instructions, and other information sent to a passenger by a tour company.

tour escort, tour leader, tour manager. *See* tour conductor.

tour operator. A company that assembles the various elements of a tour.

Tour Operator Program. An endorsement program administered by ASTA (qv) that certifies that a participating travel agency or tour operator meets certain consumer protection standards.

tour organizer. Any individual who finds people to go on tours. Distinct from a tour operator (qv).

tour wholesaler. *See* tour operator.

tour-based fare. *See* inclusive tour fare.

tourism. 1. The activity of travel for pleasure. 2. The industry based on such travel.

tourist. 1. A leisure traveler. 2. The economy class on an airline. Also referred to as "economy" or "coach." 3. The section of the plane designated for this class of passenger.

tourist card. A document issued in lieu of a visa for a short visit to a country. Typically, a tourist card does not require the person to whom it is issued to have a passport.

tourist trap. 1. Derogatory term for any attraction appealing to tourists but considered to be in bad taste or to give poor value for the money. 2. An area of a tourist destination that has become over-commercialized.

touron. *Slang.* A derogatory term for tourist, used by those in the travel industry.

tpl. *Abr.* Triple (qv).

TPM. *GDS.* Ticketed point mileage (qv).

TR. *GDS.* International transportation tax.

tracker. A person skilled in locating animals in the wild.

trade mission. 1. A quasi-governmental office of one country, located in another, created to encourage trade between the two nations. 2. An organized trip made by business representatives to explore trade opportunities in another country.

trade name. The legally protected name of a company's product or by which the company does business.

traffic calming, traffic calming device. Any of a variety of strategies used to slow traffic, usually as it enters a built-up area. Primarily European usage.

Traffic Conference Area. Divisions of the world used for the purposes of fare construction. There are three traffic conference areas (TCs): TC1 comprises North and South America; TC2 comprises Europe, Africa, and the Middle East; TC3 comprises Asia and the Pacific.

training fare. Airline fare negotiated by a corporation for the use of employees traveling for the purposes of training.

training tourist. A worker who signs up for a company training program in order to travel.

tram. A streetcar (qv).

tramp steamer. A cargo vessel with no set route, sometimes carrying passengers.

tramway. A streetcar line.

trans-canal. Referring to a cruise or other sea traffic that passes through the Panama Canal.

transcon. *Abr.* Transcontinental (qv).

transcontinental. Spanning a single continent.

transfer. 1. The transportation of a passenger between two points, such as from the airport to a hotel or vice versa, often included as an element of a tour. 2. A chit (qv) or similar device allowing a passenger to transfer from one vehicle or form of transport to another without paying an additional fare.

transient. Any person who is not a permanent resident. In some hotels, a guest who is not renting by the month.

transit point. An intermediate stop on a journey, typically one made only to change planes or mode of transportation.

transit visa. A limited-term visa issued solely to allow passage across or through the issuing country's territory.

transparency. 1. A piece of clear acetate containing an image that can be projected onto a screen; used in making presentations to groups. 2. A photographic slide.

trattoria. *It.* A restaurant or cafe.

travel advisory. A formal warning, issued by the United States Department of State, advising caution in traveling to specific countries due to political unrest, natural disaster, or other cause.

travel agency. 1. Usually used in the travel industry to refer to an ARC-appointed storefront retailer. 2. Any business that refers to itself as a travel agency.

travel agent. 1. Any person who sells travel products on a commission basis. 2. A person selling travel who meets certain minimum qualifications, which can vary widely according to who uses the term or sets the standards.

travel agent arbiter. *See* arbiter, travel agent.

travel bureau. *See* travel agency.

travel certificate. A coupon or other document that is sold with the promise that it can be exchanged for travel products and services worth more than the face value of the coupon; often of dubious value.

travel consultant. 1. An alternative term for travel agent (qv). 2. A person with specific knowledge of the travel industry hired on a contract basis to provide advice, guidance, or services to a company.

travel counselor. An alternate term for travel agent (qv).

travel intermediary. Any person or entity that assists in the distribution of travel products to travelers.

travel manager. *See* corporate travel manager.

travel partner. A travel supplier that participates in a frequency marketing program (qv) operated by another travel supplier.

traveler's diarrhea. A usually mild intestinal condition caused by adjustment to microorganisms in the water of another geographical area or by other causes associated with travel.

traveling incognito. Traveling under an assumed name or as anonymously as possible for privacy or security reasons.

travelog, travelogue. A documentary film or video extolling the attractions of a specific travel destination or group of destinations.

Travelshopper®. A simplified version of the Worldspan® GDS (qv).

travelzine. A periodical covering travel that is published exclusively on the

349

Glossary of Terms

Internet.

trawler. A pleasure boat based on the design of a type of fishing vessel.

trek. A hike, often with backpacks and typically lasting a number of days.

trekking. A category of adventure travel, typically involving visits to remote areas, with overnight lodging in tents or other minimal accommodation.

trip. In the travel industry, any journey of more than 100 miles from a person's home, regardless of whether an overnight stay is involved.

triple. A hotel room for three people.

trolley. A streetcar (qv).

Tropic of Cancer, Tropic of Capricorn. Imaginary lines that are, respectively, 23°26' north and south of the Equator, and that mark the apparent extent of the sun's journey north and south of the Equator during the course of a year. *See also* tropics, the.

tropical storm. A weather disturbance originating in the tropics (qv), with sustained winds of less than 75 mph.

tropics, the. 1. Any area where it is hot year-round. 2. The area of the globe between the Tropic of Cancer on the north and the Tropic of Capricorn on the south.

troupe. A theater group, especially one that travels from place to place.

TRPB. *GDS*. Triple with bath.

TRPN. *GDS*. Triple without bath.

TRPS. *GDS*. Triple with shower.

TRUE. Travel Retailer Universal Enumeration.

trundle bed. A bed that rolls out from under another bed.

trunk carrier. A major airline carrier, as evidenced by its extensive system of routes.

trust territory. A semi-autonomous territory that is administered by a member of the United Nations Trusteeship Council.

truth-in-advertising. A principle, sometimes enacted into law, requiring companies to be scrupulously honest in their advertising, providing accurate descriptions of products and services and omitting no material details.

TS. *Abr.* Twin-screw. Turn screw.

TSA. Transportation Security Administration.

TSEA. Trade Show Exhibitors Association.

TSI. *Abr.* Travel Service Intermediary, an IATAN term.

TSIA. Travel Service Intermediary Agency, an IATAN term.

TSI card. A photo ID issued by IATAN to those who work in IATAN-approved firms but who do not issue airline tickets (e.g. cruise-only agents).

TSS. *Abr.* Turbine steam ship.

TST. *GDS*. Transitional stored ticket record.

tsunami. Japanese term for tidal wave (qv).

TTGAC. Travel and Tourism Government Affairs Council.

TTRA. Travel and Tourism Research Association.

tube. *Brit.* 1. Subway. 2. The London Underground.

tubing. Floating down a gentle river or other waterway in an inflated car or truck innertube.

tuc-tuc. A small, open motorized taxi used in Thailand.

tug boat. A utility vessel, used in harbors to tow or move much larger vessels.

turbulence. Rough, sometimes violent, atmospheric conditions encountered by airplanes.

turista. *Sp.* Literally, "the tourist." Slang term for traveler's diarrhea (qv).

turnaround. The process of refueling and reprovisioning a plane to ready it for another flight. Also applied to ships.

turnaround point. The geographical location at which outbound travel becomes inbound travel, as on a cruise.

turndown service. In hotels, the practice of folding back the blanket and sheet of the bed in the evening, sometimes accompanied by putting a mint on the pillow or a cordial on the night stand.

turnover. 1. The periodic change of staff, as employees are dismissed, resign, or retire. 2. The periodic change of a customer base, as some customers stop doing business with a company and others start. 3. The rate at which such change takes place.

turnpike. *See* toll road.

turnstile. A rotating device through which passengers or customers pass after paying their fare or admission. Some unattended turnstiles may be unlocked only by the insertion of the correct fare or price of admission.

TV. *Abr.* 1. Turbine vessel. 2. Television.

TWB. *GDS.* Twin room with bath.

'tween decks. Contraction of "between decks." Narrow space between decks of a ship used to stow cargo.

twin. A hotel room containing two single beds.

twin-double. A hotel room with two double beds, sometimes called a double-double.

TWNB. *GDS.* Twin room with bath.

TWNN. *GDS.* Twin room without bath.

TWNS. *GDS.* Twin room with shower.

TWOV. *GDS.* Transit without visa.

TWR. *GDS.* Tower.

tying. *n.* A practice whereby an airline requires its corporate customers to use a specific GDS (qv), typically one in which the airline has a financial interest, when making bookings as a condition of receiving discounted fares offered by that airline.

typhoon. A hurricane occurring in the Eastern hemisphere.

U, u

UATP. Universal Air Travel Plan. *See* Air Travel Card.

UBOA. United Bus Owners Association, now United Motorcoach Association.

UC. *GDS.* Unable to accept request (not waitlisted). *See also* US.

UCCCF. *GDS.* Universal credit card charge form.

U-drive. *Brit.* A rental car.

UFO. *Abr.* Unidentified flying object.

UFTAA. Universal Federation of Travel Agents Associations.

UK. *Abr.* United Kingdom.

UM. *GDS.* Unaccompanied minor (qv).

UMA. United Motorcoach Association.

UMNN. *GDS.* Unaccompanied minor, where NN denotes the child's age.

UMNR. *GDS.* Unaccompanied minor.

UN. 1. *GDS.* Unable. 2. *Abr.* United Nations.

UNA. *GDS.* Unable.

unaccompanied minor. A child traveling, usually on an airline, without a parent or other adult guardian.

unchecked baggage. Baggage that a traveler retains in his or her personal control. An important distinction when liability for loss or damage is to be determined. *See also* checked baggage.

undercurrent. *See* undertow.

underdeveloped. Not having a sufficiently modern infrastructure.

undertow. A strong surface current of short duration flowing seaward from the shore, endangering swimmers. *See also* riptide.

undeveloped. Without amenities or infrastructure, as a camping area or tourist destination.

UNESCO. *Abr.* United Nations Educational, Scientific, and Cultural Organization.

uninterrupted international air transportation. Any airline flight that does not include a schedule stop of more than twelve hours in the United States.

Union Jack. The flag of the United Kingdom.

unique selling proposition. A powerful, customer-oriented statement of benefits that sets one product or service apart from all others.

Universal Air Travel Plan. *See* Air Travel Card.

Universal Time. *See* Greenwich Mean Time.

UNK. *GDS.* Unknown.

unlimited mileage. In a rental car, the absence of any per mile charge for miles driven.

unrestricted fare. A higher fare for a ticket offering maximum flexibility. Typically, unrestricted fares require no advance purchase, no Saturday night stay, no roundtrip purchase, and are fully refundable without penalty or fee.

unscheduled. Not on or according to a timetable.

unspoiled. Term used to describe tourist destinations that, in theory, have not been discovered by or overrun with tourists.

upgrade. 1. *v.* To move to the next higher category, as to upgrade a passenger from tourist to business class. 2. *n.* A coupon entitling someone to an upgrade. 3. *n.* The act of upgrading.

upper/lower. A designation indicating the use of bunk beds or berths, as in a ship's cabin or railway compartment.

upscale. Appealing to or designed for a more affluent clientele.

upwind. *adj.* Located in the direction from which the wind is blowing. *See also* downwind.

URL. *Abr.* Universal resource locator. The address of a web site (qv).

US. *GDS.* Unable to accept request (waitlisted). *See also* UC.

USCIS. U.S. Citizenship and Immigration Services, a bureau of the department of Homeland Security (qv).

user-friendly. Designed in such a way as to be easy to use or operate, especially of computers and computer software.

U-shape setup. In a meeting, a configuration in which tables are formed in the shape of a U, with chairs on the outside of the U and the front of the room at the open end of the U.

USP. *Abr.* Unique selling proposition (qv).

USS. *Abr.* United States ship.

USTAR. United States Travel Agent Registry.

USTDC. United States Travel Data Center.

USTOA. United States Tour Operators Association.

USTS. United States Travel Service. Now USTTA (qv).

USTTA. United States Travel and Tourism Administration.

usury laws. Legislation restricting the amount of interest that may be charged.

US-VISIT. A program of the Department of Homeland Security to standardize procedures for and collect information on foreign nationals applying for visas or entering the United States.

UT. *Abr.* Universal Time.

UTC. 1. *GDS.* Unable to contact. 2. *Abr.* Coordinated universal time (qv).

UTDN. *Abr.* Unattended ticket delivery network.

utilization rate. In the car rental industry, the percentage of vehicles in use during a specified period of time, figured on a system-wide or local basis.

UTR. *GDS.* Unable to reach.

UTV. *Abr.* Universal travel voucher.

UU. *GDS.* Unable.

V, v

vacancy. An empty room at a hotel or motel. By extension, any available space.

vacation hangover. The letdown or exhaustion that follows a holiday trip.

vaccination. An inoculation given to produce immunity to a disease.

valet. 1. *n.* A personal servant. 2. *adj.* Describing services such as those provided by a personal servant, as in valet parking.

validation. 1. Approval or issuance, as of travel documents. 2. The marking of a document to indicate validity or payment.

validator. A machine used to imprint tickets or other documents.

validity dates. The inclusive dates for which a fare or other offer is valid.

valise. A small piece of luggage.

value added tax. A form of taxation in which taxes are added cumulatively as a product changes hands. A common tax in Europe, which, upon application, can often be refunded to foreign visitors after their visit.

value-based pricing. The practice of charging different amounts for the same or a similar product, depending on how each customer views the value of that product.

value season. 1. Shoulder season (qv). 2. Low season (qv). 3. Any period during which lower fares or rates are offered.

van. Any of a number of forms of motorized transportation larger than a car but smaller than a bus.

VAT. *Abr.* Value added tax (qv).

v-berth. A sleeping compartment, usually small, at the bow of a boat, taking its shape from the V shape of the hull.

VDT. *Abr.* Video display terminal.

vector. The direction of motion, as of an airplane, often expressed in degrees of the compass.

veldt. The savannas of southern Africa.

velocity. Speed.

velodrome. An indoor stadium designed for bicycle racing.

vending. In a hotel, an area containing vending machines.

vendor. In the travel industry, any supplier of travel products or services.

venture capital. Financial capital provided to fund the creation or expansion of a business, especially a highly speculative business with a high potential payback.

veranda, verandah. A roofed porch.

verboten. *Ger.* Forbidden.

verification. The process of authenticating or confirming, as of a reservation.

vertigo. A dizzy sensation brought on by an inner-ear condition or a fear of heights.

vessel. A generic term for any boat or ship.

VFR. 1. *GDS.* Visiting friends and relatives. 2. Visual flight rules (qv).

VGML. *GDS.* Vegetarian meal.

via. *Lat.* By way of.

VIA Rail. Also, VIA Rail Canada, the Canadian railway system.

VICE. *GDS.* Instead of (from the Latin).

Victorian. Characteristic of the Victorian era or the late 1800s, used to describe architecture and interior decor.

video lottery terminal. A video version of a slot machine, in which the spinning reels are animated.

videoconference. A meeting in which some or all of the participants are in different locations, linked by video transmitted by satellite.

villa. *It.* A country-home. Sometimes used in the hotel industry to describe a small, separate suite or cottage.

vintage. The year in which a wine was bottled.

VIP. *GDS.* Very important person.

virus. In computers, a malicious and destructive program designed to be passed unwittingly from machine to machine via floppy disks, downloading, or other means.

visa. A document or, more frequently, a stamp in a passport authorizing the bearer to visit a country for specific purposes and for a specific length of time.

visa expediter. A person or company charging a fee to procure visas and other travel documents.

visa support. 1. Any documentation, such as a letter of invitation from an approved organization or a receipt for confirmed bookings, required by a foreign government before a visa will be issued. 2. The act of providing such documentation.

Visa Waiver Program. A system whereby citizens of designated countries are allowed to enter the United States without a visa.

vis-à-vis. *Fr.* Literally, "face to face." 1. In regard to. 2. Compared with.

visitor's visa. A tourist visa.

vistadome. A car on a train featuring a glassed-in, domed ceiling, offering an enhanced view of the passing countryside.

visual flight rules. A set of procedures that govern the piloting of a plane when weather conditions allow the pilot to *See* the ground and the natural horizon and maintain distance from other aircraft. *See also* instrument flight rules.

VLA. *GDS.* Villa.

VLT. Video lottery terminal (qv).

volume incentive. An extra commission or other inducement offered by a supplier to a travel agency to increase sales.

voucher. 1. A coupon or other document, either prepaid or given free, entitling the bearer to certain goods, services, or discounts upon presentation. 2. An exchange order (qv).

VPN. *Abr.* Virtual private network.

V-shape setup. *See* chevron setup.

VUSA. *GDS.* Visit USA fare.

VWP. *Abr.* Visa Waiver Program (qv).

W, w

Wagon-Lits. European company providing sleeping car services on trains.

wait list, waitlist. 1. *n.* A roster of names of those wishing passage on a full flight or other trip, usually honored in order of listing in case of cancellations. 2. *n.* A group of people waiting for cancellations. 3. *v.* To place someone on such a list.

waiver. 1. A written acknowledgment by a passenger of his or her declining something, as insurance coverage. 2. A document used by a travel agency and signed by the customer indicating that certain forms of insurance or other protection have been advised or offered. 3. The formal acknowledgment of dismissal of a requirement.

wake. The trail of waves left by a ship.

wake-up call. In a hotel, a telephone call delivered either by a person or a computerized system to a guest's room at a prearranged time.

walked. *adj.* In the hotel industry, term used to refer to a guest lodged in another property at the hotel's expense because no room was available for his or her use.

walkie-talkie. A portable radio communication device with limited range.

walk-in. In a hotel, a guest who arrives without a reservation. In a travel agency, a customer who arrives unannounced, especially a new customer.

walkout. A labor strike.

walk-up. In the airline industry, a passenger who purchases a ticket shortly before flight time.

walk-up rate. *See* rack rate.

wanderlust. A desire to travel.

WAPTT. World Association for Professional Training in Tourism.

WATA. World Association of Travel Agents.

water closet. Toilet. Usually *Brit.*

water table. A point below the surface of the land, below which the earth is saturated with water.

water taxi. A boat used for public transportation, typically in urban areas on lakes, rivers, or other bodies of water.

waterfront. The section facing the sea. A harbor area.

waterline. 1. The line on a ship's hull to which the sea reaches. 2. Any of a number of lines drawn on a ship's hull indicating the point to which the sea will reach when the vessel is fully loaded.

watershed. 1. The area drained by a system of rivers. 2. The crest of a ridge or mountain range, marking the point at which water will flow in the opposite direction.

WATS. *Abr.* Wide area telephone service. A form of long-distance telephone service that is purchased in bulk at lower rates.

wave season. A period of time, roughly corresponding to the month of February, in which cruise lines promote bookings through increased advertising and promotion, discounts, and other means.

way station. An intermediate or less-important station, especially on a railroad.

WB. *GDS.* Westbound.

WC. *Abr.* Water closet (qv).

w/c. *Abr.* Will call.

WCHC. *GDS.* Wheelchair (passenger immobile).

WCHR. *GDS.* Wheelchair.

WCHS. *GDS.* Wheelchair (passenger cannot negotiate stairs).

weather deck. An open-air deck on a cruise ship.

weather side. The side of a ship, either port or starboard, exposed to the prevailing winds.

weather tourism. Recreational travel undertaken to view or experience sever weather phenomena such as tornados and hurricanes.

weather warning. An alert issued by meteorologists indicating that a dangerous weather condition is either imminent or is actual occurring.

weather watch. An alert issued by meteorologists indicating that conditions are such that a dangerous weather condition is possible but not imminent.

web. Informal term for the World Wide Web (qv).

web-based. *adj.* Available via or accessed through the Internet, as a booking engine (qv).

web browser. A software program enabling users to navigate the World Wide Web (qv) and the Internet.

web fare. A fare available only on the Internet and usually only at a specific web site.

web site. Informational or commercial computer files posted on the Internet and viewable from remote computers.

webmaster. The person designated to maintain a web site.

webzine. A periodical that is published exclusively on the Internet.

weddingmoon. A trip on which the marriage ceremony is conducted in the honeymoon location.

weigh anchor. In sailing parlance, to get under way or to cast off from a mooring.

well brand. *See* house brand.

wet bar. In a hotel room, a bar or counter area with running water, used for preparing drinks.

wet landing. A beach arrival on a small boat that requires passengers to step into the water and wade ashore.

wet lease. Rental of a crewed and provisioned boat or vessel.

w/fac. *Abr.* With facilities.

wharf. A dock (qv).

whistle stop. 1. Traditionally, a very brief stop on a railroad. By extension, any brief stop. 2. A very small town.

white cap. A wave with a frothy top, especially one whipped up by the wind.

white-knuckle flyer. *Slang.* A person nervous about flying.

white-knuckler. *Slang.* A derogatory term for a short commuter flight on a prop (qv) aircraft. By extension, any rough airline flight.

whitewater rafting. A group recreational activity using multi-passenger,

inflatable rubber boats, typically steered by a professional guide, to travel down rivers with numerous rapids (qv).

WHO. World Health Organization.

wholesaler. Any company that sells to retailers as opposed to the general public. A tour operator (qv).

wholesaler rate. A non-commissionable rate for a product such as a hotel room that is extended to tour operators (qv) and packagers (qv).

wholetailer. A company that wholesales travel product to the trade but that also sells directly to consumers. The term is a combination of wholesaler and retailer.

wide-body. An aircraft designed to carry large passenger loads, widening the body of the plane to allow for more seats and an additional aisle.

widow's walk. A raised platform or high porch on the roof of a house, usually in a coastal town, originally designed to provide a view of ships far out to sea.

will-call, will-call window. A place in a terminal, lobby, theme park, or other venue where customers can pick up previously ordered tickets or other documents.

winch. An electrical or motorized device used to wind ropes, used in lifting cargo.

wind chill, wind chill factor. A calculation that takes into account the effect of the wind to provide a reading of the apparent temperature (as opposed to the actual temperature as registered on a thermometer).

wind shear. A violent and sudden downdraft of wind that can be fatal to airplanes landing or taking off.

windjammer. 1. A sailing ship. 2. A type of sailed cruise ship designed to resemble the merchant ships of the late 1800s.

windlass. A winch used to raise and lower a ship's anchor.

windward. In the direction of the wind.

wire transfer. The electronic transmission of funds from one bank to another; used to make payments to foreign suppliers.

WK. *GDS.* Was confirmed.

WL. *GDS.* Waitlist (qv).

w/o fac. *Abr.* Without facilities.

WOAG. *Worldwide Official Airline Guide.*

workshop. Seminar (qv).

World Heritage Site. A natural or man-made attraction designated by UNESCO as a treasure worth preserving for future generations.

World Wide Web. A global network of computers using hypertext technology to create a world-wide depository of information.

Worldspan®. A global distribution system (qv).

wrapper. *Slang.* A tour operator that purchases a basic tour package from another supplier, adds (or "wraps") some additional elements, and then sells the resulting package under its own name.

Wright amendment. A 1979 federal law designed to protect the then new Dallas-Fort Worth airport from competition by nearby Love Field. The law restricted flights from Love Field to destinations in Texas and nearby states.

write off, write-off. 1. *v.* Deduct, as from one's income tax. 2. *v.* Regard as hopelessly lost or damaged. 3. *n.* An expenditure that can be deducted from one's income tax.

WTCIB. Women's Travellers Center and Information Bank.

WTO. World Tourism Organization.

WTRVW. *GDS.* Water view.

WTTC. World Travel and Tourism Council.

Glossary of Terms

X, x

X. *GDS.* Connection.

XA. *GDS.* Animal and plant health inspection fee.

XBAG. *GDS.* Excess baggage.

xenophobia. Fear or hatred of foreigners or things foreign.

XF. *GDS.* 1. Cancelled phone. 2. Passenger facility charge (qv).

XL. *GDS.* Cancel. Cancel waitlist (qv).

XLD. *GDS.* Cancelled.

Xmas. *Abr.* Christmas.

XN. *GDS.* Cancelled name.

XO. *GDS.* Exchange order.

XR. *GDS.* Cancellation recommended.

x-ray. A baggage screening technology.

XS. *GDS.* Cancelled segment.

XSEC. *GDS.* Extra section (qv).

XTN. *GDS.* Extension.

XX. *GDS.* Cancelled.

XY. *GDS.* Immigration INS fee.

Y, y

Y discount fare. *See* selling fare.

YA. *Abr.* Young adult.

yacht. A luxury sail or powered vessel.

yacht broker. A person engaged in the buying and selling of recreational sailing and motor vessels, typically larger, more expensive models. *See also* charter broker.

yaw. A deviation in a ship's course, such as that caused by a storm or heavy seas.

YC. *GDS.* Customs user fee.

yield. Revenue per statistical unit. For example, an airline's yield would be stated as the average revenue per mile per paying passenger.

yield management. The practice of adjusting prices up or down in response to demand in order to control yield. This process is usually computerized.

YMCA. *Abr.* Young Men's Christian Association.

YMHA. *Abr.* Young Men's Hebrew Association.

yogwan. A traditional Korean inn.

youth fare. A fare for young people. The definition of "youth" varies among suppliers but generally ranges from 12 years of age to 22 or 25 years of age.

youth hostel. *See* hostel.

yurt. A dome-shaped Mongolian dwelling. Any construction patterned on such a dwelling.

YWCA. *Abr.* Young Women's Christian Association.

YWHA. *Abr.* Young Women's Hebrew Association.

Z, z

zebra. *Brit.* Parallel white lines on a road indicating that oncoming traffic must yield to pedestrians.

zenith. The highest point.

zephyr. A gentle breeze.

zeppelin. 1. A blimp (qv). 2. One of a now obsolete class of lighter-than-air passenger airships.

zero-zero. Used to describe weather conditions of no ceiling (qv) and no visibility.

ZIP code. In the U.S., a five- or nine-digit number used to facilitate the delivery of mail. "ZIP" is an acronym for zone improvement plan.

Zodiac. A brand of motorized, rigid-bottom, inflatable boat often used for recreational outings and wet landings from cruise ships.

zoning. Municipal laws or regulations regulating the type and size of buildings that can be erected and activities undertaken in specific areas.

zoo, zoological park. A park displaying wild (as opposed to domesticated) animals.

ZP. GDS. Flight segment tax.

Travel Trade Publications

Annals of Tourism Research
Elsevier Science
6277 Sea Harbor Drive
Orlando, FL 32887
www.elsevier.com
Quarterly; $194/year for individuals.
This scholarly journal brings a "multi-disciplinary approach" to studying the social sciences aspects of tourism in an effort to develop "theoretical constructs," whatever that means.

Association Meetings
The Meetings Group
10 Fawcett Street
Cambridge, MA 02138
866-505-7173
meetingsnet.com/associationmeetings
Bi-monthly; free to qualified subscribers, $57/year to others.

ASTA Agency Management
1101 King Street
Suite 200
Alexandria, VA 22314
703-739-2782
Monthly; free to ASTA members, $36/year to others.
This is the magazine for members of the American Society of Travel Agents who receive it as part of their membership dues. Covers travel industry trends (the ecological impact of increased tourism, what's new in automation, etc.) and agency issues (why agents are cutting back on fam trips). Also features how-they-did-it success stories.

ASU Travel Guide: The Guide for Airline Employee Discounts
1525 East Francisco Boulevard
San Rafael, CA 94901
866-483-5056
www.asutravelguide.com
Membership site; $39.95/year.
Features paid listings by hotels, tour operators, airlines and others offering discounts and other deals to airline employees.

Bank Travel Management
401 West Main Street
Lexington, KY 40507
(888) 253-0455
www.banktravelmanagement.com
Bi-monthly; included in $395/year membership in Bank Travel; $20/year to non-members.
Aimed at banks that offer travel incentive programs for their senior (50+) depositors.

Bus Tours Magazine
9698 West Judson Road
Polo, IL 61064
815-946-2341
www.bustoursmagazine.com
Bi-monthly; $15/year.
Provides information on destinations and attractions for an audience of motorcoach tour operators.

Business Travel News
VNU Business Media
770 Broadway

New York, NY 10003
847-763-9050
www.btnonline.com
23 times/year; free to qualified corporate travel purchasers; $119/year to others.
Covers the business travel industry.

Corporate and Incentive Travel
Coastal Communications
2650 North Military Trail
Boca Raton, FL 33431-6309
561-989-0600
www.corporate-inc-travel.com
Monthly; free to qualified subscribers, $60/year for others.
Targeted at corporate meeting planners and those who serve the industry.

Corporate Meetings and Incentives
The Meetings Group
132 Great Road
Stow, MA 01775
866-505-7173
Monthly; $87/year.

Cruise & Vacation Views
25 Washington Street
Morristown, NJ 07960
973-605-2442
www.e-travelnews.com
Web-based publication; free.
Covers the leisure market, with an accent on cruising. Also contains helpful articles on selling techniques and industry issues.

Cruise Reports
25 Washington Street
Morristown, NJ 07960
973-605-2442
www.cruise-report.com
Monthly; $39.95 to $69.95 depending on mode of delivery.
Reviews and rates cruise ships for an audience of travelers and travel agents.

Cruise Week
503 Crooked Creek
Wilmington, NC 28409
800-593-8252
www.cruise-week.com
Weekly; $79 (email) or $125 (fax)/year.
A two-page faxed newsletter "covering the top cruise-related news items of the week."

Destinations
American Bus Association
200 13th Street NW
Washington, DC 20005-5923
800-283-2877
www.buses.org
Monthly; $25/year.
This sleek magazine tracks trends and tour destinations and attractions for a primary audience of motorcoach operators.

eTourism Newsletter
www.etourismnewsletter.com
Free.
Covers the online side of travel marketing.

The Fam Connection
P.O. Box 820
Castroville, CA 95012
206-888-4890
www.famconnection.com
$29/year; $40/two years.
A regularly updated online or email service that lists "hundreds of fam trips and industry discounts for Travel Professionals."

Fam Facts
717 St. Joseph Drive
St. Joseph, MI 49085
269-982-2907
www.famfacts.com
Monthly; $24.95/year; $44.95/two years.
A newsletter listing familiarization trips, agent incentives, contests, complimentary hotel rooms, and such. The price of the subscription includes a directory of "hundreds of pages of discounts."

Going On Faith
401 West Main Street
Lexington, KY 40507
(888) 253-0455
Bimonthly; Free to qualified subscribers, $20/year to others.
For organizers of religious travel and pilgrimages.

Group Travel Leader
401 West Main Street
Lexington, KY 40507
(888) 253-0455
www.grouptravelleader.com
Monthly; free to qualified subscribers,

$39/year to others.
"National newspaper for senior group travel." The organ of Group Leaders of America (GLAMER).

Insurance Meetings Management
Coastal Communications
2650 North Military Trail
Boca Raton, FL 33431-6309
561-989-0600
www.corporate-inc-travel.com
Bi-monthly; free to qualified subscribers, $40/year for others.
Aimed at the senior insurance company executive.

Jax Fax Travel Marketing Magazine
48 Wellington Road
Milford, CT 06460
203-301-0255
Monthly; $15/year, $24/two years.
A thick, information-packed monthly that focuses on what's available from various travel suppliers. A gold mine of information on deep-discount consolidator fares. Just look up the destination you (or your client) wants and find out who's offering the best deal. Also features information on the latest in cruises, tours, and fam trips.

Meeting News
VNU Business Media
770 Broadway
New York, NY 10003
847-647-7987
646-654-5000
www.meetingnews.com
18 times/year; free to meeting planners, $79/year to others.
"The newspaper for meeting, convention, incentive and trade show professionals."

Recommend
5979 NW 151 Street
Miami Lakes, FL 33014
800-447-0123
305-828-0123
www.recommend.com
Monthly; free to qualified subscribers.
"Helping travel agents sell travel" is the subtitle to this publication.

Successful Meetings
VNU Business Media
770 Broadway

New York, NY 10003
646-654-5000
www.successmtgs.com
Monthly; free to qualified subscribers.
The magazine's stated goal is "to help our 75,000 subscribers be proficient and effective as meeting, incentive travel, and convention planners."

Tourism Management
Elsevier Science
655 Avenue of the Americas
New York, NY 10010-5107
212-663-3730
Quarterly; $165/year for individuals.
"The leading international journal for all those concerned with the planning and management of travel and tourism."

Travel Advance
2645 South Bayshore Drive
Coconut Grove, FL 33233
305-858-5024
Daily; $695/year.
A daily newsletter for top travel executives.

Travel Agent
One Park Avenue
New York, NY 10016
212-951-6600
www.travelagentcentral.com
Weekly; free to the trade, otherwise $79/year.
Slick, weekly newsmagazine in the mold of *Time* or *Business Week*. Bills itself as "The National Newsweekly of the Travel Industry." Provides a good overview of the industry and its trends with an emphasis on reporting (as opposed to reprinting press releases). Profiles of agencies sometimes provide good how-to tips.

Travel Bound
401 West Main Street
Lexington, KY 40507
859-253-0455
www.grouptravelleader.com
Bi-monthly.
"The official magazine of the African American Travel Conference."

Travel Courier
310 Dupont Street
Toronto, ON M5R 1V9
CANADA

Sources of Additional Information

416-968-7252
www.travelpress.com
Weekly: $25/year.
A "product driven" magazine for the Canadian travel industry.

Travel Industry Indicators
P.O. Box 6616
Miami, FL 33154
305-868-3818
www.travelindicators.com
Monthly; $95/year.
Tracks and analyses statistical trends in the travel industry with easy-to-read graphs in no-nonsense newsletter format.

Travel New England
256 Marginal Street
East Boston, MA 02128
617-561-4000
www.travelpublications.net
Monthly; free to qualified subscribers, $50/year to others.
"For the New England travel professional, including wholesalers, hotels, and leisure and business travel professionals."

Travel Press
310 Dupont Street
Toronto, Ontario M5R lV9
CANADA
416-968-7252
www.travelpress.com
Weekly; $48.15/year.
Provides general industry coverage of interest to travel agents.

Travel Trade
15 West 44th Street
New York, NY 10036
212-730-6600
www.traveltrade.com
Weekly; $10/year.
A no-nonsense business-oriented weekly tabloid — it likes to call itself "the business paper of the travel industry." Among its better features are a lively Letters to the Editor column and the "Business Features Showcase" with tips and suggestions from industry pros.

Travel Weekly
500 Plaza Drive
Secaucus, NJ 07094.
800-360-0015

www.travelweekly.com
Weekly; free to the trade.
A lively, glossy, tabloid style publication that combines travel industry news (who's doing what) with regular features on specific destinations (which can alert you to tours and cruises you might want to sell). There are regular supplements that give extended attention to various destinations (Hawaii and Europe are the most frequent, but less familiar areas like the Maya region of Central America are covered, too).

Travel World News
50 Washington Street
South Norwalk, CT 06854
203-853-4955
www.travelworldnews.com
Monthly; free to qualified travel agents, $25/year to others.
Similar to *Jax Fax* in look, feel, and layout. Covers the usual mix of industry news, new tours by region of the world, consolidator fares, cruises, fams, and so forth.

TravelAge West
9911 West Pico Boulevard
11th floor
Los Angeles, CA 90035
310-772-7430
www.travelagewest.com
Weekly; free to qualified agents.
Published in regional editions, this magazine-sized weekly features general travel industry news, with a regional focus. One nice feature is the Discount Corner, listing discounts available to travel agents. There is also a separate listing of fam trips as well as seminars being offered around the country.

Vacation Agent
3131 Route 38
Suite 11B
Mount Laurel, NJ 08054
877-727-0035
www.vacationagentmagazine.com
Monthly; free to qualified subscribers.
"The 'How to' resource for the vacation-selling travel professional."
Each issue has four sections covering resorts, tours, cruises and destinations.

Consumer Travel Publications

Andrew Harper's Harper Collection
P.O. Box 300
Whitefish, MT 59937
800-235-9622
www.andrewharpertravel.com
Irregular; $250/year.
In a loose-leaf leather binder, this 500-page publication serves as a travel encyclopedia for the upper crust. Updates to various sections are sent periodically. Subscription includes access to an online database.

Andrew Harper's Hideaway Report
P.O. Box 300
Whitefish, MT 59937
800-235-9622
www.andrewharpertravel.com
Monthly; $360/year.
The granddaddy of luxury travel newsletters. Harper (not his real name) tours super-luxury resorts, hotels, and spas and writes unbiased and highly opinionated critiques. The circulation of this 8-pager is held to 15,000 to heighten the exclusivity of the letter and there is sometimes a waiting list for new subscribers. The articles can serve as useful sales aids when dealing with well-heeled clients.

Belize First
Equator Travel Publications
287 Beaverdam Road
Candler, NC 28715
bzfirst@aol.com
www.belizefirst.com
Free online.
A web site focusing on travel, life and retirement in Belize and elsewhere on the Caribbean Coast of Central America and Mexico." Subscriptions includes, books, online access, and an email newsletter.

Best Fares
1301 South Bowen Road
Arlington, TX 76013
800-576-1234
www.bestfares.com
Monthly; $59.95/year.
Tom Parsons is the guru of the travel deal. His monthly magazine tracks every promotion and plays every angle to give readers the lowest fares possible.

Budget Travel
530 Seventh Avenue
New York, NY 10018
800-829-9121
646-695-6700
www.frommers.com/features/
Bi-monthly; $14.97/year; $24.95/2 years.
Arthur Frommer, the original guru of budget travel, is the editor in chief and that says it all.

Caribbean Travel and Life
460 North Orlando Avenue
Suite 200
Winter Park, FL 32789
800-588-1689
407-628-4802
www.caribbeantravelmag.com
Bi-monthly; $23.95/year.
A glossy magazine covering the Caribbean area in much the same way as *Travel & Leisure* covers the world.

Conde Nast Traveler
P.O. Box 57018
Boulder, CO 80322-7018
800-777-0700
www.cntraveler.com
Monthly; $12/year.
A glossy monthly with an emphasis on the upscale travel experience. Appeals to the well-to-do traveler and the not-so-well-to-do dreamer.

Cruise Travel
990 Grove Street
Evanston, IL 60201-4370
847-491-6440
www.cruisetravelmag.com
Bi-monthly; $19.97/year.
A magazine for the frequent cruiser. Each issue features a cruise, ship, and port of month. A directory issue is published in January. Discounts for CLIA agents.

The Discerning Traveler
504 West Mermaid Lane
Philadelphia, PA 19118-4206
800-673-7834

215-247-5578
www.discerningtraveler.com
Bi-monthly; $50/year.
This newsletter is a labor of love by a husband-wife team. Each issue focuses in-depth on one vacation area on the East Coast. Back issues (which come with updated information, when available) may be ordered separately.

Entree
P.O. Box 5148
Santa Barbara, CA 93150
805-969-5848
www.entreenews.com
Monthly; $75/year.
A luxury travel newsletter that describes itself as "uncompromising and confidential."

Family Travel Times
40 Fifth Avenue
New York, NY 10011
212-477-5524
www.familytraveltimes.com
Bi-monthly; $49/2 years.
Online newsletter devoted to family travel, with reports from parents.

Gemütlichkeit
UpCountry Publishing
288 Ridge Road
Ashland, OR 97520
800-521-6722
www.gemut.com
Monthly; $59to $79/year.
An 8-page newsletter covering German-speaking Europe (primarily Germany, Austria, and Switzerland), with an emphasis on itineraries and hotel/ restaurant suggestions.

Golf Odyssey
P.O. Box 3485
Charlottesville, VA 22903-0485
800-225-7825
www.golfodyssey.com
Monthly; $97 to $247/year
An 8-page newsletter that anonymously covers golfing resorts around the world. Subscription includes online access to their interactive web site.

Gourmet
4 Times Square
New York, NY 10036

800-365-2454
www.gourmet.com
Monthly; $15/year.
Upscale travel to go along with all that rich food.

InsideFlyer
1930 Frequent Flyer Point
Colorado Springs, CO 80915
800-209-2870
www.insideflyer.com
Monthly: $45/year ($12 for Internet
  access only).
Randy Petersen and company track the ins and outs of frequent flyer programs. Subscription includes online access to subscriber-only section of the web site.

The International Railway Traveler
2010 Edgeland Avenue
Louisville, KY 40204
800-478-4881
www.trainweb.com/irtsociety
Bi-monthly; $85/year.
A 16-page newsletter with an emphasis on foreign train itineraries and rail pass updates. Subscription includes member-ship in the Society of International Railway Travelers.

International Travel News
2628 El Camino Avenue
Sacramento, CA 95821
800-486-4968
www.intltravelnews.com
Monthly; $24/year, $40/2 years.
On a pennies-per-word basis, *ITN* has to be the best buy in travel magazines. Printed on cheap newsprint-like paper, this 100-pager appeals primarily to older, more adventurous travelers. Written largely by its readers, a good source of first-hand information.

Islands
Island Publishing Company
6267 Carpinteria Avenue
Carpinteria, CA 93013
800-284-7958
www.islands.com
8 times/year; $11.97/year.
From the South Pacific to the Mediterranean, with an upscale accent.

La Belle France
P.O. Box 3485

Charlottesville, VA 22903
800-225-7825
Monthly; $119/year, $205/two years.
An newsletter covering luxury hotels and restaurants in France, especially Paris.

Las Vegas Advisor
3687 South Procyon Ave.
Las Vegas, NV 89103
(702) 252-0655
www.lasvegasadvisor.com
Monthly; $50/year.
A 12-page newsletter with an emphasis on "deals" in the gambling capital of the world. 72-hour access to the "members-only" sections of the web site is $5.

Mature Traveler
P.O. Box 1543
Wildomar, CA 92545
800-460-6676
Monthly; $29/year.
12-page newsletter featuring discounts, destinations, and tips for the 50+ traveler.

National Geographic
National Geographic Society
1145 17th Street NW
Washington, DC 20036
800-647-5463
www.nationalgeographic.com
Monthly; $19/year.
The original magazine of world exploration, with lengthy articles, superb photography, and world class maps.

National Geographic Adventure
[same as *National Geographic*]
10 times/year; $15/year.
Aimed at the adventure travel niche.

National Geographic Traveler
[same as *National Geographic*]
Monthly; $18/year.
Covers the world, much in the style of *Conde Nast Traveler* or *Travel & Leisure*, although with perhaps more of an outdoorsy sensibility.

National Geographic World
[same as *National Geographic*]
Monthly; $20/year.
National Geographic for kids.

Passport Newsletter
5315 North Clark Street
Chicago, IL 60640
800-542-6670
www.passportnewsletter.com
Monthly; $99/year.
A newsletter with an emphasis on brief reviews of upscale hotels and restaurants. Each issue contains two removable Special Reports on a North American and foreign destination. Subscription includes access to the web site.

Porthole
Panoff Publishing
4517 NW 31st Avenue
Fort Lauderdale, FL 33309-3403
800-776-7678
www.porthole.com
Bi-monthly; $20/year, $30/2 years.
Glossy magazine that covers the cruise industry from the passenger's perspective.

Rick Steve's Europe
P.O. Box 2009
Edmonds, WA 98020-2009
425-771-8303
www.ricksteves.com/subscribe
Monthly; free in the U.S. and Canada.
Rick Steve's "back door" philosophy in articles about European travel. Also available online.

Shoestring Traveler, The
P.O. Box 847
Scottsbluff Nebraska 69363
308-632-3273
Bimonthly; $45/year.
A 32-page magazine on budget travel worldwide with an emphasis on courier travel.

Transitions Abroad
P.O. Box 1300
Amherst, MA 01004-1300
866-760-5340
www.transitionsabroad.com
Bi-monthly; $28/year.
Focuses on "affordable alternatives to mass tourism," including living abroad.

Travel and Leisure
1120 Avenue of the Americas
New York, NY 10036
800-888-8728

212-382-5600
www.travelandleisure.com
Monthly; $20/year.
A slick, thick, luxurious look at the world
of (generally) luxury travel, with an accent
on good writing and honest appraisals.

Travel and Leisure Golf
1120 Avenue of the Americas
New York, NY 10036
800-888-8728
212-382-5600
www.travelandleisure.com
Monthly; $20/year.

Travel America
990 Grove Street
Evanston, IL 60201-4370
847-491-6440
www.travelamerica.com
Bi-monthly; $19.97/year.
Covers a broad range of tourist destinations
and activities in the United States. Each
issue features a tour, city, and resort of
month.

Travel Books Worldwide
P.O. Box 162266
Sacramento, CA 95816-2266
916-452-5200
Ten times a year; $39/year.
This 14- to 24-page newsletter lists a
hundred or more travel books (with
complete publisher information) received
for review each month and reviews
between 12 and 25.

Travel Companions
Travel Companion Exchange
P.O. Box 833
Amityville, NY 11701
631-454-0880
www.whytravelalone.com
Bi-monthly; $48/year.
Travel safety and health tips for single
travelers with hundreds of listings of
those seeking travel companions and
partners.

Travel Holiday
1633 Broadway
New York, NY 10019-6708
800-937-9241
www.travelholiday.com
10 times a year; $17.94/year, $31.94/two
    years.

A somewhat less glamorous version of
Conde Nast Traveler and *Travel & Leisure*,
with an accent on how-to information
and tips.

Travel Smart
40 Beechdale Road
Dobbs Ferry, NY 10522
914-693-8300
www.travelsmartnewsletter.com
Monthly; $39/year, $69/2 years.
Newsletter offering short bits of
information on travel tips, low fares, hotel
discounts, last-minute deals, and the like.
Also runs what to do-see-eat features on
destinations, with an emphasis on the
U.S.

TravelLady Magazine
www.travellady.com
Weekly; free.
Online travel magazine with an accent on
luxury and romance.

TravLtips
P.O. Box 580188
Flushing, NY 11358
800-872-8584
www.travltips.com
Bi-monthly; $20/year, $35/two years.
Reports on freighter trips and other long-
term, low per diem cruises by some of the
28,000 subscribers who've taken them.
TravLtips is also a retailer and wholesaler
of freighter cruises.

Vacations
5851 San Felipe Street
Houston, TX 77057
713-974-6903
www.vacationsmagazine.com
Quarterly; $9.95/year.
"America's best source of affordable, new
vacation ideas."

Travel Industry Reference Books

Alternative Travel Directory
Transitions Abroad Publishing
800-293-0373
www.transitionsabroad.com
Annual; $20.

Ferrari Guides' Gay Travel A-Z
Ferrari International
602-863-2408
Annual; $30.

Hotel & Travel Index
Northstar Travel Media
www.hotelandtravelindex.com
Free online service.

Intelliguide Professional
Northstar Travel Media
www.intelliguide.com
Online subscription service.
$91.25/month; $995/year.

International Travel and Health
World Health Organization
www.who.int/ith/
Bi-annual; $22.50, free online.

OAG Publications
OAG
800-342-5624
www.oag.com

 OAG Africa Flight Guide

 OAG Air Travel Atlas

 OAG Cruise and Ferry Guide
 Quarterly; $237.

 OAG Desktop Guides
 North American and worldwide
 editions.

 OAGexpress
 Printed Timetable
 Monthly; $6.58, month.

 OAG Executive Flight Guide
 Printed timetables.
 Monthly: $119/year.

OAGflights
Online lookup service
Annual subscription: $199.

OAG Flight Atlas
Semi-annual; $68.
OAG Flight-Finder for PDAs
North American edition.
1 year license; $99.

OAG Flight Guides
Various editions.
Monthly; $449.

OAG FlightDisk
Software; North American and
 worldwide editions.

OAG Guide to International Travel
Quarterly; $90.

OAG HotelDisk
Software; four regional editions.

OAG Pocket Flights Guides
Four regional editions.

OAG Rail Guide
British rail schedules
Monthly; $299.

OAG Travel Planner
Windows CD-ROM; $349.

OAG WorldMate for PDAs
Annual: $70.

OAG World Airways Guide
Two volumes, available overseas
only.

Official Cruise Guide
Northstar Travel Media
800-360-0015
Annual; $79.

Official Meeting Facilities Guide
Northstar Travel Media
303-470-4445
Semi-annual; $79/year.

*The Travel Agent's
Complete Desk
Reference*

Official Travel Industry Directory
Travel Agent Magazine
212-951-6600
800-598-6008
Annual; $39.

*Personnel Guide to Canada's Travel
    Industry*
Baxter Publishing
416-968-7252
pguide.baxter.net
Bi-annual; $60.

Resorts and Great Hotels
World Publishing
805-745-7100
www.resortsgreathotels.com
Annual; $20.

Single-Friendly Travel Directory
Connecting Solo Travel Network
604-886-9099
www.cstn.org
Annual; $28 (includes bi-monthly
    newsletter).

Specialty Travel Index
Specialty Travel
800-442-4922
www.specialtytravel.com
Bi-annual; $10.

Star Service
Northstar Travel Media
800-776-0720
www.starserviceonline.com
$199/year.
Online edition is $199 for single user.

Weissmann Travel Reports
(See Intelliguide Professional)

World Travel Guide
SF Travel Publications
800-322-3834
Annual; $159.

Books about travel & the travel business

Sources of Additional Information

Note: Some of these books are out of print. You may be able to find them at your library.

Allen, Robert C., *Creating Hawaii Tourism*. Honolulu: Bess Press, 2004.

Anolik, Alexander, *The Law and the Travel Industry*. San Francisco: Anolik, 1990.

Aris, Stephen, *Close To The Sun: How Airbus Challenged America's Domination of the Skies*. Evanston, IL: Agate, 2004.

Berger, Arthur Asa, *Deconstructing Travel: Cultural Perspectives on Tourism*. Walnut Creek, CA: Altamira Press, 2004.

Bethune, Gordon, *From Worst To First: Behind the Scenes of Continental's Remarkable Comeback*. New York: John Wiley & Sons, 1999.

Biederman, Paul S., *Travel and Tourism: An Inudstry Primer*. Upper Saddle River, NJ: Prentice Hall, 2007.

Boniface, Brian, and Chris Cooper, *Worldwide Destinations: The Geography of Travel and Tourism*. 5th ed. Newton, MA: Butterworth-Heinemann, 2009.

Borocz, J., *Leisure Migration: A Sociological Study on Tourism*. New York: Elsevier, 1996.

Boyd, E. Andrew, *The Future of Pricing: How Airline Ticket Pricing Has Inspired a Revolution*. New York: Palgrave Macmillan, 2007.

Braidwood, Barbara et al., *Start and Run a Profitable Tour Guiding Business*. Seattle: Self Counsel, 2000.

Bravos, Brooke, *Cruise Hosting*. Sausalito, CA: Travel Time, 1992.

Brooks, Joyce, *Around The World in the Middle Seat: How I Saw the World (And Survived) As a Group Travel Leader*. Branford, CT: Intrepid Traveler, 2002.

Bruner, Edward M., *Culture on Tour: Ethnographies of Travel*. Chicago: University of Chicago Press, 2004.

Buckley, Ralf, *Ecotourism*, Cambridge, MA: CABI Publishing, 2009.

Buckley, Ralf, et. al., *Nature-Based Tourism*, Cambridge, MA: CABI Publishing, 2008.

Bryant, Carl L. et al., *Travel Selling Skills*. Albany: Delmar Publishers, 1992.

Burke, James F., and Barry P. Resnick, *Marketing and Selling the Travel Product*. 2nd ed. Albany: Delmar Publishers, 2000.

Cartwright, Roger, and Carolyn Baird, *Development and Growth of the Cruise Industry*. Newton, MA: Butterworth-Heinemann, 1999.

Cassidy, Maggie B., *Taking Students Abroad: A Complete Guide for Teachers*. Rev. ed. Brattleboro, VT: Pro Lingua Associates, Inc., 1988.

Colbert, Judy, *Career Opportunities in the Travel Industry*. New York: Checkmark Books, 2004.

Crouch, Geoffrey I. et al., *Consumer Psychology of Tourism, Hospitality and Leisure*. Cambridge, MA: CABI Publishing, 2004.

Dallas, Melissa, and Carl Riegel, *Hospitality and Tourism Careers*. Upper Saddle River, NJ: Prentice Hall, 1997.

Davidoff, Doris, and Philip Davidoff, *Worldwide Tours: A Travel Agent's Guide to Selling Tours*. Upper Saddle River, NJ: Prentice Hall, 1990.

Davidoff, Doris, and Philip Davidoff, *Sales and Marketing for Travel and Tourism*. 2nd ed. Upper Saddle River, NJ: Prentice Hall, 1994.

Davidoff, Doris, and Philip Davidoff, *Air Fares and Ticketing*. 3rd ed. Upper Saddle River, NJ: Prentice Hall, 1995.

Davidoff, Philip G. et al., *Tourism Geography*. 2nd ed. Upper Saddle River, NJ: Prentice Hall, 1995.

DeSouto, Martha Sarbey, *Group Travel*. 2nd ed. Albany: Delmar Publishers, 1993.

Dervaes, Claudine, *Careers in Travel (video)*. Tampa: Solitaire, 1998.

Dervaes, Claudine, *Travel Dictionary*. Tampa: Solitaire, 1998.

Dervaes, Claudine, *The Travel Training Series*. 10th ed. Tampa: Solitaire, 1998.

Dickinson, Bob, and Andy Vladimir, *Selling the Sea: An Inside Look at the Cruise Industry*. 2nd ed. New York: John Wiley & Sons, 2007.

Doganis, Rigas, *The Airline Business*. New York: Routledge, 2005.

Egger, Roman, and Dimitrios Buhalis, eds., *eTourism Case Studies*. Newton, MA: Butterworth and Heinemann, 2008.

Fay, Betsy, *Essentials of Tour Management*. Upper Saddle River, NJ: Prentice Hall, 1992.

Foster, Dennis L., *Sales and Marketing for the Travel Professional*. New York: Macmillan, 1991.

Foster, Dennis L., *The Business of Travel: Agency Operations and Administration*. New York: Macmillan, 1991.

Foster, Dennis L., *Destinations: North American and International Geography*. 2nd ed. New York: Macmillan, 1994.

Foster, Dennis L., *First Class: An Introduction to Travel and Tourism*. 2nd ed. Westerville, OH: Glencoe, 1994.

Freiberg, Kevin and Jackie, *Nuts! Southwest Airline's Crazy Recipe for Business and Personal Success*. Toronto: Texere, 2001.

Friedheim, Eric, *Travel Agents: From Caravans and Clippers to the Concorde*. New York: Universal Media, 1992.

Gagnon, Patricia J., and Shelly M. Houser, *Travel Career Development*. 8th ed. Wellesley, MA: ICTA, 2005.

Garin, Kristoffer A., *Devils on the Deep Blue Sea: The Dreams, Schemes, and Showdowns That Built America's Cruise-Ship Empire*. New York: Plume, 2006.

Gibson, Philip, *Cruise Operations Management*. Newton, MA: Butterworth-Heinemann, 2006.

Goeldner, Charles R. and J. R. Brent Ritchie, *Tourism: Principles, Practices, Philosophies*. New York: Wiley, 2008.

Gittell, Jody Hoffer, *The Southwest Airlines Way*. New York: McGraw-Hill, 2005.

Gold, Hal, *The Cruise Book: From Brochure to Bon Voyage*. Albany: Delmar Publishers, 1990.

Goldsmith, Carol, and Ann Waigand, *Building Profits with Group Travel*. San Francisco: Dendrobium, 1990.

Gorham, Ginger and Susan Rice, *Travel Perspectives: A Guide to Becoming a Travel Professional*, 4th ed. lbant: Delmar, 2006.

Gordon, Alastair, *Naked Airport: A Cultural History of the World's Most Revolutionary Structure*. Chicago: University of Chicago Press, 2008.

Greenberg, Peter, *Hotel Secrets From the Travel Detective*. New York: Villard, 2004.

Greenberg, Peter, *The Travel Detective Flight Crew Confidential*. New York: Villard, 2002.

Greenberg, Peter, *The Complete Travel Detective Bible*. New York: Rodale, 2007.

Gregory, Aryear, *The Travel Agent: Dealer in Dreams*. 4th ed. Upper Saddle River, NJ: Prentice Hall, 1993.

Hall, Colin Michael et al., *Food Tourism Around the World: Development, Management and Markets*. Newton, MA: Butterworth-Heinemann, 2003.

Hall, Colin Michael et al., *Safety and Security in Tourism*. Binghamton, NY: Haworth Press, 2004.

Hall, Colin Michael et al., *Wine Tourism Around the World*. New York: Elsevier, 2002.

Hanlon, Pat, *Global Airlines: Competition in a Transnational Industry*. Newton, MA: Butterworth and Heinemann, 2007.

Havers, Richard, and Christopher Tiffney, *Airline Confidential: Lifting the Lid on the Airline Industry*. Charleston, SC: The History Press, 2007.

Howell, David W., *Principles and Methods of Scheduling Reservations*. 3rd ed. Upper Saddle River, NJ: Prentice Hall, 1992.

Howell, David, *Passport: An Introduction to the Travel and Tourism Industry*. Albany: Delmar Publishers, 2002.

Hudman, Lloyd, and Richard Jackson, *Geography of Travel and Tourism*. 4th ed. Albany: Delmar Publishers, 1999.

Ivanovic, Milena, *Cultural Tourism*, Juta Academic, 2009.

Jung, Gerald, *A Practical Guide to Selling Travel*. Upper Saddle River, NJ: Prentice Hall, 1993.

Kirkwood, Tim, *The Flight Attendant Job Finder and Career Guide*. River Forest, IL: Planning/ Communications, 2003.

Landry, Janice L., and Anna H. Fesmire, *The World Is Waiting Out There: An Introduction to Travel and Tourism*. Upper Saddle River, NJ: Prentice Hall, 1994.

Laws, Eric, *Managing Packaged Tourism*. Albany: Delmar Publishers, 1997.

Long, Lucy M., *Culinary Tourism (Material Worlds)*. Lexington, KY: University Press of Kentucky, 2003

Lumsdon, Les, *Tourism Marketing*. Albany: Delmar Publishers, 1998.

Maisel, Sally J., *Cruising Solo: The Single Traveler's Guide to Adventure on the High Seas*. Van Nuys, CA: Marin Publications, 1993.

Makower, Joel, *The Map Catalog*. 3rd ed. New York: Random House, 1992.

Mancini, Marc, *Access: Introduction to Travel and Tourism*. Albany: Delmar Publishers, 2004.

Mancini, Marc, *Conducting Tours*. 3rd ed. Albany: Delmar Publishers, 2000.

Mancini, Marc, *Cruising: A Guide to the Cruise Line Industry*. 2nd ed. Albany: Delmar Publishers, 2003.

Mancini, Marc, *Selling Destinations: Geography for the Travel Professional*. 5th ed. Florence, KY: Delmar Cengage, 2009.

Maurer, Ed, *Internet for the Retail Travel Industry*. Florence, KY: Delmar Cengage, 2002.

Maxtone-Graham, John, *Crossing & Cruising: From the Golden Era of Ocean Liners to the Luxury Cruise Ships of Today*. New York: Scribner's, 1993.

McCormack, Mark, *Hit the Ground Running: The Insider's Guide To Business Travel*. Beverly Hills: New Millennium, 2005.

McDonnell, Ian, eTravel and Tourism: Marketing and Management Techniques. Newton, MA: Butterworth-Heinemann, 2009.

McKerchner, Bob, *Cultural Tourism*. New York: Routledge, 2002.

Middleton, Victor T. C., and Jackie R. Clarke, *Marketing in Travel and Tourism*. 4th ed. Newton, MA: Butterworth-Heinemann, 2009.

Mill, Robert C., *Tourism: The International Business*. Upper Saddle River, NJ: Prentice Hall, 1990.

Mill, Robert C., and Alastair Morrison, *The Tourism System: An Introductory Text*. 5th ed. Dubuque, IA: Kendall/Hunt Publishing, 2006.

Miller, Mary Fallon, *Cruise Chooser*. St. Petersburg, FL: Ticket To Adventure, 2001.

Mitchell, Gerald E., *The Travel Consultant's On-Site Inspection Journal*. Englewood, FL: G.E. Mitchell & Associates, 1990.

Mitchell, Gerald E., *Global Travel and Tourism Career Opportunities*. Charleston, SC: BookSurge, 2007.

Mitchell, Gerald E., *How to Start a Tour Guiding Business*. Charleston, SC: BookSurge, 2005.

Mitchell, Gerald E., *Travel The World Free As An International Tour Director*. Charleston, SC: BookSurge, 2007.

Morgan, Nigel et al., *Destination Branding: Creating the Unique Destination Proposition*. Newton, MA: Butterworth-Heinemann, 2004.

Morris, Karen et al., *Hotel, Restaurant, and Travel Law*. 7th ed. Albany: Delmar Publishers, 2007.

Morrison, Alastair, *Hospitality and Travel Marketing*. 3rd ed. Albany: Delmar Publishers, 2001.

Sources of Additional Information

Nash, D., *Anthropology of Tourism*. New York: Elsevier, 2001.

Nickerson, Norma P., *Foundations of Tourism*. Upper Saddle River, NJ: Prentice Hall, 1996.

Nwanna, Gladson I., *Americans Traveling Abroad: What You Should Know Before You Go*. 3rd ed. Baltimore, MD: World Travel Institute Press, 2004.

Nyy, Linda, *Vacation CounSELLing*. Upper Saddle River, NJ: Prentice Hall, 1992.

Oppermann, Martin, ed., *Geography and Tourism Marketing*. Binghamtom, NY: Haworth, 1997.

Page, Stephen, *Tourism Management*. Newton, MA: Butterworth-Heinemann, 2003.

Payette, Douglas A., *So You Want To Be a Travel Agent*. Upper Saddle River, NJ: Prentice Hall, 1995.

Pearce, P.L. et al., *Tourism Community Relationships*. New York: Elsevier, 1996.

Plunkett, Jack W., *Plunkett's Airline, Hotel & Travel Industry Almanac*. Houston: Plunkett Research 2008.

Poustie, Mark et al., *Hospitality and Tourism Law*. Albany: Delmar Publishers, 1999.

Raza, Ivo, *Heads In Beds: Hospitality and Tourism Marketing*. Upper Saddle River, NJ: Prentice Hall, 2004.

Reiff, Annette, *Introduction to Corporate Travel*. Albany: Delmar Publishers, 1994.

Richards, Bill. *History of Tourism in the UK*. Newton, MA: Butterworth-Heinemann, 2005.

Ryan, C., and S. Page, eds., *Tourism Management*. New York: Elsevier, 2000.

Schmidt, Gary, *101 Ways to Sell Travel*. Oakdale, MN: Travel Publishing, 1996.

Schmidt, Gary, *The Ultimate Guide to Fees*. Oakdale, MN: Travel Publishing, 1998.

Schwartz, Roberta, and Debra J. MacNeill, *Travel Sales and Customer Service*. 2nd ed. Wellesley, MA: ICTA, 1999.

Semer-Purzicki, Jeanne, *International Travel, Fares, and Ticketing*. Upper Saddle River, NJ: Prentice Hall, 1997.

Semer-Purzicki, Jeanne, and Robert H. Purzycki, *Sails for Profit: A Complete Guide To Selling and Booking Cruise Travel*. Upper Saddle River, NJ: Prentice Hall, 1999.

Semer-Purzicki, Jeanne, *A Practical Guide to Fares and Ticketing*. 3rd ed. Albany: Delmar Publishers, 2001.

Shaw, Stephen, *Airline Marketing and Management*. Ashgate ublishing (UK), 2007.

Smith, Melanie, Health and Wellness Tourism. Newton, MA: Butterworth-Heinemann, 1999.

Sorensen, Helle, *International Travel and Tourism*. Albany: Delmar Publishers, 1997.

Starr, Nona, and Sybil Norwood, *The Traveler's World: A Dictionary of Industry and Destination Literacy*. Upper Saddle River, NJ: Prentice Hall, 1996.

Stopher, P., and M. Lee-Gosselin, *Understanding Travel Behaviour in an Era of Change*. New York: Elsevier, 1996.

Swarbrooke, John, and Susan Horner, *Business Travel and Tourism*. Newton, MA: Butterworth-Heinemann, 2001.

Syratt, Gwenda, and Jane Archer, *Manual of Travel Agency Practice*, 3rd ed. Newton, MA: Butterworth-Heinemann, 2003.

Teo, Peggy et al., *Interconnected Worlds: Tourism in Southeast Asia*. New York: Elsevier, 2001.

Thompson, Douglas, and Alexander Anolik, *A Personnel and Operations Manual for Travel Agencies*. San Francisco: Dendrobium, 1993.

Todd, Ginger, *Selling Travel 1-2-3*. Indianapolis, IN: Travel Careers, 1996.

Travel Industry Association of America, *Adventure Travel Report*. Washington, DC: TIAA, 1998.

Travel Industry Association of America, *The Mature Traveler*. Washington, DC: TIAA, 2000.

Travel Industry Association of America, *The Minority Traveler.* Washington, DC: TIAA, 2003.

Travel Industry Association of America, *The Travel Marketer's Guide to Social Media and Social Networking.* Washington, DC: TIAA, 2007.

Vladimir, Andy, and Dickinson, Bob, *The Complete 21st Century Travel Marketing Handbook.* Upper Saddle River, NJ: Prentice Hall, 2004.

Vogel, Harold L., *Travel Industry Economics.* New York: Cambridge University Press, 2006.

Vukonic, B., *Tourism and Religion.* New York: Elsevier, 1996.

Wang, Ning, *Tourism and Modernity.* New York: Elsevier, 2000.

Ward, Douglas, *Complete Guide to Cruising & Cruise Ships 2009.* New York: Berlitz, 2008.

Webster, Susan, and Ralph G. Phillips, *Group Travel Operating Procedures.* 2nd ed. New York: Van Nostrand Reinhold, 1993.

WHO staff, *International Travel and Health 2005.* World Health Organization, Geneva, Switzerland, 2005.

Weissmann, Arnie, and Kevin Gillespie, *Travel Around the World.* 2nd ed. Austin, TX: Weissmann Travel Reports, 2000.

Wensveen, John G., *Wheels Up: Airline Business Plan Development.* Pacific Grove, CA: Brooks Cole, 2004.

West, Jim, *The Essential Little Cruise Book,* 4th ed. GPP Travel, 2008

Williams, Gary, *Handbook for Distance Learning in Tourism.* Binghamton, NY: Haworth, 2005.

Wills, Deb, and Debra Martin Koma, *PassPorter's Open Mouse for Walt Disney World and the Disney Cruise Line: Easy Access Vacations for Travelers with Extra Challenges.* 2nd ed. Ann Arbor, MI: PassPorter Travel Press, 2007.

World Travel & Tourism Council, *Travel and Tourism: A New Economic Perspective.* New York: Elsevier, 1995.

Zvoncheck, Juls, *Cruises: Selecting, Selling & Booking.* 2nd ed. Upper Saddle River, NJ: Prentice Hall, 1994.

Books for the home-based business

Arden, Lynie, *The Work-at-Home Sourcebook.* 9th ed. Boulder, CO: Live Oak Publications, 2005.

Attard, Janet, *Business Know-How: An Operational Guide for Home-Based and Micro-Sized Businesses with Limited Budgets.* Avon, MA: Adams Media, 1999.

Attard, Janet, *The Home Office and Small Business Answer Book.* New York: Holt, 2007.

Attard, Janet, *The Home Office and Small Business Success Book.* New York: Holt, 1996.

Berner, Jeff, *The Joy of Working from Home.* San Francisco: Berrett-Koehler, 1994.

Brabec, Barbara, *Homemade Money: Starting Smart.* New York: M. Evans & Company, 2003.

Center for Self-Sufficiency, *Home Business: How To Find or Locate Information on Home Business.* Denver: CSF, 1993.

Clouse, Michael, and Kathie Anderson, *Future Choice: Why Network Marketing May Be Your Best Career Move.* Seattle: Candlelight, 1996.

Complete Home-Based Business Sourcebook. New York: Macmillan, 1996.

Cornish, Clive G., *Basic Accounting for the Small Business.* 9th ed. Seattle: Self-Counsel, 1993.

Davidson, Jeffrey, *Marketing for the Home-Based Business.* 2nd ed. Holbrook, MA: Bob Adams, Inc., 1999.

Debelak, Don, *Marketing Magic: Action-Oriented Strategies That Will Help You Find Customers, Promote Your Products or Services, Create Exciting Marketing Plans*. Holbrook, MA: Bob Adams, 1997.

Dudley, George W., and Shannon L. Dudley, *The Psychology of Call Reluctance: How To Overcome the Fear of Self-Promotion*. Dallas: Behavioral Science Research Press, 1986.

Edwards, Paul, *Home-Based Business For Dummies*. New York: For Dummies, 2005.

Edwards, Paul, and Sarah Edwards, *Making It on Your Own*. New York: Tarcher/Putnam, 1991.

Edwards, Paul, and Sarah Edwards, *Best Home Businesses for the 21st Century*. New York: Tarcher/Putnam, 1999.

Edwards, Paul, and Sarah Edwards, *Making Money with Your Computer at Home*. 3rd rev. ed. New York: Tarcher/Putnam, 2005.

Edwards, Paul, Sarah Edwards, and Laura Clampitt Douglas, *Getting Business to Come to You*. 2nd ed. New York: Tarcher/Putnam, 1998.

Edwards, Sarah, and Paul Edwards, *Secrets of Self-Employment: Surviving and Thriving on the Ups and Downs of Being Your Own Boss*. New York: Tarcher/Putnam, 1996.

Eisenberg, Ronnie, *Organize Your Home Office*. New York: Hyperion, 2000.

Engel, Peter H., *The Soho Desk Reference: A Practical A to Z Guide for the Entrepreneur Small Office/Home Office*. New York: Harper Collins, 1997.

Eyler, David R., *The Home Business Bible*. New York: Wiley & Sons, 1994.

Fishman, Stephen, *Home Business Tax Deductions: Keep What You Earn*. 4th ed. Berkeley, CA: Nolo Press, 2007.

Fuller, Cheri, *Home Business Happiness*. Lancaster, PA: Starburst, 1996.

Gerber, Michael E., *The E-Myth Revisted Rev Ed: Why Most Small Businesses Don't Work and What to Do About It*. New York: Harper, 2005.

Germer, Jerry, *Complete Guide to Building and Outfitting an Office in Your Home*. Cincinnati: Betterway, 1994.

Goldstein, Arnold S., *Starting on a Shoestring*. 4th ed. New York: Wiley & Sons, 2002.

Gordon, Kim, *Growing Your Home-Based Business*. Upper Saddle River, NJ: Prentice Hall, 1992.

Gray, Douglas A., *Have You Got What It Takes: The Entrepreneur's Complete Self-Assessment Guide*. Seattle: Self Counsel, 1993.

Henry, Maxye, and Lou Henry, *101 Tips for Running a Successful Home Business*. Lowell House, 2000.

Holtz, Herman, *The Complete Work-At-Home Companion*. 2nd ed. Rocklin, CA: Prima, 1994.

Home Office Computing Staff, *Home Office Computing Handbook*. Blue Ridge Summit, PA: TAB Books, 1994.

Home Office Deductions: Tax Tips for Individuals. Chicago: Commerce Clearing House, 1993.

Hopkins, Tom, *How to Master the Art of Selling*. New York: Warner, 2005.

Hopkins, Tom, *Tom Hopkin's Guide to Greatness in Sales*. New York: Warner, 1993.

Kamoroff, Bernard, *Small Time Operator: How to Start Your Own Small Business, Keep Your Books, Pay Your Taxes & Stay Out of Trouble!* 8th ed. Laytonville, CA: Bell Springs Publishing, 2004.

Kamoroff, Bernard, *422 Tax Deductions for Businesses and Self-Employed Individuals*. 7th ed. Laytonville, CA: Bell Springs Publishing, 2008.

Kanarek, Lisa, *101 Home Office Success Secrets*. 2nd ed. Franklin Lakes, NJ: Career Press, 2000.

Kanarek, Lisa, *Organizing Your Home Office for Success*. 2nd ed. Dallas: Blakely Press, 1998.

Kern, Coralee Smith, *Run Your Own Home Business*. Lincolnwood, IL: NTC, 1998.

King, Dean, and Jessica King, *Paper Clips to Printers: The Cost-Cutting Sourcebook for Your Home Office*. New York: Viking Penguin, 1996.

Lesko, Matthew, *Everything You Need to Run a Business at Home*. Kensington, MD: Info USA, 1996.

Levinson, Jay, and Seth Godin, *Guerilla Marketing for the Home-Based Business*. Boston: Houghton-Mifflin, 1995.

Lonier, Terri, and Lisa M. Aldisert, *Working Solo*. 2nd ed. New York: John Wiley & Sons, 1998.

Lonier, Terri, *The Small Business Money Guide: How To Get It, Use It, Keep It*. New York: John Wiley & Sons, 1998.

Lonier, Terri, *Smart Strategies for Growing Your Business*. New York: John Wiley & Sons, 1999.

McQuown, Judith H., *Inc. Yourself: How to Profit by Setting Up Your Own Corporation*. 10th ed. Franklin Lakes, NJ: Career Press, 2004.

Meadows, Carl, *How To Organize Group Travel For Fun and Profit*. 2nd rev. ed. Littleton, CO: ETC Publishing, 2002.

Nicholas, Ted, *How to Form Your Own Corporation Without a Lawyer for Under $75.00*. Dover, NH: Upstart, 1996.

Olsen, Nancy, *Starting a Mini-Business: A Guidebook for Seniors*. Sunnyvale, CA: Fair Oaks, 1988.

O'Shea-Roche, Annette, *Partners at Work and at Home*. Seattle: Self-Counsel, 1994.

Parlapiano, Ellen H., *Mompreneurs: A Mother's Practical Step-by-Step Guide to Work-at-Home Success*. New York: Berkley, 1996.

Phillips, Barty, *The Home Office Planner*. San Francisco: Chronicle Books, 2000.

Phillips, Michael, and Salli Rasberry, *Marketing without Advertising*. 6th ed. Berkeley, CA: Nolo Press, 2008.

Pinson, Linda, and Jerry Jinnett, *The Home-Based Entrepreneur*. Dover, NH: Upstart, 1993.

Pinson, Linda, and Jerry Jinnett, *Target Marketing: Researching, Reaching and Retaining Your Target Market*. 3rd ed. Chicago: Dearborn Trade, 1996.

Pinson, Linda, *Keeping the Books*. 7th ed. New York: Kaplan Business, 1998.

Porter Henry, *Secrets of the Master Sellers*. New York: AMACOM, 2007.

Quigley, Mary, and Loretta Kaufman, *Going Back To Work: A Survival Guide For Comeback Moms*. New York: St. Martin's Griffin, 2004.

Ries, Al, and Jack Trout, *Bottom-Up Marketing*. New York: NAL-Dutton, 1990.

Robbins, Anthony, *Awaken the Giant Within*. New York: Simon & Schuster, 1992.

Robbins, Anthony, *Giant Steps*. New York: Simon & Schuster, 2001.

Roberts, Lisa M., *How to Raise a Family and a Career Under One Roof*. Moon Township, PA: Bookhaven, 1997.

Rosenbaum, Alvin, *The Complete Home Office: Planning Your Work Space*. Bergenfield, NJ: Studio Books, 1995.

Truex, Leslie, *The Work-at-Home Success Bible: A Complete Guide for Women*. Cincinnati: Adams Media, 2009.

Weltman, Barbara, *The Complete Idiot's Guide to Starting a Home-Based Business*, 3rd ed. New York, Penguin, 2007

Williams, Kitty, *Essential Soho Websites: Small Office/Home Office Online Treasures*. Manakin-Sabot, VA: Hope Springs Press, 2001.

Yoho, Dave, and Jeffrey P. Davidson, *How To Have a Good Year Every Year*. New York: Berkley, 1990.

Zbar, Jeff, *Home Office Know-How*. Chicago: Dearborn, 1998.

Zbar, Jeff, *Your Profitable Home Business Made E-Z (CD-ROM)*. Deerfield Beach, FL: Made E-Z Products, 2000.

Zelinsky, Marilyn, *Practical Home Office Solutions*. New York: McGraw-Hill, 1998.

Ziglar, Zig, *Secrets of Closing the Sale*. Grand Rapids, MI: Revell, 2004.

Ziglar, Zig, *Over The Top*. Nashville: Thomas Nelson, 2007.

Major Publishers of Travel Guides

Access Guides
www.accessguides.com
Detailed guides to major cities.

Avalon Travel Publishing
www.travelmatters.com
Publishes Rick Steves guides, Moon
　　Handbooks, Foghorn Outdoors, the
　　Living Abroad series, and others.

Berlitz Publishing Company, Inc.
www.berlitzpublishing.com
Publishes *Berlitz Pocket Guides*, city guide
maps, along with an extensive line of
foreign language phrase books.

Blue Guides
www.acblack.com
Publishes a series of destination guides
　　that combine the practical and the
　　scholarly.

Bradt Travel Guides
www.bradt-travelguides.com
British publisher of guides to exotic
　　locales. Distributed in the U.S. by
　　Globe Pequot.

Cadogan Guides
www.cadoganguides.com
British publisher of literate destination
　　guides.

Cheap Eats and Cheap Sleeps
www.chroniclebooks.com
Guides for budget travel in Europe, now
　　with a *Great Eats* line of books.

Countryman Press
www.countrymanpress.com
Publishers of regional U.S. travel
　　guides.

Culture Shock! Guides
www.gacpc.com
Publishes destination guides with an
　　emphasis on customs and etiquette.

Damron Lesbian and Gay Travel Guides
www.damron.com

Eyewitness Travel Guides
Dorling Kindersley Publishing, Inc.
www.dk.com
Sumptuouskly illustrated destination
　　guides, including the *Top 10* guides to
　　cities.

Fodor's Guides
www.fodors.com
Publishes *Fodor's Gold Guides, Baedecker
Guides, Compass American Guides*, and
Karen Brown's Guides.

Footprint Press
www.footprintpress.com
Publishes guides to hiking, biking, and
　　other outdoor activities.

Frommer's Travel Guides
www.frommers.com
Pioneering publishers of the *Dollars
　　A Day* series, now publishes a wide
　　variety of destination, activity, and
　　lifestyles guides.

Gingko Press
www.gingkopress.com
Publishers of the *Eat Smart* series of
　　dining guides.

Globe Peqout Press
www.globepequot.com
Publishes an eclectic assortment of
　　worldwide destination guides,
　　including the *Falcon Guides* outdoors
　　series, and distributes for several
　　other publishers.

Hunter Publishing
Publishers of the *Adventure Guide* and
　　Alive Guide series, with a primarily
　　Caribbean focus.

Insight Guides
www.insightguides.com
Publishes *Insight Guides* and *Insight
Pocket Guides with Maps*.

Interlink Publishing
www.interlinkbooks.com
Publishers the *Travellers History* series
　　as well as *The Traveller's Companion*

series, the *Business Traveller's Handbooks*, and the *Charming Small Hotels* guides.

The Intrepid Traveler
www.IntrepidTraveler.com
Publishes in-depth guides to Walt Disney World, Universal Orlando, SeaWorld, and central Florida.

Karen Brown's Guides
www.karenbrown.com
Guides to hotels, B&Bs, and inns of Europe, California, Mexico and elsewhere. Published by Fodor's.

Knopf Guides
www.randomhouse.com/knopf/travel/
Upscale guides to major world cities and other destinations.

Let's Go Guides
www.letsgo.com
Student-written budget travel guides to major tourist destinations.

Lonely Planet Guides
www.lonelyplanet.com
Publishes the *Travel Survival Kit* and *on a Shoestring* series as well as walking guides, city guides, and phrasebooks.

Michelin Guides
www.viamichelin.com
Publishers of the legendary *Red Guides* to restaurants and the *Green Guides* to major tourism destinations.

Moon Travel Handbooks
www.moon.com
Hip destination guides. An imprint of Avalon Travel Publishing.

National Geographic Guides
www.nationalgeographic.com/ destinations/
Publishes guides with an emphasis on National Parks and the outdoors.

Off The Beaten PathGuides
(See Globe Pequot Press)

Pineapple Press
www.pineapplepress.com
Publishes books about Florida, including guide books.

Rough Guides
www.roughguides.com
Publisher of destination guides in the Lonely Planet mold, as well as maps, and phrasebooks.

Time Out Guides
www.timeout.com
Hip, youth-oriented destination guides, primarily to major cities.

A Traveller's History of . . .
(See Interlink Publishing)

Travel Publishers Association
www.travelpubs.com
An association of smaller travel publishers. The web site contains links to member publishers' sites.

Travelers' Tales
www.travelerstales.com
Publisher of collected short travel non-fiction and destination guides.

Ulysses Travel Guides
www.ulyssesguides.com
Publishes guides for independent travelers, including the *Ulysses Travel Guides*, the *Green Escapes* series, and *Bird's Eye View*, a free Internet-based series.

Woodall's
www.woodalls.com
Publishes books on camping and RVing.

Zagat Survey
www.zagat.com
Publishes guides to restaurants and other leisure activities.